D0085641

To the Golden Door

Give me your tired, your poor,
Your huddled masses yearning to breathe free,
The wretched refuse of your teeming shore,
Send these, the homeless, tempest-tossed, to me:
I lift my lamp beside the golden door.

EMMA LAZARUS (The New Colossus:
Inscription for the Statue of Liberty,
New York Harbor)

To the Golden Door

THE STORY OF THE IRISH IN IRELAND AND AMERICA

by George Potter

WITH ILLUSTRATIONS

GREENWOOD PRESS, PUBLISHERS
WESTPORT, CONNECTICUT

Library of Congress Cataloging in Publication Data

Potter, George W
    To the golden door.

    Reprint of the ed. published by Little, Brown,
Boston.
        1. Irish in the United States. 2. Ireland--
Famines. 3. Ireland--Economic conditions.
4. Ireland--Emigration and immigration. I. Title.
[E184.I6P6 1973]   917.3'06'9162   73-3928
ISBN 0-8371-6862-7

Originally published in 1960 by Little, Brown and Company, Boston

Reprinted with the permission of Little, Brown & Company

Reprinted in 1973 by Greenwood Press,
a division of Williamhouse-Regency Inc.

Library of Congress Catalogue Card Number 73-3928

ISBN 0-8371-6862-7

Printed in the United States of America

To Erna

Acknowledgments

My husband spoke often of the kindness of many people in helping him in the preparation of this book and I am happy to acknowledge for him his gratitude to them — a gratitude which he often expressed to me and which he fully intended himself to express had he lived. Among those to whom he felt most indebted were the following:

John C. A. Watkins, Publisher, *The Providence Journal*.

The Members of the Board of Directors, The John Simon Guggenheim Memorial Foundation.

Dr. C. P. Curran, Dublin.

Dr. Seamus H. Delargy, Director of the Irish Folklore Commission, Dublin.

Dr. R. J. Hayes, Director, National Library of Ireland, Dublin.

Dr. James B. Hedges, Professor of History, Brown University.

Dr. David J. Jonah, Librarian, Brown University Library.

Dr. I. J. Kapstein, Professor of English, Brown University.

Tadhg Murphy, Folklore Commission, Dublin.

Thomas P. O'Neill, M.A., Assistant Keeper of Printed Books, National Library of Ireland, Dublin.

Clarence E. Sherman, former Librarian, Providence Public Library.

Stuart C. Sherman, Librarian, Providence Public Library.

Dr. R. C. Simington, Dublin.

Dr. Philip Taft, Professor of Economics, Brown University.

Thanks is also due Virginia Ley Fales for her precise and patient typing of the manuscript.

ERNA C. POTTER

Contents

(Illustrations appear between pages 184–185, 216–217, 376–377, and 408–409)

PART ONE

Where They Came From

. . . there is no land in the world of so long continual war within himself, ne of so great shedding of Christian blood, ne of so great robbing, spoiling, preying, and burning, ne of so great wrongful extortion continually as Ireland.

English State Paper, 1515

Good God! have mercy on poor Ireland.

Ireland's Welcome to the Stranger
by Asenath Nicholson

The Top o' the Morning

BILLY CARBERRY, in his new shoes, walked miles with the other Irishmen from northeast Philadelphia to join in the St. Patrick's Day parade in Philadelphia, then hobbled home, and when he got home they had to cut the shoes off his feet. The priest said, "Poor innocent men." An Irishman named Kennedy, the first to live in Fall River, Massachusetts, walked fifty miles to Boston and fifty miles back at least once a year, to attend the then nearest Roman Catholic church. An Irishman (apparently a young man) wrote to the Boston *Pilot* that he was tired of the blathering of what the Irish in America were going to do to England — let's go over and fight, he wrote: "I'm ready."

These Catholic Irish emigrants had carried with them to nineteenth-century America a strong cultural identity shared through the patron saint, a deep devotional faith and a hatred of England.

Their first historian in the modern manner, the seventeenth-century Geoffrey Keating, had written: "To give a regular account of the first inhabitants of Ireland, I am obliged to begin at the creation of the world." They saw nothing extravagant, though New York of the 1830s raised an eyebrow, in the insistence of a local Irish controversialist that Adam and Eve spoke Irish in the Garden of Eden.

Keating had read the early manuscripts, in which Ireland was rich, and hesitated to go behind the record, but the critical examination of modern Irish scholarship is unraveling the golden threads woven by the learned men of Christian Ireland a thousand years before to bind the men of Ireland together in a common kinship. Their object was to find a common ancestor of the diverse races which populated Ireland and symbolize the cultural unity that was felt throughout the island.

There had been a succession of invasions into Ireland before the world Christian era, but the last, somewhere between 150 and 50 B.C., had imposed its rule and impressed its culture upon the previous inhabitants. These tall, fair-haired and aristocratic Gaels, of the once powerful Celtic-speaking peoples on the European mainland, had come from Gaul and, being of the Iron Age, were more advanced than the people they found in Ireland.

Instead of hewing to the fact that the dominant Gael was the Johnny-come-lately, these ancient learned men pushed his appearance in Ireland some two thousand years back and then by genealogical fictions had the older races descended from the recent Gaels, in an arrangement that was apparently satisfactory to all. In their aim "to unify the country by obliterating the memory of the different ethnic origins of the people" and "to endow all the septs [families] which possessed any importance in their day with a common [Gaelic] origin," they invented the father of the race, one Mile, or Miletius, of Spain. The proudest boast of an Irishman was that his family descended from "the true Milesian stock."

Moreover, the fashioning of genealogies was achieved in such a way as to accommodate itself to the traditions of the land and in such a framework as to solidify the unity by the highest sanction then available, namely, the Old Testament. What the early Irish scribes did was to borrow the story of the Children of Israel, with some Latin scraps of learning, and make it their own, back to "the creation of the world," to fill the vacuum of the misty past.

The key words to describe Gaelic — or native — Ireland are "cultural unity." The spell of the island itself lay on the people. Mrs. Alice Stopford Green, the Irish social historian, described it:

> It is a striking fact that from the first, national feeling in Ireland centred not in the race, but in the island itself, the home of all its people. They were united by the bond of a chivalrous loyalty to the common land, which from the old days down to modern times has been constantly personified and called by the name of a woman.

This "sonship to the land," she wrote, was "the earliest and most passionate conception of nationality in the 'dark ages' of Europe." It radiates through Gaelic literature — the sheer joy of the physical feel of the countryside, the woods, the lakes, the streams, the song of the birds, the earth itself.

Isolated Ireland, the outermost frontier of Europe, had escaped the domination of the Romans and though Agricola, the conqueror of Britain, had looked at it over the narrow waters and had been told by an Irish exile that he could conquer it with one legion, that legion was never dispatched.

In consequence, Gaelic institutions evolved directly from Aryan origins in the mists of prehistory, and the memory of the race, as well as its evidences, was not erased by the dynamic civilizing energy of the Romans.

The important point about Gaelic society is that it was different in its major shapes from the societies of western Europe which emerged from Roman and Teutonic conjunctions.

It was an unprogressive, static society, locked in institutions which warred against change, backward-looking, in love with the past, parochial in attachments and outlook. It was rural and uncommercial, having neither cities nor towns; it lacked the civil offices of the Roman system; it had its own code of written law, called Brehon, but no legislature, and enforcement of judgments was left to public opinion. The family, or sept, constituted the basic unit of society: families, starting with the great-grandfather and extending through four generations to include relationship up to second cousins, held property in common, and inheritance was not by individuals but by the family group under the system of gavelkind. Although a school of Irish scholars disowns the word, the social structure closely resembled the tribal.

The Gaelic world had its own language, which was nationwide, a proud possession, one of the original languages of Europe, and Ireland was the first of the western European nations to turn the language of the people into a national literature. A native and distinctive literature, including the rich cycle of legends, was the highest point of its cultural progress. Imaginative power seems to have been the gift possessed in outstanding measure by the peoples to whom the name Celtic is attached.

The basic political, or territorial, unit of the Gaelic structure was the *tuath,* the independent and self-sufficient commune, of which there were between eighty and one hundred, each ruled by a king. There were enough kings in Gaelic Ireland to furnish ancestors for the Irish-American claimants to descent from a royal line, only that Irish kings (with the exception of the powerful families) had about the majestic status of county commissioners.

Gaelic Ireland never developed politically beyond the state of local autonomy: it was interested in the ward, not the national capital. It resisted with the force that local attachments and loyalties can generate every centralizing tendency by ambitious kings or the foreigners. This overriding particularism, reinforced by the family pride and jealousy of the petty territorial kings, frustrated the evolution toward the feudal centralized state which was taking place elsewhere in western Europe.

The kings rarely ceased warring on one another. "Any page of the Irish Annals," wrote Eoin MacNeil, the modern scholar, "will suffice to exemplify how from the sixth to the sixteenth century the personal fortunes of rulers and magnates counted in public affairs above everything else." They contended within their domains with kinsmen. "O'Conor Don was constantly at war with O'Conor Roe," wrote one historian, "and both with O'Conor Sligo." They left as a heritage the bitter factionalism of the counties in later Ireland.

A half century before Gaelic Ireland went down under the captains of Elizabeth, the powerful leader of the North, Shane O'Neill, was issuing the prideful ultimatum: "My ancestors were kings of Ulster and Ulster is mine and shall be mine." In the middle of the sixteenth century, it was still Ulster, not Ireland.

As genealogists, the Irish made the Daughters of the American Revolution look like scrubby amateurs. A caste of poets (or learned men) peculiar to Gaelic Ireland, the like of which in character, power, and influence is not found in the history of other nations, were the genealogists of kings and noble families, hereditary in post, their persons untouchable and their settlement of estates comfortable. Never, anywhere or at any time, have poets (or bards, as they were later called) had it so good as in Gaelic Ireland. They were the recorders of deeds as well as the colleges of heraldry, singing the names and glory of the ancestry of the noble families they served.

No body of men, even to the day of their poverty-stricken decline, was so responsible for keeping alive the Irish sense of oneness in blood and culture and the uniqueness of the Gaelic tradition. They were the custodians and the guardians of its title-deeds.

2

The Irish Face of the Church

THE IMPORTANT DATE in Gaelic Ireland — "*the* crucial date," one student calls it — is 432 A.D., the coming of St. Patrick. When he died thirty years later, pagan Ireland was well on the way to being

Christianized. Patrick's conquest was more enduring than that of any of the invaders — Dane, Norman, and English — who swarmed over Ireland; he captured the spirit, and his impress has remained the characteristic of the race. The Irish made of St. Patrick, wrote Mrs. Alice Stopford Green, "the very embodiment of the national soul, its surety and defender." What he wrought originally came overseas in the miserable holds of nineteenth-century emigrant ships, in the hearts and minds of the Irish passengers, to be passed on in America to their children and their children's children.

St. Patrick was not an intellectual or even a learned man, as he himself admitted; on the other hand, he was no fanatic. Probably the best word to characterize his successful mission in Ireland is "understanding." He knew the secret of all great colonizers, which is to merge and not impose the new idea.

What St. Patrick did was to blanket druidism, the pagan rites of the Gael, by the Christian religion without disturbing the Gaelic secular institutions or challenging the vested interests of the rulers. The Gael as Christian remained a Gael; and the Church became as natural a part of the Irish landscape as the fields, meadows, hills, woods, and bogs. The Gael stopped chanting pagan incantations and began singing hymns. He discarded the pagan names of the great seasonal feasts and observed them in honor of the saints. The wonder-working of the druids became the miracles of the new holy men. Relics supplanted the old magical charms. "No other race," said Renan, "showed such originality in its way of taking Christianity."

One hundred years after the death of St. Patrick, the Church had the Irish face of the faithful.

St. Patrick followed the Roman ecclesiastical organization of bishop, cathedral church, diocese and parish, the practical and efficient order inherited from imperial Rome, but the Irish had their own ideas of what they wanted and in due time, far removed from the watchful eye of Rome, the Irish Church, in structure, discipline and administration, was conformed to the Gaelic ways, though one hundred per cent orthodox in doctrine.

The Gaelic world took the new religion with all the zeal of the converted and its own temperamental disposition towards excess. Under Eastern influence, transmitted through Gaul, the Irish adopted the primitive Church of the desert, asceticism as the rule, the hermit as the ideal. Enraptured and penitential individuals built rude retreats, generally near the sacred places of the old pagan dispensation, and, in due course, followers came to share their austere life.

The first cenobitic enthusiasm was tempered in time by another Gaelic passion — that of learning; and out of the original huts grew the great Irish monastic schools, one or two approximating universities, which received students from England (Alcuin was trained at Clonmasnoise) and the Continent, and in turn sent their missionaries and scholars abroad in the Golden Age. And for centuries the monastery, rather than the church, was the typical Irish religious institution. The ruins of the abbeys which today dot the Irish countryside are reminders of Ireland's long monastic past.

The successful fusion of pagan and Christian Ireland released energies that burst forth into achievements that won Ireland the name, ever precious and ever remembered, of "the isle of saints and scholars."

The work of the Irish missionaries and scholars, from the sixth to the ninth centuries, in spreading Christianity to Britain and to the heartlands of Western civilization and keeping alive classical learning in areas where darkness had settled, was the greatest contribution of the Irish to Western culture. In the midst of the Saracen threat, Ireland and Scandinavia, as Arnold Toynbee has pointed out, were the reservoirs of Christian strength from which a fight back could be made had Mohammedanism won a military victory.

The Irishness, if you will, of the Irish Church was a source of deep anger to a group of twelfth-century clerical reformers, most of whom had been educated abroad and compared unfavorably its unneat state with the great Universal Church in England and on the Continent. Secularization of the Church had appeared in the eighth century. As with kings and chieftains in the political sphere, control by succession of the multiplied monasteries was confined to the blood-line families to which the founders belonged, thus honoring the solid Gaelic custom of keeping good things within the circle of relatives. After a century of agitation and effort, the reformers won and the major goal was attained: conformity of the Irish ecclesiastical organization to the Roman.

The humble character of the Irish Church, in contrast to the splendor of the medieval Church on the Continent, was not better illustrated than by the example of its titular head, Gelasius, Bishop of Armagh, walking to Dublin to receive the new decrees of the reform-

ers' council accompanied by his cow, which furnished him milk on the
journey.

A new order of national heroes grew out of the monastic organization
of Christianity in Ireland — the saints. "Emain and Tara [symbols of
pagan Ireland] had passed away," wrote James F. Kenney, the historian
of the early Irish Church, "but Armagh and Kildare [sees of St. Patrick
and St. Brigid] were to endure forever."

2

Ancient Gaelic Ireland left a deep impression on the Irish mind, in
the shaping of which it played so enduring a part. It was the period of
the heroic age — of the legendary warriors who had become as flesh
and blood in the thoughts of the Irish: Cuchulain, Maeve, Finn Mc-
Cool and his warrior Fianna, of Ossian, Oscar and Diarmuid. It was the
age of the great kings — Art, Cormac, Niall and Brian Boru, whose
mention evoked the long continuity of the race. It was the era of the
saints, honored names to a people who scaled their religion as life's
worthiest value. It was the day of the scholars, like John Scotus
"Eriugena," John the Irishman, the neo-Platonist schoolman, a bold
thinker and precursor of medieval scholasticism, and the two Irish
scholars "who came in a trading ship to France, and stood with the rest
of the merchants crying in the fair that they had wisdom to sell." It was
the age when the Irish from the perimeter of Europe strung a hundred
and more monasteries through the land of the barbarians on the mainland and beat a pilgrim's path down to Rome, "walking the world" for
the love of God.

3

Ireland's Isolation Is Broken

THE SILENCE of the watery wastes around Ireland was disturbed in the last years of the eighth century by the longboats of the
Norsemen, who came first as raiders and then as settlers. The Danes, as
the Irish called them, introduced the corporate idea in Ireland by building the first towns: Dublin, Wexford, Waterford, Cork, and Limerick;

and the Danes brought out of his petty principality in the fastness of
north Munster the "only Irish king who has acquired a position in
European history," Brian Boru. By his will, strength, and diplomacy, a
man who knew what he wanted, which happened to be what Ireland
needed, Brian, for the first and last time in the Gaelic world, united Ireland under one command; and when Brian had his name inscribed in
the *Book of Armagh* as Emperor of the Irish, this, said the historian
Curtis, "was the greatest moment in the history of native Ireland."
Brian set the pattern for a national life, but he died at the moment of
high triumph, when his national army on Good Friday, April 21,
1014, defeated the Danes and their allies from the Orkneys and asserted Gaelic supremacy over the invaders. A fleeing Viking had split
Brian's head, and that axe shattered the tenuous political unity held together by his dominance. They waked Brian for twelve days, gave him
the greatest funeral Gaelic Ireland had ever seen, and before the
mourning sighs had quieted, the kingly factions were at it again.

2

The great medieval period was for Ireland four hundred years of barren and sterile civil war in which any possible development was stifled
by a combination of clashing arms and miserable foreign rule, at the
end of which an official English state paper would say, in 1515,
"there is no land in the world of so long continual war within himself,
ne of so great shedding of Christian blood, ne of so great robbing,
spoiling, preying, and burning, ne of so great wrongful extortion continually as Ireland."

It began with Irish treachery in the great twelfth-century sellout.

Dermot MacMurrough, King of Leinster, trained by an old abbot in
the heroic sagas and filled with the dream of elevating his house to the
high kingship, was expelled for the cruelties of his ambition and turned
to Henry II, the Angevin King of England, for help. The large mind of
Henry grasped the opportunity to serve two purposes at once. He had
contemplated the conquest of Ireland and, to that end, had armed himself with the sanction of the English Pope Adrian IV on the pretext of
reforming Ireland to Christian ways; and he wanted to get rid of some
Norman nobles in the marches of Wales, part Welsh by intermarriage,
down at the heel, and hatching traitorous schemes. Dermot was referred
to these adventurers, and Ireland was vigorously shocked out of its isola-

tion by a king of England who could speak no English, by an English Pope in Italy, and by Norman freebooters leading an army of Welsh and Flemish archers out of Wales in 1170.

Right at the start the major fact of England's relationship to Ireland through the long centuries of forced association was established. Richard de Clare, the Earl of Pembroke, known as Strongbow, the Norman leader, might have gone on to be king of Ireland, which would have been good, had not Henry, who disliked ambitious feudal barons, appeared in Ireland in 1171 with an army and speedily asserted his own supremacy. England could make its military power decisive in Irish affairs whenever the chips were down. And, as Dean Swift so bitingly put it, "eleven men, well armed, will certainly subdue one single man in his shirt."

England failed to make a complete conquest of Ireland, as William the Conqueror had in England, but effected, in Trevelyan's striking phrase, "a lodgment in medieval Ireland, and hung on like a hound that has its fangs in the side of the stag." England was too weak to govern Ireland but strong enough to prevent Ireland from governing itself — that was the tragedy of the incomplete Anglo-Norman invasion.

3

After the initial shock of the invasion, Ireland entered into a long period of civil war within civil war within civil war, like a Chinese magic box. King continued to fight king in the traditional Gaelic manner; the native Irish pressed against the Anglo-Norman nobles; and the kings and chieftains slashed at the settlements of the English colonists. King Richard II at the end of the fourteenth century aptly described the harried country as divided among "the wild Irish, our enemies; English rebels; and obedient English."

An interesting thing happened to the descendants of the Norman invaders. The original Fitzgeralds, DeLacys, DeBurgos, and FitzStephens disdained the native Irish; their offspring and heirs looked upon the "wild Irish" as but little removed from barbarians; yet they had by the time of Elizabeth, in the words of the poet Edmund Spenser, "degenerated from their ancient dignities and are now grown as Irish as O'Hanlon's breeches." Or, in Dr. Lynch's more famous and inspired phrase, *Hibernis ipsis hiberniores,* that is, they were more Irish than the

Irish. They spoke Irish, intermarried with the Irish, and adopted Irish customs. "The triumph of Irish civilization," wrote Kenney, "was greater than that of Irish arms."

They resisted English rule as directed from Dublin by viceroy and parliament, on one hand; they held off the encroaching Irish, on the other. Hence, in their middle position, they were described as "rebels" to differentiate them from the Irish "enemies" and the "obedient" English.

The "obedient" English were the official class and settlers and traders, an enclave of foreigners surrounded by hostile Irish and proud and sullen Anglo-Norman nobles, hewing tenaciously to the English language and ways, uninterested in Ireland except as a means to fatten their own purses or further their careers.

"Like a spear-point embedded in a living body," wrote Lecky, this English rule of the Pale "inflamed all around it and deranged every vital function."

4

The decrees of this Anglo-Ireland ran only to the narrow confines of the borders it could safeguard — the Pale, as it was called. To conquer Ireland required an expenditure which England balked at underwriting; and the ferocious Irish were rolling back the spread of the first invasion. So England limited its commitment to the Pale it could defend, and engaged to dam by law the magnetic absorbing power by the Irish of the English; in other words, as they saw it, to stop the English from sliding into the Irish bog, "degenerating" into "mere," that is, pure Irish.

This intention was written into the notorious Statute of Kilkenny in 1366 — a medieval predecessor of Hitler's Nuremberg laws and the early application of the "No Irish Need Apply" advertisement.

Those who wished to remain in the English Pale under English law were forbidden to intermarry with the Irish, to use the Irish language, law, and dress. They were ordered to drop Irish names and substitute English. Irish clerics were shut out from English cathedrals, benefices, and religious houses. Irish poets, rhymers, and minstrels were not to be entertained, Irish games were not to be played or horses ridden in the Irish style. The Statute of Kilkenny was an arrogant expression of English cultural superiority over the Irish manner of life, which it subjected to the criminal code. It established that separation of races, with the Irish segregated as inferior, which confounded future relationships in Ireland and it was an ingredient of Irish hatred.

While the medieval world was abustle with activity, Ireland retrograded. Perhaps the most telling illustration of its backwardness is that not one university was founded in Ireland during the medieval age.

5

Everywhere were the humble native Irish, the cowherds, the laborers, the servants, the drawers of water, and the hewers of wood, the most useful of all the classes, whose broad backs supported the primitive economy.

George Siegerson, the Irish historian, has described their continuing state:

> The English and Irish combatants looked down on them as hinds and churls, unfit for fighting, but apt to produce rent and cattle. Disinclined for war and revolts, if not pressed into them by intolerable oppression, they remained, even through Cromwell's transplantations, the one comparatively fixed element in Irish social history — a settled substratum.

These humble workers were the reservoir of Irish strength and endurance. Their untutored minds, in which Catholic devotionalism overlay remnants of pagan magic, were the attic of Gaelic traditionalism; they were the repository of the old ways, investing the past days (regardless of how horrible they may have been) with the aura of a golden age.

4

The Irish Meet the Tudors

As THE MEDIEVAL PERIOD was drawing to a close, Ireland, though still divided and without a common focus for a national patriotism, had, except for one small semicircle looping inward from the Irish Sea, absorbed the Anglo-Norman invasion. But on August 22, 1485, at Bosworth Field, a Welshman, Henry Tudor, Earl of Richmond, smashed the Yorkist king, and great events were in the making for England during which Ireland was once more undone. Wrote Kenney:

> In the year 1500 English rule in Ireland . . . hardly extended thirty miles from Dublin. In 1603 the English king's writ ran undisputed from Malin Headland to Cape Clear. By 1700 every trace of the old Irish states and of their political and legal systems had disappeared.

Up to the sixteenth century Ireland had no history, strictly speaking: there was no nation, and events were local. The coming of the Tudors changed that. The Tudors decided to take Ireland in hand. The unwillingness of the Irish to be taken in hand forms the story from now on.

2

The Tudors loved power, order, money, and their own way; and as their calculating and intelligent gaze observed Ireland, they saw nothing in that "inconstant sea nymph," as Davies, the English Solicitor General in Ireland under James I, described it, to command their several affections. The fault with Ireland, they concluded, was that it was Irish; the way to redeem it to "humanity and civility," ran their logic, was to make it English.

But there was not one solid area of common ground from which a start could be made for a peaceful reconciliation between two civilizations that, neighbors by geography, were as far apart in other respects as the poles. England under the Tudors reached an advanced state in political unity, social homogeneity, and material progress, but these advantages were not the line of division which set off one land from the other. Irish civilization, in its fundamental orientations, was different and distinct from English. By origin, race, laws, language, tradition, scale of values, way of life, and, after Henry VIII's break with Rome, by religion, Irish civilization vibrated with refusal and rejection at whatever point English civilization impinged upon it.

The clash of the two civilizations during the sixteenth century unfolds a ghastly, bewildering, and murderous scene as confused as a panoramic picture of an old land battle, with foot soldiers mingled indistinguishably in melee, cavalry dashing out of side woodlots, standards raised in footless direction, and all around the dead and the dying.

The clash was bloodily played out against the tumults of the larger

European stage where the issue of Gaelic survival became entangled with the power politics of the Reformation, at the end of which England was victorious and Protestant, and Ireland defeated and Catholic.

3

Henry VIII did not contemplate a conquest of Ireland by violence when he turned his attention to its matters, but decided that Ireland could best be won "by sober ways, politic drifts, and amiable persuasions."

His plan was to feudalize Ireland with English law by the cooperation of the Irish chiefs made over into English lords by patents of nobility and by charters confirming them as sole landlords of their territory. For their own part, they would put away (as would their people) Irish things — names, dress, manners, customs, language.

What started out as a painless absorption under Henry became, as Irish resistance hardened under English pressures, a cold and sordid scramble for the fine Irish lands. Rebellion was provoked that its suppression might serve as pretext to share out Irish properties. Elizabethan adventurers, giddy for glory and gain, put their undoubted reckless courage on the point of the sword as the surest way to wring profits from the Irish land booms, saying that what they had grabbed without law they would hold by force.

4

Ironically, it was the Tudor Catholic Queen Mary who introduced into Catholic Ireland the hated engine of dispossession — the plantation of Irish lands by English settlers. Mary's ardent Catholicism was not so all-embracing as to include the Pope's faithful Irish children. In tormenting them, she was devoutly English and, according to Philip Wilson, historian of the period, had she lived twenty years and the harassing policy of her lord deputy been continued, "the Irish would have been the most violent Calvinists in Europe."

Mary, in 1556, seized the lands of the tumultuous O'Mores, O'Conors, and O'Dempseys, chieftains of their little nations, bordering on the Pale, moved the Irish tenants to the undesirable boglands, set the good lands out to the English, and placed King's and Queen's counties (renamed in honor of herself and her Spanish husband, Philip) under

English law. This was the pattern which later and more drastic confiscations followed, though this first settlement failed.

The Desmond revolt, divided into two phases, 1569-1573 and 1579-
1583, interests us for the policy into which the Gaelic chiefs and the
descendants of the Anglo-Normans had been forced by the invasion of
English rapacity on their lands. Father Ronan, the historian of the
Reformation period in Ireland, has stated it succinctly:

> The position . . . was that if the old Celtic system was to be
> saved, if the Catholic Church was to be preserved in Ireland, the
> whole country must combine, and thus combined must appeal to
> Spain and Rome for help in the struggle that was now inevitable.

This weight-of-power idea from now on haunted the Irish mind. It
rested on the premise that Ireland lacked sufficient resources in men
and arms to throw out England and that the balance must be sought
among the Catholic powers of Europe — Spain, France, or Rome —
the "Wine of the Royal Pope" and "Spanish Ale," as the poets expressed
it.

The Desmonds, sprung from the first Anglo-Norman Fitzgerald,
owned a half million acres of land in the south of Ireland and, though
ennobled, lived like great Gaelic chieftains. A group of English adventurers, gentlemen of Somersetshire and Devon out to make their fortunes, Gilberts, Chichesters, Carews, Grenvilles, and Courtneys, petitioned the Queen for permission to move in on Ireland, seize land by
title claims and hold it by force.

The resisting Desmonds, along with a small force of Italians and
Spaniards, were bloodily crushed and their rich estates confiscated in
the second spoliation of Irish lands: some two hundred thousand acres
were put out to plantation to the English — "undertakers," as they
were called. While many English undertakers resigned the task as hopeless in turbulent Ireland, a number remained in Cork, Kerry, and Limerick, the old Desmond country.

5

Elizabeth had held to the policy of her father — "sober ways,
politic drifts, and amiable persuasions" — and for the same reason: she
hated to spend money in any circumstance and she hated particularly
to throw money down the Irish boghole. She had to be dragooned into

consent for military suppression of the Desmond revolt. But no uncertain fluctuations troubled her last fateful act in Ireland once a firm commitment had been made in her mind and will to extirpate the "Arch Traitor" Hugh O'Neill, Earl of Tyrone and lord of the combined Irish forces of the North in Ulster.

Hugh O'Neill was the last, and, by many, thought the greatest of Gaelic chiefs. Educated in England, a modern man in outlook and feeling as compared with the run of Irish chieftains, acquainted with the facts of high-power politics and the making of war, he embodied in the defeat that was the Gaelic national patriotism that might have been.

At the heart of the Tyrone rebellion, which extended over nine years, was the mutual distrust of the Gael and the Englishman. O'Neill saw the dilemma of the Gael: to submit tamely to English rule meant a lingering but inevitable destruction of Gaelic life; to resist, invited the same ruthless fate as the Desmonds'.

His country, Ulster in the north, the most Gaelic part of Ireland, was the last fortress of the native Gael and, when it fell, Gaelic Ireland went into the grave.

O'Neill and his allies fought well and obstinately. O'Neill came the closest to making a national Gaelic rally of the chieftains, but it was far from complete. England sent her best captains to rough it with O'Neill, after the failure of Elizabeth's favorite Essex; and the wisest and the best, Mountjoy, found the successful way to fight a war in the difficult province of Ulster: guerdon it with fortresses, lay waste its provisions and choke and starve it to death. But the final defeat did not come in Ulster. O'Neill and O'Donnell, his strong Ulster ally, broke through the English blockade to relieve the hemmed-in Spaniards who had landed in Kinsale in the south of Ireland — exactly the wrong place to set down their expedition — and the Ulster forces were themselves routed, on Christmas Eve, 1601, helping the foreigners who had come to help them.

Elizabeth's arms, money, will, and pride had shattered a two-thousand-year-old civilization beyond repair. Gaelic Ireland was dead and Catholic Ireland took its place. Of the wreck of Gaelic institutions, Catholicism survived.

5

The Irish Reject the Reformation

THE ROMAN CATHOLICISM which Irish emigrants carried with them to America in the nineteenth century was the product of the victory by the Counter-Reformation in Ireland over the attempt by England to impose Protestantism on a hostile, stubborn, and rebellious people through political coercion. Given the nature of the Irish and the circumstances of the forced conversion, the attempt was doomed from the start, and in its course a merger between the Gaelic Irish and the Old English, as the colonists of English blood and the heirs of the Normans were called, was effected which would have been remote, if not impossible, but for the common defense of their religion.

The Gaelic Church needed reorganization from the ravages of medieval commotion, but none of the conditions which underlay the Reformation in Europe existed in isolated Ireland. Since there was no organized state in the Gaelic parts of Ireland but local autonomies, the intimate association of Church and State which distinguished medieval Europe did not obtain. The pomp and grandeur of the medieval Church on the Continent was not found in the Irish countryside. As Gaelic Ireland was poor, so also was the Gaelic Church. No prosperous prelacy contrasted with the poverty of the people to raise the cry of ecclesiastical abuses. Instead, there was a clergy close to the people, as old Gelasius with his traveling cow had been, and the closing of the monasteries dispersed the begging friars among the poor, "secure of a ministry which no one was willing to share with them." There was no emerging middle class seeking its place in power at the expense of ancient clerical property and privilege.

There was no education worth the mention. There was no university as seed ground for doubts or critical examination of creed: Bishop Tanner wrote in 1571 that "not a hundred Irishmen in all Ireland have been infected with heresy."

Irish priests, zealous, disciplined and trained under the stern dispositions of the Counter-Reformation, were taking spiritual laxness into their hands, as Spenser observed, who compared their ardors with the idleness of the ministers of the new faith of England:

> Wherein it is great wonder to see the odds which are between the zeal of Popish priests and the ministers of the Gospel. For they spare not to come out of Spain, from Rome and from Rheims, by long toil and dangerous travelling hither, where they know peril of death awaiteth them and no reward or riches are to be found, only to draw the people unto the Church of Rome.

The religious reforms of Henry VIII came to Ireland in a manner that offended the people into refusal and rejection — as part of the political deal with chiefs to Anglicize the country, looking to the eventual proscription of everything Irish, including religion.

It took the capricious and stupid intervention of Henry's new ministers in Ireland administering the official religion to bring home to the shocked Irish just what the change meant to the old ways they did not want changed. Articles to which the Irish attached great veneration (instruments of superstition and idolatry, the new ministers called them) were desecrated. In direct violation of the principle established as fundamental by the Continental reformers, who taught the new religion in the language of the country, the English reformers used the English language, though only a small minority of the people understood it; and when that fact became apparent, the use of Latin as an alternative was permitted, "a language," Lord Clare later observed, "as intelligible to the congregation as the English."

The best men of the English Reformation could not be persuaded to go to Ireland. Administration was entrusted, for the most part, to either time-servers or fanatics, with a deep hatred of Popery. If the new religion they preached was abhorrent to unshakable Irish orthodoxy, the caliber of the new clergy inspired the Irish with ferocious contempt. "If the Irish wist how," one reformed bishop was told, "they would eat you."

2

As Catholicism fashioned an Irish nationalism, so an English nationalism attached itself to Protestantism. In Ireland, Catholicism was the means by which the Gaelic identity was preserved. In England, Protestantism was identified with English liberties threatened both at home and abroad by Catholic power.

Henry VIII's new religion was essentially Catholicism trimmed of Rome to accord with the will of a national absolute monarchy. Mary, his daughter by Catherine of Aragon and wife of Philip of Spain, willed the restoration of the old religion, including allegiance to the Papacy, when she reached the throne, set the fires of persecution burning, and earned for herself the name of "Bloody Mary." Mary's deeds were to be remembered and Catholicism reviled for hundreds of years, even on the frontiers of an expanding America, because a literate man recorded them in John Foxe's *Book of Martyrs*. The Irish as Catholics, though Mary loved them not, were to suffer for her acts perpetuated in John Foxe's book and incorporated in the general indictment of Catholicism. As one historian wrote:

> For the burnings did more than anything else to generate the "unthinking, ferocious, and almost indelible" hatred which generations of otherwise tolerant and short-memoried Englishmen were to nourish towards Rome. Not for nothing was Foxe's "Book of Martyrs" to become the most widely read and possessed of English classics, nor a score of memorials to testify to Protestantism's fiery confirmation.

The long war of nerves between Elizabeth's England and the Catholic power of Europe, coming to explosion in the Armada expedition, coincided with the vigorous efforts of the Catholic Counter-Reformation to infiltrate, penetrate, and win back Protestant England, involving plots against the life of the Queen. Philip of Spain and the Pope became hated and feared names; Jesuit was synonymous with secret agent, spy, and traitor, eager to undermine the security of England for foreign masters; Catholic power was dreaded as the international conspiracy from which England might be undone; and Catholicism represented all that was un-English.

In this way, Protestantism was identified with — and Catholicism against — the national cause of England, and wrapped up in the evolving intense patriotism.

6

Ireland Is Confiscated

GAELIC IRELAND laid down its life upon the submission in 1603 of the Irish chiefs to the English, and the process was accelerated of clearing the ruined structure and wiping out its traces. English law supplanted Irish law, and the English judicial system, with courts, justices, sheriffs, and juries, was installed everywhere.

2

If the sixteenth century wrote a black page in the Catholic Irish story, the seventeenth was to write a blacker still. Irish hopes quickened on the accession of the Stuart, James I, thought secretly sympathetic to the Catholic cause, as successor of Elizabeth. But James, left with the problem of what to do with Ireland, solved it by creating the enduring Irish problem, the Ulster Settlement.

O'Neill, O'Donnell, the leading men of Ulster, and their families had fled abroad, fearing that greed for the lands restored to them would soon be the cause of attainder, trial, and imprisonment. A flare-up by a minor Irish chief was the pretext for the English to declare Ulster forfeited — six counties embracing some five hundred thousand acres. The English carried out a resettlement project that, avoiding the mistake of Elizabeth's large and unwieldy grants of the Desmond confiscation, parceled out Ulster in estates of one thousand, fifteen hundred, and two thousand acres to the undertakers. To forestall absenteeism, it was stipulated that the estates must be worked by English or Scottish Protestants (King James especially favored his subject Scots), who would build and live on the ground they cultivated and act as an English military garrison in Ireland.

An alien farming class, mostly Scottish and English sectaries, the extremest and most confirmed Protestants, was established in Ulster where the Gaelic tradition had survived the longest. The trespassing of Scottish and English Protestants upon Catholic land poisoned the confiscation with a religious party bitterness that time only deepened. The division of the country on the most incendiary of all possible lines, the religious, was well under way. Religion had become politics.

3

The Ulster confiscation, though bitter, was but the entrance to the dark valley Ireland went through under Oliver Cromwell.

The Cromwell Terror summed up in one fierce period all the ravages visited by alien hostile rule upon Ireland during the long centuries of forced association; it was a concentration of malignancy, more vicious by its cloak of godliness. In 1952, General Eisenhower, campaigning in New England for the presidency of the United States, offhandedly mentioned the name of Oliver Cromwell with praise, and almost instinctively the Catholic Irish reacted with the shock of outrage and protest. Three hundred years in time and a country separated several thousand miles in space had not effaced the memory of Cromwell from the blood of a people he had hurt. The "curse of Cromwell" is fixed in the Irish vocabulary, no matter where the scattered race dwells. Ireland still says, "Cromwell, though dead for others, survives for me."

4

The English Civil War opened a war front in Ireland with a general uprising in Ulster in 1641 when the dispossessed Catholic Irish chieftains struck to redress their grievances and get back their estates by force. The maddened Irish fell upon the Protestant planters in what the Puritans called the "great massacre" of hundreds of thousands, later whittled down by historians to some ten thousand, and on the basis of which the Puritan Parliament pledged the lands of Ireland to investors for funds to put down the rebellion. The Old English Catholics in Ireland, who feared that their estates were next in line for confiscation, joined with the native Irish in an uneasy and suspicious alliance, each side with its own army.

In England, the Puritan Parliament had found its leader in Oliver Cromwell. In the summer of 1649, Cromwell landed in Ireland with an army of intense sectaries and in a campaign that gave no quarter to the Irish battered down the rebellion, leaving the trail of the merciless executioner and despoiler behind him. After Cromwell had murdered the surrendered garrison at Drogheda and finished off the innocent civilians, men, women, and children, he wrote to Bradshaw, President of the Council:

> Truly, I believe this bitterness will save much effusion of blood through the goodness of God. I wish that all honest hearts may give the glory of this to God alone, to whom the praise of this mercy belongs.

The priests were his especial quarry: he pitilessly put them to death at Drogheda and at his next stop, Wexford, where he repeated his bloodletting. He took Waterford and ordered New Ross to surrender. Asked there if he would permit liberty of conscience, he replied:

I meddle not with any man's conscience, but if by liberty of conscience, you mean liberty to exercise the Mass, I judge it best to
use plain dealing, and to let you know that where the power of
Parliament of England have power that will not be allowed of.

The Protestants of Ireland rallied to the side of Cromwell; in March,
1650, Kilkenny, the seat of the Irish Confederacy, surrendered and
in May Cromwell returned to England, leaving to his son-in-law, Ire-
ton, the mopping up of the last Irish resistance from retreats in the
West.

Now came the Cromwellian Settlement. All Ireland was declared
forfeited. The lands of Roman Catholics in the three provinces of
Ulster, Leinster, and Munster were planted with Protestants, and
Roman Catholic proprietors who could not clear themselves of complicity in the rebellion were transplanted to the unfavorable province
of Connacht (hence the phrase, "To Hell or Connacht") and to
County Clare, of which it was said "there is not water to drown a
man, wood enough to hang one, nor earth enough to bury him." The
confiscated lands were parceled out to the investors who had financed
the war — the Cromwellian settlers who became the Protestant Ascendancy — and to Cromwell's soldiers in lieu of pay.

Catholic military officers and men who elected to follow them were
granted permission to take service in foreign armies, and companies
marched off to ships for Spain, France, Austria, and the Republic of
Venice, with the bands playing, "We return, we return no more" —
thirty-four thousand of the best men in Ireland, lost forever to the
country of their birth but to add to the fame of their land under foreign ensigns.

The waifs of the war, women of marriageable age, young girls and
boys, were rounded up, at so much a head, from the pauper houses or
the roads of the countryside and shipped off to the lonely planters in
the West Indies as hands, servants, or for whatever other uses the
owners saw fit, or unfit — altogether some six thousand of these poor
derelicts.

Out of the Cromwellian Settlement came the Catholic Irish nation,
as so eloquently described by the English historian Gardiner:

The hand of the Englishman was everywhere felt, with the result
that the spirit of Irish nationality had never risen higher than on
the day when its outward manifestation seemed hopelessly broken
to the ground, because it found a home in the breasts of all who,

from whatever race they might be descended, were treated as outcasts on account of their devotion to the Roman Catholic religion. Two centuries before the English sovereigns had been confronted by a congeries of Irish tribes. The English Commonwealth was confronted by an Irish nation.

7
The Conquest Is Completed

DURING THE BRIEF PERIOD of the Commonwealth, the Irish clergy, the particular bane of the Puritans, were harassed and persecuted; a statute of Elizabeth was revived and they were given twenty days to get out of the kingdom; a group was rounded up and banished to penal islands off the west coast of Ireland. The priests were described, with wolves and Tories (native Irish guerrillas), as the beasts of which Ireland must be rid; and one of the deepest impressions left on the Catholic Irish mind, remembered even to the present, was that the head of a wolf and the head of a priest brought the same bounty.

The Irish had met with nothing but ill-fortune from the Stuart line, and James II, the last Stuart king, who tried to turn back the clock in England, upheld the tradition. William of Orange, the Dutch champion of the Protestant cause on the continent and the undying foe of Louis XIV of France, married to James's daughter, Mary, was welcomed in England in the bloodless revolution of 1688-1689 before which frightened James fled to France. James picked up courage, money, and a staff of officers from King Louis and landed in Ireland on the way back, he hoped, to the throne. The Irish faithfully came to the support of the Stuart as the rightful *de jure* king in the Williamite war, 1689-1691. Ireland became a battleground of the larger war between France and the Augsburg-Orange alliance. At the Boyne and at Aughrim, more than the future of Ireland was at stake — it was whether Louis was to fix his absolutism on Europe. But William won, leaving a name "of glorious and immortal memory" to be toasted at Orange celebrations in Ireland, and James retired, leaving in Ireland literally a bad name which cannot be repeated here. The so-called Williamite Confiscation of the lands of the defeated Catholics followed.

Patrick Sarsfield, the Irish commander and a venerated name among the Irish, capitulated at Limerick under honorable terms. The Irish army led by its commanders, the aristocratic leadership of the country, both Catholic English and Irish, sailed off to take service in France and on the Continent — and once more, as at the end of the 1641 rebellion, the energy and the intelligence which Ireland needed so badly was drained off, its veins opened. Fourteen thousand men were thus emigrated from Ireland.

"The youth and gentry of the Irish," said Sir Richard Cox, "were destroyed in the rebellion or gone to France; those who are left are destitute of horses, arms, money, capacity, and courage. Five out of six of the Irish are insignificant slaves, fit for nothing but to hew wood and draw water."

That was the judgment upon which the victorious English government and its allies, the new landlord class in Ireland, acted to keep the Irish as hewers of wood and drawers of water in as vicious and shameful legislation as ever was written by a civilized nation after tearing a treaty into scraps of paper — the penal code from whose scars Ireland is yet to be healed.

This did not break the Irish spirit; instead, out of "the constant pressure of sufferings that draw men to the unseen world," as Lecky said, "Catholicism acquired an almost undivided Empire over the affections and imaginations of the people." It made the Irish the most zealous Catholics in Europe.

The Irish and English Catholic holders of land who remained, with some exceptions, were submerged to the peasant level. Arthur Young, the great English student of Ireland, writing in the last quarter of the eighteenth century, said:

> Upon the whole, nineteen-twentieths of the kingdom changed hands from Catholic to Protestant. The lineal descendants of great families, once possessed of vast property, are now to be found all over the kingdom in the lowest situation, working as cottars.

A peace had finally settled over an Ireland that had been in tumult and rebellion since the Normans first set foot on its earth in the twelfth century, but it was "the ghastly tranquillity of exhaustion and despair. . . . The iron had entered the soul. The memory of past defeats, the habit of daily enduring insult and oppression, had cowed the spirit of the unhappy nation."

2

The penal code was not the product of religious fanaticism. What makes the penal code so infamous is that it was the use of religious discrimination as cold and calculated policy to maintain the economic, social, and political supremacy of a minority vested interest in a country not its own and assure the degradation of its ancient inhabitants.

Edmund Burke immortally characterized it:

> A machine of wise and elaborate contrivance, and as well fitted
> for oppression, impoverishment, and degradation of a people and
> the debasement in them of human nature, as ever proceeded from
> the perverted ingenuity of man.

The penal code, most of it written in the Irish Parliament, was wicked in itself, but its evil was compounded by the broken honor of the English in violating the Treaty of Limerick, which allowed Catholics a tolerance in religion, to establish it. William of Orange might have fulfilled that treaty but the English Parliament, the enemy of the Catholic Irish, had its way over the new king, who shrugged his shoulders.

The code was not written in one statute. It was begun in the reign of William; made "ferocious" (Burke's word) under Anne; and completed under the first two Georges. Rather than examine it chronologically, one can study it better in the perspective of its purposes.

The category which struck the Catholic Irish with the most horror aimed at the destruction and betrayal of family life. A Catholic owner of land was prohibited from bequeathing it as he pleased; the land had to be divided among his sons on equal shares, much in the same way as the old Gaelic law of gavelkind, but for a different reason: the purpose was to break up Catholic landholding by subdivision, making each holding smaller by successive inheritances. But (and this was the poisonous part) if the eldest son apostatized and renounced the Catholic religion, he became the sole owner of the property and immediately his father was inhibited from placing impediments on it; the father became the creature of the Protestant son; the son could disinherit the father.

Another category shut out Catholics from all departments of civil life. The Catholic could not vote. He could not become a member of parliament, or of local government. He could not be a member of the bar or sit on the bench or act as a magistrate. The grand jury was barred to him as were the vestries. No Catholic could serve as sheriff or solicitor, and the humble offices of gamekeeper or constable were by law denied him. He could not own arms, and to make sure he did not possess arms, his house was subject to raid. The army and the navy were closed to him. He could not possess a horse valued at more than five pounds, and a Protestant could claim a horse from a Catholic by paying him five pounds, no matter the real value of the animal.

The law, it was stated on two occasions, "does not suppose any such person to exist as a Roman Catholic."

A third category looked to the perpetuation of the landed interests in the hands of Protestant owners and the confinement of the Catholic Irish to the soil as tenants or laborers. No Catholic could buy land or inherit it or receive it as a gift from a Protestant. He could not hold a mortgage on land, or hold life annuities, or take a lease for more than thirty-one years. He was restricted in the lease to a profit that did not exceed one third of the rent — he received one penny out of each three earned: if the profit went beyond the one third permitted and the Catholic did not report it for a corresponding increase in rent, the farm passed to the first Protestant who made the discovery. If a Catholic secretly bought back his own forfeited estate, or any land owned by a Protestant, the first Protestant who informed on him became the proprietor of the land.

The next category sinned against the light and the spirit. The proscription on education, Lecky pointed out, was "universal, unqualified, and unlimited." The Catholic could not attend a university, in the upper reaches, and on the bottom was denied reading and writing. A Catholic could not keep a school, act as an instructor, or serve as private tutor — ten pounds was the reward for uncovering a papist schoolmaster. He could not send a son abroad to be educated. Schools open to him were proselytizing academies, their purpose to undermine his faith.

Checks were enacted to stop a Catholic from improvement or self-reliant enterprise. To prevent his carrying on trade in the cities, a burdensome tax, the quarterage, was imposed on him. A Catholic employer, save only in the linen trade, could not train more than two apprentices: skilled work was thus denied him. And as to shove his inferiority down his throat, a Catholic could not live within the confines of Limerick or Galway: squalid Irishtowns grew up outside the walls of the cities.

Direct legislation against the Roman Catholic Church sought to wither away the clergy and make its ministrations difficult and uncomfortable. To suppress the Church completely would have raised a popular revolution; besides, the strategy of the penal legislation was stated in the titles of the several acts — to "prevent the further growth of Popery." Under successive acts, the priest had to register; he could say Mass only in his own parish; and he could not have the assistance of a curate. If an unregistered priest was taken, he was subject to branding on the check. Neither chapel bells nor a cross could adorn a Catholic church, and violation of the prohibition against pilgrimages to holy wells brought the humiliation of a public whipping.

All Catholic archbishops, bishops, deans, vicars-general, and members of the regular orders were commanded to leave the country by a certain date, and fifty pounds was the reward to the discoverer who turned one up. If a dignitary returned after he had been banished, he was liable to be hanged, disemboweled, and quartered. By striking at the hierarchy, the lawmakers hoped to destroy the organization of the Church, and by the removal of faculties reserved to bishops, such as ordination, squelch a new generation of clergy. But bishops, as felons, defied the law or, merged with the peasants, carried on their functions in disguise, certain that no Catholic would move his lips or point his finger in betrayal.

3

In consequence of this calculated persecution priest and people were tied together in a unity sealed by the common lot of suffering, sacrifice, and the alien brand of parish — a relationship that has endured in the unbreakable compartment of the Irish mind and soul.

As Lecky said of the loyalty of the people:

> They clung to their old faith with a constancy that has never been surpassed, during generations of the most galling persecution, at a time when every earthly motive urged them to abandon it, when all the attraction and influence of property and rank and professional eminence and education were arrayed against it. They voluntarily supported their priesthood with an unswerving zeal, when they were themselves sunk in the most abject poverty, when the agonies of starvation were continually before them.

English policy, as Philip Wilson has pointed out, was responsible for the authority of the priest among the people, though the English characterized the Irish as the most priest-ridden people in Europe. English policy had eliminated the native aristocracy and leadership, shut the natives out from landed property, denied them education, merged the priest and people by common oppression, and insulted the sentiments of the people by a constant parade of anti-national feeling, so that patriotism and Catholicism were synonymous and the clergy became the recognized and accepted leaders of the Catholic Irish.

4

The destruction of their social order in the sixteenth and seventeenth centuries and the usurpation of their lands forced the Gaelic people to make hard accommodation to a new set of conditions under the worst circumstances. The amazing fact is that, though subjected to a vigorous and ordered culture, they remained essentially Irish.

The Anglicization of the courts and the flood of settlers mixing with the Irish on farms and at markets and fairs spread the use of English. The Irish learned it principally from the Cromwellians. They applied to the new language the rhythm, the peculiar constructions, and turn of phrase of the Gaelic; they translated into English the poetic quality of the Gaelic and retained the racy native idiom in its expression. The mixture of English and Irish produced the brogue, which once fixed retained the old-fashioned English of its origin.

During the last fifteen years of the sixteenth century, there entered into Ireland, how and when are not definitely known, the potato, which was revolutionary in its impact. By 1657, according to George O'Brien, the Irish economist, the potato was the staple food of the poor, the index of a low living standard.

8

The Protestant Century

IN THE EIGHTEENTH CENTURY, Catholic Ireland went underground to that hidden Ireland which the Irish writer, Daniel Corkery, unforgettably pictured as "a paralytic body where one half of it is dead or just dragged about by the other." The Irish peasantry was the last element of a once intact society to hold to the old Gaelic loyalties and the remnants of the old Gaelic life.

In the eighteenth century, it was the turn of the Protestants to show a resistance to English government, and it was the time, too, when the name of America grew in influence.

In a series of measures, starting with the Act of 1660, the English Parliament regulated the sizable Irish export trade practically to a standstill; stopped the importation of Irish cattle, sheep, swine and their products; hit at competitive Irish shipping and destroyed Irish trade with the colonies. But the hardest blow was the erasing in 1698 of the Irish woolen trade, which doomed Ireland to agricultural production and excluded the industrial revolution.

In protest, a small group of Anglo-Irish began an agitation which broadened into a fight for the legislative independence of Ireland.

Jonathan Swift, William Molyneux, and Charles Lucas, advocating Irish right to free trade and free laws, laid the intellectual groundwork for the later struggle of Catholic Ireland with England. The efforts of these men were qualified, in that the liberty they asked for themselves was not to be extended to the Catholic Irish. Nevertheless, the indivisibility of liberty here worked its fertile ways, and the Catholic Irish eventually benefited.

In the final quarter of the eighteenth century, under the pressures of the American Revolution, another Anglo-Irish generation won a short-lived legislative independence. (Ireland had had an ancient parliament of nobles, but it could not be called, or its legislation adopted, without the consent of the king and council in London.)

A small group of Protestant aristocrats held five sixths of the landed property and controlled the government, law, revenue, army, navy, magistracy, local governments, and the whole patronage of Ireland. General political corruption was open and unashamed, from bribed ministers at the top to self-serving local rule at the bottom. Ministers had their price in money or titles; patrons filled the pension lists to groaning with followers; seats in parliament were on the cash-and-carry basis. Corruption grew luxuriantly in the soil of Protestant aristocratic Ascendancy Ireland. The eighteenth century was the age of grandeur for the Anglo-Irish Ascendancy, in architecture, letters, and the drama, but it was hell for the Catholic Irish.

The Dissenters, Protestants of the nonconformist conscience, mostly

Presbyterians, despised the Catholics and were themselves despised — and abused — by the Established Church Protestants. They were the poor relatives in an unrecognized branch of Protestantism, generally of humble stock, descendants of the Scottish settlers who had been planted in Ulster by James, to whose number had been added farmers come from Scotland at the turning of the eighteenth century (not less than fifty thousand families from 1688 to 1715), and a commercial and industrial class in the towns.

Their lot was not an easy one. A sacramental test kept them from office and property qualifications from the elective franchise. Their enterprise was stricken by the blow to the Irish woolen industry. They were rack-rented, tithed, and subject to famine and depression.

Economic adversities urged them to emigrate from Ulster to America — for essentially the same reasons that moved the Catholic Irish in the nineteenth century. Between 1730 and 1770, more than half the Presbyterian population of Ulster came to America, contributing a strong stock to the new country.

The Catholics, in the meantime, had started to win relief from the penal laws. Because the Catholic Irish were (at long last) completely indifferent to the fate of the Pretender Stuart's uprising in Scotland in 1745, the Lord Lieutenant, Chesterfield, of the famous Letters, relaxed the enforcement of the religious clauses and, as a concession (the English needed manpower), Catholics were allowed to join the English army.

Emboldened by the relaxation of the penal laws — but not too emboldened — three Catholic Irish gentlemen, in 1756, organized a Catholic Committee to petition humbly for the redress of Catholic grievances and began a movement that broadened in the next century into the constitutional agitation for self-government in which the Catholic Irish in the United States cooperated vigorously.

This was a timid, almost apologetic, bid, cautious and unaggressive. In the early 1760s, however, in Munster, where Irish spirit was always high, the Catholic Irish peasants, made desperate by despotic circumstances, broke out in local organized action against the enclosure of lands that by long Gaelic custom had been common and against tithes and rack rents. They wore white shirts as protective disguise and hence their name of "Whiteboys," the successors of the Tories and Rapparees, who were the partisan irregulars, and the predecessors of the agrarian secret societies. The outbreaks were local and economic, without political or religious affiliations; but they started a form of rough justice in self-protection and redress of grievance, in lieu of impartial justice in courts, that was to flame in guerrilla warfare for the next hundred years.

At the same time, the harassed Dissenters in the north of Ireland similarly took the law into their own hands for the same reasons as the "Whiteboys" in the south. As "Hearts of Oak Boys" and later as "Hearts of Steel Boys," they resisted physically, through organized secret societies, the oppression of rents, tithes, and other economic abuses.

This Protestant movement assumed a sinister aspect with the organization of the "Peep-of-Day Boys," so called from their early morning attacks upon the Catholic Irish to look for hidden arms and to intimidate the Catholics from bidding in leases and other economic penetrations. Catholics fought back by joining themselves into a secret society named the "Defenders." This private war lost its economic character and emerged as a struggle of primitive religious passion out of which the Orange Order, named after William of Orange, dedicated to the Protestant succession to the throne and anti-Popery, was formed in 1795. To the disgrace of the government, this religious feuding was encouraged and subsidized by agents to keep Ireland divided and to frustrate the revolutionary movement of the United Irishmen.

The tragedy was that this connived religious division came at the time of — and in consequence of — the merger (for the first and last time) of Catholics and Protestants under the spell of republican idealism for the goal of a free and republican Ireland.

The independent Irish legislature, established in 1782, repealed the remnants of the penal laws — with one major exception: Catholics could not hold seats in parliament, though they could vote, hold land, sit on the grand jury, and enjoy other civil rights.

The foremost fighter for complete Catholic emancipation (and a consistently loyal friend to the degraded Catholics) was the Protestant Henry Grattan, an idealist of generous and decent instincts. He was a magnificent orator of emotional power, who gave to the Catholic Irish a vocabulary of freedom. Grattan's greatest service was that his deeds softened the bitterness of penal-day recollections and offered to the Catholic Irish the example of Protestantism at its best.

The Society of United Irishmen, conceived in the early 1790s by a small group of liberal Protestant Dissenters in Belfast in the north as an expression of republican hope, had been joined with the Catholic Committee for Irish freedom. Suppressed by the government, it had gone underground to become a revolutionary secret organization.

The French Revolution sparked in Ireland the ideal of an Irish republic established by physical force as the alternative to a diseased parliament that could not reform itself of corruption and would not grant full freedom to the Catholics. A young Protestant lawyer, Wolfe Tone, embodied that ideal.

Theobald Wolfe Tone, descendant of Cromwellian stock, came the closest in rebellious spirit to the old Gaelic chieftains, and this character attracted to him in his day, and in later generations to his memory and ideal, the unreconstructed Gael in every land. He was a true revolutionary, an advocate of no bargaining, no trafficking, with the English, who he said would never relinquish their hold on Ireland unless driven out by force. He was a tempered realist and understood that the weight-of-power had to be called in from abroad to make up the Irish deficiency in men and resources. He kept always before his eyes a plan for a united Ireland, not a Catholic Ireland or a Protestant Ireland. As an individual, he was the unusual revolutionary: he had a merry sense of humor and a bright gaiety which, contrary to the popular belief in the general wit of the Irish, did not sit well with the dour, serious-minded, and ponderous middle-class Catholic leadership. It was the humble peasant Gael who best appreciated this facet of Tone's nature.

Wolfe Tone is very important in any study of the Catholic Irish in America. His was the name invoked by that segment which repudiated peaceful agitation as an approach to Irish freedom and stood for revolution and physical force. He was the godfather of secret brotherhoods, republican organizations and, in short, the Fenian ideal. He was the direct ancestor of republican Ireland.

There is no need here to go into the details of Tone's tragedy, the bloody repression of the 1798 uprising, and his own suicide as a captive of the English. His tenacity and persuasiveness won the aid of the French and three separate fleets were sent with troops to aid the Irish, each expedition ending in disaster. The English government, informed through spies of every move of the United Irishmen, knocked the rebellion off balance by striking first with wholesale arrests and then put it down in the several areas where it appeared, particularly in

Catholic Wexford, the scene of the hardest and bitterest fighting, with bloody ruthlessness, which in Wexford was answered with equal ferocity by the peasants led by priests.

After the '98 rebellion, the ground was cleared for what Lord Clare, the leader of the Anglo-Irish oligarchy, and William Pitt, the English leader, wanted — the ending of Irish parliamentary independence and the Union of Ireland with Great Britain. That consummation was achieved in one of the most monumental acts of corruption in all history, when an Irish parliament was bought and delivered on the hoof.

The Act of Union was completed in the year 1800. Irish history from now on is the story of the fight to undo the Act of Union. In that fight the United States became the staging area for Irish hopes as Spain, Rome, and France had been in the three preceding centuries.

9
Across an Irishman's Heart

AN OLD IRISHMAN in Mullingar, recollecting the past, was speaking: "The man that said the following knew what he was talking about. He said let any man go down to hell and open an Irishman's heart there; the first thing writ across it was land."

Some romanticists talk of the Irishman's *mystique* of the land, as though unseen ties bound the one to the other. Some relate the land to national patriotism or to deep sentimental attachments, in the sense of Alice Stopford Green's Irish "sonship" to the land. But the old man of Mullingar was talking of land in the down-to-earth meaning of the Galway peasant who told the 1836 Poor Inquiry Commission: "They may as well take my life when they have taken my land."

The Catholic Irishman, said Daniel O'Connell, the Liberator of Catholic Ireland, "cannot live unless he gets land. A livelihood and not profits constitutes the Irish tenant's great object." People without access to land starved slowly: "Great numbers die prematurely," the great Bishop James Warren Doyle, the first of strong nineteenth-century Catholic prelates, told a parliamentary investigating commission in 1825; "they get weak and feeble; then they lie in bed, and gradually die off."

Twenty years later they were dying on the highways, by the side of roads, in fields, cabins, and in fever hospitals, of starvation and the diseases that wait on famine, in thousands, quickly, not like the unfortunates Bishop Doyle described, wasting away.

The wretched conditions of the Catholic Irish fill a literature of travelers' accounts, economic surveys, reports, newspaper columns, and, in particular, the fat and numerous volumes of investigations by British parliamentary commissions, with cross-examinations of the highest public officials down to the humblest peasant testifying to a state of misery without parallel, to their knowledge, in the contemporary world.

2

Meanwhile Irish babies were being born faster than the Irish were dying, in a population increase during a period of fifty years in pre-Famine Ireland that possibly no other Western nation proportionately could equal for any half-century span. The lives of the poor were not long and men and women aged early, but Irish fecundity was stronger than the grave.

K. H. Connell, who made a scholarly analysis of the uncertain population figures of eighteenth-century Ireland, estimated the number in 1791 at 4,753,000. The 1841 Census, the last before the Famine, counted the population at 8,175,000. Also, in the sixty-five years before 1845, at least 1,750,000 had emigrated to England or America, enlisted in the British army, or taken service with the East India Company.

Yet with this fantastic jump in population in the space of a half-century, Ireland was "entirely dependent for its support upon an agricultural area which had been found barely sufficient for its needs when it was a third less numerous."

3

Land had one meaning to the bulk of the Irish — the potato. The intimacy of the Irishman with the potato was no caricature. In pre-Famine Ireland, the world of the Irish spun around the potato; it was, like the sun, synonymous with life. He ate potatoes in the morning; he ate potatoes at noon; he ate potatoes at night.

"Whenever you go into a poor man's cabin, and inquire for him," said Father Mathew, the temperance apostle, "the answer always is, that he is digging the potatoes. If you ask where his wife is, she is always washing the potatoes, or boiling the potatoes."

The potato kept the Irishman alive but it was also his badge of inferiority and economic degradation. "The potato," said McCulloch, the Scottish economist, "is the lowest class of food that has hitherto been raised in Europe." The potato for two hundred years had fixed the standard of living for the dispossessed and proscribed Catholic Irish at the lowest point permitting of subsistence, and regulated other matters of daily living, like housing, clothes, and conveniences, at the same marginal level.

The Irish had been forced to accommodate themselves to the lowest subsistence standards of the potato because the produce of their labor — the cereal crops and livestock — was drawn off for export to support the landlord system which oppressed them.

The potato furnished the largest amount of food on the smallest surface of gound with the least sustained effort. A laboring man required, generally, seven pounds of potatoes at each meal, and a barrel (280 pounds) was necessary weekly for himself and family: an acre of good ground would provide sixty barrels of potatoes a season. But it was an "uncertain root," as Father Mathew called it: there had been bad failures of the potato in 1822 and in 1831 and regional failures periodically, from poor weather and plant rot.

Without knives or forks, the people expertly skinned the jackets from the boiled potatoes with a thumbnail overgrown for the purpose, ate them from the hand, and washed them down with skimmed milk or buttermilk, savoring the "lumpers," the inferior potato in common usage, with a little salt — "the bit and the sup," the meal was called. When times were hard (and always among the poorest), water was the drink with unsalted potatoes.

"As time went on," wrote Salaman, "the sequence — poverty, potatoes; larger families, more potatoes, and greater poverty, became ever more firmly established, till nothing but revolution or catastrophe could break it."

4

Several important statutes contributed to boosting the population by putting an increasing number of Catholic Irish on smaller holdings of

ground. Foster's Law, for example, adopted in 1784, a measure of domestic protection, switched Ireland, which from about the third decade
of the eighteenth century had been predominantly pasturage, requiring
little labor, to more profitable tillage farming, requiring considerable
labor. People began to take the place of cows on the land.

The system of absentee landlords had given rise to an intermediate
class of factors known as middlemen, who took long leases from the
owners uninterested in the land except for an easily collectible income. The poor Catholic Irish tenant, cottier, or laborer lacked both
the capital and the knowledge to undertake on his own account any
sizable farm for tillage cultivation. The middleman was greedy for the
profits from tillage. He had no incentive, however, to invest capital to
improve or to exert himself in the exacting management of land he did
not own. It was easier and more profitable to divide up a leased estate
and sublet pasture and waste land for tillage to land-hungry people at
the highest rack rent.

The populating of land by increasing the number of farms on an
Irish estate encouraged large families. The paternal attachment of an
Irishman for his children and his desire to keep the family together in
close association led to his subdividing the farm among them, in the
ancient tradition of gavelkind, by sharing it among all. Thus, in due
course, the standard of living of the inheritors deteriorated with each
generation as they crowded on a farm for a livelihood that would have
provided a degree of comfort for one family.

Further apportionment of smaller lots to larger numbers was directly encouraged by a statute enacted in 1793 by the Irish Parliament
as a concession to the Catholic Irish. It endowed with the franchise
those hitherto proscribed by their religion. The minimum requirement
to possess the vote was a freehold lease with an interest of forty shillings, or more, value. In other words, if a man swore his holding to be
worth at least forty shillings to him, he was entitled to register and
vote. The Protestant Ascendancy certainly never intended, or permitted, the forty-shilling freeholder to be an independent man to cast
his ballot as he pleased for the candidate he favored. It was to the personal and political interest of the proprietor (or middleman) to create
and control as many freeholders as could be crowded on his property,
regardless of economic consequences, by leasing them small pieces of
ground in return for their votes.

The Napoleonic wars speeded up the conversion to tillage. The price of grain shot up because of the demands of war and the accompanying inflation. After 1806, England protected the market for Irish cereals. The sweet feel of profits stimulated intensive and more extensive cultivation, and no price seemed too high for leases in the fierce competition for land. The Catholic Irish mass shared in the prosperity to the extent of employment and easier access to the potato patch. The real beneficiary from the war's artificial boom, so far as the Catholic Irish were concerned, however, was the population figures.

5

The Catholic Irish poor married early, sometimes even before they had bought a bed. When a boy took a fancy to a girl, he also took his chances about future provision for her, marrying "as soon as he can get a cabin or a room for her." Couples entered into marriage with only the "amount of marriage fees, a stool, and a pot to boil potatoes in."

An Irish laborer, testifying before the 1836 parliamentary commissioners, said:

> The young man says to himself, I am here under the lash of my father, and there are seven or eight children on the floor with me, and I am starving along with them, and striving to earn for them, and it is little use to strive, we are in misery together; so I will take up with some girl, and I will have a house of my own, and we will live for ourselves; the longer I am waiting the worse I am getting. . . . so they marry without any fear of being worse off than before; for when he has no work, if he is ashamed to beg himself, the wife and children will beg and support him; or if he chooses to take a fling out of the country to some other part of Ireland, or the English harvest, they will all support themselves by begging till he comes back.

As Bishop Doyle said, "They say of marriage, as of other changes in their life, that 'it cannot make them worse,' but that it may give them a help-mate in distress, or at least a companion in suffering."

A Galwayman in 1835 testified to the blithe spirit in which the poor entered marriage: "If I had a blanket to cover her I would marry the woman I liked; and if I could get potatoes enough to put into my children's mouths, I would be as happy and content as any man, and think myself as happy off as my Lord Dunlo."

What manner of society was this that had produced a man, representative of his state in life and with obviously no dull or boorish intelligence, who expressed hope for no other existence than the one which would make him as content as a noble lord — a wife, children, a blanket and potatoes?

I O

The Hierarchy of Oppression

THE OLD IRISHMAN of Mullingar intelligently put into a few simple words the essentials of the wretched landlord system which the Catholic Irish could not forget when they emigrated to America.

> The landlord would take the grabber as his tennant and let the unfortunate man who made the holding worth grabbing to the grabber go without any compensation. But more and more money was the objective of the Irish landlord no matter what source it came from. The grabbers and the middle men were the real bane to the Irish peasant farmer. The landlords in themselves were not so bad nor could be so bad without the aid of the grabbers and the middle man.

The Irish peasant invariably responded gratefully to the just landlord. But such were the exception rather than the rule. Fear and distrust on one side, hatred and oppression on the other, were the links, said Bishop Doyle, which connected the peasantry and gentry of Ireland. The most baleful influence the Cromwellian landlords brought to Ireland was the shopkeeper spirit of mercantilism — the inflexible will to squeeze the utmost profit out of what was to them a colonial people and land.

Indifference to everything but the income of their Irish properties was nurtured by the system of absentee ownership. About eight thousand people, the most important of whom were absentees, held the title-deeds to the property of Ireland.

A witness testified to a parliamentary commission in 1830 that about three million pounds of rental from Ireland was spent annually in other countries; and a writer in the London *Economist* in 1845 put the drain by absentees as between six and seven million pounds a year.

The drain of rentals from Ireland was not the evil genius of absenteeism; its blight was, as Arthur Young saw so clearly, "the damp on all sorts of improvements and the total want of countenance and encouragement which the lower tenantry labor under."

In England, the owner of farms built houses for the tenants, spent money for outbuildings, improved his property by proper fencing and draining, kept up repairs, added to its fertility by constant manuring and regular rest. A landlord who violated the understood canons of decent relationship between owner and tenant, or who took unfair advantage, by a technicality or otherwise, of his tenants speedily suffered the penalties of social ostracism among his own caste.

"Lord," exclaimed the poet Spenser speaking of Ireland, "how quickly doth that country alter men's natures!" A landlord in Ireland would countenance, or himself commit, offenses that would bring him the cut direct in England. The tradition of absolute mastery over the peasants was bred into the Irish landlord.

Landlords did not rent farms in Ireland; they rented land. The tenant had to provide for himself, make his own repairs, care for his own fencing and drains, build his own outbuildings, undertake his own improvements, and use his own implements; and his reward was either a higher rent because of the improvements wrought by his sole capital — his own muscles — or an ouster to make room for a man ("the grabber") who would pay a higher rent.

2

The representative of the absentee proprietor on the estate or in a Dublin office was called the agent, often regarded as the "landlord" by the Irish tenant. Agents, if they had it not, soon acquired the custom of the country — racketeering the peasants for their own pockets. "And how much do you propose to give to myself?" was the invariable question of the agent when the tenant came to renew his lease. Or the bribe took the form of what was called a "compliment" — presents for wives, daughters, mistresses, in the form of money. "Get all you can!" a landlord had said to his agent who had inquired concerning prerogatives.

The next in this hierarchy was the resident landlord, the frequently impoverished heir of the eighteenth-century hard-drinking, hard-riding, and hard-living squireen ("the vermin of the kingdom," Arthur Young called them), debt-ridden, living in the dilapidated "big house," trying to keep up the front of his class, immortalized by Maria Edgeworth in *Castle Rackrent*.

The middlemen constituted the most hated and despised class in Ireland — the scavengers among the exploiters of the poor. "Bloodsuckers," Arthur Young called them. To Bishop Doyle they were "the worst description of oppressors that the curse of Cromwell has produced in Ireland" and their torture "the most cruel that has ever been afflicted on any people." Chart, the social historian of Ireland of the first quarter of the nineteenth century, wrote that as a class they "displayed all the cunning, avarice and knavery now to be found, say, amongst the lowest type of professional moneylender."

Under the penal laws, Catholics had been shut out from the long leases which enriched the middlemen, but with the relaxation of the code, Catholics who had accumulated wealth in grazing and the provisions trade open to them in the eighteenth century invested their money in land and became middlemen. They racked their co-religionist tenants with the same harshness as the Protestant middleman.

The farmer who sublet from the middleman or the proprietor often in turn sublet portions of his holdings, and as he was racked from above, so he racked the even smaller man below him, exacting in labor at the lowest rate possible the bulk of the rent which the inferior tenant could not pay him in money. The little farmers, an "Irish Country Gentleman" observed, "exercise the same insolence they receive from their superiors, on those unfortunate beings, who are placed at the extremity of the scale of degradation, the Irish peasantry."

The lowest forms in this system were the executioners of the will and commands of the landlord upon the peasants — the underling stewards, bailiffs, and drivers, Roman Catholics for the most part, who resembled as a class the overseers and drivers on plantations in the pre-Civil War South, "a horde of tyrants" unknown in England.

The bailiffs and drivers were the landlords' policemen; they seized the cattle or crops when rents were not paid; they were the overseers of work and the inspectors of homes; they were in charge of evictions and the tearing down of the cabins of the ejected. The Irish peasantry had formal curses to invoke against the bailiffs and drivers, whom they thoroughly detested.

Such was the economic hierarchy of oppression. The top landlord turned the screw and the pressure increased in severity and infliction

of pain the lower it depressed the wrack, a systematic, cruel, and inhuman squeezing to wring out profit, a vicious landlordism supported and protected from the consequences of its own evils by the
power of the English government. Grattan called the hierarchy "a
subordination of vultures."

3

After the peace of 1815 Ireland underwent a transition period.
The collapse of the war boom tumbled grain prices. The prosperity of
the war years had accustomed proprietors and middlemen to an in-
flated standard of living which they fought to maintain in the post-
war deflation keeping up artificial wartime rents. The peasants could
not meet the rents; the proprietors put further encumbrances on
their holdings; and the middlemen began to fall into bankruptcy.

This distressed condition forced both the proprietor and the middleman to review the situation. The change generally decided upon was,
by cold and impersonal economics, sound for the proprietor and entrepreneur, but it had the cruel face of a death warrant to the people
against whom it was directed. The decision was to consolidate the
small farms (the Catholic Irish cursed the word "consolidation" and
called it "extermination") into larger tillage holdings or into pasture-
land for the grazing of cattle — in either case to push redundant people off the precious land. This process of consolidation was also called
"clearance." In growing America "clearing the land" meant making
the wilderness fit for human use and habitation. It had a diametrically
opposite meaning in Ireland: to "clear the land" was to throw off the
people and throw down their habitations and make a wilderness for
the grazing cow by the depopulation.

The raising of the freehold qualification in 1829 from forty shillings to ten pounds ended the usefulness of the manufactured voters and
speeded up the process of eviction. No political reason now prevailed to
keep peasants on the land.

A growing consciousness in England of the dangers in this calloused
pauperization of an increasing population — the prospect of wholesale
destitution without any relief except individual benevolence — demanded governmental action to soften the transition. Economists proclaimed that the swarming of Irish pauper workers, evicted from the
land, into English factories at reduced wages threatened the stand-

ard of living of the British workers and the substitution of the potato economy of Ireland for the bread economy of England, with unwholesome social consequence.

Therefore, the English government in 1838 established a Poor Law — or workhouse system — in Ireland on the basis of a report by George Nicholls. One general statement about the peasantry in Mr. Nicholls's report stood out to sum up all statements of the wretched economic and social condition of pre-Famine Ireland. He reported in 1837 that "the condition of their mode of living is unhappily so low, that the establishment of one still lower [the poorhouse] is difficult."

I I

"Ill-Fed, Ill-Clad, Ill-Lodged"

WHEN FRANKLIN D. ROOSEVELT cast around for a phrase to describe the depression-ridden United States, he found it in pre-Famine Ireland. James Bicheno, modeling his language on Dean Swift's, said in 1829 that the condition of the peasant had not changed since Swift's days — "scantily clad, wretchedly housed, miserably fed, and grievously rack-rented." George Cornewall Lewis, in his *On Local Disturbances in Ireland* (1836), described them as "ill-fed, ill-clad, ill-lodged."

The state of pre-Famine Catholic Ireland declined from generation to generation. "Each succeeding generation," wrote Lord Dufferin in 1865, "was accustomed from infancy to a lower standard of living than that which had satisfied their fathers." A peasant reckoned himself a successful and lucky man if he left the world no worse off than when he entered it.

It can be made as a general statement that the hope of the Catholic Irish mass before the Famine was not to go ahead but to stop from going back.

2

The small farmer was never secure on his meager bit of ground. A custom had developed over the years in Ireland which gave the landlord tremendous power over his tenants. It was known as the "hanging gale." When a tenant took a lease he was not called upon to pay one half year's rent until he owed two. Thus, the tenant was technically in arrears at all times and, therefore, subject to ejectment if the landlord wanted the property.

But the most calloused abuse by the landlord of his ownership was the practice of putting farms up for "cant" (or public auction) when leases expired. No matter how faithfully a tenant had paid his rent, how dutifully he had observed regulations, or how well he had improved the property by his own labors, he was in constant danger of being outbid for his farm by the "grabber" upon the expiration of the lease.

Moreover, in the Catholic parts of Ireland, predominantly in the three provinces of Leinster, Munster, and Connacht, the tenant was not entitled to compensation either for improvements brought by himself or for the good-will of the farm in the event of his losing it. He was told to get out to make room for the new tenant. This taking advantage of the helplessness of the Catholic Irish tenant mounted into a universal grievance and was a root cause of later intense political nationalism. In the fourth province of Ulster, with its sizable Protestant population, the situation was different. The "Ulster custom" allowed for compensation when a lease was given up. The landlord discrimination between a Protestant farmer and a Catholic farmer reminded the people in the provinces outside Protestant Ulster of their inferior status.

3

Hard experience had taught the tenant the penalties of improving the property he leased or hired and the self-interest of slovenliness. If he improved the property, his rent was raised! If he on his own initiative whitewashed the walls of his cabin or put in a window, or if by his labors he increased the productivity of the soil or managed to get an extra pig, or even if he appeared in a new suit or his daughters had stockings, his rent was raised. Progress and improvement, instead of being encouraged by the landlord for his own interests, were penalized. This upside-down system withered the character, destroyed the initiative and squelched the ambition of the Catholic Irish tenant.

A classic story told of the industrious family which leased waste land at the foot of a mountain, improved it and were dispossessed for a "grabber" who offered higher rent. The family moved farther up the mountain, repeated the same hard work and fell victim to another "grabber." They moved successively higher and higher up the mountain, improving as they ascended and, in turn, being outbid, until finally they were settled at the peak and what happened after that is left, like their position, in the air.

The competition for the limited amount of land was so intense that a tenant paid a rent which reduced his standard of living to the lowest common denominator and even then left him in debt. An old Irish woman grimly and bitterly described the lot of the small farmer: "We had to squeeze the seeds and eat the hearts out of the rotten potatoes in order to make up the rent for the landlord."

4

Probably the bitterest memory the Catholic Irish emigrant carried with him to the United States centered on eviction scenes. A consolidating, or "improving," or "exterminating" landlord cleared not one or two tenants and their families, but whole villages; and, as Mr. O'Brien pointed out in the House of Commons, "the chasing away of 700 human beings, like crows out of a corn field, amounted to total depopulation." On the larger estates the number of evicted ran into thousands. Sharman Crawford, a liberal Protestant Irish reformer, showed from parliamentary returns that from 1838 to 1843, inclusive, ejectment proceedings had been taken against 356,985 persons. During the period of the Famine and in its train (1845-1852), evictions mounted rapidly as rent arrears piled up.

After legal notice of dispossession had been served on the tenants for a set date, the sheriff, or an assistant, arrived at the head of a body of uniformed troops and police, to exercise force if eviction met with resistance. The ejected stood around in groups by their dislodged, pathetic household articles, the men bursting with impotent rage, the women wailing and weeping, the children with bewildered and frightened faces, trying to help the aged, and the dispossessed bed-ridden were exposed to God knows what future. Voices mingled prayers and curses with tears. A crowd of laborers, often paupers brought from afar, either deroofed the cabin by firing the thatch or leveled it to the ground, to make it uninhabitable against the later crawling back by the evicted. The soldiers and police then regimented the evicted from the estate itself and left them huddled on the road with nothing but the sky of Ireland over their heads. If the impulsive Irish lost control of themselves and challenged the armed authorities, the outcome was inevitable: fists and rocks were poor weapons against guns and bayonets.

The stories of evictions told by parents to their boys and girls in the United States perpetuated the memory from generation to generation. Maguire, the Irish journalist who visited his countrymen in America after the Civil War, met a man whose conscience would not permit him to go to confession because he could not stamp out of his mind the hatred of, and passion for revenge against, the landlord who had evicted his family in Ireland and smashed their cabin.

Each eviction case swelled the problems of a disorganized social system and invariably eviction pushed the dispossessed into a lower social and economic status. The evicted tended to drift into towns. In the suburbs were cabins without lofts, of some twenty by thirty feet, divided by a partition in the center. Evicted families seeped into these cabins where they took not a room but a *corner* of a room while they looked for work, with three or four families crowded into a space barely sufficient to turn around in.

5

A man evicted from a holding was fortunate if he became a cottier, the lowest class of landholders, a grade between the small tenant farmer and the day laborer. A cottier hired a cabin and a small piece of ground for potatoes from a farmer or a middleman, sometimes added ground for the grazing of a cow, if he could hire a cow, which he kept until she calved. The typical cottier paid the farmer not primarily in money, but in labor, generally at the lowest going rate — the so-called "truck" system. The rent was enormous, more than fifty per cent a year of the cost of the cabin and three times as much for the land as the farmer or middleman paid the proprietor.

6

The pig made up the difference between the amount of the cottier's rent and what he had worked out by his labor.

The pig played the part in the antediluvian economics of Ireland

that gold does in delicate international trade — the balance of pay-
ments. The Irishman and his pig became stereotyped companions for
jokes and humorous cartoons. Travelers were both amused and
shocked by the morning appearance of an Irish family from their
cabin followed by the pig and poultry, like Noah and the beasts
emerging from the ark on Mount Ararat. Inglis, the English traveler
in the middle 1830s, was astounded at the home companionship of
the Irishman and the pig, living together within the same walls.
And why hadn't he that right in the cabin, he was told, "since it's he
that pays the rint." As Inglis came to understand the economics of
depressed Ireland, he blessed the snout in the cabin and pitied the
wretches without a pig. An Irish peasant, it was observed, "would as
soon think of eating the landlord himself as of eating the pig."

Like gold, there was always a market for the pig, and he meant
cash money. He was not costly to feed; he was not delicate in his
appetite, content with potato peeling, potatoes too small for human
consumption and offal; he did not require care, being an individualist who looked after himself. The profit from a pig was reckoned
at thirty shillings after a year's care — a sizable amount of money in
pre-Famine Ireland.

7

Cottier laborers west of the Shannon — where work was extremely
scarce — journeyed to England for the harvest to find the money
for their rent: they could be seen in hordes journeying the Great
Western Road between Connacht and Dublin. The "spalpeen," as he
was called, was a familiar figure in England's and Scotland's rural
areas, barefooted, always hurrying from job to job to save time,
which meant money, and welcomed by the farmer without whose
labor he could not get in his crops. The "spalpeen" walked from his
home west of the Shannon to Dublin, paid his passage across, and
then walked from job to job, and landing in Dublin again, walked to
his home. (The Catholic Irish were great walkers to save the fare of
transportation; they would have walked to America, one man said, if
they could.)

The money earned in England paid for the rent of his cabin and
piece of potato ground. (Robert Ross of the Bank of Ireland in 1830
estimated these "spalpeens" brought back between £70,000 and £80,-

ooo annually.) He planted his garden in the spring and, when the time arrived to go harvesting, he locked up the cabin, and his wife and children put the wallet on their backs and went begging potatoes to keep them until he returned. On a certain date they were reunited, the potatoes were dug and stored, and with food laid by and the rent paid, the year was considered successful.

8

It would seem that the bottom had been reached with the cottier, but a substratum existed — the laborer, described by the Devon Commission as "the most wretched among the many wretched classes in Ireland." Let Mrs. Nicholson, the generous-spirited and humane Christian evangelist from America, describe the sight she saw in Galway in the 1840s and familiar over rural Ireland:

> I saw a company of men assembled in a square, and supposed something new had gathered there; but drawing nearer, found it was a collection of poor countrymen from distant parts, who had come hoping on the morrow to find a little work. Each man had his spade, and all were standing in a waiting posture, in silence, hungry and weary, for many, I was told, had walked fifteen miles without eating, nor did they expect to eat that day. Sixpence a day was all they could get, and they could not afford food on the Sabbath, when they could not work. Their dress and their desponding looks told too well the tale of their suffering.

Mrs. Nicholson said: "Good God! have mercy on poor Ireland."

9

The piece of ground which stood between the superabundant laboring poor (cottiers and day laborers) and starvation in a system which afforded only intermittent work was called "conacre," an institution peculiar to Ireland.

Conacre (derived from a contraction of "contract acre") concretely meant the ground itself but the Devon Commission defined its common usage as "the taking of land merely for the crop or for the season." The relationship between the man who rented the land and the man who used it was not that of landlord and tenant. Rather conacre was a permit or license (limited to eleven months) for the use of land under certain conditions.

The cottier, with his cabin and patch, did not always possess sufficient ground to raise the potatoes required to feed his family, and the laborer earned so little so uncertainly in wages that his income lacked the power to buy enough food for his family. Conacre bridged the gap in these instances.

A farmer or middleman or land jobber let out small parcels of land, usually from an acre down, at a high price for one season's use to cottier or laborer. Commonly, the man who let out conacre manured and prepared the ground while the man who hired it seeded, planted, weeded, cultivated, and dug the potatoes. The farmer himself benefited from the return in labor or cash and also in the "heart," that is the fertility, the ground drew from a crop of potatoes as preparation for the subsequent grain. The laborer hired the ground for two reasons — food for the family needs and employment, which he otherwise would not have in a work-scarce country.

Conacre started under the penal code, in the days of Queen Anne, when the law restricted a day laborer to two acres of ground for his subsistence. After the law passed into obsolescence, conacre continued as necessary in a country with a surplus population unable to find steady work.

Conacre measured Ireland's uneconomic and backward state.

10

The Irish peasant's knowledge of money was as scarce as the feel of it in his pocket. Daniel O'Connell's testimony that "Money is an article that the Irish peasant knows excessively little of" echoed Jonathan Swift's observation a century previous that among the tenantry "money is a thing unknown." "Land, not wages," said George Cornewall Lewis, was his chief means of support and the potato stood in his mind for capital. "The man," said O'Connell, who knew his people well, "who gives twenty shillings in potatoes, cannot give ten shillings in money." As late as the middle 1840s, William Meade, a land proprietor and barrister of Cork, told the Devon Commission that "scarcely any of the better class of farmers give any money to their laborers." Only the gentry paid money wages, he said.

Unfamiliarity with money reached classic proportions when people in Galway pawned it.

Money had a virtue of its own to the Irish peasants, and they were extremely harsh and unfeeling with one another in money dealings. "I have known," said Daniel O'Connell, "persons who would be perfectly ready to die for each other in personal quarrels, as harsh about a shilling or a sixpence as if they had no previous acquaintance with each other whatever." The Catholic Irishman was generous-hearted in most respects but drew the line at ready cash. A close Irishman made the proverbial tightfisted Scotsman appear openhanded.

1 2

The Poor Supported the Poor

LAND CONSTITUTED almost the sole means of employment in Ireland. The industrial revolution passed Ireland by on its journey from England to the United States because the English Parliament and the kept legislature in Dublin, during the eighteenth century, had systematically strangled any industrial development.

The unemployment figures in agricultural Ireland stagger the mind with depressing digits. The Irish Poor Inquiry commissioners in 1836 reckoned the number of persons simultaneously requiring relief in Ireland during thirty weeks of the year at not less than 2,385,000, of whom 585,000 were out of work and in distress, and 1,800,000 dependent on them.

The extensive and comprehensive investigation by the Devon Commission arrived at the conclusion that "the deficiency of constant remunerative employment is the chief evil from which the laborers of Ireland suffer."

Work! That cry echoed through pre-Famine Ireland. The hard-bitten Earl of Kingston, who personally managed his sizable estate in County Cork, spoke of the "vast desire" of the people to get employment, adding that laborers "will work for any thing whatever they can get; I have had some offered to work for me for threepence a day, stout able men, and glad to get it." Furthermore, he said, no prejudice was shown against any occupation of any description; they took the meanest and dirtiest jobs to get work.

"The idleness seen among many, when working for those who oppress them," wrote Arthur Young, "is a very contrast to the vigor and

activity with which the same people work when themselves alone reap
the benefit of their labor."

The American employer discovered the Irish emigrant's capacity for
hard work as a laborer; and it was as a laborer, not as a skilled worker
or even as a farmer, that the Catholic Irishman came across the Atlantic.

2

The descendants of the Catholic Irish in America, as well as students
of immigration, have wondered why the Catholic Irish emigrants remained in the cities or struck out for canal and railroad labor jobs
instead of taking farms, as would seem natural for a people from an
overwhelmingly agricultural country.

But the fact is overlooked that the bulk of the Catholic Irish population in rural Ireland were not farmers, as America understands the
word. They were laborers. "All they know how to do is to dig," exclaimed John Leslie Foster, an Irish member of the House of Commons
and an intelligent observer of the people. The composite picture of a
rural worker in Ireland would show a man with a spade. He dug to
plant his potatoes; he dug to raise them from the ground; and when
he was not digging his own patch or conacre, he dug for the farmer
who employed him. He had small occasion to learn the science of
farming as a small tenant, cottier, or laborer interested only in a potato
crop. What the Catholic Irish emigrant knew about farming as practiced in America could be put into less than one eye. The strong and
successful farmers did not, as a rule, emigrate.

If the industrial revolution had planted factories and shops in Ireland, the Catholic Irish rural masses would have flocked into them.
They were looking for work; they had no peasant's love of the soil as
the soil: in that respect, they were not true peasants. And if the industrial revolution would not come to Ireland, then the Irish had to go
to the industrial revolution, and this they did — to England and America.

When the Catholic Irish emigrant arrived in America and found
that work was available at laboring or in industry and that, moreover,
he was paid in ready money, in cash, not in kind, the thought of going to the land and the farm disappeared from his mind. In the light
of his background, is there wonder that he remained in the cities or

joined up with canal or railroad gangs? What he wanted was a job that paid him in ready money.

3

Sir Thomas Larcom wrote that in rural Ireland "it was the Poor who supported the Poor," adding, " 'The bit and sup' was never withheld in the poorest cabins to the wretched wayfarer and they had little else."

The benevolence of the Irish poor towards the Irish poor shines with a beautiful and warming light in the dark midst of squalor and poverty. It transfigured the race and lifted them to a level of nobility that must ever be honored. It flowed naturally and simply, without calculation or reserve, from a generous and kind heart that, oppressed and victimized, moved impulsively in a common humanity for fellow suffering. The beggar solicited a pittance "for the honor of God," and the giver responded with the thought that before him stood "a God send." To deny him would be to shut the door in the face of God. The poor Catholic Irishman never stood closer to the highest religious sentiment than when he put a hand into his own slim basket and shared potatoes with the beggar on his threshold.

Families left potatoes by the turf fire at night to keep them warm in case a beggar came out of the darkness. "There was a disposition in the peasant," said John R. Barry, a magistrate of Cork, "not to allow any person to be destitute, so long as he has a *potatoe* to divide with them." Families kept their doors open at mealtime as an invitation to a passing beggar to enter and share the potatoes.

"Charity is the alpha and omega, the sum total of all that makes the man or woman, with these people," wrote the American Mrs. Nicholson, adding that "when they give, they give unsparingly from their pittance, and when they receive, they do it with much thankfulness, when the smallest trifle is offered, as when the donation is quite bountiful."

The middling class of farmers set aside a certain portion of their fields to plant potatoes for the poor. John Browne of Limerick estimated that there were five hundred thousand farmhouses falling in this category, and that each contributed on the average a ton of potatoes each year in support of the poor. And half of them, he added, were just a cut or two above the wretched cottier.

Bishop Doyle had seen farmers of the strong class — with holdings
of from two hundred to three hundred acres — "distributing on a
morning, with their own hands, assisted by a serving maid, stirabout
[a meal mush] to upwards of 40 to 50 paupers, and doing so not for
one day, or two, but regularly during a whole season of distress," and
he continued: "I could not, if I were to speak till the sun went down,
convey a just picture of the benevolence prevailing in the minds and
hearts of the middling class."

The same spirit of benevolent charity towards the hungry was extended to orphan children, widows, the lame and blind, to the sick,
in whatever form the poor could make, regardless of personal sacrifice.
Bishop Doyle said of the charity of the poor to the poor:

> You cannot be amongst the poor for a single day, particularly if
> you discharge the office of a clergyman in visiting the sick, without
> witnessing the exercise of it in the most touching manner. In visit-
> ing a poor creature in a hovel, where sickness and misery prevail,
> we find the creature surrounded by poor neighbors, one of whom
> brings him a little bread or meal, another brings a little meat, or pre-
> pares a little broth or soup, and they all comfort him with their con-
> versation and society. If the clergyman be expected, they put the
> little place in order, or seek to make it clean, and their expressions
> of sympathy for the poor creature in disease are such as console
> one's heart in the midst of that distress.

Bishop Doyle described a characteristic of the Catholic Irish that any
race would be proud to inscribe upon its national banner:
"When the Irish, who are a warm-hearted people, find distress near
them, they approach to it and seek to relieve it."

But this wise, great, and understanding man knew that, in the disorganized and unhinged state of society in Ireland, "when the hearts
of men are moved greatly, even to good, they are liable to be easily
moved also to evil."

1 3

The Midnight Legislators

THE EVIL which Bishop Doyle dreaded had the same
source as the word which the Mullingar Irishman would find written
across the heart of the man in hell: land. The Irishman who willingly

shared his last potato with a beggar would murder, or conspire to murder, a man who tried to take his land, without the slightest pity for the victim or remorse for the dead. "The Russian government has been called despotism tempered with assassination," wrote Froude. "In Ireland landlordism was tempered by assassination."

The Catholic Irish had no trust in the law or administration of justice. The Rev. William O'Brien, a pastor in County Cork, put the case simply and bluntly: "If you tell an Irishman that he will receive justice in a court of justice no matter what your religion is, he will not believe you." The lower orders, explained the Roman Catholic Bishop of Armagh, are "of the opinion, that the laws were not made for their protection; they know no parts of them, *except the penal and punishing parts.*" Every oppression among the Catholics, Daniel O'Connell pointed out, was double-barreled: "It is an oppression in itself and oppression from an enemy."

Impotent of political rights to correct inequity, convinced that the courts were engines of discrimination, certain the law operated against his interest and conscious that superior force upheld the system, the Catholic Irishman joined in secret conspiracy to regulate by force or intimidation the conditions of occupancy of land for his own protection. The people established a rude rump government for their protection against "landlord law."

Sir Thomas Larcom grasped the root causes of Irish disaffection in the landlord system and made this penetrating analysis of the local disturbances in Ireland:

> No one can be the apologist for crime so frightful, so injurious to the country in all its relations, but looked at from this point of view, are they not resolvable really into action of self-defense. "You take my life, if you take that whereof I live." A man threatened with eviction, in a society where from the absence of a mixed industry land is looked to as the only source of subsistence, thinks by killing the threatener of his life, he saves his own and that of his family. There are in fact two codes of law in force and in antagonism — one the statute law enforced by judges and jurors, in which the people do not yet trust — the other a secret law, enforced by themselves — its agents the Ribbonmen and the bullet.

The support by the Catholic Irish rural masses of this "secret law" of violence testified to the desperation of their lot: the strict morality of their private lives made room, under the conscienceless law of survival, for the immorality of the gun. They said in justification: if we do not resist in the only language understood by our tormentors, that of force, we shall be exterminated. This was their reply to the country gentleman who put off every proposal for the relief of the peasantry with the argument: "When they are turbulent, do not yield to them; when they are quiet, do not agitate them."

Larcom called the agents of this "secret law" by the name of Ribbonmen, the members of an extensive Catholic Irish secret society. The use of "Ribbonism" to characterize rural disturbances was common, but it was not a precise description. The accurate name for local organized violent resistance was Whiteboyism, derived from the prototype of the Munster peasant uprising in 1761.

Whiteboyism assumed various local titles in the several parts of Ireland: "Levellers," "Carders," "Rockites," "Lady Clares," "Terryalts," "Whitefeet," and "Blackfeet." Probably the name most familiar in the United States is the "Molly Maguires," copied directly from a local Whiteboy organization in Ireland by Catholic Irish coal miners in Pennsylvania. The local leader usually signed himself "Captain Rock," from an early Whiteboy pseudonym, or "Captain Right," or "Captain Moonlight," or "Captain Starlight," or "Captain Dreadnought," or "Lady Clare," or "Molly Maguire."

2

Certain characteristics distinguished Whiteboyism from other sources of disturbances in Ireland. It was local in organization and had a definite local objective. It served no political ends. It had no sectarian exclusiveness in executing its purposes: "The Whitefeet are most liberal people," explained Father Nicholas O'Connor of Maryborough, "for they make no distinction between Catholic and Protestant." If its demands were satisfied, Whiteboyism remained passive until an occasion of grievance breathed life into it again.

George Cornewall Lewis, the English publicist and politician, gave the most perceptive interpretation of this indigenous Irish institution in his excellent book *On Local Disturbances in Ireland:*

> The Whiteboy association may be considered as a vast trades' union for the protection of the Irish peasantry: the object being, not to regulate the rate of wages, or the hours of work, but to keep the actual occupant in possession of his land, and in general to regulate the relation of landlord and tenant for the benefit of the latter.

Whiteboyism aimed to prevent and punish eviction "and the taking of land over another's head."

3

Local circumstances dictated other particular objectives. In Clare and Galway, when the more profitable cattle trade turned land from tillage into pasture, combinations were organized to force landlords into setting aside conacre potato ground; and at night hundreds of determined men turned out with spades to dig up lush fields and, by spoiling them for grazing, make them useful only for conacre.

A common practice was the beating of "strangers," the spalpeens who came from other counties in harvest time seeking work in competition with local laborers, and frequently at lower wages. A "stranger" to an Irishman was another Irishman who did not live in the immediate locality or, at least, in the same county.

The consolidation, or clearing, of estates provoked increasing resistance and heightening violence. From 1815 through the Famine, the growing number of evictions encountered the organized opposition of the peasantry and their illegal agents, the Whiteboys, in a running war — called "agrarian outrages" by the English.

The local combinations followed a pattern of procedure in crude approximation to the legal course of justice. In a local case to be judged, the members met in secrecy. After the merits — or demerits — of the case had been discussed, often heatedly, a judgment was made to act and in what manner, or not to act. Such deliberations were part of what was called "legislating." A large landowner, noting the rising number of attacks in his neighborhood and adopting a good-natured, live-and-let-live attitude, wrote to a friend: "I have just ploughed up seven acres of good land [for conacre], which I have given to the boys (the Whitefeet), and I am on the best terms with these new legislators."

If a decision called for action, a warning notice was issued to the man to be coerced or intimidated, pasted on his door or left on his table by a stealthy confederate. Sir Francis Hopkins was an "improving" landlord. He received this warning:

> Sir Francis Hopkins, there did a Man come to look for you one
> Day with what you might call a boney Brace of Pistols to shoot you;
> and if you do not be lighter on your Tenants then what you are

you shall be shurely shot, so now we give you timely Notice; and
if you dont abide by this marke the Consequence.
So nomor at preasant.

Robert Brabazon, a landlord, received this notice:

It is requested, Mr. Robert Bropstin, that you will take notice,
and give now Grass to Farrell or two [to] Bryan Owlin or two
Owen Kugan; or if you do [not] you will be punished according
to the Regulations of our venurable Boar [Board], which will be
regularly attended to in all Parts of this United Kingdom called
Ireland.
Given under my Hand this 3rd Day of May 1838,
C. A. T. Rock.

The attempt at legal phrasing, in imitation of some "hedge lawyer"
and designed to give a formal cast to the underground "legislating,"
marked many notices. Mr. Brabazon was murdered.

4

"In case a man takes land that another has been ejected from," a
witness told the Devon Commission, "he is very sure to be injured."
That was the unforgivable sin, for which the violent beatings and
murder stood justified in the eyes of the people. That sat at the very
heart of "agrarian outrage" as the common grievance. When served
notice by the Whiteboy organization, a landlord or middleman set up
precautions in strong guard, if he was wise. But the tenant who took
the farm "over another's head" became a sitting duck open to the
attacks of the organization. He lacked the means for ample protection.
His buildings were subject to fire, his beasts to maiming, and himself
to punishment.

A man in the neighborhood of Cashel, County Tipperary, who had
been evicted from his holding for arrears in rent, replied when asked
his feelings towards the one who would be put in his place:

To be sure I would have a bad feeling to him; and why should
not I? The devil a much of the world's bread he would eat after it
any way, as I would die to have his life or any one like him, that
would step in to take the bread out of my wife's and children's
mouths.

The same psychology obtained in Ireland towards the man who had
taken another's land as in the concentration of hostility in modern

labor unionism upon the strikebreaker or the "scab." If the "scabs" prevail, the whole system of unionism is threatened. If a man could take land from a dispossessed tenant without punishment, the resistance to the "landlord's law" would break down and put the mass of rural Ireland at the mercy of a harsh order.

5

If a decision was made to murder an obnoxious landlord, the combination went a "distance" (a "distance" in Ireland in those days might be only twenty miles or the next village) to solicit an assassin, fearing recognition if one of the local members undertook the murder, although shootings were done in broad daylight by a man well known in the neighborhood, protected by the silence of the people.

Systematic oppression over the centuries had blunted moral and humane sentiments regarding violence over land occupancy into a hardened impersonality. Thus a man who otherwise enjoyed the reputation of quiet behavior and decent conduct would commit brutal violence or kill for the cause. Aubrey de Vere, a landholder, could discover "no marks of ruffianism" in the faces of Whiteboy leaders.

"They are said to be reckless of life," wrote Sir Thomas Larcom. "Is that true? . . . Are they not careful of the young? — of the aged? — of the sick? — are they not proverbial for hospitality? hospitality of the poor for the poor." Then Larcom made a statement, paraphrasing Edmund Burke, which other Englishmen with no particular axe to grind had observed of the Catholic Irish and which helps to explain the contradiction of vicious brutality committed by and supported among a naturally warmhearted and kindly people. "Of no country," Larcom put down in his notebook, "can it be more justly said than of Ireland — 'Their vices are imposed upon them — Their virtues are their own.' "

6

The peasants gave moral support and sanction to the Whiteboys with their whole heart, and closed ranks solidly in protection of a man sought by the law for an act of violence. The law officers and the English professed to believe that this unanimity of sentiment was imposed by intimidation and fear of retaliation. But the sympathy of the people for the murderer was rather to the cause which had produced the murder than to the crime itself.

The Irish peasants drew a sharp distinction between crime arising from the occupancy of land, which they did not consider crime but self-protection, and crime for self-gain. Sir Thomas Larcom, using England as a basis of measurement, pointed out that "in comparing the criminal tables of England and Ireland it will be found, as might be expected, that crimes of violence or crimes against the Person, blacken the Irish chart while crimes against property exceed in England. In murder, attempts to commit it, homicide, and maiming of cattle, for example, the numbers in our [Irish] calendar will be found more than double those of England, in proportion to our population, while in Larcenies, Arson, and Embezzlement, England greatly exceeds us, and in forgery and other crimes against property the proportion is three times greater in England than here." The crimes of Ireland arose from the particular economic, political, and social condition there. These crimes, wrote Samuel Lover, belonged rather to history than to the Newgate Calendar.

A man came into a community and asked for sanctuary, saying that he was "on his keeping," that is, he was being sought by the police for a crime in connection with the cause. The wall of protection at once closed around him. The chief constable, anxious to lay hands on this particular fellow and knowing the immunity he enjoyed by right of the cause, spread the word that his crime had not been a Whiteboy offense, but rape. The next day he was turned over.

A man "on his keeping" could pass from one end of Ireland to the other with the certainty that no peasant to whom he appealed for sanctuary would betray him to the authorities. Lewis told the story of a Tipperary laborer who could not find work in his own neighborhood, moved to another, and gave out the story that he was a murderer. He received work. Later it was discovered that the story was entirely fiction. *The Playboy of the Western World* by John Millington Synge was written around this familiar theme.

The people considered the police their enemy, not their friends or protectors, and connived to thwart them in their duties. Speaking of a police chase after certain assailants, a shopkeeper of Sligo said: "If there were a hundred police after them, it would be of no use; the people will come upon the road, and meet the men [the assailants], and mix with them. The police will start after them; the four men will divide; they run after them, and if they catch any one it is the wrong man. They say, 'That is him,' or 'That is him,' and they get hold of the wrong man. That is quite common."

A body of police came to a cabin one morning to arrest a peasant, and he fled through the countryside as naked as the day on which he was born. As the police gradually gained on the tiring man, he darted into a cabin by the roadside and, in a few brief moments, a naked man appeared running like a deer, fresh and untired, quickly outstripping the wearied police. The tiring peasant had asked aid of the occupant of the cabin who, speedily stripping himself, had taken the other's place, with no questions asked.

7

The most hated word in Ireland was "informer" or, in the technical language of the courts, "approver." In politics, "informer" carried hated memories. Informers had infiltrated the ranks of the United Irishmen in the 1790s, rising to high place, and for pay kept the government aware of every movement of the society. A visitor to the Dublin produce market noticed that one horse received tender affection and choice niblets and, when he inquired the reason, was told that this was the horse which hauled the cart carrying "Jemmy" O'Brien, a notorious informer, to the gallows for a murder he had committed.

In a society which looked to illegal and secret action for its self-defense against a stronger and oppressive power, mutual faith and trust were implicit in its operations, just as respect for the law upholds the system where even-handed justice runs. An informer in a society like the Irish was similar to cancer cells in the human body, a deadly menace. As Lewis wrote: "A man who takes land over another's head may be spared; but a man who has given evidence to convict a Whiteboy may (in the language of threatening notes) 'make ready his coffin.' "

8

The Ribbon Society, or Confederacy, unlike Whiteboyism, vowed a patriotic and political purpose, professed a national organization and appealed to the conspiratorial nature of the Irishman, with an oath of secrecy, passwords, grips, recognition signals, and a general air of mystery, its headquarters and leaders unknown to the rank and file. In organization it followed the general structure of the United Irishmen, starting with the parish society and going upward through the baronial and county committees to the Grand Lodge in Dublin, with membership confined exclusively to Roman Catholics. The society disguised itself under such formal names as the Shamrock Society or the St. Patrick's Fraternal Society. It is difficult to determine to what extent Ribbonism engaged in Whiteboy terrorism and the line of demarcation. Unfortunately for history, its secrecy precluded accurate information, in the form of records of its workings.

The Ribbon Society was the parent in Ireland of the most influential of the Irish-American organizations, the Ancient Order of Hibernians; it was the model upon which the secret societies of Irish laborers on American canals and railroads were formed; it was the fountainhead as well as the recruiting ground of Irish revolutionary societies in the United States; and it was the nexus, among the early Catholic Irish emigrants, between the United States and Ireland.

9

One form of violence indulged in by the people had nothing to do with the occupancy of land or patriotic politics: the faction fight. This institution, peculiar to Ireland, was defined by Colonel J. J. Kennedy, head of the royal police, as "The fights which took place in Ireland in consequence of the quarrels arising from local circumstances, increased by one family joining another and taking the part of another."

"In this country," wrote Richard Lalor Sheil, the distinguished Irish advocate, "a man who chances to receive a blow, instead of going to a magistrate to swear information [prefer charges], lodges a complaint with his clan, who enter into a compact to avenge the insult — a reaction is produced, and an equally extensive confederacy is formed on the other side." It was "a point of honor," added Sheil, not to have recourse to any of the legitimate sources for redress.

Faction fighting followed its own Marquess of Queensberry code, and surprise and ambush were not part of the rules. When an injured man appealed to his clan for redress, the faction leader called up all the relatives and their friends — his "back" or "backing," as his following was known. A negotiator met with the chief of the rival clan, setting a date and place for the battle and completing arrangements. The battle lines were drawn, preliminary maneuvering — or "wheeling" — followed for position, and then came the shock of combat of the two bodies armed with hurtful weapons, like shillelahs, fighting until one side retired. The English authorities stood aside on the premise that if Irishmen fought among themselves their energy and unity would be drained from fighting the alien rule.

The Roman Catholic bishops and clergy thundered against the secret societies and the criminal conduct of the local combinations: they interfered to stop faction fighting and condemned it from the altar. Ecclesiastical exhortation under the conditions which prevailed in Ireland was, as Sheil said of excommunication in politics, "of no avail." Priests received threatening notices and some were personally attacked for their sermons, or they were subjected to planted rumors of being in the pay of the government or a "landlord's priest."

14

Landlord's Law in the Courts

EVEN THE HEAVENS, the Catholic Irish believed, opened their wrath against the courts of justice; and the people imagined that "the approach of the judge to the county-town is accompanied by bad weather, rain, storms, and all the anger of the elements."

The record over the centuries warranted their conviction that a court boded no good for the Catholic Irish. English justice in Ireland was not the monument of integrity, equality, and impartiality its reputation had won in the sceptered isle nor was the judge, as proclaimed by Coke, the "lion beneath the throne"; the law was a jungle beast in the sister isle. The law in Ireland, said Lord Denman in a famous phrase, was "a mockery, a delusion and a snare."

"Judges, sheriffs, magistrates, crown counsel, law officers — all are Protestant," wrote Richard Sheil in 1828. "The very sight of a court of justice reminds them [the Catholic Irish] of the degradation attached to their religion." In the north, magistrates publicly raised the Orange toast to the memory of King William. In Dublin, sheriffs gave rigid pledges before taking office of their loyalty to the code of religious and political discrimination. Throughout Ireland, declared Daniel

O'Connell, the peasants had the impression that "in all cases where they are before the magistrates, it would be better for them to be Protestants than Catholics."

If two Catholics appeared against each other as disputants in a case, or if two Protestants were similarly arrayed, the course of justice ran smoothly and was evenly dispensed. But when a Catholic stood on one side and a Protestant on the other, whether in a civil or a criminal case, "all the passions and prejudices are excited," as Bishop Doyle wrote, and justice became sectarian and partisan.

2

Just as the Catholic Irish, feeling outside the evenhanded protection of the law, turned to Whiteboyism to safeguard their occupancy of the land and to the faction fight to settle their own private grievances, so they resorted to craft, guile, deceit, cunning, and wiliness to thwart the course of stage-managed injustice in the court. They turned a native intelligence, sharpened in wariness under the penal laws, to shrewd ingenuity and facile dissimulation to outwit the courts at their own game.

They had observed in their own relationship with courts that matters went by favor rather than right. Being a sharp-witted people, they set their sails to the prevailing winds and themselves exploited the system of favor. This they called "interest." Daniel O'Connell told the 1825 investigating commission that the Irish peasant believed that "unless he has what they call interest, he has no chance of success before any tribunal." An old Irish adage advised that "a word in the court was better than a pound in the purse." A composite picture of Ireland in a court of law would show the nation busily employed "pulling strings."

If a man became entangled with the law, his relatives and friends immediately set in motion the machinery of "interest," beseeching the landlord, the agent, the politician, the priest, everyone they believed had power and influence, to put in a "word" for Pat or Owen. A magistrate rarely blinked his eyes in surprise if he found himself showered with gifts of fowl and eggs from the relatives and friends of a man soon to stand trial. One of the benefits of belonging to a strong faction was that it frequently enjoyed the protection of its "interest" by a magistrate. In return, the magistrate expected the free labor of the faction in digging, planting, and harvesting. A magistrate who set himself out for "interest" was apparently no less respected for his susceptibilities. The people had more faith in the "interest" of a partisan magistrate than they had in the law of the land. They had more trust in the personality of a human being than in the impersonal workings of the law.

3

The fertile imagination of the peasant and his total distrust of the rigged courts perfected the alibi as a weapon of widespread and artistic use to circumvent the law. Put Paddy forward, wrote Carleton, the Irish novelist, "to prove an alibi for his fourteenth or fifteenth cousin, and you will be gratified by the pomp, pride and circumstance of true swearing. Every oath with him *is* an epic — pure poetry, abounding with humor, pathos, and the highest order of invention and talent." Even Paddy's "*extempore* oaths possess all the ease and correctness of labor and design."

One magistrate testified that persons to swear alibis could be rounded up without difficulty at any time and without pay. The extensive interrelationships of families, with connections far and wide, furnished an endless pool of alibi-swearers, loyal to the blood.

Their multiplicity and character had brought oaths into general disrepute among the people. Up to 1829, the formal political oath calumniated the Catholic religion and the Pope, and to take it a man necessarily compromised his religious beliefs, which was its purpose. In Ireland, said Wakefield, "an oath is the test on the most trifling concerns of life." O'Connell's story of the man who took an oath in the morning not to tell the truth during the day reduced the system to absurdity.

If perjury was considered fair play in the courts, the Roman Catholics among themselves on points of honor abided by the sworn word. A man went into church and there swore before his fellows that he had not informed or that he had not stolen; and he was believed. In their own village courts, where small differences were settled, an oath on a Bible or a crucifix held sacred binding power, to be violated at the risk of one's immortal soul.

Even in the courts, conscience-smitten Catholic Irish employed a technicality to avoid the sin of perjury. Instead of kissing the Bible, or the Book, as it was called, a witness kissed his thumb which held it, satisfying his mind that he had not taken an oath — "a kind of smuggler in morality," Carleton called him, "imposing as often as he can upon his own conscience."

The Crown officials felt that they were punching a pillow, or sieving the ocean, in trying to draw a disinterested or impartial petty jury. It seemed that every Irishman was related to every other Irishman (a magistrate said that "in Ireland people have a great many connections"), and how to keep relatives out of the jury box presented a continuing problem, as did intimidation of witnesses and suborning of evidence. A riot occurred in Carlow, when a party rescued cattle that had been seized for tithes, during which the magistrate and sheriff were hit by stones. A jury acquitted the accused leader: he had a brother on it.

The "rescue" was an institution in rural Ireland and a fertile source of disturbance. A "rescue" party could be gathered in a brief time to waylay and seize the cattle a tithe-collector had impounded. The police never knew whether or not they were to haul an arrested man safely to the jail: almost in the twinkling of an eye, so deep was sympathy for a man arrested, a "rescue" party, materialized out of nowhere, might pounce, even though the members neither knew the prisoner personally nor his offense. A "rescue" party on trial hardly needed relatives on a jury for acquittal.

4

The Irish loved litigation, as the Elizabethans and Cromwellians had noted centuries before. Irish men, and women, were constantly having the law upon one another, generally for petty offenses — the trespassing of a cow or fowl, a small .debt, engagements about cattle, disputes over the boundaries of farms, shopkeepers' bills, injuries to animals, and the like. Quite often the court costs amounted to considerably more than the sum at issue, but money was not the stake: a streak of vindictiveness ran through the race that, when aroused, could not be dampened down without personal satisfaction; a wandering hen would bring to furious boil the latent ill will of two neighbors, often women, and off to the courts they would hustle to get their satisfaction, called "rights." A touchy sensitiveness, arising from the insecurity of a people kept in an inferior state, manifested itself as "pride," and to offend against that (or to believe that it was being offended against) set to burning the fires of malice whose sparks constantly smoldered in an Irishman's being.

A breed of curbstone lawyer, known as a "hedge attorney," sometimes a schoolmaster with a smattering of the law's jargon, counseled the peasants. What he lacked in law he made up in knowledge of the Irish character. He used polysyllabic legal terms to impress the uneducated clients, and flattered the overheated feelings of a man bringing action by setting out the case in the most violent terms which his knowledge of the law permitted, such as "feloniously milking a cow" or "feloniously digging potatoes." Simple trespass became "burglary."

An Irish county court, as described by O'Connell, resembled Bedlam: "the plaintiff and the defendant and their wives and their witness are all bawling, at the same time the attorney screaming. There is no poetry in saying, that justice is frightened away." The accused one day arose from the table, where prisoners sat, and heaved a rock at a witness, knocking him flat, and the hurrying police found him prepared with another by his chair. A witness, asked to point out a man accused of a serious offense, came forward with the rod, tapped the man on the shoulder, saying, "How are ye, Johnny?" And a woman witness, in temper, did not hesitate to strike over the head with the rod the man she was accusing.

Self-protection over the years had developed in the Catholic Irish a skill for the evasive and noncommittal answer which bordered on artistry; and the examiner who tried to pin one down to a yes-or-no answer only beat his head against genius.

5

The Catholic Irish used all the native ingenuity of the race to oppose and thwart the "landlord's law," but the law itself they loved, sometimes as a game, sometimes as a challenge to wits, sometimes for its majesty denied to them as a people and, above all, they loved it because it centered in human relations and personality. Nothing human was ever alien to a Catholic Irishman. The Irish bar, both Protestant and Catholic, was noted in Europe. It was particularly resplendent in its orators and wits: an Irish lawyer had to be smart to stand up to the sharp and subtle Irish mind, not least of all in the unlettered peasant. The Irish emigrant ships brought to the United

States a breed of lawyers, also a people who knew what the word "interest" meant, also a people acquainted with politics.

15

Old Hands at Politics

A FAMILIAR SIGHT at election time in Ireland during the first three decades of the nineteenth century was the procession of men straggling along a country road, headed by an officious-looking superintendent, astride a mule or horse, on the way to the polling booths in the nearest town not *to vote* but *to be voted* as a bloc according to the instructions of the landlord or his agent — "with as little ceremony," wrote Wakefield, "as the Jamaica planter would direct his slave to the performance of menial duties."

These were the forty-shilling freeholders, who, for the lease of a piece of Irish earth or a hovel bartered to the landlord or middleman the vote created by the lease, taking oath, which a court clerk amenable to the landlord's interest accepted without inquiry, of a forty-shilling profit in the lease, over and above the rent charge, which the electoral qualifications required.

The whole business was saturated with corruption. Land not worth two shillings was leased to make a forty-shilling freeholder, who compounded the landlord's original fraud by his own oath for which the landlord paid the legal fee. Forty-shilling freeholders' votes were sold to the highest bidder, and the middlemen, especially, conducted a profitable traffic in them. There is the story of the landlord who sold his forty-shilling votes first to one candidate and then to the other, and told his tenants, who asked him how to vote, to shop around for the highest offer they could get for themselves.

The corrupt construction of Irish society made politics synonymous with "interest," not public, but private. The emergence of the national cause for freedom among the Catholic masses revived the idealism of the earlier Protestant and revolutionary patriots, but even that burning and noble zeal had to contend with the opportunists and self-seekers.

The great and the wealthy ran Ireland politically like Tammany Hall in its worst days. Had they not sold their own country for money and titles in the Act of Union with England and, as one rogue said,

thanked God they had a country to sell? Their very rascality, wrote
O'Neill Daunt, O'Connell's secretary, "was of magnificent dimensions.
There was no paltry peddling about them." A gentleman was thought
no less a gentleman because he dealt, like merchandise, with the votes
of his tenants or purchased his parliamentary seat as he would a horse
or a new wing for his big house.

2

The Irish peasant saw direct evidence of corruption by the politically
powerful within the small horizons of his village or townland, in the
workings of the grand jury. He might not know what his bartered vote
led to in the English Parliament in faraway London, but he knew for a
certainty that the new road was a "job," in which the local magnates
had not-too-clean fingers. It is not without pertinence that the word
"jobbing," the turning of public trust to private advantage, had its wid-
est circulation, if not its origin, in Protestant-Ascendancy Ireland.

The grand jury was not confined in Ireland, as in the United States,
to returning true bills in criminal cases. Its more important duty was to
sit as a county council, fix the county tax, and vote "presentments," that
is, appropriations, for county public work — roads, bridges, embankments, and the like.

Public works went by favor, not by merit or necessity. The Royal
Canal had been cut in the wrong direction, that it might pass near a
great man's property. Barracks were erected to create a market for an adjoining estate. Embankments were built to enhance the holdings of a
favored person. Roads were made for the convenience of a man of consequence, not for public benefit. Militia companies were raised to provide commissions as officers for favored individuals.

Grand juries pursued no investigation if a member, with a contract
to make a road, pocketed the cash money and employed his own farmers, cottiers, and laborers, deducting the labor from the rent or paying
them in food. A road could be built without the passing of a shilling
in cash from the contractor to the workers. The tenants, victims of
this truck system, even besought the landlord to get a road contract to
enable them to catch up on rent arrears by their labor. The chain of
corruption, said Art O'Connor, ran "from the Castle to the Cabin."

3

Each election contest in Ireland turned itself into a minor civil war. Elections had always been turbulent in that country. Even the whole-souled patriotic Grattan had been set upon by a Dublin mob in an election contest. During the Irish pollings, "one could scarcely hear a word," as was said of a Dublin contest. "I do not think any election where there is a contest could be held safely in Ireland . . . without a strong military and police protection being afforded," said a stipendiary magistrate. Magistrates themselves strapped on arms at election time.

The Catholic Irish took politics seriously — and vigorously. Their racial vehemence of character made them unqualified partisans; their strong feelings were intolerant of political opponents (there were instances of Catholic Irishmen who refused to work for employers with political opinions they disliked); and their swift tempers translated sentiment into strong-arm measures. The peasantry of Ireland, said John Cahill, a magistrate of Tipperary, himself a Catholic, are "very warm politicians; not that I mean to say that they perfectly understand the bearing of every question; but they are very warm in support of that which they believe to be for their interests."

Intimidation, the instrument of Whiteboyism, was the popular weapon with which they enforced their will at the polls. "Intimidation," said Lewis, "is a favorite mode of pursuing any object in Ireland." A magistrate explained that "if a Roman Catholic votes contrary to their wishes he is a more obnoxious person than the Protestant, inasmuch as they think that it is natural for a Protestant to go with his own cause, but they consider that it is extremely unnatural for a Roman Catholic to vote against his religion and his party." A Catholic landlord, who was active for the Tories against the Catholic party in Carlow, was condemned by O'Connell as "an apostate to his religion and to his country, and they ought to throw dead dogs into his grave."

In Sligo, armed parties visited houses and advised the inmates of the consequences if they failed to vote for certain candidates. "Molly Maguire" notices warned voters whose allegiance was in question. Priests vowed they would post in the chapel the names of men who voted against the cause. At polling places, partisans armed with sticks, bludgeons, and similar blunt instruments stood on watch as a threat to voters whose hearts were not "honest." It often happened that a polling place

was seized and only sympathetic voters allowed to register their preference.

Riots, bloodshed, clashes with the police, raids on audiences listening to candidates making their pleas for votes, pitched battles between
tenants committed by their landlords — a contested Irish election was
never a tepid affair.

4

Besides intimidation — the mob method in politics — the Irish knew
the shady practices of politics and, being an ingenious people, invented
a few of their own, Protestant and Catholic alike. Instances were
frequent of persons voting on freeholds whose owners were dead —
"very frequent," a man from County Mayo admitted. No man dared
to run for office unless he and his agents were prepared to spend
money like water for refreshments, not water. "Personation," that
is, voting fraudulently in another's name, was probably the most
common electoral offense; and since the polls kept opened for five days,
the elector who did not appear early discovered too often that his vote
had been declared by a repeater or floater. Around election time, rumors
slandering a candidate were sedulously spread — and in Ireland, rumors
had the speed of wind in circulating through the countryside; these
were countered by slanderous rumors spread in behalf of the slandered
candidate against the candidate who had slandered him. In Mullingar,
a placard appeared calling on Protestant landlords to dispossess every
Catholic from their lands, "driving to Hell or Connaught hundreds of
the superstitious and priest-ridden generation," and proclaiming that the
sacrifice was worth the blood that would flow. The placard, of course,
was a canard. Partisan clerks at the election booths handled the crowds
so slowly, and in such a fashion, that opposition voters were shut out.
The patron of Galway borough, one Daly, finding an opposition to his
interest, marched a regiment of soldiers stationed in a barracks nearby
into Galway and had them made voters. They voted for his friend, who
was elected.

5

Politics in Ireland was the agency through which the race hoped to
redress the multitudinous wrongs for centuries heaped upon them and

to further the "cause." A magistrate defined the "cause" in pre-Famine Ireland: "good government, good juries to try them if they are accused of offences, impartial magistrates, the same justice for a man who happens to have particular religious opinions and for a man who happens to have a contrary religious opinion." In other words, they were striving for an equal status under the law with the ascendant Protestants.

1 6

Catholic versus Protestant

IT WAS A PROVERB among the Catholic Irish that for a man to be happy in this world and in the next, he should live a Protestant and die a Catholic. The wry neatness of the proverb contained the Catholic Irishman's certainty that the good things in this life belonged to the Protestants, but that priority in bliss would be his reward in the next. "King Number is Catholic, and is strong too," wrote a correspondent of an American newspaper. "King Power is Protestant, and is stronger."

"English" and "Protestant" were synonymous; the Irish word *Sassenach* meant both Protestant and Englishman. John S. Rochford, a resident magistrate of County Carlow, drew a discerning summary from history:

> I think that the hostility which existed from the Irish to the English, was, at the Reformation, changed from the Catholic to the Protestant; that all those, whether of English or Irish descent, who continued Catholic, conceived themselves as Irish; and all those, whether of English or Irish descent, who had changed their religion and become Protestant, were considered as English; and that which was originally Irish and English, has now come to be Catholic and Protestant.

It was taken prima facie by the Catholic Irish peasants that a Protestant was a person of English antecedents. The word "Protestant" meant specifically a member of the Established Church; evangelical and other sects were specifically labeled as "Dissenters." But the Catholic Irish never doubted they all were Protestants.

Deep in the Gaelic mind was the memory that the land once belonged to his ancestors, that the Protestant English and Scots were usurpers, and that the true Irish nation was the Catholic Irish nation.

Yet there was no conscious or declared objective among the mass of Catholic people to drive Protestants out of Ireland or take revenge upon them because of their religion.

The idea of religious pogrom would have appalled them. W. C. Taylor, the Protestant historian of the Irish civil wars, in giving justice to "this maligned body" of Roman Catholics, declared that "on the three occasions of their obtaining the upper hand, they never injured a single person in life or limb for professing a religion different from their own." They protected the Protestants who had fled from England to escape the persecution of the Catholic Queen Mary Tudor; the Kilkenny Confederation, which developed from the 1641 uprising, legislated religious toleration; and the King James Parliament, in the Williamite times, drew up an act of perfect religious toleration. The Catholic Irish agitations aimed not to destroy Protestantism, but to gain rights denied to Catholics.

2

Ireland presented the anomaly in nineteenth-century Europe of being a land where parties divided on religious lines, when even the countries of Luther and of Calvin had subordinated theology to the secular state. But the situation in Ireland will be misunderstood if the word "religion" is taken in the meaning of doctrine as the cause of division. Religion marked social, economic, and political boundaries. It was observed to Wakefield that "the term Catholic is not a mark of religious distinction, but of every distinction whatever." And T. F. Lewis said: "I do not think that if the question of religion was all, the people would quarrel very much about religion; the religion is rather the mark by which parties are distinguished who are hostile upon other grounds than the cause of the quarrel." Bicheno thought that religious differences "have only been an exasperating cause to widen the breach which was already created" and that they had become "representative of all grievances."

The Protestants enjoyed the superiority of caste. Protestants of the same economic circumstances as a Catholic farmer or peasant, though ignorant and vulgar, looked down upon Catholics as an Indian Brahman would upon an untouchable. "Every Protestant cobbler and tinker," wrote O'Neill Daunt, "conceived himself superior to the Catholic of ancient lineage and ample inheritance." The Catholic addressed a Protestant, no matter how lowly his station, as "Mister." The lower orders of Protestants resisted strenuously any concessions to the Catholics, fearing their privileged position as Protestants would be endangered and Catholics placed over their heads.

The distinction between Protestant and Catholic colored and poisoned the relationships of life. The Catholic Irish were made to feel their inferiority in whichever direction they turned. The landlord thought that Catholicism, as did Charles II of the Presbytery, was not a religion "for gentlemen." The majority of Protestants "would as soon marry an African, or a female of Kamschatka as a 'papist.'" Protestants did not use the word "Catholic"; the word "papist," with all its historical connotations, was substituted, and carried "as much contempt along with it, as if a beast were designated by the term."

3

In the northern counties of Ulster, where more of a population balance existed between Protestants and Catholics, and Protestants were both peasants and farmers, the Orange-Catholic antagonism was open and ready to break out into violence with bitterness reminiscent of the Reformation.

The Orange society was a secret society, exclusively Protestant, with an elaborate ritual, passwords,* and signs, sworn to uphold the Protestant succession in England, the Act of Union, and keep down Irish Catholicism. The Orangemen, recruited principally from the middle and lower orders, were the storm troopers of militant Protestantism, "intolerably presumptious, insolent and offensive" to Catholics, wrote Newenham. Respectable Protestants shunned the Orange Order as respectable Catholics the Ribbonmen: according to the historian W. C. Taylor, "experience proves, that, in Ireland, hatred of Popery is more violent the lower we descend in the scale of rank, wealth or intelligence."

The Orange assumptions outraged every sensibility of the Catholic Irish. The toast of the Order — "The glorious, pious and immortal memory of the great and good King William," who had saved Ireland from "popery, brass money and wooden shoes" — and the Orange

---

* One of its passwords, "The Great I Am hath sent me to you," filtered into the vocabulary of the Catholic Irish. "He thinks he's the Great I Am" was used scornfully by Catholics toward one who put on airs or assumed pretensions beyond his capacities; it was frequently heard in America.

songs, "Boyne Water" and "Croppies Lie Down," of the 1798 Rebellion, flung in the faces of the Catholic Irish the reminder of defeat.
Orange flags flying from Protestant churches on holidays flaunted an
alien religious power. The Orangemen originated the offensive slogan
"To hell with the Pope!" shouted to the beating of Orange drums
with such vehemence that the blood ran from the fists of the thumpers.
   On the anniversary of the Battle of the Boyne, troops were gathered
from the other sections of Ireland to maintain order in Ulster. But the
July 12 anniversary was not the sole occasion of sectarian riots. Maxwell
Hamilton, Crown Solicitor for the Northeast Circuit of Ulster, a hotbed of Orangeism, described the familiar pattern of an Orange "walk":

> For instance, let me suppose the case of a number of Orange-
> men who choose to walk in a procession through some village in-
> habited by many Roman Catholics. In walking in procession they
> are decorated with various badges, music and insignia. The Orange
> flag is perhaps waved into some Roman Catholic's face; stones are
> then thrown at the procession party, who of course repel the attack.
> The destroying or wrecking of the whole village probably follows.
> The Protestants, being beaten out of town by the Roman Catholics
> (who rise in great numbers for the occasion), get the worst of it;
> their flags are probably taken from them; their drums are trampled
> upon and broken. They come back in a day or two, having collected
> all the forces they possibly can, and avenge themselves. That creates
> of course a great deal of private animosity between the parties who
> have been engaged in the conflict, and they will some time or other
> have their revenge for any particular injury they each received dur-
> ing the affray.

   Lives were lost, blood flowed freely, heads were cracked in this
senseless fury of sectarian passion. The English government, or its representatives in Dublin, had not been loath to stir up the latent antagonisms to keep Ireland divided, but Ulster history, as Ford, the chronicler
of the Scotch-Irish in America, has written, "is unbroken in its continuity, and it has transmitted to our own times feelings, interests, prepos-
sessions and antipathies derived from the sixteenth century." The religious wars did not end for Ireland with the Treaty of Westphalia.

The Faith of Patrick

THE ROMAN CATHOLIC CHURCH had emerged from its penal bondage poor and shabby in its material establishment but stronger than ever in spiritual endowments, loved by the people with the deepest attachments of affection and loyalty. In common adversity, Church and people had come to an insoluble unity which no other circumstances could have wrought.

Beaumont, the traveling companion of De Tocqueville in the United States and probably the most penetrating observer of pre-Famine Ireland, peered with insight to the heart of this relationship, writing:

> The Irish people exists in its Church; there alone it is free; there alone it is sure of its rights; there it occupies the only ground that has never given way beneath its feet.

He characterized the priesthood as the "most national body in Ireland," belonging "to the very heart of the country." The Irishman, he said, "believes there is nothing permanent or certain in this world but his religion which is coeval with old Ireland, — a religion superior to men, ages, and revolution. . . . To an Irishman there is nothing supremely true but his creed."

Ironically, it was the French Revolution, which scourged the Roman Catholic Church in France, that set the Irish Catholic Church back on the road to recovery and established its modern foundations. Under the eighteenth-century penal laws, because education was denied to the Catholic Irish, the priesthood received its training in colleges abroad — in France, Belgium, Italy, Spain or Portugal. Association with people of other nations had given these priests a wider outlook than the narrow skies of Ireland permitted and softened the angular Irish nature somewhat, but the fear of invoking the penal laws made them timid and satisfied with carrying on their priestly duties inconspicuously, without drawing attention to themselves by championing Catholic rights.

Edmund Burke, the inflexible enemy of the French Revolution, persuaded the Protestant Ascendancy in Ireland and the English government that it might be dangerous to continue to train Catholic

Irish priests in France from which they would return with Jacobinical principles, and that it was time anyway to educate Irish priests in their own country. In consequence, the Royal College of Maynooth was established in 1795 by a small public grant — and from that moment, the Church started to lift its head from the penal yoke.

For the first time since the Tudors, young Irishmen who from their calling were destined to positions of leadership among the people were trained as a body. They exchanged ideas and discovered that the son of a peasant from County Monaghan related the same experience of hardship and oppression in his district as the son of a peasant from County Kerry. The seclusion of their lives in Maynooth stirred the sparks of national feeling and restricted their interests to the Church and Ireland.

The establishment of Maynooth and diocesan seminaries elsewhere, in combination with the political struggle for Catholic Emancipation, was a revolutionary force in translating the meek, timid, and servile eighteenth-century Irish hierarchy and clergy into an aggressive, assertive, and strong-willed body in pre-Famine Ireland — the "modern" priests, they were called.

The Protestant Archbishop of Dublin regretted the passing of the old penal-day priests. They were better educated, he thought; they were then under the patronage of gentlemen, imbibing their ideas, and eternally grateful to their benefactors for preferment; their withdrawal abroad for some time "from the scene of fermentation and party" was by its nature advantageous. But in Maynooth, he went on, "the student still breathes . . . the atmosphere of inflammation"; he kept up a connection — "not a wholesome one" — with friends he knew before he entered the seminary. Maynooth as at present conducted, the Archbishop concluded, was "not favorable to tranquillity" nor to "principles of sound civil allegiance."

One magistrate explained that he used to dine with the old priests, but the new Maynooth lot were inclined to keep aloof from the gentry; and James Glassford, a commissioner of education, thought the Maynooth men more strenuous in opposition to, and less tolerant of the measures of, the Protestant clergy than the old priests. "Maynooth," said the London *Times*, "contains scarcely any gentlemen." The "modern" priests were disturbing the settled — and unequal — order.

Bishop Doyle, thirty years after the start of Maynooth, described the new priests as "energetic, active, laborious, shrewd, and intelligent

. . . filled with zeal in the discharge of their duties." Their offices and connections, he continued, "mix them up and identify them with the people; they are acquainted with, and take an interest in the domestic concerns of almost every family; they possess the full and entire confidence of their flocks; they are always employed; there is nothing dull or quiescent about them."

The busy and hard-working Irish priests of the home-trained new school had little time for scholarship, books, or literary pursuits. They were practical men consumed with a passion for building, or, as Bishop Doyle eloquently put it, "cleansing the holy places, rebuilding the sanctuary, making new vessels for the sacrifice and worshipping most devoutly at their half-raised altars."

The most familiar sight in rural pre-Famine Ireland on Sunday mornings was the dense crowds outside a chapel, standing or kneeling in sun or rain, because the mean little eighteenth-century church, which resembled a cow barn, could not accommodate them. The penal restrictions upon Catholic churches, which limited their numbers; the poverty of the people, which inhibited improvements and repairs; the tremendous growth of population, which outgrew the capacities of the little churches — all these imposed upon emancipated Catholic Ireland the difficult task of rebuilding the physical plant of the Church from scratch.

2

Abuse of the Catholic Church by other sects was as frequent and expected as the rains in Ireland. It ranged from the comparatively temperate description of the Church by Archbishop William Magee of the Established Church as a "gloomy, erroneous, exclusive, and intolerant superstition" to the more rugged "a limb of Antichrist" of the Dissenters to the vulgarity by the street-corner evangelical of "the old whore" and "the mother of all abominations."

The English mentality of the Counter-Reformation period had persisted. Beliefs imputed to the Catholic Church included such articles as that it was lawful to murder a heretic, that no faith need be kept with a heretic, that princes excommunicated by the See of Rome might be deposed or murdered by subjects, and that the Pope held superior jurisdiction in the realm: echoes of the Elizabethan age reverberated down the centuries.

The Catholic peasant thought things were being carried too far when, in addition to supporting the aristocracy, the government, the army, the local roads and his own Church, he had to support by legally imposed tithes a Church in whose creed he did not believe, whose services he did not attend, whose parsons in the overwhelmingly Catholic areas were absentees — "nine-tenths of the people," said O'Connell, "are compelled to contribute to the Church of the one-tenth."

The Catholic Irishman saw the wealthy, even magnificent Church Establishment and compared it with the miserable hovel where he worshiped. He saw the comfortable sinecures of the Establishment, distributed among the favored, with a handful of worshipers and compared them with the pittances of his own hard-working priests. He noted that the Protestant Archbishop of Armagh, with an income of £20,000 a year, left an estate of £130,000, while the Roman Catholic Archbishop of Dublin, Dr. Troy, with an annual income of £800, died worth about tenpence.

In 1831, emboldened by the victory of Catholic Emancipation, six million Roman Catholics resolved not to pay the tithes to the Church of six hundred thousand Protestants. Failure to pay made the property of the recalcitrant subject to seizure, and it was not edifying to see a cow impounded for tithes protected by sixty men of the 12th Lancers, five companies of the 92nd Highlanders, a strong force of police, and two pieces of artillery. The mode of collection was hardly uplifting: the parsons, not relishing the obnoxious task, sold the rights to a tithe-proctor, a breed with all the instincts of a shark.

The Tithe War waged back and forth, climaxed in the little village of Rathcormac, County Cork, when police and soldiers, headed by one Archdeacon Ryder, appeared to collect a tithe of forty shillings from a Widow Ryan. Peasants rushed to protect the widow and in the fighting twelve were shot dead. The next year, 1835, Ireland's Chief Secretary Drummond denied military assistance to the parsons, and in 1838 the English government enacted a tithe composition measure.

The law favored the Established Church with measures which irritated the Catholic Irish. A priest could not hold services at a grave in the local cemetery, which had once been Catholic property, without the permission of the minister, who fixed the time: the Catholic clergy boycotted this petty tyranny of the law. The Catholic population was taxed for new churches of the Establishment and repairs of the old, and the support of the clerk and sexton. A Catholic prelate or priest could not, by law, wear the vestments of his office outside the confines of the church, in public procession, for example.

The Irish Catholic priest could not help plunging into politics when political action looking to Emancipation was the sole means of ridding his Church of such excrescences imposed in the first place by politics.

The word "proselytism" acted upon the Catholic clergy with the same impact as "informer" upon the Catholic peasant. The Established Church, Bible and religious societies in England, and the evangelical sects felt that their "white man's burden" in Ireland laid it upon their consciences to redeem the benighted papists from superstition and idolatry, remove them from under the maleficent spell of the priests, and convert them into good and moral Christians, that is, Protestants. Some landlords, like Lord Farnham, took it upon themselves to persuade their tenants of the virtues of Protestantism — and the wisdom of "turning," as the Catholics called conversion.

What these societies tried to carry out essentially was the old and unsuccessful Tudor policy of turning the Catholic Irish into good English Protestants — and the rejection in the nineteenth century was just as vigorous as in the sixteenth. As a parish priest in County Meath told Wakefield: "The poor cannot be tempted." Catholicism was so settled in their bones that without it, they would not have been Irish. Catholicism so satisfied the deepest needs of their nature, that they accepted it simply and without questioning.

The Catholic Irish believed that no member of their Church was converted to Protestantism without a material consideration. Daunt wrote:

> The universal conviction on the minds of the lower order of Catholics was that nobody "turned" . . . except for lucre, and that an enormous fund existed, under the control of the Protestant leaders, for buying up the religious beliefs of all the Papists who were willing to conform.

Apostasy, wrote Beaumont, was "the greatest of crimes in the sight of the Irish peasant." The Irish recoiled from an apostate not only as a lost soul, but as a betrayer of the race: he had, in effect, "informed" on his own people by a shameful desertion. Disgrace was visited upon his family, and the long Irish memory stored his name. One of the reasons the Catholic Irish still are so meticulous about refraining from meat on Friday (though that original reason has been forgotten) is that in Ireland to eat meat on Friday was a public profession of apostasy.

Hunger or distress drove some Catholic Irish to the Protestant minister "during the dear [critical] months of the year for support," according to the Rev. Thomas Costello of County Limerick, but they returned
to the chapel when the crops came in. Daunt tells of a "convert" on the
estate of Lord Bandon in County Cork, who "turned" to hold his lease
when that nobleman decided to plant a Protestant colony.

> "But you'd lose your poor soul!" remonstrated a man.
> "Och, — maybe not — maybe not. I expect God won't take me so
> short entirely but that I may quit them all and go back to mass once
> more before I die."

The "convert" added that, in protection of his soul, he shut his ears to
the prayers and services in the Protestant church and said his Catholic
prayers to himself. One day, suddenly taken ill, he sent a messenger for
the priest for the last rites. "But, hark ye!" the double-dealing invalid
warned, "tell his Reverence not to come up till after dark, for fear any
of the Protestants should see him and tell the minister." The priest refused to come.

On Lord Farnham's missionary estate, some Catholics were "converted" three or four times a year to get soup, potatoes, and clothes.
Proselyters intensified their missionary work during the Famine period
with the establishment of feeding stations, from which spread the words
"Souperism," to describe the commercial process of conversion, and
"Soupers," to characterize both the converters and the converted. Zealous landlords built Protestant churches and schools on their estates,
and made attendance a condition of tenantry: converts under duress
often distressed the minister by saying the Rosary during the Protestant
service. When word arrived from County Cavan that Lord Farnham's
exertions had borne the rich fruit of 1483 conversions, Archbishop
Magee traveled forth to confirm the new flock, only to find forty-two.

The evangelicals conducted conversion raids with both persistence
and energy upon the Catholic flocks, supported with funds from England. Walls carried anti-Catholic placards, and controversial literature
was liberally distributed. Itinerant colporteurs called Scripture readers,
who were often converted Catholics, talked to the Catholic people and
distributed Bibles. Finding the door of a cabin open, they entered to receive the traditional polite welcome and hospitality of Catholic Ireland to the stranger. They passed the time of the day with the family
and, after a while, asked permission to read a chapter of the Bible, ex-

plained its meaning and, if the man of the house was agreeable, left literature. The priests, possessive of their people, gathered their flocks around them and exclaimed, "The wolf is on the track!" They preferred not to underestimate the material and political power of Protestantism in Ireland, where Catholicism was synonymous with poverty. Children taken into foundling homes whose parents were unknown were registered and reared as Protestants. Houses of industry, dispensaries, and hospitals were nurseries of Protestant proselytism. Charity to the Catholic Irish carried a meaning of Protestantism.

Evangelists tried to preach publicly in the country towns in competition with horns blown loudly by boys or above the catcalls of the faithful Catholics. Sometimes the local priest appeared to challenge vigorously the assertions of the preacher, and the excitement-loving Irish relished the war of words; or he came hustling up with his blackthorn stick to drive the curious away, leaving the missionary alone with his Book.

3

Distrustful of superiors, the Irish peasants trusted the priests. Friendless in a hostile atmosphere, they felt the priests were their friends. Disdained and despised by the ruling castes, they found comfort in the regard of the priests. A landlord would think it outrageous to mix with them, but the priest took them by the hand.

John Cahill, the Crown Prosecutor for County Tipperary, admirably summed up the relationships between priests and people:

> There are very kindly feelings between them; they visit them when they are sick, and speak of religious subjects with them, and advise with them on all their affairs; they are continually among them. If a poor man wants a favor asked of some great man, he gets the priests to ask that favor of him; if he is in distress or difficulties, he goes to his priest, and looks upon him as his friend or protector.

The priest came from much the same social and economic background as the people to whom he ministered; the wretched cabin held no shock for him. The people frequently felt the priest's power but rarely his patronizing. The priest was their doctor, and his medicine chest was part of his traveling equipment. The people conferred with the priest on business affairs as well as on family troubles. On his dying bed, the Irishman sent for the priest to make his will: the will was associated with the last rites; hence, the belief that drawing a testament drew on death. They asked his advice on the wisdom of emigrating, and carried with them his character reference. For those who could not read or write, he read their letters or penned their messages. Emigrants sent money to their families through the priest.

The people were tied closely to him by the great events in a peasant's life — a christening, a wedding, a funeral. The peasants' hearts overflowed with gratitude at the response of the priests to sick calls, upon which they were "frequently exposed to the most imminent danger of losing their health and lives in visiting, at night, the wretched hovels of the peasantry, where nothing is found but misery and contagious disorder." Bishop Doyle once angrily cut short the excuse of a priest that he had neglected a sick call because he lacked a horse. "Horse, sir!" exclaimed the bishop, "and a poor dying soul at stake: you should have mounted a cow if no other mode of conveyance had presented itself."

Obedience by the people was automatic in the spheres where the people thought the priest had rightful authority. But in politics, they would struggle even against the priest were he to oppose them. A priest who too vigorously upheld the existing system was called a "landlord's priest," and stories circulated that he was either a spy or in the pay of Dublin Castle. In political matters, the priest more often reflected the views of the people than led them. The authority of the priest diminished if he interfered with what the people thought was to their interest. If the issue arose, the people supported their local priest against the bishop, and even against the Pope. O'Connell spoke out of the peasant's heart when he said he took his religion from Rome and his politics from home.

4

The Church in this period had neither the resources nor the personnel to provide regular services for all the Catholics in rural Ireland. People traveled, by horse or on foot, for miles to attend services on Sunday and feast days, but this was out of the question for Catholics who lived in scattered and remote villages. Twice a year, starting Easter and Christmas, a priest traveled on regular schedule to the outlying bounds of the parish on what were called stations, to hear confessions and give

Communion. There he also collected the parish dues — a shilling or two from a man and wife. In the absence of the services of a priest regularly, the people kept up their relationship with the Church by a public saying of the Rosary each Sunday, and it was the common custom of households to close each evening with the Rosary. The binding power to the Church, as well as the religious comfort to the people, of the Rosary in remote rural Ireland cannot be stressed too strongly: it was the golden link of the people with a Church whose priests they saw only twice a year. And the people called a priest, in Irish, *soggarth aroon*, or "priest dear."

18

A Look at the Catholic Irish

THE STEREOTYPE of the "stage Irishman" libeled the Catholic Irish people. Compare the buffoonish Shauns and Paddys of the caricature with the picture of the Catholic Irishman whom Daniel O'Connell lifted from his penal crouch, as drawn by a writer in the Boston *Pilot* in 1847, who caught the harsh lineaments of that penal-scarred soul:

> He was a suspicious, shrinking man: strange, unintelligible emotions were always on his countenance; and he turned his eyes askant whenever you looked into his face. He seemed to be thinking, and contriving, constantly, without any apparent motive. You felt you could not open your heart to him; for he never did to you: if in low rank, he plied you with transparent flattery; if he was of middle life, he was still breaking off a conversation mysteriously. And old men, his contemporaries, who have gained his confidence, and reached the bottom of that deep, dark, narrow heart, have declared that they could find in it no human faith, or hope. There was so much distrust and despondency within him, let him be as honest as he might, yet in political enterprises they dare not trust him; sheer despair had laid him open to corruption.

Calculated oppression had scarred the Catholic Irishman, deeply and hurtfully. "All the faculties of his soul that despotism has touched," wrote Beaumont, "are blighted; the wounds there are large and deep. All this part of him is vice, whether it be cowardice, indolence, knavery, or cruelty; half of the Irishman is a slave."

Over the centuries of subjugation, the Catholic Irishman had evolved a character to fit him for survival in a hostile environment. The contented and comfortable masters and preachers, who talked of principles, called this invidious character immoral and blamed the absence of scruples upon his religion, which failed, they said, to inculcate correct teachings.

The moral standards of a people tyrannized by an alien power are not those which prevail where government is by consent of the ruled. For the Catholic Irish to obey and honor the laws fashioned for their oppression, was to tighten the bonds of inferiority and acquiesce in the serfdom. To give unquestioning allegiance to the power which ruled them was to betray their own nature, wanting freedom. To accept humbly a social system which exploited them to the margin of an uncertain and low subsistence, was to compound their own poverty. To reconcile themselves to institutions which insulted their religion and held them in disdain as a people was to be a slave.

The soul of the Catholic Irishman seethed with sedition and rebellion. He loved the songs which proclaimed undying hatred of the English and the old stories of outlaws and heroes, interchangeable terms. He bought and learned by heart the disloyal ballads peddled at fairs. He reveled in speeches boiling with treason and preferred the priest to talk on political subjects than preach religious or moral homilies. But he had the earthy peasant wisdom and instinct of prudence to understand that an unarmed peasantry could not throw off a government that was brutal in the exercise of force or stand up to his masters who, by lifting a finger, could call that force to their side or, worse still, deprive a man of his livelihood.

Their alien rulers deprived them of the things which separate a man from a slave, including their self-respect; and that, like denying them education, was a sin against humanity. Arthur Young, with brutal candor, described the relationship between master and worker in the last quarter of the eighteenth century:

> A landlord in Ireland can scarcely invent an order which a servant laborer or cottar dares to refuse to execute. Nothing satisfies him but an unlimited submission. Disrespect or any thing tending towards sauciness he may punish with his cane or his horsewhip with the most perfect security; a poor man would have his bones broke if he offered to lift his hand in his own defence.

In self-protection, the Catholic Irishman put on a mask of dissimulation and deception; evasion became a shield; craft and wiliness crept into his nature; and he made an art of the cunning. "And why wouldn't we be cunning?" a ragged messenger asked of a pair of travelers who accused him of the trait. *"Isn't it our strength?"* They delighted in stories that exalted a man's quick wits in outsmarting another, or his cunning in extricating himself from a difficult situation. But in accordance with the law of his nature, the Irishman carried these defense weapons to extremes. Flattery gushed from him with the overwhelming luxuriance of the tropic of Capricorn: laborers ever praised their masters because they dared not speak out, noted Wakefield, lest "some bird of the air should tell the master" and they lose their sixpence or eightpence a day. If they petitioned, they went to their knees to deliver it. Their fingers were constantly to their hat, tipping it; and they lowered their eyes in the presence of the gentry, fearing to offend with the stare or direct glance. Their voices took on a whine, and "we are so poor" was standard on their lips. Their heads were bowed as they walked, and their language was timid: "they receive as a favor," wrote Beaumont, "what they ought to demand as a right." A landlord, for his part, rarely granted a concession as a right; it was always a favor; and the peasant could not relate an act of justice to the law: it came from the kindness of the man who gave it.

Servility and a consciousness of inferiority impressed upon the Catholic Irish by all the agencies of alien domination damaged the spirit of a people whom a Donegal landlord thought "a quiet, inoffensive race, and naturally civil and kind in their manners." Compensation, in turn, carried the Catholic Irishman also to extremes, and boasting and bluster often expressed inner insecurity and doubt: "as he has a master, he is a flatterer," reported the sharp-eyed Beaumont, "and full of insolence when he is not cringing."

The Catholic Irishman thought honestly with his emotions and schemed with his mind. For centuries a prey, he built up the characteristics — distrust, suspicion, secrecy, and cunning — of the hunted.

2

The English, who knew less about the neighboring Irish than about the Hindus or Zulus thousands of miles away, blamed Irish racial characteristics for their social degradation. Yet the Irish peasantry, as Lewis pointed out, were not, on the whole, "an ignorant and illiterate class, as compared with the same rank of persons in other countries";

and Bicheno found in them none of the sogginess, sullenness, and boorishness of Continental peasants. The London *Quarterly Review* admitted that the race was endowed with natural capacities of no mean order — unequaled, perhaps, among northern peoples for quickness of imagination, fertility and ingenuity of device.

Even modern critical examination of past Irish patriotic assumptions cannot break down the conclusion regarding the cause of the evils of the social state in Ireland reached by the Frenchman Beaumont, in 1839:

> Consider attentively the character of the Irishman, analyze his virtues and his vices, and you soon recognize that every one of his dispositions, good or bad, is directly derived from the state of Irish society since the Conquest, and that this social state has either originated his inclinations, or at least given them direction and development.

The Gaels had little feel for trade and commerce; they held the merchant in rather low estimate. The Milesians, ran one prideful saying, were "scholars, poets, priests and warriors"; while in contemptuous contrast the Ulstermen were "weavers, shopkeepers and merchants." The Catholic Irish, said Chart, "rarely exhibit the combination of qualities which make for industrial success. They lack the keen interest in money-making, the sharp eye for a chance of profit, the readiness to submit to sacrifices in the hope of a distant reward, the stubborn endurance of a self-imposed task, which characterise the Englishman, Scotchman, and Ulsterman."

It is a striking fact that the Catholic Irish, almost as a race, rejected commercial careers for their children. A prosperous trader or dealer destined his son for the Irish bar or for landholding. Everyone, no matter how poor, said Matthew Barrington, Crown Solicitor for Munster, wanted his son a priest, or an attorney, or a lawyer. Father John Kelly of Mitchelstown, County Cork, observed that the generality of the Catholic Irish considered every person employed by the state, whether military or civil, as a kind of gentleman, and deferred to him as such with awe and reverence. An officeholder received respect withheld from a shopkeeper, an interesting background for the avidity with which the Catholic Irish sought the public payroll in the United States. With the peasant, noted O'Connell, "the situation of a police man is an extremely valuable one."

3

The closely knit loyalties of family life made the home the center of the Irishman's small world. Robert O'Callaghan, an inspector of barracks, thought that Irish children were "more inclined to support [their parents] than almost any people I have ever met with," and Bicheno added that "they feel it to be an obligation from which they can never be released." This abiding sense of family obligation was the most important instrumentality in transplanting millions of Catholic Irish to the United States; and it also held back many who had the urge to go but refrained because of the duty to care for aged parents.

The hospitality of the race was proverbial. O'Halloran, the historian, illustrated with an example the essence of this fine Catholic Irish virtue. Speaking of the middling and poor in Munster and Connacht, he said:

> Their houses are open for all poor strangers. As soon as one enters and places himself by the fire, he looks upon himself and the people look upon him so much as one of the family that he will rise to welcome the next comer.

It was not alone the Catholic Irishman's instinctive hospitality which distinguished a kindly nature; "he will make you feel the acceptance of a favor or kindness he bestows to be a compliment to himself rather than to you," wrote William Carleton. "The delicate ingenuity with which he diminished the nature or amount of his kindness, proves that he is no common man either in heart or intellect; and when all else fails he will lie like Lucifer himself, and absolutely seduce you into an acceptance of his hospitality or assistance."

4

Among themselves the Catholic Irish had a standard of pride that, though it did not wear a plume, held tenaciously to a dignity which was often excessive and also pathetic, under the circumstances. A man in the harsh season was too proud himself to beg for potatoes, and sent his wife to a distant area lest the family lose caste. Laborers testified before an inquiry committee that they preferred to work for a farmer at four shillings than receive five shillings on a public project if the stigma

of pauperism was attached to it. A revealing paragraph in a statement
by the Poor Law Inquiry commissioners highlights this pride:

> Notwithstanding the wretchedness of so many of the laboring
> classes, there is a deep rooted aversion to let others know their priva-
> tions, and they generally suffer in silent resignation, unless the
> benevolent mind of a neighbor suspects, or his searching eye discov-
> ers, the want which is concealed within the walls of the cabin. If he
> has a potato himself, relief, but secret, immediately follows.

This pride manifested itself strongly in a man's sensitivity to his
good reputation or the name of his clan. A man might strike an Irish
man without provocation and afterwards receive forgiveness; but "if another shall breathe but a hint, however remote but premeditately, that
he is perfidious," neither forgiveness nor generosity could be expected:
brooding on the insult to his reputation often mounted to the point of
brutal savagery in reprisal.

A creature of emotions and feeling, the Irishman had an impulsive-
ness which was as rapid and as wild as a summer's squall, quick to take
offense where it may be none was intended and as quick with an outburst of generosity it may be he could not afford. Touching sentiment
and harsh cruelty moved in the same orbit. "The Irish are not philoso-
phers as a rule," noted James Connolly, the Irish labor leader; "they proceed too rapidly from thought to action."

5

It may be that this emotional instability was the source of the intemperance which rode Ireland like a curse. (Ireland gave the word
"whiskey" to the English language.) Increasing knowledge of alcohol-
ism from modern studies points to a relationship between compulsive
drinking and emotional disturbances — a flight from reality, a compelling sense of inadequacy, frustration, a feeling of inferiority and insecurity. If unsteady emotions hasten a man to the glass, then the
Irishman fulfilled the specifications outlined by modern psychology as
the root causes of excessive drinking. It was assumed as a patent fact
that his poverty drove the Irishman to drink to forget the misery which
surrounded him. Without doubt this judgment carried validity, but
evidence showed that the Irishman drank more heavily when in a
prosperous state, that is, comparatively speaking. The hardest drinkers
in Catholic Ireland were the small farmers possessed of money on

market and fair days; the so-called tradesmen, or skilled workers, such as stonemasons, carpenters, tailors, and the like, with money wages; the colliery workers with a steady wage; and the fishermen with shillings in their pockets. The peasant was not rated a hard or consistent drinker for the simple reason that he could not afford it.

"The impression left by a perusal of the evidence," concluded a report of the 1836 Poor Inquiry Commission, "is, that the male rural population, though guilty of excess at fairs, markets, and wakes, are not habitual drunkards," and it noted that the "females are generally exemplary for their abstinence from stimulating whiskey." An Irish magistrate, writing in 1825, thought that "the lower orders of Englishmen are as much addicted to drunkenness as the same class of Irish." Then he made an observation that Americans were to discover for themselves: "The Irishman however is more noisy when he is drunk."

Great dreams became realized when the Irishman drank; his superiority to the world manifested itself, in his own mind; he could call into being the world of his imagination, different from the unkind and often bitter realities; and he felt powers within himself to bring down the sneerers and scoffers. The temporary victory in drink over frustration, insecurity, and the sense of inferiority, which constantly dogged him, probably accounted as much for the Irishman's intemperance as any of a score of other factors.

On the other hand, the Catholic Irishman who hated drink became intemperate in his fanaticism. As in so many departments of an Irishman's nature, he was a stranger to the balance of the mean in his emotions.

For a spell, from 1839 on, Ireland took the pledge from Father Theobald Mathew, a gentle Capuchin of Cork City, saintly and naïve, working a modern miracle with the race, who, reports showed, improved noticeably in a material way but, other reports indicated, became sullen, morose, and irritable from the strain of abstinence.

6

The general conjugal fidelity and reputation for chastity among Irish women were often cited to the honor of the race. The director of a survey in Ireland remarked to Frederick Page, the Deputy Lieutenant of the English county of Berkshire, that the eight hundred men under him, mostly soldiers, employed all over Ireland had almost all married there in consequence of the chastity of the women. Wakefield wrote that the easy and unreserved manner of Irish women deceived the English regiments stationed in Ireland after the 1798 Rebellion, who conceived the merry eye and the squeeze of the hand to be indications "of further favors." Where "the heart is uncorrupted," as in Ireland, he said, it is pure and "their virtue so well guarded as to be in no danger."

The Irish wife was often the brains, the manager, the savings bank, the realist for the notional and unrealistic husband. Landlords and agents preferred to give leases to widows than to male petitioners for the ground. The Irish woman had a hardy spirit, an undaunted courage, and, in asserting herself, an uninhibited brass. She was in the forefront of food riots. The police would rather face the wrath of the menfolk than the tongue — and bricks — of the women. "Remember your soul and liberty!" a wife shouted to her husband, imprisoned for debt and promised freedom if he voted Tory: the husband went back to jail. Husbands were warned not to return to the cabin if they voted for the landlords against O'Connell in the famous Clare election. When the men of the Irish Confederacy in 1847 failed to appear to rescue John Mitchel, the patriot, from his captors, it was Irish women who threw bricks at the soldiers carrying him in shackles to the transportation vessel.

7

Uneducated himself but eager for knowledge, the Catholic Irishmen held in the highest, even awesome, respect the fellow who could read and write. The word "scholar" was used among the unlettered Catholic Irish in a cavalier fashion, to say the least. Upon investigation it was often found that the "scholar's" claim to the name rested on the achievement of reading a newspaper.

The naturally inquisitive Irish relished the newspaper, regardless of its date. It was the popular medium of education among the people, where books were a rarity. "We have seen children desert their marbles, lads their game at hurley, and lovers their sweethearts," wrote Hall, "all for the sake of hearing the news. When the paper is finished, the elders talk it over, and the younger listen, and their habit raises up a race of politicians."

The incessant chatter of parents on politics and the unceasing political activity that attended O'Connell's leadership placed politics high in the interests of Catholic Ireland, which looked to it as the road to release from alien rule. But the nature of the Catholic Irishman gave him an affinity with politics as a practical affair more than as the science of government. The realities of existence had forced him to be a shrewd judge of human nature: his relationship with the landlord or agent had taught him to examine the face for the mood of the man to determine what line of attack to assume in pursuing the object he had in mind; he carefully probed to find out the superior's opinion that he might agree with it; he had developed a formula of circumlocution that aimed to get and not give information; his acquired suspicion kept his guard up at all times; his cynical experience instructed him that men are more often moved by interest and favor than by principle; his wiliness in anticipating and his ingenuity in thwarting danger to his own concerns were the products of his hard life.

The Catholic Irishman inclined to place all affairs on the basis of personal relationships: we have already heard of his axiom that a word in the court was worth a pound in the purse. His business dealings went by personal relationship; his life was guided by the personal relationships of family or clan; he did not inquire if the cause of an opposing faction had right on its side: his loyalty was to his own faction; and he expected loyalty to himself similarly, whether his cause was just or unjust. An Irishman felt almost instinctively the character of a man he met for the first time, whether he could be trusted as "one of us" or whether he had to be watched. He was not, as O'Connell had said, "a speculative character." His interest, first, last, and always, was in other human beings, fulfilling his native inquisitiveness, a quality essential to success in practical politics.

This was the secret of the Catholic Irishman as a politician: that he knew human beings and what moved them, and that he felt for them (or at least gave the appearance of feeling) the sentiments which they felt for themselves. The massive natural virtues of the Catholic Irish — hospitality, sympathy, and loyalty — were instruments that a leader knew how to play upon; also the reverse of the coin — malice, vindictiveness, and the long Irish memory.

8

As a personality the Catholic Irishman was an individualist, almost to the point of anarchy, positive in his beliefs, even though wrong, and emphatic in his expression, bordering constantly on belligerency; he loved to take the contrary side, often for the sake of contrariness; he disliked the rising because advancement in others implied to his mind a non-recognition of his own merits; he doubted the value a man placed upon himself, or the world placed upon him, preferring his own judgments, generally critical; he was no quick yea-sayer, more often a vigorously nay-sayer.

In this respect, a local historian observed in the Catholic Irish of the nineteenth century the same human failing that a seventeenth-century student thought pertinent to comment upon — their jealousy of one another; "but it is supposed," continued the local historian, "that this vile attribute is supplied only against their own countrymen or countrywomen, and expressly towards neighbors and relatives. It is so to speak, in inverse ratio to the degree of kinship or acquaintance, and it would appear that scarcely, if ever, there is jealousy by an Irishman towards a stranger or foreigner whatever may be the latter's degree of success or good fortune." This jealousy clawed at them: no race was more warmheartedly sympathetic with a man who was down and none more ready to clabber him when he was on the way up. It entered into their humor.

9

The broad farcical element, which characterized Irish humor to other peoples, did not express the comic genius of the race nor did the famous "Irish bull," which had its source in incomplete mastery of an alien language and literal translation of constructions that were correct in the original Irish. Authentic Irish humor had its roots in the quality of mind which distinguished the Gael throughout his history — imagination. This was best found in the solemn, serious, and straight-faced treatment of an absurdity. In the latter part of the 1830s, the Chinese government took strong measures to suppress the opium trade, invoking the opposition of the British, who were making a profitable enterprise of it. Two Chinese officials, Commissioner Lin and Lord High Admiral Kwan, were prominent antagonists of the English in the opium war. The Tipperary *Free Press*, under the heading "Irishmen in China," solemnly undertook a discussion of the two Chinese:

> It is said that the Chinese Commissioner Lin and the Lord High Admiral Kwan, are both natives of the County Waterford, the former having dropped the first letter of his name (Flin) and the lat-

ter (Quan) spelling his name differently, in order to assimilate with those of the country of their adoption. This fact would account for the bitterness manifested in all the attempts hitherto at negociation; the deep sense of wrong continued for centuries by England towards Ireland, may have actuated these Irishmen in high station to revenge the insults of their native land, under the shadow of a violation of the laws of the Celestial Empire.

Others picked up the theme and embellished it — with a straight face.

This playing with the outlandish and incongruous delighted the funny bone of the Irishman. John Gaynor, it was said, was a grand old middle-class farmer — a magnificent storyteller. He would tell of the cock blackbirds that took to feeding on corn, and the corn fermented in their craws and turned into whiskey. The birds got drunk and merry, and could be heard in every glen and garden whistling the "Cruiskeen Lawn."

O'Connell's off-beat humor reflected the comic sense of his race. In a speech at Galway, he told the audience that the English Chartists had asked him: " 'Have not the English ill-treated you for 700 years?' 'Only 672,' said I." Always with a straight face.

Historically, the Irish had venerated the fighting man and in their disarmed state of the conquest they transferred their respect to the "strong boy," the athlete powerful with his fists or gifted in wielding the faction stick or fleet of foot or nimble at hurling. They never doubted their prowess, in a fair field, over the English, and, lacking that field, they got back at the English with their humor.

What enthralled the Irish was the constant jibing and joshing among themselves, preferably personal in nature and not without malice. The use of malice by an Irishman against another (behind his back) defeated its end unless the language raised a laugh. With his sharp instinct for human failings, a mimicking Irishman could destroy in the eyes of others the pompous or the pontifical in an Irishman who assumed pretensions. Their genius for the apt nickname showed both the spirit of malice and of precise observation. The edge had been whetted in the give-and-take of a naturally talkative people, in the contest of native wit, that whiled away the long nights by the fire in a cabin.

10

But great as was their individuality as a temperamental character-istic, it did not extend as a racial trait to self-reliance. A sympathetic English observer wrote:

> The Irish peasant finding his own resources so limited, crushed and fettered as he has been for so great a number of years, has ac-quired a slavish habit of looking to any one rather than to himself for assistance. His energies of mind and body are all directed to the services of others; he has no idea of working for himself, beyond the narrow limits of his potato garden.

He looked to the family faction, as his forebears had looked to the clan, for redress of personal grievance or wrong. He looked to the land-lord, the agent, or the priest for advice and assistance. He looked to the magistrate as a person, not to the law, for his interest, not justice. He disliked to be alone, or work alone, or travel alone: he felt his own individuality best when he was with other Irish. He was accus-tomed to taking orders and directions, not giving them. He was, by the force of circumstances, habituated to working for others, not strik-ing out on his own. He had developed a sense of dependency upon others that was a handicap to his individual progress.

There is a passage in one of Carleton's short stories which excellently sums up the Irish gregariousness and mutual dependency:

"Well," said Andy Morrow, "I should like to know if the Scotch and English are such *heerum-skeerum* kind of people as we Irishmen are."

"Musha, in troath, I'm sure they're not," says Nancy, "for I believe that Irishmen are like nobody in the wide world but themselves; quare crathurs, that'll laugh or cry, or fight with any one, just for nothing else, good or bad, but company."

1 9

The Invisible World of Ireland

SAMUEL BOURNES was a landlord of Cromwellian anteced-ents in Rossport, County Mayo, a man of business often at odds with the Catholic Irish laborers. In improving his house and ground, he was confronted with a strike by the men. They downed their shovels and stood sullen and abusive before him, because his plans called for tampering with a well and a tree they respected as sacred. The spirit of his Roundhead ancestors arose in him: "If you and your kind," he said, "were less addicted to superstitions and ghostly beliefs and carried out your work in a practical and sensible manner, you would be much better off."

Mr. Bournes's "practical and sensible" eyes could not see the invisible world which was as familiar to his Catholic Irish workmen as the river, the road, and the waving grain. Mr. Bournes had not listened at night to the old people and their tales of "superstitions and ghostly beliefs" related with the conviction of truth, confirmed by their own experiences, and sanctioned because they "had" (heard) them from their own fathers and grandfathers. Mr. Bournes did not believe in the powers that had hovered over Gaelic Ireland from the time that was beyond any man's memory.

The superstitions of the Catholic Irish peasantry were characteristic of the intense folk life of a people steeped in tradition and ancient culture. In the backwash of a Europe that had been transformed, on an island shut off from modern influences by the English conquest, denied access to education, isolated rural Ireland kept the memory, unbroken and in direct succession, of its older life. The Irish language was a reservoir of the past as well as a medium of communication. Oral tradition, uncontaminated by books and undiluted by alien ideas, conserved the old beliefs from generation to generation: in this sense rural Ireland, in its outlook, was both primitive and innocent. The people were devout Roman Catholics and had an unshakable faith in the supernatural. The pagan heritage had also been saturated with the supernatural. Because they had not been exposed to unbelief or skepticism or scientific rationalism, the unseen world was as real to them as their poverty-stricken lives. Besides — and this is the key — they were an imaginative people. With their abiding sense of the supernatural, they saw no inconsistency in blessing themselves with one hand and spilling a bit of milk on the ground for the "good people" with the other.

If our minds can forget the unhappy surroundings, we can see in the folkways and the superstitions of the Catholic Irish the outlines of an artistry that the misery obscures.

If we try to understand the superstitions, not as the besotted unenlightenment of a hopelessly ignorant peasantry but as the outlet for the imagination of a people strangled in normal development by circumstances dictated from a foreign land in a harsh and unfeeling despotism, the prevalence of supernatural spirits takes an artistic shape that holds validity by the continuing interest of poets, including the greatest of the modern poets, Yeats, himself an Irishman but not a Catholic. The English conquest had not stripped the race of its original feel for the poetic.

The fairies that dwelt in Ireland — "the grass is full of them," a piper said — were a projection of the character of the people — mischief-loving, fond of dancing and singing, great at sports, gentle until aroused, full of wiles and tricks, called the "good people," who themselves liked to be called "the gentry." Of course they spoke Irish: "What else would they talk?" a woman replied to Lady Gregory. While there were malevolent and malignant creatures among the invisible hosts, the Irish fairy world stands forward by the absence of grossness and the sinister apparitions which other races have conjured up in their experience. The witch, for example, was rare, and the devil had no place in the fairy universe. "Fallen angels" was the characterization by the Catholic Irish of the spirits, although their origin was pagan.

The grace and delicacy in the concept of the little creatures represented an idealization of the invisible world rather than a fearful perversion of human characteristics. Their little forms were so lithe that when they danced upon a dewdrop it trembled but did not break. Fairy music, once heard, haunted the mind with its loveliness; and the highest praise of a fiddler was that he had snatched his art from the wee folk: the people could dance all night without tiring to his tunes. And the fairies took the blame for many a stumble and repose in a roadside ditch after a man was "overtaken," which was the Irish euphemism for the late stage of drunkenness. The Irish preferred the poetry of unreality to the prose of fact.

Strange things happened in Ireland. Fairy raths, or forts, fairy rings and fairy paths were inviolate ground, and if a road took an unnecessary turn in building, it was because the people refused to cut through a traditional fairy path. It might be a wandering cow or a prowling dog or an untethered donkey at night which sent shivers of apprehension through a lone Irishman walking, or weaving, along a lonesome road, but to his imagination the sounds became the next day the rustlings of the "good people." Many stories told of the numerous fights to rescue cattle the fairies were driving away. Fairies "struck" people for offending against them, and the unfortunate victims were crippled or took to their beds and died. If a fairy were attached to, or a captive of, a family, he would leap from his confinement when carried over a bridge, to float away on a wave playing on his pipe. When a person sneezed, it was the custom of whoever was handling food to cast a bit on the ground as propitiation: at milking time, a little was spilled for the "good people" as was a cupful of the first draw of the poteen still.

The supremely successful creation of the Irish imagination was the leprechaun, or (in Irish) pygmy, called the cluricaune in County Cork, the luricaune in County Kerry, the luridadawne in Tipperary, and the logheryman in Ulster, the shoemaker of the fairy world, the custodian of its crocks of gold, a merry, whistling fellow given to drink. He associated himself with families, preferably of the old Roman Catholic aristocracy. One had been in a family for five hundred years and was highly respected because of the ill-treatment he gave Cromwell and Elizabeth. The universal appeal of this little fellow made him an invisible export of Ireland and the name of "leprechaun" synonymous with Irishman in other lands. Translated from his native haunts, the tiny figure became cloying and commercial.

As deeply ingrained in the tradition of the people as belief in fairies was the cry of the banshee, an invisible agency which Sir Walter Scott, a fine student of folklore, called "one of the most beautiful" of "Irish fiction." The banshee, a woman, belonged to the ancient Catholic families of Ireland, though Mr. Harris, a Quaker, was reputed to have one associated with his family. When death approached the member of a family, the banshee took up her wail, not as a warning because death could not be escaped, but as a notice and as a lamentation, a fearful and harrowing sound, it was reported by those who had heard it, a cry of piercing sorrow.

2

Among the poor, the "keen," or human lamentation by the living for the dead, contained the poetry and music that was every Irishman's heritage. (Geraldus Cambrensis in the twelfth century said the Irish always expressed their grief musically.) It was the wail of sorrow which the Irish shared with the Jews and the Arabs, and probably had its origin in an Eastern land whence it was carried to Ireland by the dispersing Celts. Those who have never heard the "keen" must satisfy themselves by imaginative re-creation and find in it poetic drama of high order: a poor cabin, the only light the steady glow of candles, shadowy people sitting in the obscurity beyond their range, and an old woman, usually a professional "keener" but sometimes the wife or mother of the dead man, rocking to and fro and pouring forth in cadenced shrieking voice an improvised oration reciting the virtues of the man stretched in death on a table or rude box covered with a sheet.

> Cold and silent is thy bed. Damp is the blessed dew of night; but the sun will bring warmth and heat in the morning, and dry up the dew. But thy heart cannot feel heat from the morning sun: no more will the print of your footsteps be seen in the morning dew, on the mountains of Ivera, where you have so often hunted the fox and the hare, ever foremost amongst young men. Cold and silent is now thy bed.
>
> My sunshine you were. I loved you better than the sun itself; and when I see the sun going down in the west, I think of my boy and my black night of sorrow. Like the rising sun, he had a red glow on his cheek. He was as bright as the sun at midday: but a dark storm came on, and my sunshine was lost to me for ever. My sunshine will never again come back. No! My boy cannot return. Cold and silent is his bed.
>
> Life-blood of my heart — for the sake of my boy I cared only for this world. He was brave; he was generous; he was noble-minded; he was beloved by rich and poor; he was clean-skinned. But why should I tell what every one knows? why should I now go back to what never can be more? He who was everything to me is dead. He is gone for ever; he will return no more. Cold and silent is his repose.

This is part of a "keen" composed by an illiterate mother at the waking of her son, Florence Sullivan, hanged at the beginning of the nineteenth century in Cork for singing treasonable songs. Its simple dignity was not unusual: the generality of "keens" followed this pattern; and the character of the Irish language, in which it was sung, lent itself to expressive and poetical words and phrases.

The moment of the "keen" at the wake and during the funeral was the time of solemn truth. Otherwise, the wake in peasant Ireland was a social affair, where laughter and boisterousness obtained more than shows of sorrow.

People accustomed to the studied solemnity of the customs of other people at the occasion of death were shocked and horrified at the doings of an Irish wake and termed them savage and barbaric. But the Catholic Irish did not think that way: they deeply understood the sorrow of the family left behind — death was a sacred and holy thing for them; but the sociability of the wake was calculated to make the widow forget her sorrow and troubles and distract the thoughts of the grief-ridden. From the time that a death was known, the person left had little time to be alone with her sorrow: the cabin was filled at all times with the coming and going of visitors, and friends were expected to sit up all night during the usual two days' waking; tobacco was provided, and talk filled in the hours.

It was considered disrespectful not to attend a funeral, even though the dead person was unknown to those who joined the procession. An English commissioner, sitting as a member of the Poor Law Inquiry in the 1830s, saw several funerals of common laborers or of their wives followed to the grave (three or four miles distant) by from twelve to twenty farmers on horseback and two hundred or three hundred laborers and others in cars (carriages) or on foot, "scarcely one of whom had any kind of connexion with the deceased and many did not even know him or her. As the funeral passed some of the inmates of most of the cabins on the road sallied out to join us, although they could not tell the Assistant Commissioner who it was they were thus going to follow to the grave."

3

The Irish peasant, who rose to the heights at a wake or funeral, warded off death with superstitious charms, and fought sickness both with charms and the homemade remedies with magical properties concocted by old men and women who knew the secrets of cures. There was a charm for every ailment, from chin-sickness (whooping cough) to the bite of a mad dog. There were wishing stones and cursing stones; there were amulets to ward off evil; there were rites to propitiate the invisible forces; there were fairy women who had the secrets of undoing the wounds of the little folk.

The peasants mixed together the old pagan magic and the Roman Catholic religion. A folk cure for the mumps suggested: "Take nine black stones [nine was the pagan mystical number] gathered before sunrise, and bring the patient with a rope round his neck to a holy well — not speaking all the while. Then cast in three stones in the name of God, three in the name of Christ, and three in the name of Mary. Repeat this process for three mornings and the disease will be cured."

A belief, universally held since time immemorial by the Irish, was that the wicked man received punishment, often in kind, for his evildoing. Dermot MacMurrough, the betrayer of Ireland to the Normans, died of an "intolerable disease" and without the last rites. Pope Adrian, who authorized Henry to annex Ireland, died by swallowing a fly in a glass of water. A bad landlord, who charged the people too high a rent, was said not to have had a pipe of tobacco at the finish. Hard punishment came particularly to those who persecuted a priest. A prosperous farmer said that he must hasten to the courthouse "to see the shackles going on the priest" and he made a similar remark during the trial. The priest is reported to have told him: "You hurry home and may be you will find enough to do there." On reaching home, he found his child drowned in a well.

Lady Wilde, the mother of Oscar and an assiduous folklorist, expressed in rather overwrought language, but essentially a fair statement, the relationship of the Irish peasantry to the unseen world that lay around them:

> All the solitudes of the island were peopled by these bright, happy, beautiful beings, and to the Irish nature, with its need of the spiritual, its love of the vague, mystic, dreamy, and supernatural, there was something irresistibly fascinating in the belief that gentle spirits were around, filled with sympathy for the mortal who suffered wrong or needed help.

The people believed that the fairies followed the emigrant to America: "You'll travel far," Biddy Leary, a cure woman, told Lady Gregory, "but wherever you go you'll not escape them." But in the crowded slum tenement houses, by the looms, boilers, and forges of factories, along the canals and railroads, amidst the bustle of city streets, the fairies of the pleasant countryside, the ruined castles, the furze-covered hills, and open skies found (and wanted) no haven in America. A leprechaun would have sobbed to death in New York's Five Points or Boston's Fort Hill.

4

Did the Irish really believe in fairies, or were they up to their old pastime of treating the absurd seriously? One woman made a classic answer: "Oh, I wouldn't believe in the fairies, but it is not harm to believe in fallen angels!" Or the characteristic instance told by Sean O'Faolain of the West Cork woman who, when asked if she believed in fairies, replied: "I do not, but they're there!" Devout Roman Catholics though they were, a corner of their minds kept room for the paganism that was older than Patrick.

5

Eloquence, such as the mother's "keen," came naturally to the Irish tongue, the inheritance of an imagination that had filled the native language with poetic images and metaphors. Other races seemed earthbound and prosaic in their ordinary speech beside the most common Irish lad, told to go on an errand early in the morning: "I'll be off at the flight of night," he replied.

The language of the ordinary peasant was the true oratory of Catholic Ireland. Being a natural man, he was not afraid of poetry in expression, and being a countryman, he called upon nature for his metaphors. "I would be proud to live on your honour's land as long as grass grows or water runs," said a cottier asking for a lease of the landlord.

The Catholic Irish were the only people in Western civilization who used the invocation of religion in their everyday speech. The mention of one dead was invariably followed by a prayer: "The heavens be his bed this day," "Heaven rest his soul," "The angels spread his bed this night," "Lord have mercy on him." Hall overheard a beautiful expression: "God's blessing be with his soul, and give him the everlasting repose of Heaven and our own souls, at the last day." The citing of a boon was followed by "thanks be to God." People greeted each other in the name of Mary, Patrick, or Brigid. A newcomer entering a house, where others were gathered, always exclaimed: "God save all here!"

Their language was rich in terms of affection and endearment, freely used and without inhibitions. Translated into the English, this became "blarney," the excesses of emphatic and unrestrained natures. No Irish-

man thought another Irishman was using precious or artificial language when the first said, "It's an opening to the heart to see you." Nor
was it thought out of the ordinary to sprinkle exchanges in conversation with *cushla ma chree* ("pulse of my heart") or *vick machree*
("son of my heart") or *mavourneen dheelish* ("my sweet darling").
The Irishman was not being effeminate when he called his male companion "darling": he was merely translating from the Irish.

As no race exceeded the Catholic Irish in religious invocations or
terms of endearment, so also did they take first place in their power —
and use — of curses: like the saint of old, they loved cursing. There is
none like Paddy for cursing, wrote Carleton. "His imprecations are
often full, bitter, and intense. Indeed there is more poetry and epi-
grammatic point in them than in those of any other country in the
world." He rose to the heights of virtuosity of language in the evils he
called down on the head of an enemy, believing that a curse, no matter
how uttered, "will fall on *something*" and that it hovered for seven
years over the head of the accursed, "like a kite over its prey." The
Catholic Irishman showed an ingenuity of invention (and a flexi-
bility of conscience) when he devised a curse that would bring bad
luck without, at the same time, violating his religious scruples: a gym-
nastic moralist was he.

2 0

Emergence from Penal Bondage

THE DYING VOICE of the old Gaelic culture, in the peasant
poets of the latter half of the seventeenth and deep into the eighteenth
century, was glorious — "perhaps," wrote Douglas Hyde, "the sweetest creation of all Irish literature." While these poets lived as peasants
and recited their lines in miserable cabins, the note they struck was a
nostalgic yearning for the old Gaelic aristocratic order. The peasants,
speaking and understanding Irish, nourished this poetry as their tradition. The common Irish of the four provinces, wrote Hyde, "deprived
of almost everything else, clung all the closer to the Muse."

Starting in the latter part of the eighteenth century, with the relaxation of the penal laws, and accelerated by the powerful influence
of Daniel O'Connell, the Catholic Irish drew away from the old Gaelic

aristocratic tradition and values, and peasant standards took their place in the Catholic Ireland that was beginning to assert itself. The gradual relinquishment of the Irish language and the increasing use of a foreign tongue, English, had the effect of alienating the people from their cultural antecedents.

Ireland demonstrated that a people lose living communication with their native culture when they adopt an alien language. Jeremiah Curtin, the American of Irish descent who pioneered in the study of folklore and journeyed among the Irish taking down the stories and superstitions of the old people, said: "I did not meet a single person who knew a myth tale or an old story who was not fond of Gaelic and specially expert in the use of it, while I found very few story-tellers from whom a myth tale could be obtained unless in the Gaelic language; and in no case have I found a story in the possession of a man or woman who knew only English."

But the process of de-Gaelicizing had been inevitable since the breakup of Gaelic society after the defeat of the chieftains and the forcible imposition of English institutions.

The poetry was the wake-song of the old order. In time, the Gaelic aristocratic relationship became a memory. The vacuum in the peasantry was actively filled by the "modern" native-trained priests of Maynooth and other Irish seminaries, vital, aggressive and assertive. They pressed upon the people who had lost their old culture, their aristocracy, their leadership, and were rapidly losing their language, a system of Catholic morality and discipline that has since dominated as the cultural nourishment of Catholic Ireland.

They carried through a renaissance of practical Catholicism upon the ruins of the destroyed Gaelic culture, and they asserted a vigorous leadership, when the last restraints of the penal laws had been removed, that had once been held by the aristocracy. They were removed from the peasants by their education and by their priestly office, but their tastes and prejudices reflected the body of the peasantry in which the great bulk of them had originated.

Contemporary with the entrance of the native-trained priests as a vitalizing force in the lives of the people was the rise of Daniel O'Connell to dominion over the minds of the peasantry and the introduction of the people to a political consciousness for which hitherto they had had no need, since the government of Ireland had been conducted on the premise of the nonexistence of the Catholic Irish peasantry.

Thus, two powerful forces — an intensified and self-conscious Catholicism and a growing awareness of, and interest in, politics as a means to the end of Irish nationality — gradually filled the vacuum after the withering away of the old culture.

The decline of the use of Irish as a language and the substitution of English had a vulgarizing effect upon the tastes and dignity of the peasant. He had not lost his Irish nature, but he had lost the old guiding marks. Contrast the poetry of eighteenth-century Owen Roe O'Sullivan — "Owen of the Sweet Mouth" he was called by the peasants — or the lyricism of Egan O'Rahilly with the sentimental, tawdry, and buffoonish ballads and songs popular in English in the nineteenth century, and the picture is clear of the change that had come over a people by the usurpation of their language by an alien tongue. Even the folk tales had lost their imaginativeness and become contrived stories shot through with homiletic design. Nobody laughed so uproariously at the "stage Irishman" as the untutored peasant Irish, whose fathers and grandfathers knew by heart the poetry of Owen Roe O'Sullivan.

2

Daniel O'Connell exploited the symbolisms of Gaelic Ireland that had high place with the peasants in order to forward his political agitations, but he lacked true sympathy with the native culture. No man of his generation did so much to eliminate the Irish language and force English upon the people as O'Connell. He was a man to whom the practical and the utilitarian were the criteria of action and decision. He foresaw that English, as the language of affairs, was inevitable and that Irish had value only in a cultural sense — and he accepted the inevitable, indeed hastened it, for the new spirit of nationality he was forging for the Catholic Irish people. The old culture, in which he had been steeped as a boy, was to his pragmatic mind unrealistic if Ireland were to rise to modern statehood. He believed his people would find a new expression and a new culture in an atmosphere of political freedom.

3

Daniel O'Connell was the first modern man to use the mass of a people as a democratic instrument for revolutionary changes by peaceful constitutional methods. He anticipated the coming into power of the people as the decisive political element in modern democratic society. What O'Connell did in the forty-five years of his political activity — a tremendous job and a tribute to his genius — was to transform a people from a state bordering on servitude, uneducated, inchoate, groping for new attachments, into a democratic race — so democratic that no other political ideology has ever seriously tempted them.

He educated them by his unceasing agitation and pounded into their heads a few simple ideas; he created of them a public opinion which he directed; he made them aware, for the first time in their history, that humble and neglected people could be invested with a public character; he taught them to use the elective machinery for their own benefit. And they sensed that O'Connell's purpose drove for an equality under the law from which they were excluded, and would give them a dignity and self-respect that English and Irish oligarchical rule had denied them. Indeed, the Catholic Association, which O'Connell founded as the agency to promote Catholic Emancipation, was the "first fully-fledged democratic political party known to the world."

O'Connell took the leading role as a layman in an ecclesiastical issue that had far-reaching bearings on the future of the Catholic Church, both in Ireland and in the United States. For centuries, the people had supported the Roman Catholic Church out of their pittances, while the Established Church was endowed. A move by William Pitt to subsidize the Catholic clergy as part of the Act of Union bargain had failed. After the Act of Union, the English government thought it advisable to revive the matter of Church and State. Negotiations were started for the removal of Catholic disabilities — removal of the prohibition to sit in Parliament being the most important — and, in order to attach the Catholic clergy to the throne, the stipulation was made that the throne would hold a negative power over the appointments of bishops — the so-called Veto — to prevent Irish nationalists from membership in the hierarchy, in return for which the clergy would be subsidized. Some of the older and timid bishops leaned to the project; and the Holy See, grateful to the English for the war upon Napoleon, who held the Pope a prisoner, favored the Veto, through a cardinal who was a caretaker of papal affairs in the absence of the Pope.

O'Connell fought the Veto fiercely, rallied to his side the anti-Veto bishops and the Maynooth clergy and defied Rome, in the end making his opposition prevail. Thus, the reviving Irish Catholic Church entered upon its period of renaissance free and independent of state intervention. It was not beholden to the state for financial support of its clergy, and it was not subject to the will of the state in the appointment of bishops. Despite the timid bishops and by the vigor of O'Connell's fight, the Church in Ireland landed on the popular side.

4

There was nothing of the romantic and reckless sword-and-cape rebel about O'Connell: he was a hardheaded, practical, and ingenious Irish lawyer, who planned and acted within the letter of the law, on its border most of the time, in order to change the law. He threatened to retire from leadership if a drop of blood was spilled, and preached that a man who committed a political crime gave strength to the enemy. He was prepared to bargain, negotiate, and concede; he was willing to play hard practical politics, for the ends he sought for Ireland. He forced the suspicious and secretive Irish peasants to trust him; and they, on their part, contributed their pennies for his personal support so that he could be free for a public life: his enemies for this called him "the big beggarman" and "the king of the beggars." He was the tribune of the peasantry; he proclaimed that he was the servant of the people of Ireland and that he gloried in that servitude.

5

O'Connell was born in the midst of feudal Irish life in wild southwest Kerry in 1775, the son of a small Catholic landlord and the nephew of the most prosperous smuggler in the area, who ruled his retainers like an Irish chieftain. A member of a large family, he had been fostered, in the ancient Irish way, by a sheep herder and his wife, and as a lad spoke nothing but Irish. His wealthy uncle had sent him for education to France, from which he fled when the French Revolution broke out. As a student of law in London, he read deeply in radical political literature — Paine, Godwin, and Jeremy Bentham — which made an ineradicable impression on him. He was a devout Catholic and a sincere libertarian. He hated religious intolerance and persecution, and would not keep silent when his Catholic brethren in France persecuted Protestants. He fought the See of Rome when, for political reasons, it supported England against Irish claims. As a member of Parliament, he was found on the side of all measures that had the content of liberty.

His hatred of slavery everywhere amounted to a passion, and on this score he was absolutely uncompromising. He was a leader in the fight for emancipation of the West Indian slaves; and every Irish member in the House of Commons was on his side. This inflexible detestation of slavery by O'Connell made him a controversial figure in the United States and, as we shall see, divided the Catholic Irish community in this country.

O'Connell's enduring and ultimate political objective was repeal of the Act of Union and restoration of Irish self-government under the British monarchy, to which, as a constitutional monarchist himself, he gave undeviating fidelity. He eschewed the use of physical force for the objective of a republican Ireland, which had been the pursuit of Wolfe Tone and the United Irishmen; and the continuing contest between the followers of O'Connell's constitutional procedures and the physical-force men divided the American Irish as it did the Irish in Ireland for generations.

But it was brought home to him that Catholic Emancipation must precede the grim struggle for repeal. In wresting political leadership for the contest, O'Connell organized the peasants as his main supporters.

The Catholic nobility and the wealthy Catholic mercantile class hoped for Catholic Emancipation as a means of social recognition and a public life. O'Connell wanted to lift up the whole people. His gifts reached their highest point as a demagogue, in the sense of moving masses of people. A big-framed man, alive with energy, with a leonine head and features which coarsened as he grew older but which were dominated by a handsome pair of gray eyes that flashed bubbling humor and passion, he embodied the Catholic Irish concept of a king. His generosity was kingly; he walked the streets of Dublin followed by a "tail," a ragged court that lived on his beneficence and sang his praises; he commanded any audience before which he made an appearance, even the British House of Commons. His good humor and good nature struck a deep responsive chord in the people.

He knew the Irish people as probably no other man had ever known them. When he appeared in public in the gaudy robes of Lord Mayor of Dublin, the first Catholic Irishman to hold that office in two hundred years, he winked, pointed knowingly at the outfit, and in other ways signified to Tim and Shaun that he was still one of the boys despite his apparel: he knew what their reaction would have been had he assumed a pomposity in keeping with his attire.

He mixed broad Irish humor with a recital of facts to educate the people. He always drew a roar when, upon interruption, he commanded: "Put a potato in that calf's mouth." His power of abusive language and invective was used without shame and brought out all the snobbery of the English, who thought him "no gentleman" — which bothered O'Connell not at all: had he played the English gentlemanly game in Parliament, he would have betrayed the Irish cause. He could not resist personalities: "And then there is Cresswell Cresswell," he said speaking of a politician, "the fellow with two Cresswells, as if one was not bad enough." Of the Tory Radical Oastler, he said: "Oastler! Why, there is not an honest Tipperary horse that would have him in the same stable with him."

He chastened, bullied, wheedled and, above all, he flattered his Irish audiences, laying it on with a trowel. In every speech he would play upon this note at least once, and often as the conclusion:

> Oh, how I delight in admiring my native land, with her people, brave, generous, and good — faithful, temperate, and moral — they crowd round the sacred altars — they throng the sacred rails when the holy sacrifice has concluded — they behave kindly, nobly, and affectionately to their wives and children. Oh, nature has given them a country fit to live in and be happy, and shame, shame, on the man who does not struggle to make her free and legislatively independent.

In 1823, O'Connell established the Catholic Association, pledged to work for Catholic Emancipation, with a few followers and under the constant threat of the English administration to suppress it. The Catholic hierarchy and clergy stood in a gingerly relationship to him until Bishop James W. Doyle openly approved O'Connell and his design.

Then O'Connell formed an alliance with the Irish Catholic Church in an organization that, for practical political skill and efficiency, stands even today as a masterpiece in effective party management. The surest way to reach to the last peasant in the most remote parts of Ireland was through the Catholic parishes. O'Connell's organization was based on the parish, with the priests and local worthies as its agents. The messages, speeches, and propaganda of the Catholic Association reached the people from the priests on the altar or in the gatherings outside the chapel after Mass.

The people were asked to finance the association, by two divisions: membership was taken by the better-circumstanced at the annual subscription of two guineas, and by associates, the peasants, at one penny each month, collected by the priests or by local workers. The inclusion of the peasant's penny was a touch of political genius: that penny gave the peasant a personal interest, often at a sacrifice, which he would not have had were he but a spectator; he felt that he was part of a great national movement and that he was important in it.

The details of the fight for Catholic Emancipation need not be retold here, but after O'Connell had been elected to the House of Commons from County Clare, in 1828, by the peasants who risked eviction to vote their convictions, the issue was handed straight to the Duke of Wellington, premier, and Robert Peel, Home Secretary and expert on Irish affairs: Catholic Emancipation or civil war. The Iron Duke frankly told the House that the granting of Catholic Emancipation, begrudgingly as it was given, was preferred to a civil war which the old warrior hated.

In 1829, the Catholic Irish were freed of the last shackles of the penal laws, when George IV with a sour face bowed to Wellington, Peel, O'Connell, and the Irish peasants.

The formation of an association in the United States to aid O'Connell in this struggle was the first appearance of the Catholic Irish as a community, with mutual interests, on the American scene in the nineteenth century and the first consciousness of the American people that a Catholic Irish element was now a part of the growing population of the new Republic.

PART TWO

How They Got Across the Ocean

> . . . the principal freight from Ireland to the United States consists of Passengers.
>
> Thomas Wilson, United States Consul in Dublin, to Secretary of State Monroe, February 17, 1816

2 1

Ways and Means

THE IRISH-BORN BRITISH CONSUL in Boston in the early 1840s, Thomas Colley Grattan, explained that in Ireland among "the small farmers, artisans, and peasantry, the United States are considered as a sort of half-way stage to Heaven, whither some of the kindred and friends of almost every family have already repaired" and send back descriptions of the new land as "the very 'El Dorado,' " in comparison with Irish hardship.

Mr. Grattan, a talented literary man, expressed rhetorically the sentiment more characteristically put by a young Catholic Irish emigrant from County Limerick who had taken a farm in Ohio and written to his father in 1836: "Now I can tell you as a fact, that a poor man in Ireland could not do better than come here, for it is the truth of a good country."

The mind of the Irishman might pant for this paradise, but the hard fact of the $12.50 to $25 passage money over the Atlantic's three thousand miles qualified the constant testimony of a disposition on the part of the Irish to emigrate by the equally constant phrase, "if they had the means." But as the flow of Catholic Irish emigration got under way, slowly at first, following the Napoleonic wars, an increasing number found the way. As was said in Ireland that the poor supported the poor, so it was with Catholic Irish emigration that the poor helped the poor.

Montaigne recounts that, after the Emperor Conrad III had successfully besieged the Duke of Bavaria, he consented to no milder condition than the gentlewomen of the town might leave with so much only as they could carry on their backs. "Whereupon," wrote Montaigne, "they, out of magnanimity of heart, presently contrived to carry out, upon their shoulders, their husbands and children, and the duke himself. . . ."

Every Irish emigrant to America* carried, potentially, upon his back other Irish men, women, and children. The first spade the Irish laborer plunged into the American earth or the first broom the Irish girl hefted over the American household floor was dedicated to the snugging together of the dollars for the remittance or the prepaid passage to those left behind. The American dollar was the magic carpet by which the Catholic Irish made their way to America — the consistent and enduring element in the Irish migration.

The Catholic Irish emigration was conducted almost solely by the people themselves through their own enterprise, that is, they achieved what was then the difficult job of transferring themselves from one country to a distant land over the water without systematic organization or state assistance.

The British government in 1823 settled 568 and in 1825 an additional 2024 men, women, and children, overwhelmingly Roman Catholics, from the County Cork area in Canada out of public funds, but the cost of this experiment totaled so high that the government thereafter adamantly resisted the pleas of emigration theorists, the recommendations of parliamentary commissions, and even the pressures of Irish Famine distress for assisted Irish emigration.

The British government's official connection with Irish emigration restricted itself to laws to protect emigrants from the inhuman abuses of the trade and an administrative service of agents, established in 1834 in the principal ports of England, Ireland, Canada, and New Brunswick, for the enforcement of laws and regulations concerning passenger ships. The intervention of the government was mildly confined to that degree of humanitarianism consistent with low emigrant fares; yet this laissez-faire policy, though it countenanced the filth and human misery of an emigrant voyage, had the overall beneficial effect of making possible the departure of Irish men, women, and children who otherwise, with better accommodations and higher fares, would have been, as the British emigration commissioners sensibly said, "prevented from going at all," and it coincided with the means of the Irish emigrant, whose "whole object," said a British harbor official in 1854, was "cheapness," or as Emigration Commissioner Elliot expressed it more formally, "to secure economy of transit."

No benevolent organization of consequence with private funds

---

* In this section, the word "America" includes British North American parts as well as parts in the United States.

existed in Ireland or England to assist the Irish to emigrate systematically and conveniently. (The Irish Pioneer Emigrant Fund of Vere
Foster, a gentry idealist and true friend of the Catholic Irish, had in the
1850s assisted some four hundred selected young to emigrate in *eight*
years.) The American Irish emigrant societies made it emphatically clear
that they could not, lacking funds, afford financial help to emigration
from Ireland. "There is one obvious fact about emigration to America,"
said an old Irishman, "and it is that the Irish people paid for it out of
their own pockets."

2

The Earl of Durham, in his 1839 report on Canada, described emigration to that country, considerably made up of Irish passengers, as "without forethought, preparation, method or system of any kind," and James
B. Forsyth, a witness before the Durham Commission, testified that its
want of system gave it "a vagrant character."

Individualistic Catholic Irish emigration appeared as the epitome of
desultory disorderliness — an aimless wandering away of hapless people
from a hopeless situation to an unknown and uncertain future. The
Germans, with their instinct for regimentation and order, had a *Gies-
sener Gesellschaft* or *Teutonia-Orden* or a German-American Settlement Society in America or state assistance or noble patronage on the
other side for systematic group emigration. Passengers on a typhus-
ridden Irish emigrant ship in Quebec quarantine watched a Bremen
ship coast by with healthy emigrants on deck singing a charming hymn
"in whose beautiful harmony all took part." A party of over a hundred
Swedish emigrants, just landed, passed through the streets of Boston,
the women and children in wagons, the men on foot, carrying American
and Swedish flags, on their way to a farm settlement.

Several group colonizations organized and led by Irish parish priests
came to grief, one through the indiscipline of the emigrants at Liverpool and another by attrition along the Mississippi. The most grandiose
scheme of Catholic Irish colonization, conceived by John Godley, idealistic son of a Connacht landlord, the plantation of a New Ireland in
Canada under the leadership of the clergy, endorsed by a formidable
list of Irish nobles, gentry, and landlords, to be jointly financed by
private subscription and government loan, was savagely chewed to
pieces by the Irish hierarchy as a diabolical plot to "exterminate" the

Catholic Irish and tossed into the wastebasket by an unsympathetic British ministry. The Irish disposition to anarchic individualism warred against systematic group colonization.

Despite the casual disarray of the Catholic Irish emigration, it contained within it a deep foundation of order, even logic, in accordance with the traditional Irish pattern. The individual Irishman was tied by inflexible bonds to the complex of intricate family relationships extending beyond immediate consanguinity which imposed duties and responsibilities that could be avoided only by his own shame and the censure of an opinion he respected. His responses to these family obligations were almost instinctive, above rationality, to be honored by the call of blood to blood.

So it can be said of Catholic Irish emigration that while as a physical fact it was individual, one by one or two by two, the addition ultimately made a family emigration to America. Behind the young Irish farm laborer or servant maid who set off alone for America was a waiting family, and behind them the friends.

A letter from a poor railroad worker in Peekskill, New York, to his family in Ireland holds its simple power more than a century later and sums up in unlettered articulateness the heart of Catholic Irish emigration:

> Beekskeel march 8th 48
> My dear and loveing wife and children I Received yours of January 20th 1848 which gave me to understand that yous were attacked by a Severe Fever but thanks be God that yous are Recovered and well as I am at Preaset thanks be to his kind merceys to us all be on the watch at the Post Office day after day I wont delay in Relieveing yous as it is a duty encumbered on me by the laws of Church and I hope God will Relieve me. I work on a Railway at 8 shillings per day and pays 18 Shillings per week for my Boarding this is a good Country for them that is able to work and nother person. So I will be able to pay yours passage withe the help of God on the First of August next the sending of this sum of money to yous Compells me to let it be Back tel then and i long to see that long wished for hour that I will Embrace yous in my arms there is nothing in this world gives me trouble but yow and my dear Children whoom I loved as my life. Be Pleased to let me know how my two sons is Patrick and Franciss and not Fergetting my dear Father and mother Friend and neighbours not Forgetting your sister Bridget thank God she was to mind yous in your sickness and sorrows which i will never forget to her i expect to go to newyork on the 17th of march to send you this Bill of Six Pounds which you will

Get Cash for in the Provensil Bank of Ireland I will send it in the
Revd Patrick ogara is care For you I feel very sorry for sorry for
my Brother Francis that lived at St. John I Fear he is dead.

  dont answer this letter tull you Receive the next in which the
money will Be for you.

  Keep your heart as God spareed you, so long you will be shortly
in the lands of Promise and live happy with me and our children.

                            No more at Pressent
                    From your Faithful husband till death
                                  Thos Garry

  I was ready to go to york to pay Passge for you and the children
but I consider yous would not stand the wracking of the sea till
yous be nourished for a time.

This warm human letter preserves the spirit which animated the
fortunate Catholic Irish who had arrived in America to move with
vigor and willing self-denial towards assisting family and friends to
emigrate.

Tom Power held thirty acres of Irish land in a County Limerick townland which had been in his family for seven generations. He was
married and the father of ten or eleven children, the youngest four or
five years old. He and his family were evicted, and Tom made the decision to go to America. He was able to borrow the passage money for
himself — £2 10s. — and stocked enough potatoes and bread to provision himself on the voyage. Familial piety gathered around the distressed couple and their children. His wife's sister and her husband,
who were childless, undertook to support Mrs. Power and the children
in Tom's place until he had made his way in America. In a period of
from eleven to twelve years, Tom Power brought out the entire family,
one by one, to America.

John V. Stewart, a landowner in Counties Clare and Donegal, told
how the uncle raised the passage money in 1845 for the son of a pauper
widow with six children. During the Famine years of 1846 and 1847,
the young Irishman sent enough money from America to keep the
family alive, and in 1848 he forwarded £24 for their emigration.

An up-and-coming Irish woman found it no use to remain in Ireland
and starve. Leaving her six children and "the old man" behind after
scraping up passage money, she landed at St. John, New Brunswick,
and wandered into Maine as far as Portland, where she took up hard
labor, principally washing, and by frugality earned enough to bring out
two of the children. She toiled on, and secured the passage for two

more. She toiled on, and the last two arrived in 1833. "And now," she said, "I'm going to send for the old man, and then we shall all be here."

Not all members of a family group emigrated. A brother or a sister or a grown or married son or daughter might prefer to remain in Ireland. The pattern of the separated family, some in America and some in Ireland, was familiar all through the years of Catholic Irish emigration. Out of a household in a Dingle Peninsula townland, sons left in each generation for the United States, as many as fifteen in four generations, and to illustrate the span, some were killed in the American Civil War and one fought in Korea.

3

Rev. Thomas Costello, a County Limerick parish priest, when asked in 1825 how the Catholic Irish got the money to emigrate, replied that the passage was paid by friends in America, who made arrangements with the master of a returning vessel. Advertisements solicited this trade. The first of its kind in the *Truth Teller,* an Irish-American weekly started in New York in 1825, appeared on February 25, 1826, announcing the passage from Cork to New York of the ship *Liverpool* about the first of the following May, with the advice:

> Those who are desirous of engaging passage for their friends, are requested to apply to Captain Alexander Robinson, at the counting room of Messrs. John F. Murray & Sons, No. 2, Exchange Buildings, between the hours of three and six, p.m. — N.B. Passage money to be paid at the time of engaging.

This method of bringing out relatives and friends had long been used by the Ulster Irish in their eighteenth-century emigration. What is significant in the *Truth Teller* notice was that a shipping house thought it opportune to advertise in a paper directed exclusively to the Catholic Irish in the United States.

Captains of vessels in the Irish trade carried money from the Irish in America to relatives and friends back home; and Alexander C. Buchanan, then an Irish-born timber merchant in Canada, wrote in 1828 that he had frequently seen in Quebec and other ports "poor fellows who have proceeded a distance of 400 or 500 miles to find a captain of a ship or some other person" to convey remittances. He thought that about two thirds of the passages from Ireland to the United States were paid for in the United States and that more money would be remitted if the emigrants enjoyed better facilities.

This cumbersome method of sending money was supplanted by the organization in 1829 of the remittance business in connection with shipping agencies. Samuel Thompson, of the pioneering family in packet emigration, advertised the opening of an office in New York where not only passages could be secured but "drafts on Liverpool, payable on demand, can also be furnished." The multiplication of combined passage and exchange houses in New York, with growing representation in communities where the Catholic Irish were settling, testified, in the 1830s, to the fact that as Irish emigration increased to America, so did Irish remittances and prepaid passages.

4

It remained, however, for Mathew Carey of Philadelphia, an exile from Ireland, publisher, pioneer American political economist, and the then most distinguished Catholic Irishman in the United States, to reveal in figures the extent of Irish remittances. In a series of public letters to Bishop John Hughes of New York in 1838, he praised the Catholic Irish for "the extraordinary and almost incredible sacrifices made in the shape of remittances, on the altar of parental, filial, and sisterly affection — three times out of four, probably by persons in needy circumstances and depending upon scanty wages for support."

Mr. Carey received replies from only five of the houses he queried, two in New York, two in Philadelphia, and one in Baltimore; yet these five had transmitted to Ireland, in 1835 and 1836, the sum of $314,975 in small drafts. The New York house of Abraham Bell & Co., of which Jacob Harvey, the worthy Irish Quaker, was a member, added the information that in eight years, 1830 to 1837, inclusive, it had remitted to Ireland no less than $354,933. Then, belatedly, Roche Brothers & Co., a New York Irish-American firm, organized in 1836, which dealt almost exclusively with the Catholic Irish, informed Mr. Carey that in 1836 and 1837, the latter a depression year, it had remitted a total sum in small drafts of $281,485 to Ireland. On the basis of the figures returned, Mr. Carey projected a sum of $800,000 remitted by the Catholic Irish in America for the period covered.

These sums, Mr. Carey stressed, were sent by laboring men earning from 75 cents to $1.25 a day, when they could get work, and female domestic servants earning $1.25 a week.

The American remittances attracted the attention of Robert Murray, chief officer of the Provincial Bank in Ireland, who wrote to Sir Robert Peel on January 1, 1847, that they had been annually increasing since 1837 until, in 1846, they reached a sum he estimated at $725,000; and the unsentimental Scotsman said that "such a beautiful story of un-forgotten affection" was probably not to be found "in the world records of human attachment." But Jacob Harvey in New York, with more complete figures, in a letter to the New York *Post*, dated January 21, 1847, placed the 1846 Irish remittances at $1,001,650.

This recording for the year 1846 — the first full Famine year in Ireland — is the first mention that the supposedly improvident and indolent Catholic Irish had as a group, at what must have been back-breaking sacrifice, passed the million mark in remittances — a phenom-enal sum for the times and from a group that then formed the lowest free-labor category.

Starting in 1848, the British Colonial Land and Emigration Commis-sioners annually published figures of Irish remittances, "confessedly very imperfect," they explained, because of the secrecy of some banks and mercantile houses and inability to get at the sums which passed through private hands.

The sums were immense: $2,300,000 in 1848; $2,700,000 in 1849; a jump to $4,785,000 in 1850; $4,995,000 in 1851; then up to $7,020,-000 in 1852; $7,195,000 in 1853; $8,650,000 in 1854, which was the peak year in connection with the Famine emigration. After 1854, with better conditions in Ireland, remittances leveled off to $4,000,000 to $5,000,000 in 1855 and 1856, and then to $2,000,000 to $3,000,000 in 1857, 1858, 1859 and 1860; and they declined to $1,870,305 in the first year of the Civil War.

From 1848 to 1861, inclusive, Irish emigrants remitted the breath-taking known sum of $59,236,555 to their native land. John F. Maguire, an Irish journalist, after talking with bankers in America, estimated that the Famine emigrants had in twenty years sent $120,000,000 to pay emigrant passages and support parents and relatives in Ireland.

In this work of "unforgotten affection," the Irish girl (she might be any age from sixteen to sixty) showed a strength of character and unself-ish devotion that ascended to nobility. She had always been faithfully mindful of filial piety, but now in America she was consumed by thoughts of suffering in Ireland. Her savings and scant monthly pittances sped with love across the sea. Lord John Russell told the House of Commons in 1851 that Irish annual remittances exceeded £1,500,000 sterling, and the Boston *Pilot* commented that "a large portion of that amount is sent by the Irish servant girl whose love of home and filial affection are bright gems in their character." P. Fitzgerald, remittance agent of West Troy, New York, related that Irish girls walked a distance of fifty or sixty miles from the state of Vermont to save a few dollars to enlarge the drafts for those in Ireland. In 1852, the hired girls of Pittsburgh remitted $53,000 in six months to the old country; and the same story was repeated in every community where the Irish settled. The comparison of the small earnings of these Irish girls with the total amounts sent to Ireland tells a story of self-denial and faithfulness that is of epic proportion in the history of the Catholic Irish in the United States.

In the power of conscience and the sentiments of poor Irish emigrants to make them forget themselves in the larger loyalty of family and race, no other emigrant peoples to the United States matched this admirable and unselfish record.

Standards of comparison make the achievement even more impressive. The Patriotic Fund in England, established after the Crimean War in 1854 for its sufferers and subscribed to throughout the prosperous British Empire, amounted to only $7,500,000. When the Free Church of Scotland broke from the historic Establishment in 1843, Scottish wealth throughout the world rallied to build the new edifice, but the total sum collected after three years was $5,000,000. "These sums," said Nicholas Waterhouse to a meeting of English social scientists in 1858, "are not to be compared with the annual remittances of the Irish emigrants," and he added:

> If we look back through the pages of American history from the present to the day when the "Mayflower" first sighted that wild New England shore, we shall find no more magnificent spectacle than this — the work not of the great, the rich, or the mighty, but of those who were poor, and needy, and destitute of all things save true hearts and strong hands.

In Mathew Carey's words of more than a century ago, "Let us pause here for a moment to reflect on this glorious display of the sweetest and most ennobling of the charities of life."

5

Not every Catholic Irishman had a relative or friend in America. The willing and eager without connections on the other side had to go, as the Irish put it, "on their own strength." "I have 11 brothers and sisters," said Thomas Buckley, a cooper in County Limerick in the early 1830s, "and if they had the means to emigrate they would not stop another day here." In the lowest economic classes, the continuing struggle was not to get means to emigrate but work to live. "Few laborers are to be found among the emigrants," explained Father Tom Maguire of County Leitrim in the early 1830s; "they are unable to pay their passage; as their earnings hardly suffice for their daily maintenance, they cannot save."

Yet the harsh economy of Ireland itself forced people to emigrate. A small farmer foresaw at the end of his lease the reckless competition for his holding by land-hungry people at prices he knew he could not meet without beggaring himself. With the landlord's permission, he sold the good-will of his lease; and the money saw him through to a passage, just about. A small farmer outbid at the expiration of his lease and unable to hire another holding sold his stock and effects for what they would bring, and was off.

Often a farmer had no choice, even though he wished to brave it out in Ireland: he received an eviction notice for arrears of rent. The landlord, satisfied to get the property, "usually forgives [the tenant] his arrears of rent, and allows him to dispose of his stock and furniture and potato crop," explained Thomas Hungerford, a justice of the peace in County Cork; "with these the emigrant pays for his passage, and that of his family."

The small Irish farmer made up a considerable part of the early Catholic Irish emigration in the 1820s and 1830s, along with the young laborer and the young male and female servant, generally themselves enterprising sons and daughters of the small farmer, with no prospects on a crowded subdivided farm. Where did they get the means? Who aided them if they had no friends in America?

Father Matthew Fullam offered an explanation generally applicable in such incidents:

> No aid, except from their friends,* who frequently distress themselves in order to send off, perhaps, the best-conducted son, in the

---

* "Friends," in this Irish use, meant blood relatives.

hope that his savings in a strange land may rescue other members of the family from the impending ruin which hangs over this ill-fated country.

Stern priests often complained of the young, "leaving their parents at home distressed from providing means for them to emigrate, and from the loss of their assistance." But there were also the young who yearned to emigrate and would have found the means had not loyalty and duty towards aged or sick parents kept them in Ireland.

Father Fullam's statement excellently pointed up the hope among the Catholic Irish poor of getting one member to America and starting the chain of remittances. When the Irish Poor Law came into operation, instances are recorded of families selling everything they owned to get passage money for a son or daughter and then betaking themselves to the poorhouse to wait for the American remittances.

The Irish peasants were, as Bishop Doyle had observed, great hoarders of small coins, especially the women, and the savings hidden in the thatch of the roof or buried in the ground frequently came out to pay the passage money of a son or daughter selected to start in America the transmission belt.

The Catholic Irish emigration was year after year, as a general statement, a young one and with small individual capital: the husky laborer and the apple-cheeked girl entered the emigrant ship, in a common phrase, "barely having enough to pay the passage."

6 ·

More than one Irishman hit the deck of an emigrant ship with the hot breath of the bailiff on his trail; and a vessel ready to pull anchor for America was the scene of a lusty free-for-all when the emigrants, though they did not know the man, fought with the police to rescue a future candidate for American citizenship who had sold a crop behind the landlord's back and decamped with the proceeds. The Rev. John Chester, a divine of County Cork, waxed wroth at farmers "who defrauded their creditors, sold off their stock, and emigrated." Their friends were delighted when one family carefully contrived false stooks of straw to deceive the landlord while they used the money for the grain to pay their passage. Justice of the Peace Bagot in County Galway told of the happy letter a mason had shown him from his two sons in America, offering to send him $250 if he would join them. The sons, laborers, had stolen money from the father to buy their emigration pass-age. If the lad sent to sell a cow at the fair did not return with the money, it was automatically assumed that he had legged it to the nearest port for America: the cause was good but the method regrettable until the first remittance forgave all. Poteen sellers had the habit of turning up in America after discovery of damning evidence by revenue agents. Observers noted that many emigrants traveled to ports at night — to avoid the landlord, one cynic said. It was all in the game of getting to America, and many a young American has looked into the honest face of his Irish grandfather and heard him chucklingly tell the oft-recounted story of the dubious means by which he snared American passage money.

Borrowing from landlords where a decent personal relationship ex-isted, or from comfortable farmers, was rather a common method of financing individual emigration. Aubrey de Vere said that his district honored the custom of the landlord's furnishing a part of emigration money, with the rest to be collected among neighbors: there was a good willingness in rural Ireland to help others emigrate. The practice of the formal petition to the landlord — to enter a grievance or request a favor — was used to ask emigration assistance, like the following from a tenant, probably written for the petitioner by a tenant "lawyer," to Major Mahon, a Roscommon landowner:

> The Honorable Petition of Honora McNamara of Churchs^t Strokestown most respectfully Informs your honour that we are de-prived of Our parents and is 5 orphans and Our passage is paid by my Brother James to New Orleans he lived many years in the Em-ployment of Major Mahon as groom and in Consequence of the passage being paid for us and fearful of losing it by not having Sufficient means to enable us to proceed to Liverpool and provide us Sea store for our Voyage we expect the humanity of your honour will be so kind as to give your Petition a little compensation for our house and it may be the means to assist us to reach our destination to our Brother as it is the greatest act of Charity to assist your Peti the Orphans to leave this distressed country
> Your Pet^t is in duty Bound to pray
Honora McNamara
> Churchstreet Strok

A notation on the petition in the handwriting of Major Mahon ad-vised the agent "to provide their Food & assist the McNamaras to America, about £6 or £7."

As consolidation of farms grew in favor among proprietors and wholesale evictions accompanied Famine distress, landlord-assisted emigration in bulk increased as an important element in the movement of the Catholic Irish to America.

7

Landlord-assisted emigration,* directed generally to British North America primarily because of cheapness, varied from the typical pattern of individual Irish emigration in that it followed the principle expressed by Francis Spaight, a Limerick merchant-shipper and landowner: Never take an individual; take the whole family or none at all.

This made sense. The inflexible conditions exacted by landlords clearing their property of surplus population in return for emigration assistance were surrender of landholdings and leveling of their cabins by tenants to prevent squatter infiltration. The bargain thus comprehended shipping of whole families.

William Gabbett, a Limerick proprietor, in 1826 knew of no landlord assistance to tenants, and Earl Fitzwilliam seems to have been the first to employ systematic emigration to clear his vast Wicklow estates, starting in 1831 and 1832. During the 1830s, landlord-assisted emigration was spotty and inconsiderable. Emigrant Agent Buchanan at Quebec observed in 1835 an increase in landlord assistance, but U. S. Consul Wilson wrote in 1836 that the number at the port of Dublin "has not exceeded . . . five or six hundred in the last five or six years."

But in 1839 the Irish Poor Law, which made workhouse paupers, generally evicted tenants, chargeable to estates, came into operation; and landlord-assisted emigration began to climb. Colonel Wyndham, son of the late Lord Egremont, who had reduced the charges on his English estate in Sussex by shipping paupers to America, started to clear his Irish properties in the west with a hundred and thirty souls assisted to America in 1839. Traditional resistance to permanent emigration in intensely Gaelic areas had stubborn roots: Connacht in the west was the last of the four provinces to feel the impulse to emigration, and then only through Famine stress. The peasants fell under the influence of stories that the colonel planned to sell the emigrants or fix them as bond slaves on his lands in Canada (he had no lands in Canada). But when

---

* For material on landlord-assisted and pauper emigration I am indebted to "Irish Emigraton During the Great Famine," by Oliver MacDonagh, in manuscript at the National Library of Ireland, Dublin.

encouraging letters came, the task was simplified; and up to 1847, Colonel Wyndham had shipped out 220 families, or 1419 souls.

Landlord assistance prior to the Famine was local and not extensive: Wandesforde sent out some three thousand from his Kilkenny estates, farmers to Upper Canada and miners to Pottsville, Pennsylvania, and the lead mines of Wisconsin; Francis Spaight emigrated the surplus tenants on his newly purchased Derry Castle estate in Tipperary; Gore Booth offered to pay the passage to America of tenants whose leases had expired and were not to be renewed; and Lords Bessborough and Ormonde assisted and encouraged emigration from their properties.

But during the Famine years, this assistance jumped upward to a peak. Oliver MacDonagh, the closest student of Famine emigration, estimated that the number reached above fifty thousand, including two thousand from the Sligo estate of Lord Palmerston and thirty-five hundred from the Kerry holdings of the Marquess of Lansdowne, two aristocratic British politicians, whose paupers and tenants dumped destitute in America wandered through the streets begging, to the indignation of republican citizens of the United States and outraged British North American officials.

Not all landlord-assisted emigrants arrived in such miserable shape, but too many did, in particular during the frightful 1847 Canadian shipments. Landlords operating on the cheap paid for passage and provisions but withheld landing money, which meant that their emigrants, poverty-stricken to start with, arrived on the other side of the Atlantic without a shilling and as objects of local charity and assistance. Some landlords, like Monsell, took exemplary care of their emigrants, but the reports of emigrant Agent Buchanan at Quebec and Agent Perley at St. John, where the bulk were sent, spoke unfavorably more often of their sorry condition than to the contrary.

Landlord-assisted emigration was a cold statistical business proposition. John Ross Mahon, agent of the estate of Major Mahon (he who was later assassinated) in the Strokestown area of County Roscommon, concisely set out the reasoning. He explained that Major Mahon's property contained two-thirds more population than it could feed. The situation was a losing proposition for both the estate and the tenants, and if the estate were to be made to show a profit, the redundant numbers had to enter the poorhouse or emigrate. Agent Mahon continued:

> The cost of keeping a pauper in the Roscommon Poor House averages about 2s.9d. per week — £7-3-0 p an: The cost of emigra-

tion averages £3-12-0 per head to Quebec, being a difference of
£3-11-0 in favor of emigration in the first year, and all other cost of
support saved.

The cost of clearing the surplus population of the townlands
named, by emigration would be £5,865-12-0, cost of support in Poor
House £11,634-10-0 being a difference in favor of emigration of
£5,768-18-0.

Approving the clearance of his estate by emigration, Major Mahon
wrote to his agent from London on June 5, 1847: "I am quite satisfied
you would not recommend my sending out another batch were it not to
my advantage to do so . . . I am quite satisfied that in your hands,
whatever is most for my advantage, & benefit of the estate will be attended to."

The words "my advantage, & benefit of the estate" were key and
dominating in landlord-assisted emigration. Yet it would be incorrect
and distorted to interpret this numerous emigration in the negative and
narrow confines of the self-interest of landlords, accompanied as it was,
in MacDonagh's words, "by some needless suffering and little generosity." Landlord-assisted emigration from Ireland was much like British
imperialism: though the motives sprang from self-interest and individual
profit, the by-products and end results of the process returned compensatory benefits to the subjects.

Thousands were enabled to emigrate who otherwise would have
been rutted in Ireland's hopeless misery. The rejected of one country
contributed their labor to the foundation works of another land, though
America, at first sight of them, was ready for a second rejection. Judg-
ing the landlords from a century of perspective, MacDonagh's conclusion has validity, that "possibly it would be fairer to appreciate such
generosity as there was and take, on its merits, the honest conviction of
many proprietors that, in improving their lands, they were also eman-
cipating tenants from misery instead of taking advantage of their legal
rights to make their lot more miserable." Certainly the assisted emigrants were grateful and "had in the long run," said MacDonagh,
"small reason to regret the opportunity that had been given." Beside the
calloused indifference of the landlords who threw thousands onto the
roads and ditches to shift for themselves, the landlords who assisted
emigration shone with benevolence.

8

The 1838 Irish Poor Law permitted the assisted emigration of paupers by a combination of taxes and landlord assessments, and its later amendment introduced greater elasticity, extending to non-inmates of poorhouses whose Poor Law evaluation was under five pounds. But the stigma of the poorhouse connection with emigration was so offensive to the Irish peasant that in four years, 1844-1847 inclusive, only 114 males and 192 females, a total of 306 souls, took advantage of the offer of assistance.

The ravages of the Famine years, however, changed the picture. Young girls and children, orphaned by the death or the "desertion" to America of parents and relatives, were forced into the poorhouses. The removal of some fifteen thousand inmates, mostly girls and children, principally to America in the peak years, March 1851 to March 1855, at a cost to poorhouses of $85,000 annually, could technically be called a pauper emigration, but in actual fact that would be a misnomer. Adverse circumstances had stranded them in poorhouses; they were not poorhouse material; they were far superior to landlord-assisted emigrants. Buchanan, in his report from Quebec for 1851, spoke favorably (among others) of the "clean, healthy condition" of these young females and reported the praise of shipmates of "their conduct and behavior on the voyage." Workhouse superintendents were not above sneaking in among the acceptable a resident barge or harridan, the aged, hopeless drunks, or some of the sickly, as the agent at St. Andrew's furiously testified, but these seem to have been exceptions. The girls speedily melted away from both colonial and American ports into employment, and the children were taken into the arms of parents or relatives to whom they had been assigned. After 1855, this pauper female-children emigration faded into insignificance.

9

There was a saying in Ireland that what the letter from America contained was more encouraging to emigration than what was written in it. The depressed and worsening state of Ireland's economy, climaxed by the Famine, set up that impulse to emigrate, in the words of John Quincy Adams, "as keen as that of urgent want, to drive a man from the soil of his nativity and the land of his fathers' sepulchres." But the

impulse to get away from conditions offering little or no hope might
have petered out in talk and fading dreams, if the letters from America
had not offered the attractive alternative of encouragement to a better
life and future. The interplay of a bad economic system and the optimistic letter from America acted as the propelling agency in the decision
to emigrate: the token of progress in the money remittance was the
clincher — no Irishman racked for rent in the old country or faced with
eviction for arrears, or the laborless laborer, could argue against the hard
fact of the American dollar as evidence of success.

The few emigrant letters which have survived are social documents of
significance now. Strikingly, they carried little information descriptive,
or reflecting curiosity, of the new country. Bare facts and news of a personal nature, scales of wages and prices in the new land, remembrances
to relatives and friends back home, and practical encouragement to
others to emigrate made up their contents.

The litany of regards and remembrances to relatives, friends, and
neighbors was sometimes scattered through a letter, as names occurred
to the writer, and sometimes bunched, as in this letter of a son and
daughter to their family in Sligo:

> Mary Margret Joins me in sending our loves & Best respect to
> you Dearly Beloved father & Mother Brother Patt and my Brother
> Mick Uncle Martin & Wife Patt Martin John Mary and Nancy to
> Mick hart & Aunt and fammily Patt Carrane and Famely Patt
> Medrooy & fammily and to Brother James M'Leam and Mary Patt
> Martin & Wife John & Mick & all John Lowny & fammily and
> Denis Killorran & family and to Mrs. Kelly And remember me to
> her Mrs. Mulany & Daughter Mary McFolery William Teaf Mc-
> Cormick & Mrs. McGlewn & to Thomas Geraghty & family and
> How he is Getting on with his Mellons & Cucumbers & Patt Mc-
> Gowen and all the Lissadell Garden Boys

But the recurrent theme dominating letters was the urgency of the
plea to others to emigrate. It was the full melodic line of emigrant
letters. A poor emigrant, writing in 1846 to a sister in County Clare,
hammered at the "come out" note between bits of news:

> Dear sister . . . it would give me greate pleasure to think that
> you Come here, for i think you would do verry well in this Coun-
> try, for labouring men earns 10 shillings per day here in summer
> time; do what you can to Come to this country as quick as possible,
> for you would get plenty of washing to do here, And earn 4 shil-
> lings per day. Let me know how Pat Holliran and family is getting

On, and if my sister Judy [Mrs. Holliran] know that if she was here that she would get trades for them, And in summer time he [Pat Holliran] would get from 10 shillings to 12 per day . . . And my sister bridget do what she can to come here. Let my sister Ellen know that she would get from 5 shillings to 6 for making one dress here; and if she could possibly come here Let me know . . . Let me know how my Ant mary and her son Patt is; and if Anne came here she would do very well in this country, Let me know if ye Are to come. And sind me an Account if ye are to come or not. And dont be in doubt of money, and if ye dont I will remit what i can in summer, and I will sin you . . . Let my sister Mary Write to me as quick as possible, and let me know will she come, or Anny of her sisters, and i will have what I can for ye when ye come here. . . .

One young Irish lad described, in terms that would be understood (and marveled at) back home, the abundance of the new land as "every day is like a christmas day for meat," and added, in a form of Irish bull, "if I was in the old country I would come back again."

A young Irish girl, early in 1848, wrote from New York City: "This is the best Country in the world it is easy making money in this Country but hard to save it" and two months later wrote that she was "very Displaced with my brother Patrick because he did not come here because he would be do better here or [than] at home" and Mick Hayes also would do better here "or at home."

Thurlow Weed, the New York politician, talked in Ireland with a car driver with a sister in New York and a cousin in Baltimore, who had written back "that they eat the pig themselves, and have plenty of bread to their potatoes."

But not all letters were favorable. Bryan Clancy, who had had a bad trip and was sick and discouraged in New Brunswick, where he landed, wrote, "I often wished to be at home Bad and all as we were." A disgruntled Irishman wrote in 1838: "I am about three years in this country, and sorry am I that I ever saw the face on't."

Letters constituted the strongest and most impressive recommendation to emigrate, beside which such literature as emigrant handbooks and guidebooks was insignificant. The contents of letters quickly became public property: the Catholic Irish were not a people to hide good news of success; and the unsuccessful in America either did not write or disguised their failure in colored letters.

The aggressiveness of passenger agents scattered throughout Ireland, representing Irish ships and Liverpool brokers, promoted and kept before the people the idea of emigration. Placards announcing the ship sailing schedules and describing the opportunities of America in exaggerated and misleading language — land was cheap and work was ready — were posted on chapel doors, walls, cabins, everywhere they would attract attention.

To what degree talkative and energetic passenger agents in Ireland persuaded people to emigrate remains speculative.* The remittances and letters from America had created a psychological atmosphere favorable for emigration. The agent served to facilitate the mechanics of emigration rather than to germinate (or in today's jargon "sell") the idea. Once the Catholic Irish emigration was started, it had a momentum of its own.

2 2

"The Curranes and Morans Have All Gone . . ."

ARTHUR YOUNG, traveling through Ireland in 1776-1779, observed so little Roman Catholic emigration in contrast to the steady flow of Protestant Irish from Ulster to America that he concluded: "The Catholicks never went; they seem not only tied to the country but almost to the parish in which their ancestors lived." Then he visited Waterford on the east coast of Ireland: "The number of people who go passengers in the Newfoundland ships," he wrote, "is amazing; from 60 to 80 ships and from three thousand to four thousand annually."

Starting around 1765, the port of Waterford built up a sizable provisioning trade with Newfoundland over the narrowest passage between the North American continent and Europe, later exploited by the Atlantic cable and air routes. The seasonal fishing industry of Newfoundland needed strong and hardy men for its ships. Like the cottiers of the west of Ireland, in their annual harvesting trips to England and Scotland, men of the Catholic counties of Waterford, Wexford, Kilkenny, and Cork started on the provision boats for the Newfoundland fishing

---

* W. F. Adams, in his thorough but academic study of Irish emigration up to 1845 (1932), overemphasizes the role of the shipping companies and agents in their influence in stimulating emigration during this period.

ground in the spring, worked through the summer, and returned to their farms in the fall with rent money.

The Newfoundland route contributed its numbers of Catholic Irish to the United States, since the bulk of its emigrants planned to earn enough in the fisheries to pay their way to Nova Scotia or New Brunswick, some to settle in these provinces, others to go on to the States. The passage and provisioning were cheap, and a passenger "gets no more than his breadth and length upon the deck of the ship," his sea chest his bed. In 1814 and 1815, when the close of the Napoleonic wars raised the price of long-scarce fish in Europe and created a demand for labor in the Newfoundland sea plantations, from eleven to fifteen thousand Irishmen took to the emigrant route; and in the early 1830s, the very poor from the Kilkenny, Waterford, Wexford, and Cork areas still used it, hoping, as in the past, "to be able, after a season, to proceed to the United States."

Two advertisements in an Irish-American weekly, trying to locate Irishmen who had lost touch with their families or friends, typically illustrated the Newfoundland-United States route. The first was in 1835 and the second in 1840.

> Patrick Dalton, Co. Kilkenny. Sailed from Waterford in 1829. Landed in Newfoundland, stopped there one summer. Last heard of (about 3 years ago) was in Alexandria.
> John Spillane, Co. Cork, sailed from Waterford about eleven years ago for Newfoundland, where he resided until about six years ago — since that time he has been in Halifax, Boston and Providence, last heard of in Newport and understood he left lately for Illinois. A shoemaker.

Boston received a number of these Newfoundland emigrants, and the leader of its small Irish community, in the 1830s, was a mechanic in the Charlestown Navy Yard who had first landed in Newfoundland.

2

The Newfoundland emigration was an isolated movement that operated in its own orbit. The potato failure of 1822 and consequent famine in the south and northwest of Ireland was the eventful engine which set in motion the nineteenth-century migration of the Catholic Irish to other countries. Individual Catholics had dribbled in with the earlier

Protestant emigration from Ulster to America, and a number had taken the road of exile after the 1798 Rebellion.

The first outbursting in escape was to England and Scotland, among the very poor, who had no hope of striking out for America. Unlike the itinerant Irish harvesters, they settled permanently in industrial Lancashire and Glasgow and Edinburgh, in coarse work at cheap wages. It is a significant parallel that these Catholic Irish settlers in the cities across the channel rarely emigrated to America, just as their brethren who settled in America's Atlantic cities could rarely be persuaded to move to the West.

The emigrants headed for America, relatively fewer than the English migration, numbered about ten thousand a year up to 1825, said Alexander Buchanan, with more Catholics in 1825 than he had seen before coming to Canada; but Redmond O'Driscol told of the "incredible extent" of emigration in the spring of 1826: on one day he had seen three vessels sailing out of the harbor of Cork to British North America and three ready to go, with all passages sold. This Cork emigration was the product of the government-assisted emigration to Canada in 1823 and 1825: it had the effect, said Alexander Buchanan in 1828, "of opening the eyes of the peasantry of the South of Ireland" to the advantages of emigration; and he estimated that for every thousand assisted by the government to emigrate, two thousand would follow voluntarily.

From 1825 through 1830, upwards of 125,000 migrated from Ireland to America, on an annual average of twenty thousand.

Another painful Irish famine, followed by epidemic, in 1830-1831, so accelerated the decade-old migration that in the years 1831-1832 more than 130,000 departed for America and set the date, from 1830 onward, when, in the opinion of W. F. Adams, a careful student of Irish emigration, "the Irish emigrant became a recognized and important factor in American economic and social history."

In the nine years of the 1830s, 341,000 left Ireland for America in a rising graph, set back in certain years by deterrent factors: the numbers in 1833 and in 1835 were reduced by one half from each preceding year, primarily because of the cholera epidemic; in 1838, only eleven thousand emigrated because of the political disturbances in Canada and the 1837 depression in the United States. Increasing steadily, the figures reached over 92,000 in 1842 but dropped to 38,000 in 1843, which was the Repeal year of political hope in Ireland. In 1845, there was what was considered, at the time, a normal flow of emigration from Ireland — upwards of 77,000.

Up to the Famine, approximately one million had left Ireland for America, in character an increasingly Catholic Irish emigration, a fact to be noted in view of the widely held assumption that Catholic Irish emigration over the Atlantic started with the Famine. The Famine's emigration was concentrated in a few years, the pre-Famine's spread over twenty-five years.

The Famine's headlong panic flight was an emigration phenomenon not paralleled until the population uprootings of the two world wars of the twentieth century.

The year 1846 was the vanguard, with 106,000 hastening away from Ireland. Between January 1, 1847 and December 31, 1854, the emigrating Irish numbered 1,656,000, of whom 1,321,725 entered the United States, with 1851 the peak year, 254,500, never since topped.

In 1855, when the exodus had exhausted itself, the Irish emigration was reduced to 78,000, or 28.17 per cent of the Irish total of 1851, approximately the same number as the last pre-Famine year.

One famine had started the migration of the Catholic Irish, a second had accelerated the process, and the Great Famine reduced the population of Ireland by one fourth, through deaths by starvation and disease and through the far greater loss in numbers by emigration. Millions of words have been written, and will be written, of this catastrophic national disaster, the thoughts of which still shiver the national soul, but one old Irishman, years later recalling the Famine with sadness, personalized the painful wrench of the flight in one wistful sentence: "The Curranes and Morans have all gone long ago from Baile na n Gall to the USA."

3

The first movement of the Catholic Irish towards America was directed to Canada and New Brunswick for the compelling reason that the passage was much cheaper than the direct journey to the United States. In the period 1820-1835, the Catholic Irish emigration to British North America annually exceeded that to the United States. In the period 1835-1845, the balance swung the other way, but not by a wide margin. The Famine emigration, however, changed the balance overwhelmingly and permanently in favor of the United States, the numbers to British North America from 1847 to the eve of the Civil War dropping to one seventh of the total United Kingdom emigration.

The Catholic Irish had readily available for a cheap passage the timber boats, which left Irish ports in ballast and returned from the forests of Canada and New Brunswick with the deals and staves for the hogsheads and firkins of the provisioning trade, and wood for rooftrees. After the depredations of the Cromwellian magnates on once luxurious woods, Ireland was bald in the absence of trees. A lad of twenty left his native Mayo barony for the first time and saw a tree: "Lord, Father, what is that?" he exclaimed in wonderment. A fleet of timber ships, wallowing three-masted tubs, prone to founder from structural strains by the nature of their cargo and never built to consider the passenger trade, served the emigrants.

They embarked passengers to British North America lumber ports at a cheaper fare than American cargo ships to New York because, as Francis Spaight candidly admitted, "whatever we get in the way of passengers is so much gain to us," and because under British legislation they were permitted to carry more passengers per registered ton and superficial deck space than the American Congress tolerated. Moreover, their sailing schedules coincided with the emigration season: they went out in the early spring to arrive in time for the opening of the St. Lawrence and the end of the winter logging season; and that was the time of the emigrants' swarmings; every advice warned prospective emigrants against landing in North America in the fall or winter.

The once regular traffic between northern Irish and American ports, particularly New York and Philadelphia, that conveyed linens and the eighteenth-century Ulster Irish emigration from Belfast and Londonderry and returned with flaxseed and potash, had been shattered by the rise of Liverpool as the center of the American trade and the diversion of the flaxseed market from Philadelphia to Holland and the Baltic area.

It was a simple matter for Irish shipowners to rig up jerry-built berths between decks, add water, fuel, and the meager rations required by law, leaving the passengers to furnish the bulk of provisions themselves, and to collect from the growing Catholic Irish emigrant trade profitable fares for space that formerly had been wasted on the westward trip.

But Canada and New Brunswick were not the end of the route for Catholic Irish emigrants; they were the backdoor entrances for re-emigration to the United States. The dawdling British North American provinces lacked the opportunities of work and pay in the bustling, expanding United States; and, besides, friends awaited them there.

4

In *Niles' Register* of July 27, 1822, appeared the item: "*One thousand men* . . . are wanted to labor on the Erie Canal." The following week it noted: "It would appear that many more persons have arrived in the United States during the present season than in the last. A good number reach New York and other ports direct, but by far the greater part arrive via New Brunswick and Canada." This interesting conjunction helps to explain the number of Irish laborers employed in building the Erie Canal. The site of the works was within relatively easy striking distance of the Canadian border; the works needed a continuing supply of laborers; the newly landed Catholic Irishman in Canada needed a job right away at what he could do best — dig with a spade; hence, the introduction of the Catholic Irish to labor on public works.*
On September 3, 1825, *Niles' Register* reported: "During the present season, 8,122 'settlers' have arrived at Quebec . . . and have reached us in good time to help the people of Ohio to make their canals, for which hundreds of them are 'wending their way.'" A year later the same weekly wrote: "Many passengers are arrived at N. York and other ports direct from England; but many more reach the United States by way of Canada. The northern frontier swarms with newly-arrived Irish people."

The Catholic Irish emigrant routes through British North America to the United States became well established.

From St. John in New Brunswick, starting in the mid-1820s, a steamboat crossed the Bay of Fundy to Eastport in Maine, which was the transshipment point for Boston and the New England states, and for New York, Philadelphia, and Baltimore by coastal vessel. Later steamboats supplanted sail, and the ancestors of thousands of New England Irish arrived in Boston from Eastport on the well-known steamboat *Admiral*. To avoid the Massachusetts requirement for bonding of passengers by sea, masters of vessels landed an unknown number, in un-

---

* The term "public works" means canals, railroads, and sizable construction jobs, not necessarily governmental undertakings.

watched harbors, in an illicit traffic in Irishmen: as early as 1823 the master of a Belfast, Maine, schooner was arrested for smuggling Irishmen into Massachusetts. Many walked to their New England destinations or in search of work along the route from the New Brunswick border. Before leaving County Sligo, men were heard to declare they planned to walk from Quebec to New York. The town of Concord, New Hampshire, buried an Irishman who died while walking from the Canadian border.

If an American tracing the progress of his Irish ancestors to America runs into a blank wall, let him remember that no records of crossings over the border from British North America were kept, and the savings from illegal Massachusetts entrance by water were more important to them at the time than the genealogical disposition of their descendants.

Interestingly, Boston was not an important direct emigration receiving port for Catholic Irish until Enoch Train started his line of packets in 1844 and the Famine numbers poured in. David Henshaw, collector of customs for Boston, reporting in 1836 that comparatively few emigrants arrived from Great Britain, said: "The principal emigration is of the Irish population, by way of Nova Scotia, New Brunswick, and Eastport in Maine"; and British Consul Grattan, in 1843, noted "a considerable increase" in emigrants at the port in the last two years, "chiefly from the Provinces of New Brunswick and Nova Scotia."

5

Quebec was by far the most important port of arrival in the British provinces for Catholic Irish emigrants, but the re-emigration distribution to the United States began at Montreal, which they reached by steamboat up the St. Lawrence, a distance of 180 miles. One route led a short distance by land to St. John's, then by boat across Lake Champlain to Burlington, Vermont, for New England, and to Whitehall, whence to the Troy and Albany areas and down the Hudson to New York City. A second route led from Montreal to Kingston by way of Prescott (opposite Ogdensburg) or by Ottawa (formerly Bytown) and the Rideau Canal. Kingston was a jumping-off place across Lake Ontario for northern New York and, by way of the Welland Canal, for Niagara and Buffalo. At Buffalo, the flow of both Canadian and Erie Canal emigrant traffic joined for transshipment to ports on Lake Erie — Erie, Cleveland, Sandusky, and Toledo — and the West. At Cleveland, connections were made for Cincinnati, Pittsburgh, and Louisville, and at Toledo, for parts of Indiana. Those headed through Canada for Michigan, Indiana, Illinois, Wisconsin, Iowa, or Minnesota could push forward, on a third route, to Windsor and Detroit.

The use of the British provinces route to the United States by great numbers of women and children, unaccompanied by the male head of the family, developed from the persistent pursuit of the Catholic Irish for cheapness of transit. This passage was cheaper but, in addition, the state of New York imposed a head tax of two dollars uniformly on all alien passengers, regardless of age, children as well as adults, and the total New York reckoning for a man with a large family ran into money. The male head, therefore, embarked for New York, leaving the rest of the family to come out by the St. Lawrence, "trusting, in many instances," wrote Dr. Douglas, Quebec Medical Superintendent in 1842, "to receive assistance on their arrival there to enable them to proceed" to join him.

6

A queer twist in the mechanics of Catholic Irish emigration was that vessels proceeding directly from Irish ports went to the British provinces, while Irish emigrants heading directly for the United States left from Liverpool.

Two events combined to turn Catholic Irish emigration for America towards Liverpool. First was the introduction in 1823 of steam navigation between Ireland and England, which quickly developed by its expeditious transport of Irish cattle to the English market. Where sailing packets took from two to four days, and often a week, for a passage from Dublin to Liverpool, a steam voyage took fourteen hours. Next was the establishment in 1828 of steerage for emigrants in the American packets engaged in the Liverpool trade. The notice calling attention to the first advertisement of the new steerage packets summed up the revolution in the passenger trade as it bore upon Catholic Irish emigration:

> The facility of crossing the channel from ports in Ireland where there are seldom any direct communications with the United States, and the dependance which may be placed on *punctuality* in sailing from Liverpool, will materially lessen the expenses of emigrants, and enable them to bring their families to a country where honest industry is fairly remunerated.

EMBARKING AT LIVERPOOL

The advantage in a set date for sailing to emigrants, who had to furnish their own provisions, guaranteed the success of the new order from the start. An Irish emigrant going to America on a margin which called for the tightest economy was in a precarious situation if, on arriving from the interior at a port town, he had to cut into his food reserves and into his skimpy resources for lodgings, in the event a transient ship was delayed. (Sometimes they sailed as much as a month later than their advertised date.) With a packet ship, he could arrange departure from his townland to coincide with the date set for sailing. As the 1820s turned into the 1830s, Catholic Irish emigration from Liverpool heightened, and in the 1840s the great English port had a near-monopoly on the trade. Nine tenths of the emigrants out of Liverpool to the United States were Catholic Irish, and four fifths of them sailed on American ships.

7

Emigration followed the cargo trade routes, never the other way. American ships carried raw cotton for the hungry maws of Lancashire's mills, and returned with England's textiles, hardware, cutlery, iron rails, and the Irish. Irishmen were on one deck, iron rails in the hold, and the two met again on American earth to vein the expanding country with railroad tracks. Debarking the Irish at New York, the ships then proceeded to New Orleans, completing the Cotton-Irish triangle. British-registered ships in the American emigrant trade followed the same procedure, except that the timber vessels turned north for the British provinces.

In 1843, American shipowners began to build their cargo ships with an eye to emigrants. They installed permanent berths in place of the improvised arrangement between decks thrown up at Liverpool and dismantled at New York. They increased the size of ships and added an extra deck to accommodate greater numbers. Whereas the ship *Nicholas Biddle* arrived in New York from Liverpool with 214 emigrants and the *Powhatan* with 208 in May, 1842, the liner *Washington* from Liverpool landed 956 emigrants in New York in April, 1852.

Just as Catholic Irish emigrants were loaded with the cargo at Liverpool, so they were discharged at New York with the cargo. New York was so far and away the greatest receiving port for Catholic Irish emigrants to the United States, from the very beginning of the migration, that citing figures for other ports merely highlights the predominance of New York. As in Massachusetts, some masters avoided the New York alien tax by landing the Irish at Perth Amboy in New Jersey, leaving them to straggle into New York City. New Orleans was a distant second as a receiving port: Catholic Irish bound for Mississippi River landings and Western states used the New Orleans route. Boston was third, with a heavy influx during the Famine years.

The Americans earned this trade by their progressiveness and more humane treatment of Catholic Irish emigrants: even the British admitted the superiority of American emigrant ships, captains, and crews. The emigrant ships out of Irish ports were the worst of all in every respect and never improved to the end of sail.

8

John O'Connell, son of Daniel O'Connell and a member of the British House of Commons, proclaimed that emigrant ships under British register should at least be as good as the ships which transported convicts to Australia. Vessels which had just brought in a cargo of guano, hides, or old rags, "in unwholesome and offensive condition," were pressed into emigration service without being cleansed and whitewashed. Stephen De Vere, an Irish gentlemen reformer and idealist, made a trip as an emigrant on a ship with gunpowder to the Quebec garrison. A ship that had carried coolies from Madras to the West Indies the year before was translated into an emigrant ship to America.

The American laws concerning passengers were more severe than the British and tried particularly to prevent the great evil of the emigrant trade — overcrowding: a captain who risked piling in more emigrants than the law allowed faced the menace of confiscation of his ship by American authorities if the number over the law exceeded twenty. American law aimed to enforce better ventilation below decks, healthier conditions of sanitation, and separation of the sexes in steerage.

But no law, as the English emigration commissioners admitted, could stop the frauds practiced on Catholic Irish emigrants, who suffered from an organized racketeering relatively as vicious as the thuggery of New York's waterfront in modern times.

2 3
The Voyage

JOHN BESNARD, the weighmaster of Cork City, was an honest and decent man. After observing the business ethics of emigration for twenty years, he said: "Nothing would induce me to go into the American trade, unless I could see it put on such a footing as would enable a man to conduct it on Christian principles."

Mr. Besnard's ten-foot-pole attitude towards the emigrant trade was explained concretely by the Liverpool correspondent of Dublin's *Freeman's Journal*: "From the very first application they [Irish emigrants] make relative to their passage to the moment of their setting foot on American soil, those with whom they have to do, with perhaps some few exceptions, make it a point to gull and deceive them." And, as will be seen, the same gantlet of swindling was resumed in America.

The typical Catholic Irish emigrant was as unsophisticated and innocent of the world as any person would be who had not set foot out of the confines of his native village in his life. More Catholic Irish emigrants had seen New York, Boston, Philadelphia, or New Orleans than had seen Dublin. He was filled with warm affections from the simple friendship tokens of relatives and neighbors, who had rallied around to bid him Godspeed, pressing his hand with a firm grasp while tears of sentiment stood unashamed in saddened eyes. It may be that the women of the village had brought as contributions a supply of hard oaten cakes — the journey-cakes of the Irish emigrant — baked and baked until each one "was like a slate there; an' it was as good when they got there as when they left." Or a collection of potatoes had been made for him in the townland. His friends had walked a way with him (the famous "American wake" was a development of a later period) to the traditional spot — a ford, a hill, or a crossroads — where emigrants departed for ships.

The breaking of personal ties was the hardest wrench for the warm-hearted and affectionate Catholic Irish emigrants. Irish-Americans later, at St. Patrick's Day celebrations, grew lugubrious over the piece of Irish earth, or sod, the emigrant supposedly carried with him to rest by his side on that day he was buried in alien soil. This pleasant fiction was the product of Irish romantic sentimentalism in America, like the numberless melancholy songs about the Irish exile in America, composed in Ireland by men who had never been out of their native land. The departing emigrant had little room in his scant belongings for a piece of Irish earth, let alone inclination to carry away a piece of sod that had denied him a living.

They had had the blessing of the priest and trusted implicitly in the Lord, the Virgin, and the Saints to carry them safely over the waters to their new homes. And so when they arrived in Liverpool, they were, as the American Captain Knight of the *New World* described them, "like a lot of sheep surrounded by wolves." The greater number of these emigrants, said Sir George Stephen of the Colonial Office,

> . . . are of the most simple and ignorant character; they will believe anything; they are extremely credulous; they will find themselves in a strange place, and they are disposed to attend to every word that is said, and to give up to it; consequently, there could not be a more convenient prey, as it were, to those who are disposed to defraud them.

They gave their confidence to a perfect stranger who came up to them in Liverpool and, in an honest brogue, inquired, "How are you, Jack Dimpsey?" They did not suspect that a confederate of the "man-catcher," as the breed was called, had sent prior information from Ireland of this particular batch of emigrants or had mingled with them on the channel passage to Liverpool to find out their names and their capital.

2

The Catholic Irish emigrant got the first taste of what lay ahead of him on the channel crossing from Ireland to Liverpool, where he was packed in a steamer without cover on an open deck, exposed to bad weather and the cold, drenched with the spray of rough water, the companion of cattle and pigs for the English market. John Besnard had "Christian principles" in mind when he indignantly burst out:

> The parties who take them over get 10s. a head for the convey-
> ance of these poor people from Cork; they do not get half the money
> for pigs, and yet the pigs are comfortably lodged between decks,
> because they are of value to somebody, while these poor people are
> not looked after at all.

The managing director of a channel steamboat company, when asked if the stench was not bad when the poor emigrants were lodged in the open space abaft the funnel, which on the previous voyage had housed pigs, replied: "The class of deck passengers are not so fastidious as to that."

The old slave-shipping Liverpool, now the heart-pulse of that world-wide commerce which made Victorian England wealthy, bustled with life, vigor, and rough color along its four miles of docks, and out in the Mersey ships of every description waited to discharge cargo or depart to every spot in the world. Of all seaports of the world, wrote Herman Melville, who visited it as a sailor before the mast in 1837, "Liverpool, perhaps, abounds in all the variety of land-sharks, land-rats, and other vermin," more sharks than Jack found at sea, and particularly fond of Irish emigrant fare. One would have to go far to come upon a parallel of conscienceless scavenging to equal the mean pickings of the Liverpool refuse upon the small coins of poor Irish men and women, "whom a successful fraud not merely deprives of some superfluity, but reduces to destitution."

The great American shipping houses and English shipowners divorced themselves almost completely from direct dealings with the emigrant passenger trade. They sold space between decks for a flat sum to Liverpool brokers, who conducted the retail business of filling the cargo ships with emigrants. These brokers opened branches or commissioned agents in the United States to deal in prepaid passages and Irish remittances, and in turn local representatives were appointed in cities with large Irish settlements. The reputation of these Liverpool brokers was, with a few exceptions, so smelly that William Tapscott, himself the head of a large firm, ruefully admitted that "a respectable man hardly likes to say he is a passenger-broker."

The "Jack Dimpsey" man-catchers or runners or the porters (called the "Forty Thieves"), who wrestled the chest or luggage from the emigrant by sheer force in spite of the latter's protests, and then grossly overcharged him, were either lodging-house keepers or in their employ. The Liverpool emigrant lodging house, a vile, filthy, overcrowded pest-hole, which the medical superintendent at Quebec insisted was the main source of the disease Irish emigrants carried into ships, grew out of the strictly enforced prohibition of the dock commissioners against lights and stove fires on berthed vessels, which required emigrants to repair to the lodgings in lanes and alleys until the hour of embarkation.

The lodging-house keeper or runner constituted himself the guide of the trusting emigrant in the preparations for the sea voyage. He led his charge on the rounds of passenger agents along Waterloo Road, their headquarters, seeming to bargain for the cheapest fare when his aim was the highest commission; next at the provisioning dealer's, where the emigrant was overloaded with short-weighted, poor quality food, on the warning that ships barred passengers without a certain quantity of food. (This overstocking was a swindle less injurious to the emigrant than a practice of the masters of Irish ships in urging the emigrant to understock, so that when his supply ran short at sea he was forced to buy from the ship stores at extortionate prices.) The third stop was at the store where gimcrack cooking, water and other utensils ("Scarcely a passenger who does not take a chamber pot with him") were fobbed off on the emigrant, again under the caution that the ship required them.

Told that his English money was worthless in America, the emigrant was now "dollared." His ignorance was exploited by the money changer to exact an exorbitant commission or to pass off on him foreign coins twenty per cent below the dollar's value or the heavily discounted American shinplasters.

These sharks who preyed on the credible Catholic Irish emigrants were, for the most part, Irishmen themselves. The whole system of lodging houses and attendant abuses was so outrageous that seventeen American captains of well-known packet ships petitioned Lord Grey, Colonial Secretary, for the establishment of a depot to accommodate emigrants from the time they landed until they sailed, and offered to contribute to its maintenance out of their percentage of passage money, but the government took no action. Private attempts to establish emigrant depots were destroyed by lodging-house keepers and their runners with the tolerance of Liverpool's officialdom.

If the Catholic Irish emigrant arrived at Liverpool with a passage paid for in Ireland the previous winter or prepaid in America at a price lower than the going fare, he was delayed in Liverpool until the rush was over and prices had dropped or shunted to an inferior ship. Thirty emigrants were forced to take passage for Quebec when they had purchased tickets for New York: it was either that or make up the difference in price out of their small capital.

But the genuinely heartbreaking fraud was the worthless passage: a hundred emigrants from Ireland arrived in a batch in Liverpool to be told that their tickets were fraudulent. The numbers who constantly had to take the sad route back to Ireland, their small capital dissipated, their misery compounded, testified to the perfidy of which human beings are capable on the defenseless and wretched poor.

Another fraud which cried to heaven for punishment was deception of the ignorant regarding destination in America. Patrick Gormley, a Liverpool passenger agent, was fined and his license revoked for selling David Harrigan, his wife, and two other females tickets to St. John's, Newfoundland, instead of St. John, New Brunswick; a poor illiterate woman was persuaded that the shortest route to Quebec was by way of New Orleans; and runners, with ships to fill, told the innocent that Boston was the nearest port to Mobile. The *Montreal Packet* was advertised to sail from Dublin to New York, and 186 persons bought tickets for the American port but instead were landed at St. John, New Brunswick; the aroused passengers brought legal proceedings and forced the owner to complete the journey to New York.

Buchanan at Quebec was convinced that this chain of fraud "accounts for the number of improvident emigrants who annually arrive at this port."

The heritage of Liverpool to countless Catholic Irish emigrants was a long-remembered bitterness at the impositions on their ignorance and helplessness; it often remained longer than the memory of the voyage, which was hardly a holiday cruise.

3

After undergoing a perfunctory medical test for infectious diseases, which the Irish learned to beat in dubious cases by having healthy Timmy take his place in line with the ticket of sickly Paudeen, the emigrants, in great confusion and with much noise, scrambled on board the vessel with their luggage but not until the precious cargo had been stowed.

The names of these Irish emigrant ships have long been forgotten, but in their day they were household in the Irish communities in America: the famous Liverpool packets to New York — *Isaac Webb, Queen of the West, Yorkshire, Isaac Wright, New World, Constitution, Star of the West*; the Boston packets — *Washington Irving, Governor Davis, Daniel Webster, Frank Pierce, Parliament,* and *Chariot of Fame*; and the ships out of Irish ports to British North America — *Idea* of Galway, *Perseverance* of Dublin, *Maria Brennan, Borneo, Jessy, Energy* of Limerick, *Clifton* of Cork, *Active* of Londonderry, *Bruce* of Newport, *Pomona* of Sligo. And Catholic Irish came over on the *Mayflower* — from Ballyshannon.

The Catholic Irish traveled light: the Irish emigrant, said T. W. C. Murdoch, an emigration commissioner, starts for America with "just the clothes he stands up in, or scarcely more." Even though the Irish had capital, they put on the semblance of poverty, to beat their way as cheaply as possible. This peasant closeness was an obsession with them. They sewed money in their clothes and suffered hardships before parting with it: "they will sometimes starve for a week," said a Quebec forwarder, "rather than produce it," and the emigration agent at Hamilton, Canada, declared that some of the Irish applicants for relief "were found to be possessed of sums varying from £10 to even £200." One emigrant known to have considerable capital appeared on the streets of Cork begging in an outfit as tattered as the poorest cottier's. Agent Buchanan at Quebec was constantly torn between his suspicion of Irish secretiveness about money and his decent wish to relieve genuine distress when he was appealed to for assistance.

While the ship was being towed from the dock out into the stream, the systematic search for stowaways began. They were found hidden in barrels or chests, sometimes dead; they were prodded out from under bedding, beneath sails, behind luggage piles, within dark nooks and corners. Martin Dooley had successfully hidden himself with provisions

SEARCHING FOR STOWAWAYS BEFORE DEPARTURE FROM LIVERPOOL

on the ship *South Carolina* from Liverpool; Dr. Moriarty, the port physician of Boston, amputated his mortified legs.

4

The ship rested in the stream until the routine of the roll call had been taken of the passengers, to check the tickets and uncover deceptions and frauds, as described in the *Illustrated London News*:

> Sometimes an Irishman, with a wife and eight or ten children, who may have only paid a deposit of his passage-money, attempts to evade the payment of the balance, by pleading that he has not a farthing left in the world, and trusting that the ship will rather take him out to New York for the sum already paid, than incur the trouble of putting him on shore again with his family. Sometimes a woman may have included in her passage ticket an infant at breast, and may be seen, when her name is called, panting under the weight of a strapping boy of eight or nine years of age, whom she is holding to her bosom as if he were really a suckling.

A ticket calling for a boy under twelve at half fare would be produced by a strapping lad of nineteen who could lift a plow by the handle.

"They are a difficult people to manage for their own good," sighed an harassed official, to which the berthing clerk of an emigrant ship could nod vigorous assent. He had hardened himself to their complaints, protests, grievances, demands, and wants and opened his ears only when he heard the clinking coins of a tip.

He was used to Catholic Irish requests for indiscriminate berthing, men and women of different names asking to be put together in the same berth, married and single men and women packed without distinction of sex. Dr. Lancaster, medical chief at Liverpool, spoke of this as a common occurrence; yet he had never heard from captains or doctors on ships of any impropriety. They described it as "a surprising thing" and one "which could not occur with any other class of people than the Irish."

The Catholic Irish, belligerently vigilant of the chastity of their women, had devised a system for the care of single women in the careless berthings of emigrant ships — the male protector. Devout Catholic parents were more worried over the virtue of their daughters than of the dangers of the deep. If no brother were going out, the parents arranged for the departure of a single girl with a male cousin or relative or neighboring friend, in whose honor they had complete trust, or in the charge of a married couple. "It is true," said the Irish men, "that if we are not satisfied that our women are to be exempt from disturbance or annoyance, we prefer sleeping in the same berth with them," pending a total separation of the sexes in emigrant ships.

But the voyage was difficult in other respects than indiscriminate mixing of the sexes for the unusually modest Irish women. Sympathetic passengers isolated and screened off a woman giving birth; and thoughtful American captains arranged schedules so that women could have privacy in use of improvised toilets. It was hell, however, to be on a ship with an indifferent captain and a coarse crew.

5

Mrs. Chisholm once exclaimed that shipowners were accustomed "to make a large profit and to put people in a small space." Except on ships built for the emigrant trade, the space between decks ranged from five-and-a-half to six feet. And, remember, the majority of these ships were under a thousand tons, often nearer five hundred. Double tiers of berths were rigged along the sides of the ship on a deck squeezed in between the main deck and the hold, each berth to hold four adults, each adult to have the eighteen inches required by law. Thus four persons slept in a compartment of six feet by six feet — "they have not much more than their coffin," said an official. Since each emigrant provided his own bedding, often not of the same width, strife was constant over the distribution of space, with many "a stroke struck" during the voyage. A board nine inches high separated one tier from the other, but the bedding raised the berths to a common level, "so that," said Sir George Stephen, "all down both sides of the steerage deck, men, women and children are lying in one promiscuous heap apparently on the same platform."

At the start of the voyage, Irish fiddlers speedily bowed away the sadness of leaving the old land behind in the merry rhythm of clogging feet in jigs, reels, and hornpipes. But this gaiety was brief. Within twenty-four hours, as the ship struck the ocean's swells, the moans and groans of seasick Irish ran the scales of lament. There was none to help them, and when they finally clambered out of their berths in the befouled air they were weak and exhausted, their mouths thick from the lack of water and their bodies wracked from lack of nourishment: the crew had been too busy getting the ship taut for the passage to distribute supplies systematically.

When the ship plunged into heavy weather, the hatches, which were the inlets of fresh air and light, were battened down, often not speedily enough to save the emigrants and their bedding from a drenching. In the darkness of the steerage they pictured the worst and, "frantic in despair," wrote Rev. Bernard O'Hara, a passenger, "their cries were loud enough to rise above the storm and reach to Heaven." John Mullawny (Maloney), a member of the lay Third Order of St. Dominick, resigned himself to the end in a bad storm and as he wrote to his father:

> . . . all the passengers Gave up hopes of being Safe but I had Confidence in the lord and the Blessed Virgin Mary and My holy father St. Domnick that the [they] would not see us perish I was one night that I did put on my habbit and surplis and went round all My friends and neighbours to leave them the last farewell i went to my bead and Gave Myself up to the lord But thanks Be to God we arrived safe on land.

This same spirit of resignation tolerated, even accepted, a state of affairs that also reached to heaven. "We had not been at sea one week," wrote Herman Melville, "when to hold your head down the fore hatchway was like holding it down a suddenly-opened cesspool." The harbormaster's boatman at Quebec had no difficulty, at the distance of gunshot, "in distinguishing by the odor alone a crowded emigrant ship." The emigrants had no inclination for cleanliness, except when disciplined by a stern captain; not all captains cared, and the Irish were difficult to manage. Explaining that "many inconveniences . . . must remain inseparable from the passage by sea," the British Commissioners of Emigration wrote, "it is not to be expected that these poor people can have the same habits, or command the same means, of cleanliness, as persons more favorably situated." Stephen De Vere, on the other hand, said the steerage conditions demoralized the passengers, and they had neither the heart nor the will to exert themselves. The emigrant lost his self-respect and elasticity of spirit: "he no longer stands erect."

The law ordered twenty-one quarts of water each week for passengers (both for drinking and washing), which, when on short supply because of leaky or spoiled casks, caused frightful suffering and raised threats of mutiny. The law also required a minimum of food that was "not sufficient for the sustenance of any human being" — one pound of breadstuffs daily or its equivalent in potatoes up to 1847, when the ration was increased to a pound and a half. An English official said that this diet would keep an Irishman alive, but not a Sussex laborer. Passage certificates specifically warned emigrants to bring along their own supply of food and not to depend upon what was called the "parliamentary diet."

Grates, called "cabooses," were set up on the main deck, and passengers lined up with their supplies to cook their own food. The "cabooses" were few, and each individual required at least fifteen minutes to heat his food; passengers often waited from morning until late in the afternoon for their turn, except when they tipped the attendant; and children and old men were pushed aside in the scramble to use the stoves. Many, dismayed at the delay or unable to stave off the pangs of hunger, ate their oatmeal raw, with unhappy consequences.

Every emigrant ship was a potential pesthouse. The typhus that was endemic in Ireland, or the diseases carried aboard from a dirty Liverpool lodging house, became "ship fever" and took its toll in sickness and death. Stephen De Vere's account of his passage on an Irish emigrant ship to Quebec in the 1847 fever year is classic in its description of the stark horror of such a ship at its worst:

Hundreds of poor people, men, women, and children of all ages, from the drivelling idiot of ninety to the babe just born, huddled together without light, without air, wallowing in filth and breathing a fetid atmosphere, sick in body, disspirited in heart, the fevered patients lying between the sound, in sleeping places so narrow as almost to deny them the power of indulging by a change of position, the natural restlessness of the disease; by their agonized ravings disturbing those around and predisposing them, through the efforts of the imagination, to imbibe the contagion; living without food or medicine, except as administered by the hand of casual charity, dying without the voice of spiritual consolation, and buried in the deep without the rites of the Church.

The captain added to the debasement by a profitable traffic in grog, which American captains strictly prohibited on their ships.

6

Yet despite the unhealthy conditions of emigration steerage, the mortality, with the exception of certain bad years, was surprisingly low. The fact which keeps intruding itself on the attention of the student, who examines the considerable evidence on the unsanitary emigrant ships, is not the number of deaths from disease but the disembarkation of so many hundreds of thousands alive. In the retrospect of our present-day emphasis upon personal hygiene, the numbers who arrived in America — and healthy — after an Atlantic passage on an emigrant sailing vessel seems to prove the validity of miracles.

The mortality figures of early emigration are not available in reliable form, but Alexander Buchanan wrote in 1828 that of the six thousand emigrants he had shepherded in fifteen or sixteen voyages to North America, not more than six adults died. The years of the cholera plague, 1832 and 1834, were known to be costly in emigrant lives. But from 1841, when accurate figures for the Canada emigration were first published, through 1846, out of the 173,564 who embarked from United Kingdom ports, the total mortality, on shipboard or in quarantine, was 1107, or 0.63 per cent of the whole.

The mortality of the 1847 emigration to British North America (almost wholly Irish) was the worst on record. The bare figures need no language to point up the devastation among the fever-hagged emigrants, debilitated by lack of nourishment from the potato failure and demoralized in spirit to the point of indifference to death. There died on the passage — 6116. There died in quarantine — 4149. There died in the hospitals of the provinces — 7180. The total number who died out of the 86,812 embarked was 17,445, or 16.33 per cent of the whole. In contrast to this figure of one death for each six embarked, the New York figures for total emigration in 1847 showed one death for every 145 embarked.

The 1848 Canadian mortality (one per cent) and the 1849 (2.73 per cent) revealed a considerable reduction but was still abnormal. For 1850, 1851, 1852, and 1853, the percentages wavered around the 0.5 per cent figure and so on, in relatively small percentages of mortality as remedial legislation improved accommodations, until the coming of steam limited deaths on passages to normal expectancies.

Except in 1847 and the bad New York cholera year of 1853, which hit the Germans harder than the Irish, the emigrant ship was not altogether the death wagon which popular belief held (and still holds) it to be. The term "coffin ship" was a product of 1847. The victims were taken in large measure from among infants and children, who on

PASSING THE TIME WITH A DANCE BETWEEN DECKS

land probably would have been spared, and from among the aged, for whom the wracking voyage was too much.

The general discomfort and vile conditions of the voyage to a people like the Irish, unaccustomed to the sea, need no further details, but the many testimonials inserted in the Irish weeklies in America by thankful emigrants for a pleasant voyage, and gratitude to captains and crews for attention and care, reveal another side of the emigrant passage that has been obscured by the classic horror stories.

The complaints of the Catholic Irish, who were no restrained grumblers, were directed not to the discomforts and mean circumstances, but to the sparsity and foulness of the water allowance, the short weight and bad quality of the food rations, the mistreatment and brutality by mates and crew and the indifference of masters to their protests, and extortionate prices when their own food supplies ran out. Sometimes, as in the case of the *Normandie,* when actual starvation took place, or the *Charles W. Sears,* when the water supply ran low, the details are blood-chilling; but there are pleasant pictures of Peter Nolan of Kerry catching a fish off the Newfoundland banks or emigrants jigging gaily in the holds or sunning themselves on the main deck in the fresh, salt air during a quiet passage.

7

The pale rider exacted far more lives by disease on emigrant ships than by wrecks or fire at sea. Again the record must be read in the context of ships crowded to the law's limit, and frequently beyond, with sometimes only two lifeboats on a hulk that would today be condemned by an inspector merely at a glance, and without the present rigid precautions for the safety of passengers. And again the record of lives lost is surprisingly low when set against what Robert Albion calls "the grim possibilities" and the fact that hundreds of thousands were safely landed. One reason was that the Catholic Irish emigrating season coincided with the usually fair weather of spring and summer; it was not until the winter of 1846-1847 that the Famine panic introduced the taking of passage in the off, and potentially violent, season.

Outside the tiny hamlet of Cap de Rosiers (Cape of the Roses) on the Gaspé Peninsula is a small clearing in the woods by the side of the road. In that clearing, on a base of granite blocks, stands a monument facing the Atlantic. The curious passer-by who stops will read on its face:

> Sacred to the memory of 187 Irish immigrants from Sligo wrecked here on April 28th, 1847. Ship "Carrick" of Whitehaven. 87 are buried here. Pray for their souls.

This simple memorial, erected by the parishioners of St. Patrick's Parish, Montreal, better than any grandiose monument, stands as a vigil over all the humble Catholic Irish emigrants who were lost on their way to the land of promise and for whose souls the generations are asked to pray.

8

The Catholic Irish who landed in America before the Civil War came on sailing ships. While in the 1850s the steamship was supplanting sail and forecasting the later great emigrant trade (William Inman in 1851 had his eye on it with steerage passage in the steamer *City of Glasgow*), the price still remained beyond the means of the Catholic Irish. The Civil War marked the transition from sail to steam for the Catholic Irish and the passing of the American merchantman which had carried so many thousands to the United States.

April and May were the recommended months for the emigrant to take passage. The average length of voyage on a sailing ship from Liverpool to Quebec was six weeks, and from Irish ports it was four days shorter; from Liverpool to New York, the passage averaged five weeks. No guarantees existed that a sailing ship would reach her destined port in the average number of days. During July and August, which emigrants were advised to avoid, the prevalence of southwest winds made for "a tedious passage." The horror stories of ships which ran low, or out, on food and water during an overextended passage from storms or mishaps at sea, forced the enactment of legislation requiring sailing ships to store a supply of water and sea stores sufficient for ten weeks.

The price of passage fluctuated from time to time according to the demand, season, cost of foodstuffs, new legislative requirements or restrictions, and changing economic conditions; but there was one constant factor which worked to keep the price down — the intensive competition of shipping agencies. Before organization entered the emigrant trade, the cost on regular cargo vessels was prohibitive to the Catholic

Irish emigrant: in 1811, for example, the rates from Londonderry to New York between decks varied from $50 to $60. Twenty years later the price from Liverpool to Quebec was $20, and from Cork $12.50; from Liverpool to New York, it was $25; from a western port of Ireland to Quebec, it was even cheaper — $10. In 1851, the passage price from Liverpool to New York, on the average, was $17.50, with the packet ships charging a higher fare, and from Liverpool to Quebec about five shillings cheaper.

As a rule, the fare to New York ran higher than the fare to the British provinces, but over the years the New York price had been brought within competitive levels with the British North American price from Liverpool. The passage fare from Irish ports to British North America ranged around $12.50. These, of course, are rough approximations: the brokers charged as much as the traffic would bear when the demand was high — at one time in 1847, the fare from Liverpool to New York was $35 — and what bargain they could strike when the demand was spotty.

The price from ports in Scotland ranged from $15 to $17.50. One third of embarkations from the Clyde was Irish, not Irish who had settled in Scotland, but emigrants from the north and west of Ireland.

2 4

The Emigrating Catholic Irishman

THE CATHOLIC IRISH EMIGRANT left his native land with no intention of returning, except as a visitor should he have the means. He came to make a permanent residence in America, unlike so many among the later or "new" immigrants from other lands, who hoped to find the savings to spend their last days in the old country. Daniel O'Connell called emigrant ships "ocean hearses," because the Catholic Irish who embarked on them never returned to Ireland.

2

Catholic Irish emigration was essentially a country, village, and small-town emigration. The people came from townlands, villages, and parishes with melodious and sweet-sounding names that fell with pleasure upon the Irish ear (as they do today) and invoked association of the Gaelic past, of saints, scholars, chieftains, and of legends, like Skihanach, parish Ballyshedy, County Cork; Balegknock, parish Movreach, County Kerry; Kinnilligh, parish Crosherlaugh, County Cavan; Balligooney, parish Lisdowney, County Kilkenny; or like Ballymenagh, Lisroughnagh, Ferriter Ballyughtreagh, Rathkeal, Kilraghtish, Doornana, Tullgullen, Mannonorag, Taughmacconnell, Kilcolman, Tamla Acrilla, Clogheen, Drumleagh, and Carricktouhal. An Irishman in America, asked where he came from, replied with the name of his townland, parish, and county.

3

The emigrating Irishman wore the clothes of his nation, the costume associated with the "stage Irishman." Kohl described it amusingly but not inaccurately — "the French company dress coat, with its high useless collar, its swallow tail hanging down behind, and the breast open in front." With this coat went "short knee breeeches, with stockings and shoes." The costume was made "of a coarse gray cloth called 'frieze,' from which the coats themselves derive the name of 'frieze coats.' " The hat was "a strange caricature of a beaver or silk hat," and Pat "pinches and flattens and twists" it "into a fashion of his own. He pushes up the brim away from his face in front, while behind it soon hangs in festoon fashion." When the crown fell in, a pack-thread kept it together; when it collapsed, the owner continued to wear it.

The Irish emigrant, dressed in native fashion, was a familiar figure in American port towns before the Civil War, looking like a displaced member of the French Academy with a brogue, who had taken to the hard and dusty refugee road. He speedily cast off this anachronism and dressed himself in the American manner: "i had to buy splendid cloathing," one wrote home, "for there would be no respect for you if you did not go respectable."

4

A story that entered into the mythology of Ireland was of the number of emigrant families that were blown right back to the port from which they embarked when, within sight of America, the wind changed. They got word to neighbors, who made up new bundles of oaten cakes and went to the port and presented them to the back-blown emigrants. Then they re-embarked and reached America safely.

5

The sadness of departure among a highly emotional people touched deeply the families and friends left behind, much more than the emigrants, who were speedily caught up in the contagion of excitement and confusion and the strange faces soon to be new friends; and one who remained wrote down a scene in a leave-taking from an island off the coast of Kerry:

> . . . the bright May morning with the summer sun shining in the heavens: the birds singing in the hedges, and the cuckoo's call echoing in their ears, as the sad procession wended their way down to the emigrant ship — men, women, and children — the very old and the very young — filling the clear summer air with their wails and lamentations.

With the quick adaptability of the race, they set about the work of making a new home in the United States, and what befell them is now part of the vast history of the many-peopled Republic.

PART THREE

What Befell Them in America

. . . it is the truth of a good country.
Letter from a Catholic Irish emigrant
in Ohio, 1836

2 5

The Best Poor Man's Country

REV. EDWARD EVERETT HALE, author of *The Man Without a Country,* called the Catholic Irish the race without a future. It was not that he meant to be uncharitable, but he had a theory that the Catholic Irish were a washed-out people. Within the scope of recorded history, he explained, the great Celtic race, once the fee-holder of Western Europe, had been defeated and pushed ever westward by peoples pressing upon it from the east until the last sizable body of pure-blooded Celts stood at bay in Catholic Ireland, the western perimeter of Europe. There it paid the penalty for its unmixed blood — successive defeats.

Now the final catastrophe had come not by force of arms, asserted Mr. Hale, but by "the competition of the well-composed English social system," which it could no more successfully withstand than its progenitors the disciplined legions of Caesar. The historic retreat of the Celtic race had no land westward for refuge, only "a plunge into the sea." But fortunately Providence had intervened with American cotton ships going westward at cheap passage rates. Mr. Hale continued:

> The Irish emigration, then, is the dispersion, after its last defeat, of a great race of men, which, in one way or another, has been undergoing defeat for centuries. . . . They are fugitives from defeat, or . . . fugitives from slavery. Every Irishman who leaves Ireland for America seems to be as really driven thence . . . as if he had made a stand in fight at the beach at Galway, and had been driven by charged bayonets into the sea.

If this view be correct, reasoned Mr. Hale, the pure Celtic race was "at this moment useless in the world" and "for His active purposes the Almighty has done with it."

This was a neat intellectual rationalization of the tremendous phenomenon, in the form of the Irish Famine emigration, then overwhelming the ports of the United States and British North America, a nice pattern put together from wide reading by a bookish man. It had one fault — the Rev. Mr. Hale did not know the Catholic Irish.

A year before, a young Roman Catholic priest in the Boston diocese, native-born of Irish parents, gave a talk on the same subject — the Celtic Exodus, as the emigration was called at the time. But he interpreted the design of Providence for the Catholic Irish differently from Mr. Hale. The Irish, declared Father John T. Roddan, are like the Jews, indestructible. He continued:

> Ireland has more lives than the blackest cat; she has been killed so many times that her enemies are tired of killing her, and there she is, as provoking as ever, ready to be killed again.

Sir Robert Peel once sighed that Ireland had always been his greatest difficulty, and an English parliamentarian, out of patience with the eternal Irish Problem, had suggested a final solution: sink the whole island in the Atlantic for twenty-four hours.

As Father Roddan saw it, the Almighty had not done with the Catholic Irish but had opened America to them. "God made Ireland need America," he said, "and He made America an asylum for Ireland. And He will reward this great country, because it has done a work for Him." The reward, the zealous young priest prophesied, would be conversion of America to the True Faith: "It is certain," he declared, "that a majority of Americans in the year 1950 will be Catholics."

Events have a way of reinforcing the ancient admonition on the inscrutability of Providence.

But if the insights of Mr. Hale were awry in the gloomy future he predicted for the remnants of the Celtic race, his common sense was sound in giving a good whack to the native American cries to turn out the swarms of pauperized Catholic Irish emigrants. His plea for Americans to receive and welcome these emigrants was singularly free from the conventional abstractions of America as the refuge of the persecuted and the haven of the oppressed. It derived from Yankee down-to-earth horse sense, which was the genius of seeing the obvious. These Catholic Irish emigrants, ran Mr. Hale's argument, will take over the manual labor of the country and release our own laborers for higher-grade duties; by this method our civilization will be advanced. The displaced Americans will be pushed up into higher categories — foremen,

bosses of farms, railway agents, machinists, inventors, teachers, artists
— which they could not reach unless an available body of cheap hand
labor existed. This hard manual labor must be done, and without the
Irishman's spade "the whole fabric of our civilization [must] be degraded."

Thirty years later, Thomas R. Hazard, the Shepherd Tom of the
readable *Jonny Cake Papers* of Rhode Island life, probated the judgments of Mr. Hale. Though their coming seemed to face the American
laborer with ruin, he wrote, the Irish actually "fourfolded the wages
and made bosses of the Yankee laborers" and now it was the turn of
the Sons of Erin to be lifted on the shoulders of the new immigrants.

2

The circumstances of his background in Ireland disqualified the
Catholic Irish emigrant from any work but the hardest and coarsest labor in the new land. Uneducated, accustomed to a marginal existence,
a stranger to the refinements, thankful for a job at cash wages, he entered into the lowest stratum of free white labor as the hewer of wood
and drawer of water, with his sole capital a brawny back and two
strong hands, under conditions of comfort and consideration by employers decidedly less favorable than a humane plantation owner arranged for his Negro slaves, who were property and therefore expenda-
ble only at a monetary loss. There came with the mass of laborers, of
course, Catholic Irishmen of education and trained skills — teachers,
clerks, and artisans; but a common complaint was that competition with
the favored Americans in employment forced the higher economic class
of the Irish into the ranks of rough labor.

America needed — and needed badly — the hard manual labor of
which the Catholic Irishman was capable. The editor of *The Shamrock*, an Irish-American publication in New York, argued early in 1817
that emigration was clearly in the national interest:

> . . . we have wildernesses to be cleared, canals and roads to be
> made; we may vote supplies for internal improvements, money may
> be raised but if the laborers cannot be obtained the work will remain
> undone. The farmer settled comfortably on his plantation or the
> mechanic placed at his loom will not put by their regular avoca-
> tion to earn their money in public employ. This must be done by
> the newly arrived emigrants, or the work will not be done.

Native American labor expected a higher wage than the emigrant laborer; and the free Negroes, who offered a labor pool, were not satisfactory for rough work, according to an employer in Chester County, Pennsylvania, who wrote in 1816: "For since [the War of 1812] commenced we have been under the necessity of hiring the blacks and we are heartily tired of these creeping [i.e. slowly moving] creatures."

The Boston *Morning Post*, in 1836, related that the Irish endured many kinds of labor and exposure "which would soon destroy the health of a Yankee" and added that "the laboring class of the native American population . . . is not sufficiently numerous to answer one half our demands for manual labor." The black population, "once so much more numerous than at present in this part of the country," had gradually sunk into oblivion because "the Irish, whose labors were found more serviceable, have taken their places, as railroads are fast taking the place of canals."

The "indolent Irish" had been a characterization fixed on the race by the English in Ireland that America inherited. Superficial observation gave it currency in America for two major reasons. One was the frequent spells of unemployment the Irishman suffered from the nature of his manual work — inclement weather, cyclical depressions, and job competition. On this score the description was unjust because of elements beyond the individual Irishman's control. The other was the shiftlessness of a ragtag and bobtail minority, noisy, dissolute, troublesome, gravitating to public relief, which unfairly settled a distorted reputation on the race in the minds of people often initially prejudiced.

After the chronic unemployment of his native land, with its concomitant distresses, the Catholic Irishman leaped to the work opportunities in America, no matter how hard and coarse, as a blessing. An Irish emigrant in Cincinnati shoveling out large stones summed up a common attitude by saying that America was a rare place for a working man: "'Deed it is, sir; a man that can do hard rough work, and keep from drink, need never look behind him." America, said another, "is the best poor-mans country in the world."

The Catholic Irish emigrant made himself synonymous among the discerning with hard work at low wages and unpitying exploitation. Ralph Waldo Emerson in Concord wrote to Henry Thoreau on September 8, 1843:

> Now the humanity of the town suffers with the poor Irish, who receives but sixty, or even fifty cents, for working from dark till

dark, with a strain and a following up that reminds one of negro-driving. Peter Hutchinson told me he had never seen men perform so much; he should never think it hard again if an employer should keep him at work after sundown.

General Swartwout of New York, in reclaiming marshlands from the sea, had employed Germans, English, Swiss, Yankees, and the Irish but "had found, at last, that when real hard labor had to be performed, when wet and cold had to be faced, none would work like the Irish." The shrewd general had also uncovered a secret of the Irish nature — that a good word given to an Irishman "did more than a handful of dollars upon any body else."

The intelligent Emerson also made a shrewd observation in elementary economics that accounted for the relatively slow progress of the Irish in status — the strongest competitor of the Irish laborer was another Irish laborer from the pool which emigration kept filled up. Emerson said:

> But what can be done for their relief as long as new applications for the same labor are coming in every day? These of course reduce the wages to the sum that will suffice a bachelor to live, and must drive out the men with families.

The Catholic Irishman not only worked hard but dangerously. The bones of many Irishmen lay encased in the foundations of the material America they helped to build. The death, in 1836, by drowning in Lake Champlain of an Irishman who tried to rescue a Methodist minister set up a chain of reflection in the mind of a fellow Irishman:

> How often do we see such paragraphs in the paper, as an Irishman drowned — an Irishman crushed by a beam — an Irishman suffocated in a pit — an Irishman blown to atoms by a steam engine — ten, twenty Irishmen buried alive by the sinking of a bank — and other like casualties and perils to which honest Pat is constantly exposed, in the hard toils for his daily bread.

Safety precautions were negligible; the worker took the risks as part of the day's job; if he became disabled by accident, the burden fell on public charity or the good hearts of his friends.

America had virtues with compelling appeal to the Catholic Irishman. It was a land blessed with an abundance of food, in comparison to the intermittent famines endemic in Ireland and the single diet of potatoes. Hezekiah Niles told the incident of an Irishman boarding at a farmhouse:

The farmer used often to say to his wife — I am tired of wheat bread, or of corn bread, or of buckwheat cakes — of beef and of pork, and the like; give us a change. Ah! said the Irishman "I then thought it strange, that a man should be tired of having enough of any of these things."

Or the story Michel Chevalier, the French traveler, had picked up, which, apocryphal or not, made a sound point:

An Irishman, who had recently arrived, showed his master a letter which he had just written to his family. "But, Patrick," said his master, "why do you say that you have meat three times a week, when you have it three times a day?" "Why is it?" replied Pat; "it is because they wouldn't believe me, if I told them so."

A republican American, narrating the same story, would not have used the word "master" to describe the relationship of employer to employed. That word had small status outside the slave states. To the American the use of distasteful "peasant" comprehended an aristocratic society, and it found no lodging in the national vocabulary. O'Connell called the massed Irish audiences "peasants" to their faces with no reaction of resentment; "peasant" was a fighting word of contempt in the United States. The Irishman could hold his head higher by the simple fact of his presence in the new land. Mathew Carey wrote to his fellow countrymen abroad that no man was obliged "to crouch to fellow mortals, nor to submit to insolence or stripes from him." An American, he continued, enjoyed security of person, a light tax, a chance to hold property free and clear, and no law enforced support of the clergy, a state different from that which obtained in Ireland.

But there were grave and persistent inhibitions in republican America imposed on the Catholic Irish not included in Mr. Carey's favorable bill of specifications. They were members of a different and exotic religion which overwhelmingly Protestant America associated, as an inheritance from the Reformation and from England, with idolatry and superstition in worship and with despotism and tyranny in policy. They were poor; and America, bouncy and optimistic, hewed to the social assumption that poverty flowed from defective and vicious individual character. The Catholic Irish joined the popular political party as zealous and vigorous partisans and had visited upon them the contumely of press, pulpit and other agencies in the service of conservative forces. And finally, though they spoke English, the brogue marked them as "foreigners" and "aliens."

It will seem strange to American descendants that for a long period their ancestors were described in newspaper stories as "an Irishman" or "a foreigner" and classified in public documents as "aliens." The relationship of "aliens" with crime and pauperism was generally applicable to the Catholic Irish as the particular source of offense. "If a swindler, thief, robber, or murderer, no matter what his color or country," wrote Patrick S. Casserly of New York, an Irish schoolmaster, in 1832, "commit any nefarious or abominable act, throughout the Union, he is instantly set down as a native of Ireland."

An uncomplimentary description of the Irish by a political enemy received wide circulation:

> The children of bigoted Catholic Ireland, like the frogs which were sent out as a plague against Pharaoh, have come into our homes, bed-chambers, and ovens and kneading troughs. Unlike the Swedes, the Germans, the Scots, and the English, the Irish when they arrive among us, too idle and vicious to clear and cultivate land, and earn a comfortable home, dump themselves down in our large villages and towns, crowding the meaner sort of tenements and filling them with wretchedness and disease. In a political point of view, what are they but mere marketable cattle.

When a political orator or a hostile newspaper referred to "Pharaoh's frogs," the words required no further explanation.

The stereotype of the Catholic Irish, when they started to arrive in numbers as emigrants, had been fixed in the American impression from several sources. The lingering prejudice against the Protestant Irishman of the eighteenth century as turbulent, fractious and hard-drinking attached itself to the Catholic Irish emigrant for the same reasons. Americans saw the Catholic Irish through the eyes of English writings as the cabin companions of the pig, disturbers of the peace at fairs, lawless and rebellious, steeped in ignorance and superstition, whom the English (again from their own version) had tried unsuccessfully to civilize.

The Americans also adopted the other attitude of the English toward the Catholic Irish, that of condescending amusement at buffoonish characters, who preferred play to work, improvident, happy-go-lucky, with quick and ingenious wits, the standard "stage Irishman" of the theater and novels. The American press pinned comic anecdotes and jokes on the Irishman as the central figure and made the "Irish bull" a part of American humor. But papers which indulged in Irish-baiting as a stock in trade savagely burlesqued the race, like this reprint from the *Albion* in 1825 of the Irishman at home:

> Upon a Sunday he appears in his loose mantle in the House of God, which you know, sir, is an ould bit of a blanket skewered under his throat, and neath the smile of his priest who comes and axed him all about his children, and their concarns — and then the honest son of Aaron answers his priest with pride, and boasts of his having saved a penny in the week to idicate his children — their heirs to his potatoe patch.

The Americans mocked all foreigners, not the Irish alone, and had caricatured sterotypes of the dumb German, the prancing, perfumed Frenchman, and the superior-aired Englishman.

A practice of baiting the early Irish emigrants indulged in by rowdy elements was "Paddy making." An effigy dressed in rags, its mouth smeared with molasses, sometimes wearing a string of potatoes around its neck or a codfish to mock the Friday fasting and with a whiskey bottle stuck out of one pocket, was set up in a public place on the eve of St. Patrick's Day and in the morning the outraged Irish charged it. Mayor DeWitt Clinton prohibited "Paddy making" in New York City by ordinance in 1812. The Irish in Baltimore cut down the mast of a vessel on which one dangled, and in Utica it led to an all-day riot in which two Irishmen lost their lives and others on both sides were badly injured.

3

On April 2, 1830, an advertisement appeared in the New York *Courier and Enquirer* which proclaimed a more sinister form of prejudice: "No Blacks or Irish need apply," the notice of a work opportunity specified. Or as a variant in the *Journal of Commerce* of July 8, 1830, put it: "Wanted — A woman well qualified to take charge of the cooking and washing of a family — any one but a Catholic, who can come well recommended, may call at 57 John-street." Or as worded in the New York *Evening Post* of September 4, 1830: "Wanted. — A Cook or a Chambermaid. They must be American, Scotch, Swiss, or Africans — no Irish."

These curt notices, usually in connection with domestic services, reflected a growing consciousness of the new element in the social structure — the Catholic Irish emigrant. Such declaration of unabashed

discrimination was hardly so hurtful as the silent conspiracy of employers not to hire Catholic Irish help. An applicant's obvious Gaelic name
or the sound of his brogue barred the door to employment, regardless
of his personal qualities or qualifications, frequently on the justification
that American or Protestant Irish help would not work by his side.
"While some Americans preferred to hire natives of specific countries,"
writes Robert Ernst, a student of pre-Civil War immigrant life in New
York City, "no other immigrant nationality was proscribed as the Catholic Irish were."

The words, terrible to the race, "No Irish need apply," became
etched in the memory and left a heritage of bitterness, as well as of
sadness, among people who had felt their cutting slash and were sensitive to the connotations of rejection they carried.

The racial exclusiveness charged against the Catholic Irish as an indictment of their incapacity to assimilate with American institutions
was not entirely of their own making. The newcomers naturally sought
out the areas of their countrymen in the new land. When their friendly
overtures to Americans were coldly rebuffed and their excess of enthusiasm in exaggerated language was marked off as silly Irish blarney,
they withdrew within themselves and continued their native tradition
of separateness. If an Irish family moved into a neighborhood, the exodus of non-Irish residents began. Among the first Catholic Irish settlers,
the huddling together followed a law of mutual self-protection against
physical assault by native Americans or Orange Irishmen. The very
people who refused to accept them led the pack in the cry of Irish exclusiveness. The door was pointedly slammed in their faces, and then
their clannishness was damned.

Yet — and this is an interesting twist — the Catholic Irish did not,
in their own minds, consider themselves as "foreigners" or "aliens" in
America. They characterized the Germans, the Swiss, or the French as
"foreigners" and held themselves superior to the races which did not
speak the English language: the fact of the linguistic identity with
America undoubtedly made the distinction, though the quick adaptability of the Catholic Irish to the United States, which they took to with
a natural affinity, entered into their attitude. Like later emigrant peoples, they were conscious of and impressed by the presence of Americans as the native stock, there before them and to whose institutions
they were sympathetic and wished to conform.

These inhibitions, contributed to by the Irishman's drinking, fighting, political assertiveness, and poverty-stricken social circumstances, put the race through a harsh and painful purgatory. But they were not so damaging in the face of the eventual remedial strength of American free institutions as either to demoralize the Catholic Irish or discourage further emigration. Only once did a movement arise among the Irish to transfer themselves out of the United States and that died quickly of its own repugnance. Under tremendous pressures, not once did the national Congress tamper with the naturalization laws in this period to make the emigrant a second-class citizen, though individual states tried to degrade him; and the idea of barring or restricting emigration to a land crying for population was never seriously entertained even by the declared enemies of the emigrant — the Native Americans and the Know Nothings.

4

The Catholic Irish were the first emigrants in the nineteenth century to feel the impact of that vigorous resistance to the "stranger" or the "foreigner" which has persisted in the American character since the original colonization; and the survival of the Catholic Irish minority in an atmosphere of hostility such as marked particularly the pre-Civil War period furnished a test, if any evidence be now necessary, of the wisdom and the tough-fibered strength of the American Constitution, to which the Catholic Irish appealed for the protection of their civil and religious rights in troubled times and in the name of which they could depend upon a solid core of generous and decent American opinion for support. It also testified to the "blackest cat" durability of the Catholic Gael.

26

The Long Leap to the Cities

THE CATHOLIC IRISH, when they clambered aboard an emigrant ship, carried, with certain exceptions, a prejudice against farming. It spelled out the string of their woes — poverty, unemployment, famine, unrewarding labor, eviction and a dismal future. They needed a job with cash wages as speedily as possible, having little or no capital,

and their want urged them to concentrate in the larger cities and
towns, following the Irish country custom of wandering to the nearest
large town looking for work and food as laborers when dispossessed
from estates, farms, or little cottage patches.

They therefore tended to linger at the ports of landing along the Atlantic seacoast. If times were good they were quickly taken into the labor force, and if times were untoward they became subjects of private
generosity or public charity until an upturn.

For a race which never knew cities until the Danes, Normans, and
English came and which anciently had savage delight in raiding and
burning them, the Catholic Irish took to American cities with an affectionate attachment. They bridged in one evolutionary leap the transition from backward and lonely villages on the outermost edge of Europe to the humming and gaudy cities of the new world. By ordinary
standards, they should have been bewildered and confused at the
abruptness of the change, and many were, but great numbers within a
relatively brief time had not only caught on to the ways of the city but
were taking in hand the latest shipload of greenhorns with the easy
familiarity of old residents; indeed, a common grievance of native-born
Americans was that the Irishman still with the dew of Galway on him
had no hesitation, and lacked no self-assurance, in showing natives
how to do things right.

The material improvement of the Catholic Irish undoubtedly would
have been more rapidly advanced, their purgatory of slum life avoided,
and the antagonism of native Americans to their piled-up numbers in
the cities minimized had they seized the opportunity, as the first sizable
wave of nineteenth-century emigrants, to settle on the ample and cheap
land. But the unfortunate heritage of subjected Ireland and their own
natures acted as impediments. Economic disability — the need of immediate work and the lack of capital to buy land and tide them over the
estimated three years to clear and work a farm — played its part in
their preference for cities.

The Irish temperament, unfitted for lonely life, shuddered at the
prospect of a wilderness clearing without Irish fellowship. A Catholic
Irishman, writing from Ohio in 1831, noted the small number of Irish
holding farms in comparison with the Germans. The German emigrants, he observed, unacquainted with the language and unqualified
for commercial business and social intercourse except among their own,
were forced to go into employment "where loquacity is dispensed with"

and hence they settled on the soil. The Irish, however, he said, were the reverse — "a social, warmhearted people, with a natural aversion to solitude or exclusion from society." So they chose "rather to be making a little money, and live on a moderate subscription, than retire into what they look on as a wilderness, and sit down for life deprived of the society of friends and countrymen, and their everyday acquaintances, which they enjoy in cities."

In the cities, the sound of the familiar brogue, their own included, was around, the church within striking distance, and gregarious excitement, constant gossip and merry sociability never wanting. The Catholic Irish loved crowds, noise, and footless movement. They loved cities. They were an urban people without knowing it in Ireland.

2

The conditioning of Ireland had stunted in them the "go-ahead" drive which animated native Americans. The brunt of life's struggle in Ireland, as has been shown, was not to go ahead but to stop from going backward. If he worked steadily and received wages regularly in the United States, the Irishman held himself to be so much better off than he ever could have been in the old country that he inclined to settle contentedly in his lot and thank Providence for his good luck. "Unfortunately for our countrymen," wrote an Irishman who had taken a farm in the West, "they are too content to 'live from hand to mouth.' This unworthy contentment is one of the fruits of that infamous government in Ireland — crushing the souls out of the people in every way — morally as well as physically. If we could be seized with a *speculative discontent,* it would be the best thing in the world for us."

Americans noted the stagnation of the Irish in city life and ascribed it to the characteristic backwardness of the race. But Americans, who had never known a food shortage, let alone periods of famine, were strangers to the psychology of a people who had lived constantly under the shadow of hunger.

3

When Catholic Irish emigration started to accelerate in the 1820s, the newcomers set a few simple patterns of location that generally obtained in the future course of the migration.

The powerful and consistent force in distributing Catholic Irish throughout the country was labor on roads, canals, and railroads. Each public work left a residue of Irish along its course, who, ambitious to abandon the vagabondish life, sought out local employment. The demands of growing industry for unskilled and rough labor drew the Irish to mills, factories, forges, and construction work.

Irish emigrants who landed in Canada or New Orleans, without friends or relatives to go to, proceeded along the emigrant routes across the northern border or up the Mississippi looking for work. Countless emigrants started walking from wharves, hoping to find jobs along the way: it was a maxim in America that if a man walked far enough into the interior he was certain of finding work, and the farther he went, the higher his wages.

Following an Irish custom, Irishmen enlisted in the Army when work was scarce and, upon the expiration of enlistments, many settled in the communities near the fort from which they were discharged: the pioneer Catholic Irishman in Chicago was a soldier from Fort Dearborn.

Irishmen working as day laborers in Northern cities went to warmer sections during the winter months when outdoor work — and a day's pay — shut down. It was not uncommon for a married Irishman in New York or Boston to leave his wife and children in the care of friends and go far away for a job during hard times, exactly as he would in Ireland if pinched by distress; and if he liked the new place, the family was sent for.

A familiar sight in America in the early period of emigration was a group of Irish laborers walking the roads looking for employment under a leader of their own choosing, just as Kerry or Cork harvesters wandered in bunches into neighboring counties seeking a day's earnings and food, or Connacht cottiers set off yearly to England and Scotland for the harvest.

A knot of young Irishmen from the same townland in Ireland — three, four, or five "comrades," as they called themselves — indulged their itchy feet in America and, being unmarried, thought they "would look around" the country before lighting. If one "parted" from his comrade or comrades and found work opportunities, he wrote, or had a letter written for him, to his friends to come to New Orleans or St. Louis or the Susquehanna or along the Erie Canal.

The chances and changes of the wide United States separated families that in Ireland would have held to the traditionally close-knit household. A family with members dispersed to three or four corners of the United States was not at all unusual.

Once an Irishman had settled, the nesting routine for his family and friends in the old country began and the remittance went overseas. The cluster, or "huddle," as the Irish called it, was in the making. An old Irishman described the process: "Emigrants from the same village or district usually settled down in the same city or town in the States where their relatives or friends or neighbors had preceded them, thus forming little colonies."

4

The Irish boarding house, such as Mrs. McAlpin's, welcomed the unmarried young and emigrant families without relatives or friends. In the larger settlements, boarding houses catered to emigrants according to their county origins, in the Irish tradition of county separatism. Thus, a Kerry emigrant sought out a boarding house maintained for Kerrymen, and a native of Cork looked for a Cork family.

Outside of the solace of mingling with people from the same county, the emigrant had practical reasons for his choice of boarding house. Resident lodgers held themselves under obligation by honored tradition to help the newcomer from their own county to find work and acquaint him with the ways of the new land. News of friends was more likely to be had, or messages left, with fellow countymen. There he found that Dennis had gone to the Erie Canal, and if he followed he inquired at a county boarding house along the waterway of the whereabouts of Dennis. In time, as emigrants distributed themselves, an Irishman could travel from one end of the country to the other and in each city or town locate an Irish boarding house, or an Irish family happy to give him shelter.

The emigrants brought with them the familiar Irish names: Maurice, Hugh, Michael, Bernard, Patrick, James, Thomas, Cornelius, Timothy, Daniel, Dennis, Francis, Martin, John, Christopher, Eugene, Charles, Peter, Anthony, Matthew, Edmond, Joseph, while the common names for women were Mary, Mary Ann, Catherine, Bridget, Ellen, Johanna, Margaret, Honora, Elizabeth, Julia, Hannah, and Eliza.

"I need not say," Father Roddan once remarked, "that the Irishman carries the name of his country written indelibly upon his face." God's hand stroked upward as He made the Irish nose.

They introduced into the United States the plaintive Irish tenor, Irish jigs, sets and reels, and the Irish crying jag. The sad Irish melodies, which the Americans loved, and the rowdy Irish ballads, which the Gaels had by heart, entered into the nation's repertory. They brought with them a love of talk — "gab," if you will — and of loud and emphatic oratory. They leavened rather stodgy American life with buoyant good nature, outpouring affability and generous cheerfulness; also when pushed, they pushed back. If they were "Pharaoh's frogs," at least they did not croak. The Catholic Irishman may have been, as John Randolph, the eccentric Virginian, described him, "this bog trotter, with his spade on his shoulder, and his wheel barrow in his hand," but he was sprightly and lively.

If the angels in Heaven were stormed with familiar voices coming from a different direction on earth, that was the Irish moved to America saying their prayers.

27

They Managed to Get Around

THE DEPOSIT of eighteenth-century Catholic Irish had been in Pennsylvania, where Penn's Charter permitted exercise of their religion, and in Maryland, the mother of the Roman Catholic Church in the United States. But New York had superseded Philadelphia as the transatlantic port of Irish commerce and emigration, and in 1815 Mathew Carey placed two thirds of all the Irish-born in the United States in Pennsylvania and New York.

During the next three decades, internal redistribution and accelerated emigration had spread Catholic Irish colonies from New England to Texas, then a part of Mexico, without disturbing the population supremacy of Pennsylvania and New York — indeed, they increased in numbers with each ship arrival — so that Famine emigrants, starting to come late in 1845, could find relatives and friends in the several parts of the United States. An emigrant who landed between 1820 and 1845 and wanted to "look around" before settling down might like the

Irish companionship in Massachusetts or might think opportunity wider in St. Louis, and America grew conscious of the Gaels in its presence, a cross-section of whom can perhaps best be pictured by a journey through the United States.

2

The admirable Bishop Cheverus, first prelate of the Boston diocese (created in 1808), on leaving for his native France in 1823 recommended that the New England see be relinquished and merged with New York, so discouraging seemed the prospects of Catholicity. But in 1831 Bishop John England of Charleston prophesied that "the land of steady habits will, before the lapse of half a century, be a land in which the Catholic Church will extensively flourish!"

By the accident of geography — the relationship of the first large port on the Atlantic coast south of Canada to the emigration terminals of New Brunswick, Halifax, and Newfoundland — Boston developed into one of the most sizable Catholic Irish cities in the world. The Irish came to Boston as the earlier Pilgrim emigrants to Plymouth: it was a first American landfall.

In 1818, a number of Irish laborers were expressly imported to work on the construction of the Mill Dam, the first of the artificial roads built by private capital to connect Boston of the peninsula with the mainland. The reclamation of peninsular Boston from coves, inlets, and ponds by filled-in land required the rough labor which was at hand in the growing Irish population, down from British North American ports on coastal vessels or on foot. The Irishman with a hod, a spade, or wheelbarrow became familiar on the Boston landscape, which his labors were changing.

They settled along Hamilton and Broad Streets in the Fort Hill area overlooking Boston Harbor, the eighteenth-century residence of Boston shipmasters and men of commerce, now in decline, politically denominated as Ward 8. They grouped in the North End, Ward 9, centered around busy Ann (now North) Street, the readymade clothing district, where Andrew Carney, a County Cavan emigrant, started as a tailor and rose to be the wealthiest Catholic Irishman in New England by 1845, from the successful readymade clothing firm of Carney & Sleeper and banking and insurance interests. Along Ann Street, ambitious Irishmen opened shops to service fellow countrymen and, with higher economic status, joined the Charitable Irish Society, the first Irish society in America, founded in 1737 and reincorporated in 1809 to remove the obnoxious clause which confined membership to Protestant Irish. These men took pride in holding office in the charitable societies of the Church, and many had been present in the Cathedral of the Holy Cross on that memorable St. Patrick's Day, 1833, when for the first time the choir broke forth into the recessional, "Hail Glorious Apostle!" written by an Ursuline nun of the Charlestown convent and arranged by Thomas Comer to a national air of Ireland. The Boston *Jesuit* predicted correctly that the hymn will "undoubtedly be sung annually, on the Feast of St. Patrick, in many of the churches of the United States."

The recognized lay leader of the early Boston Irish community was neither wealthy nor prominent but a humble and competent mechanic at the Charlestown Navy Yard, Daniel O'Callaghan, who had landed in Boston from his native Wexford by way of Newfoundland. He did the hard work in a fund-raising campaign to build a little church in Waltham. He plowed through bitter snowstorms to attend meetings in behalf of Catholic Emancipation in Ireland. The Charitable Irish Society felt it had honored itself by electing this artisan as president. He was chairman of the protest meeting against the violent press attacks on the Boston Irish in 1834. A self-educated man, he lectured on ancient Irish history to raise funds for the Young Catholic's Friend Society, organized to clothe poor Irish children kept from Mass by proud Irish parents ashamed of their rags.

O'Callaghan's name added no great deeds to Catholic Irish fame but he represented a not unusual type of first-rate Catholic Irishman, self-taught, intelligent, hard-working, with a native dignity, who, strong in character, faithful in religious duties, ardent in devotion to Ireland, loyal to the oath of American citizenship, set an example to his people and by his conduct helped break down the barriers of prejudice against the Catholic Irish.

Every community where the Catholic Irish settled knew the O'Callaghans: they were the salt of the earth, the village Hampdens and the "mute inglorious" Miltons of the Catholic Irish, forgotten in their alien graveyards because the simple achievements of ordinary good men rest with their clay; yet in their lifetime they were the responsible chieftains conscious of the need to set their people to the pattern of the adopted United States. They believed that a good Catholic made a good American, and as a citizen he need not lose his affection for Ireland.

An obituary notice in 1849 of a County Clare emigrant to the United States in 1819 could be applied to all the early O'Callaghans:

> He was an ardent lover of old Ireland and everything Irish, and he cordially participated in every thing done here for the benefit and assistance of the unforgotten land of his birth. And it was his honor during his life and we hope it is now his reward, that he was a consistent and devoted Catholic.

Boston, as an emigrant center, formed one of America's labor reservoirs upon which road, canal, and railroad contractors drew. It was also a Hub, in a different sense from a radiating center of culture and letters: from Boston the Irish fanned out to other parts of New England for work. In 1824 Michael Reddy, newly arrived from Ireland and dissatisfied with Boston, walked to Providence, where he found a job, which he left in 1825 to labor on the Blackstone Canal. A year later the waterway had been completed as far as the little village of Woonsocket in Rhode Island and here Reddy remained to be the first Catholic Irish settler.

They went likewise to the quarries in Quincy and the factories in Canton and Foxboro, to the farms in Dudley, and to the tanneries of Salem. The distribution of the Catholic Irish in New England was from Boston outward as well as from the New Brunswick-Maine emigrant route southward.

James Kavanagh, a lad from County Wexford, landed in Boston with a companion about 1781, presumably on a coastal vessel from Newfoundland, and moved to the opportunities opening in remote Maine, then a part of Massachusetts. He settled in Newcastle on the Damariscotta River and prospered as a shipbuilder and trader in lumber with the West Indies. He is remembered as the father of Edward Kavanagh, a leader of Jacksonian Democracy in Maine, the first Catholic of Irish descent elected to the legislature of a New England state, the first sent from New England to Congress (1831-1835), and the first to be a New England governor (as lieutenant governor he succeeded the governor elevated to the United States Senate).

At the opposite end to the gentry life of the Kavanagh family in the big house on the Damariscotta was the ramshackle settlement of poor Catholic Irish laborers in the model mill village of Lowell built by Boston capitalists. In April, 1822, a gang of stout Irish laborers, thirty in number, bossed by Hugh Cummisky, a contractor, walked the twenty-five miles from Charlestown and began digging the foundations of the Merrimack Company's cotton textile factory — "in reality the first settlers of the town," as a historian of the Lowell textile industry described them. Joined by others, they re-created in this pleasant Yankee countryside an Irish village that would not have been out of place in Galway or Mayo. By the side of the Suffolk Canal, on a little more than an acre of hired ground, the Irish pioneers staked out a settlement of rude shanties, variously called "the Acre," "New Dublin," and "Paddy Camp Lands," with such names as Dublin and Cork for the streets. They built a church and, uniquely in the United States, public funds supported their Irish schools, with instruction in the Catholic faith by Catholic teachers, an arrangement permitted because, since Church and State had not yet been separated in Massachusetts, sectarian schools received public moneys. Native American workers resented the intruders and, on the night of May 18, 1831, the Irish, with the women using their aprons as the arsenal of bricks, drove off the natives who had concerted battalions to wipe out "the Acre" in the famous "Battle of the Bridge."

That was the same year Bishop England noted:

> It is a fact that the creation of manufactories in New England has done more in a few years to provide for the wants, for the morality and for the religion of the Irish Catholic emigrants, than any other occurrence in the United States.

North of Boston in Massachusetts, Yankee employers preferred to hire native-born workers to the Irish. In New Hampshire, the total Catholic population in 1835 numbered 387, the lowest in the six New England states, but by 1842 it had almost quadrupled and, with the building of the railroads and the opening of the textile industry in Manchester, the Catholic Irish poured in. Vermont, the most tolerant and kindly of the New England states toward the Irish, welcomed them as workers on farms, in the local factories, and in quarries: in 1835, Vermont had the largest Catholic population in the New England states next to Massachusetts, 5620 souls, Irish and French Canadians.

In western Massachusetts, Catholic Irish came, as in Lowell, to dig the foundations of factories and remained to work in them. South of Boston in Massachusetts, his countrymen followed the first Irish settler of Fall River, Patrick Kennedy, the walker mentioned at the beginning of this story, who arrived in 1822, and they worked in the textile mills, as in Taunton nearby. The early Irish settlers in Providence were cloth printers from County Donegal; Irish laborers came in numbers, with the building in the 1830s of the Boston-Providence railroad, and settled near its terminus in Fox Point. Irish laborers were employed in erecting Fort Adams in Newport and in the Portsmouth coal mines.

Connecticut, like New Hampshire, was a wilderness for the Catholic Irish in the early period. Bishop Fenwick in 1830 dedicated the first Catholic church in the state at Hartford before a large congregation "consisting principally of the respectable Protestants of the town." In 1835, the state's total Catholic population, mostly Irish, numbered 720, but in 1844 it had jumped to 4817. The notable Irish family in the state was the Ryans, three sons of a prosperous cloth manufacturer in Kilkenny, who, with another Ryan, no relation, in 1836 purchased a woolen mill and established a successful business.

3

New York City was the front and center of the Catholic Irish in the United States, the capital city of the race, with a Gaelic population that eventually was larger than Dublin's, the nerve-center of the movements to assist Ireland in the struggle for self-rule, the citadel of Irish Democracy, the haven of Irish exiles, the reservoir of wealth as well as the quarters of the most degrading poverty, the head to which the American Gaels looked for leadership and direction, the seat of what was to develop into the most fabulous see, outside Rome, of the Roman Catholic Church.

One reason alone gave the city its Catholic Irish strength — it was the greatest receiving port of Catholic Irish emigration.

In 1820, there were approximately 25,000 Catholics, mostly Irish, in New York City; their numbers were doubled a decade or so later; and in 1844 a speaker at an Irish rally called it "the most Irish city in the Union." Cobbett estimated in 1824 they comprised one sixth of the population, but more faith can be placed in his judgment that the Irish did four fifths of the hard labor in the city. George T. Strong noted in his diary that, on a hot May day, Wall Street was "encumbered with bricks, blocks of stone, and huge Irishmen." They built the Harlem Railroad and the Croton Aqueduct; they laid the pipe for the gas mains; they leveled the hills; they remade the city. They drove the hacks and drays, enjoyed a near-monopoly on stevedoring and long-shore workers, and competed for shipyard jobs.

In this early period, the Catholic Irish were spread throughout the city: collectors were appointed for every ward in the city if a fund was to be raised for an Irish cause. But the largest cluster was in the Sixth Ward, with a heavy concentration in the so-called Five Points area on filled-in swampland, and in the adjoining Fourteenth Ward on the lower East Side. One particularly noxious warren was an old brewery remade into small living quarters, an offense against nature. Being poor and often without work, the Catholic Irish emigrants lived where their small means permitted, jammed into run-down residences, cheaply built tenements, which began to appear in the early 1830s, or improvised shanties in alleys and courts, piled into garrets and cellars, with primitive sanitary facilities, without water except from a common pump, the first to suffer from an epidemic and the most widely ravaged by fatalities because of congestion and the accumulation of abominations: one third of the entire number of cholera cases in the city in 1832 was in the Sixth Ward. Another affliction harmed them: increasing emigration tended to fix their hard bonds; the living conditions of the Catholic Irish had degenerated in the 1850s from the 1830s. Slums by then had become an institution.

Far removed from this emigrant life was old Dominick Lynch of a gentry Galway family, called by General Washington "the handsome Irishman," who had come to America in the eighteenth century, made a fortune in the Spanish and shipping trades, speculated successfully in land (he settled Lynchville, which later became Rome in upper New York), signed the address by Catholics to President Washington, and served as trustee of the first Catholic church in the city. His son Dominick, an exquisite, a leader of New York society, brought the first Italian opera company to the city; another son, James, was president of the Utica Insurance Company, a Whig alderman and a judge; and a third son, Edward, married the daughter of Dennis McCarthy, a successful liquor dealer, in what the parents would consider a good match, merging Irish prosperity in a precedent honored by succeeding generations of the affluent.

Cornelius Heeney, a penniless emigrant, amassed wealth in the fur trade, first as partner with an illiterate German porter, John Jacob Astor, the founder of the great Astor fortune, and later on his own, and he distributed his fortune generously on Catholic charities and good works in Brooklyn. James Kerrigan, from County Donegal, made a famous leather product known as "Kerrigan's Morocco"; William O'Brien conducted a clearinghouse for insurance claims and a private bank; John Costigan went on from selling books to be a railroad superintendent; Hurley, the hatmaker, had a standing order for three new hats yearly from General Lafayette; Andrew Cooper, the soapmaker, was the first Catholic Irishman to be elected to the New York General Assembly; James Cunningham was an early dealer in Catholic religious publications.

But the representative Catholic Irishman, of historical stature in the story of the race in America, was Thomas O'Connor, who shared with Dr. MacNeven the leadership of the New York Catholic Irish community in its early period, a man who made up in solid worth what he lacked in flamboyancy and, wanting color, has been neglected by time.

Thomas O'Connor is remembered now as the father of Charles O'Conor (the son adopted the ancient Irish spelling), the eminent counselor, who broke the Tweed ring. Yet for more than fifty years O'Connor was the soul and voice of the New York Catholic Irish lay community, its statesman in factional disputes, organizer for Irish causes, the good right hand of Bishop Hughes. Rarely was a meeting held for a Catholic or Irish interest that O'Connor did not play a leading role, as chairman, officer, or speaker, during his long life, which ended in 1855. He held it a matter of conscience to aid the poor emigrant and try to raise his status. Tammany made him a sachem. Perhaps the only show of personal affection by Charles O'Conor, unbending, dour, and distant, with cold eyes, was toward his father, whom he venerated.

O'Connor had been a '98 rebel and the oath of membership in the United Irishmen had been given him, so tradition ran, by Wolfe Tone himself. He was a well-educated man when he landed in New York in 1801, trained, it is believed, by his relative, O'Conor of Belangare, the famous eighteenth-century Irish antiquarian; certainly he was the finest Irish scholar of his day in New York.

The checkered lives of *The Shamrock*, the first Irish American weekly, which he established, now discontinued, now revived, bespoke the good intentions of the proud O'Connor to write the story of Ireland for uninformed Americans, instruct his countrymen in correct republican principles and organize them for the War of 1812, explain

the doctrines of the then strange Roman Catholic Church, and find
work for Irish emigrants. His career was intertwined with the best of
Catholic Irish endeavors in New York City.

Thomas J. Brady was a revealing example of the career an educated
Irishman could make in the United States and of the start such a man
had over his unlettered fellows, still benighted by the penal laws. As
an Irish schoolmaster, a familiar figure in America, he was proficient
in Latin and Greek, and professionally translated from French, Spanish, and Italian. He studied law and was admitted to practice. But he
was also the teacher of his son, James T. Brady, who adorned the
American bar, a man of exceeding charm and grace, polished by the
cultivated household in which he had been reared. Education was
the prime difference between the Bradys and the laboring Catholic
Irish emigrant, as with O'Connor and his son. It needed the contrast
of the United States to underline the real damage to the Catholic
Irish of the penal laws — denial of education. It took several generations in the United States for them to catch up on the eighteenth-
century retrogression suffered by the lack of education.

In the world of the emigrant, apart from the wealthy and educated
Catholic Irish, social distinctions started to appear with the improved
economic status of individuals. The emergence of the so-called "lace
curtain" Irish set showed itself in the first Erina Ball on St. Patrick's
Eve in 1831 at Masonic Hall, at which the high price and strict limita-
tion of tickets assured a select attendance, warning away the unwanted "Paddies." The inauguration of Erina Balls in other cities, or
similar affairs under a different name, usually marked the lineaments of
a middle-class Irish society. Social snobbery — towards fellow Irish
noticeably — was endemic in the Catholic Irish nature and broke out
at the first lift of economic improvement.

4

Across the river in Brooklyn village a small community of Catholic
Irish (less than one hundred householders in 1822) had, despite their
poverty, built a small church in 1823. They worked in the Brooklyn
Navy Yard, as carters to handle the freight of the port, as day laborers,
or as farmers. They huddled together in a district by the Navy Yard
and along the waterfront. By 1826, they had formed the Erin Fraternal
Association and were celebrating St. Patrick's Day. Before 1823, they

traveled by ferry to attend St. Peter's in New York and on a Sunday morning trudging through the sand along the shore was Patrick Mc-Closkey, an emigrant from the north of Ireland and a small shopkeeper, with his family, holding by his hand the young son, John, who was to be the first cardinal of the Roman Catholic Church in the United States. George McCloskey, the milkman, had two sons who entered the Church, one of whom was consecrated as Bishop of Kentucky and the other was the first head of the American College in Rome.

5

Of the estimated 100,000 Catholic population of the state of New York in 1825 at the opening of the Erie Canal, 50,000, almost entirely Irish, lived along the water route from New York City to Buffalo, the Lake Erie terminus of the canal.

The construction of the great Erie Canal, started in 1817 and completed in 1825, stretching more than 350 miles across New York State from Albany on the Hudson to Buffalo on Lake Erie, was the proving ground of Catholic Irish labor and the source of settlement along its route. The coincidence of the first massive public works in the United States with the first flood of Catholic Irish emigrants brought together unskilled workers who needed jobs and a project which needed a large labor force — a "capital road from Cork to Utica," as it was once toasted at a gathering of Irishmen. That road ran more by way of Quebec-Montreal to Troy, Albany, and Oswego than through New York City.

Here the Catholic Irish began a work pattern that henceforth would weave the network of canal and railroad communications which made the United States of imperial stature.

The Irish were not present in numbers in the first years of the work: "three-fourths of all the laborers were born among us," the canal commissioners reported on January 25, 1819. But the work of the Irish had been singled out for mention in the report of the previous year, which stated that "three Irishmen . . . finished, including banks and towing paths, three rods of the canal, in four feet cutting, in the space of five and [a] half days," which returned them "the very liberal wages of one dollar and eighty-seven cents per day." The Irishman's capacity for difficult and hazardous work was tested during 1819. Then the Montezuma marshes, out from Syracuse, raised difficulties, not least of which

A group of worshipers at a Scalán (Mass Station) in rural Ireland

IRISH TENANTS BEGGING AN ESTATE AGENT FOR A REDUCTION OF RENT IN HARD TIM

A MEETING OF THE RIBBON SOCIETY.

was the infestation of armies of mosquitoes more terrible than if they had carried banners. Here the Irish went forward with the work under appalling conditions that proved their hardihood; and contractors welcomed the increasing number of Irishmen who poured in from emigrant ships: they became synonymous with the building of the Erie Canal.

The canal produced a class of Irish contractors and subcontractors. The canal commissioners early concluded that the most politic mode of proceeding with the work was to parcel out contracts for small sections to responsible bidders rather than concentrate it in the hands of a monopoly or a few large contractors. Ambitious Irishmen bid for sections, varying from forty rods to three miles, and since the state of New York advanced sums for a contractor to set up with teams, implements, provisions and other essentials and covered monthly payrolls, the Irish canal contractor was born along the route of the Erie. When the main canal was finished in 1825, Irish contractors kept together cores of fellow countrymen and bid for sections on new canals which the Erie had inspired. Later, these same contractors and other Irishmen, who had moved upward from laborers, turned railroad contractors. They were a numerous and, generally, a respected class.

The Erie and the branch canals it spawned in New York required great numbers of men for maintenance and operation, and the Irishman settled along the routes where his shanty was a familiar sight. The booming cities which the Erie had raised from villages gave work to Irish canal laborers. They were saltmakers around Syracuse. They found employment in quarries: the Irishmen were particularly skilled in all branches of stonework. They went into the forests as choppers and they hired out as farmhands. They added to the populations of Albany, Troy, Utica, Syracuse, Rome, Auburn, Rochester, Lockport, and Buffalo, in the last place loading and unloading the lake ships and rearing up a tough, hard-fighting, hard-drinking breed of lake sailors.

The roaming Irish mission priests made the line of the works their parishes while the canal was under construction, saying Mass in the shanties of the workers. The dollars of the canal workers helped build the parish churches that grew with the congregations along the waterway. Out of the parish churches and the mission activities of the priests rose the sees of Albany, Buffalo, and Rochester. As Thomas D'Arcy McGee, the Irish-American journalist, expressed it, these poor, rude Irishmen were not only building a canal, they "were working on the foundations of three episcopal sees [and] opening the interior of the State to the empire of religion, as well as of commerce."

The name of Devereux represented Catholic Irish wealth and prominence throughout the area. In 1802, John C. Devereux, born to a gentry family in County Wexford, established himself in the little town of Utica as a merchant of dry goods and groceries after having been a dancing master in Massachusetts and Connecticut. Joined in 1806 by his brother Nicholas, the Devereux family extended their interests to include banks (Nicholas represented the Bank of the United States), a brewery, a woolen mill, and the Utica & Schenectady Railroad. John was so highly esteemed that under the new city charter in 1840 he was elected the first mayor of Utica. Nicholas, with friends, purchased four hundred thousand acres of land in Allegheny and Cattaraugus Counties and encouraged Irish emigrants to colonize there. They endowed the Roman Catholic Church generously, and their names stood firmly linked with the growth of Catholicity in central New York.

Thomas McCarthy settled in Salina (now Syracuse) in 1808 to become its pioneer merchant and a saltmaker; Patrick Lynch, Irish-born son of a farmer in DeWitt, opened a dry-goods store in Syracuse and spread his interests to include salt, iron, land, and banking; the tight-fisted Thomas Doyle, who had worked on the canal, prospered as a manufacturer of salt but continued to smoke a clay T. D. pipe.

Troy, on the Irish emigrant route from Canada as well as the westward-turning point of New England emigrants, was a particular gathering place for County Limerick Catholic Irish, who, in 1824, organized the St. Peter's congregation.

The Rochester cluster of Catholic Irish, principally canal workers, settled around the log cabin of James Dowling, built in 1817 by the pioneer Irish settler, and naturally called Dublin, with the first Catholic church raised in 1821. The first daily newspaper in Rochester, the *Advertiser,* started in 1826, had as editor a young Catholic Irishman from Carrickmacross, County Ulster, Henry O'Reilly, who had learned the trade of printer in New York. Perhaps, wrote a local historian, "no one individual has made a deeper and more lasting impression upon the early history of Rochester than Henry O'Reilly." He was the community's first historian, active in all public affairs and leader of the town's Jacksonian Democracy. With James Wadsworth, the squire of Geneseo, he conducted a campaign which led to a reform of the public school system. He was the founder of the "O'Reilly lines," the telegraph company which engaged in a long war with the rival Morse company, and the first lessee of a territory extending from Philadelphia westward for the magnetic telegraph. Rochester was the home of Patrick Barry, who built the Mt. Hope Nursery into the largest in the United States, was horticultural editor of the famous *Genesee Farmer* and a pioneer scientific fruit grower, a nationally recognized authority on fruit trees.

In northern New York were found Catholic Irish, who, unlike city laborers and factory workers, liked to farm; indeed, the predominance of agriculture at the time of their early arrival left no choice. They made settlements in their own colonies, from Plattsburg, a community grown around some Catholic Irish migrants from Boston, to the largest grouping in Ogdensburg on the St. Lawrence, on the emigrant route. Scattered through western New York were other Irish farming townships.

6

New Jersey, like Connecticut and New Hampshire, lacked a considerable Irish population until the 1840s. The Irish built a little church in Paterson in 1822, attended by a priest from New York who was once stoned, and in 1834 the pastor in Newark was the only resident priest in the state. The first clash between the native-born and the Irish occurred in 1834 — an attack upon Newark's first St. Patrick's Day parade.

7

Philadelphia was the great funneling port of eighteenth-century Protestant Irish emigration, and the comparative trickle of Catholic Irish emigrants found in Pennsylvania a sullen tolerance for their religion. At the outbreak of the Revolution, the Catholic Irish mercantile community in Philadelphia, including Thomas FitzSimons, a signer of the Constitution, the Moylans, one of whom was Washington's aide-de-camp, and John Barry, the Revolutionary naval captain, held a respected place. Philadelphia was the center of the United Irishmen in America and the exile resort of Wolfe Tone, Dr. Reynolds, A. Hamilton Rowan, Napper Tandy, and Alderman John Binns, who, remaining, became a leading political figure in the state and agitator for Irish freedom.

8

Philadelphia was the home of another Irish exile, Mathew Carey, at his death in 1839 the most distinguished Catholic layman in the United States. Any list of eminent Catholic Irishmen would have to list Mathew Carey close to the top, and it would be no unwarranted avarice for Celtic fame which assigned him a place as a great American in his many-sided usefulness.

Mathew Carey landed in Philadelphia on November 15, 1784, as an exile on the ship *America,* secreted aboard in Dublin disguised as a woman to escape the law for an attack on the injustices of English rule. Five years before, his father, a prosperous baker, had sent him to exile in France when a pamphlet by Mathew, then nineteen, on the oppression of Roman Catholics set the nose of the Irish Parliament to twitching. He worked in Benjamin Franklin's little printing shop in Passy, a village outside Paris, and later with Didot *le jeune,* the famous typographer.

The Marquis de Lafayette had sought out the young exile in France for information on Irish affairs, and in his exile in Philadelphia. Carey was sent for by Lafayette, then visiting Mount Vernon, and presented with $400 to begin life in the new country.

With this windfall, Carey started the *Pennsylvania Herald* (he had edited a paper in Dublin) and began to build circulation by the novelty of reporting in full the proceedings of the House of Assembly, in the English newspaper fashion. A duel with a rival editor, who called Carey a "foreign renegado," laid him up with a wound for fifteen or sixteen months. Recovered, he undertook the publication of the *American Museum,* a kind of eighteenth-century *Reader's Digest,* "intended to preserve the valuable fugitive essays that appeared in newspapers." It was a critical success (Washington was one of its admirers), but an economic failure.

He turned his attention fully then to the bookstore and publishing house he had established in 1785: he had been a bookseller in Dublin. From 1785 to 1817, as sole owner, and from 1817 to 1824, as active head, he carried on the greatest publishing and book-distributing business in the United States. He printed the first American edition of the

Douay (Catholic) Bible. "No other publishing firm, even in proportion to its size," wrote Bradsher, a biographer, "published so many works of native production between 1787 and 1824." His list included Noah Webster, Philip Freneau, Percival the poet, Parson Weems, Irving, Cooper, and John Neal; and his house first printed Dickens and Scott in the United States.

Carey's prodigious energy and capacity for sustained work (he was lame) fired the enthusiasm of his convictions, along with a quickly touched sense of indignation, into a career of public usefulness, with no ambition for public office (rather unusual in an Irishman). He showed no ardor for fame; he unselfishly gave himself for good works; he breathed and lived public spirit; he indulged a warranted self-pity — that those who benefited by his endeavors returned no appreciation and others remained indifferent to the high causes for which he strove.

From 1793, when he was an effective member of the committee on health to combat the yellow fever plague, until his death, his prolix pen was unceasing in reasoned advocacy of important issues. He worked and wrote in behalf of relief for Greek rebels and the movement to colonize free Negroes in Africa, to which he regularly subscribed money. He brought an active intelligence to bear upon the increase of public charities and upon prison reform. He agitated for the Pennsylvania canal system. He was an early sponsor of kindergarten schools. He belabored the men of property indifferent to wretched social conditions and he showed, with a devastating array of statistics, the shortsightedness of employers in enforcing an iron law of wages; his pamphlet on the wages of female workers was a classic in social thinking for the times.

His pragmatic mind understood that improvements, whether in wages and working conditions or care of prisoners, produced a general social benefit. His thinking, while not original, was far in advance of his time.

Perhaps his best-known service was as vigorous propagandist for the American System, in which he became interested during 1819; and he turned a hitherto neglected side of his talents to distinctively American thinking, as contrasted with the European principles of Adam Smith, Malthus, and Ricardo, in the field of political economy, deserving the title of the first American political economist, whose flashes of insight probed the forming character of the national economy. His admiration for the English productive system, and his experience with the deliberate stifling of unprotected Irish industry to furnish a British market outlet, guided him to the thesis that a well-rounded American economy required the growth of industry under protection. In contrast with the grim pessimism of English economists, he radiated a healthy optimism for the future of the United States, sensing the difference between an untapped continent with a vigorous people animated by free institutions and the inhibitions of old European societies. For thirteen years, as a disciple of Hamilton and a documenter of Henry Clay in the political field, Mathew Carey was the moving spirit in societies to promote American industry, and the Carey pamphlets reflected (which will seem strange today) the difficult struggle of industry to get accepted against the hostility of agricultural and commercial interests.

Carey's fine Americanism had not obscured his love of Ireland. The sorry plight of emigrants, during the passage and on their arrival, moved him to leadership in the organization in 1790 of the Hibernian Society in Philadelphia, the first for the relief of emigrants. Outraged by an exaggerated account of the "massacre of 1641" in Ireland, he carefully studied the historical material and in 1819 published *Vindiciae Hibernicae; or Ireland Vindicated,* in which, from Protestant sources primarily, he disproved the old Puritan propaganda and set the affair in truer perspective. He wrote a handbook as an inducement for the Irish to emigrate and, in a series of public letters addressed to Bishop Hughes of New York, defended the merits of his Catholic Irish fellow countrymen against contemporary calumny.

Carey carried his racial origin like a banner: "I glory," he wrote, "I feel a pride in the name of an Irishman" and asserted that no other nation, under the circumstances of vile rule for six hundred years, "would have preserved the slightest ray of respectability."

His son Henry (1793-1879), whom Mathew carefully instructed, has been described as the "leader of the only group that can be said to constitute an American school of political economy" and as "an original thinker of power." Henry retired early from the publishing house to devote his attention to writings on political economy. Like his father, he rejected the "dismal science" of the English classicists and even more than Mathew he articulated the optimism and buoyancy of the United States, which, with his intensely American nationalism, contributed to the American sense of bounciness.

He anticipated much of modern economic thinking, particularly the mutual benefit of harmony to capital and labor and to the national gain, with increased productivity the aim, from which the worker would profit through higher wages without destroying the capitalist's incentive to invest, since his returns would rise with higher output. This thinking ran contrary to the contemporary concept that profits rose with lowered wages. He refuted Malthus by his theory that man's inventiveness would increase the means of subsistence for a growing population. He was an early advocate of conservation of national resources. Like Mathew, he was a strong protectionist but not before undergoing a period of hand-holding with laissez-faire. His dislike of England was part Irish and part American political economy.

9

The presence of Catholic and Protestant Irish from the embattled north transplanted ancient antagonisms to the streets of Philadelphia, which were compounded by native American dislike of the Irish. In 1825, a battle broke out on the high seas on an emigrant ship between Catholic and Protestant Irish and was renewed on arrival in Philadelphia, with friends of both sides joining in. Three years later, in August, native Americans mistook the banner of the craft of Irish weavers for the flag of Ireland and started a riot in which several persons received gunshot wounds: the contest really had its origin in an incident two days before the outbreak when a member of the Philadelphia watch entered an Irish tavern where a woman lay dying, demanded food and drink, abused the Irish present, and was shot to death. The anniversary of the Boyne in 1831 precipitated an extensive riot by the procession of Orangemen, in violation of a promise to the mayor, which excited the Catholic Irish, and brickbats and huge chunks of coal flew through the air and off Catholic and Protestant heads. Counselor Sampson came out of retirement to defend, without fee, the arrested Catholic Irish.

A year later, Rev. Michael Hurley, rector of St. Augustine's Roman Catholic Church, voluntarily gave up his residence as a hospital for cholera sufferers, and thirteen Sisters of Charity came to Philadelphia from their home at Emmittsburg, Maryland, to nurse the stricken. Two of the nuns died. Twelve years later St. Augustine's Church was burned by a native American mob.

10

Irish history walked the streets in the person of John Keating, grandson of Geoffrey Keating, commander of a company of horse at the siege of Limerick, who, at the surrender of Patrick Sarsfield, had gone to France with the army of James II. John, an officer of the Walsh-Serrant Irish regiment in the service of France, had been stationed in Santo Domingo at the outbreak of the French Revolution. When the National Assembly dissolved the royalist armies, John came to Philadelphia with the exiled French colony and, at his death in 1856, was described by his countrymen as "the last survivor of the Irish Brigade," a link in America with the old aristocracy that had gone to its grave with Sarsfield.

In the light of the subsequent fate of the Catholic Irish in America, it was ironic that the first extended, well-documented, and substantial vindication of the United States against the calculated and patronizing sneers of British writers came from the pen of Robert Walsh, son of a Baltimore merchant, a Catholic Irish emigrant. In Philadelphia in 1819 appeared *An Appeal from the Judgments of Great Britain respecting the United States of America,* a fat volume that at once summed up the virtues which entitled the United States to respect and, from the works of British writers, painted a black and melancholy picture of miserable conditions in Britain. This study by one of the first graduates of Georgetown College and the son-in-law of Jasper Moylan, the great Philadelphia merchant, was in effect a declaration of American independence from literary subserviency to Britain and pushed Walsh into the contemporary forefront of American letters. The work made a tremendous impression on the country and may very well be considered a contributing element to the American sense of nationalism.

Unlike Mathew Carey, whose publishing house addressed itself to a general audience, Eugene Cummiskey, an emigrant to Philadelphia from County Tyrone, printed books for a Catholic audience and was the first publisher of Catholic works in the United States, including the Bible with Haydock's notes, Lingard's *History of England,* and Butler's *Lives of the Saints.* Prayer books, missals, catechisms, works of piety and devotion, theological studies and translations of Catholic works from other languages rolled from his press.

II

Pennsylvania in 1826 authorized a sizable program of internal improvements to establish communications with the lakes and the then western country and conquer the barrier of the Alleghenies to Pittsburgh and the Ohio. The Pennsylvania anthracite industry, which dated from 1820, needed to find outlets at the Hudson and at Philadelphia.

Irishmen came as diggers of canals and remained as diggers of coal, attracting fellow countrymen to the great tier of eastern Pennsylvania anthracite coal counties centered in Wyoming, Carbon, Schuylkill, Luzerne, and Northumberland counties. They worked on the Delaware and Hudson Canal, the coal waterway to the Hudson, and dug the Lehigh Canal from Mauch Chunk to Easton, forty-two miles south. They labored on the famous gravity railroad that carried coal from Summit Hill to Mauch Chunk and, as miners, were to make Summit Hill an Irish principality. Strange-sounding names like Mahoning, Packerton (also known as Dolansburg), Pottsville, Tamaqua, Newquehoning, and Shenandoah (pronounced "Shanadore" by the Irish) started to filter back to Ireland. This mining area later earned notoriety after the Civil War from the secret society of the Molly Maguires, which started to send threatening notes to coal operators as early as 1848.

Irish laborers on the Chenango and North Branch Canals took wild lands to clear for farms in Pennsylvania's northeastern county of Susquehanna in the 1820s and 1830s on the easy terms offered by the agent, Edward White from Limerick, described as "an Irish gentleman," married to the eldest sister of Gerald Griffin, the Irish novelist. Flourishing settlements grew up in Middletown, Silver Lake, Friendsville, and Choconut Townships.

Armies of Irishmen worked on the great Pennsylvania Canal from Philadelphia to Pittsburgh: Rev. Michael Curran was mission pastor for canal laborers from the resident Harrisburg church dedicated in 1827, while Rev. Bernard Keenan, who had come from Ireland with Bishop Conwell of Philadelphia in 1820, served in St. Mary's, Lancaster, for fifty-four years, the fountainhead of Catholicity in that area.

Irishmen labored on the Portage Railroad, started in 1831, the engineering marvel of the day, which carried passengers and freight, including canal boats, from the canal terminus at Hollidaysburg by a series of inclined planes to the top of the Allegheny Mountains and lowered them down the western slope, in another series of inclined planes, to Johnstown, from where the Pennsylvania Canal ran to Pittsburgh.

12

Catholic Irish had settled on the eastern slope of the Alleghenies, in northern Cambria County, following the first pioneer, Captain Michael McGuire, a veteran of the Revolution, who donated a large plot of ground in "McGuire's Settlement" to Bishop Carroll, and there Father Demetrius Gallitzin, the early missionary, a Russian prince converted to Catholicism, established a station on the crest of the Alleghenies called Loretto.

Catholic Irish from County Donegal had by 1795 started a colony in the wilderness at Donegal Township in Butler County, and later congregations in Butler and Armstrong counties descended from these pioneers. Catholic Irish had worked on the two great pikes, or roadways, through Pennsylvania leading to the western country and made homes along the thoroughfares. Also Catholic Irish had filtered from over the Maryland border: Franklin County in the early 1820s contained the largest Pennsylvania Catholic population second to Philadelphia.

13

Only fifteen souls, mostly Irish, attended the Mass said in Pittsburgh by Father Gallitzin in 1804, but Rev. Charles B. McGuire in 1829 laid the cornerstone of a church which, when dedicated in 1834, was perhaps the largest in the United States — 175 by 70 feet, with four double Gothic doors, fifty-seven stained glass windows, and capable of holding twenty-five hundred persons.

Father McGuire, descendant of a lineage family in County Tyrone, had been educated on the Continent and, as a Franciscan friar, remained in the Low Countries until the proscription of the clergy in the French Revolution. He had been sentenced to the guillotine but escaped through the sacrifice of a devout Catholic. He taught theology at St. Isidore College in Rome and once more had to flee with the arrival of Napoleon's troops. The King of Bohemia sent him to attend a member of the royal family in Brussels, where he ministered to the dying brought in from the battle of Waterloo. A cardinal gave him a letter to the Archbishop of Baltimore, who assigned him to the western Pennsylvania missions whence he arrived in Pittsburgh in 1820. An urbane and cultured man, steeped in Continental Catholicism, in love with the ceremony and liturgy of the great churches of Rome, a confidant of royalty, he dreamed of the Gothic and the panoply of the ancient rites in the raw town of Pittsburgh among the poor Irish, accustomed to the log-hut chapel or Mass in a stable.

Father McGuire's friend was Colonel James O'Hara, a native of Ireland, the first big businessman in a city that produced many men of great affairs, a knowledgeable army contractor and the founder of the glass industry in Pittsburgh. O'Hara had been educated by the Sulpicians in Paris, it was said, but somewhere along the line in the new country he had drifted away from the Church, as was the case with so many Catholic Irish in the wilderness.

14

On the bank of Neshannock Creek deep in western Pennsylvania lived an early settler of Mercer County, John Gilky, educated for the Catholic priesthood but retired to the life of a hermit in a little cabin he occupied for forty years. He experimented with potato seed and produced the famous Mercer potato, sometimes called Gilkies, which, said a contemporary account, was a blessing to millions and added millions to the wealth of the United States. "The poor solitary exile, from the Emerald Isle," said the account, "has done more to benefit mankind than many a hero of a hundred battles."

15

The diary of Rev. Patrick Kenny, Irish-born mission priest in the Wilmington area of Delaware during the first four decades of the nineteenth century, drew a picture of a Catholic Irish type with which Americans became acquainted, often at the expense of their patience. As was not uncommon at the time, Father Kenny farmed for his support, and his hired helper was Patrick Haw, described in the diary as "this Irish Indian Savage, Drunkard, Egg & cider sucker," who if he received his just deserts would be "in his proper lodgings Botany Bay." Patrick Haw was one of those ham-handed Irishmen likely to do the wrong thing from a misunderstood direction, a sudden inspirational notion or their own cross-grained perversity. Experience with this type made one employer declare he dared not hire an Irishman lest the quarry he owned fall on the Gael's head. During Father Kenny's absence, Patrick cut down the willow tree which shaded the springhouse, for no apparent reason, and his employer wrote in the diary that "old Patrick" was "the most destructive digger, or mower of walks therein of every thing except a full grown flat Dutch cabbage, or a potato stalk in blossom." Once after a spree, which was another weakness, Patrick had to be bled, and he told the priest "his blood is so thick, it would not come out." His blood was only one of Patrick's thicknesses.

The Irish worked in the DuPont and other powder mills along the Brandywine. Father Kenny set down in his diary for January 30, 1823:

> Garesche's powder mill blew up. John Kelly, only 2 months from Ireland where he left his wife and 7 children Dead. Also Wm Duffy and Wm Delany — all catholics. 4 Irish Cath wounded.

16

Maryland meant the Carrolls. Among the direct descendants of Charles Carroll, who arrived in Maryland in October, 1688, as Lord Baltimore's attorney general, were Charles Carroll, a signer of the Declaration of Independence, his cousins, Daniel Carroll, a delegate to the convention which drew the Constitution, and John Carroll, first bishop of the Roman Catholic Church in the United States. By right, the name of Carroll enjoys pre-eminence among the American Catholic Irish.

Charles Carroll of Carrollton, the Signer, died in 1832, the last of the great figures of the Revolution, surrounded with awe and majesty, nationally reverenced. Yet the young Carroll received his education in French Flanders, Rheims, Paris, Bourges, and London because he could not be instructed in colonial Maryland by teachers of his own religious faith; and when he returned, after sixteen years abroad, the law prohibited him from voting or holding public office: he was a Roman Catholic. The lot of his father, Charles Carroll of Annapolis, had been in his generation even harder: he could not hold office or vote; he could not practice law; he could not attend church services of his faith or publicly teach young children; he paid tithes to support the Church of England and, for a time, double taxes because he was a Roman Catholic. Though he was considered the wealthiest man in colonial America, he was subject to English penal disabilities against Roman Catholics, as was the lowliest peasant in Ireland.

The heritage of Charles Carroll made him a natural foe of England, but his American patriotism was a finer compound than sterile hatred: he believed in liberty and he risked his neck and the largest fortune in America in that cause. Religious disabilities had left his father embittered; the son, with his passions under tight control, said: "We remember and forgive." He did not explode, as would have his father, when a well-meaning friend suggested that since all religions were indifferent to the Creator, Carroll might as well, for the sake of his own career, embrace the religion of his fellow countrymen. Carroll replied: "What, then, do you advise me to quit a false religion & adopt one equally false, & this merely to humour the prejudices of fools, or to be on a footing with knaves? I have too much sincerity and too much pride to do either, even if my filial love did not restrain me." But he expressed a determination to serve his country in a private capacity, notwithstanding his disabilities on account of religion. With sensitive objectivity, the experience of his family had not soured Charles Carroll against the detractors of his faith but against religious fanaticism: "knaves & bigots of all sects & denominations I hate and despise," he said. It was paradoxical that while Carroll could not enjoy the political rights of Protestants, his controversy with the strong advocate of England's course made him the leader of the patriotic party and first citizen of colonial Maryland. Though other colonies seemed dubious of Maryland's putting forward a Roman Catholic as champion of American rights, Carroll hoped, according to his biographer, Ellen Hart Smith, "to win them over, to convince them that a man's religion was his own business, and his own privilege."

Charles Carroll's services as a patriot are a part of American history. In 1792, the Federalists were prepared to offer him the candidacy of President of the United States if George Washington declined a second term. He was as representative an American as the descendant of a Puritan divine and accepted as such. A man so mean or prejudiced as to challenge Carroll's Americanism because he practiced the Catholic religion would have been openly hissed. Carroll himself was too broad-gauged and equitably philosophical ever publicly to recall the harsh trials of the family because it believed a man's religion was his own private affair. Toward England, after the Revolution, his attitude was the same as toward colonial anti-Catholicism: "We remember and forgive."

17

Baltimore had supplanted colonial Annapolis in the nineteenth century as the chief commercial center of Maryland, and the Catholic Irish, long settled in the colony, "had become sufficiently numerous by the last of the eighteenth century," according to one historian, "to play an important part in the social, commercial and professional life" of Baltimore. Luke Tiernan, come from Ireland in 1787, was representative, a leading merchant and shipowner, active in civic affairs, a founder of the Hibernian Society in 1816, a Baltimore signer of the petition to Congress for an Irish colony in Illinois, a trustee of the Roman Catholic Cathedral and zealous in the American movement for Catholic Emancipation.

The poor Catholic Irish in the Fell's Point waterfront section, the famous old St. Patrick's parish, were added to by the steady flow of emigrants into Baltimore with the start of construction of the Baltimore & Ohio Railroad in 1828 and the Chesapeake & Ohio Canal in 1829, and the rise of churches along the routes meant permanent settlers.

In 1837, Bridget Gibbons of Gay Street, who had come to Baltimore with her husband Thomas by way of Canada from County Mayo, watched President Andrew Jackson, then close to the end of his second term, in a carriage parade through the streets of the city. She held a child, three years old, high in her arms that he might look upon the famous man. Years later crowds gathered on the streets of Baltimore to pay their respects on his return from Rome of the same child, now the famous James Cardinal Gibbons, the pride of the American hierarchy.

18

Before the period of canals and railroads, Irish had pushed into western Maryland as laborers on the road to Cumberland, and with the start of the National Road to the Ohio they were hired at the emigrant wharves and put to work wearing the national costume they had arrived in — hard hat, swallowtail coat, tight knee breeches and heavy brogans, described as the "immortal Irish brigade — a thousand strong, with their carts, wheelbarrows, picks, shovels and blasting tools," paid six dollars a month.

Among the subcontractors on the road after Congress ordered it extended through Ohio was John Sheridan, an emigrant from County Cavan, who lodged his family in the Catholic settlement of Somerset on the National Road. On March 6, 1831, his wife Mary was delivered of her third son, named Philip, remembered in history as the Union cavalry general. (In Ireland, the old people vowed Phil had been born in the old country.)

19

The Catholic Irish name most prominently identified with Washington was that of James Hoban, a gifted artisan from Dublin, who won the design contest for the President's House and rebuilt the White House after its destruction by the British in 1814. In addition, he designed and erected the State and War offices and was one of the superintendents in the construction of the Capitol — a Kilkenny man by birth and at his death, in 1831, described as a patriarch of the capital city of the United States. He was a friend of Thomas Carbery, great-grandson of a 1730 Irish emigrant to Maryland, a prosperous contractor and sixth mayor of Washington.

At Georgetown lived the widow of Wolfe Tone, and in his declining days the exemplary Counselor Sampson resided in the pleasant town with his daughter, who had married the son of Wolfe Tone, employed in the topographical department of the government.

20

The building of the great canal running north and south the length of the state drew Irishmen from the Quebec emigrant ships to Ohio, and, by 1830, they constituted a noticeable part of the population, though smaller than the German emigrants. They located in growing towns, like Youngstown, Defiance, and Toledo, built their shanties as pioneers in Dayton, and found work on farms. A nativist newspaper in 1836 raised an uproar against the Catholic Irish canallers because, as red-hot Democrats, they were influencing elections in Shelby County.

But their sizable concentration was in Cincinnati, clustered in the river wards, where in 1829 they formed a Catholic Emancipation society and read, starting in 1831, the English-language *Catholic Telegraph*, founded by the Irish-born Bishop Purcell. Charles Dickens, who came to America in 1842, wrote in his *American Notes* of the Grand Temperance Parade he had watched in Cincinnati, observing:

> I was particularly pleased to see the Irishmen, who formed a distinct society among themselves, and mustered very strong with their green scarves; carrying their national Harp and their Portrait of Father Mathew, high above the people's heads. They looked as jolly and good-humoured as ever; and, working (here) the hardest for their living and doing any kind of sturdy labour that came in their way, were the most independent fellows there, I thought.

21

The appearance of the Catholic Irish in Indiana coincided with the start of the Wabash-Erie Canal in 1832. While the temperance people expressed surprise at the capacity of the Irish canallers for drink in the whiskey shanties, which moved forward with the work, it was also noted that "the growth of the Catholic Church along the canal corresponds more or less exactly with its progress." Textile mills in the northern part of the state employed the canal laborers who wanted a settled home.

22

The opening of the Erie Canal encouraged Irish who wanted to get out of the cities of the East to follow the migrant route of the Americans to Ohio, Michigan, Wisconsin, Illinois, and farther west. G. A. O'Keefe, formerly an attorney in Cork, urged the Irish, in 1829, to come by the way of the Erie Canal to Michigan Territory where they would be welcomed. In the 1830s, they had their own "Irish church," the Holy Trinity, in Detroit, which by the time of the Famine had a sizable Irish population. Travelers saw them on lake steamers, huddled together with their scant belongings, their poor state contrasting with Americans, journeying to the then Western country.

Catholic Irish pioneered with the miners who dug lead in the area that encompassed northwestern Illinois, northeastern Iowa, and south-western Wisconsin where the three states now touch. Galena, then larger than Chicago, resembled an Irish village in the middle 1820s: the first recorded survey of mineral lands along the Fever River was made for two Irishmen in 1825; the first mention of the name of Galena was in a mining permit issued in 1826 to another pair; the first grand jury, convened in 1827, had as members P. Hogan, John Foley, Michael Murphy, James Foley, Michael Coe, Michael Finley, James Lynch, and Owen Riley; the first license for a Fever River ferry was granted to John Foley and Abner Fried; the first will recorded in Jo Daviess County was that of Patrick Markey; the first indictment in the circuit court was against Michael Dee for assault and battery with intent to murder. A township occupied by the Foleys was named Vinegar Hill after the site of the 1798 Rebellion battle.

The Irish moved over into Dubuque when the territory was opened, and in 1835 Father Samuel Mazzuchelli, a mission priest, found some two hundred Catholics there, mostly Irish. Early Dubuque contained a considerable Irish settlement, with its leaders active in civic and po-litical affairs. One Irishman was active in a different way, made Dubuque history and attracted national attention. Patrick O'Connor, a violent and unruly man, in 1834 killed his partner, George O'Keefe. Since Dubuque lacked the apparatus of justice, the citizens formed themselves into an impromptu commonwealth, arrested O'Connor after a coroner's inquest, empaneled a jury, allowed the accused to challenge members and to select a friend as counsel, called witnesses and, at the conclusion of what his countrymen admitted was a fair trial, hanged him — a procedure the Eastern press praised as a rebuke to usual frontier lynch law.

Lead attracted Catholic Irish to neighboring Wisconsin, and an 1829 map of the region included Murphy's furnace, Kirkpatrick's fur-nace, and Keho's diggings; even before these locations, Dublin was an Irish colony, north of the village of Shullsburg, on the borders of what were known as the Irish Diggings.

23

Dr. William B. Egan, an Irishman, described as "physician, lawyer, real-estate operator, and politician," was the original Chamber of Com-merce booster of Chicago, incorporated as a town in 1833 and boasting a population of between three and four thousand in 1835. His tireless talk envisioned the growth of the muddied-street hamlet into a great city. Naturally, for his efforts in promoting it, he delivered the oration of the day at the breaking of ground on July 4, 1836, for the Illinois and Michigan Canal and, naturally, Irishmen were recruited from emigrant ships to dig it. When cash for payrolls was tight, the laborers received their pay in scrip convertible into land holdings. Speculators bought up this scrip at heavy discount from the needy Irish, and years later the Catholic Irish historian of the canal shook his head sadly at the criminal throwing away of their golden opportunity by the laborers. But many took land, and from Chicago southwest through Joliet, Seneca, Ottawa, LaSalle, and across to Kane and McHenry counties and down the Illinois River as far as Peoria, the Catholic Irish made a wide band of settlements on canal land. Their gregarious instincts returned many to expanding Chicago and by the terminal of the canal they gathered in the Bridgeport section. In time, from additions to the nucleus of canal workers, Chicago had a distinctly Irish coloration.

24

On St. Patrick's Day, 1827, Captain May of the steamboat *Shamrock* fired three rounds at dawn in honor of the patron saint, and the Irish of St. Louis proceeded to celebrate, the high spot being a banquet which turned into a rally for General Jackson. Two years before, the Protestant inhabitants of the town presented Rev. Mr. Neil, the Catholic pastor, an address on his leaving for Ireland on a fund-raising trip.

The Catholic Irish enjoyed a status of equality in this raw frontier early St. Louis denied them in the East, where "settedness" prevailed; and "the Irish crowd" relished the Jacksonian spirit of nondiscrimination. Luke Lawless, lawyer and judge, brother of "Honest Jack" Lawless, the radical O'Connellite, was the close friend of Senator Thomas Benton and twice acted as second in Old Bullion's duels. Jeremiah Connor, benefactor of Bishop DuBourg, gave Washington Avenue to the town out of his extensive land holdings — a donation worth millions of dollars today — and was president of the Erin Benevolent Society organized in 1818. The father of Bishop Timon was a merchant. Thomas Brady and John McKnight were partners in trading, and the Catholic Irish formed a respectable part of the business community.

But John Mullanphy was the outstanding Catholic Irishman in St. Louis, considered the richest man west of the Mississippi. He had left Ireland to be a subaltern in the Irish Brigade in France disbanded by the French Revolution. He came to the United States and prospered as a merchant and trader on the frontier, making his largest coup in cotton. Andrew Jackson seized Mullanphy's cotton in New Orleans for barricades against the British, and at Mullanphy's protest stuck a gun in his hand saying that if the cotton meant so much, go out and defend it. Those stacked bales behind which the Americans fought in the Battle of New Orleans, as vividly presented in the art of the time, were undoubtedly the Irishman's. Sensing that the War of 1812 was coming to an end, Mullanphy stationed himself on the post road at Natchez and when the rider appeared with the news of peace, he hustled into a waiting boat and had himself rowed to New Orleans. With two days' advance notice, Mullanphy bought up every bale of cotton he could lay his hands on at four cents a pound, chartered a vessel, and shipped his holdings to Liverpool where it sold at thirty cents a pound. Mullanphy was extremely generous as a benefactor of the Roman Catholic Church in St. Louis, and his eccentric son left a will, in which he set up a liberal fund for the assistance of emigrants through St. Louis, that made legal history in the long wrangle over the disposition of the fund after the purpose for which it had been denominated had become obsolete.

25

Bishop England, in 1840, warned his fellow Irishmen:

> Our southern states are the worst places to which an Irishman can emigrate, except he is a merchant with *good capital*, a mechanic in the way of building or tailoring (with as much spare means as would support him for a couple of months), steady habits and untiring industry.

Southern planters frowned on mixing white men as workers in the fields with Negroes. Irish labor in the South was employed in work on which valuable Negroes could not be risked, such as digging canals; and Irishmen had to compete with free Negroes in the cities and larger towns. There was little inducement for the Irish to go South, except to New Orleans, although at the opening of the Civil War they constituted the largest foreign-born group in the South.

New Orleans was the largest Catholic Irish settlement in the South. "If it had not been for the constantly recurring epidemics," speculated one writer, "New Orleans might have been as much an American Dublin as Boston or New York." In one epidemic of yellow fever which took 7001 lives, 3569 were Irish.

Before the Civil War, New Orleans was second to New York as the largest emigrant receiving port in the United States, and Irish passengers were numerous. One student writes: "In 1830 with 49,826 inhabitants and in 1840 with 102,193, New Orleans had a population that was almost half foreign; of these foreigners, the Irish were, by far, the largest immigrant group."

New Orleans carried a distinctively Continental Roman Catholic tradition with its French Creoles and Spaniards. Those native-born Americans in the North who accused the Catholic Irish of incapacity to be assimilated to American ways because of their religion never observed the interesting and revealing laboratory in New Orleans. They rejected entirely (as they were rejected by) the French Creole civilization and entered vigorously into the American life of the city, preferring American ways to the French Catholic tradition.

Out of a little settlement in the vicinity of St. Mary's and Tchoupitoulas Streets, by the landing where the hard and tough "Kaintuck" rivermen disposed of their crocodile-like flatboats, developed the Irish Channel, a slice of the Emerald Isle at the mouth of the great river. Along its banks the Irish built their shanties with lumber from the broken-up boats that had served their purposes on the down voyage. A Northern visitor in the winter of 1835-1836 described an Irish cluster as "a row of unpainted, black, ancient-looking, wooden buildings, which sat back some thirty feet from the street, and were walled about by a high, close board fence, with an entrance opposite each tenement."

Tchoupitoulas Street, with its saloons, boarding houses and oyster bars, was the O'Connell Street of the Irish. There Thomas Diamond kept the Louisiana Hotel, where the Third Ward Democracy Club talked politics and planned strategy. There the Irish shopped at St. Mary's Market, modeled on the familiar French markets. Along it walked Irishmen, still with their swallowtail coats and brass buttons, and the Irish women wearing the native hooded cloak. As emigration increased, the Irish spread out from the settlement along the river.

They worked as laborers on the five-mile levee constantly menaced by the encroaching river. They drove the drays: the same Northern

visitor estimated that upward of two thousand Irishman followed this
employment. They were in and out on canal work and later built the
railroads. They competed in the market with the Negro, "whose true
position," one observer noted, "the Irish laborer has usurped, and who
hates an Irishman as he hates death." But they were not so successful
in displacing free Negro skilled labor: Olmstead, the observer from the
North, was told it was not unusual to see an Irishman carrying the hod
for a Negro mason.

Many of the Irish had prospered into middle-class status: Cardinal
Gibbons as a boy had lived in New Orleans with his uncle, a substantial merchant. The Catholic Irish had their own church by 1833, divorcing themselves from the French.

They speedily fell into politics and were an important element of
the Democracy of New Orleans and Louisiana. Their flair for politics,
their quick knowledge of its practical workings, and their intense
partisanship, accompanied by violence at the polls, aroused the nativist
sentiments against them. New Orleans was a hotbed of Native Americanism directed against the Irish but they fought back with vigor and
had behind them the organized Democracy.

Irishmen worked on the river steamboats as firemen and stevedores,
and it was from these jobs that they dropped off to settle in towns, like
Natchez, along the Mississippi, which was a great Irish emigrant route.

26

In 1829, two ships, the *Albion* and the *New Packet*, sailed from
New York for New Orleans with Catholic Irish on their way to take
up homes in an Irish colony that was to be established in San Patricio
on the River Nueces in the Mexican state of Coahuila and Texas. Two
Irishmen, John McMullen and James McGloin, had come to Matamoros in Mexico by way of the United States and there had taken
wild land in a grant from the government as empresarios, on condition
they develop it with colonists. McGloin journeyed to New York and
persuaded a body of Catholic Irish emigrants to try their luck in the
country of Catholic Mexico. McGloin returned a few years later, according to a notice in the *Truth Teller* of October 5, 1833:

> Such settlers as intend to proceed to the colony of Messrs. Mc-
> Mullen and McGloin, are informed that the vessel chartered by

Mr. James McGloin (who is at present in town) will sail *positively* on Tuesday next the 8th instant. Persons disposed to better their circumstances, and proceed with Mr. McGloin, will receive every information by making immediate application at No. 4 Benson street.

The schooner *Messenger* sailed on October 14 with eighty-six more Irish settlers for the San Patricio colony, "in excellent spirits," according to the account.

Even earlier James Power and James Hewetson had applied for grants as empresarios on the old Refugio Mission lands, but delay by the Mexican authorities had held it up. Power, of County Wexford, had landed in Philadelphia early in the nineteenth century and, after remaining in New Orleans for twelve years, had settled in Saltillo in Mexico in 1823. Hewetson, from County Kilkenny, had been a member of the party led by Moses Austin, father of Stephen Austin, into Mexico. At Saltillo, he had met Power in the Irish colony there. With the grant authorized by the Mexican government, Power had gone to Wexford in 1833 and distributed handbills and posters in the vicinity advertising the prospects of the colony of Refugio. Catholic Irish families sold their holdings or borrowed money and in December, 1833, Power led a party of colonists on the ship *Prudence* from Liverpool.

Thus the Catholic Irish colonies of San Patricio, just below San Antonio, and of Refugio, bordering on the Gulf of Mexico, were established. These Catholic Irish colonists lived the life of pioneers and developed the wilderness; they were subject to attacks by the wild Indians, and were soon indistinguishable from the Americans filtering into the country. When the chips were down and the choice lay before them of standing by Catholic Mexico or joining in the movement for independence, the Catholic Irish were found on the side of the American Texans. The names of forty-two Irish colonists were signed to the Goliad Declaration of Independence; they fought under the Texan flag for independence; James Power was a signer of the Texas Constitution. Texas today still has a San Patricio County and one named after McMullen; and descendants of the original colonists hold pride in the part of the Catholic Irish in the establishment of Texas. It was the son of County Cavan emigrant parents, John Timon, later the first bishop of Buffalo, a Vincentian missionary, who re-established the Catholic Church in the new Republic of Texas.

The Catholic Irish did manage to get around the country before the flood of Famine emigration in a rather surprising way.

2 8

The '98 Exiles and Catholic Emancipation

THE FIRST ATTEMPT in New York City — on the night of April 19, 1825 — to organize sentiment in support of Daniel O'Connell's agitation for Catholic Emancipation in Ireland collapsed at the opening meeting. A mixup in advertisements, locating the rally in two different halls, brought out a slim attendance, which, after desultory proceedings, voted an indefinite adjournment.

It was not indifference to Catholic Emancipation which accounted for the lack of interest by the local Catholic Irish community; rather it was the general impression that O'Connell's fight had been won and English legislation to that effect only a matter of course. But the House of Lords destroyed the Emancipation bill passed by the House of Commons, and O'Connell ordered the agitation renewed.

The sense of outrage at the rejection which seized Ireland communicated itself to America, and another rally gathered in New York, on July 19, 1825, this time enthusiastically attended under the encouragement of the new weekly, *The Truth Teller*, which, established on April 2, addressed itself to a Catholic Irish audience. The principal speech that night by Counselor William Sampson set the pattern almost religiously adopted by subsequent movements among the Irish to justify their agitation on American soil for release of Ireland from England, with which the United States officially maintained friendly relations.

The name of William Sampson stirred those generous feelings of the Catholic Irish which they particularly lavished on men who had suffered for Ireland. The son of a Londonderry Protestant minister and trained for the law, he had been jailed for his open United Irishmen activities in 1798 and exiled, landing in France after the John Adams administration, fearful of alien rebels, had denied him entrance to the United States as undesirable. He had remained on the Continent for seven years and finally arrived in the United States on July 4, 1806, "just in time," he said, "to join in the festivities of that memorable and auspicious day" — and, naturally, the party of President Jefferson. He resumed his work for the Irish cause.

In this germinating speech, Sampson related the cause of Ireland to the deepest republican sentiments of the United States. "Do we forget that the cause of the oppressed is the cause of the free and virtuous?" He associated the fight for Catholic religious freedom with the American revolution for political liberty against the same foe, saying:

> It is that terror, tyranny and persecution that has made the population of Ireland so truly Catholic, and it is the knowledge of that sacrilege that places an honest man, particularly an American, on the side of Catholic Ireland.

He recalled the spilling of Irish blood in America's wars. He cited as precedents for American sympathy the subscriptions raised in the United States for the Greeks in their war of independence and the resolutions favoring the Catholic South American countries in their struggle against Spain. He invoked the debt of an expanding material United States to the humble Catholic Irish workers, asking:

> Is not this city prospering and growing by the labor of the poor Irish, who swell the capital of our rich proprietors by their hard and daily work? Do they not help to dig our canals, and to erect our works of defense?

The essentials of this speech were to resound down the years in impassioned Irish oratory.

To Dr. William J. MacNeven, the recognized leader of the Catholic Irish community in New York, was assigned the writing of the address to the people of Ireland. It was a work that everybody who knew him took for granted would be done well — too well, as it turned out.

Dr. MacNeven would have been a welcome and attractive figure in any society — intelligent, poised, courtly, a man of warm charm, stern integrity, and moral courage. William J. MacNeven was born at Ballynahowne, County Galway, in 1763, and was thus sixty-two years old when the address to Ireland was written. He was the descendant of an ancient Irish family which had lost its large property in the north of Ireland by the Cromwellian confiscations and been moved to the wild lands beyond the Shannon. "There my family lived, like others of the old race," wrote Dr. MacNeven, "in obscurity and independence —

true to their religion — full of love of Irish nationality, traditionary pride, and aversion to England."

Educated at the University of Prague and at the University of Vienna, from which he received a medical degree in 1783 at the age of twenty, he established practice in Dublin the following year. Engaging in patriotic politics, MacNeven first joined the Catholic popular party and then took the oath of the revolutionary United Irishmen and was a member of the five-man executive Directory. In 1798 he was arrested and jailed in Dublin for a year and then transferred as a state prisoner, with eighteen other leading United Irishmen, to Fort George in Scotland for three years. On his release, he served for two years in France as a captain in the Irish Brigade of Napoleon's armies, but disillusioned by the emperor's shiftiness and evasions concerning a planned invasion of Ireland, he sailed for the United States and landed in New York City on July 4, 1805, where he practiced his profession, lectured on medicine, started the first chemical laboratory in New York, and wrote and edited books and journals on medicine and chemistry.

But his busy life did not distract him from the responsibilities of leader of the growing Catholic Irish community or devotion to the Irish cause. The plight of the Irish emigrant concerned him; the welfare of the humble Catholic Irish poor was close to his heart; and, being an Irishman, he was actively interested in politics — as a Jeffersonian, of course. There was no disagreement that this Catholic Irish exile should speak for the Irish in America.

In the address, Dr. MacNeven paid American free institutions the highest praise possible: he urged the American federal union as a model to the Irish people. Recognizing that repeal of the Act of Union was then out of the question, he recommended that Ireland seek a relationship to the imperial Parliament in London that his adopted state of New York enjoyed with the national government — in other words, local autonomy or home rule. Breathing the expansive and self-confident republicanism of free America, the MacNeven address was a bomb dressed in felicitous phrase.

In due time this first expression of sympathy from an American source for the Irish struggle reached the Catholic Association in Dublin, but instead of the jubilant reception the New York Irish had expected, O'Connell, in a masterly exhibition of double-talk, put the kiss of death upon it. As was to happen so often in the coming years, the leaders on the ground in Ireland felt the need to put the checkrein on American impetuosity. O'Connell knew that the English government was seeking pretexts to smother the rapidly expanding Catholic movement; and in this game of cat-and-mouse, he had cause to dread the rough intrusions of Americans, three thousand miles away, shouting for home rule. Following his policy of one step at a time, he rejected the larger measure of freedom urged by MacNeven to concentrate upon Catholic Emancipation.

So rebuffed by O'Connell, the New York society, enthusiastically organized to spread propaganda and raise funds — "rent," as it was called in Ireland — for the Catholic Association, fell apart before the ward committees had passed the hat from door to door in New York. "It appears to be the policy of the leading men among the Irish at home," said MacNeven, "not to connect their cause, at present, with the Friends of Ireland in this republican country."

By the resignation of the New York Irish leadership, the honor of forming the first functioning society to agitate and raise rent for the cause of Catholic Ireland in the United States fell to Boston, when on April 16, 1827, the Hibernian Relief Society was established. It was not a charitable but a political organization, and its title followed the lead of the Dublin society, which had re-formed itself for political pursuits in the disguise of a relief organization to take advantage of a loophole in the English law. The Hibernian Relief Society of Boston inspired and showed the way to similar organizations elsewhere in the country.

2

In the interval between the New York collapse and the founding of the Boston society, the case for Catholic Emancipation had been taken up in public meetings at Baltimore, Washington, and Augusta, Georgia, by local bodies which called themselves Friends of Civil and Religious Liberty. These meetings avoided the political involvements of the MacNeven address and contemplated no fund-raising campaigns. While Catholic Irish participated in and shared the customary offices, these bodies represented the sympathy of native-born Americans and Protestants, including Protestant United Irishmen exiles, for the struggle of Catholic Ireland.

After Boston had set the example, the Irish in the frontier town of

St. Louis followed with a similar society in July, 1827. Early in 1828, Catholic and Protestant Irish in Philadelphia formed the Friends of the New Catholic Association and speedily gathered into auxiliary groups the Irish in the surrounding area. This society was the first to send to the Dublin Association a remittance, almost a thousand dollars, the start of the flow of American millions during the next hundred years for the Irish political wars.

An incident in Ireland shook the New York Irish out of their apathy after the Dublin rebuff in 1825. Harry Mills, holder of a small four-acre farm, had led the revolt of the forty-shilling freeholders in the County Louth election to vote in opposition to the Ascendancy candidate against the wishes of the powerful landlord, Wolfe McNeil. "I won't vote for any man that votes against the country and the religion," Mills defiantly told the landlord. Because he had paid his rent, Mills could not be dispossessed but the indignant McNeil set afire the turf pile and shouted to the openmouthed peasants, "Let the priest with his holy water put that out."

The doughty Mills hailed the landlord into court, lost the case, and was pressed for costs. All his belongings were seized, his cow, his little horse, his furniture, and "sorrow a taste of anything did they leave behind, bad luck to them, and I may say the flesh is fairly picked off my bones — and if the gentlemen of the Association don't do something for me, and send me off to America, I'm done entirely."

The voice of Harry Mills carried over the water to New York; his story was within the familiar experience of the Catholic Irish community there. A deputation waited upon Dr. MacNeven and on August 8, 1828, a meeting was held to collect a fund for the unafraid forty-shilling freeholder — "to keep," as the resolution said, "the Wolfe from the door." But the gathering did not stop with raising a hundred dollars for Mills; a second motion called for the organization of the Friends of Ireland in New York; and at a mammoth meeting three weeks later a society was formed, with Dr. MacNeven as president and Eber Wheaton, principal of the Mechanics' Institute in New York, a native-born American and sturdy-grained republican, without Irish blood or connections, as secretary.

The contagion of enthusiasm spread with the formation of society after society wherever Catholic Irish had settled as the news from Ireland grew more encouraging. A thrill ran through Irish communities when his grandson handed into a Baltimore meeting of the Irish

Emancipation Society of Maryland the subscription of, as the *Truth Teller* excitedly proclaimed in boldface type, "THE VENERABLE CHARLES CARROLL OF CARROLTON." Memories sprang alive at the note to the New York society, with a $25 contribution, from the widow of Wolfe Tone, living in Georgetown, who wrote that a speech by MacNeven "has awakened all those feelings which sorrow had overwhelmed."

But more revealing of the unshakable core of Catholic Irish strength in the United States was a letter to New York from Felix McConnell of then remote Pittsford, Vermont, enclosing $22.50, the contributions of thirteen Irishmen and one American, who had handed in 50 cents. "Our mite is small, we know," he explained, "but our numbers and means are equally so, being all (with the exception of two mechanics) laborers," adding that "Erin expects that all her sons will do their duty." Or the request of Philip F. Scanlan, a pioneer Dover, New Hampshire, Catholic Irishman, that the names of ten Irishmen in the town be enrolled, explaining that they were under the strain of taxing themselves to build a Roman Catholic church. The Irish digging the canal in Pennsylvania asked for directions in sending their contributions, as they wanted to aid "suffering Ireland by our money" and feared that Emancipation would come before they had added their mite.

In the towns along the Hudson and the newly opened Erie Canal, the response spread. From Cincinnati and Detroit came contributions and zealous sentiments, and in wild and tough Galena the Irish lead miners raised almost a thousand dollars, which a visiting Englishman described as a fund for an Irish rebellion under the guise of civil and religious liberty. The society in New Orleans collected approximately two thousand. Louisville, Natchez, and Savannah each had its joint society of Americans and Irish.

Before the news reached the United States of the victory of Catholic Emancipation, more then thirty societies had been formed in the United States, three in Canada, and one in Matamoros, Mexico, to aid the brethren in Ireland.

This was the first organized movement of the Catholic Irish in the United States to assist the Irish back home: the American associates of the United Irishmen in the eighteenth century were principally Protestant Irish from the North. It set the patterns the later and larger movements were to follow, even to the ladies' auxiliaries (the women of the

Maryland society issued an address to the ladies of America) and the inevitable factionalism: a group in Brooklyn broke off from the parent organization and set up shop by itself, and dissension had started to creep into the New York society. A national convention was in the process of making, at which time, it was reported, President Andrew Jackson would contribute $1000.

3

It happened that this movement occurred in an American breathing spell of good feeling between the anti-Catholic prejudice of the eighteenth century and the rise of anti-foreign Nativism. Hezekiah Niles, the noble old republican editor of *Niles' Weekly*, spoke in 1829 of "that sympathy and good feeling for the [Catholic Irish] which is common to almost every man in the United States" in their struggle for Emancipation. But Niles joined with other editors in opposing public agitation as interference in the domestic affairs of another country, of which a representative opinion was that of the New York *National Advocate*, written by that extraordinary personage, Mordecai Noah, who asked:

> What right have we, the American people, to interfere between the British Government and any portion of its subjects? Suppose Ireland has been misgoverned, suppose the condition of that country to be in every respect unhappy and degraded; yet what is it that entitled us to convoke public meetings and vote addresses on the matter? Sympathize as we please, be indignant as we may and all that is honorable and proper: but to obtrude our sympathy and indignation into the British Cabinet is the most absurd of all possible absurdities.

Thus early was struck that note of American objection to the use of the United States as a staging ground for the Irish cause which persisted. What would an American say, as Niles stated the case, if the English interfered in our domestic tariff concerns?

Amidst the general American rejoicing on the ending of Catholic disabilities, an ominous voice was heard. A Philadelphia clerical paper observed on the success of Catholic Emancipation: "We shall be sorry for this measure if the revival and dissemination of the trumperies and delusions of popery are to be the result of it," and warned that the pining lion (the Roman Catholic Church) was waiting in his den to recover his strength.

A solemn Te Deum Mass was sung in Philadelphia on the receipt of the King's assent to the measure; the bells of the Episcopal Christ Church rang out; the famous Liberty Bell was ordered again to proclaim freedom: it was on this occasion that the bell cracked; and the victory dinner was held in Independence Hall at the State House, the last time that room was used for a public purpose.

New York enjoyed a gala celebration, with fireworks and a Te Deum Mass after Bishop Dubois, born in France, had been nudged by the Irish into taking cognizance of the event. Everywhere the local societies met and toasted the victory. With their work done, they dissolved voluntarily one by one, with the pledge to rise again when Ireland needed help, but some reformed into Hickory Clubs to support Andrew Jackson.

The sum of more than a thousand dollars remained in the treasury, and the society unanimously voted to turn it over to the fund for the monument to be erected to the memory of Thomas Addis Emmet, the most respected of the Irish in the United States, who had died in 1827.

4

Dr. MacNeven's funeral praise of Emmet, "for the beneficial influence he has shed upon the Irish character in the United States," spoke the American sentiment for the reputations of MacNeven, Sampson, and other '98 exiles as well. Emmet was first among equals in this Irish triumvirate. To both the Catholic and Protestant Irish, said a contemporary, Emmet "stood in a relation of interest and importance, in which no man now living on this Continent stands — the very heart's-blood, the life and soul of everything Irish in America."

Thomas Addis Emmet, the son of a doctor in Cork, of a Church of Ireland Ascendancy family, had committed himself to the Catholic and to the nationalist cause not because he was a romantic idealist, like his brother Robert, but because he was a decent man who could not abide English injustice and was convinced that only by force could Ireland win freedom. He was a member of the Directory of the United Irishmen and a close friend of Wolfe Tone. For his rebellion he was smashed in fortune, and exiled forever from Ireland.

Emmet spent one year in a Dublin dungeon and then was confined in Fort George in Scotland because of the representations of Rufus

King, the American minister to England, an interference which had important political repercussions in the United States. Upon his release, he conferred with Napoleon on French aid to Ireland and, disillusioned with the emperor, he set sail and arrived in the United States on November 11, 1804. Three days later he applied for American citizenship, having resolved never to return to an unfree Ireland.

Federalist hatred of Irish rebels tried to frustrate Emmet's career as a lawyer in New York, but Governor Clinton, "a plain, stern, ardent republican, and of Irish blood," came to his side, and in time the Irish exile rose to eminence at the American bar.

A colony of Catholic Irish had clustered in Greenwich Village, then open country lying between the North River and what was later to be Jefferson Market. On July 12, 1824, the toasting day to the immortal memory of King William, a group of New York Orangemen "walked" to Greenwich Village to provoke the Catholic Irish to fight. The reaction in Greenwich Village was the same as if the "walk" had happened in the County Antrim countryside: the Catholic Irish drove the Orangemen back to the city streets. The sheriff hustled together a posse and bursting into Greenwich Village arrested every Irishman that could be laid by the heels. The arraignment on the next morning bound over a hundred or more Irishmen for "rioting and disturbing the peace." At the September session, the Irishmen were tried and were about to be sentenced on one-sided testimony.

On that same morning Emmet, who had been living in the country and had not heard of the incident, chanced to be in the court on an important case. Somebody informed him of the facts. Emmet hit the ceiling in his indignation, immediately pushed aside his own case, and strode into the courtroom to defend the unfortunate Irish laborers. When he had finished, the judge, almost with an apology, dismissed the whole brood of Irishmen without even a reprimand.

Both Americans and Irish found affection for Emmet in his own virtues, but his family name took on certain immortality and mystical adoration among the Catholic Irish people by the romantic life and death of his younger brother, Robert, in which a moving love affair with Sarah Curran, daughter of the great Irish orator, had entwined itself with the magniloquent defiance of his judges from the dock and his brave death at the hands of the executioners after an abortive and mismanaged one-day rebellion in 1803.

The story of Robert Emmet had all the elements that tugged at the sentimental heartstrings of the Irish. He was St. Joan and Don Quixote to the Catholic Irish, the confused symbol of their painful yearnings and foredoomed frustrations. Richard Sheil expressed a general sentiment when, in a letter to Thomas Emmet, he spoke of "that feeling of melancholy attachment which every good Irishman should entertain for your name."

The Catholic Irish in the United States sang as the directions ordered, "with melancholy expression," the national poet Tom Moore's nostalgic invocation of Sarah Curran, "She Is Far From the Land," or with equally forlorn sentiment the tribute of Moore, who had been Robert Emmet's friend and classmate at Trinity College, "O, Breathe Not His Name." The famous speech from the dock, concluding with the command that not until Ireland was free was his epitaph to be written, was learned by heart by the generations. "Robert Emmet" as a given name was as standard as Michael or John. American villages and counties proudly bore the name of Emmet after a local Irish politician had skillfully maneuvered in meeting or legislative hall. Next to the saint himself, his was the most toasted memory at St. Patrick's Day observances. Societies and military companies proudly assumed his name. In unofficial Catholic Irish hagiography Robert Emmet came as close to sainthood as a Protestant could ever arrive.

Americans, when they saw or thought of Thomas Emmet, remembered not only his own sacrifice in the cause of Irish liberty but also the martyred name of Robert Emmet. They respected the unselfishness of Thomas Emmet and his unusual virtue of personal disinterestedness. Thomas Emmet was the sort of man of whom men would say that if they had to be somebody other than themselves, they would be Thomas Emmet. His funeral was a public occasion in New York City, a tribute America reserved for its most honored.

The three exiles sought in America to honor the oath they had taken in Ireland: "to found a brotherhood of affection, an identity of interests, a communion of rights, and a union of power, among Irishmen of all religious persuasions." For years devoted and mindful Catholic Irish brought flowers to the grave of Emmet in St. Paul's churchyard and to the graves of MacNeven and Sampson in Newton.

The Democratic Party might also honor the memory of these three Irish exiles with flowers.

IRISH EMIGRANTS EMBARKING AT QUEENSTOWN (NOW COBH).

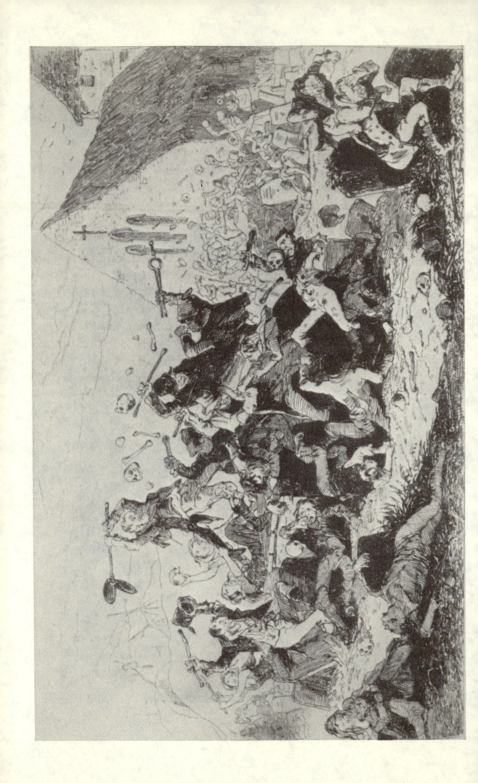

2 9

The Irish as "Ready-Made Democrats"

ON ELECTION NIGHT of November 4, 1828, supporters of
General Jackson and his ticket rushed to Tammany Hall for a jubilation, only to find it occupied by a meeting of the Friends of Ireland.
James Shea, the speaker, broke off his discourse to announce that the
gathered Irishmen would surrender to the Jacksonians not only the
room "but also their whole strength, their whole might, and their
life's-blood if necessary."

This was not Irish blarney. The Catholic Irish held General Jackson
in the worshipful veneration reserved for their own national heroes, almost as a folk figure. They identified themselves, as emigrants or the
children of emigrants, with General Jackson, himself the son of poor
Irish emigrants. Their Irish feelings rejoiced in affectionate kinship
with the military chieftain who had whipped the British at New Orleans, and their traditional regard for the fighting man gloried in his
quick pugnacity. They shared with the humble classes the conviction
that he stood for the common man and responded to the intuitive prejudices of his partisan nature, as their political chief.

President Jackson took a high place in the symbolism of the Catholic
Irish. The association of the American hickory with the Irish oak was
continually invoked. Toasts to Andrew Jackson linked him with Daniel
O'Connell in a merger of American politics with Irish national aspirations. After President Jackson had gone into retirement, his name
still had a thrilling ring to the Catholic Irish. The Boston *Pilot* noted
in 1844 that on the coming March 15 "the venerable hero of New Orleans — God bless him — will be 77 years of age."

Andrew Jackson and his administration strengthened the tradition
of Catholic Irish loyalty to the Democratic Party, which had begun
with the proscription by the Federalist Party of the United Irishmen
and of the Protestant Irish generally. The old chestnut of the Catholic
Irishman's being "agin the government" held validity in Ireland's national politics. In America the reverse was true: the Catholic Irishman
was for a government that was not "agin" him.

2

The inheritance from Ireland which made the earlier Protestant Irish, as a Federalist senator called them, "the most God-provoking democrats this side of hell!" operated similarly upon the Catholic Irish. The Catholic Irish brought with them to America a hatred of aristocracy, or anything savoring of or pretending to aristocracy, from their own grueling experience in Ireland, or of exclusiveness and class superiority. They hated a party that affiliated with English policy or aped English ways. They hated property qualifications or similar disabilities upon political equality.

The Baltimore *Republican,* a Democratic paper, answering in 1835 the attacks of the Richmond *Whig* on the Catholic Irish, recognized the attraction of the Catholic Irish emigrant, "almost without exception, as it were by instinct," to the Democratic Party:

> What to the native citizen is abstract theory, or the fruit of historical research, in relation to the encroachment of tyranny, has been to the Irish emigrant the sad nursery tale, or the mournful experience of his riper years; and therefore he is found battling manfully in the ranks of Democracy.

An articulate Irishman, writing in the Boston *Pilot* of September 24, 1836, gave further depth to the association of party and race:

> They [the Irish] have suffered too much persecution in their own country from the tyranny of an unrighteous oligarchy, and the grinding extortion of a mean and rapacious aristocracy, to have much partiality for the Exclusives in this. . . . They discriminate with a knowledge almost intuitive, the difference between the politics of the two contending parties of these States. They mark the principles of the hardy yeomanry, of the industrious mechanic, and of a certain part of what is called the middling classes: the Irish perceive that their interests are identified with these portions of our citizens, and to maintain that interest, give them their support.

A Philadelphia paper struck to the very heart of the matter. What the Catholic Irishman wanted in politics, it said, was not power but protection. When the winds of intolerance were beating around the head of the Catholic Irishman in the pre-Civil War period, the Democratic Party sheltered him and in return he gave it loyalty. It was a practical accommodation on both sides; in addition, the Catholic Irishman felt comfortable and at home within the Democratic Party: the opposition comported itself like the Ascendancy he had no reason to love in his native land. The Catholic Irish were, in the contemporary term, "ready-made Democrats" when they arrived in America.

3

The Catholic Irishman's connection with the popular party, or Democratic Party, had its genesis in one of the greatest blunders in the political history of the Republic — the Alien and Sedition Acts adopted by the Federalists under President John Adams that set the pattern and precedent for later nativist, or anti-alien, movements.

In the summer of 1798, the Federalists adopted four laws, two of which — on naturalization and sedition — aimed to stop the absorption of emigrants by the Democratic (then the Republican) Party, proscribe Protestant Irish Jacobinism, and advance the political fortunes of the Federalists. The Naturalization Law of 1790 had made American citizenship relatively easy, providing a probationary period of only two years, later revised in 1795 to five years. In 1798, the Federalists legislated that the foreign-born must reside in the United States for fourteen years before applying for citizenship and then must wait five additional years before naturalization. Harrison Gray Otis, the die-hard Federalist from Massachusetts, left no doubt against whom the measure was directed. He wrote to his wife: "If some means are not adopted to prevent the indiscriminate admission of wild Irishmen & others to the right of suffrage, there will soon be an end to liberty and property."

The Sedition Act, a gag act directed at the Jefferson-French-Irish party, operated in effect to silence and punish criticism of the government, the most effective of which was carried on by articulate Irish scribblers. The first to become entangled in the Sedition Act was an Irishman, John Day Burk, playwright and journalist. The first jailed under the law was another Irishman, Matthew Lyon of Vermont, a Protestant Irish firebrand.

"By 1798," wrote Samuel Eliot Morison, "the alliance between native democracy and the Irish vote, which has endured to this day, was already cemented."

The Alien and Sedition Acts had little direct bearing upon the small Catholic Irish minority then in the United States, but their spirit of proscriptive hostility to the alien remained a reality to the increasing numbers of Catholic Irish emigrants up to the Civil War. Democratic leaders, including the Irish, never let the Catholic Irish forget it. Three nativist movements, each in the middle of the decades of the '30s, '40s, and '50s, directed to making the alien emigrant a second-class citizen by restrictive naturalization laws, kept alive the memory of the origin of the spirit. Though the Federalist Party died with the election of Thomas Jefferson, the Democrats successfully labeled the Whigs and the first Republicans as the old Federalists under new names and made the characterization stick with the Catholic Irish.

4

An incident that made their blood boil fixed in the memory of the Catholic Irish emigrants the direct relationship of the bitter Federalist anti-alien and anti-republican policy to their own Irish national aspirations and revered leaders. In 1807, Rufus King, a staunch Federalist, ran for office in New York. The three '98 Irish exiles, Emmet, Dr. Mac-Neven, and Sampson, together with fellow United Irishmen in New York, took up opposition, and O'Connor's *The Shamrock* suggested Mr. King was undesirable. The New York Federalist press, led by the New York *Post,* branded the Irish opposition as alien meddling in affairs that were properly American. Emmet, in a public letter of April 4, 1807, asked King "whether you propose submitting to the world any explanation of your interference with the British Government, respecting the Irish state prisoners in the year 1798." King refused to reply and, on April 9, Emmet revealed the story which, besides reflecting no credit on King personally, threw a bright light on the narrow Federalist mentality.

Emmet recalled that in the summer of 1798, after the Irish uprising had been put down, some of the Irish state prisoners, that is, the arrested leaders, entered into an agreement with the Irish government to emigrate as exiles to a country mutually agreed upon in return for a general amnesty that would stop the protracted bloodshed. Upon the acceptance of the offer by all the prisoners, the suppression ceased. But it was resumed. The reason was that Rufus King, then American minister to England, had remonstrated with the British government against the sending of the Irish prisoners to the United States, on the ground, as Mr. Marsden, the undersecretary, significantly answered when pressed by the prisoners: "Perhaps Mr. King does not desire to have republicans in America." Emmet charged that the British government had seized upon King's remonstrance as a pretext to keep the Irish prisoners as long as possible in confinement, and King collusively had allowed himself to be used as a tool against the Irish. Then Emmet came to the heart of the matter that the Irish memory retained with anger:

> The misfortunes which you brought upon the objects of your persecution were incalculable. Almost all of us wasted four of the best years of our lives in prison. As for me, I should have brought along with me my father and his family, including a brother, whose name perhaps you even will not read without emotions of sympathy and respect. Others nearly connected with me would have come partners in my emigration. But all of them have been torn from me. I have been prevented from saving a brother, from receiving the dying blessings of a father, mother, and sister, and from soothing their last agonies by my cares — and this, sir, by your unwarrantable and unfeeling interference.

In short, Emmet placed the execution of his brother Robert on the soul of Rufus King, the Federalist.

The letter became an instrument of Democratic practical politics to keep alive in the Catholic Irish segment of the party the memory of Rufus King's proscriptionist role in the martyrdom of Robert Emmet. It was also a reminder that Jefferson's liberal administration welcomed the Irish prisoners after their release. Twenty years after its publication, Mr. Quigley, speaking at a St. Patrick's Day celebration in the frontier town of St. Louis, asked "where is the Irishman with but one spark of native pride, who would vote for the party which refused admittance into the United States to such men as Sampson, Emmet, Bond and hundreds of their brave but unfortunate companions of '98?"

As late as 1860, an Irish stumper in the Lincoln-Douglas campaign told a Massachusetts audience that Douglas "will carry on the principles of Thomas Jefferson, who opened the gates of freedom to Thomas Addis Emmet, Sampson, Dr. MacNeven, Wolfe Tone, and several others of the Irish patriots of 1798, who were refused passports to these hospitable shores in 1801, by Rufus King." The facts were a bit askew, but Mr. Raferty had a good Democratic heart — and a long Irish memory, more than half a century after the Emmet letter.

5

Father John T. Roddan, American-born son of Irish emigrants, was editor of the Boston *Pilot* from 1848 to 1858. Of bright intelligence and a Whig in politics, he was particularly knowledgeable in political matters touching upon his own people. "The trammels of party were first forged for adopted [naturalized] citizens at New York," he wrote in 1853.

The so-called ignorant Catholic Irishman had had wider political experience in his own country than had been the lot of emigrants from Continental European lands. He had been a part of the public opinion which made possible Catholic Emancipation; he was further educated by O'Connell's new campaign for repeal of the Act of Union. He had seen the technique of voting, often as a block of forty-shilling free-holders. He was a democratic being by virtue of Ireland's struggle to win religious and political equality. An instinct for politics, half-indigenous and half-cultivated, urged him to active participation in its affairs: he loved to talk politics. As his own needs had made him in Ireland a member of what was called the "popular" party, so his own needs in America made him "take as naturally to the democratic party as ducks take to water when they break the shell."

The Catholic Irishman required leadership in Ireland that he could trust and that would direct him; his heritage had been hardly of the character that encouraged self-reliance. The leadership was ready-made for him in the persons of Emmet, MacNeven, and Sampson, Irish patriots and stalwart Democrats in the United States, and, as United Irishmen, children of the French principles which Thomas Jefferson represented. The influence of these men, together with Thomas O'Con-nor, in directing the first flow of Catholic Irish emigrants into and holding them to the Democratic Party was in Father Roddan's mind when he described the trammels of party as being forged on the emigrants in New York.

6

But natural sympathies and indoctrination by influential leaders did not of themselves alone make — and keep — Catholic Irishmen loyal to the Democratic Party. Efficient and unceasing organization, detailed and minute, either by leaders of their own race, or Democrats who cultivated them, shepherded their inclinations to political use. None was more astute in this practical skill than Tammany Hall.

Tammany has been characterized as anti-Irish in its formative years. This assumption had its origin in the march of some two hundred

Irishmen on Tammany Hall, on the night of April 24, 1817, to force
the nomination of Thomas A. Emmet as Republican (Democratic)
candidate for Congress, which ended in a free-for-all. Tammany's opposition to Emmet was not racial but owing to his intimate friendship
with DeWitt Clinton, with whom Tammany long fought a running
battle.

In *The Shamrock* of March 9, 1816, more than a year before the
Emmet march, Thomas O'Connor, in protesting against the native
attitude toward the foreigner of "Go to the country from whence you
came if you do not like it here" (the sentiment dates back that early),
wrote:

> The Tammany Society of this city is an honorable, a noble con-
> trast to whatever is illiberal or ungenerous: patriotic and republican,
> it is composed of gratitude and hospitality. This character belongs to
> it not only in its collective capacity, it is the distinguishing fea-
> ture of every individual member.

O'Connor was too honest a man to have given such a comprehensive
endorsement of Tammany unless it deserved the good words by fair
treatment of his own countrymen.

The property qualification barred the poor Catholic Irishman from
the ballot in the early days. A New York State constitutional convention in 1821, however, extended the franchise, with Tammany and
the Democratic Party active in pushing the change, and in 1826 the
property qualification was removed. In the 1827 election, the Catholic
Irishman made a vigorous appearance on the stage of New York City's
politics.

The New York City election in the fall of 1827 was a proving
ground of General Jackson's strength against President John Quincy
Adams for the 1828 national campaign. It was a violent contest by
partisans on both sides; and the Irish emigrants joined it as Jackson
adherents with the same zeal they would have displayed in a wild
Tipperary canvass.

Stout Irishmen armed with clubs acted as bodyguards of Jackson
polling officials, and at given signals rushed supporters of the Adams
cause. In the Eighth Ward, two hundred Irishmen "were marched to
the polls by one of the Jackson candidates who walked at the head
with a cocked pistol in each hand and then without leaving the polls,
they voted three times apiece for the Jackson ticket." In the Fourth
Ward, a Kilkenny Irishman and a Vermont Yankee fought for five

hours and fifty-eight minutes in front of the polling house, which served as a pretext for Jackson officials to keep back anti-Jackson voters. "The inspectors at some of the polls," continued the account, "saw the necessity of causing a cross to be placed on the Bible," forcing the Irish to take the election oath by the method prescribed in the courts for Catholics.

Irishmen, under American direction, were following the violent election procedures customary in their own country, where, it will be recalled, every contested election required the service of the military to keep order and prevent bloodshed. Of the forty-shilling freehold class, the Catholic Irish lined up behind American leaders to vote, as they had formed a procession behind the landlord's agent in Ireland. Their intense and excessive partisanship had expression in loyalty to Jackson in the same unrestrained fashion as their unquestioning fidelity to O'Connell.

American students have too frequently taken it for granted that the Irishman's amenability to political discipline was a product of his obedience to the authority of the Church, when in fact his schooling had been at the direction of the landlords and then, when that authority had been successfully challenged, under the organizational genius of Daniel O'Connell.

This initial excursion of the Catholic Irish as a body into New York politics did not go unnoticed. The *National Advocate* professed alarm at the "foreign body in the midst of us, of alarming magnitude and overwhelming influence," adding:

> Every thing in the shape of an Irishman was drummed to the polls and their votes made to pass. . . . It was emphatically an Irish triumph. The foreigners have carried the day, and the Americans have now nothing to do but to submit to their masters with as good a grace as they can.

This was partisan nonsense. The Irish were more noticeable as foreigners in the election than numerous. But it was the first cry of the political nativist Americans against the Irish.

Among the stalwart Tammany braves was Major William Denman, editor and owner of the New York *Truth Teller*. Denman, born of a German father and Alsatian mother — on St. Patrick's Day in Edinburgh, he avowed — was a veteran of Wellington's army and encased his dwarfish form in a voluminous military cape to give himself the proper martial air. As an editor, Denman was a master of scurrility as was his

Irish-born associate, George Pepper, who wrote the first history of Ireland in the United States and loved the bottle not wisely but well. Starting as a Catholic Irish weekly to keep emigrants informed of Catholic Emancipation news, the *Truth Teller* progressively translated itself into a straight Democratic Party organ to hold the Catholic Irish vote.

The influence of the *Truth Teller* in cementing the Catholic Irish affiliation with the Democratic Party was of high importance. It had a national circulation and reached the emigrants on their way to naturalization, perhaps the only paper they read (or had read to them), setting their minds favorably towards the Democratic Party as their friend and protector, reprinting and answering assaults on their religion and race from a Whig press which, in New York particularly, matched the *Truth Teller* in violence. What was printed in the *Truth Teller* was repeated among the Catholic Irish outside New York — and the *Truth Teller* saw that the Democratic Party got the best of it. It had no competition for the attention of the Catholic Irish in the American political field. The Catholic weeklies of the period confined themselves generally to theology, controversy, and religious news. Information of a political nature centered on Irish affairs.

Indeed, the Catholic hierarchy, a conservative body, leaned in personal preference towards the conservative Whigs, and the Jackson party, according to the Baltimore *Republican,* had few friends in the Catholic prelacy. The hierarchy looked with growing apprehension upon the concentration of the Catholic Irish in the Democratic Party; it saw this political bunching as a target for political nativism to attack the Church as the agency responsible for the solidity of the Catholic Irish vote to further its own ends through politics. Most of all, it feared the label of the "Catholic vote," having the good sense to foresee the dangerous products of the "Catholic vote" or a "Catholic party" in an overwhelmingly Protestant country.

Bishop John England, who reflected the sentiment of the Catholic hierarchy on politics, addressed the Roman Catholic citizens of Charleston in 1831 and minced no words in setting forth what could be called the official policy, writing:

"I am no renegade to Ireland; but I AM NOW AN AMERICAN. . . . When upon your approach to the polls, any person addresses you as an Irishman, or a Frenchman, or an Italian, or by any appellation but Carolinian or American, his language is distraint and offensive. He is either igno-

rant, or supposes you to be so, or has some sinister view. There is a
BRIBERY OF THE AFFECTIONS. . . . There is a bribery in reminding you
of the bravery, and the patriotism, and the generosity of the Irish. And
all this is the more insulting as the object of the adulation, or the familiarity, is too plain to be mistaken. . . . I warn you of your solemn serious obligation, that in giving your vote you recollect, that YOU ARE AN
AMERICAN! A CAROLINIAN!"

7

Bishop England's excellent phrase — "bribery of the affections" —
expressed the susceptibility of the Catholic Irish nature to reward
out of gratitude political attention, consideration, and favors shown to
the race. The Catholic Irish remembered that they had been defended
and befriended by the Democratic Party when, in bitter days, their
name was a term of scorn and contumely. Even beyond the powerful
motivation of self-interest, this phrase helped to explain the attachment
of the run-of-the-mill Catholic Irishmen, with no political ambition or
no axe to grind, to the traditional Democratic Party.

The early experience of the Catholic Irish with American politics
solidified into a tradition; and the Catholic Irish character historically
had been governed by tradition. Father Roddan wrote that an Irishman "seldom changes his convictions, and when he does, the process
is a slow one. When he once gives his confidence, it is not easy to induce him to remove it. . . . Even when he is convinced that he is
wrong, he will pretend to stick to the wrong for a while, just to show
people that he has a mind of his own."

The obituary notice in 1837 of Garret Byrne, an early resident of
New York's Catholic Irish community, described him as an Irishman
of the old school, which it defined as "unchanged and unchangeable
in his principles — a warm-hearted Irishman, and ‚ an unflinching
Democrat." The tradition by that date had been well established, and
father passed it on to son.

8

The presidential campaign of 1832, which opposed Henry Clay, the
nominee of the National Republican Party, to Andrew Jackson's candidacy for a second term, "marked the beginning of many things," in

the words of Claude Bowers, "that have come to be commonplace in American politics," including the drive of the two major parties to capture the Irish vote.

The renewal of the charter of the privately conducted Bank of the United States was the issue. How was the issue to be made vivid and understandable to the Catholic Irish emigrants, at home with ward politics centering around the personality of the alderman but at sea in national affairs? The politicians found the successful formula by explaining American politics in terms of the national experience in Ireland of the emigrants.

The British and Irish people, it was explained, were loaded with a national debt, requiring annual taxes of a hundred million dollars for interest charges; they paid hundreds of millions annually to a national church; they paid for a huge standing army to keep the people down; the Irish people were "literally beggared" by oppressive laws for their enslavement. "The main agent of government in effecting all these evils is the *National Bank of England*." The Bank of the United States was the same instrument of tyranny in the United States that the National Bank of England was in Ireland.

Deep-seated prejudices were stirred in warning the Catholic Irish voters what would happen if Henry Clay were elected: a British nobility will be established that will annually draw three million dollars from the Bank of the United States; the government will be placed under the management of a score of well-born aristocrats who will ride roughshod over the laboring classes; Nicholas Biddle, president of the Bank, will elect the President of the United States without troubling the people to vote; the charter of the Bank will be renewed by which the specie will be carted by wagonloads to Philadelphia and sent to the lords and dukes of Great Britain; the Bank will reduce the price of property and thereby secure to British lords, dukes, and generals a landed estate in America.

The word "Tory," originally an Irish word, was a black word to the Catholic Irishman; it was the label of the anti-Irish party in British politics, the symbol of English injustice. It was transferred to America to fix, in Irish terms, the political antagonist of the Catholic Irish emigrant: "An Irish Tory in Ireland is sure to make a good Whig in America."

The Henry Clay and Bank party engaged in their own demagoguery to bribe the affections of the Irish. Henry Clay in the Senate in March,

1832, anticipating the coming election, had sweet-tongued the Irish in his own marvelous way. None amalgamated so quickly with the Americans as the Irish, he said, continuing:

> In some of the visions which have passed through my imagination, I have supposed that Ireland was, originally, part and parcel of this continent, and that, by some extraordinary convulsion of nature, it was torn from America, and, drifting across the ocean, was placed in the unfortunate vicinity of Great Britain. The same open heartedness; the same generous hospitality; the same careless and uncalculating indifference about human life, characterise the inhabitants of both countries. . . . And I have no doubt that, if the current of emigration were reversed, and set from America upon the shores of Europe, instead of bearing from Europe to America, every American emigrant to Ireland would there find, as every Irish emigrant here finds, a hearty welcome and a happy home!

Henry Clay, at a later date, was author of the sentiment that dogged every emigrant race in the United States, meant originally as flattery but which grew progressively obnoxious: "Some of my nearest and dearest friends [are] Irishmen," he told a St. Patrick's Day dinner.

The Clay Bank party organized an "Irish Anti-Jackson town meeting in Philadelphia," held in the State House yard on August 6, 1832, after a call signed with two thousand names, which Jacksonian Irishmen tried to break up. But the intrigue to set the Irish to attract the Irish by what amounted to an Irish party in the 1832 campaign was a maneuver that outraged the feelings of the Irish themselves and had the effect of closing up the ranks in support of Jackson. At a great meeting of the naturalized citizens of New York City held in Tammany Hall on the night of September 19, 1832, Dr. MacNeven, the presiding officer, disavowed the Philadelphia appeal to the Irish as an Irish party. "We have no pretense of confederating as Irishmen upon American politics," he said. "We hold our rights as Americans and must use them as Americans without reference to alien origins." The Irish, he went on, have found "not merely an asylum but a country in the United States." We may congregate as Irishmen to help the cause of Ireland itself, he explained, "but we must disclaim and reprobate every appeal to Irishmen, as such, at the American Hustings."

Public meetings of the Catholic Irish in Newark, Brooklyn, Albany, and Pittsburgh followed the lead of the New York meeting, disavowed the Philadelphia purpose, and renewed allegiance to Andrew Jackson.

This episode, on the fringe of the 1832 campaign, indicated that both contestants had become conscious of the Catholic Irish vote. The Clay Bank party subsidized a newspaper, the New York *Irishman,* "despised by every true son of Erin," said the *Truth Teller.* The New York *Courier and Enquirer,* edited by Colonel James Watson Webb, once a staunch Jackson paper but converted to Clay by the loans of the Bank to Colonel Webb, ran a series of addresses "to the adopted citizens" of New York, written by an Irishman of "the apostate breed," a penny-a-line "mere hireling of the Bank," said the *Truth Teller,* who would lead the naturalized Irish to the polls as "the landlords of Ireland would lead them to the hustings" and fix on them a fourteen-year alien law.

This putting the brand of "apostate" on the Catholic Irish who left the Democratic Party set up the same response of automatic feelings of betrayal in the mind of the devout Catholic Irishman as did the terrible word "informer" or the renegade from the Church. The word "apostate" took on a political as well as a religious meaning. A writer in the *Truth Teller* knew the psychology of the people he was addressing when, inveighing against the Whig candidates in 1838, he thundered:

> The Irishman that would vote for them is a Jemmy O'Brien — a traitor to his country — an apostate to his faith — and a grovelling slave amidst freemen.

The name of Jemmy O'Brien, the notorious informer in Ireland, was murderous when publicly applied to an Irishman.

The Irish of Brooklyn had resolved: "That we consider any appeal to our Irish feelings, with a view of influencing our suffrage . . . calculated to lessen our just influence, and lower our fair character." This noble counsel of perfection was directed against the anti-Jackson seceders; it would be expecting too much of human nature for the Catholic Irish politicians of the Jackson persuasion not to dwell upon Irish feelings in advancing party and personal interests, in violation of the counsel of perfection, especially when those Irish feelings were already deeply entwined with what Old Hickory stood for. The Catholic Irish, as the first of the politically conscious emigrant people, set the pattern of racial bloc voting which succeeding emigrants from other lands almost instinctively adopted under their own leadership.

Loyalty of the Catholic Irish to the principles of Andrew Jackson ran the grave risk of penalty. Being of the working class mostly, they were subjected to the pressure of employers, who as a group had attachments to the conservative interests represented by Clay and the Bank. The secret ballot was then unknown and when employers presented their employees with Clay tickets the alternative was "or else," either spoken or implied. Irish workers for Hance & Brooks, carpenters in New York's Sixth Ward, were handed anti-Jackson ballots by the foreman and informed that they would receive wages for time lost in going to the polls if they voted the anti-Jackson ticket. The Irish refused and declared they intended to vote for Old Hickory. At the next payday, they were discharged.

Yet Mr. Everett of Massachusetts, blaming the defeat of Clay on the "foreign vagrant," "brutally ignorant" and with no interest in the prosperity of the country, declared that "the majority of them could be bribed to vote for any thing or any body for a glass of whiskey!" The *Truth Teller*, taking recognition of such a charge, which was a familiar accusation in the House of Commons against Irish voters, even to the consideration, "a glass of whiskey," pointed out that opponents since the time of Jefferson always commanded more money for political purposes than the Democrats, but that the Irish remained faithful to the Democratic Party.

9

A severe test of that political loyalty cropped up in the New York City election in the spring of 1834. In September, 1833, it was officially announced that the Government would withdraw its deposits in the Bank of the United States and place them in state banks. Jackson had decided to carry the war against his formidable financial adversary and its strong-willed head, Nicholas Biddle. The Bank, as a strategical counter to impress upon the country the menace of Jackson's move, began to tighten credit in the midst of a wild speculative cycle. Jackson's lieutenants started to regiment his popular following through public meetings and endorsements. Dr. William J. MacNeven himself, on January 29, 1834, presented resolutions at a meeting of the Fourteenth Ward in New York upholding the President.

But within two months Dr. MacNeven changed his mind. The tight money policy of the Bank and the calling in of loans had started a depression which drove businesses to the wall and imposed great suffering on the poor, for whom MacNeven's heart was moved. Convinced that the removal of the deposits, which he now considered arbitrary and unconstitutional, was the major cause of the hard times, he expressed public disapproval of the Jackson course on the eve of the local elections in New York.

This political disaffection understandably disturbed the local Democratic leaders. Here was a man for whom the Catholic Irish had strong attachment, and gratitude for his services in the Irish and Catholic cause might prevail with his fellow countrymen over loyalty to the Democratic Party. But this was not Ireland. While the Catholic Irish would follow Dr. MacNeven's leadership in a cause to help Ireland, they had their own opinions on American matters. Daniel O'Connell himself was to find out that his hold on Irish affections did not reach over the Atlantic on American issues.

A public meeting of the Irish was called to disavow Dr. MacNeven. Tammany Hall was crowded to the doors and an overflow meeting held in a park nearby. The full force of the Catholic Irish political commanders was turned upon MacNeven: he had divorced himself from the affection of his fellow countrymen by associating with their enemies, who had closed the door of America to the '98 exiles (MacNeven included), who wanted to shut the Irish out from citizenship, who slandered the Catholic Irish as the "spawn of cellars and garrets."

The proof of the meeting's success came in an unlovely aftermath. An excited mob, no doubt whispered to by the calculating politicians, now certain they had quarantined the influence of MacNeven, marched to his home and outside hissed and groaned the name of a man whose life had been unselfishly devoted to their betterment. Within a year the principals in the cry against MacNeven were sponsoring resolutions in his behalf — after he returned to the party.

10

New York's Sixth Ward on the lower East Side, with reservoirs in the adjoining Fourteenth Ward, had grown in the 1830s to be the largest Catholic Irish community in the nation, and next to Ireland herself and the settlements in Lancashire and Scotland the largest in the world. There Tammany Hall, through Catholic Irish politicians, had vigorously organized a solid phalanx of Democracy. Politically ambitious fellow countrymen elsewhere in the United States noted the success of Tammany in, as well as the susceptibility of the Catholic Irish to, bloc organization.

The early successful relationship with the first flow of Catholic Irish emigrants in the 1820s and 1830s was the source of Tammany Hall's long-maintained policy of carefully organized attention to the newcomers of other races. The Catholic Irish learned from the Tammany connection the importance of the ballot, and they in turn contributed their organizational skill and an ancient shrewdness developed in Ireland in outwitting opponents. They had an intuitive knowledge of human behavior and a genuine feel for practical politics. They had, from their own experience as emigrants and sons of emigrants, a firsthand acquaintance with the feelings of newcomers.

The inclination of the Catholic Irish to value a candidate by personal qualities and identity with their own feelings was a racial inheritance. A candidate for coroner in New York in 1825 appealed for Irish support as "an honest and charitable and *poor* man," who always "evinced a special attachment to the natives of Ireland." A candidate for register was recommended as a veteran of the War of 1812 with the more compelling distinction that he had saved a girl from drowning. Their votes were urged in support of an alderman who had employed Irishmen on the roads and proved himself a friend to "the poor emigrant of Ireland, who has reached our shore in poverty and distress." A charitable heart, friendship for the poor, kindliness toward the Irish emigrant, and, if a non-Catholic, nondiscrimination in hiring Catholic help and a liberal attitude on the Church — such declarations of virtues in a candidate struck up a warming flame among the Catholic Irish.

But Catholic Irish politicians had to be constantly on the alert against the wiles of opponents of the same race, familiar with another side of the Irish nature: Dr. Christopher C. Rice, a political leader, stood up in a public meeting to deny emphatically the accusation that he was "a fine man," in the sense of one who held himself superior, and therefore indifferent to the run of the Catholic Irish.

A satire on the turbulent politics of the Sixth Ward, written in 1838, had an Irish politician urging his countrymen not to go on farms, advising:

> I tell ye not to leave the city,
> Because you know 'twould be a pity,

To see men digging farms, and doating,
Who should be in the city voting.

A great attraction of the city over the lonely country was the opportunity of the Catholic Irishman to indulge his love of politics. The
gregarious nature of the Catholic Irishman organized itself — or was
organized — in clubs of various descriptions: mutual benefit, social,
workingmen's or Irish patriotic societies. He was a born joiner, loved
the routine or factional quarrels of meetings, and indulged the long
legal frustration in his native land by a pedantic parliamentarianism in
the new country, which was balm to his feeling of importance: he was
a pettifogger of no mean proportions in the minutiae of parliamentary
procedure. Racial leaders used these clubs as a strong grasp on the
loyalty and votes of the Catholic Irish emigrants.

The Hibernian Provident Society, an early New York benefit society
that had been supplanted by the Hibernian Universal Benevolent
Society, a non-political welfare association, was revived in 1833 as a
political adjunct. Richard B. Connolly, a self-serving Cork Irishman, the
"Slippery Dick" of the notorious Tweed Ring, forwarded his political
fortunes through the Mechanics' Benefit Society and the Brian
Borihme Club, organized to honor the saints and heroes of Ireland, including one not in the hagiology — Saint Tammany. Politicians rotated as officers of the several workingmen's and artisans' societies.
Ambitious men forced their way into political notice by forming social
clubs. The Irish military companies were more political than warlike.
Politicians paid the bills for target-shooting excursions, offering trophies
for marksmanship and their voices for the Democratic Party. Felix
O'Neill, a prosperous grocer, rose to an alderman's chair by his cap-
taincy in the City Guard Troop; and "Honest John" Kelly, who reorganized Tammany after the Tweed scandal, started his political career
as captain of the Emmet Guards. Catholic Irishmen ran with the volunteer fire companies, which were political auxiliaries.

Young second-generation Catholic Irishmen were politically trained
in the Young Men's General Committee of Tammany or as secretaries
of the ruling General Committee. John McKeon, a graduate of Co-
lumbia, son of Captain McKeon, a War of 1812 hero, learned the
ropes on committees and as lawyer of Tammany clients before he
was sent to the New York Assembly in 1832 and to the 24th Congress
in 1834. Charles O'Conor, son of Thomas O'Connor, high in the
councils of Tammany, served an apprenticeship in Tammany before he

gave up political ambition for concentration on the law, and John T. Brady, the great lawyer, was active in Tammany high circles but shunned political office. Dr. MacNeven was an early Tammany leader in the Fourteenth Ward, serving a term as alderman.

II

The alderman had the status of petty king to the poor emigrant. He handled a host of minor patronage jobs, and he had influence with employers of labor. He was the intermediary for the unfortunates caught up in the law: he saw to it that they got bail and, if the charge was serious, that they were represented by counsel. Aldermen Dennis McCarthy, a prosperous liquor dealer, Thomas S. Brady, the lawyer, and Felix O'Neill, a grocer, who variously represented the Sixth Ward in the 1830s, invariably headed or organized benefits for the widow left in poverty; they arranged balls to raise funds for a man crippled at his work and with a family to support; they re-established in business men visited by bad luck. Invariably the same list of Tammany braves served as the committee for relief benefits and balls. The alderman knew everybody in the ward, and he was everywhere in the rounds of professional duty.

Of the same blood, the Catholic Irish alderman paid the greatest respect to traditions and customs. His presence at a wake or a funeral consoled the widow and brought a distinction to the household from which gratitude for his respect rarely fled. In Ireland the humble were not accustomed to such intimate attention from public officials.

The nature of the alderman had to be generous and open. The Catholic Irish loved the man who put his hand into his pocket freely and with, as they said, "a good heart." A man who carried a purse and doled out change with a sour face had no right to be an alderman.

The alderman, or political leader, assumed for the emigrant in America many of the offices attended to by the priest in a parish in Ireland. There the priest was the one educated man the peasant consulted when he scratched his head in perplexity. In the different political and social environment of the United States, the alderman had a power in his own right he could exercise for the emigrant.

The glamour of the alderman, whom they knew personally, thus filled the imagination of the Catholic Irish emigrants, and it did not wear off. Dean Swift said that Bolingbroke would have been a more effective statesman if he had had "a small infusion of the alderman." The Catholic Irish in America were weighted with an overinfusion of the alderman.

12

Granted that the "bribery of the affections" may have been calculated and returned political — and other — dividends to its practitioners, still it contemplated a sharing of humane sentiments by the powerful to a people who in their homeland had received little but a cuffing around by the powerful. This had a depth of meaning to the emigrant that only an emigrant could know. Tammany had its terrible and corrupt sins, but it provided a form of social service long before society organized it professionally, and it also had a sense of humanity for the emigrant when the world around was otherwise cold and indifferent, if not actively hostile. The same could not be said of other parties.

Politics offered a way to a higher economic and social station for the able and ambitious Catholic Irishman in a day when it was difficult to break the chains of hopeless emigrant poverty. Patrick Rice, thirty-eight years of age, a native of the neighborhood of Newry in Ireland, died on November 5, 1833. His obituary notice gives a glimpse of a career in the early Catholic Irish community of New York:

> To the merchant, he was well known in the laborious avocation of a porter, for his strict integrity, diligence and zeal; in the lower wards, as a thoroughgoing republican [democrat]. He entered into the political contests of the day — and having risen by honest thrift, to the condition of a respectable grocer, Mr. Rice distributed, with a liberal hand, a very large portion of his hard-earned means to the poor, who were the chief objects of his care, as he had no family of his own — to them his loss is indeed severe and affecting.

One thousand of his countrymen and fellow citizens followed his coffin to the grave.

Politics gave the Catholic Irishman a psychological lift for which he could not hope in a country suppressed for centuries by an alien rule — a sense of personal importance; and that was a fact of major significance in the understanding of a people from a land where bondage had served the end of humiliation.

The Catholic Irishman was introduced to American politics in the ward, and local politics long dominated his interest, to the extent that in time his name became synonymous with it. His Irish background, his own nature and American circumstances accounted for this specialized political character.

Historically, the Catholic Irishman's patriotism had been county and local. Though the Gaelic social structure had been destroyed for two hundred years, the spell of loyalty to petty king or chieftain had endured in deep parochial attachments. O'Connell had given him a sense of the Catholic nation, but intense political nationalism, an expression of unified sentiments, was a post-Famine growth.

The Catholic Irishman's "interest," as previously described, rested in his native land with local justices of the peace, magistrates, the local agent of the candidate for Parliament, and the agent of the landlord, or the landlord himself. His concerns in America were in neighborhood (ward) and local affairs. He was an ardently parochial human being, easy and at home under his own patch of sky.

His feel for politics was human and personal; abstractions, unless embodied in a personality, failed to stir responses and left him cold. He relished the factionalism of an intraparty struggle for control of a ward, in which attachments and antagonisms were clearly defined in contending individuals.

He was familiar with the mechanics of party politics from practical experience in Ireland. Tammany, for example, built from the ward upward. Electors in the wards chose ward committees of three, whose duty it was to call ward meetings and arrange for elections. These ward committees made up a general ruling committee at the top. Each ward selected delegates to a nominating committee, which selected candidates in an open convention and submitted them to ward meetings for ratification — the so-called "great popular meeting." Each ward had a vigilance committee to get out the vote, protect the voters, and conduct the general campaigning. This party political structure closely resembled the secret Ribbonmen organization in Ireland.

Regularity was the first law of the Ribbonmen; regularity was the cement of Tammany's strength. Catholic Irishmen, if ambitious, bucked the regular organization for place and preferment but within the organization, and when the fight was over, resumed party loyalty. Factionalism was forgivable; deserting to the other party brought the severest penalties. The "ignorant" Catholic Irishmen understood the mechanics of party politics often more keenly than the native-born.

Hostility hemmed the Catholic Irishman within the limits of ward and local politics. It was unusual, particularly in the settled regions of the East, for a Catholic Irishman in pre-Civil War America to hold, or even to aspire to, office on a higher level than local. In the newly opened territories, where men started from scratch and a sense of equality minimized discriminations, the Catholic Irishman had a wider opportunity to stand on merit, and since his numbers were fewer, nativist antagonism lacked the virulence aroused by the crowded congregations of emigrants in the seaboard cities.

The fact was that the Catholic Irishman in the East generally had to depend upon the votes of fellow Catholic Irishmen to elect him to office: the second-generation wealthy Kavanagh, elected to Congress from Maine, was an outstanding exception. The frequency with which non-Irish voters scratched an Irish name on a Democratic ticket raised constant protest: an "O" or a "Mc" set a voter's pencil to work. The party expects us to go down the line for a Democratic ticket, the Irish complained, and so we do, but the party displays no similar staunchness toward an Irish name on the ballot. We do not ask support for a candidate because he is a Catholic Irishman, they said, but it is unfair to penalize him because he is a Catholic Irishman. They objected, also, to the cultivation by the party of the Irish when the weather was fair and walking on the other side of the street at the appearance of storm clouds. The public excitement over the burning of the Charlestown convent in Massachusetts in 1834 and the lacing of the Irish character by the Boston press after the New York election riots of the same year concentrated public hostility on the race, and the Democratic leaders prudently took shelter. In 1835, previous to the November election, the naturalized Irish of Boston met and adopted a resolution that, in the light of existing circumstances, "we are determined to stand neuter in the approaching State election, as we cannot confide in either of the parties into which the Common-wealth is divided."

In the 1836 election in New York, at a time of rising nativism, Thomas O'Connor, Alexander Stewart, a Protestant Irishman, and John McKeon, American-born of Catholic Irish ancestry, ran 1500, 1000, and 200 votes, respectively, behind their Democratic co-candidates on the same ticket. In one instance, the name of McCall, a presidential elector, not an Irishman, and described as one of the best Democrats in the State of New York, was scratched — "spotted," as the term was — and the words "No Irish" written on the ticket. "They put their mark on him who bore the name of Mc——," it was said. The *Truth Teller,* stressing that Democrats had struck at "every thing that can be called 'Irish,'" warned that scratching of the Irish must stop or "farewell to the party."

As the growing Catholic Irish vote became concentrated in districts and wards, the solid bloc was powerful enough to elect an alderman or councilman and sometimes members of the state legislature. Their leaders speedily learned that if a Catholic Irish constituency was essential to elect one of their own to a small office, that same constituency by its size became worthy of courting for its weight by party leaders, and hence could wield influence in larger affairs. This meant an amount of patronage, but also it meant friends of the race in high office and therefore protection against hostile onslaughts.

The 1840 Democratic national platform carried a plank favorable to the emigrants, and each four years up to the Civil War repeated the sentiment. The Whigs, on the other hand, consistently alienated the Catholic Irish by alliances with nativist movements.

13

The Sixth Ward of New York City received its "bloody" title from the election riots of 1834 and the "ould" was added to fix the blame for the disturbances on the Irish. The outbreak introduced the Catholic Irish to the country, now growing conscious of this spreading emigrant element, as political brawlers through the outraged cries of the Whig press against Jackson's foreign mercenaries.

On the first day of the three-day balloting, as was then the electoral practice, a small frigate named the "Constitution" mounted on wheels paraded through the streets, and passing McDermott's Sixth Ward Hotel, both a polling place and Democratic headquarters, the rough sailors who manned it in the pay of the Whigs jeered and taunted the Jacksonians. The invasion invited retaliation. Led by George Strong, a fierce Tammany brave, a Democratic mob stormed the Whig committee room, bloodied twenty party workers and left the place a shambles.

That night a vast meeting of outraged Whigs organized voluntary battalions to keep order in the Sixth Ward and early the next morning stationed themselves before McDermott's Hotel. In the middle of the morning, the Whig barge advanced towards the hotel and incited opposition, in the course of which a sailor bludgeoned an Irishman. Like a hurricane, "coming from nobody knew where and going to nobody knew whither," his fellow Irishmen rushed to the attack with bricks and clubs. Special election constables answered a hurry-up call and arrested the Gaels in spite of a spontaneous Irish rescue party. Whig threats against "the damned Irish" as the cause of the rioting were unconcealed.

On Thursday morning rioting was resumed, but the course of events is not clear from the contradictory reports. A pro-Irish account said that the Whig roughs tried to close the Sixth Ward polls to Irishmen and Jackson supporters. Disregarding the mayor's commands, the Irish, swinging shillelahs, fell upon the Whigs, who retreated, "closely pursued by the Faugh a Ballaghs" (the name of the Irish regiments in France), in the direction of the Whig headquarters, out of which Whig partisans poured and knocked down every Irishman they came upon. The other story, anti-Irish, was that the Irish attacked the barge of the sailors in front of Masonic Hall and when the Whigs rushed to the help of the tars, the Irish swept through the hall with murderous fury.

Whigs broke into Broadway gunshops and the report spread that the United States Arsenal was to be seized. The mayor called out the city militia and, in the meantime, peaceable men had taken possession of the Arsenal before the crazed partisans could seize it. The appearance of a detachment of infantry, bayonets affixed to muskets, and two squadron of cavalry quieted the mobs and ended the riots.

"It [the past election]," said the New York *Journal of Commerce*, setting the tone for the Whig press elsewhere, "was merely an affair of *Americans*, for the choice of *their own rulers;* and yet *foreigners* must needs work themselves into a fury, and attempt to settle the question by club law." Charging the Irish with ignorance of American institutions and hatred of all government and with being herded to vote in their own land "under the management of LORDS and PRIESTS," the *Journal of Commerce* continued:

> We have among us a large number of native born COLORED PERSONS, *whom the laws prohibit from voting, but who, at least many of them, are attached to our institutions, and are intelligent, and in*

many respects FAR BETTER QUALIFIED *to participate in our elections than the persons of whom we have been speaking.*

Hezekiah Niles wrote that the arrested "were nearly all Irishmen . . . the victims of persons 'behind the scenes,' less *brave* but more *cunning* than they." This explanation in extenuation of the Irish struck an unusual note among the uniform anti-Irish bitterness in the Whig press. The New York *American* called the Irish "riff-raff"; the *Courier and Enquirer* said they were too low for attention. In an election contest in Albany the next month, the Whig "bullies fought the Irish wherever they could find a single one going peaceably about his business without company or cudgel to protect him."

The Boston press was so violent that the Catholic Irish community gathered in public meeting to protest the attacks. The Boston *Atlas* was especially vicious. It compared the "bullies and bravadoes" of New York to the Catholic Irish leaders of the Democrats in Boston, "who if they had the *strength* and *courage* equal to their baseness and breeding, would *first destroy the property of every honest and industrious citizen, and then* DRAG THEM AND THEIR WIVES AND THEIR CHILDREN TO THE SCAFFOLD." *The New England Review* wrote that "with some praiseworthy exceptions" the Catholic Irish constituted "the most corrupt, the most debased, and the most brutally ignorant portion of the population of our large cities."

Catholic Irish speakers at the Boston meeting pointed out that vicious and weak men existed among all races, but they did not condemn the Yankees for their bad members, as the whole Irish race was being slandered for its paupers and lawbreakers. Indeed, one speaker said:

> To the credit of the citizens of Boston, be it said, they as a body behave towards their Irish fellow-citizens as Christians and Philanthropists — and we on our part, reciprocate the feeling. On no occasion have we attempted to exercise any undue influence over them.

But they made it clear that their attachment to the Democratic Party was not to be weakened by the violence of Whig attacks.

14

The election riots of 1834 were an element entering into the initial cohesion of the several forces that, emerging as the native American movement, gave new life and shape to sentiments as old as the colonies. The part of the Irish in the outbreaks acted, in a measure, as a precipitant. The movement had been taking shape from a variety of directions, even before the election, and its several ingredients spelled trouble for the Catholic Irish.

3 0
Under the First Nativist Guns

EMIGRANTS PILING IN from Europe, starting in the 1820s, revived a prejudice against the stranger and his different ways that had had early roots in the colonies — the "hostility," as Scioto, the student of nativism in New York, defined it, "to every non-American influence that could clash with the settled habits of the American community."

With clarification after diffuse beginnings, antagonism came to center upon the Catholic Irish as the prime source of friction. They felt the force of the native American opposition so vigorously — more than other emigrant peoples — that before the excitement exhausted itself they had settled into the conviction it was directed against them solely.

From the beginning of the American Revolution to the close of the Napoleonic wars, the prolonged period of battle raised a barrier against European emigration. A new and homogeneous generation of Americans, unfamiliar with the emigrant, entertained a general and generous willingness to accept and absorb newcomers into a spacious land.

The initial rumblings of native Americanism were provoked with a rising sense of indignation at the calculated policy of dumping English poorhouse inmates upon America, shipped at parish expense to be rid of the cost of their maintenance, and the practice of some German states in disposing of convicts by transportation to our shores. At first the anger was directed at England, but in the 1830s, when bad European economic and political conditions raised the flow of emigration to a tide, the particularized protest against English widened to include foreign paupers as a whole.

A memorial in 1837 prepared by the mayor and aldermen of New York stated that during the past seven years, 296,259 emigrants had arrived at the port of New York. In 1835, the total population of New York numbered 270,089. Thus, in a period of less than a decade, the count of foreigners who had poured into New York exceeded by 26,170 the total population of 1835.

"This country," reported the commissioners of the New York alms-house, "has become the great receptacle for the miserable outcasts from European society."

They presented a social problem, herded in the cities under conditions of squalor, spreading disease. They filled the streets with beggars, whom America had not known before. They were disorganizing the homogeneity of the country, the nativists asserted.

2

The breaking down in emigrant-receiving cities of almshouse figures by place of birth of inmates showed that, of the noticeable increase in foreign paupers, natives of Ireland predominated, often in singular excess. The foreign population of the Boston almshouse had jumped 115 per cent from 1829 to 1834, while the native-born had decreased by 10 per cent; in November of 1835, it reported 306 foreigners, nearly all Irish. Of the 870 foreigners in the New York City almshouse on November 1, 1834, natives of Ireland accounted for 305. There were 1303 from Ireland alone among the 1895 foreign-born in the Philadelphia almshouse during 1834. The trustees of the poor of Baltimore reported to the City Council that, during 1833, natives of Ireland and Germany under their charge exceeded the American-born. The Louisiana Charity Hospital admitted 4287 foreigners in 1835, of whom 2354 were Irish.

These reports told the story of the casualties of the flight from the Irish famine of 1831 and pestilence of 1832. Emigration to Canada in 1831 jumped three and a half times over the figures of 1827, and accounts from Montreal in that summer pictured the sorry conditions: hospitals filled with sick emigrants, a tent colony improvised to accommodate the overflow, hundreds sleeping on the beach at night.

A violent nativist publication asserted in 1836 that were it not for "lazy and vicious emigrants from England and Ireland" we could "dispense almost entirely with our prisons, our penitentiaries, and our alms-house establishments," and blamed the large number of paupers in the New York City almshouse on "the poormasters of England and Ireland." (There were no poormasters in Ireland at this date; Ireland had no Poor Law.) The Irish answered that they did not come to the United States to beg, but to avoid begging in Ireland: they hoped to better their condition in the underpopulated United States by work, in contrast to Ireland where there were too many people and too little work.

The Catholic Irish poor tried to take care of their own distressed, as they had in Ireland: they had not lost their instinct to draw near suffering and relieve it. "We hesitate not to say," wrote the New York *Evening Post* in 1838, "that there is more charity exercised by the poor Irish than by any other class of our population." Those who ended in the almshouse became public statistics; there were no statistics of the numbers saved from public charity by the native benevolence of the Irish poor. The *Truth Teller,* in defending the readiness of the Irish to tackle work, was not dealing in cant when it proclaimed that the Catholic Irish, so long as they commanded one cent, shrank from depending for support on public charity. The tradition of the shame attached to pauperism had not fled the people.

The Catholic Irish emigrants, in general, arrived in the country close to the margin of destitution and struggled constantly with poverty thereafter. They worked for low wages and in uncertain employment; they had scarce provision against misfortune or sickness. If they landed from emigrant ships sick or without means or friends to whom to turn, as many did, the almshouse was a refuge until they had established themselves. A widow with a large family or a wife left straitened with children while her husband sought work in a distant part gravitated towards public charity. The *Philadelphia Gazette,* commenting on the Boston complaint that in one week in September, 1835, of the thirty-seven admissions to the poorhouse twenty-nine were Irish, wrote:

> The Bostonians deride the fate of the Irish — they make their name an exponent for barbarity — they send them to labours that produce but little rewards and early death; and they expect that their wives and children shall be blessed with dowries and patrimonies like those of the New England yeoman, who are lords of the soil, and who chooses his own labour and fixes his own price.

Let Boston look, it said tartly, to the immense profits from Irish labor.

The commissioners of the New York almshouse stated that in the winter of 1837-1838, seven tenths of the applicants for outdoor relief were Irish women whose husbands were out of the city, but the commissioners added the husbands were "very particular to be here to vote at the spring election." It should be explained that a nativist city government was in power.

Invariably the initial charity established by the expanding Catholic Church was an orphans' home, but the Church, like the emigrants, had slender resources in its early days to care for its needy. If possible, orphans were distributed among relatives or cared for by neighbors, as in Ireland, under the ancient custom.

The quick assumption of the nativists that the size of the Catholic Irish population in almshouses related to a predisposition for an easy living at the expense of the taxpayers knew not the individual pride of the poor, who chose an existence often harsher than the low-grade security of the poorhouse rather than surrender in the struggle. Nor did they know the nature of the Catholic Irish to whom the poorhouse held a terror more realistic than even poverty: shut off from their fellows in an almshouse, they would miss the gregarious brotherhood of an Irish neighborhood: the loss of freedom of personal movement to a Catholic Irishman was as terrifying as the prospect of Hell's fires.

The nativist indictment of the Catholic Irish for pauperism conveniently overlooked, defenders said, their hardy brawn laboring for material improvement of the country on jobs repugnant to the native-born. The *Truth Teller* struck a note constantly repeated by the Catholic Irish in justification against nativist attacks:

> Irish emigrants are as useful a body of men as can come into a country, because they effect the great bulk of all the hardest labour, and contribute above all others to the wealth, and greatness of the country. Turnpikes, rail-roads, and canals throughout the whole Union attest the industry of the Irish labourer, and his great importance.

The Catholic Irish felt that the public cost of maintaining their paupers was very small in contrast to the wealth they were helping to create by their labor. They also reminded detractors of the head tax emigrants paid to support alien paupers. But the tight-minded nativist saw the emigrant in wholly unfavorable terms, often brutal: the editor of the New York *Courier and Enquirer* described a shipload of Irish emigrants just landed as "live stock."

3

The nativists brought the Catholic Irish up on a more comprehensive and serious charge than pauperism. They were Roman Catholics and, as an article in the *North American Review* in 1832 said, "the word

Catholic was synonymous with guilty." Indeed, according to nativist theology, Roman Catholicism induced pauperism.

Spiritually, intellectually, culturally and emotionally, America was the child of the Reformation. Though the sects differed in ways of church government and points of theology, they had, by origin, agreement on the common distinguishing element of their several professions of faith — a protest against the Roman Catholic Church, marked in the colonies, except Pennsylvania and Rhode Island, by proscriptive statutes against the Roman Catholics.

The noble sentiments of the Declaration of Independence, the revolutionary alliance with Catholic France, and the liberal articles of the Constitution quieted, without eradicating, the anti-Catholicism of the eighteenth century. Dr. MacNeven, in 1807, had noted with some surprise that in the land of liberty he encountered a religious partisanship with which he had been well acquainted in Ireland.

Up to the close of the first quarter of the nineteenth century, the United States had been too busily occupied with its own political and economic problems and the second war with England to be distracted by religious differences, except such intramural political offshoots as the Federalist clergy's attacks on Thomas Jefferson. The greatest single reason for peace on the religious front, however, was that Catholic emigration had not started to flow in numbers to attract attention.

But there were stirrings in the branches. The rise of a religious press, starting with the Boston *Recorder* in 1816, opened an avenue for anti-Popery. It was a custom of the country for the secular press to insert anti-Catholic barbs as a matter of course, without causing the eyebrows of its readers to rise. Bishop John England in Charleston launched the *Catholic Miscellany* on its career in 1822 to explain Catholic principles to a people he conceived as more misinformed than bigoted.

The extension of prejudice against Protestant Irish in the colonies and during the Federalist "reign of terror" to include now the Catholic Irish was noted by the *Truth Teller* in 1826:

> It is impossible even *here* to look around us without encountering *prejudice* against Irishmen, and especially Irish *Catholics,* on every hand and in every quarter. It really seems so strongly to have fastened upon the public mind, that even education itself, with all its expanding power, has been unable to supplant it.

Bishop England, in 1826, found the source of this anti-Catholicism in the English antecedents of the United States. The degradation of the

Catholic up to the time of the Revolution, he thought, stemmed from British policy, contrivance, example, and law. "The feelings of nations," he wrote, "do not suddenly or very quickly subside, much less become altogether different. Only half a century has passed away since this was the case, and it could hardly be expected that all this feeling could be forgotten by this time." The ancestors of Americans had persecuted Catholics, he continued, and Americans could not, and did not, consider their ancestors bad men. It was his observation that gentlemen used words offensive to Catholics, like "Popish priests" and "Romish bishops," in an unthinking way, without meaning to be unkind.

The Americans had established their independence of England without losing the strong English strain in their character and nature. Given this strain, it was human that there should be a reaction to the Catholic Irishman not alone on the score of his religion, but also of his race. "Irishmen have never been favorites with the Anglo-Saxon race," a nativist writer explained, "and it is undoubtedly true that the same feeling which has existed for centuries towards them in England, has, in a more modified and less illiberal form, all along pervaded the Anglo-Saxon race in this country."

4

There seemed to be in Bishop England's analysis in 1826 an optimistic implication of the eventual dissolution of anti-Catholicism with the passing of time. Instead, it was systematized in 1830 for greater effectiveness.

The prospectus in November, 1829, of a new religious journal, *The Protestant,* clearly outlined the offensive which ministers of the evangelical persuasion intended to unlimber against the "Beast," that is, the Roman Catholic Church:

> To inculcate Gospel doctrines against Romish corruptions — to maintain the purity and sufficiency of the Holy Scriptures against Monkish traditions — to exemplify the watchful care of Immanuel over "the Church of God which he hath purchased with his own blood" — and to defend the revealed truth which [a long list of reformers] have approved against the creed of Pope Pius IV and the canons of the Council of Trent — and no article will be admitted into the Protestant, which does not contribute to these desirable results.

This publication, designed to appeal to native American sentiment, was edited by a parson born in Scotland and another from the Canadian circuit.

The integrity of *The Protestant* was put under a grave shadow by a calculated deception upon its editing by a Philadelphia priest born in Ireland, John Hughes, later to be the archbishop of New York. Soon after its appearance, Father Hughes, writing under the pseudonym of "Cranmer," furnished *The Protestant* with a series of letters with "alarming reports of the progress of Catholicity" in Pennsylvania, exaggerated statistics and preposterous accounts of Catholic ceremonies. The editor of *The Protestant* liked the "Cranmer" letters: "We hope," he commented, "our correspondent will supply us with plenty of his *Gospel* ammunition, and it shall be discharged so as to produce the desired results," and he later vouched for the author as a Protestant. After four months of this deception, Father Hughes revealed himself as "Cranmer."

Father Hughes had made his point in exposing *The Protestant,* but the trickery also exposed the Church to the lively suspicion that dubious means were not above employment in striking at opponents, and Catholics themselves expressed disapproval of Father Hughes's deception, the most vociferous being the Irish-born Father Thomas C. Levins, pastor of the Cathedral in New York. Father Hughes later expressed his regret that he had written the "Cranmer" letters.

The rancor of the heated exchanges between two strong-willed Irish-born priests bespoke the troubled state of the infant Roman Catholic Church in the United States that had broken out in its most violent form in the public scandal of the fight between lay trustees and ecclesiastical authority during the 1820s in Philadelphia. The issues as defined, ex parte, by the trustees gave ammunition to the nativist assertion that Roman Catholicism was incompatible with the free institutions of the United States.

5

The tenet that the Roman Catholic Church was the unalterable foe of civil liberty and, therefore, un-American in character formed a keystone of nativism. It adapted to American political circumstances the belief which dated back to Elizabeth's England that a Roman Catholic owed no allegiance to a heretic (Protestant) prince and that no oath bound his conscience when the claims of a state upon his obedience conflicted with the Papacy. A report in 1830 on a sermon at the Park Street Church in Boston by Dr. Lyman Beecher, a leader in shaping the politico-religious form of nativist anti-Popery, concisely set forth this belief:

> He unhesitantly asserted, that he never could look upon a Roman Catholic in the light of a fellow citizen! That such was the power of the Pope and Priests over the conscience of a Catholic, as to induce him easily to break through any oath that interest, or any other consideration may have induced him to take!

The common indictment that an Irishman could not be believed on his oath derived from such doctrine. "All the evidence of every Papist living or dead," wrote the *Protestant Vindicator*, a successor of *The Protestant*, "is not of more weight than a puff of wind; for in all matters connected with the papal craft, it is absolutely impossible for a genuine Papist to speak the truth, or swear to the truth, if his statements will in any way injure Popery and its Priests."

If the priest so exercised power over a Catholic's conscience as to command it on the bedrock matter of loyalty to country, then it followed that the priest directed the Catholic's vote; and as Catholic Irish emigration swelled in the 1830s, the charge mounted that the priest led the Irish voters in hordes to the polls. In New York City, Bishop Dubois took the pains of issuing a public statement that he himself never interfered in politics and held his clergy to the same rule. But you could never believe a Papist priest and, moreover, there were the whispered instructions in that mysterious box, the confessional, which itself bothered and excited the nativists no end.

Persistent in the native American folklore was the expected appearance at almost any moment of the Pope with an invading army, here to be joined by his Catholic Irish legions.

The doubts cast upon the undiluted loyalty to the country he had adopted as home for himself and his children stirred the Catholic Irishman to fervent professions of patriotic devotion. The Catholic Irish *Sentinel* of Boston, in 1835, expressed the feelings of the race in the context of the charge:

> We can tell our dishonorable maligners, that if the Pope's army were to invade the country to-morrow, that every Catholic Bishop and Priest in the Union would, as in duty bound, stimulate all

Catholic citizens to repel the foe, "the strangers to the common-wealth of Israel," — and to defend the American freedom.

In the later and more bitter phase of the nativist movement, Catholic Irish spokesmen, instead of waiting for the Pope and his army to come of his own accord to conquer America, in effect personally invited him to appear if he dared. One Captain Hogan of a Boston military company declared that if the Pope of Rome did come to the United States with hostile intent, we would not kiss his toe (as we are supposed to do) but plant a bayonet in his breast. A Catholic Irishman in charge of a militia company made the point of loyalty even more impressive by including Daniel O'Connell with the Pope as a possible invader (it was not clear where O'Connell was to get an army or why he should lead it to America) and serving notice of the duty of every citizen "to lose his life in repelling the foe."

6

The questioning of the compatibility of the Roman Catholic with the free institutions of America was one prong of the dual politico-religious arraignment by the nativists. The other was the standardized anti-Popery inherited from Europe — "a very ordinary type," one Catholic Irish scholar called it in 1831. The literature of conventional anti-Popery is as voluminous as it is repetitive. The *Jesuit*, a Boston Catholic weekly, summarized in 1830 the high points of the anti-Catholic attacks with material gathered from religious journals, where, it said, any one

> . . . will every where find our religion denominated *Popery*; our-selves, *Papists*; the venerable Head of our Church, *Antichrist*; Rome, the place of his residence, *Babylon*; our worship, *superstitious, idola-trous* and *Pagan*; our ceremonies, *trumpery, mummery*; he will find it asserted over and over again, spite of all we have said to the con-trary, that we *worship idols*; that we fall down before and *adore* wooden gods; that we *deify* the Virgin Mary; that we *pay money* to the *priests* to have our sins forgiven us; that we acknowledge the Saints to be our *Mediators*, instead of *one Mediator, the man Jesus*; that we *despise and forbid* the circulation of the Bible; that we wish to keep the people in ignorance; that we are laboring to have the INQUISITION established in the country; nay, that we have already succeeded in establishing it; — and one of these *veracious* editors, can, if he think proper, even name the very Bishop at the South, who has received the appointment of GRAND INQUISITOR.

It was no secret to the well-informed in those circles which went in for that kind of stuff that Bishop John England of Charleston — the most gentle and charitable of men — had received the appointment from the Pope of Grand Inquisitor for America and that the site of the Pope's residence in the United States had already been selected. The Vatican was to be located in the pork-packing city of Cincinnati.

7

The establishment of *The Protestant* in 1829-1830 was but one manifestation of an evangelical revival within American Protestantism akin to the New Light excitement of Jonathan Edwards in the eighteenth century. The revival was the emotional expression of a vigorous drive of organizational energy among the several Protestant sects to shake religion out of complacency into fruitful purposefulness. Starting in 1824 with the organization of the American Sunday School Union, the activists spread out to establish the American Bible Society, the American Tract Society, and the American Home Missionary Society. The zeal for reform included a movement for stricter observance of the Sabbath, a temperance crusade, war against tobacco and, in the New York Magdalen Society, redemption of, in the phrase of the day, "fallen women." Pressure upon Congress by the evangelical reformers for legislation to prohibit the transportation of mail on Sunday, when measured with the other activities, convinced suspicious Catholic Irishmen that the object aimed at was union of Church and State.

Conversion of the misguided straying in the darkness and despotism of Popery naturally contemplated lessons in its errors. Catholics in Ireland were familiar with this under the name of "proselytism" or, in more colorful terms, "The wolf is on the track!" Stories started to appear in Catholic and Irish weeklies of indignant Catholic Irish stubbornly rejecting the gift of Bibles, stuffing tracts inside the stove, and refusing to barter their faith for jobs. Whether the story was true of missionaries appearing on Monday to take back the shoes from the Irish children who failed to appear at Protestant schools on Sunday, or whether it was an adaptation of a familiar tale in Ireland, one must take into account its general currency.

The most striking figure of the evangelical revival was the Rev. Charles G. Finney, a lawyer converted by a "mighty baptism of the Holy Spirit" after a religious indifference in youth, a powerful preacher of the dread of God's punishment, who became a national figure by the excitement his intensity aroused at evangelical meetings during the decade of 1825-1835, starting in the Utica, Auburn, Rome, Albany, and Troy areas of New York State. The Catholic press issued a warning against the fanatical sect in Troy called "the Finnyites, from the name of the founder, a miserable Impostor, an insignificant driveller of a lawyer." The people he proselyted "were every where known by the deadly hatred they constantly bore to the Catholic Church."

In 1832, the Rev. Mr. Finney came to New York City, the center of the Protestant New Life movement, where the Broadway Tabernacle, the Madison Square Garden of pre-Civil War days, was erected particularly for his talents. Here were true-growth fundamentalists in religion and the full-blown anti-Papists.

Here anti-Popery was organized and systematized through the New York Protestant Association, religious journals, and sympathetic secular newspapers. Aggressive anti-Popery took to public meetings for wider audiences than church congregations, with sponsored lectures on such subjects as "Is the Roman Hierarchy that man of Sin and Son of Perdition, who was predicted by Paul in his second Epistle to the Thessalonians?" Catholic priests challenged speakers at meetings and engaged in set controversy through the columns of the *Truth Teller*. Public debates between Catholic and Protestant controversialists extended through the 1830s: Fathers Levins and Power and Dr. William Brownlee of the Dutch Reformed Church in New York; Bishop Fenwick and Lyman Beecher in Boston; Father John Hughes and Rev. John Breckinridge in Philadelphia; Bishop Purcell and Rev. Alexander Campbell, founder of the Campbellite sect, in Cincinnati; Bishop England and Rev. Richard Fuller in Charleston.

Catholic Irishmen harmed the cause of their Church by bringing muscular Christianity to bear upon theological dialectics. An excited crowd broke up a Protestant Association meeting at Baltimore in 1834 and set to flight the speaker, the Rev. Samuel B. Smith, an apostate priest. The next year, a collection of Catholic Irishmen interrupted a New York meeting addressed by Messrs. Finney and Brownlee on the subject, "Is Popery Compatible with Civil Liberty?" and broke up the furniture. See, proclaimed the jubilant anti-Papists, it's true what we have been preaching: the Catholic Church will not abide civil liberty.

Bishop Dubois immediately cautioned Catholics against "attending at the meetings, taking part in or notice of their proceedings, or in any

way interrupting them, how uncharitable soever they may be." Other
bishops issued similar warnings and the hierarchy formally established
aloofness as official policy.

8

The anti-Popery campaign of charges based on impure doctrine and
the political despotism of Catholicism took a nasty turn with the publication, after the burning in 1834 of the Charlestown convent by a nativist mob, of *Six Months in a Convent* (issued in March, 1835), an in-
nocuous work which became a best-seller overnight and alerted the
knowing to the great popular interest in the mysteries of nunneries,
preferably to the orgies supposed to be held within their walls. A
shameful incident in Pittsburgh in the summer of 1835 underscored
the lurid imagination of the public and willingness to believe the
worst of convents. Acting on a matter of internal discipline, the Bishop
of Detroit, their superior, had ordered the members of a St. Clare convent near Alleghenytown, a suburb of Pittsburgh, moved elsewhere. It
happened that some weeks before Father John O'Reilly, pastor of St.
Paul's Church in Pittsburgh, had left on a vacation. Rumor connected
his absence with the removal of the nuns and put the stamp of vice
and infamy upon it. His loyal congregation took legal action against the
publication of the rumor, and Father O'Reilly hastened back to ask the
Protestants of the city for a fair hearing. The rumors were proved without any foundation whatever, but an ugly state of mind had shown itself.

Ecclesiastical freebooters in New York gathered for a killing at the
appearance of the Rev. William K. Hoyt, a Canadian, with a woman
who had a story to tell. The joint enterprise from the lower depths of
religion produced a work that stands as a monument to human gullibility, *Awful Disclosures of Maria Monk, as exhibited in a narrative of
her sufferings during a residence of five years as a Black Nun in the
Hotel Dieu Nunnery in Montreal,* published in New York in 1836.

It was a Gothic tale of seduction and murder in the Hotel Dieu
Convent of Montreal, all of which Maria witnessed and was a part
of, she vowed. She told of the Mother Superior instructing young nuns
to obey the lustful demands of priests, who came from their residence
by a subterranean tunnel. Babies born of the unholy wedlock were first
baptized and then strangled, and their bodies disposed of in a pit. Nuns

who resisted were suffocated to death between feather beds. Maria had fled the convent, she said, because she was to have a child by a Father Phelan and wanted to save it from death. (Prints were peddled of Maria Monk, with a priest standing behind her with a baby in his arms, with the caption "Maria Monk and Old and Young Father Phelan.")

An affidavit speedily appeared from Maria's mother, to the effect that the girl had not been right in the head since she stuck a slate pencil into it at the age of seven, that she was notorious for telling ridiculous but plausible stories, and that the Rev. Mr. Hoyt had offered Mrs. Monk a hundred pounds if she would swear that Maria had been a nun, which she refused. It developed that Maria Monk had been a prostitute and had been an inmate, not of the Hotel Dieu Convent, but of the Magdalen Asylum, an institution for wayward girls in Montreal. The father of her child was a local Montreal boy.

The *Truth Teller* had immediately discredited the book on internal evidence and showed that, if an ordinary check had been made by the authors and publishers, the manufactured story would have fallen of its own lies. Two respectable Protestant clergymen, with permission of the Bishop of Montreal, had thoroughly inspected the Hotel Dieu Convent, even the sheltered quarters of the nuns accessible to none but their own membership, and reported their conviction that the book was untrue. The complete demolition of the Maria Monk story and of a sequel printed to capitalize on the popular interest came from Colonel William L. Stone, editor of the *Courier and Enquirer,* who happened to be in Montreal in 1836, listened to Montrealers, both Protestant and Catholic, express amazement that the Americans could be such yokels as to put any faith in the book, and received permission from the French Bishop of Montreal to inspect the convent.

Though evidence from numerous sources accumulated of its complete falsity, the book continued to sell: "the three hundred thousand copies of the *Awful Disclosures* sold prior to the Civil War and the editions which have appeared since that time," wrote Ray Allen Billington, the historian of the anti-Catholic crusade, "justly earned for it the questionable distinction of being the 'Uncle Tom's Cabin of Know-Nothingism.' "

9

The Maria Monk fiction and the spate of imitative disclosures it bred touched the Catholic Irish at a sensitive nerve. The thought of immorality among priests and, above all, among nuns was as alien as it was abhorrent to their nature. The Catholic Irishman thought no less of the priest for being overfond of the bottle; he might grumble at the pleading of the priest for more money to build more things; he respected the sternness of a priest enforcing discipline upon an impulsive people with sound whacks. But the ancient austerity of the Irish drew a sharp line at sexual irregularity among the clergy. As for waywardness of nuns, sooner would the Irish accuse their own mothers. The immoral happenings described by Maria Monk and her school simply were not in the experience of the Catholic Irish.

The best expression of American Catholic Irish sentiment on sensational works calculated to degrade the Church on the score of clerical immorality had been written by Mathew Carey in 1826 in an address to the Protestant clergymen of Philadelphia, who had recommended the "disclosures" of an apostate Spanish priest:

> Permit me to ask, gentlemen, have you ever discovered in the conduct of your Roman Catholic fellow citizens, either individually or collectively, anything that warrants the odious character of their religion, in the book, the circulation of which you have so zealously aided by the authority of your respectable names? . . . Suppose its whole contents, so far as regards Spain, Portugal, and Italy were true, and most of it is probably untrue; and suppose, further, that it is right and proper that the chain forged from time to time for nearly three hundred years by avarice, ambition, bigotry and persecuting for the Roman Catholics of Great Britain and Ireland, should remain forever, how does this apply here? . . . Can you lay your hands on anything in the United States, from Maine to Georgia, and from the Atlantic to the Mississippi, like the scenes depicted in those countries, whether true or false?

10

The New York Whig press, through which ran a strong strain of the old Federalist exclusivist spirit, expressed anti-Catholic prejudices but they were part of a political vocabulary directed against the foreign emigrant, notably the Catholic Irishman, who was also a confirmed

Democrat. Editors, reflecting a common American attitude, were inclined to think of the Roman Catholic Church more as a European political system than as a Christian faith.

Theorizing that the Roman Catholic Church was a political system, Samuel F. B. Morse in 1834 fashioned the fundamental ideology that governed the nativist movement and gave it political orientation.

Morse today enjoys an honored place among American immortals for his invention of the electric telegraph, but as a younger man he was an original crusader in the native American movement. An unhappy incident in Rome had soured him against what he called the Papal system. Watching a religious procession from an unobtrusive spot, he was knocked on the head and violently cursed by a papal soldier, who put a bayonet to Morse's breast, for not removing his hat at the passing of the Host. Out of this came the *Foreign Conspiracy Against the Liberties of the United States,* the nativist manifesto. It was first published in 1834 as a series of articles in the New York *Observer,* and in 1835 it appeared in book form, and was widely read in both media.

The pattern Morse worked out in *Foreign Conspiracy* to make an American case against Roman Catholicism as a subversive political agency was an extraordinary, almost a precise, parallel, in structure, substance, even in language, to the contemporary American case against international Communism. Morse's argument, passionate, labored, and repetitive, boiled down to these essentials:

An international conspiracy existed in Europe among the reactionary despotisms of the Holy Alliance, headed by Catholic Austria, to subvert the liberties of the United States. The Holy Alliance, which had enslaved the groaning peoples in its satellite captivity, could not rest secure so long as the free United States stood in contrast at all points with absolute government.

The United States was not to be attacked and conquered by the sword; there were other weapons. "Who among us is not aware that a mighty struggle of *opinion* is in our days agitating all the nations of Europe; that there is a war going on between *despotism* on one side, and *liberty* on the other?"

How was the design of Austria to subvert the United States to be operated? There was in Austria an organization, the St. Leopold Foundation, "ostensibly a religious object," which raised funds for the Catholic Church in the United States, its patron the Emperor of Austria, its guardian the evil Prince Metternich. This society was the creature of the

Austrian government. And the Pope was a puppet of Austria and followed orders.

Morse explained that his remarks had nothing to do "with the *purely religious* character of the tenets of the Roman Catholic sect"; his subject matter was "altogether political."

The agents (the Fifth Column) of the Austrian emperor were the Jesuits, "the most wary order of ecclesiastics," who came and went between Austria and the United States to carry out the design, with funds from the St. Leopold Foundation. These Jesuits concealed their anti-republican sentiments, the better to lull suspicions. The Catholic Church in America professed to ally itself "with the *democracy* of this land; it is loudest in its denunciations of tyranny, the tyranny of American patriots! it is the first to scent out oppression, sees afar off the machinations of the native *American* Protestants to unite church and state! and puts itself forth the most zealous guardian of civil and religious liberty!"

Despotism worked in secret. On the other hand, the United States worked in the open; we had no passport system, no secret police, no censorship, espionage, or control of thought, no examination of the mails, no secret inquisitorial courts. We should only ourselves subvert the free institutions if we tried to match despotism with the instruments of despotism. We tolerated all sects, including "that solitary sect, the Catholic, which builds and supports its system on the destruction of all toleration," which worked "in the light of Protestant toleration" in order to destroy it. Our strongest defense against this planned subversion was to strengthen our moral and intellectual life and, by enlightenment, thwart the dark aims of Popery.

The Jesuits were getting control of education. The priests controlled the votes of Catholics through the confessional and voted them as a body in a deal with unprincipled demagogues for advantages to the Austrian design. The disturbances on canals and railroads were carried on by the Catholic Irish to upset the good order of the Republic and present to watchful Europe the spectacle of republican anarchy. Police were unable to quiet these rioters; they obeyed only their priests, who could now tell their masters, "we already rule the mob." The Irish clanned together as Irish, when they should know no other name than Americans, "and every means has been used and is still used, *especially by Catholics,* to preserve them distinct from the American family."

Catholic strength increased by the steady flow of emigrants, ignorant, benighted, the tools of despotic monarchies. Every "unlettered Catholic emigrant . . . that comes into the country, is adding to a mass of ignorance," difficult to eradicate by republican institutions. We were the "dupes of our own hospitality," which will eventually turn us out of doors.

Then Morse stated the enduring heart of native American policy:

> Our naturalization laws were never intended to convert this land into the almshouse of Europe. . . . No, we must have the law amended that NO FOREIGNER WHO MAY COME INTO THE COUNTRY AFTER THE PASSAGE OF THE NEW LAW .SHALL EVER BE ALLOWED TO EXERCISE THE ELECTIVE FRANCHISE.

The cold war, conflict of ideologies, subversive political infiltration, enemy Fifth Columnists, the Wooden Horse tactics, the difficulty of fighting totalitarianism in a democratic society, the suspicion of the alien, the appeal to one hundred per cent Americanism — the familiar elements of today's headlines were set out by Morse in 1835. There can be no compromise, he declared: "Our religion, *the Protestant religion,* and *Liberty* are identical, and liberty keeps no terms with despotism."

Morse's manifesto showed more ingenious inventiveness than warrantable substance. He had arranged conjecture, assumptions, unrelated facts, bad history and overwrought imagination into a cause of special pleading.

II

His identification of "the Protestant religion and Liberty" seemed to Morse as obvious as the noonday sun, as it would be to both the educated and the uneducated Protestant American, and this included men of generous good will and wide tolerance.

But the Catholic Irishman, out of his own bitter knowledge, identified "the Protestant religion" with a system as despotic as Morse described the sinister evil of Austrian absolutism. He had known political Protestantism at first hand in Ireland, and it had as much relationship to the "Liberty" Morse proclaimed as a stone lying in the road. The Irish associated political Protestantism with an oppressive Ascendancy, landlords, injustice, religious discrimination, and their own poverty. They were still bearing the assaults, blows, and insults of Protestant Orangeism. They hated kings, emperors, dukes, and princes for reasons well founded in history. To think that they wanted to make the Emperor of Austria the ruler of America, when they had left Ireland to escape the blight of a monarchical system, was not only an offense against common sense; it was cant and hypocrisy.

The Protestant American pictured the Roman Catholic Church in terms of a medieval tyranny, the persecutor of heretics, the inquisitor of the free conscience, the ally of Spanish and Austrian obscurantism. The Irishman knew Catholicism as the anvil for the hammer of Protestant persecution. His priests had been hunted like beasts. His fathers had attended Mass in secret places with watchers posted on the alert for soldiers with bayonets. His grandfathers had been denied education because they were Catholics and turned out of their ancient lands by the fact of their religion.

Yet, with their whole history crying out against the unfairness of the accusation, the Catholic Irish were included in the general indictment of Roman Catholicism as despotism. It was difficult to find a meeting of minds.

12

Thus, in the middle 1830s, native Americanism had taken its main ideological form, built around a few central ideas. It was anti-foreign and anti-Catholic, personalized in the Catholic emigrant, the Irishman in particular. But so long as the deeply grounded principle of religious liberty prevailed, not the slightest chance obtained of resurrecting the old colonial penal laws against Catholicism, and so long as the country needed population and cheap labor, no possibility could be entertained of restricting the free flow of emigration to the United States. The way to save the country, then, was to revive the Federalist expediency of the Alien and Sedition Acts and strike through restrictions on the naturalization laws that would deprive the emigrant of political status and remove his influence in political affairs.

Major Mordecai Noah, editor of the New York *Evening Star*, said in 1835, as indirectly quoted by the *Truth Teller*, that the American people "are willing to receive Irishmen here — to give them a place on the soil — to give them the protection of the laws of this country — and to permit them to share in the liberties of the Union, but they must take no part in the government, aspire to no office, and claim no part of the rights of the American citizen."

What infuriated the nativists was the enthusiasm with which the Catholic Irish threw themselves into partisan politics, the noise they made in shouting up their favorite candidates, the assertiveness of their political opinions and their readiness to back up their views with physical force, and their belligerent rejection of the idea that in politics they should conduct themselves like well-behaved servants grateful for the privilege allowed them of voting, on the assumption that the native-born were endowed with a priority over the naturalized.

The nativist method to eliminate the emigrant from politics called for a revision of the naturalization laws to extend the probationary period of the applicant for citizenship from five years, then the legal requirement, either to fourteen years, the term that had been fixed by the Federalists in the John Adams administration, or to twenty-one years.

13

The three-day New York election riots in 1834 and the breaking up of the Brownlee-Finney Protestant Association meeting in March, 1835, set in the excited climate of anti-Popery agitation, induced men who thought like Morse to put their heads together for means to curb the Catholic Irish.

In June, 1835, anti-foreign sentiment politically organized itself in New York City into the Native American Democratic Party to promote a program of opposition to officeholding by the foreign-born, to pauper and criminal emigration, and to the Catholic Church. Tammany countered this movement by a meeting of American citizens in the Irish Sixth Ward to uphold the virtues of the foreigner. But in the fall election Tammany failed to nominate a foreign-born candidate, despite which the Catholic Irish went straight down the line for the party. Tammany had observed in the Five Points riots during the summer the bitterness of anti-Catholic Irish sentiment in the city.

Gangs of nativist toughs had for some time concentrated upon the Catholic Irish as legitimate prey. Young American butcher boys, running in gangs, took sport in beating the Irish as hated foreigners. Low-life native Americans, uneducated, filled with prejudices, a cut above or in the same economic category, were consistently the turbulent antagonists of the laboring Irish. Resentment, if not the fear, of economic competition for work with the Irish entered into this hostility, a theme constantly played upon in nativist literature. The complaint was not so much that the Catholic Irish deprived them of jobs as that the Irish accepted lower wages and, with the reservoir of emigrant labor, forced and kept down the scale of wages.

Yet the Irish came under attack from an opposite source, the employers, for a different reason: their strikes, or "turn-outs," for higher wages. "Our citizens," declared a nativist mayor of New York in 1837, "had no serious turn-outs — no riotous parades — no conspiracies against the business and families of quiet, industrious and honest operators, until after officious interference by mischievous strangers." The previous year, Irish stevedores had struck for higher wages and a number of their leaders had been jailed for rioting.

A meeting had been called for Tuesday, June 23, 1835, by a Catholic Irish politician to form a military company under the name of the O'Connell Guards in the Sixth Ward. With the spirit of nativism active, "the making of an *Irish* regiment out of American citizens," as the organization plan was dubbed, filled the mouths of demagogues with hot words. The Irish have determined to put down the natives, it was said; they were organizing the O'Connell Guards to that end.

The meeting never got together. On the Sunday before the date set, the gathering tension exploded in a series of riots in different parts of the city between the natives and the Irish that continued for three days. In the ferocious fighting that took place early Sunday evening in Pearl Street, near Chatham (now Park Row), in the Sixth Ward, an innocent passer-by, Dr. William McCaffrey, a respected physician, father of a large family, an Irishman and a Whig, was knocked to the ground by a stone while hurrying to a patient, trampled upon, and died soon after his rescue. The appearance of the mayor ended the riot.

Nobody had respect for the watch, as the haphazard police force was called, and certainly the Irish had no reason by experience to expect even-handed treatment, or even protection, from them.

With the memory of the burning of the Charlestown convent by a mob fresh in their minds, the Catholic Irish, fearing an attack upon St. Patrick's Cathedral, prepared their own defenses. The street approaches were torn up and barricades erected with wagons and carts. Under the leadership of a brace of powerful men, grim-faced Irishmen moved into the church itself and the adjoining cemetery and, armed with weapons of every description, set themselves for a nativist attack. A mob of rioters, heading for the cathedral, wavered and stopped and then retreated before the fortified line the Irish had established. On Monday night, the rioting again picked up, with the nativists making a frontal attack upon the Green Dragon, a public house near Broome Street, which they wrecked. The mayor once more appeared, accompanied by prominent citizens and the police, but the mob action was not dispersed until a great amount of blood had been shed. On Tuesday night, mobs again broke loose and continued the wrecking. But quiet gradually settled upon the strife-torn streets when news circulated that the meeting to organize the O'Connell Guards had been called off.

The New York *Herald* blamed the Irish for starting the riots. An account from an Irish source, after describing the scenes of mob activities as looking "like those of a town taken by an enemy," painted a black picture:

> Gangs of butcher's boys, dissipated young men, idle vagabonds, and sanguinary desperadoes, were seen walking up and down, with savage yells of "down with the Irish," coupled with horrid blasphemies against their religion; here breaking the doors, windows and furniture of some obnoxious European; there brutally knocking down every foreigner found in their way; again, hurling stones at the Orphan Asylum, and threatening to burn the Cathedral, to the great consternation of the whole city.

14

The Whig press, spokesman for the minority party in New York City politics, had in rasping language attacked, abused, condemned, and mocked the Catholic Irish since the Jackson victory in 1832, but the object was more to serve political than anti-Popery aims by the exploitation of anti-Catholic prejudice. The local Whig Party struck an alliance with the native American party in the fall election of 1835 and showed considerable strength. In 1836, a presidential election year, the nativist Americans, many of whom were Van Buren Democrats, avoided association with the Whigs and, as an independent party, nominated Morse as candidate for mayor in the municipal election, but he polled only some 1500 votes out of a total of 30,000, demonstrating that the party could not stand alone. The Whigs appreciated that their best hope for local victory lay in using the native American party to attract nativists away from the Democrats. In 1837, the native Americans nominated Alderman Aaron Clark for mayor with an out-and-out anti-Irish, anti-Catholic address, which declared:

> What mean the extended league of Irish societies through your land? What mean the systematic effort of these Foreigners to keep themselves distinct from the American people? . . . What motives move them to vote? What appeals stir them? Not American but foreign interests, the interests of Ireland. . . . The foreign politician, distinguished in a cassock, is behind the curtain, and moves the wires. He it is who governs them. He speaks the name of the candidate, and his flock is ready with their colored ballots. They rally as Irishmen, not as Americans; they rally under the green banner, not the stars and stripes.

The meeting approved a program calling for a residence of twenty-one years by aliens before naturalization, exclusion from public office of all but native Americans or naturalized citizens of twenty-one years' residence, and a registration of voters to end electoral frauds.

The Whigs established a complete fusion with the nativists and, aided by an economic depression, elected Clark mayor and put into office a nativist-tinged council. The consequence of this sizable victory in New York City was the extinction of the first native American party in politics, absorbed by the Whigs.

It was during this time that Patrick S. Casserly publicly disavowed the Whigs, and his experience was a Catholic Irish mirror of the times. Casserly, a graduate of Dublin's Trinity College, proprietor of a classical academy in New York, translator of Longinus, a prolix contributor of opinionated articles to the Catholic and Irish press under the name of "Sarsfield," had studied American politics before he emigrated in 1828 and concluded that Federalist-Whig principles were correct. He had been vice-president of a Whig convention of naturalized citizens. But the anti-Catholic and anti-Irish agitation brought him to renounce "all connection with the illiberal, intolerant, and persecuting" Whig Party of New York and join the Democratic Party. He had had enough.

The Clark administration proceeded to kick out the Democratic officeholders, down to the lowliest Catholic Irish lamplighter, including Major Denman of the *Truth Teller*, who had been the city's printer. The Board of Aldermen authorized the Commissioners of the Almshouse to transship, with their consent, alien paupers who were, or were likely to be, public charges, with "at the same time . . . no prejudice to the cause of humanity." Despite its solicitude for "the cause of humanity," the Clark administration raised the head tax on emigrants from one to ten dollars and then barricaded the entrances to New York City when masters of vessels, to avoid the tax, dumped sick and diseased Irish emigrants at Perth Amboy and other places in New Jersey, which had no alien tax, without accommodations, sometimes landing them up creeks in the mosquito-infested marshes to find their own way in a foreign land. But this brutality had a beneficial consequence, in awakening responsible Catholic Irish to the need of a society to protect emigrants.

15

Dr. William MacNeven, with Thomas O'Connor and Major Denman of the *Truth Teller*, had, in 1829, revived the Shamrock Friendly Association, an early emigrant society, under the name of the Union Emigrant Society to assist newcomers into jobs. It confined itself to the functions of an intelligence office and successfully placed hundreds of Irish emigrants on public works, in domestic service, and with farmers. But, always short of funds, it appealed to the Common Council for a small appropriation, arguing that by finding work for the unemployed it saved the city the cost of supporting them at public expense. The Council rejected the petition on the ground the society encouraged emigration and, in the debate, revealed a strong anti-Irish prejudice. Because of this refusal, the Union Emigrant Society closed its doors, lacking private means to continue.

The disgraceful punitive policy of the Clark nativist administration towards emigrants, together with mounting frauds practiced on them, turned the attention of the New York Catholic Irish to another attempt at organization. The kind words on emigrants by Governor William H. Seward in his message to the state legislature in 1839 aroused activity and late in May of that year the Irish Emigrant Relief Association was announced. Its prospectus detailed a typically Irish grandiose plan — on paper. Its performance seems to have been confined to meetings at the Apollo Saloon on Broadway and a drive to scare up members and raise funds. Within a few weeks its secretary resigned, pleading the pressure of business, but the expressed hope of the *Truth Teller* that "the designs of the illiberal or the treacherous may never be engrafted upon an institution which has charity and the general good for its only object" suggested that the society had fallen into self-interested hands.

The closing of the columns of the *Truth Teller* to its proceedings proclaimed a repudiation of the society, and it fell apart. Later inquiries into the disposition of its funds ran into a blank wall.

The prosperous part of the Catholic Irish community, with a few exceptions, showed no great interest in the welfare of the poor emigrant class except as it operated through the charitable agencies of the Church. The emigrant world itself felt under no constraint to support an organized effort to assist newcomers, but it faithfully honored the Irish code of individual help to relatives and friends just arrived: the impersonality of a social welfare society struck the Irish imagination negatively.

Fortunately a Catholic Irishman of substance, Robert Hogan, a merchant, who merits a place of high recognition in the American Irish story for a fine social conscience and usefulness, thought that "Irishmen holding a social position" were under obligation to care for their poorer emigrant countrymen. As President of the Friendly Sons of St. Patrick, the elite New York Irish society, he had become acquainted with emigrant abuses, particularly in remittances to Ireland, and on December 9, 1839, he wrote for advice on the formation of an emigrant society to Dr. MacNeven, who responded encouragingly.

A man of lesser character and dedication than Hogan would have despaired at the wall of apathy and indifference he encountered. A year and two months after he addressed Dr. MacNeven, he finally issued a call for a public meeting on February 18, 1841, with the approval of Bishop Hughes. The handful of the faithful in Irish good works rallied, but the general attendance was small. Despite discouragement, Hogan persisted and on March 22, 1841, he announced the formation of the Irish Emigrant Society, with Dr. MacNeven as president and himself as vice-president.

Immediately the society came under vigorous open attack and a malicious underground whispering campaign — by the Irish themselves. Professional Democratic Catholic Irish politicians, who had with calculation been excluded from place in the society, smeared its sponsors as "aristocrats." The class dislike and distrust by the emigrants of the Friendly Sons of St. Patrick, from whose membership came leaders of the society, was invoked to discredit the new organization. The poison tongue of "Slippery Dick" Connolly, the shady politician, hinted that the funds of the society would disappear like those of the dissolved Emigrant Relief Society. The whisper was planted that the "aristocrats" intended to send emigrants to Jamaica to take the place of the emancipated slaves and to dump land speculations upon the innocent Irish emigrant. Vested interests in robbing the emigrant along the waterfront joined in blackening the honest intentions of the society. The patriotic Irish society formed to aid O'Connell's political campaign in Ireland feared the competition of the emigrant society for funds.

Hogan proved indomitable and plowed ahead (at one time the society had only $30.35 in its treasury) and then the tide turned, with the proceeds of a gala ball to replenish the exchequer and the grant of five hundred dollars from the board of aldermen. Poor emigrants started to attend its meetings, and Horace Greeley threw his influence on its side.

On November 12, 1842, it was proclaimed that the society was no longer an experiment, and its useful work in protecting and finding work for the emigrants, meeting incoming ships, and handling remittances began to show returns. Thanks to the courage and determination of Robert Hogan, the most successful of all Irish emigrant societies was prepared for its task when the flood of Famine emigration started half a decade later. Singlehanded he had braved and defeated the mean prejudices of his professional Irish countrymen for the good of the people of his own blood.

16

The first phase of the native American movement had quieted down by the time the New York Irish Emigration Society started, but the inspiration of the New York native American party had encouraged nativist endeavors elsewhere.

Early in 1837, Henry Clay, by request and not in sympathy, presented to the Senate a petition by fifty-seven inhabitants of Wurtsboro, Sullivan County, New York, asking for the disfranchisement of Roman Catholics because their creed was inconsistent with the principles of American government and "it is there intention Sooner or Later to out number the Protestants at the Ballor Box and if that Should Ever be Realized we need no look for any laws more mild than have been Realized in France Spain and Portugal." It denounced the Pope as "the most desperate Potentate and Persecutor of Protestants on the face of the whole earth" and asked for public inspection of nunneries every six months. Other petitions, less illiterate but of the same nature, appeared.

Now, in the light of this primitive and crude anti-Catholic nativism, there came an interesting and certainly surprising development. The first nativist organization with a declared ambition to be national in character, the Native American Association of the United States, was formed in Washington on July 11, 1837 — and its moving spirit was a Roman Catholic, Henry J. Brent, of an old Maryland family, who had been educated at a Catholic college, Mount St. Mary in Emmittsburg. And on the rolls of the association were found "the names of many highly respectable members of the Catholic Church."

The purpose of the association was to unite Americans "as brothers to sustain the strength and purity of their political institutions" and establish a national character free of foreign pollution. To that end it asked the cooperation of all native-born Americans for the repeal of the naturalization law entirely and the exclusion of all foreigners from office, whether under the federal or the state governments, vowing to hold guilty any public officer who placed a foreigner in a job while there was a competent native willing to fill it.

Its constitution divorced the association from any connection "with any religious sect or denomination, leaving every creed to its own strength, and every man untrammeled in his own faith." Its newspaper, the *Native American,* while it printed violent attacks on foreigners, drew the line sharply at anti-Catholic agitation. A memorial to Congress from petitioners of Washington County, New York, against the introduction of "foreign Catholics" into the United States, brought a rebuke from the paper: "This is outrageous — we will not hold with these particularizing sectarians for one moment in their particularizing patriotism." And it denied any right to stigmatize fellow Christians.

Nativism among settled Catholics illuminated the basic anti-foreign character of the movement, at least in its origins. The membership of the New Orleans Native American Association contained Catholic Creoles. On several occasions in the course of the nativist movement, the question arose of divorcing it from the anti-Catholic issue, the better to concentrate on restricting the foreigner. Robert Walsh, editor of the *Quarterly Review* and son of a Catholic Irish father, favored a longer period of probation for aliens. Indeed, the spirit of nativism insinuated itself within the walls of the Church for a time.

If the Washington Native American Association barred anti-Popery, it did not spare its rods on the back of the Catholic Irishman. The official organ drew a distinction between the Irish of an earlier period and the new — and undesirable — Irish emigrants. After the Emmets, Sampsons, and MacNevens, it said, "emigrants became of less moral worth." It reprinted stories derogatory of the Irish: an Irish woman begged bread, "For the honor of God," from a passing stranger; he loaded her with groceries for herself and her brood of children; a snooper followed her into a grog shop where she exchanged the supplies for rum. The Irish, it reported, were taking jobs from honest Americans. The Irish were "too foolish to govern — they are too strong to be governed. Are these people then fit to govern us?" it asked. It reprinted the handbill circulated in the New York municipal election of 1839 and which became a show piece of nativist propaganda:

> IRISHMEN, to your posts, or you will lose America. By perseverance, you may become its rulers; by negligence, you will become its slaves. Your own country was lost by submitting to ambitious men. This beautiful country you gain by being firm and united. Vote the ticket, ALEXANDER STEWART, Alderman, EDWARD FLANAGAN, for Assistant — both true IRISHMEN.

The Irish, "foolish" though the nativists thought them to be, were not so foolish as to distribute such a handbill or seek Irish votes in that manner or language: it had all the appearance of a typical campaign canard, with which the Irish became familiar. The Irish anecdote of course appeared: " 'What kind of a country is this?' said an Irishman, who attempted to pick up a stone that was frozen to the ground. 'You let your dogs run loose, and tie your stones.' "

"In the name of God," it cried, "do we want these people here?"

17

On July 2, 1838, the select committee of the House of Representatives, to which the several petitions and memorials of individuals, societies and of the cities of Boston and New York had been referred, issued a report through its chairman, which, incorporating the substance of the petitions, made an extremist attack upon foreign emigrants and recommended a bill restricting the naturalization law. The House refused to take action, and the first round of the fight to penalize the emigrant ended.

18

The Bamber case, which developed in February, 1838, proved that if the Whigs wanted to line up with the native Americans, the Democrats intended to stay with the Irish; it confirmed also the fact that with increasing emigration Catholic Irish political strength was on the rise in New York City and could not be disregarded.

The Bambers, County Antrim Protestant Irish, a violent and willful family of a father and three sons, had shot and killed a constable in 1830 while resisting arrest. John, the father, and James, a son, had escaped to New York. Documentary testimony was forwarded from Ireland to the British consul in New York, who had them apprehended, and secured from Governor William L. Marcy their surrender to British authorities for trial in Ireland. Marcy apparently handled the matter in routine fashion, but the Bambers sought out Alderman Brady of the Sixth Ward for advice. A protest meeting was held in a public house, resolutions censuring Marcy were passed, and a committee of prominent Irish political leaders was appointed to handle the case. The best Irish lawyers of the New York bar volunteered their services and, calling on Governor Marcy in Albany, presented evidence which induced that skillful politician, not unmindful of the Irish vote, to reverse his decision and free the Bambers. An enthusiastic meeting of their countrymen gathered in City Hall Park to greet the released Bambers "with most joyous acclaim."

But in a relatively brief time the Bambers, cheered as Irish heroes, were damned as Orangemen: they had been reached by the Whigs and issued a pamphlet recounting their persecution at the hands of Governor Marcy. It developed that they were not only traitors against the Democratic Irish who had secured their release, but that they had been informers against their Catholic neighbors in Ireland. When the Whigs attempted to make the Bamber case a political issue in the fall campaign, a committee of Catholic Irishmen called on Governor Marcy and, with a great flourish, endorsed his release of the Bambers and exonerated him from all "foul imputation" of political enemies.

19

In that election, William H. Seward was chosen Whig Governor of New York and, after the din of nativist pursuit, the Catholic Irish, to their great joy and surprise, heard a friendly voice speak in kind terms of the emigrants in his message to the legislature. Governor Seward urged in effect a new deal for the belabored emigrants: that they not only be welcomed and naturalized without regard to creed or place of birth, but also that they be admitted in good faith into the membership of the American family on the same footing as the native-born.

Though the Catholic Irish politicians unsheathed Democratic knives against Seward, whom they suspected of seeking votes, the Catholic Irish heard this new note like a voice in the wilderness. It received a particularly warm welcome especially in the land of the Pilgrim and the Puritan where the Catholic Irish had been going through an ordeal, in one instance an ordeal by fire.

3 1
"The Icicles of Yankee Land"

THE IRISH ON THE *Maria Eliza,* from Cork to St. John, caught in an ice floe and carried to Greenland, received a more hospitable welcome from the Eskimos than the Irish who came to Boston received from the Yankees.* The Catholic Irish could not have settled in any section of the United States less inviting to their prospects.

"New England, taken on the whole," said Grattan, the British consul in Boston, "is the hardest soil for an Irishman to take root and flourish in." Or as Thaddeus Murrough said to Dorah Mahony in Lowell: "The people here don't like our folks at all at all." A Boston newspaper in 1836, commenting on an appeal from New Orleans that if New Englanders did not want the Irish, Louisiana could put them to work at good wages, wrote: "There, Irishmen, pack up your duds and be off. We can spare you very easily."

From the outset, the self-sufficient Yankee nation looked upon Catholic Irish emigration "as an intrusion, and resented as such." The Catholic Irish were made to feel in New England, as a British statesman had characterized them in relation to old England, that they were "aliens in race, language and religion."

It was an ironic (and harsh) twist of fate that the Catholic Irishman

* The word "Yankee'" is used here in its original meaning of native-born New Englander of English stock.

who left his native land to escape the thralldom of the English settled in New England amidst the purest Anglo-Saxon stock in the United States — a stock, moreover, from which Oliver Cromwell had sprung. He had disavowed the Cromwellian Ascendancy by the Shannon and the Lee but in New England encountered the "aristocracy of yeomen," in the phrase of William A. Leahy, by the Charles and the Connecticut. As nowhere else in the United States, the old Celt and Saxon opposition was re-enacted in New England.

The English character of Boston struck the foreign traveler. While the majority of Americans denied that they were English, the Bostonians, he observed, "consider themselves, and pride themselves, as being peculiarly English."

The population of New England was the most homogeneous in the United States, and Boston, commented Mathew Carey, "has as few foreigners as perhaps any town in the world." A writer in the *North American Review* in 1834 chided an English visitor who had written a book unfavorably analyzing the New England Yankee. The same charges you have brought against the New Englander, he said, were the mirror of the English character to the world — excessive gravity, external coldness and reserve, exclusive devotion to gain, an indisposition to be amused and an overweening estimate of their own advantages, political and personal.

Within New England, the solid yeomanry outside Boston thought the people of Boston put on airs. Sylvester S. Southworth, the plebeian editor of the Providence *Literary Subaltern*, visited Boston and was distressed by what he found there. "The citizens of Boston," he wrote, "make unbounded pretentions to plain republican simplicity, and yet a more confirmed race of aristocrats never existed." There was in their manner, he noted, "a frigid kind of aristocratical feeling, which is excessively repulsive, and well calculated to offend those, who would approach them, with gentlemanly, yet not obstruse or indelicate freedom, and extend to them the naked hand of honest, yet justly provoked friendship." Boston, this Rhode Island Yankee concluded, was nice to visit "but not a place that I would like to live in."

2

New England was the stronghold of the orthodox in religion. The vigorous but narrow strain of the original Puritan had shaped the character of New England. The Roman Catholic Church loomed in the minds of the orthodox as the mighty medieval despotism, the unchanging enemy of their American liberties as it had been of the Protestant liberties of their forefathers in England. Though the bulk of the orthodox in New England had not set eyes on a Papist until the appearance of the Catholic Irish, they knew him through Foxe's *Book of Martyrs* and the sermons of the minister, to whom anti-Popery was as much an article of faith as any doctrine of the creed. They saw the Irishman with a hod on his shoulder as both the agent of the Anti-Christ in Rome and his victim in the darkness of superstition; they felt the need both to suppress and save him.

The Dudleian Lecture at Harvard set the intellectual tone for the orthodox. It was founded in 1750 by prosperous Paul Dudley "for the detecting and convicting and exposing of the idolatry of the Romish church; their tyranny, usurpations, damnable heresies, fatal errors, abominable superstitions and other crying wickedness in her high places." The widow of Deacon Ingersoll in Stockbridge was no doubt in her ordinary affairs a good and kindly woman but when somebody suggested to her that Mass be celebrated in the small shop she had rented to one of the town's first Irish settlers, she exploded: "The shop turned into a Cathedral! No, I would rather burn it!" Father P. J. Lenihan heard a Pascoag, Rhode Island, native open up on the Irish and Catholics: they were the dupes of priests; they came to confession and gave the priest money and he forgave their sins but the priest could forgive them as much as his horse; he denounced Ireland and regretted that "good old England" was not treating the Irish half as they deserved. "It is said," reported a serious-minded New Englander, who prided himself on his intelligence and goodness, "that a few days since [this was in 1835] in one of our manufacturing villages, a priest came from the city, and in the course of the afternoon pardoned seventy dollars' worth of sins; — a very profitable half-day's job!"

George T. Curtis, representative of the finest spirit of Boston, just and decent, addressed the Charitable Irish Society in Boston on St. Patrick's Day in 1841 and asked the members "not to be as you are by national temper — impatient" in the matter of open antagonism to the Roman Catholics, explaining candidly:

> There are causes for the existing position of Catholics in a Protestant country, long anterior to the present age, which you people should look at, and looking at which, their good sense will enable

them to make allowances. Such a contest as that which began and was carried on in the Reformation, for ages, could not but leave much bitterness, for many other ages, behind it. Here too, you are to remember that to all this is to be added the peculiar traits of the Puritans. You know that our fathers fled, not merely from the Church of Rome, but because, to their consciences, the Church of England was too like that of Rome, to be tolerated by them; and you will not wonder, therefore, that some traces of that feeling have descended to their children.

It happened that the three sects — Unitarian, Quaker and Protestant Episcopal — least antagonistic to Roman Catholicism were small in numbers in New England in comparison to the orthodox Calvinists. The sects which had drawn their spiritual strength primarily from Geneva remained the most virulent in anti-Popery: the original Puritan reformers, who willed to cleanse Elizabeth's reformation of its Popish trumpery, had been schooled at Geneva; and John Knox had the true Geneva fire in his belly.

3

When the Catholic Irish first came to New England, the influence of Puritan piety still obtained. Christmas was an ordinary workday: shops were opened for business and plants operated. Thanksgiving was the New England religious feast day in place of Christmas, and each year, in accordance with the custom of the Puritan theocracy, a day was publicly proclaimed by the Governor of Massachusetts of "humiliation, fasting, and prayer" — a substitution, the Catholic Irish said, for the observance of Good Friday. The secular influences of a growing commercial center and the spread of non-theological Unitarianism reduced the ascendancy of the orthodox clergy in Boston from its former dominance, and a rising middle class was spreading itself among other denominations of the Protestant faith. But a robust Protestant spirit reigned supreme in the northeastern corner of the United States.

In this stronghold of the old orthodoxy, an older faith started to raise its crosses among the weathercocks on the steeple of meetinghouses. Perhaps the oldest story that contrasted Roman Catholicism and Protestanism in New England centered around these symbols. A Protestant asked a Boston Irishman why his church had not a weathercock, as the Protestants had. "For a very plain reason," the Irishman is reported to have replied. "You do well to have weather-cocks on your Churches, for they are like your faith *veering about with every wind of Doctrine;* but our Cross, like our Faith, is stedfast and immoveable."

Boston Protestants on their way to Sunday church observed with varied feelings the sight of Irish men and women, with beads in their hands, kneeling on the hard pavement outside the Cathedral of the Holy Cross or rising in unison as they followed the celebration of Mass inside where every inch of space was occupied by worshipers. The true built-in Yankees of Sandwich on Cape Cod gaped in frank curiosity at the unprecedented procession that started from John Doyle's tavern on Sunday, September 19, 1830, and passed through the main street to the little church the Catholic Irish had built. Never before had they set eyes on a Roman Catholic prelate and here was stout Bishop Fenwick of Boston, dressed in full pontificals, come to dedicate the church, attended by Father Barber, the New England convert, and in the line every Irishman in the vicinity, some of whom had walked eighteen miles from Wareham to participate and who would have something to talk about on the long trek back. A writer in the Boston *Daily Advertiser* warned Bishop Fenwick and Father O'Flaherty, who were carrying on a theological debate with Rev. Lyman Beecher in 1831, to keep in their place: "Let the Roman Catholic Bishop and his Colleague," he said, "reflect where they are. They are not in corrupt and profligate Rome, where such outrages are no offence." A preacher, speaking of the increase of Catholics in Boston, exclaimed: "Oh that the wide Atlantic had for ever separated us!"

A self-contained, self-centered and self-satisfied culture, narrowly Protestant in religion, Anglo-Saxon in its dispositions and aristocratical in its surety of superiority, cold in exterior, standoffish in temperament and provincial in its attitudes, came face to face with the invasion of this tight small world by the Catholic Irish, who were as different in vital respects as visitors from Mars. It would have been a counsel of perfection to expect that the New England Yankees, traditionally content to live among themselves without the presence of strangers, would take these foreigners to their breasts in the spirit of the Declaration of Independence and of the Constitution. They believed they had the most advanced culture in the United States and now it was disturbed by a race they disliked and stubbornly, like the English, refused to try to understand.

The movement to convert Catholic Ireland to Protestantism by converting the Catholic Irish in America was an instance in point. The

Boston *Recorder* seriously undertook such a campaign in 1835. Some five million Catholics in Ireland, it argued, were headed for perdition because they obeyed the Pope and his priests instead of God "and degrade themselves with whiskey-drinking, fighting and other vices." The bulk of the laboring class that came to this country were Irish, and it was in their conversion that the redemption of Ireland must be sought. The Catholic Irish "are essentially one nation, whether in this country or in Ireland." Note the Irish news in the papers; observe how the Irish are constantly writing home; witness the emigrant funds remitted to Ireland and the advertisements soliciting this business. Suppose a hundred thousand, or even ten thousand, Catholic Irish were "really converted to Christ" in the United States. The consequence would be ten thousand letters to Ireland preaching the Gospel in every part of that country. These letters from the loved ones in the United States sooner or later would take effect upon the people in Ireland and reform would come from within. How can the conversion in the United States fail to win Ireland? Moreover: "By the conversion of Ireland, the danger of Roman Catholic ascendancy in the United States would be annihilated at a blow."

The saints would have to gird for the contest, though. A minister in a New England town invited an Irishman to his church, but the Irishman excused himself by saying he had no good clothes to wear. The minister gave him a new suit, but the priest stopped the Irishman from attending the services. When the minister asked the Irishman if he should not judge for himself, he received an answer typically Irish, obvious to every Irishman but beyond the comprehension of the minister. *"If he* [the priest] *tells me wrong,"* the Irishman said, *"the worst is his own. He must answer for it, not I."*

The incident was revealing of the obtuseness of the orthodox clerical mind to the psychology of the Catholic Irish race: if the penal laws in Ireland had failed dismally to change their faith, what hope had an orthodox minister who insulted their faith and the priests while attempting to persuade them to the light? Orthodox New England marked off to incorrigible superstition and benighted ignorance the refusal of the Catholic Irish to see what appeared to be the obvious: the advantages, moral and material, of the enlightenment that followed the torch of the reformed faith. "It is almost in vain," wrote a conventional New Englander, "to argue with an Irish Catholic. He is impervious to reason."

How could the Yankees hope to understand the Catholic Irishman when their experience had never encountered the undisciplined imagination of the true Gael, like the one who told a sober-sided New Englander of how a priest turned a man into a cow? The genuine Yankee, though he wore a coat of reserve, was as inquisitive as a crow; and this particular one had maneuvered a good-natured and friendly Irishman into conversation, resolving, as he admitted, "that I would try to make known to him 'Christ and him crucified.' " The Yankee told the Irishman that the priests deceived the people, and the Gael responded that the priests could perform miracles, which was more than the parsons could do. One had been worked in his own father's house in Ireland, he avowed:

> There were a great many hundred people there. And there was a man who was mad with the priest. He saw the priest going by, and he went out and cursed him. The priest told him he had better stop; and he would not stop. He swore and cursed the priest, and all the people heard him. Then the priest turned around and said to all the people, "Now do you look and see God punish this man for his sins." Then the priest looked at him, and pointed at him with his finger, and said a few words that nobody could understand, and the man was turned into a cow. And the people were all frightened, and looked at the cow, and while they were looking, her horns grew out *two miles high into the air.*

The Irishman had not seen this happen, "but my father did, and I never knew him to tell a lie in my life!" The Yankee admitted that he had been worsted and changed the subject, checking off to superstition what might have been a vigorous pull on his leg.

How could the Irishman, for his part, hope to understand the Yankee when the latter had facets of character that struck the Irishman as not only remote but distasteful and hypocritical, of which the story Julian Hawthorne told of his father and of his uncle, Horace Mann, was an instance. Nathaniel Hawthorne, the author, once admitted in the presence of Mann, an earnest and humorless spirit, that he occasionally smoked a cigar. "Did I understand you to say, Mr. Hawthorne, that you actually use tobacco?" asked Mann in a state of great excitement. "Yes, I smoke a cigar once in a while," was the reply. Mann, a great admirer of Hawthorne's genius and for whom he held deep affection as a man, rose from his seat and paced the room in agitation, torn between the principle that tobacco was an evil and his feelings for the writer as a human being. Principle won, and he exclaimed in a voice filled with censure, "Then, Mr. Hawthorne, it is my duty to tell you that I no longer have the same respect for you that I had" and strode from the room.

Such moral attitudinizing on a simple creature comfort like tobacco struck the Catholic Irish as the sheerest cant. To place the duty of disliking tobacco above a warm human attachment for a man violated, to the Catholic Irishman, the code of personal loyalty and sacrificed natural feelings. Projected into other fields, this moralizing on human frailties indulged by the Yankees appeared to the Catholic Irish as pharisaical.

4

The Catholic Irish had an instinctive distrust of reform and of novelty. The optimistic belief of advanced Boston thinkers in the perfectibility of man did not jibe with their religious creed of the constancy of the old Adam in frail and weak human nature. They had brought from Ireland the suspicion that the man who came to do good was a proselytizer in disguise and sought conversions. Their conservative traditionalism looked with disfavor on new ideas or the disruption of old patterns. They had a temperamental distrust of the professional reformer, intolerant of standards not his own: "busy bodies," the Irish called them, "who care not so much to ascertain what is right, as to run on their own account, without pausing to inquire whether they are sent or not." The numberless notional "isms" nurtured in New England tickled the Irishman's funny bone. Who's superstitious now, he exclaimed in glee, when sedate Bostonians gathered solemnly to listen to a lecture on phrenology or participate in spirit-rappings?

The Catholic Irish introduced a relaxed sabbatarianism among a stern sabbatarian people and thereby another barrier to understanding was raised. The Catholic attitude was that Sunday should "be truly the Lord's day, devoted especially to His worship, but not destitute of social enjoyments such as becomes a pious Christian."

The Irish filled the streets of their sections on Sunday, visiting with one another, talking and sometimes quarreling, the children playing games with vigor and shouts, and the men making the rounds of the *shebeens* for a pious drink. Relatives and county men gathered together for a handshake, and the Irish were not a people for keeping their presence quiet. The solemn New Englander fumed at what he considered a desecration of the Lord's Day. He also misconstrued the Irish custom of invoking the name of God in common speech as swearing and blaspheming. An old school deacon who had hired an Irishman asked him when he was going to start. "By the help of God I will commence next Monday," was the reply, and the deacon discharged him, saying he would have no man work for him guilty of such profanity.

The clannish exclusiveness of the Catholic Irish bothered the Yankees, themselves an exclusive people. We hear a great complaint against the Irish, wrote the Boston *Pilot* in 1839, "because they do not mingle with the people among whom their lot is cast, because they adhere to favorite customs, and enjoy their national likings and antipathies without the consent of the majority. But what does all this amount to, but that they set the Yankees an example which they would do well to follow, *in minding their own business.*"

5

The conduct of the Yankees toward the Irish intruders had not been such as to impress the newcomers with the desirability of adopting the customs, manners and feelings of the people of New England. We should be "very sorry," wrote the *Pilot,* "to see the hearts of that free and generous people chilled by an embrace with the icicles of Yankee land."

The frigid or hostile reception of the Catholic Irishman in New England threw him deeper into the segregation of clannish exclusiveness. Consul Grattan recognized this, observing:

> He gives his hand — and an Irishman's hand almost always has his heart in it — but the cordiality of his grasp meets a cold return. He speaks in the fulness of sincerity; but no voice responds in the same key. His uncouth air, his coarse raiment, his blunders and his brogue are certainly unattractive or ludicrous, to those who consider him only a machine for doing the rough work of the state, or as an object of political speculation. The Irishman soon sees the fact of his position; for he is sensitive and shrewd beyond most men; and it may be imagined how keen and how bitter is his annoyance. No man is sooner than an Irishman thrown back on his own feelings. The recoil is in proportion to the exuberance; and in the same degree in which they are originally warm and social, they become morose and gloomy when thus repelled.

The extravagance of the Irishman's proffer of friendliness, of his sentiments, emotions and language, offended the taciturn and unemphatic Yankee as insincere blarneying: people did not wear their feelings on their sleeves in New England. The howling and jollification of Irish wakes seemed barbaric to the tightly reined Yankees. The compensatory boasting of the Irish that everything was better in Ireland than in the United States and the often expressed wish to return to the dear old land appeared deceitful, or at least big-mouth talk, when the same people who voiced this open nostalgia were even then buying passages to bring brothers, sisters, relatives or friends to the United States from the country for which they heaved loud sighs. "All my countrymen agree with me that Ireland is much superior to America," wrote the author of a satire on anti-convent literature at the time of the burning of the Charlestown convent, "and my wonder is that none of them ever go back to it."

"It is to most New Englanders," a Yankee wrote in 1835, "a subject of unceasing astonishment where these locust legions of Irish emigrants can come from." The increase of Irish-born paupers had stirred both the Boston and Massachusetts authorities to initiate limiting action by national legislation. In 1834, it was publicly charged "that one-tenth of our Irish population are either paupers or criminals," which brought a spirited rejoinder from the Catholic weekly, *The Jesuit,* demanding proof and charging that in Protestant eyes pauper and criminal were synonymous. They lived in "contented degradation," asserted the Boston *Atlas,* and they preferred this mode of subsistence "to the cultivation of the luxurious soil, acres of which might be purchased with the frugal savings of a month." Sneers at their poverty were common: the "hatless and shoeless Irish," "the green jacket of the woodsawyer," "the tattered shawl of the washwoman." An articulate Irishman, asking the Yankees to try to remember that the Catholic Irish emigrants were victims of the system in Ireland, shrewdly penetrated to New England thinking in relation to the mass of the poor:

> In sight of the thousands of Irishmen who throng our cities, and whose peculiar national characteristics point them out clearly and at once, as being the children of misfortune and oppression, Americans have too long been apt to couple their appearance in his imagination with his own countrymen, placed under similar circumstances, and draw inferences unfavorable to the man.

The Irishman, he continued, performed services that Americans would not be submitted to and hence, from these circumstances, it was supposed that he lacked independence and a manly spirit.

"They dig our docks, and excavate our railroads, and scour our brasses," wrote a New Englander who disliked the Irish. "We do not know what we should do without them. We do not know what we shall do with them." The hardheaded Yankee employer liked a reservoir of cheap labor more than he disliked the Irish. The Yankee man of business never let his personal sentiments interfere with money-making.

The deepest grievance of the Catholic Irish against the Yankee nation, next to its deep-seated anti-Catholicism, centered on the iron law of economics enforced on the race. As early as 1839, the *Pilot* voiced the resentment of the Catholic Irish:

> Have they [the Irish] not had abundant evidence that the Yankees only love foreigners as the hunter loves the deer — and that they have sought and still seek but to obtain their services at the lowest possible valuation, and then strip them of their hard earnings by treachery and fraud!

A few years later the same paper declared that the Catholic Irish had "received from New England nothing but the scant liberty to spend our sweat upon her barren fields, or to strain our vigor in her manufactories" and that the emigrant of today was under no compliment to the Yankees, who were, after all, the emigrants of yesterday.

The economic exploitation of Catholic Irish labor by the New Englanders was a continuing process because fresh batches of emigrants from Ireland kept a fluid labor surplus available at cheap wages. This and the inability of Irish help to stand out for better conditions because of the paper-thin marginal reserves between them and destitution gave the employer an advantage he did not scruple to wield. The Irish felt that the Yankees overworked and underpaid them and then in such instruments as the company store squeezed further profits out of their hard day's work.

The Irish memory fixed upon the darkling picture of the Yankee "skinflint," softened by recollections of individual acts of kindliness, and firmly believed that great New England fortunes, in the textile industry particularly, had been built on their sweated backs.

6

A companion grievance was the feeling that his race and religion impeded the rise of the Catholic Irishman to more favorable economic status. No matter his merits or qualifications, he sensed an uncovenanted conspiracy on the part of the Yankees to keep him in the role of "hewer of wood and drawer of water." The words of the Protestant Irish patriot Grattan were quoted in point: "The original sin of his birth will never be forgiven him."

Get naturalized and educate your children! These were the sovereign remedies advocated by the Church and by his leaders to earn that respect for himself he now lacked.

Through naturalization political power would come, his leaders preached. Those who now sneered at the Irishman would appear, hat in hand, bidding for his favor when he enjoyed the franchise. They described the franchise as the one potent weapon to break the thrall of his inferiority in New England and smash through the barrier to economic improvement and social and political recognition. With the ballot, one man wrote in 1834, Irishmen, with the hod on their shoulders, "would then be represented, we should boldly and proudly take our stand among the citizens of Boston . . . in a word, we would be respected."

7

But Boston and New England in general had other ideas, and the success of the Yankee political dynasts in retaining ascendancy over the floodtide of emigration was a phenomenon in the history of American politics. The Yankee was as smart, resourceful and imaginative a politician as ever managed an election or adorned a legislative chamber. The Irish, with their gift for the game, never underestimated or minimized the capabilities of the Yankee politician. The breed of Sam Adams, which had outwitted the British governors, reproduced itself each generation. The Yankees furnished a distinguished list of statesmen to the nation in numbers out of proportion to the population of the six states, and they produced a race of local political bosses as bold as they were shrewd. Their job was to protect the property interests of New England from assaults and when corruption was necessary they knew where to find the money and how to distribute it.

They surrounded and isolated the Catholic Irish vote — a maneuver to which the Irish contributed by their clannish huddles; but they struck hands with it when the conservative nature of the Catholic Irish coincided with the conservative interests of the Yankees. They made concessions only when forced by circumstances they could not control.

The record in Boston spoke for itself. The Catholic Irish by 1844 formed one fourth of Boston's population, to the number of thirty thousand; by 1853 there were seventy thousand, or two fifths of the whole. Yet, as Leahy pointed out, "this great mass of citizens was wholly unrepresented in the government. It was not until 1857 that it obtained a common councilman, Mr. John H. Barry. Its first alderman, Christopher A. Connor, was not elected until 1870; its first congressman, Patrick A. Collins, until 1882, and its first mayor, Hugh O'Brien, until 1884." It was not until the second decade of the twentieth century that an American-born Catholic Irishman, David I. Walsh, was elected first as Governor and then as United States Senator. Illinois and California had Catholic Irishmen as Senators before the Civil War.

8

The Catholic Irish thus came as intruders and remained a foreign body to homogeneous, Protestant and Anglo-Saxon New England. The story of the Yankee-Irish conflict in New England is not pleasant but it is not black. The clash did not break out into bloodshed — a tribute to a sense of justice and decency among the cultivated New Englanders and the remarkable forbearance and patience of a naturally impulsive race, who obeyed the injunctions of their maligned priesthood. Individual instances of compassion and helpfulness by Yankees are as vivid a part of the Irish memory as the darker shadows. A Catholic Irishman in 1834 agreed that the Irish were insulted, "but with respect to the more enlightened part of the community, I will say that Irishmen, *individually,* are respected, are found trustworthy, and in many situations the utmost confidence is placed in them, whilst *collectively* as Irishmen . . . they are despised and insulted." The distinction thus drawn was fundamental.

The Catholic Irish source material of the period is singularly free of expressions of hatred for the Yankees. Anger, resentment, irritation, a sense of grievance in which self-pity is mixed, a feeling that the Irish were getting the rough end of the stick unjustly, yes; but no hatred such as was reserved for English rule in Ireland. Even in 1834, when the Boston press lashed the Irish unmercifully for the New York election riot, the public protest meeting adopted a resolution of confidence and faith in the good citizens of Boston. They adopted means familiar to them in Ireland of expressing gratitude to Yankees who befriended them. Since the town clerk of a New England community owned no field to be cut by their voluntary labor, the Catholic Irishmen, wanting to pay their respects for this man's kindliness and considerate treatment, insisted that they bear his coffin to the graveyard on their shoulders — the one tribute they felt did honor to his memory.

The fact was that the Catholic Irish entertained deep respect for the good qualities of the Yankee — or the "American," as they called him. An Irishman who had moved to Philadelphia because he could not abide the intolerance of a New England country town later admitted he admired the perseverance, the capacity for hard work, frugality and the integrity of the genuine Yankee. "Let the Irish-Americans take pattern by the Yankees," wrote the editor of the *Pilot*. "Let them imitate the energy, patience and prudence of his character." Such holding up the virtues of the Yankees for emulation was familiar in Catholic Irish households. Josiah Quincy and Josiah Quincy, Jr., were cited as examples of honorable citizens, of spotless integrity, who postponed private interests to the public good. John Ryan, the successful wool manufacturer of Norfolk, Connecticut, wrote a series of articles advising his fellow Catholic Irish how to accommodate themselves to the peculiar circumstances of New England, and the sum and substance of his discourse was: Look to the Yankee as a model for self-improvement and economic progress. In anger at what he called the "Irish lip-orators for Ireland," a writer said, in effect, that a couple of smart and persevering Yankees on the spot in Ireland would do more for the cause than the whole brood of spouters.

9

The Yankees were a difficult people — and so were the Catholic Irish. The Yankees were stubborn, tenacious and narrow. The Irish were positive, assertive and belligerent; put out the door, they came in the window. The Yankees were jealous and solicitous of their rights, for which, they said, they had fought. The Irish were content with nothing less than full equality in these rights and made the air ring with their protests when the Yankees claimed a priority in them. The Irish were not a docile people; they seethed full of trouble, noise, argument and dispute; there was fire in them, open hearths, as against the cold reserve and tight-lipped monosyllabism of the Yankee. Hit at, the Irishman hit back. The Boston press, both secular and religious, with notable exceptions, belabored and ridiculed the Catholic Irish; the Catholic Irish press, starting with the Catholic weekly, *The Jesuit*, entered the lists with the shillelah of the faction fight and taught the sarcastic Yankees lessons in Dublin scurrility. But except where the Catholic religion was concerned, the *Pilot* displayed more good nature and humor toward Yankee detractors than did the Boston press towards the Irish.

10

Before entering into a recital of the indignities to which the Catholic Irish were subject in Boston and New England, it is well to distinguish, as the Catholic Irish of the day did, among the several categories of Yankees.

The Yankees of wealth and position, called the Brahmins, were, generally speaking, indifferent to the Catholic Irish and certainly not openly hostile to them. They were conscious of a growing Catholic Irish community in Boston, but as a world apart from their interests and affairs; they rarely came into direct contact with it and the fixed prejudices they held with the region against the Catholic Irish were, for that reason, unaggressive. As men of property they found the Catholic Irish emigrants useful as low-wage workers, though they grumbled at the social problems and the cost in taxes from the poverty of the newcomers. In one relationship the Catholic Irish were close to the Brahmins. Irishmen drove their carriages and tended their gardens; Irish servant girls took over care of the kitchen and chamber. In time, the Catholic Irish became an indispensable part of the household of the Brahmins, and the mutual loyalty of the one to the other formed lifelong attachments.

The social gulf between the Catholic Irish and the Brahmins was unbridgeable. Andrew Carney, the successful clothing manufacturer, enjoyed the respect of the business community for his steady habits, good moral character and unostentatious behavior. "His business transactions," wrote the Boston *Pilot* in 1844, "throw him into contact with native capitalists; they receive him with a cold politeness if he traffics with them, but in a social life they shun him as a plague." No evidence exists that Andrew Carney was ambitious for a social life; had he been, the door was still closed against him.

The word "Brahmin" has become a convenient latter-day label to describe indiscriminately the antagonism of the Yankee nation to the Catholic Irish. The characterization is both untrue and unfair. The Brahmin, as a Boston capitalist, exploited the Catholic Irish workman, but the Brahmin, as a civilized human being, defended the Catholic Irish and acted as a buffer in their behalf when religious and racial prejudice ran wild. The intervention of Brahmins to befriend and help the Catholic Irish when it seemed that all hands were turned against them made a record of civility in an otherwise unhappy chapter of the story of the race in the New England states. The decent and just Boston Brahmin was a man without peer in the United States. He needed not to love the Catholic Irishman to stand against his being persecuted.

The middling class of Yankees — the overseers and executives, the local officeholders, the small businessmen, the big men in the small towns, the solid church people and the men and women with the small outlook of rural New England — had an open and cold hostility to the newcomers. They respected order too much to participate in acts of violence against the Catholic Irish, but they had no scruples of conscience in condoning outbreaks after they happened. They departed from a neighborhood when an Irishman moved in. They favored the separation of their own brethren from the Irish in hospitals and asylums. They discriminated against the Irish when they were in positions of authority. Their eyes turned bleak when they looked upon a group of Irishmen. They were singularly without charity in their attitude and conduct towards the Irish and disposed to censure those among them who had charitable sentiments. "The Irish could work," wrote the social historian of Holyoke, "but as creatures from a different world they could scarcely expect to mingle with the natives . . . the line was drawn not between capitalist and laborer, well-to-do and poverty-stricken, but between Protestant American and Catholic immigrant." They made life difficult for the Catholic Irish in ways short of violence but icily cruel.

The lowest order of Yankees took to open violence against the Catholic Irish. This particular order, which came into closer touch with the body of Catholic Irish than the other two classes, was the distorted image of the strong qualities in the Yankee nation. A meaner-spirited or more cussed creature than the ignorant and narrow Yankee — the "gone-to-seed" Yankee — of the lowest economic category would be hard to find. He was as ornery as a mean horse, with his own people as well as with the foreigners. Compassion for fellow human beings had been drained out of him. A purposeless stubbornness characterized his nature. The moral fiber of Pilgrim and Puritan had gone flabby in him while the ancestral lack of generosity to an opponent had hardened. He was bigoted without the sectarian's justification of belief in his own creed; he was, generally, not a steady churchgoer. His forefathers formed the mobs which Sam Adams manipulated so skillfully and he made up the anti-Catholic Irish mobs. He was essentially a lawless man, preferring to take the law in his own hands — and he had a lively sense that the law did not run for the Catholic Irish.

In 1826, an Irishman stole a chain from a Boston truckman, the drayman of Boston's narrow and tortuous streets. No law was summoned. The Irishman was seized and covered with a sheet of tar, goose feathers and flour. This first encounter heralded a long spell of enmity by the rough and formidable Boston truckmen against the Irish.

II

The early Irish colonies in Boston, small in numbers, were subject to assault by Yankees of the working order. On the night of June 19, 1823, after a quarrel between individuals during the day, the first Yankee sortie invaded the Irish section in Ann Street and hurled stones through windows. Three years later, on the nights of July 11, 12 and 13, 1826, Yankees turned Broad Street into a shambles and repeated the damage in the other Irish section of Pond, Merrimac and Ann Streets in the North End in three days of rioting. Public authority made an ineffectual attempt to stop the Yankee rabble and, though warned by the Irish, neglected to take strong precautions on the third and worst night of mob action.

Outside of Boston, the Catholic Irish suffered the gang assaults of antagonists in Lowell, Portland and Bangor. In the last-named place, on the ground that emigrants took bread out of the mouth of the native-born laborer, the Yankees went on a rampage of several days, destroying and burning the homes of the Irish and beating every Irishman they laid hands on, until the better elements organized themselves into law-and-order forces.

In the spring of 1834, the Boston Irish felt so isolated that the suggestion was made that they engage "a professional friend" to plead their cause and defend their rights. There was pathos implicit in this sense of being cut off from the rest of the community. They held a dignified meeting in May, 1834, to protest against the calumnies visited upon their heads for the violence of the Tammany Irish in the New York City election. Three months later the most shocking outrage against the Roman Catholic Church in New England occurred — the burning of the Ursuline convent in Charlestown across the river from Boston.

12

The conflagration that lighted the historic countryside of Middlesex County on the night of August 11, 1834, originated in low religious and racial prejudice excited into riotous deed by rumor which the remedy of fact failed to overtake because of tragic frustrations. In terms of drama, it seemed that an evil *deus ex machina* had determined that the Ursuline convent must be burned to the ground, and it used human credulity, cowardice and innocence to aid in the work. The destruction of the convent was, in the words of the best Catholic historian of the affair, "the most disgraceful outrage ever perpetrated in New England and the most tragic event in the history of the Church here."

The Ursuline female seminary was first established in Boston in 1820 by Bishop Cheverus, and the quality of its teaching attracted a growing attendance, so that in 1826 the plot called "Ploughed Hill" in the western part of Charlestown that is now Somerville was purchased, renamed Mount Benedict after Bishop Benedict Fenwick, and on its summit a three-story brick building was finished in 1827, to which two large wings, enclosing a courtyard, were added in 1829.

The convent stood in historic territory. The next eminence to Mount

Benedict was Bunker Hill. Through this Middlesex County had galloped Paul Revere. Here was the great Charlestown Navy Yard.

A narrow and provincial Yankeedom inhabited Charlestown. This "nunnery" (it was never called a convent) had been, an apologist explained, "pushed into the midst of a decidedly Protestant people," who resented its presence as "wholly *foreign*," founded by "*foreigners*," built by "*foreign* money," and directed "by the spiritual subjects of a *foreign* potentate, the Pope."

Yet this "foreign" convent drew its body of students principally from the families of substantial New England Protestants, who preferred the genteel Catholic training for their daughters to the Puritan discipline from which, as Unitarians mostly, they had revolted — a galling disposition to orthodox teachers. At the time of its burning, the convent had in residence forty-four pupils, from six to eighteen years of age, principally Protestant young ladies with sound Yankee names like Parkman, Endicott, Adams, Danforth, Penniman and Storer against which names like Mary O'Brien and Elizabeth Maguire, along with the French names of Millicent Dublois and Suzanne Perrault, sister of the French-Canadian rebel leader, stood out. The number of Catholic girls at no time had exceeded ten.

The Lady Superior, a convert to Catholicism, had been born Mary Ann Ursula Moffatt in Canada and taken the name in religion of Mary Edmond St. George, an unusual woman of stout heart, good humor and infinite tactlessness. She had an aristocratic contempt for the lower order of Yankees, whom she called *canaille;* and this scorn ruled her judgment when the warning flags of danger from the mob waved vigorously. At the convent she had a staff of ten — professed nuns, novices and helpers — and a couple of Irishmen for work on the grounds and in the stables.

The lower order of natives in Charlestown and Middlesex County and over in Boston were both fascinated and repelled by the convent — that "mysterious institution," they called it. Its seclusion and privacy agitated their curiosity — for the worst. Their noodles were filled with lurid tales imported from the European continent of sinful orgies carried on within its walls, of helpless women confined against their will, of underground vaults and secret disposal of bodies of innocent victims. Convents, they believed, should not be allowed to exist in a free country and, besides, the Catholics and the Irish were a set of damned rascals and scoundrels.

It was not alone the Charlestown convent which raised the resentment of the native stock. In 1829, a church had been erected for the expanding Catholic Irish population, with Father Patrick Byrne, a native of Ireland, as pastor. Two years later Bishop Fenwick purchased a site on Bunker Hill for a Catholic cemetery, opened, said the selectmen of Charlestown, without the consent of the public authorities, and even as the convent burned he awaited the outcome of a legal suit against Charlestown for permission to bury the dead there.

The ill-restrained feelings of the Charlestown natives broke into open violence against the Catholic Irish on Thanksgiving in 1833. Some Irish families were holding a dance in the tavern of Roger McGowan when a "party of idle Americans," in the words of the *Boston Transcript*, "for the sake of sport," invaded the house, insulted and abused the Irish who were "innocently amusing themselves," as the New York *Truth Teller* put it, and in the course of the slugfest one of the natives was killed. Several nights later, the original rioters augmented by supporters to the number of some five hundred returned to the battle and, in spite of the efforts of the selectmen and marines from the Navy Yard, leveled McGowan's house.

A flow of rumors kept the convent in the public mind. Eight years before the convent was burned, a snoopy neighbor and declared enemy of foreigners, John Runey, who was to play a central role in the tragedy, presented himself to the Lady Superior to inquire about women confined against their will and served notice that if Massachusetts had no law on the statute books to free them, he would make it his business to see that they were freed. In 1830 a story appeared in a Boston paper that a young female orphan had been inveigled into the Ursuline convent "after having been cajoled to transfer a large fortune to the Popish Mass-men."

The following year the *Jesuit* branded as a lie a report going the rounds of the Calvinistic press that a pious young lady had "eloped" (the old-fashioned word for escaped) from the Mount Benedict institution. The religious *Boston Recorder* kept up a running campaign to warn off Protestant parents from entering their daughters in the convent. A preacher from another part of Massachusetts appeared in a Charlestown pulpit and said in the course of his sermon: "A nunnery in Charlestown! a nunnery in Charlestown! I am astonished that the people of Bunker Hill suffer one stone to remain standing on another."

But the most grievous harm to the convent's reputation was the stories circulated by a young Charlestown woman. Had she lived today, Rebecca Theresa Reed would have expended her sentimental fantasies and urge for self-dramatization upon Hollywood or autograph-hunting of personable young crooning stars. In the circumscribed and unromantic life of a limited-interest Yankee town, Miss Reed looked for glamour and excitement in the novelty of the Roman Catholic Church and change from the drabness of her poverty-stricken youth in the mystery of the foreign nunnery. Father Byrne had instructed and baptized her in the Catholic faith and through his intercession the Lady Superior, much against her better judgment, consented to accept Rebecca as a charity scholar in the convent, that she might be trained to set up a little school as the means of her support.

The discipline of the convent dispelled her romantic notions and she lacked the application for study. The Lady Superior had decided to notify her at the end of six months to seek a career elsewhere. Miss Reed herself felt the call back to the world.

After a little more than four months in the convent, on January 18, 1832, Miss Reed "eloped" melodramatically. Instead of leaving by the front gateway, which was open, Miss Reed "escaped" by climbing over the fence, to the amusement of the Lady Superior and pupils watching from the windows. In this way nuns fled from European conventual dungeons in lurid anti-Popery literature. Unhappily she fell and skinned herself.

Miss Reed was no Maria Monk, except in one characteristic: she told imaginative stories that fell plausibly upon ears attuned to unfavorable reports. She made no representations of immorality in the convent, but dwelt on harsh penances imposed on the nuns, of their prostrating themselves before the bishop, of the bishop's request of a dying nun that she find out in Heaven why a bag of gold he needed to build a college had not descended to him. She acted out before attentive audiences scenes she said she had witnessed in the convent and gave similitude to her mummery by mumbling in what the credulous thought to be Latin. Her decision to leave the convent, she said, came when she overheard the bishop and the Lady Superior discussing plans to kidnap and transport her secretly by carriage to Canada.

Threats were common that the convent should come down. The most serious menace that overhung the convent came from its neighbors, the brickmakers employed in the yards which adjoined the Mount Benedict seminary. They were recruited from New Hampshire, then perhaps the most narrowly anti-Catholic state in the Union. A rough, tough, hard-drinking and obscene crew, they hated Catholics, Irish and foreigners with the unreasoning hatred of ignorance and credulity.

The workman most respected by the brickmakers was John R. Buzzell, a native of New Hampshire, the demonic energy of the mob which destroyed the Charlestown convent. Buzzell, then twenty-nine, was a man of tremendous physical size, six feet six in height and built in proportion, famed throughout the countryside for his strength and agility, a wrestler and bruiser of fearful power.

Bad relations prevailed between the brickmakers and the convent. They sneered at the nuns on their evening walks and offered to help the young lady students escape. In June, previous to the calamitous August night, Peter Rossiter, a gardener and watchman employed by the convent, an Irishman of surly disposition, had roughly handled a young American girl he caught taking a short cut through the convent grounds, according to the story that spread, though Rossiter later denied it. Buzzell, called "Old R," took upon himself the role of rustic cavalier, caught Rossiter off the convent grounds and so unmercifully beat the Irishman as to lay him up for nine days. Rossiter refused to take legal action: "I did not *prostitute* him," he explained, "for fear that he might waylay me, and take revenge."

Buzzell boasted around that there wasn't an Irishman he couldn't lick, and he offered to take on three at a time. The story of the fight circulated through the low life of Charlestown and Medford and to the firemen of Boston, and Buzzell became a local Ajax — the beater of Irishmen. He had shown the Irish "how things of that kind were settled in this country."

Like a paraphrase of a Greek drama played in this outwardly pleasant and peaceful Yankee countryside, the event which fused prejudice, antagonism, rumor and ingrown regionalism into tragic explosion originated within the convent.

Sister Mary John, born Elizabeth Harrison of Philadelphia, member of the Ursuline community for thirteen years, was second in command of the Mount Benedict seminary. Toward the end of July, 1834, the Lady Superior noticed Sister Mary John's state of agitation. As a teacher of music, she had an assignment load that today seems incredible: she gave fourteen lessons a day, of thirty-five or forty minutes each. She broke under the strain, became (as she said) "mentally deranged," or, in the medical language of the day, was seized with "brain fever."

On the afternoon of July 28, 1834, Sister Mary John "eloped" from the convent, appeared in the home of Edward Cutter, a brick manufacturer, across the road from Mount Benedict, and asked to be driven to West Cambridge (now Arlington) to the residence of Mr. Cotting, whose daughters had attended the seminary. Snooping John Runey, a selectman of Charlestown, with a farm down the road from the convent, was pressed into service and, with Mrs. Runey, drove Sister Mary John to West Cambridge and on his return told the anxious and disturbed Lady Superior of what had happened. Bishop Fenwick, speedily informed, drove out that night to the Cotting home, but Sister Mary John refused to see him and the next morning he dispatched her brother, Thomas Harrison, an engraver in Boston, who got her consent to talk with the bishop. The same afternoon she returned to the convent with the bishop where she was placed under the care of Dr. Abraham Thompson, its physician.

The "elopement" might have passed off with no untoward consequence but for two things: the suspicious inquisitiveness of the Yankee neighbors and the wall of protection and silence the convent attempted to throw around the sick Sister Mary John to avoid the occasion of a public scandal.

Mrs. Runey, as much a busybody as her husband, had hurried back to the Cotting home on the day after the "elopement" and was present when the bishop met Sister Mary John. According to the story Mrs. Runey and her husband spread around Charlestown, the bishop told the sister she was perfectly free to leave the convent after two or three weeks upon the recovery of her health, which was consistent with the rules of the order that members could return to the world upon their own wish. But, said Mrs. Runey, Sister Mary John took her aside and begged, if she had not been released in two or three weeks, "to make a stir about it" and take action to find out what her condition was. The Lady Superior informed the Runeys and the Cutters when they began inquiring that Sister Mary John could not receive visitors.

Suspicion and rumor leaped over the wall of aloofness the convent erected around Sister Mary John and what the eyes could not see the tongues found to be the worst. Over the weekend, about a dozen brickmakers held a rump meeting at the schoolhouse near the convent and discussed plans for burning or, as they said, "taking it down." No decision was arrived at, but four nights later a larger gathering of thirty accepted the advice of Alvah Kelley, owner of the brickyard immediately adjoining the convent, not to act until the three weeks supposedly set by the bishop for the release of the nun had passed.

There is evidence of these two meetings in Charlestown, but apparently a parallel and more widespread conspiracy to destroy the convent had developed in Boston among the firemen and their friends, and perhaps the truckmen. The details of the burning of the convent revealed not the spontaneous uprising of a mob but a strategy worked out in advance and timed for a given signal.

The selectmen of Charlestown officially took notice on Monday, August 4, of the rumors of the conspiracy by seeking the counsel of Joseph Tufts, a reputable lawyer, who himself had not heard the gossip — which indicated the distance of separation between the upper and lower classes of Yankeedom. He inclined, in a "it can't happen here" manner, to minimize the threats. This opinion was shared by the Lady Superior upon being informed of the rumors: for all her shrewdness, she confronted the affair from the beginning with an unworldly innocence, governed by a serene confidence that since the convent had committed no offense against law and morality it was not accountable to a crowd of peeping bigots.

A reporter picked up the rumors from a chat with the tollgate keeper on the Medford Pike, and on Friday afternoon, August 8, the following item, loaded with dynamite, appeared in the *Boston Mercantile Journal*:

> Mysterious. —— We understand that a great excitement at present exists in Charlestown, in consequence of the mysterious disappearance of a young lady from the Nunnery in that place. The circumstances, as far as we can learn, are as follows: — The young lady was sent to the place in question to complete her education, and became so pleased with the place and its inmates, that she was induced to seclude herself from the world and take the black veil. After some time spent in the Nunnery she became dissatisfied and made her escape from the institution, but was afterwards persuaded to return, being told that if she would continue but three weeks longer she would be dismissed with honor. At the end of that time, a few days since, her friends called for her, but she was not to be found, and much alarm is excited in consequence.

This was the first notice in the press of the growing Charlestown excitement. Its distortion of the background of Sister Mary John, its incendiary inaccuracy and its publication without a check of the facts added irresponsibility to the mischief brewing. The story was copied by other Boston papers on Saturday morning, and on Saturday afternoon a statement by Bishop Fenwick appeared in the *Boston Transcript* denying the truth of the account in the *Boston Mercantile Journal* and promising a true presentation of the facts on Monday.

On Saturday night, Edward Cutter, who had read the "mysterious lady" item, accompanied by his brother Fitch, called at the convent with the hope, he said, of interviewing Sister Mary John, so as to counter the mounting ugly spirit of the community. The Lady Superior, previously on friendly terms with Cutter, burst out in anger against him. She blamed Cutter for sending Sister Mary John to West Cambridge instead of informing the Lady Superior first — an act for which she could not forgive him. "No, you sha'n't see her," she exclaimed; "I'll not gratify you so much." Then she continued in mounting ire:

> You may bring on your mob as soon as you please. *You*, Mr. Cutter, *you* have applied to the *selectmen* for a mob to tear down our buildings, and you and Runey are to head it, I am told. *But there will be a retaliation. The Bishop has twenty thousand of the vilest Irishmen at his command, and there will be a retaliation. You will have your houses torn down over your heads, and you may read your riot act till your throats are sore, but you'll not quell them.*

The Lady Superior testified in court she had used the threat of twenty thousand "brave" not "vilest" Irishmen to tear down the property of Cutter and others in reply to his warning that the convent might be burned.

After her passionate outbreak had spent itself, the Lady Superior ushered Sister Mary John into the room, and the convalescent nun told the visitors that not only had she recovered in health but also, of her own will, she wished to remain in the convent. Edward Cutter was now so satisfied of the true state of Sister Mary John that he offered to write an account of his visit for the Monday morning Boston newspapers in the expectation it would end the excitement.

Now the Charlestown selectmen once more entered the confused and disturbed picture. Early on Sunday morning, August 10, a handbill, in writing, had been found posted in Charlestown:

To the Selectmen of Charlestown!
    Gentlemen — It is currently reported that a mysterious affair has
lately happened at the *Nunery* in Charlestown. now it is your duty,
gentlemen, to have this affair investigated *immediately;* if not, the
Truckmen of Boston will *demolish* the Nunery thursday night —
August 14.
    Boston, August 9, 1834.

The date, "Thursday night, August 14," ran like a counterpoint
through the affair; subsequent testimony gave validity to the assumption that Thursday night had been fixed by the plotters for the deed.
What caused the time to be advanced to Monday, August 11, or
whether the Thursday date was deliberately publicized as a false scent
to cover up an agreed earlier date, we shall never know.

A second handbill appeared in Charlestown on that Sunday:

> Go ahead!! To arms!! To arms!! Ye brave and free, the Avenging
> Sword unshield!! Leave not one stone upon another of this curst
> nunnery that prostitutes female virtue and liberty under the garb
> of holy Religion. When Bonaparte opened the Nunnerys of Europe,
> he found crowds of Infant sculls ! ! ! ! !

Samuel Poor, a selectman, constituted himself a committee of one to
inform the Lady Superior that something should be done to allay the
excitement, producing the handbill as evidence of public sentiment.
"She treated the information with indifference and contempt," Poor
later reported, "and said she did not care a straw about it . . . Her
own innocence would protect her. She also said that she could send
her own man to the rail-road, and *raise five hundred Irishmen in fifteen
minutes,* and *the Bishop could raise twenty thousand Irishmen,* adding,
'and you know how they are uncultivated.' " She refused to believe
any grounds for apprehension existed.

Nevertheless, she consented to an inspection of the convent by the
entire board of selectmen on the following afternoon, Monday, August 11. The Lady Superior, at Poor's request, brought in Sister Mary
John, and she, at the suggestion of the Lady Superior, showed Poor
through the building from the top to the bottom, except one room
where a nun seriously ill with consumption rested. Poor was satisfied
that nothing was amiss at the convent and said he would write a statement for the Boston press to substantiate and fortify Cutter's statement.

Bishop Fenwick did not prepare a statement, concluding that one by
a Protestant would carry greater weight. Now the demon of frustration

started to work. Late Sunday afternoon, Cutter took his statement to the office of the *Morning Post* and was informed that the piece, "to which *no material importance* was attached at *that time*," as the editor later explained, was too late for the Monday edition (the papers going to press early on Sunday) but would be inserted on Tuesday morning. Selectman Poor, undiscouraged by the failure of Cutter, whom he met in Charlestown, also visited the *Morning Post* with his own statement and was told the king himself could not stop the press. These were unhappy portents.

Whether the publication of the Cutter and Poor notices on Monday morning would have prevented the destruction of the convent that night is a doubtful issue in the light of the grim sequence of events which unfolded a set determination to carry out the conspiracy, regardless of the true state of affairs in the convent.

On that same Sunday, Rev. Lyman Beecher preached his famous sermon — the plea to save the Mississippi Valley from the threat of an increasing Catholic emigrant population — in three different churches in Boston. The coincidence of the Rev. Mr. Beecher's Sunday anti-Popery sermonizing with the Monday night burning of the convent has since linked his name with the tragic conflagration on no other evidence than the coincidence itself. Dr. Beecher has the guilt of sectarian rancor to answer for, but it is incorrect and unfair to accuse him of inciting the Charlestown-Boston mob to riot, as earlier Catholic historians spread on their pages and later writers repeated.

Dr. Beecher had been absent from Boston for two years, and returned on a money-collecting trip shortly before the outrage. He had no knowledge, he testified, of the excitement in connection with the convent, which is credible in view of the ignorance among the upper classes generally of the stirred feelings among the lower. The sermon, which is still available, had in it, as Dr. Beecher stated, nothing of "mobocratic tendency" and had been preached and read for several years without mounting riots. Dr. Beecher made the strong point that the church people of Boston, still less the audiences of his three Sunday sermons, were not found among the hooligans and ne'er-do-wells who made up the mob. It is true that Dr. Beecher was a vigorous anti-Popery preacher, but that is a far remove from throwing a brand, or inciting a brand to be thrown, into the convent. Historians shy away from "guilt by coincidence."

The entire body of selectmen of Charlestown, accompanied by the two Cutter brothers, appeared at the convent on Monday afternoon, August 11, at three o'clock to inspect the convent. Sister Mary John herself was the guide (the Lady Superior disdainfully took no notice of them) and for three hours they dutifully and thoroughly poked into every nook and corner. They found nothing amiss or suspicious.

Ironically, the official report of the selectmen designed to allay public excitement was published the day after the convent was burned.

On the same afternoon of Monday, August 11, Levi Thaxter of neighboring Watertown drove into Cambridge to consult with his friend, Judge Fay, concerning the rumors abroad of an attack upon the convent. This was news to the judge, and as both had daughters in attendance at the convent they thought it wise to investigate on the spot and remove their children if danger seemed to threaten.

Between eight and nine o'clock, groups had gathered near the convent's main gateway. Judge Fay listened to the talk, uniformly hostile to Catholics, convents and the Irish. One man described the convent as a secret society for which there was no law in the country. Another said that "if the Catholics get the upper hand of us, they will crush us to the earth." The men mentioned Thursday as the time "they guessed the convent would come down." Edward Cutter circulated among them with the story of his visit to the convent and of his talk with Sister Mary John and tried to persuade them to go home. They knew of the visit of the selectmen to the convent that afternoon and that even then John Runey was in Boston with the selectmen's report to be published the next morning. Judge Fay was later of the opinion that knowledge by the ringleaders of the corrective stories to appear in Tuesday's morning paper had forced a decision to attack the convent on Monday night instead of the scheduled Thursday.

Moving from group to group was Buzzell, with a large club in his hand, breathing fire against the Irish, boasting of the Rossiter beating and, said Judge Fay, "in a special humor to fight an Irishman if he could find one." If his reminiscences of that night told to a reporter more than forty years later were accurate, Buzzell had already accepted leadership of the riot. In the morning, a fellow workman, returning from Boston, had told Buzzell: "They are coming out of Boston to take down the nunnery tonight." That night a stranger came to the house where Buzzell boarded, said there were thirty men outside ready to go to the nunnery and asked Buzzell to take command. "You are the man who licked Rossiter," said the stranger, "and just the man to lead us."

Buzzell consented. He was the key man in the joining of the parallel conspiracies to attack the convent, if his memory as an old man was true: details in his reminiscences were confused.

Judge Fay and Mr. Thaxter, being assured by Cutter that he could disperse the groups and knowing that Runey would soon return from Boston to assist in keeping the peace, felt no reason for apprehension and drove away, leaving their children in the convent. Some of the groups also departed, and there were mutterings about returning on Thursday night.

But the crowd in front of the gate, instead of dissolving, grew larger, and about 9:30 cries were heard from the Medford road, "Down with the convent! Down with the convent!" and a mass of figures surged up the pathway to the circular drive in front of the main building. The Lady Superior, after giving the order for the children to be collected for flight if necessary, appeared at a second-story window in response to the mob cry for the "figurehead" (a short time before a partisan crowd had chopped off the figurehead of Andrew Jackson from a naval vessel in the Charlestown Navy Yard). Unafraid, she demanded to know what the invaders wanted. To see "the nun that had ran away" came the response. But the demon of frustration again got in his licks. At the moment her presence might at least have divided the councils of the crowd, Sister Mary John fainted dead away from nervous excitement. The Lady Superior reported this and told them to come the next day, warning the mob it would be the cause of the death of the seriously ill nun. "So much the better" was the reply. To their impudent taunts she returned barbed insults. "She was," said Buzzell, "the sauciest woman I ever heard talk." Threatening to return on Thursday, the crowd departed, and the Lady Superior, thinking the menace ended, instructed the sisters and the children to return to the dormitories.

The massed figures, however, returned for a second parley. A young novice, Sister Mary Bernard, born Grace O'Boyle in Ireland, innocently told them from a window that the convent had no male protectors but talked so persuasively that several in the mob spoke up and offered her their protection. Then the Lady Superior appeared in another window, charged the mob with drunkenness and told them stoutly she depended upon the protection of God.

At the foot of the hill, the hard core of the conspirators, certain there would be no resistance to an attack on the convent, gathered in a caucus around Buzzell and, deciding to go ahead that night, lighted tar barrels in Alvah Kelley's brickyard and a blaze leaped up to the particularly lovely August night. In the nearest church steeple, the bells, at that time the fire alarm system, pealed and the warning was picked up by other church bells.

The Charlestown engine companies halted on the Medford road and watched or, as their accusers charged, waited for the real action to start as knowing accessories. The stage awoke to the drama when Engine Company 13 of Leverett Street in Boston came running up, the regulars of the company, at that time serving without pay, followed by the volunteers and friends. Before the establishment of trained municipal fire departments, cities depended upon the volunteer departments, the hangers-on and the citizenry generally to put out fires. These companies were both social and political organizations with great power among the commonalty, the firehouses the neighborhood gathering places and in Boston the center of anti-Irish prejudice.

When Engine 13 appeared, a number of men, variously estimated at from fifty to one hundred, sprang out from hiding places in the shrubbery and seized its ropes. There was nothing spontaneous about this act. The men had smeared their faces as disguise, and they reminded onlookers of Indians: apparently the story of the Boston Tea Party was still lively in the minds of the plotters. They hauled Engine 13 up the convent roadway, attended by the crowd which had come out from Boston, with the mob of the curious following. Just in front of the convent it was halted and a voice sang out, "Off badges, and go ahead!" This voice was later identified as that of Prescott Pond, a volunteer member of the company and brother-in-law of Rebecca Reed.

The Lady Superior instructed the nuns to awaken and lead the children to the summer house in the garden in the deep rear of the grounds and told the older girls to take the younger by the hands, to calm them and keep them from being separated. She then herself, deliberately and with courageous self-possession, went through every room in the three-story building to make sure that none of the children was left behind. The nuns had with great effort assisted to safety the sister then in the last stages of consumption.

The storming of the convent door took place at 11:30. The leaders of the party then did the one act of decency in an otherwise indecent exhibition of mob passion: they searched the convent from cellar to top floor, even going out on the roof, to make sure that no females remained in the building. They told an ineffectual selectman who had been borne inside the building by the initial rush that they would hurt none of the females but the convent, that hated symbol, must come down.

Looting and destruction started at once. Windows were smashed from the inside or by stones from outside. Desks, drawers, cabinets and cupboards were torn open and anything thought of value stuffed in pockets: a thousand dollars in the Lady Superior's desk, which she had failed to reach, disappeared. One Yankee picked up a piece of gilded wood: "I've got one of the *idols* they used to worship," he proclaimed. A book came hurtling through a window. "Here goes the Bible," the man who threw it shouted. "Set fire to it with a torch." With yokel humor, some pranced around in the garments of the nuns. Buzzell donned the bishop's robes he found in the lodge, "in the spirit of deviltry," he recalled, but they were stripped from his back to make fire torches.

The furniture and adornments were thrown out of windows. Three pianos came crashing to the ground, followed by a harp and other musical instruments. The convent was stripped of all movable articles, except inflammable material.

At 12:30 the firing of the convent began with a torch lighted from Engine 13. The incendiaries set about their work in several parts of the building and speedily the shooting flames lighted up the faces of the active mob and curious onlookers. One hour after the first torch had been applied, the roof of the convent fell in.

The firing party did not stop with the main convent building. The chapel, the bishop's lodge, the farmhouse that had been the original school, the stables and the barn were each set to burning. One incendiary prided himself upon his humaneness by saving a hen from the burning barn. Marvin Marcy, son of a hotelkeeper, a sandy-haired boy whose girlish face had yet to feel a razor, set the low-lifes to howling with laughter by a mock auction of the bishop's valuable library and then destroying the books before the lodge was burned. Even the tomb at the foot of the garden was not inviolate: the rusty lock was torn off, men pushed their way in, name-plates on the coffins were stolen, and one coffin was ghoulishly broken open, exposing the remains.

The offense which most shocked Catholic religious sensibilities was the desecration of the Sacrament. Two of the nuns had ripped the mahogany tabernacle from the altar and hidden it among the vines, where a party of marauders discovered it. They opened the ciborium and scattered the sacred wafers in the fields. It became a fixed tradition among the Catholic Irish that these violators all came to a horrible end, and one man who had been showing the wafers in the drinking places of Charlestown committed suicide a few days later, it was believed.

At dawn, the once imposing convent building and its neat companion buildings were black and smoldering ruins.

If the selectmen of Charlestown had had gumption, said Captain Quinn of Engine 13, a straightforward man not involved in the conspiracy, the disaster would not have happened, and he gave his opinion that a dozen or fifteen resolute men could have stopped the mob. Only one obscure hero, a Colonel Amory of Charlestown, acted vigorously to break up the mob. The selectmen were more fearful of the mob than the mob was of the selectmen. There was a total abdication of responsibility by the town authorities. Enough fire companies from Charlestown, Boston and Medford were present to flood Mount Benedict with water; not a drop was pumped. No riot act was read, no effort made to call assistance. No magistrate appeared or, at least, spoke up; and the strongest action on the side of the law was an order by a tipstaff to a young lad to go home, when the destruction was complete.

Edward Cutter came with helpers to lead out the frightened huddle of nuns and children from the rear garden, though the Lady Superior, still angry with him, refused to accept the refuge of his home and found shelter in a neighboring farmhouse.

One young student walked to Charlestown for the early morning stage and at Boston proceeded to her home in Dorchester. Later she vividly remembered the walk along Sea (Federal) Street, "which swarmed with Irish, as I passed unnoticed among the little Pats and Bridgets that played in the gutter, and crowded the sidewalk in front of the shanties where they lived."

The little Pats and Bridgets were to tell their own little Pats and Bridgets of what happened on the night of August 11, 1834, but the real root of the long Catholic Irish bitterness was not alone what happened that night but what failed to happen after that terrible ordeal of fire in New England.

13

The respectable elements of Boston were shocked at the lawless deed on the soil of the Puritans, "themselves flying from the religious persecution in the old world," as the outraged Boston *Atlas* expressed it. "Never," reported the *Jesuit*, "did the destruction of any one place excite so universal a burst of disapprobation, and so general a sympathy, among the upper classes of society, and so deep and intense a feeling." Regret at the persecution of the Catholics was mixed with concern over the infamy that would be attached to Massachusetts.

Mayor Theodore Lyman, Jr., of Boston called a meeting of citizens at Faneuil Hall, where the eminent Josiah Quincy, Jr., read a set of resolutions and the old Federalist Harrison Gray Otis emerged from retirement to express the shame felt by decent men and women. One resolution pledged "the Protestant citizens of Boston . . . to unite with our Catholic brethren in protecting their persons, their property, and their civil and religious rights." By authorization the mayor appointed a representative committee to bring the rioters to justice. George Bond, barely controlling his indignation, moved that the committee find ways of raising funds to repair the convent damage. Similar meetings were held in Charlestown and Cambridge.

It remained for Bishop Benedict Fenwick to set the example of dignity under terrible stress, even of majesty, and certainly of Christianity. The spiritual leader of poor and humble Irish laborers, he stood up in the robes of an ancient authority and spread a radiance that shamed the incendiary flames. At the lowest point of the fortunes of the Roman Catholic Church in New England, it reached its highest eminence through his greatness.

On the three railroads under construction radiating from Boston to Worcester, Lowell and Providence were employed thousands of rough and quick-tempered Irish emigrants. Reports spread through Boston on Tuesday afternoon that these Irish railroaders were hastening into the city to avenge the desecration of their religion and to stand by their countrymen in case of further mob excesses. Bishop Fenwick sent out six priests in different directions to check the march. That evening at the Cathedral of the Holy Cross he walked out on the altar before a congregation of silent faces that in the shock of sacrilege looked to him for direction, and opening the Book of the Gospels he read from the fifth chapter of Matthew:

You have heard that it hath been said, an eye for an eye, and a tooth for a tooth.

But I say to you not to resist evil: but if one strike thee on thy right cheek, turn to him also the other:

And if a man will contend with thee in judgment, and take away thy coat, let go thy cloak also unto him.

And whoever will force thee one mile, go with him the other two. . . .

You have heard it hath been said, Thou shalt love thy neighbor, and hate thy enemy.

But I say to you, Love your enemies: do good to them that hate you: and pray for them that persecute and calumniate you . . .

After describing the beauty and utility of the Ursuline convent and denouncing the conduct of the mob, he asked: "What is to be done? Shall we say to our enemies, you have destroyed our buildings and we will destroy yours? No, my brethren, this is not the religion of Jesus Christ — this is not in accordance with the spirit of that blessed religion we all profess. Turn not a finger in your own defense, and there are those around you who will see that justice is done you."

Bishop Fenwick had confidence in the good will of the best Bostonians and ample proof of their decent intentions. A group called on him in the sad hours and "offered to rebuild the convent at once. If possible they would efface every vestige of the violence of that infuriated rabble even before the tidings could reach beyond the limits of the state." But the bishop refused the private generosity. He faithfully abided by the principle that since the catastrophe resulted from the failure of public authority, common justice demanded that the state make proper restitution.

The convent had been destroyed by "the basest and vilest portion of the people"; the influential and wealthy had sought to wipe out the infamy by their benevolence; the bishop was yet to encounter the middle portion and rural Massachusetts as represented in the legislature — the Great and General Court of Massachusetts.

The Catholic Irish of Boston strictly observed the bishop's good advice. Two weeks later the Boston *Galaxy* remarked: "The Irish population have been remarkably orderly and quiet." Francis J. Grund, then a professor at Harvard, described the burning of the convent as sufficient to provoke the "utmost temper and worst passions." Yet not for one moment had the tranquillity of the city been disturbed, and he gave full credit "to the moderation of the Irish, and the forbearance which they manifested in an appeal to their better feelings." (It is ironical that the nativists later cited the restraining influence of Bishop Fenwick in a touch-and-go crisis as an example of the total command of the clergy over the Catholic Irish.)

The week that began with the burning of the convent was the most violent and tense in Boston since the Revolution. On the night following its destruction, a mob, gathering at the rumor of the descent of Irish railroaders, skirmished in the vicinity of the Cathedral, well guarded by strong Irishmen, and then rushed to Charlestown to complete ravaging the convent by tearing down trees, uprooting vines and destroying the remains of the fence, while a company of lancers, protecting the property of Edward Cutter, watched. The military waited in Faneuil Hall for a riot call. The students of Harvard formed a defense force against a rumored attack by the Irish on the college. Volunteer patrols tramped through the streets of civilized Boston, and citizens remained at home at night behind tightly locked doors. At the weekend peace returned to Boston and Charlestown.

Nothing was salvaged from the convent, not even the insurance of $12,000 on the building and $2,000 on the furniture, which was void under the circumstances of the fire; indeed, in consequence of the convent riot, insurance on Catholic property increased fourfold in Boston; underwriters were not sure engine companies would pump water on burning Catholic church property. The total damage was set at $50,000.

After the initial shock of the outrage had worn off, intolerance took a second wind, this time in the middle portion of the population, in the last analysis the unrelenting foes of the Catholic Irish and the least forgivable for their cold spite because they could not plead the ignorance and the gullibility of the rabble. They argued the case in justification of the convent's destruction through a representative sheet, the Boston *Whig*, started in September, 1834, asserting that sympathy for the nuns tended to "build up a system of miscalled religion, abhorrent for its impiety and ignorance." A large audience thus awaited the issuing in March, 1835, by a Boston publishing firm of *Six Months in a Convent* by Rebecca Reed, written by Benjamin Hallett, a Boston editor and politician. Hallett hacked it out to cash in on the widespread appetite for anti-Popery literature whetted by the burning of the convent. It became a best-seller overnight, though unlike *Maria Monk,* which it inspired by the sales success, the account was not lascivious; it was dull in comparison to the *Awful Disclosures* and rather prissy in a Yankee way. The Lady Superior replied point by point, and Hallett then replied to the Lady Superior. An anonymous wag put a period to the controversy by *Six Months in a House of Correction,* a broad-axed satire upon Rebecca Reed's original story.

The Boston *Whig* challenged the report of the mayor's investigation committee issued on September 20, 1834. The committee, which candidly stated they were "*unanimously* opposed to [Roman Catholic] characteristic tenets," completely absolved the convent of the injurious misrepresentations unjustly attributed to it, traced the imputations to the stories of Rebecca Reed, characterized the burning as "an event of fearful import as well as of the profoundest shame and humiliation," advocated strengthening of laws and procedures against a similar event in the future and recommended public indemnification of property losses.

14

Twelve men were indicted for burglary and arson, in the old-fashioned language of the Massachusetts statute, "not having the fear of God before their eyes, but being moved by the instigation of the devil." They were principally artisans — brickmakers, shoemakers, bakers and carpenters — and included Buzzell; Pond, the brother-in-law of Rebecca Reed; Alvah Kelley, the brickyard owner, and Marvin Marcy, the lad who mock-auctioned the Bishop's library. Others carried such typically Yankee names as Sargeant Blaisdell, Isaac Parker, Nathaniel Budd, Jr., Aaron Hadley, Ephraim G. Holwell, Benjamin Wilbur, and one, undoubtedly a descendant of Protestant Irish stock in New Hampshire, had the Celtic name of Thomas Dillon.

The Commonwealth of Massachusetts vigorously prosecuted the case amidst an openly hostile opinion and in the face of threats and intimidation. But after the acquittal, to great popular jubilation, of Buzzell, the ringleader, in a trial which started on December 2, 1834, before Chief Justice Lemuel Shaw and two associates of the Supreme Court, public interest waned. Sixteen witnesses placed Buzzell on the scene, but the defense attorneys effectively exploited anti-Catholic feeling, which was their trump card, and the freed Ajax held a reception on the green outside the courthouse. In two subsequent trials, either acquittals and disagreement were the verdicts, except for Marvin

Marcy, the irresponsible lad who went to the scene for a lark and was the least involved in the conspiracy, who was found guilty and sentenced to hard labor for life. Bishop Fenwick started and headed a petition for his pardon; the Lady Superior wrote to the Governor pleading for the boy; and the public generally forwarded petitions to the effect that a disgraceful injustice had been done in his case. Within a year, he received a pardon.

With the conclusion of the third trial in June, 1835, the curtain dropped on the events of the riot itself, but a new chapter opened in the affair.

15

The bitter feelings that the Boston Catholic Irish community kept under control at the burning of the convent would have been dispersed had the Massachusetts legislature done justice in the generous spirit of the Brahmins and liberal Protestants. The long, searing memory of Charlestown developed not solely from the deed itself but rather from the intolerant spirit in which indemnification of the convent was rejected by the legislature. That memory contributed to the shaping of the Boston Catholic Irish mentality.

From the many evidences of a Protestant sense of shame and outrage, the Catholic Irish were in a conciliatory mood, in the same sense as Charles Carroll in reference to the unhappy state of Catholics in colonial America: "We remember and we forgive." The Catholic Irish nature was susceptible to the magnanimous gesture. Before the sequel of Charlestown had run its course, the Catholic Irish concluded that the bulk of opinion in the state condoned and felt satisfaction at the destruction of the convent.

At the convening of the Massachusetts legislature in January, 1835, Bishop Fenwick presented a petition for indemnification of the Ursulines with the plea that the protection they had a right to expect had not been given. This plea was ironically underscored by a bill the Bishop had received the previous November from the Charlestown Board of Assessors for taxes of $79.20 for the convent land and buildings. "If this be not HARD, to use a common phrase," sighed the *Jesuit*, "we know not what HARD is."

A select committee of the Massachusetts House of Representatives brought in a divided report. The majority, headed by Mr. Kinnicutt of

36 WHAT BEFELL THEM IN AMERICA

Worcester, favored the payment of indemnity, not as a legal right (no
statute then existed to cover the circumstances of the mob destruction)
but to secure life and property in the state, reaffirm the principle of
religious liberty and soften the disgrace on the state's name. The minority report, presented by Rev. Joseph Field of Claremont, engaged
in no such highfalutin nonsense. It believed that "the recommendations of the majority interfere with the oath of allegiance prescribed by
the Constitution which declares that no obedience shall be paid to any
foreign potentate" and argued, in sound no-Popery vein, that public
indemnification would put the stamp of approval upon the mischief of
this foreign-controlled religion and that this "Protestant state" could not
undermine its constitution by admitting a culpability, of which it was
not guilty, by a payment to the nuns. The subsequent debates on the
report showed the speeches in favor of indemnification but the votes
overwhelmingly — 412 to 67 — against payment. Boston and the larger
town with Catholic populations made up the yea vote; the orthodox
centers in small-town and rural New England held firm against the
"foreign nunnery." The Catholic Irish Democrats of Boston, in protest
against the conduct of the legislature, boycotted the fall elections in
1835.

The Fenwick petition was the first and the last time the Roman
Catholic diocese of Boston officially petitioned for the redress of damages. It drew the mantle of silence around itself and withdrew from an
unequal contest.

The Bunker Hill monument, built by the subscriptions of the public, was nearing completion, and this testament to American liberty
looked westward on the ruined face of the convent — a contrast which
gnawed at the liberal Protestant conscience. The Unitarian *Christian
Examiner* in 1840 thought the rebuilding of the convent should have
priority over the monument. "Nothing less," it said, "can make our
peace . . . with ourselves, and the spirit of our insulted Constitution,
our violated Faith." It stated what was now apparent — that the refusal
of justice to the Catholics rested "on the part not of a few, but of the
whole body of our people."

In 1841, a petition headed by John Greenleaf Whittier, the Quaker
poet, asked the Massachusetts legislature for indemnification of the
convent — a move solely by liberal Protestants, in which the Bishop
and the Catholics stood aside. The dissenting minority against indemnification in the first committee report had now become the major-

ity and argued that it was not expedient for the state to remunerate the convent since the issue was a local affair, while the minority held that the state was morally responsible for damages. This minority report brought to the front two signers who deserve remembrance in American Catholic Irish history. George Ticknor Curtis, the son-in-law of Justice Story of the United States Supreme Court and brother of Benjamin R. Curtis, also a Justice of the Supreme Court, turned into a crusader for justice to the convent and for his principles was penalized by the Whigs. The Rev. George Bradburn, a Universalist minister and representative from Nantucket Island, never failed once, by word or deed, to struggle for fair play toward the convent and the Catholic Irish minority. But the legislators nodded their heads in approval when Ichabod Lindsey of Charlestown compared the rioters to the heroes of Bunker Hill and admitted the duty of government to protect religious worship, "but it is not its duty to protect a man in keeping, under the cloak of religion, his 'three hundred wives and seven hundred concubines.' " The petition was pushed aside.

George Curtis returned to the fight in the legislature of 1842 with the indemnification petition of George Bradburn and as chairman of a select committee called all his legal acumen into a formidable argument in the report, concluding with praise of the Catholics for their poise and the shame on the state of the Charlestown ruins: "They have not spoken, they have not written," he said, "but the mournful dignity of their silence, made eloquent by this index of their wrong, is more touching and more persuasive than the most persuasive appeal." The petition was pushed aside.

The most imposing effort by liberal Protestant opinion to force indemnification to a favorable issue was started late in August, 1842, with a petition headed and circulated by Abbott Lawrence. The name of Abbott Lawrence, merchant prince and capitalist, was perhaps the most respected in Boston for character and integrity; he was, of all the members, the embodiment of the Boston Brahmin. The petition was signed by such representative Bostonians as Harrison Gray Otis, James T. Austin, Charles Sumner, James Russell Lowell, George Bancroft, Charles Francis Adams, Wendell Phillips, and William Lloyd Garrison.

The Democratic Party carried the state in the 1842 canvass, electing the governor, lieutenant governor and majorities in both houses of the legislature. The victory of the party, upon which the Catholic

Irish, asserted the *Pilot,* "have claims . . . which it will be perilous for them to forget," together with the imposing Lawrence petition, gave rise to hopes of a just settlement in the next General Court. The Catholic Irish were a buoyant people by nature: "I hope," toasted a member at the St. Patrick's Day dinner in 1843, "that the next St. Patrick's Day, we may hear and see the nunnery rebuilt and Ireland free."

The message of Democratic Governor Marcus Morton to the General Court was the first setback: he was profoundly silent on the convent issue. The Lawrence petition was formally presented; it did not seek indemnification but merely asked for an official inquiry into the facts of the burning of the convent. The House, Democratic though it was, exultingly rejected even an inquiry into the facts and turned down the Lawrence petition by the overwhelming vote of 204 to 73. The Senate made a gesture of adopting an order for an inquiry, knowing what its fate would be in the House. Who were worse, asked the *Pilot,* the Charlestown mob or the "viler mob" of the House? The Catholic Irish were now, it continued, "citizens without protection, taxpayers without a government, and Americans without a country." Only one refuge remained — the ballot box.

Immediately after the rejection of the Lawrence petition, a large body of the Catholic Irish gathered at the Odeon Hall, on March 23, in response to the call to "take into consideration the conduct of the Legislature in relation to the convent claim." Eight annual messages by three different governors had failed to mention the convent; three legislatures had kicked out the redress of a wrong "with indecent haste"; both Whigs and Democrats had failed to pursue justice.

A week later at the Masonic Temple, with a larger and highly enthusiastic attendance, the Catholic Irish of Boston organized as a separate bloc, not as a separate political party and not as a Catholic party, which would be "monstrous," said the *Pilot,* to join with Protestant friends to support those candidates in either of the two major parties who would pledge in advance to further the convent claim and to withhold support from candidates who showed hostility or kept silent. A state committee was named to press the campaign in every part of Massachusetts. It was estimated that eight thousand Catholics were registered voters in the state. The convent question had now become a political issue, unhappily.

The attempted pressure bloc was a failure. By the middle of July, the *Pilot* complained of the indifference and apathy that had crept into the state organization. The reluctance of Irish Democrats to break from party regularity brought upon their heads the condemnation of the *Pilot* as deserving of "ignominy and insult." The hopelessness (not to speak of the economic retaliation that might ensue) of challenging Yankee candidates on the convent question in localities outside of Boston and in the larger towns was apparent to their small Catholic Irish communities. A Boston newspaper threw into the Catholic Irish midst the suggestion of treachery by a prominent leader, who, it charged, had sold out on the convent question for a Democratic nomination to office. "Hereafter," said the *Pilot,* meaning after the election, "we shall have some interesting revelations about the *public spirit* of the state executive committee." The revelations never appeared.

The Whigs, normally the majority party in Massachusetts, wrested control from the Democrats and now, said the Irish, we shall give them a chance to speak up for convent indemnification, but not a word did their Governor Briggs in his message say on the subject. The opposition phalanx held its lines and in a debate on the Lawrence petition, which had again been presented, one particularly barrel-charred No-Popery man added insult to injury by proposing that if the convent were to be indemnified, so should a house of ill-fame which a mob had torn apart in New Bedford. Though the legislature pleaded it had no time for the convent issue, it spent two days in debate on the protection of clams and grouse and "if," said the *Pilot,* "the convent sufferers were clams, they would have protection."

By an extraordinary coincidence, Bishop Fenwick died on August 11, 1846, the anniversary of the burning of the convent — "on the very day," noticed the *Pilot,* "on which he had drank the bitterest chalice of affliction during the whole course of his apostolic labors." Bishop Fenwick never recovered in spirit from the shock of the convent calamity. A weariness seemed to have come over him. He had stood up to the crisis with the fortitude of the true gentleman and by his conduct had made the Church he loved respected by the judicious. He did not live to feel the healing balm of Dr. George C. Shattuck, a sterling Yankee, who in his will left five hundred dollars to Bishop Fenwick's successor "in token of my sense of the great injustice done by the unindemnified destruction of the Ursuline convent in Charlestown." This was an act of classic piety that merits a warm place in the Catholic Irish memory.

The demagogue Ben Butler of Lowell, who had seen the flames of the burning convent from his home, came the closest, in the 1853 session of the Massachusetts legislature, to wringing victory from the successive defeats of convent restitution since 1835. Under his smart politicking, a bill granting indemnity had been pushed to a third reading but over the weekend rural Massachusetts had been heard from and, as the *Commonwealth* said, the orthodox Whig members from the back areas did not stand the fire. On reconsideration, the measure was killed by the narrow margin of nine votes.

That year, with the Know-Nothing movement on the increase, the *Pilot* dropped the curtain on the sad tale of the sequel of the convent's burning; "It may be ten, twenty or thirty years hence," it predicted, "but the day of an honorable settlement will surely come, and, although Massachusetts cannot afford to wait, Catholics can."

To this day Massachusetts has not made restitution, not even of a token nature, such as the state made in expunging the exile of Roger Williams three hundred years later.

The Bunker Hill monument was dedicated in 1843 with eloquent phrases on liberty by Daniel Webster, and spectators, by a glance, could take in the wreck of the convent on the next hill. The ruins stood un-relieved, as a sad testament of what intolerance teamed with willful credulity can wreak, until 1875, when Archbishop Williams of Boston sold the land.

16

Less than a year after the burning of the convent, the Boston *Sentinel,* the secular successor of the clerical *Jesuit,* asked why "the lower classes of the citizens of Massachusetts" showed such intolerance of the Catholics and Irish. A mob at Wareham, a Yankee village on the approach to Cape Cod, had on May 17, 1835, interrupted Mass being celebrated in the hotel for the Irish workers in the local nail factory and threatened to destroy "the Popish priest." In October of the same year, a crowd of nativists, led by a temperance fanatic, had at the other end of New England driven a small colony of Catholic Irish out of Concord, New Hampshire.

In Boston, gangs of young rowdies tormented the Irish for their sport, and the insulting sneer of "Paddies" invited physical combat. The destruction of the convent failed to appease the anti-Catholic Irish malice of the lower orders. The prickling harassment exploded into a pitched battle on Sunday afternoon, June 11, 1837, in the Broad Street riot, with the old enemies of the Irish, the Boston volunteer firemen, at the center of the brawl, seeing "no other way of vindicating American muscle and independence," said a contemporary report, "than by breaking the heads of their fellow-citizens."

A scuffle between some Irishmen forming a funeral procession that Sunday afternoon and members of an engine house nearby so agitated an officer of the company that he sounded the alarm bells for help. At this, the Irishmen disengaged themselves and fell in behind the moving procession. Not far from the junction of Sea (Federal) and Summer Streets, in the vicinity of the present South Station, Company 9, answering the alarm, swung around the corner at breakneck speed and skidded to a stop, the running firemen swerving the engine before it crashed into the rear of the funeral march on the way to the Charlestown Cemetery.

The Irishmen feared the company intended to break up the funeral and seized the ropes of the engine. The firemen fell upon the Irishmen, and the Irishmen swung back in a free-for-all. Six companies of firemen joined Company 9, together with straggling members from other companies, and pressed the Irish back into their own Broad Street district. Messengers, swifter of tongue than accurate in information, spread the word that the firemen had killed an Irishman and destroyed the hearse and coffin. The disrupted funeral procession, strengthened by Irish auxiliaries, including the women, who fought fiercely, took a stand but, outnumbered, retreated southward along Broad Street.

Infuriated firemen assaulted the tenements looking for Irishmen who might have taken refuge, and piled up considerable damage. But loafers, ruffians and wild-spirited lads, who followed the firemen, wreaked the worst vandalism. They looted what was of value and smashed the Irish quarters, broke up furniture, tore out grates and ripped open beds to scatter the contents into the street until the next morning Broad Street was ankle-deep in feathers and straw.

Mayor Samuel A. Eliot — father of the president of Harvard — appeared early and with the courage the Irish respected tried to impose his authority, only to be knocked down. He sent out a call for military, but since the members were dispersed on Sunday, the horsemen and infantry did not move down State Street into Broad until between six and seven o'clock. With Mayor Eliot, the aldermen and the city council in line with the militia companies — an impressive sight, people afterward said — order was restored.

The hearse proceeded by itself to the Bunker Hill cemetery and the poor departed soul entered into the grave unattended by friends. Three Irishmen of the fourteen people indicted received sentences, but no Yankee was punished. In consequence of the Broad Street riot, Mayor Eliot forced a paid fire company upon an unwilling Boston and later a modern police system was established.

17

A Catholic convent burned and the Irish district stripped — Boston indeed expressed violently its sentiments on the intruding and unwanted Catholic Irish. The Boston City Council and the Massachusetts legislature had initiated action in the political field to restrict the franchise and make more difficult the entrance into the United States of the Catholic Irishman. The foreshortened Yankee definition of an American excluded the Irish, even unto the second generation, from honorable participation in the duties of citizenship and set the ground for the most humiliating experience yet of the Boston Catholic Irish community, a cold, calculated and deliberate insult, a nativist American slap across the mouth.

Among the military companies which had suppressed the Broad Street riot marched the recently organized Montgomery Guards, a company of second-generation and of naturalized Irishmen, named in honor of General Richard Montgomery.

The company had been formed for the praiseworthy purpose of militia service and association with the life of the city and state; it was an affirmative expression of a will by the Irish to be Americans. Pride of race and sentimental attachments to the motherland prompted a distinctively green uniform, on their caps the emblem of the eagle bearing a harp symbolic of amalgamation, their motto: "Fostered under thy wing, we will die in thy defence." Each member wore a piece of lace in the form of a shamrock sprig. A deep psychological necessity urged the Catholic Irish to express membership in the American community in terms of their racial identity — a pattern consistent with emigrant peoples; but the means of fulfillment through this symbolism struck highly nationalistic America as unpatriotic and unsatisfactory hyphenation.

The membership of the Montgomery Guards was described by the *Boston Mercantile Journal* as "Men of good character and respectable standing in the community." More than half of the company's roster of forty-five were American-born and the rest either naturalized or at least had taken out first papers. Each had the economic status to be able to purchase his own uniform. The captain, elected by the company, was a Protestant of old New England stock, William S. Baxter, a later convert to Catholicism, and membership included several Protestants.

The Montgomery Guards, chartered in January, 1837, made their first appearance in public during the Broad Street riot, where they were entrusted the all-night assignment of sentinels of the peace and conducted themselves as a militia company, not as Irish partisans. Indeed, the Boston *Atlas* welcomed the Montgomery Guards not only as an example to the Irish who brawled among themselves but as a source of strength, it said, in quelling Irish disturbances: "One hand will be made to wash the other," it remarked in shrewd Yankee practicality.

But amidst the laudatory comments crept in a note of unease; some feared the presence of an armed Irish company (forty-five members) as a menace to American institutions and some bluntly damned the Irish character of an American militia company. The ill-will against the Montgomery Guards rose strongest among the Yankee noncommissioned officers and rank and file of the other militia companies and they held talks among themselves about putting down the damned Paddies.

Tuesday, September 12, 1837, was Brigade Review Day, when all the local militia companies rendezvoused on Boston Common for drill and maneuvers in a day-long military display. The ten companies forming the Light Infantry Regiment were in the process of coming into line, with the older companies taking their positions first, when the Montgomery Guards, the newest company, swung last into their assigned place. There was a rumble of undertones and at the command of a noncommissioned officer the City Guards, defying the orders of their officers, left the parade line. With the flag flying and the drum beating out "Yankee Doodle," the company marched through the city streets to its armory, contemptuously refusing to stay on the same ground with the Irish company. Four companies immediately left the Common after the City Guards and at noon a fifth also departed. Six militia companies thus staged a mutiny against the Commonwealth of Massachusetts and military law in a flagrant and public insult to the Irish.

At six o'clock the remaining companies were dismissed and the

Montgomery Guards started the march back to their Dock Square armory. With the Irish company separated from the other militia outfits, "a gang of worthless wretches," in the words of the *Boston Mercantile Journal,* hooted and assaulted the green-uniformed men. Paving stones, glass bottles, anthracite coal and clubs flew through the air and, though none of the Guards was killed, a number were painfully wounded and their uniforms bespattered with their own blood from the missiles thrown by Americans.

The discipline and forbearance of the Irish company was extraordinary. Though armed with muskets and bayonets, they kept their formation intact and with eyes straight ahead marched without break or resistance back to their armory. How they were able, as Irishmen, to keep their tempers seemed "a marvel" to Consul Grattan. While the Montgomery Guards passed through Tremont Street under attack, the Boston Lancers clattered down School Street in sight of the assaulted company but offered neither assistance to the Guards nor resistance to the mob.

The next morning a thoroughly aroused public opinion, this time on the side of the Irish without qualification, roared its angry disapprobation. Baltimore and Savannah held public meetings in protest against the disgraceful treatment of the Montgomery Guards; newspapers throughout the country pilloried the name of Boston; Irish military companies in other cities forwarded resolutions of comfort to the Montgomery Guards.

Four of the rioters were brought to trial, and three received sentences of three years at hard labor, and the other, two years. But in the more important test of punishing the mutineers, Governor Edward Everett, of distinguished name and career, lost his guts, in plain language, and weakly submitted to the forces which whispered it would cost votes to punish Yankees to give justice to the Irish.

Though high officers of the militia advocated punishment to restore discipline in the service, and officers of the six companies were arrested for negligence and complicity, the commander of the brigade refused to press charges.

Governor Everett, after months of pulling and hauling, ignobly straddled the issue. He disbanded the six companies of mutineers but without public censure. In due time, after the affair had quieted down, a reorganization of the militia permitted the revival of the disobedient companies under new names: the City Guards, which originated the mutiny, became known as the City Grays and wore their old uniforms.

Then, in response to the pressure of the disobedient companies and their supporters, Governor Everett revoked the charter of the Montgomery Guards. He had no legal ground for the revocation; he could cite no cause — of insubordination or neglect of duty or dishonorable conduct; every consideration of law and fair play, as well as the soldierly behavior of the Irish under great stress, demanded that they be upheld. He justified himself on the plea of public order. He cited the apprehension that the corps could be sustained only by force, and that its reappearance would be the signal for outrages of a dangerous character.

Grattan, the British consul, was disappointed at Everett's lack of character. The transaction, he wrote, "was a test of his capacity for public affairs, and of his moral courage. Its consequences were fatal to his political career. They not only deprived him of the attachment of the Irish inhabitants of the State, but must have lost him the confidence of even the native citizens, who saw that he possessed, if not the fury of a partisan, at least the weakness of a participator. He was to all intents and purposes an accessory after the fact." After the Montgomery Guards affair and the letdown of the Irish by the Whig Governor Everett, the *Pilot* in 1838 advised its readers: let's vote the Democratic ticket; that party has treated us better.

Grattan tried to persuade Everett to attend a St. Patrick's Day dinner, to which he had been invited courteously but without cordiality, as a means of conciliating the Irish. Later, he confessed to Grattan that he could not venture to confront the ill-used Irish even as their guest and under the sure protection of their hospitality.

After the revocation of their charter, the Montgomery Guards issued a public statement that manfully stated their side of the controversy but ended with the stated determination "never to shoulder a musket in the militia of this Commonwealth WHILE THE COUNTERSIGN IS PROSCRIPTION." But the Boston Catholic Irish later re-formed their ranks in the militia and again they felt the rebuff of proscription, as we shall see.

A resolution of the Montgomery Guards of New York to the disbanded company in Boston, however, set the deepest sentiments of the Catholic Irish toward defense of their adopted country. In the flamboyant rhetoric of the day, the resolution said that the Irish would be ready in the hour of the country's danger and "we know that the American flag when blended with the proud colors of the Montgomery

Guards will never be backward at an onset — never surpassed; and that that flag will never be abandoned, deserted, or forsaken, whilst Irish Americans feel the pulse of life under a green coat."

The gravestones of the Mexican War and the Civil War later bore testimony to the profound reality behind the high-sounding words.

18

These were harsh and trying years for the Catholic Irish in Boston and New England, and even tolerant Vermont joined in the violence with the incendiary burning of St. Mary's Church in Burlington in May, 1838.

The Catholic Irish had borne the trials with patience and forbearance — and had, in the familiar Yankee phrase, "hung on." The slugging attacks by Yankeedom on the Church had tightened loyalty to the ancient religion, called back the wavering and wayward, and deepened affection and attachment to the one mooring that gave the Catholic Irish spiritual strength in the new land.

Further tribulations lay ahead, but the Catholic Irish were better prepared to defend themselves. They were increasing in numbers and gaining political influence. A minority was winning economic strength. A stronger backlog of friendliness was building among the Yankees, but still a small minority in contrast to the stubborn prejudices of the majority. The Catholic Irish were coming to learn that the Constitution was on their side.

In the meantime, Catholic Irish emigration was steadily pouring into the United States and large numbers continued to be drained into the service of building canals and railroads. The conditions of that unsettled life gave the Catholic Irish race a reputation for violence and lawlessness and was an important chapter in their American story.

3 2

Irish "Strollers" on Public Works

CAPTAIN MARRYAT, the English novelist and traveler, observed in his *Diary* in the late 1830s that the "emigrants most troublesome, but, at the same time, the most valuable to the United States, are the Irish." Without the Irish, he continued, "the Americans would not have been able to complete the canals and railroads and many other important works."

The conjunction of "troublesome" and "Irish" developed in considerable measure from the disturbances on public works. While "Irish riots" drew public attention and censure, little notice (and then unfavorable) was paid to the economic origins of the disturbances. The reasons Americans, and even at times the Catholic Irish press, cited to account for the troubles — Irish abuse of American liberty, combativeness, overindulgence in liquor or county factionalism — missed the point that the Irish workers resorted to a form of primitive and inchoate labor unionism in self-protection against harsh conditions of employment, including fraud, and for better wages. Lacking the machinery of bargaining and the disciplines of organized unionism, they used violence to enforce demands or redress grievances. The Irish had their side of the story, not so footless and distorted as opinion of the time made it out to be. Behind the "riots" lay as unconscionable and relentless an exploitation of unprotected labor as American history affords. More than self-pity caused Irish canal and railroad workers to compare their lot with Negro slavery — unfavorably.

Thomas O'Connor had foreseen in his New York *Shamrock,* even before the Erie Canal was started, that a program of internal improvements offered the best work opportunities for his unskilled Irish countrymen in the United States, but he conceived the hard labor as a means to build up savings for eventual settlement on the land. This concept dominated the best Catholic Irish thinking decade after decade, but with too many Irish emigrants canal and railroad labor became an end in itself. They journeyed from job to job on public works, and had fixed on them the name of "strollers."

"Employment certainly on the canals and public works is a happy thing for the needful to have on their arrival," wrote an Irishman in 1829; "but it appears to me that when once embarked in this they never think of anything else. They spend summer after summer on these canals, and in the end they find themselves just where they set off."

The public works that burgeoned under the example of the Erie Canal clamored for laborers. One thousand men were wanted for the Delaware and Hudson Canal in 1825 and a year later three thousand were advertised for. One thousand men labored on the Ohio canal system in September, 1825, and a few months later their numbers had jumped to twenty-five hundred. The Delaware and Chesapeake employed twenty-five hundred in 1826 and five hundred hands were digging the Blackstone Canal from Providence to Worcester.

In July, 1826, *Niles' Register* reported that no less than 102 canals were made, making, or projected in the United States.

Agents met incoming ships to hire emigrants for public works. Irish grocers, who also sold liquor, allowed their countrymen to run up bills and bargained with contractors to supply laborers from these debtors. Saloons acted as labor recruiting offices. Contractors, wanting sober men, sought the offices of Rev. John Power, pastor of St. Peter's Church on Barclay Street. The Union Emigrant Society, in its short life during 1829, placed 1162 idle in work, mostly on canals.

Contractors placed advertisements in the New York *Truth Teller* to reach into the New York Catholic Irish emigrant pool, of which the following, the first in 1829 and the second in 1833, were typical:

> Wanted immediately, 40 Stonecutters by Wm. & Michael Byrne & Co. who reside in Harrisburgh, Pa, to work in the neighborhood of Harrisburgh, on the Pennsylvania Canal, to whom liberal wages and constant employment will be given for one year at least.
>
> Wanted on Delaware and Hudson Canal about 1000 laborers to whom liberal wages will be given. Application to be made on John C. Dunn, inn keeper, Anthony Street, New Brunswick, N.J. There are three steamboats leaving New York for New Brunswick and canal is within short distance of wharf.

But unscrupulous contractors speedily took advantage of the response of Irishmen to work opportunities. If they needed five hundred laborers, they advertised for a thousand and then used the surplus to beat down the wages of the five hundred they hired, as well as the wages of the men already employed. Many labor "riots" on public works originated in resisting this sharp practice.

2

As early as 1826 appeared the fraud of absconding with the payroll by public works contractors, which became familiar to victimized Irishmen and the root cause of numerous canal and railroad disturbances. About the middle of December, 1826, stories circulated that the "wild Irish" had rampaged and considerably damaged the works of the sixteen-mile canal from the Savannah to the Ogechee Rivers in Georgia. Inquiry revealed that a pair of contractors had "eloped" with $700 owed to the workers, principally Irish, together with the savings entrusted to them, leaving the laborers destitute, and that the "damage" consisted of roughing up another subcontractor from whom the Irish tried to squeeze information of the whereabouts of the embezzlers.

The system of letting out subcontracts by the principal contractor, which originated on the Erie Canal, lent itself both to absconding and the sweating of labor. If a subcontractor, operating on a shoestring, ran into difficulties, he solved his problem by disappearing with the wages owed the workers. Since the uncertain profits of the subcontractor depended upon the amount of work he could wring out of the laborers at the lowest wages and the cheapest accommodations he found for them, life on the public works was hard.

Tyrone Power, the Irish actor and ancestor of the moving picture star, saw the Irish laboring on the canal connecting Lake Pontchartrain with New Orleans in the first half of the 1830s, and he painted a vivid — and terrifying — picture of the conditions under which they worked:

> I only wish that the wise men at home who coolly charge the present condition of Ireland upon the inherent laziness of her population could be transported to this spot, to look upon the hundreds of fine fellows labouring beneath a sun that at this winter season was at times insufferably fierce, and amidst a pestilential swamp whose exhalations were fetid to a degree scarcely endurable for a few moments; wading amidst stumps of trees, mid-deep in black mud, clearing the spaces pumped out by powerful steam-engines; wheeling, digging, hewing, or bearing burdens it made one's shoulders ache to look upon; exposed meantime to every change of temperature, in log-huts laid down in the very swamps, on a foundation of newly-felled trees, having the waters lying stagnant between the floor-logs, whose interstices, together with those of the side-walls, are open, pervious alike to sun, wind, or snow. Here they subsist on the coarsest fare, holding life on a tenure as uncertain as does the leader of a forlorn hope; excluded from all the advantages of civilization; often at the mercy of a hard contractor, who wrings his profits from their blood; and all this for a pittance that merely enables him to exist, with little power to save, or a hope beyond the continuance of the like exertion.

Power contemplated the number of Irish lives that might be spared if the employers only showed them a decent consideration and could not find heart to tax them for forgetfulness in cheap whiskey. The jigger of whiskey, as indispensable a part of the day's work as the spade or the leveler, provided bracer and medicine alike. As one annalist noted:

> At that day the idea of constructing a canal without whiskey would have been viewed as preposterous. . . . Every shanty was supplied with whiskey which cooled them when it was hot, and heated them when it was cool; that was good in prosperity or adversity, in sickness and in health, before breakfast in the morning, and on retiring to rest at night; in a word, an article that possessed specific virtues at all times.

The contractor supplied whiskey as a routine of the work. The jigger, a dram of less than a gill, was downed first at sunrise, when the work started, then at ten o'clock, another at noon, and the last on the job at supper time. Some contractors offered six whiskey breaks a day. The whiskey was not a solace given in good heart; the jiggers supposed that the Irishman's shovel flew into the work after a belt of whiskey and that without it he grew morose and idling.

3

With increasing numbers of Irish workers, accounts appeared of "riots" on the public works. In the spring of 1829, Irish laborers on certain of the Pennsylvania canals struck for better pay or, as one paper reported it, "combined to enforce higher wages." The strikers not only laid down their tools but to buttress their demands tried violently to restrain the laborers who continued to work. The strikers were suppressed by force, the ringleaders jailed and condemned as foreigners "who have yet to learn respect for the laws."

The building of public works resembled the settlement of the frontier. Thousands of men lived a rough life away from civilized centers, quartered in the flimsy barracks of shanties.* They had no

---

* A master of English prose described the Irish public works shanty. Henry Thoreau bought for $4.25 the shanty — "considered an uncommonly fine one" — of James Collins, a railroad worker, for the boards to build his house by the side of Walden Pond. "It was of small dimensions, with a peaked cottage roof, and not much else to be seen, the dirt being raised five feet all around, as if it were a compost heap." The window was deep and high. "Doorsill there was none, but a perennial passage for the hens under the door-board." Inside, it "was dark, and had a dirt floor for the most part, dank, clammy, and aguish, only here a board and there a board which would not bear removal." The "board floor extended

CHIEF ENGINEERS' OFFICE CHESAPEAKE & OHIO CANAL;
CUMBERLAND, 13TH APRIL, 1850.

*To the Contractors for the
completion of the Chesapeake & Ohio canal,
their Agents, and Sub-contractors.*

YOU are directed not to employ upon your works any of the following named persons, viz :---

Lawrence Burns, mason,
Richard Keefe, stone cutter,
Nicholas Hughes, stone cutter,
George Biggs, stone cutter.
James Mulligan, stone cutter,
Henry Carter, mason,
Dennis Nolan, mason,
Jeremiah Reide
Lawrence Swift
John McSweeney
Thomas Nugen
John McGinty
Edward Conner
James Watson

~~Martin Monro~~
Michael Keenan
Patrick Murray
Michael Cunningham
Martin Rudy
Patrick Bannan
Patrick Murray
Peter Lavelle
Hugh McCaffry
Edward Riely
Mark Kilroy
Patrick Roach, and
William McCormick.

CHARLES B. FISK, Chief Eng.

Blacklist of workers, mostly Irish, on the Chesapeake & Ohio Canal

amusements or diversions except as contrived by themselves, working, drinking, gambling, and fighting hard, among themselves and with inhabitants along the line. "The laborers on our canals and roads, chiefly raw foreigners," wrote a comfortable editor in settled surroundings, "are hard to convince that they live under a government of laws."

4

Charles Carroll turned the first spadeful of soil on July 4, 1828, and work began on the Baltimore & Ohio, the first great railroad project in the United States, with hordes of Irish laborers taking over from

under the bed" and the cellar was "a sort of dust hole two feet deep." "There was a stove, a bed, and a place to sit, an infant in the house where it was born, a silk parasol, gilt-framed looking-glass, and a patent new coffee-mill nailed to an oak sapling, all told." *Walden*, Riverside Library Edition, pp. 47-48.

the delicate hands of the aged Signer. In the summer of 1829, exaggerated reports spread of "several dangerous and disgraceful" riots on
the works not far from Baltimore. One or more contractors had absconded with wages owed the laborers, left penniless, many with
families. The company's directors, with "some wholesome fears . . .
for the safety of the work," as an Irishman expressed it, distributed
a small percentage of the defalcated sum among the men to quiet the
excitement and agreed to protect their interests with the contractors
in the future.

Two years later, toward the end of June, 1831, Truxton Lyon,
a contractor, disappeared owing the workers $9000 in current and
back wages and the savings given him for safekeeping. The company
wanted to settle for $2000 but the men, brooding over the swindle and
agitated by leaders, went into a blind frenzy and started to tear up the
tracks they had laid. The superintendent persuaded them to stop with
the offer to go into Baltimore to confer with the directors. He returned
with the sheriff, who was hardly interested in the argument of the
spokesman, Hugh Reily, that the destruction, if wrong in law, held
in justice and that the company was morally bound for the contractor's
embezzlement.

The sheriff issued a riot warrant in Baltimore to Brigadier General
Steuart, and at night militiamen boarded a train furnished by the
company. This was the first time in history that troops moved by railroad — a hundred Maryland militiamen to put down Irish laborers.
The military arrived at the shanties of the workers when dawn was
breaking, surprised them in their beds and arrested fifty, including
Reily. They were marched through the streets of Baltimore to the tune
of martial music and jailed. Brought before a local judge and examined, thirty-seven were released as tools of the leaders, who were
remanded. The company immediately sent out plentiful supplies of
food to the workers and their families. "A new contractor came out and
finished Lyon's job," wrote the historian of the B & O. "Whether his
workmen were ever fully paid is not in the records."

Niles' Register found it difficult to suppose that the "wrong-headed"
Irish could believe such acts of violence would pass unpunished.
"The Irishman's heart generally is, and always would be, in the right
place," the editor continued, "but the oppression which he suffered at
home has not yet ceased to have effect upon his head — and, though
his person has been transferred to America, it takes him some con-

siderable time to shake off those prejudices and habits that belonged
to and influenced him in the land of his birth. . . . Let us then pass
over as easily as we can, the doings of the great majority of these men,
and charge them to the account of British domination." That judgment failed to contemplate that the Irishman responded violently in
Maryland for the same reason he struck back in Ireland — a feeling
that his superiors would not show him justice.

In the middle of August, 1831, a parcel of twenty Irishmen cooled
their heels in the jail of New Market, in Maryland's Frederick County,
on the line of the B & O, after a hassle with colored laborers. Now
appeared on American soil the transplanted traditional institution of
old Ireland — the rescue party. Four hundred Irish laborers responded
to the blood clan call and proceeded in a body to liberate the cooped
Gaels, but forehanded preparations had arrayed to meet them the
county's high sheriff, the local militia — and Father John B. Mc-
Elroy, Roman Catholic pastor of Frederick. With Father McElroy at
their head, the soothed Irishmen formed an orderly procession, returned quietly to their shanties and resumed work the next day. The
grateful B & O presented the priest $100 for charity for his pacific
intervention.*

The quieting influence of the clergy on Irish overwrought feelings in
disturbances made many a native American head shake with misgivings. Father Curran had pacified Irish rioters in 1830 at Harrisburg.
"The magistrate there had been abused, and his authority trampled
under foot," wrote the outraged *The American Traveller,* "when the
Catholic clergy were allowed to magnify the influence of the Church,
in contrast with that of the state, by coaxing and conjuring down the
turbulent spirit of these disorders." Better to use the utmost severity of
the law, it advised, than suffer the interference of priests:

---

* Father McElroy, an interesting figure, had at the time of the incident been in
Frederick since 1822 building St. John's Church and planning for St. John's
Literary Institution, an academy, orphan asylum, and first free public school in the
town. A native of Brookeborough, in the northern county of Fermanagh, he had
come to the United States after a limited education in Ireland and worked as a
bookkeeper at Georgetown College. He entered the Jesuit Order as a lay brother
in 1806 and was ordained eleven years later. He was named as one of the two
chaplains to the Irish troops of General Zachary Taylor in the Mexican War. His
outstanding achievement was the founding of Boston College in 1858, which he
opened in 1860 and served as president during 1861-1862. For seventy-one years he
was a member of the Society of Jesus and died, blind and in retirement, in Frederick, which he loved, in 1877.

If the throes of *ignorant foreigners* who are drawn together by the favorable opportunities for profitable labor in our great public works, *can* be taught the supremacy of our laws *in no other manner, let them learn it at the point of the bayonet,* and if hecatombs of them should be sacrificed in restoring peace and order, it were far better than to have their excesses conjured down by the bloodless, but not harmless mummery of a priest — by the influence emanating from the triple-crowned monarch of Rome.

5

President John Quincy Adams turned over the first soil to symbolize the start of work on the Chesapeake & Ohio Canal — a waterway from the Potomac to the coal mines of Cumberland in Maryland and thence, according to plans, to the Ohio River — on the day Charles Carroll performed the same ceremonial act in Baltimore for the railroad.

The number of public works in progress in the United States and Canada made labor scarce and wages high; and the Chesapeake & Ohio Company wanted to build the canal on the cheap. On November 18, 1829, its President Mercer circularized the American consuls at Cork, Belfast, and Dublin, asking for the distribution of notices which stressed the advantages of work on the canal to the laboring poor of Ireland, "who . . . have, at this moment, a year of scarcity presented to them," he wrote. He solicited the good offices of the American minister in London, James Barbour, in the hope the British government might countenance the emigration from Ireland "of three or four thousand hands . . . with their priests, if they could come along with them." Neither application brought the cheap Irish labor he wanted. He applied in 1829 to the newly formed Union Emigrant Society for five thousand laborers, and three schooners departed from New York in August with three hundred mechanics and laborers for Georgetown.

The company's account books designated these men as "New York Laborers," and the Georgetown Trustee of the Poor, in the second week of August, 1829, told a pathetic story. Almost hourly he was called upon "to relieve the Labourers coming into town, from the Line of the canal sick and destitute of the means to procure medical aid or the common necessaries of life." These poor Irishmen had been picked up from the street perishing and several had died, "more from a want of food than as a consequence of disease." He felt that the responsibility for their care rested with the source which had brought them to the works — the canal company. A firm of contractors, Boteler & Reynolds, described to the company the sorry condition of the laborers from New York, for whom they had had to buy clothes, the cost to be deducted from their wages. "In furnishing clothes to these men," advised the secretary of the company in a reply typical of the C & O's calloused attitude towards labor, "please to be very limited in the supply — merely doing what is indispensable."

The winter wages, from November 1 to March 1, for laborers ranged from $8 to $9 a month, with deductions for time lost by inclement weather, and board, but if bad weather stopped work, "we board them free of expense." After April 1, wages rose to from $10 to $12 a month, with board.

As on other public works, contractors absconded with the wages of the laborers. Often the men waited two months for pay because of the company's constant financial difficulties. Contractors intended that the men should labor from the rising of the sun to the going down thereof: one asked the company to build the shanties closer to the works, as too much time was lost from employment by the distance the men had to go for meals. Aches and fevers during the unhealthy

AN IRISH WORKER'S PAY VOUCHER

season, July through August, so depleted the work force that in 1832 the company took the extraordinary measure for the times of hiring a physician to examine the shanties, recommend precautions and care for the sick in order that the progress of the canal might not be delayed.

But late in August of that year, cholera, which had reached the United States from an Irish emigrant ship at Quebec, struck the works of the Chesapeake & Ohio, and man after man died, "turning black and dying in twenty four hours in the very room where his comrades are to sleep or to dine." Early in September, information reached the company's office that "the poor Exiles of Erin are flying in every direction." The flight from the plague turned into a rout, and as a letter described the scene:

> The poor creatures, after seeing a few sudden & awful deaths amongst friends, straggled off in all directions through the country; but for many of them the panic came too late. They are dying in all parts of Washington County [Maryland] at the distance of 5 to 15 miles from the river. I myself saw numbers of them in carts & on foot making their way towards Pennsylvania.

Thomas F. Purcell, a company engineer, a decent and humane man, who consistently had a heart for the Irish, wrote of the demoralization of the workers:

> Humanity is outraged by some of the scenes presented; men deserted by their friends or comrades, have been left to die in the fields, the highways, or in the neighboring barns & stables: in some instances, as I have been told, when the disease has attacked them, the invalid has been enticed from the shandee [shanty] & left to die under the shade of some tree.

The company established some ramshackle hospitals as temporary quarters — planks for bunks, some blankets and straw for stacks, "and as few and as cheap articles for the Hospital at Harpers Ferry as possible," as President Mercer directed. The company required laborers to contribute 25 cents each month as their share of the upkeep of the Harpers Ferry Hospital, intended to be permanent, and itself appropriated the lean sum of $500 to meet the panic emergency along the whole line of the works.

The authorities of Hagerstown refused to permit the burial in St. Mary's Catholic Cemetery of the bodies of four Irishmen brought from the canal, and prohibited future burials of plague victims. The next year, in August, cholera struck again and once more Hagerstown closed the cemetery. Purcell recommended that the company purchase suitable lots for a burial ground, but the board of directors demurred: this was outside their line of duty, they explained. In a burst of benevolence, however, they authorized the engineers "to use any waste ground owned by the canal company for the interment of persons dying upon the works of the Company."

No records are available of the number of Irishmen employed by the canal company who died in the cholera epidemics of 1833 and 1834. The company had more important matters to attend to than dead laborers.

The Catholic Irish laborers on public works everywhere (as well as the Irish crowded in unhealthy city garrets and cellars) severely felt the scourge of the death plague, from the Harlem railroad in New York to New Orleans whence came the brutal report that "the poor Irish canal diggers were dying like rotten sheep."

6

In the terminal period 1820-1840, labor unionism in the United States was taking shape against powerful resistance. But the Catholic Irish on the canals and railroads had brought their own form of labor unionism with them from Ireland, in secret societies modeled on the Ribbonmen and in the terroristic practices of the Whiteboy local organizations.

It was inevitable, given the iron law of wages on canals and railroads and the harsh working conditions, that the Irish should turn in self-protection to a system familiar to them in the old country. The defenses of a subjugated people were moved structurally intact to America.

The typical public works Irish secret society had its origin on the Delaware & Hudson Canal in 1827 or 1828 and spread to other works. The familiar Ribbon paraphernalia appeared on this side of the Atlantic — hand-grips, passwords, recognition signs, and oaths of secrecy. Rumor reported its headquarters to be in New York and, as in Ireland, the directing heads were said to be saloonkeepers: Bishop England was certain that grog-sellers organized and exploited the secret societies. Local representatives managed the society's affairs on individual public works, and walking delegates from headquarters collected dues, organized branches, and carried the time-to-time changes in pass-words. It enforced its own secret dominance by intimidation and physi-cal violence. "It is a state of things," wrote Commissioner George Bender of the Chesapeake & Ohio Company, "which puts the laws of the country, as they at present stand, to positive defiance."

As among the Whiteboys in Ireland, the secret society in America had economic objectives: better pay, redress of grievances against un-scrupulous contractors, and protection of the jobs of its members, even against fellow Irishmen. The 1834 riots on the Chesapeake & Ohio Canal furnished an early — and classic — example of the crude economic and labor union lineaments of the secret society.

This disturbance originated in the will of an Irish secret society to impose the principle of what is now the closed shop against the mem-bers of a rival Irish secret society it considered interlopers. It will be recalled that in Ireland harvesters who walked from their own county to another seeking work were driven out with physical violence by spontaneous local combinations got up to maintain a county monopoly upon employment.

In the winter months on the canal, with the work force reduced, contractors took advantage of the surplus pool to engage laborers at lower wages. A group of Irishmen from the south of Ireland, banded together in a secret society known as the Corkonians, watched Irish-men from County Longford in the north of Ireland called the Far-downs,* also organized in a secret society, laboring at jobs that could (and should) be filled by Corkonians, and they schemed to put a stop to this taking of bread by the Longford men out of the mouths of Corkonians.

If they drove the Fardowns off the works, the Corkonians would enjoy a monopoly of the jobs and, by the forcibly created labor short-age, be able to dictate higher wages to the contractors. Accounts of the riotous proceedings that followed ascribed the cause, severally,

---

* A "Fardown" was an Irishman from one of the northern Irish counties. Though Protestant strength was concentrated in the north of Ireland, the word "Fardown" had no religious overtones. Tradition traced the origin of the word to the ninth century when children from the east, south, and west of Ireland went to the center of learning, Armagh, in the northern province, which was "far down" from the rest of the country and hence its inhabitants were generically called "Fardowners." Since the other provinces could not compare with the excel-lence of Armagh as a seat of learning, jealousy arose and the anti-intellectuals, as it were, used "Fardown" in a sneering and contemptuous way and the tradition carried over the centuries.

to non-payment of wages, discharge of workers or dissatisfaction with pay, but the real motive was comprehended by Resident Engineer Purcell, who said "the quarrel had nothing to do with money transactions" and was "the result of a regular organization . . . the ultimate object being to expel from the canal all except those that belong to the strongest party and thus secure for the remainder higher wages."

The focal point of the 1834 disturbance was the village of Williamsport on the Potomac, a few miles southwest of Hagerstown near the Pennsylvania border. The Corkonians were bunched in a labor gang near Dam 5 above Williamsport and the Fardowns around Dam 4 below the village. The war exploded on January 16, 1834, with the fatal beating in Williamsport of a Fardown laborer by a gang of Corkonians in the campaign of intimidation.

On January 24, the Fardowns took to the offensive. Fiery leaders rallied an army of three hundred Longford men on the dam below the village and started on the march, armed with guns, clubs, and helves. They explained to the nervous inhabitants of Williamsport that they intended no violent purpose but planned to make a show of strength to the Corkonians and demonstrate that they could not be driven from the works. In the vicinity of Williamsport they picked up reinforcements, swelling their numbers to between six and seven hundred.

They proceeded to the stronghold of the Corkonians at the upper dam and on the crest of a hill in a field three hundred well-armed Corkonians were drawn up in battle formation awaiting them. The Longford men might well have contemplated confining their appearance to a show of strength, but the Cork men naturally assumed they had come for war and began the attack. Several volleys were exchanged and a number fell dead. The Corkonians, outnumbered two to one, retreated in a rout. The Longford men, their passions murderously agitated, pursued the fleeing Corkonians and mercilessly committed mayhem on the less fleet of foot. The Corkonians sought shelter in the woods where many were overtaken and put to death. The bodies of five were found in one place with bullets through their heads. The wounded lay scattered all over the battlefield.

At ten o'clock that night the victorious Fardowns paraded through Williamsport, marched quietly to their quarters below the town and went to bed in their shanties.

The next morning, the sheriff of the county, who was also head of the militia, arrived in Williamsport with two companies of Hagerstown volunteers and added their strength to the local military organization. Then an interesting event took place. Messengers, sent to the warring headquarters to seek a reconciliation, returned with deputies selected by the respective societies empowered to draw peace terms. On the Monday night following the bloody fighting, these deputies sat down in Lyle's tavern in Williamsport with magistrates and leading citizens of the village and drew up a "treaty" which *Niles' Register* described as "somewhat of a novelty in diplomatic history." The unusual document, made and concluded on January 27, 1834, read:

> Whereas great commotions and divers riotous acts have resulted from certain misunderstandings and alleged grievances, mutually urged by two parties of laborers and mechanics, engaged on the line of the Chesapeake and Ohio canal, and natives of Ireland: the one commonly known as the Longford men, the others as the Corkonians; and whereas it has been found that these riotous acts are calculated to disturb the public peace, without being in the least degree beneficial to the parties opposed to each other, but on the contrary are productive of great injury and distress to the workmen and their families —
>
> Therefore, we, the undersigned, representatives of each party, have agreed to, and do pledge ourselves to support and carry into effect the following terms of the agreement:
>
> We agree, for ourselves, that we will not, either individually or collectively, interrupt, or suffer to be interrupted in our presence, any person engaged on the line of the canal, for or on account of a local difference or national prejudice, and that we will use our influence to destroy all these matters of difference growing out of this distinction of parties, known as Corkonians and Longfords . . . and we further bind ourselves to the State of Maryland, each in the sum of twenty dollars, to keep the peace towards the citizens of the state.

The "peace treaty" was signed by twenty-eight deputies, fourteen from each faction, with sturdy Gaelic names like Timothy Kelly, William O'Brien, Michael Collins, Jeremiah Donovan, Murty Dempsey, Michael Tracy, Garrett Donohue, and Daniel Murrey.

The citizens of Williamsport placed no great faith in the paper treaty, and on January 28 the representative of the Williamsport area in the Maryland House of Delegates introduced a resolution asking the President of the United States to order federal troops to the recently disturbed line of the canal. President Jackson directed the Secretary of War to dispatch at least two companies of regulars as expeditiously as possible. On the basis of this order, a modern historian makes out a case that Andrew Jackson was the first American President to use federal troops to break a strike.

7

By 1836, the Irish secret societies had established the Whiteboy system in full force along the line of the Chesapeake & Ohio Canal works.

The "midnight legislators" held court in the Potomac Valley as the Whiteboys did in County Cork or County Tipperary. An aggrieved laborer told his story at a meeting and if the adjudicators concluded that he had made a case, the decree issued of the measure and mode of punishment. Execution was not entrusted to men in the jurisdiction of the rump court which had "legislated" on the matter but, as in Ireland, enforcers were called in from a distance, usually the neighboring section, who carried out the assignment and then melted back into their own shanties. The meeting which they had served sent men, when called upon, to return the favor at the distant job. As Commissioner Bender of the Chesapeake & Ohio Company explained it: "If [the punishment] is to be executed at the 'round top' [a section of the works], or above there, it is assigned to men below. If to be executed at Millstone point, then to persons from the round top."

Anonymous letters notified the contractors of the will of the "midnight legislators," warning of punishment if the decree were not obeyed. A placard directed to the contracting firm of Montgomery & Little was typical — it was found posted on the door of Montgomery's office, stealthily left during the night.

> Mr. Montgomery & Mr. Little.
> Sirs, Take notice.
> that we give ye a civil notice Concerning your Manager Mr. James Reynolds that you will discharge him out of your employment so as that it will save us Some trouble for coming here a distance I come from the round top to save trouble Because we respected you and your partner without giving ye a regular notice. But any laboring man that will work under the said James Reynolds let him mark the consequence hereafter . . . a fair Notice I give ye without no more trouble if Reynolds leaves the tunnel in 6 or 8 days time after this notice will be no more trouble

Experience had taught the contractors of the risk they ran to laugh at, neglect, or brave out the anonymous warning notices. The notice on the firm of Montgomery & Little was relatively undemanding — the discharge of a boss who had incurred the wrath of the secret society. Some contractors against whom judgment had been reached by the "legislature" received notice to give up their contract entirely and their laborers to quit employment. John Daily, a contractor, had brushed aside a warning placard; his carts and tools were thrown into the river and he was compelled to quit under a threat of death. The common form of bringing an enjoined contractor to heel was through the boycott of his job by the laborers. Laborers received warning not to work for P. Crowley, and none dared: if they disobeyed the edict they were visited at night by a party and severely beaten. Contractors sometimes leagued themselves with the leaders of the secret society for their own interests. Crowley had been served notice to get off the job in order that another favored by the conspirators could get it. Such corruption could not help entering into an organization that lived in secrecy and by strong-armed methods. A contractor named Tracy was attacked through warning served on his laborers, who immediately quit and the work stopped. Tracy apparently set his teeth to defy the secret society. He was severely beaten and his life attempted when, sitting in his shanty one night talking to a priest, fire was set to a train of powder under it, and both barely escaped destruction.

No man dared to give testimony in a court of law if agents of the society were arraigned for a deed; even men beaten refused to name their assailants. An Irishman had been historically conditioned against the role of "informer." But multitudes came forward to furnish an alibi for a man on trial. The contractor Daily, who had felt the force of the secret society, blamed its enmity toward him on his refusal once to provide an alibi.

This state of affairs, even to the details, reproduced along the line of the Chesapeake & Ohio the standardized Whiteboy procedure in Ireland.

Trouble among the Chesapeake & Ohio canal workers, wrote the historian of Allegheny County, Maryland, was endless. "They were a wild set," he said, "and doubtless were treated with harshness and injustice." Up to the completion of the canal at Cumberland, the com-

pany's hard labor policy, which grew tougher with mounting financial difficulties, provoked a violent response from the Irish.

8

The enmity of the secret society to James Reynolds was inexorable.
Previously he had been compelled, under threat of death, to relinquish a Chesapeake & Ohio contract and now, as a manager or superintendent, the society again menaced him. Reynolds, like the contractors Daily, Crowley, and Tracy, who had felt the society's wrath,
was an Irishman. He had committed the unforgivable sin — he had
informed in a court of law on Irishmen in the Baltimore and Washington murders and riots in 1834.

On the afternoon of November 18, 1834, Peter Gorman, a railroad
contractor, sat casually conversing in his shanty with John Watson, a
construction superintendent, also of Irish blood. Gorman, the American-born son of a 1794 County Meath emigrant and the father of
Arthur Pue Gorman, later boss of the Democratic Party in Maryland
and a United States Senator, had been under notice of the Irish secret
society, a wing of the C & O society, in operation on the road. The
door of the shanty burst open. Eight or ten men rushed in, forcibly
dragged out Gorman and Watson and, beating the pair, left them
unconscious on the ground.

The next night, after midnight, the visitors returned. They gave
Watson, disabled on the couch, a minute to say his prayers and then
shot him four times. One Mercer, an assistant superintendent and
an Irishman, staying with Watson, was hurried outside and killed. A
third man named Callon, also Irish and an assistant superintendent,
fled in his bare feet and escaped the pursuers. A fourth occupant of
the shanty, one Welsh, received a charge of shot in his body but not
fatally. The invaders plundered the shanty.

On the following Saturday night, the party, on a mad rampage, took
forcible possession of a tavern on the turnpike halfway between Baltimore and Washington, looting it, and another group broke into a
store a mile distant and seized what goods the proprietor had left
after he had removed the greater part out of the general fear which
had seized the sparsely populated area.

During Sunday and Monday, Colonel Williams of the Anne Arundel County militia recruited a hundred citizens and asked assistance of the Baltimore militia. On the 25th a detachment of light infantry, under Colonel Campbell, himself a Catholic, arrived. In two divisions, they surrounded the 4th and 8th sections of the railroad construction and, as a correspondent reported, "we have literally swept the railroad, having taken 300 Irishmen." The next day the Irishmen, who had "passively submitted themselves to the proceedings," were moved to Baltimore and jailed. Detectives of "the most efficient character" were employed by the civil authorities of the county to help trace down the murderers.

With the area safely cleared of the Irish laborers, a large meeting of the inhabitants of Anne Arundel and the neighboring Prince George counties gathered at a tavern to pass resolutions against scenes "scarcely paralleled in the annals of our history." The blame was confined exclusively to "that class of laborers which has been generally employed on the aforesaid work, and it having been established, beyond all question, that the Irish laborers compose that class, and that they have formed secret associations, to which they are bound under the most awful and solemn oaths to keep each other's secrets, and under which association they are enabled to accomplish their hellish plots without being in danger of discovery."

Asserting that the good citizens had not received cooperation from the proper sources — that is, the railroad — to maintain law and order, they passed the following resolution:

> Resolved, That we do consider and hold the present class of Irish laborers employed on the Baltimore and Washington railroad as a gang of ruffians and murderers. . . .
>
> Resolved, That, inasmuch as by their plans of secret associations, justice and the laws are deprived of their dues, it behooves our fellow citizens to adopt such measures as will tend to their quiet and safety. . . .
>
> Resolved, That the president and directors of the Baltimore and Ohio railroad, be requested to order their agents and contractors, to discharge from their employ all such laborers as have been herein described.
>
> Resolved, That we will use all lawful means in our power to bring to justice, as many of the participators in the late murders, and all suspected persons as can be arrested. . . .

The meeting then sent a curt and peremptory letter to President Thomas of the Baltimore & Ohio saying that if the company did not take measures to protect the community "they will muster a sufficient force and drive every Irishman off the road from the Patapsco to the big Patuxent, at all hazards."

The Irish sensed the spirit of lynch law and knew the meaning of American mobs: the story of the burning of the Charlestown convent a few months previous was familiar to them. The Irish laborers, with their women and children, along the line of the works fled in all directions with their scant possessions. The authorities of Anne Arundel County, to make sure there would be no return, pulled down their miserable shanties.

"It has been a hard case on the innocent," said *Niles' Register,* "but so it is in all cases of force." Still it was necessary, continued the editor, to make an example in punishment of the Irish "for taking the law into their own hands." That echoed the sentiment of Irish landlords.

At a two-day trial in January, 1835, Owen Murphy was found guilty of the murder of Mercer and sentenced to death. And Terence Coyle (the newspapers spelled it "Coil") and Patrick Gallager were found guilty of murder in the second degree, both in the case of Mercer and of Watson, and each sentenced to eighteen years at hard labor, the sentences not to run concurrently, a total of thirty-six years in jail for the pair.

9

The most common origin of the "riots" was a strike, or "turn-out," in the contemporary term, by the Irish for better wages or in resistance to a wage cut, during which violence, often fired by liquor, showed itself in an attempt to close down the works as a means to bring the contractor to terms. The militia in the locality consistently acted as strike-breakers, with the consent and approval of the community and the press, which invariably blamed the troublesome Irish foreigners.

Mathew Carey, in a letter to Bishop Hughes in 1838, showed the other side of the picture, when fair treatment of the laborers, with an order of just discipline, maintained a state of peace. Two Irish contractors on the Wilmington & Baltimore Railroad employed between them a thousand laborers, principally Irishmen. During the two years spent in constructing the work, there were no riot, no outrage, no strikes, no disturbances; and the job was managed "with as much order and regularity as ever prevailed among such a number of men in any country." Mr. Carey ascribed this condition to the control by the contractors of whiskey and no embezzlement of the hard-earned wages of the laborers.

Irish labor trouble on the public works stood apart, as a separate episode, from the course of American labor during the period. The Whiteboy, or Ribbon, movement did not appear in factories and plants, where the Irish mixed with other peoples: it prevailed among large bodies of Irish canal and railroad workers isolated more or less from other races and, straight from Ireland as emigrants, still obedient to the influences of their native land. In one instance, it burst out in the Carbondale coal mines, with a large Irish working population, in resistance to intolerable conditions, anticipating the "Molly Maguires" of a later period.

10

Advertisements and notices of labor wanted on public works dotted, during the 1830s, the pages of the *Truth Teller,* which advised Irish emigrants to seek out such jobs. But the Roman Catholic clergy sounded a rising note of protest, of which the *Catholic Herald* of Philadelphia in 1839 set the tone: "For our own part," it wrote, "we distinctly say we do not by any means intend to recommend our countrymen to work in public works as the means of support; we regard these places as the certain destruction of many — Alas! too many." We know, answered the *Truth Teller,* that most of the Irish emigrants do not belong to that class "who come prepared to 'settle on farms.' They seek a market for their labour, that being the only capital they possess, and if they fail to find this, they are even in a worse condition here than they could have been at home." That summed up concisely the urge of necessity which propelled the Irish to public works and kept filled the paths from emigrant ships to canal and railroad jobs.

Perspective is distorted if the story of the Catholic Irish on public works is confined to riots and disturbances. The bulk of the laborers were, as one contractor wrote, "peaceable, sober and industrious," with agitation stirred up by a "ruthless and disorderly minority," in the words of the *Truth Teller* in 1839, which assumed leadership.

Along the lines of every public works, the poor Catholic Irish laborers built church after church, as they had along the Erie Canal, and the upraised cross followed after their shovels, pickaxes, and scrapers. The visit of the missionary priest for stations became the most satisfying moment of their hard and rough lives. The Rev. J. F. O'Neil, the Roman Catholic pastor of Savannah, moved from section to section of a railroad construction job in Georgia in 1838. He timed his approach to each station to meet the men as they were coming from work and addressed them as they ate supper; he heard the confessions of the men until eleven at night and then gathered them for a prayer. At daybreak he said Mass, gave Communion and preached a sermon of moral instruction. This was the usual routine of the priests who followed the line of the public works.

Sometimes the men on the public works prepared for the visiting priest what was known in Ireland as a *scalán*, an improvised sanctuary in the open, a remnant of the eighteenth-century penal days when Mass was celebrated in secluded spots by a priest in secret. Against a ledge or embankment laborers fashioned a covering, with latticed side supports, of evergreen boughs, like a stage with one side exposed, protecting or shading the priest and the rude altar from the elements. Before it, the Irish workers gathered to attend Mass, in the manner of their forefathers.

II

Ruthless contractors had, by the end of the 1830s, systematized the swindling of unlettered Irish laborers on public works. With the funneling of Irish Famine emigrants after 1845 into the railroad building boom, the opportunities to defraud and exploit them increased and so did the number of "riots."

Contractors continued to abscond with payrolls, and maddened Irish reacted with violence. A section contractor on the New York & Erie disappeared with a $1200 payroll. Melvin & Company, contractors on the Gloucester Railroad, "went off the track," with a loss of $3000 to between two and three hundred laborers. Contractors on the Central Railroad in Vermont failed to pay the Irish laborers, and the militia quelled the ensuing "riot." "While railroad contractors continue dishonest," wrote the Boston *Pilot*, "it is idle to suppose that hard-worked and cheated laborers will be anything but violent and tumultuous." The *Pilot* also sorrowfully observed the number of dishonest subcontractors who were Irish. A priest in upper New York State said that in the space of a few months no less than six contractors, two of whom

were Catholic Irishmen, absconded on the railroads his mission cov·
ered.

Contractors obliged the laborers to trade at the stores they established
on the works, at a charge up to 50 per cent over a fair price: this "store"
or "truck" system was in common use on public works. Contractors cop-
pered the business by paying the workers in due bills redeemable only
in their store. Jessop & Wilkes, contractors for the New York & Erie
Railroad, opened a dry goods store near the line and, despite remon-
strances, compelled the men to take their pay in clothes at a large sur-
charge. Being poor and necessitous, often with families, they accepted
the articles and sold them at a considerable loss. Contractors opened
their own grog shops, sold whiskey at a premium, gave liberal credit to
the men and encouraged them to drink, putting the laborers in their
debt.

The workers received wages once a month, with a percentage withheld not always recoverable when a man quit his job. If a laborer failed
to work twenty-six days during the month, his whole wage was penalized, not simply the days he had missed. If he left before the monthly
payday, he was subject to an arbitrary reduction in each day's pay owed
him. Some swindling contractors engaged men at, say, a dollar a day
but paid them a lesser sum. Contractors laughed at outraged Irishmen
who went into court for judgments against deception and fraud; they
merely appealed, and the costs, as well as the law's delay, put prosecution out of question.

Contractors tried to pay laborers in "shinplaster" money. In the winter of 1838, troops were rushed from Chicago and from Will County to
put down some four hundred rioting Irishmen, who were destroying
their own work on the Michigan & Illinois Canal. The frenzy originated in the scheme of the contractor, who received his payment in
good Illinois bank money, to pay the Irishmen in "wildcat" money, that
is, bills of distant and shaky banks purchased at a considerable discount
from their face value and unacceptable in Illinois stores.

Scoundrels exploited the Irish weakness for drink to cheat men of
their earnings. When a payday approached, the contractor, finding
himself short of funds or wanting to appropriate the wages of the men
for himself, set the stage for his knavery. Cheap rotgut was distributed
liberally at the contractor's expense and as the Irishmen felt the glow
of power inside themselves, whisperers, or agents provocateurs, played
upon their belligerent spirit to start a fight or provoke them to drive

Irishmen from another county away from the works. The law was called in and the men fled. Fearing arrest, they did not return to the job and the rogue of a contractor pocketed their pay. Newspapers carried stories of another Irish "riot."

Michael McQuaide of Utica testified that several contractors "confessed to me that they had created these rows themselves, coming on pay day, for the purpose of evading the payment of the men." He once met a contractor who, though his contract forbade the sale and use of whiskey on the line, nevertheless brought up six barrels of whiskey to his section. McQuaide asked him the reason. " 'Oh,' said he, 'don't you know that Monday next is pay day, and I have not money to pay the men, so I must get up a fight to quiet them.' " Out of a hundred and fifty men on that job only thirty showed up to claim their wages; the rest melted away after the fight. The contractor cleared $1500 by his trickery upon the impetuous and ignorant Irishmen.

A sensational case arose from the arbitrary practices of contractors in the payment of men. Large numbers of emigrant Irishmen had been attracted from the East to the works of the Illinois Central Railroad by advertisements promising $1.25 a day. Albert Story, a contractor employing between three and five hundred men on a heavy grading job, reduced the pay to a dollar a day when the winter season set in, and they struck, demanding what was owed them so they could be off to other sections.

Story paid some of the men, but on December 15, 1853, announced no more wages would be forthcoming until an error in his books had been rectified. His foreman barred the door of Story's store, which was also his office, and told the crowd outside to be off. An old man, John Ryan, a laborer described as an "irritable" Irishman, pushed aside the foreman and faced Story, saying that as the father of fourteen children he needed his money. A scuffle followed, and Story, who was drunk, fired two shots and killed the old man. Maddened Irishmen seized Story and beat him to death. Four Irishmen received death sentences for the deed, which Governor Matteson commuted to life imprisonment when convinced the men had been convicted by anti-Irish prejudice rather than the evidence, though the violent anti-Irish Chicago *Tribune* shrieked that the governor had sold out justice for the Irish vote.

The Pennsylvania Railroad kept a large force of private police along the line of its works, "for to aggravate the minds of the laboring class," said one Irishman. They "needed watching more than the poor Irishman," said another. Ostensibly, these private police served to put down strikes; instead, charged the Irish, they provoked labor trouble to prove their usefulness. What particularly irked the Irish was that they themselves paid for the cost of the private police by deductions from their wages.

12

Laborers started work at sunrise and continued to sunset, or, as one Irishman said, "until our sweat mixes with the nightly dew." When the days shortened, so did the pay: one scale governed the long days of light in the summer, another the briefer working hours of winter. Pay stopped on days of inclement weather, and if rain or snow shut down work after the men had started, the laborers lost that day's wages.

Contractors worked the men, it was said, "to the door of death." One estimate held that twenty-five out of every hundred railroaders died from causes connected with the work. Respiratory diseases were occupational hazards. Agues and fevers in unhealthy country being opened by railroads shook the strong frames of Irishmen, and intermittent cholera ravaged men packed closely together in shanties under primitive conditions of sanitation. The cave-in of embankments became the tombs of countless Irishmen and neglect of safety precautions sent them into Kingdom Come with faulty explosions. An Irishman crippled by the dangers of public works had the prospects only of the almshouse. Neither companies nor contractors felt under obligation to men injured on the works. "Will it be believed," asked the *Irish American* in 1849, "that, on the railway sections, if a man is 'blasted' by an explosion, his face and form disfigured for life, he will not only not be compensated for his personal afflictions; but if the pay of a fragment of a month be owing to him he is not considered entitled to, and will not get it, because his month is not served out!!"

The mortality of railroad laborers as compared with men in other walks of life was fixed at three to one: a workday of from fourteen to sixteen hours under a broiling sun and then a drop into the sleep of fatigue with a shirt still sweated to his back did not promise long life. The average working life of a railroader lasted seven years, it was figured. More Irishmen died on railroads, ran the common belief, than on emigrant ships.

Their pay ranged from 60 cents to $1.25 a day. The latter price pre-
vailed on Western roads opening new territory or in unhealthy climates
(Illinois, for example, where ague was endemic), as an inducement to
overcome the disadvantages. A wage scale of a dollar a day appeared
in advertisements for railroad labor, but letters from Irishmen who had
gone to the works on that promise reported the pay, in reality, to be
lower, 87½ or 75 cents daily. Out of this, the men were expected to
provide their own keep, with board advertised from $1.75 to $2 a
week.

The *Olive Branch,* a Protestant religious weekly in Boston, spoke up
in outraged humanitarianism against the lot of the Irish railroad laborer:

> There is no class of men on earth who are tyrannized over, by
> men in a little brief authority, more than Irish laborers; particu-
> larly in this case with those employed by Railroad Contractors. They
> are made to work like dogs, too many hours for human nature to
> endure, even when it has the iron sinew of the Irish laborer. They
> work for two-thirds the price of our own citizens could be induced
> to work for any circumstances, and they are abused and cheated
> in a way to disgrace human nature.

But strong American contractors and prime Irish contractors tolerated no sharp practices, worked the men hard but treated them fairly,
faced no disturbances and kept the crews intact from job to job. The
absence of trouble among Irish laborers and the want of "Irish riots"
under just contractors bespoke the source of violence. The Irish responded gratefully to decent treatment. Like the Whiteboys in Ireland,
they remained quiet without occasions of grievance.

13

The Ninth Provincial Council of the American Roman Catholic
hierarchy at Baltimore in 1840 formally condemned the secret societies
on public works and warned its communicants against membership in
them:

> As far as we can discover, the pretext is their own protection,
> but the practice is monopoly, blasphemy, insubordination, idleness,
> riot and the terror of the vicinity. This abundantly explains the
> rapid demoralization of a class that was originally virtuous, indus-
> trious, laborious, useful and peaceable. When once the custom of
> forming secret societies is established in any part of a community,

it rapidly pervades the entire, and demoralization is the necessary consequence.

Those who adhered to the secret societies were denied admission to the Sacraments.

Two years later, Bishop Hughes specifically named the two secret societies — Corkonians and Connachtmen, or the Far-ups and Far-downs — against which he had been forced to issue a pastoral letter.

Despite the Church's condemnation, secret societies flourished during the 1840s and into the 1850s. The addition of Famine emigrants to the laboring population on expanding railroad construction provided fertile recruiting ground for the shrewd Irish manipulators who had fastened themselves upon secret societies for easy profits.

These societies promised to protect the Irishman's job on a public work, but they also exploited the Irishman's love of underground organizations, with the paraphernalia of Irish Ribbonism, which they came closely to resemble, even to the inclusion of the word "Shamrock" in the names of the several societies as in Ireland. The number of these societies cannot be traced, but one had its central office in Buffalo, another was directed by a rum-seller in New York, and a third operated out of Williamsburg in Brooklyn.

The secret society, in its later phase, savored of what is today called a racket. The proceeds invited the attention of calculating operators. A society in upper New York contained seven thousand dues-paying members. Two secret societies in the coal-mining region of Pennsylvania's Schuylkill County were reported in 1847 to have collected ten thousand dollars from members. With thousands of Irishmen working on the railroads, the pickings were rich: intimidation pressed the unwilling into taking the oath and paying the initiation fee and dues.

As secret societies were organized along Irish country or provincial lines, they perpetuated the hereditary county divisions and enmities. They played upon or exaggerated county feuds as a means of holding members. Fast-talking agents, called "captains" or "tribunes," went from one end of a work to the other, "carrying exaggerated stories of how 'Far downs' had maltreated 'Connaught men,' and vice versa," or urging the members of one society to drive away Irishmen belonging to another to protect or secure a monopoly of the jobs, in this way begetting a row that often developed into a general riot.

The county fights, said the Boston *Pilot*, were "the curse of Ireland."

"We are miserably disgraced," it continued, "and can reply nothing to
the scorn of the American press. Cork men murdering Connaught
men, in a strange land! What an infernal vitality the curse of Ireland
has."

An Irishman on a railroad job in Iowa wrote that the Irish did not
fight because of origins in different counties but because they were
provoked into disturbances by contractors who used the riots as a
means to evade paying them. Dr. W. Quigley, Roman Catholic pastor
of Schaghticoke, New York, a mission priest, held the conviction, after
two years of continuous duty among Irish railroad laborers, that "fraud
and imposition and arbitrary regulation of wages" were the "sources of
most, if not all, the evils complained of."

14

Irish disturbances on public works brought into life two movements
organized to promote peace and union among the laborers, but with
different emphases.

In the fall of 1851, delegates of nine Irish organizations in New
York City, beneficial, total abstinence and laborers' societies, working-
class groups, gathered as the Convention of Irish Societies and issued
an address to their fellow countrymen. The purpose was to fight secret
societies and stop the disturbances by applying to the workers on railroads the same mixture of trades-union principles and mutual benefit
assistance that governed their own urban organizations. The Convention urged the formation of local societies on the railroad works, with
initiation fees and dues for a benefit fund. Such a society would protect members from frauds and imposition of contractors, ran the plea,
and seek regulation of workers' wages; it would help an Irishman looking for work and, if none was available, furnish him the means to proceed to the next job. By open and orderly organization and by a working arrangement among the societies, they would unite Irish workers
and merge their strength for a stand against the divisive tactics of self-
serving secret societies and conniving contractors.

In the summer of 1851, Bishop Timon of Buffalo formed the Erin
Peace Society "to promote union and peace among Irishmen, and to
prevent quarrels and strife." The gentle Timon stressed the religious
character of the society: the parish priest would be president of the

local; every member promised to say his prayers daily and encourage others to receive Communion regularly. A benefit fund would assist widows and distressed members.

Neither the Convention of Irish Societies nor the Erin, or Hibernian, Society realized the hope of national organization; indeed, each raised only a handful of branches. They worked in close communication with each other at the start, but conservative-minded clergymen began to shy away from the Convention of Irish Societies when politicians like Mike Walsh, the famous demagogue and an indifferent Catholic, began to plead its cause, and its leadership extended activities to include specific agitations on workers' hours and wages, the "truck" system and indiscriminate condemnation of contractors. Prudent clerics were sensitive to the general hostility to trade unions.

But the endeavors of the New York Convention and its allies in the up-state peace society bore good fruit when the New York State Legislature in 1853 established a ten-hour day in factories and plants and extended the benefit to workers on the railroads and canals — and Irish public works labor received protection from public authority. The cause, initiated and carried through by Catholic Irishmen, made an important first step to stop disturbances, improve the status and condition of the laborers, and narrow the sources of their grievances.

With its growth and extension, permitting a wider ministration to the public works, the Catholic Church carried warfare against the secret societies: an Irish priest was the most formidable foe of oath-bound, underground organization.

The growth and extension of the Roman Catholic Church was a phenomenon of the pre-Civil War period, thanks principally to the Catholic Irish emigrants.

3 3
The Building of the Church

THE BUILDING of the Roman Catholic Church was the greatest collective achievement of the Catholic Irish in the United States. This is said in no spirit to detract from or minimize the contributions of other nationalities to the growth of the Church. But Irish numbers predominated in the cornerstone period of the Church's history. In the early or "old" immigration of the nineteenth century, Germans and Irish made up the bulk of alien passengers, but Catholics comprised only a minority of the Germans: Shea, the Catholic historian, estimated that one fifth of the Germans who entered the United States in 1854 were Catholics.

By the Civil War, the Roman Catholic Church was firmly established, with the Irish the main builders. The driving power of the Catholic Irish people and clergy stamped the Church with an Irish character it has since retained. The simplest test of the validity of that statement is to try to think of the Catholic Church in the United States without the Irish.

"In this country," wrote Patrick S. Casserly in 1840, a half decade before the mammoth Famine emigration, "the idea of Catholicity and Ireland is so blended in the minds of the American people, as to be in a manner inseparable."

No doubts troubled the mind of Rev. Michael McCarron, pastor of St. Joseph's Church in New York City, as to where the strength of the Catholic Church in the United States lay, when in a public speech in 1851 he said:

> Is it not clear and evident that the children of Ireland coming hither in such numbers are the great element of Catholicity in this country? Is it not by means of them that the faith has stricken such deep root and is being so rapidly spread over the length and breadth of the land? Who have dug the foundations of our churches, reared and ornamented the stately edifices? . . . Who have built the Catholic colleges and universities? Who have been . . . the Priests, Bishops and Archbishops of the United States of America? Yes, the sons of St. Patrick, or their immediate descendants.

The world, said one writer, is thoroughly "possessed with the notion that all Irishmen are, should be, or might be, Catholics."

2

Sound and practical reasons fitted the Irish, in preference to Continental Europeans, to build the Roman Catholic Church in the new country governed by republican political and social institutions.

They, first of all, spoke the English language. This by-product of the English conquest turned out to be an advantage of inestimable benefit in the accommodation of the Church to the United States.

Next, their experience in Ireland had prepared them to embrace without qualification the great American constitutional principle of separation of Church and State. They had known the Established Church as a political engine of the Ascendancy in Ireland. They not merely opposed the political connection of Church and State; they hated the very idea. They had upheld Daniel O'Connell in his victorious struggle against the Crown Veto. "For my own part," said O'Connell, "I would prefer death to consenting to the degradation of Catholicity, which a union of our Church with the State would necessarily produce. . . . I am a decided advocate of the 'voluntary principle.' "

Bishop John England, the first of the strong Irish-born prelates in the United States, dwelt insistently on this theme. "Never were any principles of temporal government better adapted to the interests of the Catholic Church than those of our States and of our Union," he wrote; and though strong opposition existed to the Church, "its perfect security is found in the severance of Church and State." Since the Bull of Pope Adrian the Saxon in the twelfth century, said the Boston *Pilot*, "The Irish have always been the most Church-and-State hating portion of the Catholic world."

On the other hand, the French clergy, fleeing the Revolution or Napoleon, and the Canadian French clergy, still beguiled by monarchy and accustomed to a well-endowed Church in Quebec favored by official British policy, and the German clergy, beneficiaries of kings and princes in Bavaria, Saxony, and Baden, had not been trained in the "voluntary principle" and rather distrusted the idea of severing the Church from the State.

The Irish held it a matter of great pride that they supported their own clergy, without subvention of the state, and remembered with a fierce attachment the mutual sacrifices of priests and people to maintain the integrity of the Church during the long decades of official persecution, so that "the fine link of affectionate sympathy between the shepherds and the flock has been kept up by the mutual and reciprocal wants of the pastor and the people."

The Irish had by necessity been reared in the simplest forms of religion, in churches more cow-barns than temples, in services in the open under the sky or in hidden glen to escape informers; and "they were not appalled," as Bishop McQuaid of Rochester said, "by the wretchedness of religious equipments and surroundings in their new homes on this side of the Atlantic." Stately cathedrals, familiar to other Catholic peoples, were unknown to the Irish until after Catholic Emancipation. The priest and the altar sufficed for the early Irish emigrants, and rude surroundings had no offense to them.

The Irish, trained in the hard school of religious repression, had won religious rights by united combative agitation. It was an old story to find the Church under attack in the United States, hear the familiar strain of the anti-Popery charges and encounter the rough hand of American hostility. They girded their loins and put to use the lessons learned in Ireland. They did not need to be told that political strength brought respect for the rights of a minority, or that the friendship of Protestants of good will was a shield and a buckler. Bishop O'Connor of Pittsburgh wrote in 1842: "We find it necessary to make friends of as many as we can of liberal Protestants to protect us from the bigots who swarm here, who if they could would devour us."

The Irish were roaring anti-monarchists and, if the Continental Church represented to the American Protestant mind a political despotism, the Catholic Irish absolved themselves from any softening toward the kingly or absolutist principle by their almost unanimous association in the United States with the popular party dedicated to political equality and republican principles.

De Tocqueville, the most penetrating European observer of American institutions, had the Irish as examples when he wrote in 1835 of the Catholics in America: "These Catholics are faithful to the observances of their religion; they are fervent and zealous in the belief of their doctrines. Yet they constitute the most republican and the most democratic class in the United States." He explained that doctrinally and before the altar, Catholicism recognized no human inequality. When the Church was separated from the State, as in America, and no incentive existed to take the side of a governing aristocracy "from a religious motive," then "no class of men is more naturally disposed than the Catholics to transfer the doctrine of the equality of condition into the political world." He continued:

> Most of the Catholics are poor, and they have no chance of taking a part in the government unless it is open to all the citizens. They constitute a minority, and all rights must be respected in order to ensure to them the free exercise of their own privileges. These two causes induce them, even unconsciously, to adopt political doctrines which they would perhaps support with less zeal if they were rich and preponderant.

The Catholic clergy in America, De Tocqueville said, have not opposed this political tendency. Rather they placed the body of revealed religion in one category, to which they assented without discussion; in another they placed those political truths which they believed the Deity had left open to free inquiry. "Thus the Catholics of the United States are at the same time the most submissive believers and the most independent citizens."

3

Bishop England distrusted the French element in the Roman Catholic Church in the United States as inimical to its progress and status and as strongly promoted the Irish as the natural and logical colonizers of the infant Church. In 1835, he set out the case for the Irish against the French:

> The Irish are largely amalgamated with the Americans. Their principles, their dispositions, their politics, their notions of government, their language and their appearance become American very quickly, and they praise and prefer America to their oppressors at home. The French never can become American. Their language, manners, love of *la belle France,* their dress, air, carriage, notions, and mode of speaking of their religion, all, all are foreign. An American then says, "It might be very good, but 'tis foreign aristocracy." Trivial as this might seem, it has impeded the progress of our Religion here. And the French generally refer to France as the standard of perfection. The French clergy are generally good men and love Religion, but they make the Catholic Religion thus appear as exotic, and cannot understand why it should be made to appear assimilated to American principles.

From the establishment of the hierarchy in 1789 to 1820, there had been ten bishops and one administrator, of whom six were French, three Irish, and two American-born. The Catholic population added by the Louisiana Purchase, the French West Indies colonists ousted by the Revolution and the advent of French refugee clergymen, particularly the Sulpicians, who were the teachers in the Baltimore and Emmittsburg seminaries and were called the "Baltimore junta," gave the Church a French cast which the Irish resisted. The Irish welcomed the presence of Bishop England as the leader who would "win for them," in the words of Father Guilday, England's biographer, "what they believed they were being defrauded of — just representation in the affairs of the American Church." Since the French did not emigrate, increasing Catholic Irish numbers eventually resolved the dispute on their side.

4

Bishop John England arrived in his diocese of Charleston, South Carolina, the largest and the poorest diocese in the whole Catholic world, he called it, on the last day of December, 1820. A famous cleric in Ireland before he accepted the newly created Charleston bishopric, England became the light of the American hierarchy, of distinguished personal and intellectual stature. The bishop of the Carolinas and Georgia, with a Catholic population of ten thousand in 1836 out of a population of some two million whites and blacks spread out over an area the size of France, with two priests to assist him when he arrived, the churches shanties, the head of a poverty-stricken and comparatively inconsequential diocese, John England, in spite of these material disadvantages, was for almost a quarter of a century the most important and influential Catholic ecclesiastic in the United States.

He was an intense Irish nationalist. When consecrated bishop of Charleston in Cork, he refused to take the oath of allegiance to the government on the ground that when he reached the United States he would renounce it immediately to become an American citizen and that, in case of war between the United States and England, he wanted his conscience clear to exhort his people to arm and resist his Most Gracious Majesty to the last.

As was said of the Anglo-Norman invaders that they became more Irish than the Irish, so Bishop England became more American than the Americans. Instinctively democratic, he gloried in American institutions and spent a great deal of his time in building the intellectual framework of the compatability of Roman Catholicism with the free American society, for the benefit of his fellow Catholics and of those Protestants who would listen. He proclaimed religious liberty the noblest tower in the edifice of the American Constitution.

His Baltimore friend and biographer, William George Read, wrote that Bishop England attached "the utmost importance to what might be called the 'naturalization' of Catholicism." "He desired," explained Read, "that it should no longer be regarded as the religion of strangers; but that its ministers should be American, in principle, feeling, and habit."

The Irish Bishop England strongly developed the pattern, set by John Carroll, the first Roman Catholic bishop, of what might be called the diplomatic school of American Catholic churchmen. In an overwhelmingly Protestant nation with pronounced bias against Catholicism, he believed in the clerical soft voice and proposed to reduce antagonism by brains, character, example and the assimilation as rapidly as possible of the strangeness (or "exotic" appearance) of the Church. His course was like that of the statesman of a small country in modern international politics who wins the respect and regard of great powers by ability and skill. His method avoided a frontal attack on the creeds of the Reformation; his mission was to explain and expound Catholicism. He sought to penetrate the Protestant mind to the end of softening anti-Catholic animosity.

5

Bishop England took charge of a diocese that had been especially created to end the long internecine warfare between the priests and congregations of the Charleston-Norfolk area and the archbishops of Baltimore, climaxed by a schism, that centered essentially in the contumacy of the Irish priests and the resistance of Irish congregations to being served by a French priest. The faction-minded and nationality-conscious Irish gave the infant Church in the United States a continuing headache in the intramural struggle of episcopal authority to exercise canonical administration and discipline against the lay system of trusteeism.

The population of the Church was anything but homogeneous, and each national grouping wanted its own separate church, with priests of the same blood. The trustee system compounded the strife of national identities. The involved story of trusteeism properly belongs to the history of the Church, but the relationship of the Irish to it may be briefly filled in.

The Constitution prohibited the state from interference in religious affairs, but the state had an interest in the property of religious societies, and it required legal incorporation. Though it was inconsistent with canonical government, Bishop John Carroll consented to what was called "the Protestant system of church government" or, in another expression, "congregational ideas," by which a lay board of elected trustees managed the material affairs of each Catholic church.

Assertive trustees extended their powers beyond property and financial management to adminstration. They challenged the bishop's authority to appoint priests and the pastor's to name teachers and sextons and used the power of the purse, through control of pew rents and revenue from cemeteries, the main sources of income, to enforce their will. It took strong-willed and tough-minded Irish prelates to break the divisive factionalism of Irish boards of trustees and conform the Church in the United States to canonical practices.

The most notorious of the bishop-versus-trustees clashes, the so-called Hogan schism in St. Mary's Church, Philadelphia, spread over the decade 1820-1830. It began when the new bishop of Philadelphia, Henry Conwell, suspended Rev. William Hogan, temporary pastor of St. Mary's, because of his dubious credentials as a priest. Conwell was an old man when he came from Ireland to Philadelphia, weak, irresolute and pious; Hogan was a rogue, a glib and persuasive confidence man. The trustees defied the bishop and supported Hogan, while the church divided into pro-bishop and anti-bishop factions, and the annual elections of trustees turned into riotous brawls, the padding of the voting list, the struggle for physical control of the balloting box in the church, the calling out of the sheriff and his men, the seizure of the church by one party and the arbitrament of a Protestant umpire in disputed returns. Even with the dropping of Hogan by his faction, the struggle continued between the bishop and the trustees, reaching a peak in the forced retirement by Rome of Bishop Conwell and an appeal by two priests to the United States government to protect their rights upon their removal to Cincinnati.

In 1830, Francis P. Kenrick, a native of Ireland, who had been on the arduous Kentucky mission, was named coadjutor bishop of Philadelphia. In 1831, trustee trouble started again at St. Mary's. Bishop Kenrick, of a different stamp from Conwell, himself appeared before the congregation in cassock and with a cross on his breast and in a nononsense manner, first, as Father John Hughes exultantly wrote, broke the neck of a bad principle and, then, diplomatically refused to accept the withdrawal of recalcitrant trustees, insisting he wanted their services by his side. A new type of Irish prelate had appeared.

6

The Irish, with their traditional disposition to huddle, naturally sought out congregations of their own under priests of their own race.

A large Catholic settlement, mostly Irish emigrants, ninety-five families in two clearings, lived in Butler County in western Pennsylvania. They were not at all satisfied with the periodical visits of Father Helbron, a German priest, and on May 28, 1803, petitioned Bishop Carroll for a resident priest of Irish nationality:

> The far-off Catholic does not like to send for Mr. Hilbrun [Helbron] as he does not know how to utter himself in the English tongue or preach as would be expected from a person in his station. I expect we will be daily getting more numerous especially if we had a priest. The sectaries here of all denominations have their preachers, we are the only people left desolate of a pastor.

They preferred "if possible one that could understand the Irish language" and then with characteristic Irishism declared "we would rather depend on providence a little longer than get a German priest." Or as they probably said in their less formal way among themselves, "better to say our prayers by ourselves than have a Dutchman." Later they threatened to bring a priest from Ireland if Bishop Carroll did not honor their demand.

These early Irish placed great emphasis on preaching. They had noticed the pride of the Protestants in the preaching powers of their ministers. They thought an oratorical priest made Protestants respect them, and they felt humbled at a poor preacher of their own faith. The difficulties of French and German priests with the English language made an Irish congregation squirm with anguish.

The Irish disposition for their own Irish clergy manifested itself as vigorously in America's largest see as in the Pennsylvania wilderness. In the New York diocese, Rev. John Dubois succeeded Bishop Connolly, who had died in 1825. Father Dubois had fled revolutionary France as a refugee, and after missionary work in Maryland and Virginia, founded the famous college of St. Mary's in Emmittsburg of which he was president when called to New York. He was a fine scholar, a gentle and kindly man, a visionary who came to New York with worthy ambitions to promote the Catholic faith, but he had one handicap that was never overcome: he was a Frenchman in an overwhelmingly Irish diocese. That was the head of Bishop Dubois' offending. On merit, his appointment was admirable; as policy, it was a mistake. The Irish had expected Rev. John Power, a native of County Cork, vicar-general of the diocese and administrator after the death of Bishop Connolly, to succeed as bishop, and they prepared to give him a vigorous rally. The brunt of their disappointment and resentment fell undeservedly on the head of French Bishop Dubois.

The Irish, in effect, carried on a sit-down strike against Bishop Dubois. Bishop England, writing in 1834 to his friend Paul Cullen, later to be the first cardinal in Ireland, explained the impasse. Bishop Dubois, he said, had not a dollar nor could he raise a hundred in his diocese, and all his projects were faced with doom. Yet a bishop in whom the people had confidence and respect could annually in the New York diocese raise from sixty to eighty thousand crowns. The solution was simple, he continued:

> The people are principally Irish, and American in feeling, and they see that in the administration of the American Church the whole action is anti-Irish and anti-American. They are therefore inert.

An Irish bishop was necessary.

The imperfect command of the English language by Bishop Dubois made his preponderantly Irish congregation feel that a "foreigner" ruled the diocese. Father John Power wrote in 1829: "Doctor Dubois is thirty-six years in America, and when he attempts to give common instructions, thirty-six* out of three thousand cannot understand a word of what he says. Hundreds leave the Church and actually go into the Rum Shops while he is speaking!"

The trustees of parishes, principally Irish or of Irish descent, surrounded and ambushed Bishop Dubois. His fine plans for schools, colleges, and a seminary broke on the rock of Irish obduracy. He traveled to Ireland to raise funds for an Irish emigrant hospital which he could not raise in New York. Congregations turned their backs on clergymen, even of Irish blood, named by Bishop Dubois.

In a pastoral, issued in 1834, Bishop Dubois asked why the Irish in New York opposed him with no just cause. He cited his record, as president of St. Mary's and as bishop, to show that instead of discriminating against the Irish, he invariably favored Irish clergymen in ap-

---

* This repetition of the "thirty-six" above was clearly a slip of the pen by Father Power.

pointments. "And who are those who object to our foreign birth?" he asked. "Are they not in the same sense foreigners themselves? for the question was not why an American had not been appointed, but why was it not an Irishman?" There Bishop Dubois went to the heart of the matter.

On January 6, 1838, Father John Hughes of Philadelphia, a native of Ireland, was consecrated coadjutor bishop of New York. If Bishop Dubois failed to understand and control his sullen and resentful Catholic Irish children, Bishop Hughes understood and mastered them.

A year and a month after Bishop Hughes's consecration, the trustees of old St. Patrick's Cathedral, on February 6, 1839, ordered the removal of a Sunday School teacher appointed by the bishop but disapproved of by the trustees. A common constable duly appeared and ejected the teacher. Bishop Hughes, who had watched the bitter fight in Philadelphia under the ineffective Conwell, seized upon this incident for a showdown with the trustees.

He called a meeting of the pew-holders and put the issue up to them: whether they were willing, in a conflict, to sacrifice the doctrines, discipline, and ecclesiastical authority of their religion to their civil powers as a corporate body. Then, bringing up sentiments that would have been entirely foreign to Bishop Dubois, he contrasted the state church of England, "a gilded slave, chained to the crown," with the persecuted religion of "poor Ireland, who upheld the freedom of her faith at the sacrifice of all that men hold dear beside." He pictured the Irish in the days of the penal laws, "assembling in the solitude of the mountain or the dampness of the secret cave around their priest, for whose head the laws offered the same premium as for that of a wolf." The people were visibly moved by the strength of his oratory and his vibrations on the tenderest strings of the Irish memory. Though Bishop Hughes had still to threaten interdiction of the church and cemetery against the recalcitrant trustees, he had won the fight for all practical purposes on that Sunday afternoon.

As with Bishop Kenrick of Philadelphia, a new type of Catholic Irish prelate had appeared in the United States.

7

Attachment of Irish congregations to a pastor or priest quickened their loyalty to him against the bishop, as in Ireland. The bishop transferred Rev. John Brady, Jr., from a Connecticut town. The parishioners nailed a notice across the entrance to the church: "Let no man take this down till the Bishop gives a reason for removing Mr. Brady from his beloved congregation. Let no man dare to." St. Mary's Church in Boston was divided into warring factions, each supporting its favorite priest. To bring peace, Bishop Fenwick transferred Rev. P. O'Beirne, disliked by one party. On a Sunday afternoon, when Rev. Thomas J. O'Flaherty, a strong temperance preacher, who remained, was conducting Vespers, the O'Beirne faction hissed him and started a riot, shouting the name of their favorite and attacking the O'Flaherty supporters. One shocked parishioner was quoted as saying, in a magnificent Irishism: "I never saw such a scene since the days of Queen Elizabeth." The disturbance brought the police, and Bishop Fenwick put the church under interdict.

The congregation at Hartford rose in open revolt at the refusal of Bishop O'Reilly to permit the burial of a beloved pastor in the churchyard. The congregation of Ogdensburg, New York, disagreed with the pastor over a lawn in front of the church and threatened his life. The congregation of Chicopee, Massachusetts, attacked Rev. James Strain, described as "of hasty temperament and utterly without tact," on the altar and ripped vestments from his back. The Irish feelings showered on a beloved priest turned into fury against one who displeased them. The French bishop of frontier Dubuque threatened to interdict a church when the Irish tried to isolate it as a separate Irish church, and the Irish congregation in Chicago refused to accept a priest named to succeed their Irish pastor. In the West as in populous New York and Boston, these early Irish emigrants had their own ideas concerning the running of a church, despite bishops. As Father John Roddan traced out this trait of the Irish temperament in pastoral affairs:

> If a church is to be built, or any thing done which requires *one* leader, *twenty* start at once, and begin to pull in opposite directions. Peter will have nothing to do with it if Paul shows his face. John will not contribute a cent, if James is to hold the funds. Charles is sure that Patrick will fill his own pocket with the public money. Terence thinks that nothing will be done while Henry is a manager. Cornelius wonders why Owen has so much to say. If Michael is put at the head, Hugh goes away angry, and drags fifty after him; if Hugh is made master, Michael says that he and his party will drive Hugh off the ground.

It took a priest tougher-willed than his factious and opinionated flock
to get things done.

8

But far more representative than the sporadic outbreaks of trusteeism
was the moving story told by Rev. P. J. M. O'Reilly of the tasks of the
priests and the deep, self-sacrificing devotion of the Irish to their religion under hard circumstances in pioneering days. Father O'Reilly,
who had come to New York City in 1833 to raise funds, was pastor of
the Catholic congregation on the Hudson spread out over an area fully
fifty miles in circumference. He had been moved to build a church at
Saugerties, Ulster County, in place of a mission station, by:

> . . . the zeal which I saw the poor creatures manifest in attendance
> in the services of their religion, from which neither the summer's
> heat, nor the winter's cold, nor the dangers attendant on crossing
> the mountain cataract, could deter them. When I saw them enter
> my temporary little place of worship, from their homes beyond the
> Catskills, on the morning of Sunday, pale, wayworn, and fasting,
> having travelled all the night of Saturday, I thought I would build
> a church which would be to them a bond of union, and a resting
> place, around whose walls they might deposit in sacred security
> the mortal remains of their kindred, with the deep, enduring affec-
> tion of Ireland, which buries its heart in the "grave with those it
> loves."

The church needed a roof for completion and as his funds were exhausted, he called on his countrymen for aid. "If I fail, I do not know
them," he said, as thousands of other Irish priests said to themselves
when building a church, knowing they could depend upon the Irish to
see them through.

Bishop Barron, himself an Irishman, writing from St. Louis to Dr.
Cullen in Rome on the little support given the priests, said: "The poor
Irish with great faults on other scores give the principal support." A
visiting Irish priest wrote to the president of Maynooth College that
the Irish laborers on public works, "though they were up at the dawn,
and the shirt seldomed dried on their backs, have never refused the call
of charity."

Father O'Reilly, in his appeal, told of his plans to form a missionary
station in the western part of New York State to cover thirty-two coun-

ties in which numbers of Catholics were deprived of religious instruction by the absence of a priest.

The loss of Catholic Irish or their children to other sects by the lack of priests bothered the clergy, who for years were governed by the distorted figures of Bishop England. He wrote in 1836 that Catholicity had lost 3,750,000 between 1786 and 1836, an estimate statistically demolished by Bishop Shaughnessy.*

Bishop O'Connor of Pittsburgh wrote that in western Pennsylvania and that part of the state east of the Alleghenies the early Irish emigrants, though settled in districts removed from a church, remained staunch in their Catholic faith but their families drifted away "and, in the majority of instances, the Catholic parents were laid away in their graves by children strangers to the faith." A Catholic Irishman married a woman of another faith and, without his own church, joined the congregation of his wife, and the children were reared in that sect. The gregarious Irishman, in a community without a priest or church, gravitated to the local Protestant church as the center of its social life and there remained.

Good Catholic Irishmen joined the Masonic order as a social organization and for good fellowship without inhibition. Daniel Carroll, brother of the first Roman Catholic bishop in the United States, was a prominent Mason in good standing. James Hoban, architect of the White House and superintendent of the building of the Capitol in Washington, wore his Masonic apron on formal occasions, such as laying a cornerstone. The leading Catholic Irish of early St. Louis saw nothing inconsistent in practicing their faith and participating in the Masonic order.

9

The representative Catholic Irish priest up to the Civil War was the mission priest. As Catholic Irish emigration heightened and the people started to build their colonies over the United States, the importance of the mission priest increased and his round of calls grew more arduous. The mission was a familiar institution in Ireland, where, as previously shown, it was known as the station, the name of which persisted in the United States.

---

* Cf. *Has the Immigrant Kept the Faith?* Gerald Shaughnessy, New York: The Macmillan Company, 1925.

The design of the station was standardized. The priest had his central headquarters in a community of size with a church. From there he radiated out to serve five or six mission stations periodically, from two to six weeks apart, often longer for the distant outposts, sometimes only twice a year for a tiny congregation in a remote spot.

In the absence of a weekly service, the people were urged to gather together on Sunday and conduct their own pious observances — a "dry Mass," this was called. The instructions in 1823 of Bishop Cheverus of Boston to the Roman Catholics of Hartford set out the simple procedure:

> In the meantime, you will do well to procure a room and meet every Sunday to perform together your devotions. Let one who reads well and has a clear voice, read the prayers of the Mass, a sermon or some instruction out of a Catholic book.

The Irish, for their part, liked to gather for the saying of the Rosary, following the custom of rural Ireland.

Generally, when the congregation was small, the services were held in the house of a member, as in Ireland on the stations. The house was more often a tenement than a private dwelling or a rude log hut in the back country.

But Mass was frequently said wherever room could be found. In the course of this mission period, the priest set up his simplified altar in various and sundry places: in the basement of a tin store, in stables, in Masonic halls, in the sorting room of a woolen mill, in barns, in the residence of a French professor at Yale, in barrooms (with the bar concealed by blankets), in the attic of a hall reached by climbing through a trap door, in firehouses, in the basements of courthouses, in billiard parlors, in the dining room of an industrial company's boarding house, in Daniel Dempsey's Blooming Grove Garden in Brooklyn, in the hayloft over a stable, in blacksmiths' shops, in dilapidated buildings, and, when no sheltered place could be secured, in the open — in fields, meadows, and in the woods — "no roof under which to assemble than the broad canopy of Heaven." Priests accepted the invitation of kindly ministers to hold services for their congregations in Protestant churches. The Catholic Irish in those days resembled the primitive Christians in the places where their altars were set up.

77777

IO

But the Catholic Irish, who had come to the United States to stay, always planned for the day when they would have their own church: the mission priest had the dream of turning his mission stations into churches with resident priests.

Peter Turner called a meeting of the Roman Catholics of Brooklyn on the first day of January in 1822 and inscribed on a sheet of old-fashioned foolscap paper a petition to the bishop in New York for a church that, in concise and straightforward language, expressed for all times the yearning of the Catholic Irish in the United States for a House of God of their own:

> In the first place, we want our children instructed in the principles of our holy religion; we want more convenience of hearing the word of God ourselves. In fact, we want a church, a pastor, and a place of interment.

It was never said better.

The itinerant mission priest's schedule necessarily called for Masses to be said on week days. This meant that the Catholic Irish attended service before work. So up they were in the middle of the night to be ready for Mass at 4:30 or 5 A.M., with the dawn starting to break as the priest's "Ite missa est" was heard, soon to be followed by the sound of the bells in plants calling them to their labors at sunrise. One thing can be said of our Roman Catholic brethren, and especially of our Roman Catholic sisters, without exciting controversy, wrote James Parton, "they begin early in the morning."

There was comparatively little building of churches up to 1835, but after that date their numbers multiplied, coincident with and the result of the ever-increasing emigration, until just before the Civil War a Catholic weekly noted that hardly a week passed without the laying of a cornerstone or the dedication of a new church. When a bishop set his mind upon a cathedral or a pastor on a stone church, his first thought went to Patrick C. Keeley, the then Tiffany of Catholic architecture, born in Kilkenny, who began as a carpenter in Brooklyn and aside from instructions from his father, a builder, was self-taught. Keeley in his day designed some twenty cathedrals and six hundred churches, from Vermont to Wisconsin, hardly architectural classics but fitted to the simple and untutored taste of the Irish clergy at the time, who considered themselves fortunate that they had a Catholic to call upon: later architects, like Ralph Adams Cram, shuddered at his work.*

The people were as anxious as the priests to build churches. The clergy from time to time had to restrain the Irish disposition to make great plans without the means to carry them through. "There are about half-a-dozen of us poor Irishmen in this town, God help us," wrote one of the half dozen; "we have no priest or Mass to go to." These people felt the mood to start a church at the slightest nod of encouragement. Between two and three hundred Irishmen in a Rhode Island manufacturing village rarely saw one of the limited number of priests and "in order therefore to secure one more permanently they have determined with God's blessing to erect a church, persuaded that where there is an altar, there also will be found a priest" — a belief common with the race.

But the priest and the leading laymen of the congregation were generally sensible in procedure and when they concluded that the numbers were sufficient to undertake the task, they went about it in an orderly way, as the following item indicated:

> On Sunday, the 8th instant, after mass, a meeting, presided over by the Rev. Mr. Gibson, was held at the home of Mr. Dominic McDavitt, for the purpose of taking into consideration the most effectual means of erecting a church to meet the spiritual wants of the rising congregation of this place. A subscription list was opened, and although the greater part of the congregation was not present or apprised of it, the sum of three hundred and fifty dollars was collected on the occasion, and the following gentlemen were appointed a committee to collect funds and superintend the building, viz., Messrs. Hugh McGown, Edward McGovern, and Dominick McDavitt.

A year later, the bishop's permission having been given to go ahead, the cornerstone was laid and two years from the initial meeting the church was blessed. This was the church in Milford, Massachusetts, and the routine of its construction was generally the accepted practice.

Behind the story of the Milford church and of practically every church in the United States was heroic self-sacrifice on the part of the people, for the most part close to the margin of poverty. "If the Celt has not as good faculties for procuring a house for himself as some

---

* It is strange that while Keeley's multitudinous churches still stand, his name is forgotten, and material on him is practically nonexistent.

other races," wrote a Buffalo Irishman, "he has a better inclination to raise one for the glory and honor of God."

The Church cannot forget, said a priest in 1850, "that hundreds of churches have been erected in a few years, and the country studded from Maine to Key West and from N. York to Minnesota with convents, hospitals, schools and colleges, erected mainly in the cities, by Catholic servant girls living at six dollars a month, and in the country by Catholic laborers working on the railroads and canals, at a dollar or a dollar and a quarter a day."

The assistance of Protestants in helping to build the Church in the United States, in donating plots of land or subscribing what was then a generous gift, remains a bright memory with the grateful Catholic Irish. That in instances calculation mingled with beneficence in this generosity — principally a wish to hold a faithful Irish working population in a manufacturing town — does not detract from the overall helpfulness of Protestants to a Church whose lot then laid with the poor.

Many of the Catholic churches had originally been Protestant meetinghouses, purchased from Episcopalians, Universalists, Methodists, Baptists or other sects which were erecting new churches or, in some instances, had merged congregations. The bishop gave the building raised to the Reformation a good blessing and the Catholic Irish were in business. One enthusiastic Irishman saw in this transfer of property a reformation, under Irish auspices, of the Protestant United States:

> The weather vane is being pulled down from the best edifices of our sectarian brethren, and the Cross of Christ crucified elevated in its stead; the Font supplies, in their vestibule, the place of the accommodating umbrella stand; the altar has supplanted the *desk;* the Priest robed in the emblems of his sacred office holds the place of the smooth faced youth, flourishing his cambric and his rhetoric together.

II

Americans called the priest "the old priest," even if he was a young man, or "the Paddy priest," and his own people described him as "Rev. Mr." up until the middle of the 1850s, when "Father" came into general usage. He did not wear the black cloth and the Roman collar associated now with the Roman Catholic clergy. (The Roman collar was not worn in Ireland until the time of Cardinal Cullen, in the middle of the nineteenth century.) The Catholic Irish priest dressed like a minister, in somber-colored clothes, frequently brown, with a cravat. Father Kenny in Wilmington wore a broad-brimmed hat and looked more like a Quaker than a Catholic priest. This avoidance of distinctive garb derived in measure from self-protection, the desire of the clergy not to draw attention to themselves and suffer the taunts and insults of the hostile.

The Irish priest in pre-Civil War days was principally a builder. The buzz of the carpenter's saw and the slap of the mason's trowel had the pious sound of a litany to his ears as another church of the Holy Roman Catholic and Apostolic religion arose. There was considerable of the Irish contractor in his veins. His careful supervision watched the church rise from the basement to the spire. Parishioners joined in prayers for a speedy recovery when Rev. Daniel Hearn, building a stone church in Taunton, Massachusetts, lost his footing and fell from the scaffold, probably much to His Reverend's discomfiture not from the pain but his enforced absence from the job he had watched stone upon stone, "with singular affection."

Mostly of peasant or small shopkeeper stock, these Irish clergymen were shrewd and knowing in money matters, tough bargainers, frugal (even tightfisted) in the handling of funds, careful and precise in keeping accounts. Of their generality, it could be said of them, as it was said of the deceased Rev. Edward Farrelly, born in County Cavan: "He was not only a good, zealous, faithful priest — he was a man of excellent business habits." An obituary notice praised Father James Conway of Salem, Massachusetts, as "a shrewd, practical business man."

Bishop John Hughes, representative of the new class of clerics, spoke in characterization of them when he called himself "by trade a kind of church builder."

Increasing emigration had overwhelmed the plan of Bishop Carroll, in the first decades of the Church under the Republic, to raise an American-born, American-trained priesthood. Bishop England was the first actively to recruit priests, or candidates for the priesthood, in Ireland, and other members of the hierarchy beseeched bishops in Ireland for clergymen, or themselves visited Ireland in search of worthy clerics. By 1840, the Provincial Council proclaimed that the United States must depend upon foreign priests to meet the clamoring demands of congregations. American bishops "adopted," that is, paid the expenses of Irish students preparing for the priesthood on the understanding they would serve in the underwriting diocese. Many Irish priests, on mission work in the West Indies, presented themselves to American bishops when their tolerance to the climate had broken. Irish religious orders, particularly the Augustinians and Franciscans, sent priests to the new land. Irish priests, feeling the call of the United States, received permission of bishops to depart. In 1842, the founding of All Hallows College in Dublin, a school for mission work for young men too poor to pay the costs of the seminary training, furnished many priests and several bishops for the United States. After the ravages of the Famine, a great number of priests left depopulated Ireland to attend the refugees in the United States. The full story of the recruiting in Ireland of priests for the United States deserves the attention of detailed study.

What with the rounds of missions, building churches, and tending the needs of his flocks, the Irish-born priest had little time left for books or the amenities of life: too much remained to be done to savor the leisure of study or pleasant refinements. Nevertheless, his Irish nature inhibited him from silence when a local parson thundered against Rome, and, with *The End of Religious Controversy* by Rt. Rev. John Milner, an English priest, who had collected and answered the major anti-Catholic arguments, by his side, he thundered back, if he could persuade the local press to print the response.

As a class, generally speaking, they were stern, austere, puritanical, authoritarian, imposing on their people the same discipline they had undergone in Irish seminaries. They were inclined to be neither tender nor sensitive to the feelings of their congregations in laying down the law. They brandished the blackthorn, as in an Irish village, over the heads — and sometimes on the backs — of the imprudent and disobedient. The rod was not spared on the Irish lad in the church or school. The first rule of the Roman Catholic Academy, underneath the Boston Cathedral on Franklin Street, made that clear in 1829: "The disposition of each child is studied as far as practicable, and when mild means prove abortive, recourse is had to coercion."

The Irish accepted the disciplinary chastisement from the priests and pastors: the Irish father stern in the raising of his children (and he was a stern master) expected no less in the relationship of priest to people. But they revolted against the strong hand when it invaded what they thought were their rights. The knowing Irish clerical disciplinarian understood that it was one thing to brook the Irish nature and another to try to break it.

More often than not, the Irish priest was a holy terror after Demon Rum. He not only preached against intemperance in vehement language to raise a man's hair on his head, but he also sought out the individual drunks to whip them out of the evil into support of their neglected families. His warfare with the evils of excessive drinking never ended. He never succeeded in gaining total victory over the adversary, but he attached an evil repute to the selling of liquor.

The heritage of segregated Catholic Ireland, together with the disposition of the "modern" or Maynooth clergy not to mix freely with non-Catholics in Ireland, inclined the Irish priest in the United States to maintain, as one secular newspaper said of a departed pastor, "the reserve and seclusion common to the Catholic clergy," though, on the other hand, Father Doran in Cattaragus County, New York, who was also a colonizer and land promoter, boasted that he was "a Yankee priest." Bishop Hughes disliked priests who mingled with non-Catholics: he called them "Protestant priests." Instinct with these Irish priests was the distrust, again an Irish heritage, of Protestants as proselytizers of their flocks. They kept a sharp eye for "the wolf on the track." The Irish priests reflected the strong characteristic of the race to huddle together: in that way temptations to latitudinarianism, or a free-and-easy and liberal attitude toward Reformation sects and doctrines, would not arise and faith and morals were safeguarded.

The congregations learned to recognize one sign in Irish-born priests: a lassitude, an apathy, a complaint of illness, a drooping of the spirit. That meant one thing: homesickness for Ireland had taken possession of their pastor. The yearning to look upon the old country, shake hands with old friends and often to embrace aging parents became a physical ailment. Soon, when a substitute priest had been found, notice was given that His Reverence had departed on a trip to Ireland to recover his health or, as one explanation of such a departure put it, the physicians had stated that "the voyage and invigorating air of his native land will restore him to health in a few months," though the Irish climate was notoriously wretched. Like the emigrant who had tasted America, the priest liked to visit, not to return to Ireland: the United States was in his blood.

12

The Irish emigrant looked to the priest for leadership, advice, and direction, as in the old country; and the responsible priest took it upon himself both to explain the meaning of America and to guide the stranger in the right paths. The priest was not content merely to preach simple lessons in morality from the Gospels to his congregation; he entered into the intimate affairs of his people and sought to indoctrinate them in the principles of the country where they had begun a new life. A series of articles by an Irish-American priest directed to the Irish emigrant embodied the nature of the sermons heard from the altar.

The blessings of the United States as contrasted with conditions in Ireland were stressed:

> In Ireland a father often wept to think that his children would grow up, and never be able to rise above the conditions in which they were born. — Here there is no honor, no station, no eminence they may not aspire to, if they know enough to fill it. Your son in Ireland would be oppressed laborers, your son in America may sit in the highest places of the land.

The emigrant was bound "before God to love his chosen home" but he needed not nor should he renounce his love of old Ireland — a constant sentiment dwelt upon both by the priest and the Irish lay leader.

His first duty was to become a citizen as soon as he could:

> It is only America that holds out to the houseless wanderer the right hand of fellowship. It is only in America that he is furnished with the materials of prosperity, and bid to go on and prosper, until he stands on a level with the proud lordling, in whose presence he crouched, a few years before.

If he did not become a citizen, the priest warned, "he is guilty of ingratitude" — a terrible sin in the native Irish tradition.

The "bare fact that you are a citizen and therefore a maker of laws" would spur the desire the Irishman did not feel in his own country "to have also a direct interest in the soil, as well as in the institutions of the country." The priest then directly connected naturalization with the ownership of a home. In one village of his mission district there were 220 men in the congregation, of whom 92 were heads of families. Of these, 62 were naturalized and "I believe that nearly all of these own, or partly own, the houses in which they live." He had observed in the affairs of the mission that the greater part of the married men were naturalized while the greater part of the young bachelors remained aliens. With a suggestion that a Protestant minister would hesitate to put forward as untoward interference in private lives but to which the Irish were accustomed from their priests, he said:

> I give this advice to young women; when he proposes, ask him in the first place if he minds his duty [that is, if he is a faithful practicing Catholic]. Next place ask him if he is sober. Finally ask him if he is naturalized. If not, send him away until he adheres to it.

Once an Irishman had become a citizen, then he had the obligation of qualifying himself to be a good citizen. First, he must be faithful to God and the duties of religion: an infidel, liar, drunkard, blasphemer or dishonest man cannot be a good citizen. Next, he must provide for his own mental and physical improvement:

> Take one hour, just one hour every evening, give it faithfully to your pen, and to your reading book, and in one year you will read as well as I do, and perhaps write much better. . . . Go to school if you can; and if you cannot, get your children to teach you what they have learned.

As for politics, the priest described as shameful "an attempt to bring us to the polls as Irishmen and as Catholics" and warned against the use of Irish votes as the tools of a party. The interests of the country, he explained, "require you to vote, not as Irishmen, but as men and as Americans." Only one contingency justified their votes as Irishmen — and that was against the party which would change the naturalization laws to their disfavor and disfranchisement.

Then the priest gave a lecture on cleanliness, taking up the argument that dirt in Ireland was of despair and not of choice. "But this excuse does not and cannot be used by us in this country. There is not a shadow of justification here for a dirty house or for dirty children." The women were to blame if this condition prevailed, "and it is better for the woman to flourish a wet mop about the house every morning, than to spend the time gossiping with a neighbor." No excuse was acceptable on the score of no time: women with a houseful of children kept themselves, the house, and the children in neat order. "Sometimes," he sighed, "I do not wonder that the men run away as soon as they get their suppers, for careless women are often scolds; and the poor man runs to some place where he can have a social talk by a clean hearth."

The priest lashed out at the exploitation of Irishmen by Irishmen:

> There are a great many Irishmen in this country who live by the ignorance, the simplicity, and the vices of their fellow-country-men. It may be said that in America the Irishman has no enemy more deadly than some men who were born in the same country — perhaps in the same parish with himself. The most hard-hearted plunderer of the poor emigrant when he steps on our shores is too often an Irishman.

He vigorously urged that they leave their county fights and their prej-udices back in Ireland and stop brawling. "Ten or twelve thoughtless rioters will give a bad name to the whole Irish society. . . . Let your united action compel men either to behave themselves, or to call them-selves something else than Irishmen. If they will do neither, hiss them out of town."

This has been quoted from at length to show the personal, intimate and paternal relationship of the priest to his Irish emigrant people; it is also a revealing social document of the Irish in America.

13

Sunday was the important social, as well as religious, day in the cal-endar of the Irish emigrant. He attended Mass in the morning and Ves-pers in the afternoon. Since he and his friends, who wanted to be pres-ent, could not afford to take a day off during the work week, he was married on Sunday and his children were christened on Sunday. The Irish came in from the surrounding countryside to the local church, with much visiting and jollity among friends. After Mass, the married met outside the church to exchange greetings and gossip. The unmar-ried young men, freshly scrubbed, their faces shining, wearing their other suit (if they had one), stood in groups to eye the young, high-colored, bright-faced girls, just as in Ireland. Guests sat down to big spreads with their relatives and friends when Mass was over, and Sun-day was the big day for *shebeens* in tenement houses, garrets or cellars.

On special occasions there were charity sermons, with renowned ora-tors gracing the pulpits, for a specified charity, usually an orphan asy-lum, when the congregation was expected to contribute liberally. A board of lay managers of a Catholic asylum assumed the responsibility of raising funds for its maintenance. In 1833, in Boston, a fair was held, the proceeds of which were turned over to the asylum. New York followed the next year, and in time this annual affair became established generally in dioceses, returning sizable revenue for charitable designs.

14

The emigrants from rural Ireland carried the custom of the wake overseas with them, especially pronounced with the Famine refugees, to the mortification of the long-established Irish who had settled into a respectable state in the United States and to the shock of Americans, who surrounded death with reticence and solemnity, or to their amusement. The Catholic clergy and press angrily denounced the old custom:

> Our clergy are opposed to these useless customs, as well as every true friend of Irishmen. Let the dead have the quiet reverence, and the sorrow which are fit; but let them not be outraged by the feasting and night-watching of an indiscriminate crowd of noisy people. The old habits of Ireland will not answer here.

The *Catholic Observer* characterized wakes as "no better than public nuisances," and the Boston *Pilot* recoiled with horror "to find the dead room a scene of rioting and drunkenness." The steady Irish of Boston flushed when a sectarian paper described the spree given at the Revere House to members of Congress, who accompanied the remains of John Quincy Adams to Boston, as an "Irish wake."

15

The preparations for a funeral in rural Ireland were simple. The local carpenter made a coffin on the spot, and friends carried it on their shoulders to the graveyard, with the mourners either riding on horseback or following on foot. In American cities, Irish emigrants had to become acquainted with the undertaker, in the European custom. The first advertisement of an undertaker asking for Irish patronage appeared in the New York *Truth Teller* on January 28, 1826. It described the confusion and irresolution when death entered a family and the familiar practices of Ireland no longer prevailed. One friend volunteered his services to bespeak a coffin. Another took the assignment to order a grave opened at some designated spot. A third summoned the tailor and dressmaker. A fourth ordered the shroud, crape, and so on. A fifth engaged the hackney coachman. A sixth invited the clergyman.

All this confusion could be avoided, the advertisement continued, by employing "an UNDERTAKER." He handled all the details in proper order and everything was conducted "with the utmost decency, solemnity, and punctuality." Only one bill was offered — the undertaker's, which amounted to about twenty per cent less than the usual expenses. John L. Dillon, of 496 Pearl Street, the only general undertaker in the city, therefore offered his services.

As in Ireland, the people thought it disrespectful to the dead not to turn out in large numbers for funerals, and the hearse carrying the remains of a humble Irishman, a night watchman or baggage agent or store clerk, who had been well liked or honored for his family virtues, was followed to the graveyard by a procession of marching mourners often a mile in length, in contrast to the austerity of a Protestant funeral, with a few carriages for the family and close friends.

The funerals of the long-settled or of the second-generation Irish were conducted with dignity, decorum, and solemnity. But a "Paddy funeral" was something else again. The Boston *Courier* drew a vivid picture of a typical Paddy funeral:

> A hearse, followed by twenty-three dingy hacks, three limping cabs, two faded carryalls, and a chaise with nearly every screw in it loose, passed through Charles street, yesterday afternoon, at 4 o'clock. The hacks contained men and women, to the number of four to seven each, and the cabs, carryalls and chaise were proportionately laden. It was one of the meanest displays of human beings that has ever taken part in a funeral procession in Boston. There were three women and two men in one of the carriages; the men were smoking long pipes, which, on the score of decency towards their companions — as was supposed — were protruded through the side windows; and the women filled the air with their jangling and horse-laughter. . . . One of the cabs, in which were four unwashed buffers with bloated faces — threatened to break down, and its stoppage occasioned a general inquiry of "What the devil ails ye?" from the persons in the adjacent carriages. The whole procession was a wicked and heathenish affair, alike disgraceful to the living and the dead, and the sooner that the practice of "paddy funerals" is brought into disuse the better it will be for the Irish residents of Boston.

The Boston *Pilot*, subscribing "heartily to the sentiment of the article," contrasted the "*Irish Catholic* funeral" as a very different affair, the mourners poor but respectable, orderly, quiet, and sober, not "as disgusting a set of savages" as gathered at a Paddy funeral. "The corpse receives a very really Christian burial."

Generally the cabs and carriages of a Paddy funeral raced to the graveyard and they always raced on the return trip. If it happened that two Paddy funerals met on the road to the same graveyard, the drivers whipped their horses for a contest as to which would reach the gate first, the mourners, heads stuck out of the windows, shouting encouragement to their own and bad luck on the rival procession. In one race, the two hearses smashed together, and one was so damaged that the coffin was taken out and carried to the graveyard on the shoulders of the pallbearers. The police of the Sixth Precinct in New York City arrested a whole funeral party for racing in the streets.

The abuse which brought the authority of the Church into action against it was the imposition, become a custom, on a poverty-stricken family to hire carriages for the mourners at a Paddy funeral. A poor man was forced, "on pain of being called mean," wrote Bishop Timon, "to give his last dollar for a carriage and leave his family next day without bread." The *Catholic Telegraph* asked: "When will our people understand that in most of these instances, where survivors are left so utterly destitute, the larger the funeral the deeper the shame and the greater the disgrace." The bishops finally had to interfere, with regulations limiting the number of carriages at funerals; Catholic societies passed resolutions to boycott funerals with a long procession of carriages the family could not afford; the Catholic press kept up a constant agitation against the practice. Yet the ancient customs of Irish funerals continued to prevail against the wrath of clergy and press. After a violent dressing-down of the practices by the Boston *Pilot,* a correspondent wrote in that "if the Pulpit cannot mind [discipline] them then I am afraid that the *Pilot* (in a newspaper sense) never can."

16

The Irish loved cemeteries. The poetic muse frequently turned its stirrings to melancholy reflections on the grave, or fashioned lines on the beautiful surroundings of a cemetery. Visitors to Irish communities were invariably shown the graveyard by their relatives, and a voluntary letter writer, on a trip through the country, reported to a Catholic

Irish weekly the several cemeteries he viewed on the journey. Parish picnics were held in cemeteries. The Irish hated to have graves disturbed, and the pastor in New Bedford found a rebellious congregation facing him when he ordered reinterment in a new lot he had purchased. Boston Irish long remembered the dispute with the bishop over denial of rites if bodies were not laid at rest in a new cemetery against the wishes of people who held lots in an old cemetery and wanted to be buried with their own.

17

Bishop England died in 1842. He had been the predominant prelate in the affairs of the Church during the 1820s and 1830s, as Archbishop Carroll had been the architect in the previous period. By now the Church had established itself on canonical foundations, asserted its authority over lay trusteeism and quieted down the racial rivalries. The new generation of churchmen, particularly Bishop Hughes, set out to claim equality of rights with an aggressiveness quite different from the suavity of Bishop England. The last major work of Bishop England was a treatise explaining the Roman Catholic position on human slavery, the issue which was coming to overshadow all else in American life. The Irish took a stand on the issue that seemed strange in the light of their own history.

3 4

The Anti-Abolitionist Irish

IT WOULD BE THOUGHT that the Catholic Irish, a subjugated people, themselves emancipated from religious disabilities only in 1829, would sympathetically array themselves in the United States on the side of freeing the Negro slaves. Yet the Catholic Irish, almost to a man, were linked in the public mind with the slave power in pre-Civil War America.

Lord Morpeth, a popular Chief Secretary of Ireland, who had praised "that superior social morality of the poorer classes of Ireland over any other people," returned from America and denounced the

Irish in the United States "as being amongst the worst enemies of the Negro slaves."

The Synod of Armagh in the twelfth century had freed every captive in Ireland and since that time, as a famous Irish Quaker Abolitionist proclaimed, "a slave has never polluted our green isle." The penal laws had humbled the Catholic Irish to the lowest status, but serfdom, as known in feudal Europe, had not obtained in Ireland. Not one slave ship ever sailed from Ireland, and the country boasted it had never participated in the slave trade. A Belfast merchant attempted to form a company to engage in the slave traffic. Thomas McCabe quickly broke up the meeting with his shout: "May God d——n him who subscribes the first guinea." Every Irish member of the House of Commons voted in favor of the emancipation of the West Indian Negroes; and O'Connell said it was the Irish votes which enabled the Whigs to carry through the measure.

Daniel O'Connell, the Liberator, the worshiped leader of the Gaels everywhere, held rank as one of the foremost Abolitionists in the world, passionate and wholly uncompromising in his hatred of human slavery.

Mrs. Nicholson, the American evangelist, talked with a priest in Ireland. "His first inquiries were concerning American slavery," she wrote. "Its principles and practices he abhorred, and he could not comprehend its existence in a republican country."

What had happened to the Catholic Irish in their transplantation in the United States to change them?

"It was not in Ireland you learned this cruelty," O'Connell thundered at an Irish-American apologia of slavery. "Your mothers were gentle, kind and humane. . . . How then can you become so depraved? How can your souls have become stained with a darkness blacker than the Negro's skin?"

2

The general conclusion has been passed down from the emotion-charged pre-Civil War period that the Catholic Irish upheld slavery, whereas their own literature pointed to the more discriminating judgment that they were anti-Abolitionist. This distinction is important. A set of circumstances peculiar to the United States made the Catholic Irish emigrant distrustful and suspicious of the anti-slavery movement for reasons that impinged upon his own feelings, loyalties, and interests.

The accepted assumption maintained the Catholic Irish feared that the abolition of slavery would release the Negro as an economic competitor in the North and endanger their jobs in the lowest and roughest categories of labor. That was an easy oversimplification of a complex matter. It should be weighed among the elements contributory to the Catholic Irish attitude but not with the emphasis of preponderance which uncritical examination has placed upon it. When the prosperous and substantial Catholic Irish, with no reason whatever to fear the economic competition of emancipated Negroes, when thoughtful Catholic Irish opinion, including some of the most brilliant lawyers in the United States, when the Catholic clergy and the Catholic press held the same attitude toward anti-slavery as the common laborer, the explanation of economic rivalry becomes diluted. In fact, the Irish laborer feared the competition of another Irishman more than he did the Negro and fought more savagely with rival Irish workers than he ever did with the colored people.

Dr. T. L. Nichols, a convert to Roman Catholicism, a native of New Hampshire but vigorously Southern in his sympathies, thought their attitude on slavery stemmed from dislike of Negroes by the Irish:

> They have no sympathy with the negro. They care very little about his emancipation, and wish him as far as possible away from their vicinity. Their antipathy to the negro, which seems genuine and instinctive, and which manifests itself as soon as they come into contact with him, is more marked than that of the North Americans generally.

But the Irish also disliked the French and the Germans. They gaped at the first sight of a Negro like yokels in a big city and oral tradition in Irish-American families perpetuated the common story of the "greenhorn" ancestor who thought the first Negro he had ever met to be the devil himself.

Thomas G. Grattan pondered on their strange attitude. The poor Negro, he wrote, had done them no harm; he did not stand in their way; he "cannot presume even to an equality with them." The Negro had furnished them "no wrongs, no rivalry, and no insults to avenge." The Irish had "no early habits of thought (as the Yankees have) to make a black skin abhorrent to their taste." Why, then, this "lamentable blot upon the Irish in America," their "too evident adhesion to pro-slavery doctrines"? He could come to only one accounting:

> A galling sense of inferiority to the dominant Anglo-Saxon popu-lation makes Irishmen too happy in finding another portion over which they can in turn domineer; and they would, if possible, place the negro lower than he is, that they might on his degradation rise above the level assigned to themselves.

This psychological response by the Irish to a people they found in an even worse economic and social position than had been their unhappy lot must be reckoned with, but Grattan's analysis did not go to the roots of the matter. The core of the Irishman's position centered nei-ther in support of slavery as an institution nor in dislike of the Negro. Both were related by transference to the real source of the Catholic Irish antagonism — dislike of the Abolitionists, their friends and their allies, "the brawling tribe" who pass for Christians, as the Irish called them.

3

The initial impulse of Abolitionism was religious and moral, Protes-tant and evangelical. It came from the Great Revival in western New York in the 1820s, of which Rev. Charles G. Finney, a dissenter from orthodox Calvinism and against whom the Boston *Jesuit* had warned Catholics in 1829, was the burning-brand of inspiration.* The move-ment of "disinterested benevolence," in Finney's words, promoted a Great Awakening, a moral cleansing through emotional fervor, in his-toric evangelical fashion. It gave birth to widespread reforms and stirred intense reformist activity. Abolitionism was its most momen-tous fruit, spread in the 1830s by the apostleship of the Seventy, dedi-cated preachers of the word that slavery was a sin and that every slave-holder must be rebuked for his sin. Barnes wrote:

> From the beginning the movement had been inextricably bound up with the [Protestant] churches. The churches were its forum and the homes of its local organizations; from the churches it drew its justifying inspiration, evangelical in character — a part of the benevolent empire.

---

* For an excellent account of the origin of this movement and its fundamental relationship to Abolitionism, cf. *The Antislavery Impulse 1830-1844* by Gilbert Hobbs Barnes, New York: D. Appleton-Century Company, 1933.

Many of the consecrated of the "benevolent empire" were also anti-Popery preachers. Anti-Catholic agitators in the "Maria Monk" period of the 1830s, like Brownlee and Bourne, were vigorous anti-slavery partisans. At its fountainhead, in its very origins, Abolitionism carried to the Catholic Irish a lash as cutting to their deepest religious susceptibilities as the overseer's whip was to the back of the slave — the lash of anti-Popery.

Two New York newspapers, the *Journal of Commerce* and the *Commercial Advertiser,* described in 1833 as "the only papers which favor the class of anti-slavery disorganizers," were bitter scarifiers of Catholicism and of the Catholic Irish.

The Catholic and Irish press bristled with distrust and suspicion at this burgeoning offshoot of Protestant evangelism. The *Truth Teller,* commenting on the first annual report of the American Anti-Slavery Society in 1834, characterized the "reverend brethren" as "bigots of the most despicable character." Five years later the Boston *Pilot* was specific in its accusation: "These [anti-slavery] societies are thronged with bigotted and persecuting religionists, with men, who, in their private capacity, desire the extermination of Catholics by fire and sword."

Abolitionists of the extremist stamp joined slavery with Popery as the two evils subject to the universal emancipation they proclaimed to save the United States from moral ruin. (At a later stage, they linked Popery with slavery in another meaning, as affording comfort and support to the slave power.)

The agitation of the evangelicals, who had sought a law in Congress to shut down the United States mails on Sunday, led the suspicious Catholic Irish to the belief that their goal contemplated an established religion — a sensitive point with the race. The *Truth Teller* in 1833 warned its reader that "this ranting and crying for the liberation of the blacks is all a hoax; their ardent wish is that the Church should exercise its influence in conquering the established law of the land; they have proclaimed to their followers and devout members, that their interpretation of divine law should supercede [*sic*] the Constitution and the laws of these States."

4

The early invocation by the Abolitionists of the "higher law" than the Constitution set up fears for their own safety among the Catholic

Irish that increased as the fabric of the Union was threatened. The Constitution was the charter fortress which guaranteed them the right to practice their religion freely, and they dreaded the outcome if Abolitionists, tinged with anti-Popery, gained supremacy. The Union protected the five-year naturalization period of probation. The Catholic Irish right up to the Civil War held to the conviction that it was the anti-slavery forces in the North that threatened the Union, not the South, which, they argued, had been provoked by Abolitionist fanaticism into a counter-fanaticism in defense.

The conservative forces of the North held protest meetings against the excesses of Abolitionism, and with this conservative reaction the Catholic Irish sympathized. It should be remarked here that Catholic Irish opinion, except in the drive for political equality, in which it was radical in temper and method, was more likely than not to be found on the conservative side. The Irishman, by nature as well as by the teachings of his Church, opposed innovations, had little patience with reform and reformers and put small faith in the use of law to change or perfect human beings. The leading Catholic Irish lawyers vigorously upheld the strict construction of the Constitution on slavery, in this being at one with the conservative legal minds of the North.

The Boston *Pilot* in 1839 urged its Catholic readers to beware of the danger of contributing, even in the smallest degree, to the support of Abolitionist and anti-slavery societies:

> That we should simply caution our fellow Catholics to stand aloof from these insidious and bloody-minded sectarians is not enough. We charge them with treason to the country — as conspirators against the peace of society — and as a class of tyrants of the most dangerous and treacherous character.

5

Another consideration, which grew increasingly compelling as the lines tightened on the slavery issue, drew the Catholic Irish to the side of the opposition to Abolitionism — their political affiliation.

Catholic Irish political leaders signed the address of the Democratic General Committee (Tammany) of the city and county of New York, dated September 29, 1835, in opposition to the Abolitionists and on slavery. The substance of the address sustained the rights of the states in relation to master and slave against interference by the general

A PEASANT'S COTTAGE BEING DESTROYED AFTER HIS EVICTION.

A TENANT EVICTED AND BURNED OUT.

INTERIOR OF AN IRISH DWELLING IN NEW YORK IN THE 1850s.

THE VOTING-PLACE, No. 488 PEARL STREET, IN THE SIXTH WARD, NEW YORK CITY

government, described any attempt to weaken or sever the Union as treason, and promised cooperation to counteract the "infatuation of a few fanatical individuals."

Representative Catholic Irish opinion, especially in New York City, held a warm spot in its affections for the South. No acts of brutal intolerance, like the burning of the Charlestown convent, were committed in the South. In O'Connell's fight for Catholic Emancipation, the Scotch-Irish planters in the South had given vigorous support to the cause. Irishmen who journeyed southward had not suffered the cold hostility of Northern communities.

The Democratic Party had been consistently loyal to the Catholic Irish emigrants and continued to befriend them up to the Civil War. Southern ascendancy marked the Democratic Party as the agency of the slave power, to be borne down by the unsparing enmity of the Abolitionists and anti-slavery forces. As their strength increased, the anti-slavery forces penetrated and came in time to dominate the parties looked upon by the Catholic Irish as the successors of the Federalist tradition — Whigs, Freesoilers, and Republicans — and therefore as foes. This Northern political alignment had in sufficient instances to impress the Catholic Irish allied itself with and accepted the support of the Native Americans and, during the 1850s, of the Know Nothings. The parties which embraced both Abolitionists and Native American antagonists of the Catholic Irish strengthened the faith of the race in the Democratic Party and doubled its allegiance. If the Democratic Party gave sympathy to the cause of the South on the issue of slavery, the Catholic Irish, for reasons they thought transcended slavery, went along. So be it: they had no cause to be on the same side with the Abolitionists in a party that historically had nagged and despised them and would have reduced them to the status of the slave so far as citizenship was concerned. "The same party who would make the *negro a freeman,*" said the Galena (Illinois) *Democrat* in 1839, "would make the *Irishman a slave.*"

While the Boston *Pilot,* the best of the Catholic Irish weeklies and the most representative of Catholic Irish thinking, condemned the Abolitionists and their political allies as disrupters of the Union, never did it embrace or try to justify slavery as an institution. It urged a gradual emancipation, not the solution by violence.

Repeatedly as a theme constantly played, the Boston *Pilot* and the Catholic press generally, reflecting the views of the Church, insisted that the preservation of the Union took precedence at every turn over the abolition of slavery. This grew to be the heart of the Catholic Irish position on the issue.

6

The Catholic Irish had not that priority of interest in the issue of slavery which disturbed and divided the native-born. Starting in 1840, with the opening of Daniel O'Connell's agitation to repeal the Act of Union with England, the Catholic Irish concentrated their energies on the national cause in Ireland. "We want to make the freedom of Ireland sure," wrote the Boston *Pilot* in 1845, "before we turn our strength to the liberation of any other race." Intensely nationalistic peoples, struggling for their own freedom from an alien power, are egocentric in their ideals and aims and not inclined to be overconcerned with or diverted by similar struggles elsewhere, except to the extent that they may be turned to the advantage of the national issue. Nationalism is a single-minded — and jealous — taskmaster. What were the Abolitionists, with all their talk of freedom, doing for Irish freedom? The Irishman who asked that question replied that only two Abolitionists had joined the Repeal movement in Albany. The Abolitionists condemned the Irish for not helping to free the slaves; the Irish slugged the Abolitionists for not helping to free Ireland.

7

After 1845, the refugees from the Famine, besides lacking familiarity with the slavery issue, were consumed by their own passion — a burning hatred of England. They picked up and made their own the contention that England, for base motives, promoted the anti-slavery cause. A visiting English Abolitionist, George Thompson, had stirred a national protest among American conservatives in 1834-1835 by anti-slavery speeches, and mobs set (or were set) upon him in several places. A representative statement of this belief among the Catholic Irish carried all the conviction an Irishman could pound out, with mounting anger, against "the guilty enterprises of Britain":

> It is one of the contingent purposes of England, the darling project of her anti-slavery politicians, to create a servile war in this country, and promote a disruption of the Union. Therefore is it

that these abolition traitors are exclusively recognized in England as the American anti-slavery party; and therefore is it that they direct their efforts, not to smooth the way for emancipation, but to create foreign sympathies, and cast odium upon America, to introduce licentiousness under the mask of liberty, and to smooth the way for anarchy and destruction, to open the floodgates of war and confusion which may involve black and white in common ruin, and in which British ambition may triumph, when our adopted country, like India under Warren Hastings, has become a desert.

The Catholic Irish believed the worst against England.

The Famine refugees in the United States hated the English more and had less reason to pity the plight of the enslaved colored when one of their leaders declared, contrasting English benevolence toward the West Indian slaves with fumbling English policy during the Famine: "The [English] government gave twenty millions of British money to rescue some few hundreds of thousands of blacks from slavery, but they refused to vote ten millions to save eight millions of Irishmen from the grave."

The poverty-stricken state of the Famine refugees was so miserable that they compared their lot unfavorably with the situation of the slave, fed, sheltered, and clothed by the master. "This is a slave state," wrote a railroader from Missouri, "but the slave is treated better than the Irish." An Irishman in the coal region of Frostburg, Maryland, on strike for eleven weeks against what he called "slavery," wrote that "as we are occasionally black, our taskmasters might take the opportunity of selling or buying us before we get washed." The economic depression of the Irish worker in the very heart of Abolitionism brought out a wringing cry: "The slave population is in general undoubtedly more comfortably provided for in the way of the necessaries of life, personally more kindly regarded, and subjected to less of iron rule, than the operatives in northern factories."

Harriet Beecher Stowe had been feted in England by a landlord who had cleared his estate of people in the Irish manner, and one bitter Irishman wrote: "With our abolitionists, no suffering is worthy of sympathy, unless the sufferer has a black skin. It is time to get up an anti-white slavery society, and to write about some White Uncle Tom." Such sentiments, in which self-pity mingled with biting resentment at their own harsh treatment and neglect, set the Abolitionists and the Negroes they favored outside the Irishman's orbit of affection.

The Catholic Irish certainly had no pecuniary stake in the institution of slavery; and self-serving property interests in no way influenced their attitude. The number of Catholic Irish slaveholders was negligible.

8

Where stood the Roman Catholic Church on this issue? "The Catholic Church alone stands aloof," explained an article, "The Catholic Church and the Question of Slavery," in the *Metropolitan Magazine*, a Catholic publication, in 1856. This echoed the sentiment expressed by the *Truth Teller* in 1834:

> You do not find the Catholics attempting to stop the mails, revive the blue laws of Connecticut, or amalgamate blacks and whites; you never hear them urging on the blacks to the violation of law, or producing riots by their sentiments.

Bishop Hughes said in 1841 that "harangues about abolition" were not heard from Catholic pulpits.

Officially, the Church did not condemn slavery. Neither, officially, did the Church condone slavery. While the war of opinion raged with heightening velocity and bitterness, the Church refused to be budged from a position of neutrality, and the pastoral letter of the Ninth Provincial Council of Baltimore said in May, 1858: "Our clergy have wisely abstained from all interference with the judgment of the faithful which should be free on all questions of polity and social order, within the limits of the doctrine and law of the Church."

In the midst of a sectional controversy tearing the country apart, the Church remained prudent and aside from the whirlpool of wildly agitated feelings. There were Catholics in the North and Catholics in the South. Issues pass but the Church endures. The Church's unity and Catholicity must be preserved, even if Presbyterians, Methodists, and Baptists were splitting into Northern and Southern congregations on the issue of slavery. The Church, therefore, removed itself officially from active participation on either side in the grim issue.

The Catholic prelates in council generally followed a policy of timidity. Bishop O'Connor of Pittsburgh wrote to Dr. Cullen in Rome on July 15, 1846, concerning this extreme caution:

> At our late Council at Baltimore very little was done. It is a lamentable thing that here as elsewhere, with so many enemies around us, we are unable to take any vigorous measure to improve

our condition or indeed to preserve what we have. Everything, however, went on harmoniously. Anything and everything suggested was sure to meet with the concurrence of few or many, so that harmoniously we all agreed to let everyone do as he pleased, and do nothing together.

The Church at the time was preoccupied with a host of problems which did not press upon the longer-settled Protestant sects. The Church's population consisted in the main of Irish and German emigrants, and each incoming ship added to the complexities. Priests had to be recruited or trained for ministration to the increasing numbers; churches, convents, orphanages, schools had to be built; difficulties arising out of the transition from an old culture to the new had to be smoothed; and anti-Catholic movements put the Church in a state of siege. The Church, by force of circumstance as well as by deliberate decision, had to give precedence and preference to the emigrants over the Negro slaves. "It was the lack of connection with slavery and politics," wrote one student, "that enabled the Church to care for them so well as she did."

The Church would have applied its ancient and massive patience to the solution of slavery in the United States through the one agency it had learned to live with — Time. This principle was stated by the Rev. J. W. Cummings, a popular Catholic speaker, pastor of St. Stephen's Church on 27th Street in New York in 1850:

> The world was gradually prepared by the Church for the abandonment of slavery, but her work began in the souls of the masters. . . . Whenever the Catholic Church has fair play, she will cause the extinction of slavery, without scandal and without suddenness. She does not attempt to remove evil by inflicting greater evil. Her work gains insensibly; but its results are sure.

The thoughtful men of the Church, trained to react unemotionally to difficult situations, asked: After abolition, what? Can the social fabric stand the shock of liberating ignorant Negroes, by law denied education, from slavery without preparations for freedom? Would not the country, by speedy emancipation, exchange the evil of slavery for a still greater evil?

The Church looked upon the Abolitionists as wild and dangerous enthusiasts, risking the life of the Union for what the Church considered their maddened morality. An editor-priest of the Boston *Pilot* voiced this common feeling of Catholic churchmen in 1851:

As often as we consider this fanatical outpouring of abolitionist treason, we feel thankful that Catholics have no part in it. Nowhere has treason been preached in a Catholic journal, or praised by a Catholic speaker. When we look at the aiders and abetters of treason, we note that they are, for the most part, persons who have been busy bearing false witness against Catholics, by saying that they are disloyal to the American government. The time of trial has come, and as might be expected, the Catholics are, to a man, for the Union as it is, while their defamers are preaching, writing, and what is worse, they dare do it in the name of conscience, in the name of God.

This was in comment on the violent reaction among the Abolitionists in Massachusetts to the 1850 Compromise, especially their determination to defy the Fugitive Slave Act, "in the name of conscience, in the name of God."

"The Catholic Church in the United States," said the *Metropolitan Magazine,* "stands alone, immoveable, unchangeable, the only conservative body in the United States, the only body which does not take a partisan stand [on slavery] or send out its propagandists."

The Abolitionists had a radically different concept of the Church's lofty neutralism on the burning issue and its glacier-like remedy. "There are noble members of all sects save the Catholic," said Rev. Theodore Parker, as violent in his Abolitionism as a Southern planter in his defense of slavery. "I never knew of a Catholic priest who favored freedom in America, a slave himself, the mediaeval theocracy eats the heart out from the celibate monk." Helper, in his *Impending Crisis,* on the eve of the Civil War, washed his hands of the Catholic Irish: "We can well afford to dispense with the ignorant Catholic element of the Emerald Isle. In the influence they exert on society, there is so little difference between slavery, popery, and negro driving democracy, that we are not at all surprised to see them going hand in hand in their diabolical work of inhumanity and desolation." Antislavery sentiment in the North was absolutist — those who are not with us are against us; and the neutralist Church was listed as foe.

9

But the aloofness from the slavery issue which the Church professed had early been broken by Bishop England in a statement that influenced Catholic thinking on the subject and was not disowned by the hierarchy; hence, it was accepted as the orthodox expression of the Catholic viewpoint. The series of letters on domestic slavery had been drawn forth from Bishop England in the heat of the political campaign of 1840.

When Martin Van Buren ran for the Presidency in 1836, opponents raised the charge that he favored the Catholics (indeed, that he secretly was a Catholic) because of a courteous letter he had sent, as Secretary of State under Jackson, to the American consul at Rome in reply to certain questions asked by the Pope relative to the situation of the Catholics in the United States.

General Duff Green, editor of the Baltimore *Pilot and Transcript*, a fire-eater and blowhard, favorable to the candidacy of Whig William H. Harrison, had revived the Van Buren letter, described Bishop England as "the Inquisitor-General of the United States," and warned that if Van Buren received a majority in those places where Catholics were strong they would be punished. John Forsyth, Van Buren's Secretary of State, set out to counter Green's activity. Harrison, who was the first presidential candidate to receive anti-slavery support, had been forced on the Whig convention, asserted Forsyth in an address to the people of Georgia aimed at the whole South, by a combination of anti-Masons and Abolitionists. Forsyth associated the Catholic Church with this combination and cited the Apostolic Brief of Pope Gregory XVI in 1839 on the Slave Trade, saying that the Brief had been urged on the Pope by British anti-slavery interests working through O'Connell, then highly unpopular among slaveholders by his Abolitionist declarations. The Forsyth purpose was to stir prejudice against Harrison in the South and by tying him in with Abolitionists and a Pope supposedly favorable to Abolitionism hope to raise the wind of anti-Catholicism.

Bishop England, in the series of letters to Forsyth, published in the *Catholic Miscellany*, successfully dissociated the Pope from the alleged combination and then proceeded to demonstrate that the Pope's Brief dealt not with *domestic slavery* but with the *slave trade*, or *traffic in Negroes*, outlawed in the United States since 1808 and policed by the British Navy on the high seas as a violation of international agreement.

The Bishop of Charleston extended what started out to be a clarification of the Pope's Brief blurred by the partisanship of Forsyth into a long explanation of Catholic theology and history in relation to slavery, with liberal quotations from the Scriptures, the Fathers of the Church, and St. Thomas Aquinas, which amounted to a justification of domestic slavery. Since neither Council nor bishop challenged the orthodoxy of England's explanation, the series of letters passed as the official statement of the Catholic hierarchy. Certainly, it influenced Catholic thinking.

But though England the theologian could make a case for domestic slavery, England the man opposed it. "I have been asked by many," he wrote a year before his death, "a question which I may as well answer at once, viz: Whether I am friendly to the existence or continuation of slavery? I am not — but I also see the impossibility of now abolishing it here. When it can and ought to be abolished, is a question for the legislature, and not for me."

Not one Roman Catholic bishop in pre-Civil War days proclaimed for Abolitionism. The Catholic viewpoint, as elucidated by England, was that slavery was a natural calamity, like sickness, war or poverty, the consequence of original sin. But it denied that slavery was a sin in itself, per se, here differing fundamentally with Protestant Abolitionists, that slavery was a sin in itself. Catholic apologists could not reconcile the "higher law" of the Abolitionists, which took precedence over the Constitution in the matter of slavery, with strict morality and blamed the "private judgment" principle of the Reformation, defiant of constituted authority.

10

Instead of the simplified fear of economic competition by emancipated Negoes, a complex of elements contributed to shape the Catholic Irish attitude on slavery: a Protestant moral crusade which to the Irish had anti-Catholic implications as well as anti-slavery purposes; an unbudging loyalty to the Democratic Party that had been isolated as the party of slavery; the conservatism of the Roman Catholic Church and its official silence on the issue; the absorption of the Irish in their own national issue and their hard struggle, as we shall see, to prevent the splitting of Irish-American unity on Irish freedom by involvement in the slavery controversy; the suspicion of English subversive plotting against the Union by promoting civil strife; Irish emigrant resentment against Northern compassion for the slave while indifferent to Irish economic suffering; and, above all, the Irish loyalty to the Union

they thought menaced by the crazed fanaticism of parsons and politicians — the preachers mad and the politicians pretending to madness
for their own interests. One student, after exhaustively examining the
source material on attitudes of the New York Irish, concluded, in the
matter of slavery:

> In the main, the Irish-American position in the slavery question
> was dominated by their loyalty to the Union. . . . the majority
> took no positive stand on slavery as such. They favored making
> such concessions to the South as were needed to preserve the
> Union, but the main emphasis was on the preservation of the
> Union rather than on the defense of the institution of slavery.

The Catholic Irish enlisted in droves in the Civil War to preserve
the Union, not to abolish slavery, as Archbishop Hughes made clear at
the time.

II

Minority voices were heard reproaching their fellow Catholic Irish
for not actively taking up the cause of freedom for the slave. Bishop
Clancy, who for a time assisted in Charleston, confessed to Bishop
England that he could not in good conscience countenance slavery.
Father J. P. Dunn of Philadelphia, a forthright priest, who started the
first Free Church for the poor in that city, stood by the side of O'Connell on the slavery question. Lawrence Kehoe, a County Waterford
man, later an eminent Catholic publisher, was a staunch Abolitionist
and admirer of Seward, Senator Sumner, and Horace Greeley. William
Shannon introduced the ban on slavery in the California constitution
and Senator David Broderick of the same state vigorously opposed the
extension of slavery. Now and then a thoughtful Irishman grasped
the principle of the indivisibility of freedom, like John Lambert of
Vermont, who chided the Boston *Pilot* for seeming "to exult in a manner unbecoming one who is publicly pleading the cause of the oppressed and abused Irish people, and the persecuted Catholics" in the
case of the slave Sims, returned to bondage from Massachusetts under
the Fugitive Slave Act. How your columns would shriek and howl if
an escaped Irish patriot were seized by the United States and returned
at the demand of the English government! "As a native of Ireland, as a
Catholic Christian," he said, "I can not but feel for the whole human
race who are suffering in bondage and oppression."

"How widely different is your course from that of the great patriot, philanthropist, and statesman, and Christian, Daniel O'Connell," he exclaimed in chastisement.

12

It was a rare anomaly that the leader the Catholic Irish in the United States revered, Daniel O'Connell, was told to mind his own business and be off when he tried to influence them to support Abolitionism in America. The same people who asserted the Catholic Irish could never be amalgamated as American because they remained subject to foreign influences, urged upon them the wisdom of listening to the advice of Daniel O'Connell, a foreigner, on Abolitionism. It was not understood at the time that in rejecting the leadership of O'Connell on an American domestic issue, the Catholic Irish had become Americans and had struck their roots in American soil. They heeded his words on an Irish issue. They told him to go to the devil on an American issue.

O'Connell absolutely refused to be silent or soft-soap American public opinion on slavery. He taunted the memory of Washington and rebuked Andrew Jackson as owners of slaves. An old and precious friendship between O'Connell and Bishop England practically came to an end on the slavery issue. He said he would never visit America so long as men were held in bondage: if there was a place black enough in hell, he exclaimed, "that was the place for Americans." In 1839, O'Connell tried to force non-recognition by England of the Republic of Texas unless Texas pledged the abolition of slavery and the slave trade, and he wanted to empower Britain to make arrangements with Mexico for the creation of a state, on or near its northern border, as an asylum for Negroes to counter Texas.

Good God! exclaimed O'Connell, this "filthy aristocracy of the skin." Learn this lesson well, he told the Irish in America: "THAT ONE CAN-NOT HAVE ANY PROPERTY IN ANOTHER MAN." Instead of ridiculing the Abolitionists, join them, he urged. "The desire to procure abolition is, in itself, a virtue, and deserves our love for its charitable disposition as it does respect and veneration for its courage under unfavorable circumstances."

13

The great Repeal campaign in the United States, when the Catholic Irish gathered their strength to assist O'Connell in Ireland, was ripped and divided and torn because O'Connell refused to keep silent on the issue of slavery. The frustrations of the Irish in America, who wanted to free Ireland when O'Connell wanted to free the American slaves as well as free Ireland, turned them to cheering the Liberator in one voice and explaining to Americans in another that their great hero misunderstood the situation in the United States and did not know what he was talking about. The Repeal campaign had its other troubles, also, because its participants had not lost their Irish nature, but it was a gallant movement, in which the humble Irish laborers, the hewers and drawers of wood, showed their devotion to the cause of Irish freedom.

3 5

The Riven Repeal Agitation

DANIEL O'CONNELL organized the Loyal National Repeal Association in Dublin on April 15, 1840, with less than one hundred at the meeting and an initial membership of fifteen, a sparse inaugural reminiscent of the start of the Catholic Association seventeen years before to agitate for Catholic Emancipation. The Liberator, now over sixty-five, girded himself for the decisive struggle — repeal of the 1800 Act of Union and re-establishment of an independent Irish parliament in Dublin under the monarchy.

Catholic Emancipation had bestowed no material benefit on the Irish peasant and laborer, and the nation sank lower in the bog of economic misery. During the 1830s, O'Connell, the "member from Ireland" in the British House of Commons, had risen in reputation to be one of the great public men of Europe, but his political skill had failed to move either the Whigs or the Tories to embrace self-government as policy for Ireland. O'Connell's personal ascendancy over Catholic Irish opinion enforced a truce while he tested the English government to determine if it would give justice to Ireland. That policy of watchful waiting having failed, O'Connell concluded that Repeal had to be wrested from London by the method so successful with Catholic Emancipation — agitation of the Irish masses as a pressure threat upon the British government by peaceful means.

2

The first move to organize opinion in the United States to lend O'Connell moral and financial support for Repeal came from Boston. On the night of October 6, 1840, a group of obscure Irishmen — artisans, laborers, and small shopkeepers, including Patrick Donahoe, then struggling to keep his infant Boston *Pilot* above water — met to talk over the formation of an American Repeal auxiliary. Some had been members of the old Hibernian Relief Society, whose example had inspired this meeting. Misgivings dampened the deliberations. Why not wait until New York, with its wealth and prominent Irish names, took the initiative? Did not their own obscurity doom it? Nevertheless, they proceeded.

With a certain trepidation, they hired Boylston Hall and advertised a public meeting for the following Monday, October 12. The outcome was electrifying. Between fifteen hundred and two thousand eager-faced Irishmen, for the most part humble and poor, filled the hall to capacity. A fish packer presided; the leading Irish temperance advocate in Boston and a hack driver acted as vice-presidents; a coal and wood dealer and the assistant editor of the Boston *Pilot* recorded the meeting as secretaries. After speeches and resolutions, the meeting unanimously shouted its approval of the formation of a Friends of Ireland Society. The initial Boston response proved that three thousand miles of water had not separated the Irish from the patriotic cause.

Speedily the Boston society organized itself, issued an address to Irishmen and friends of Ireland in New England, and local enthusiasts started to solicit members in thirty-one New England cities and towns. During the week of March 29, 1841, the first draft of one hundred pounds, collected in dues and assessments from poor laborers mostly, was remitted to Dublin.

The Boston Irish had, by their activity and zeal, set an example to their fellow countrymen elsewhere, and it was not without self-satisfaction that they said: "We Irishmen of Boston boast of our priority in the formation of our Repeal Association." Until the debacle of Irish hopes in the abortive rebellion of 1848, no American Repeal society showed the same perseverance, the same dogged faithfulness, the same record of continuous effort in behalf of Ireland as the Boston Repeal Association.

The unusual success of the Boston association in avoiding, or at least minimizing, the Irish intramural faction wars which continually erupted during the course of the American movement rested in the good sense, or luck, which prompted its organizers to agree unanimously on the selection of John W. James as president. The Boston Irish, when friends from the American population were exceedingly scarce, had no warmer and truer friend than this Yankee, and the resurrection of his unselfish devotion to the cause of the disdained Irish minority pays honor to his neglected name.

James was twenty-five years old when the liberal and humane dispositions which marked his useful career as a public-spirited man attracted him in 1827 to a meeting of the Irish, a fringe portion of Boston's population, in behalf of Catholic Emancipation. With his sympathies engaged, he joined the Hibernian Relief Society and became its president.

This youngest son of a Revolutionary patriot, Sergeant Benjamin James, who had fought in the Battle of Bunker Hill, was not so much of the familiar Boston reformer stamp as the defender of the underdog and friend of measures to raise the station of the poor and the common man. He was a whole-souled Yankee Jeffersonian Democrat in a city saturated with Federalist and Whig principles, which nevertheless respected him for his integrity as a man.

Year after year he was re-elected president. Faithfully he attended every meeting, through the thin times of apathy and the moments of bursting enthusiasm, and dutifully he gave in his regular contribution of five dollars. He studied and mastered Irish history; he consumed the great parliamentary reports on Ireland; he subscribed to Irish newspapers. In 1841 he prepared an address from the Boston Repealers to Dublin which the impressed O'Connell himself read to the National Repeal Association and praised for its excellence.

While faction besieged the Boston Repeal Association, it broke on the presence of James and the massive reputation he bore with the lowly Irish in the ranks. Malcontents might slur an Irish vice-president or a recording secretary, one of their own, but invidious remarks on the good Yankee who had come into their midst invited fight. He stuck with the Irish cause through local feudings which would have sent a less dedicated man to retirement for peace of mind. He presided at the birth of the Repeal movement in the United States and he attended its wake, an honored figure and household name in every Irish community, venerated particularly by the Boston Irish because he had no self-interested axe to grind and spent himself because he believed simply that a downtrodden race deserved justice and freedom.

Protests in the American press against the Repeal campaign immediately appeared. "Is not this palpable attempt to interfere in the legislation of a foreign country," asked the Boston *Atlas*, "a direct infringement of the laws and constitution of the United States?" The Repeal orators revived the arguments of Counselor Sampson in rebuttal and avowed their prime allegiance to the United States. Administrations in Washington, secretly delighted at the twisting of the Lion's tail and not unmindful of the growing Irish vote, looked the other way.

3

Philadelphia, with its large Irish population and United Irishmen tradition, speedily followed Boston in the formation of a Repeal association at a public meeting on December 8, 1840. Less than a week later, at a meeting in Tammany Hall called by the old Friends of Ireland society, the New York Irish organized a Repeal society and named Robert Emmet, son of the late Thomas Addis Emmet, as president. Reports began to pile up of the spread of the movement throughout the country by formation of local societies.

The New York society soon fell into differences. President Robert Emmet took personal offense at a slur upon the men of 1798 by O'Connell, the first manifestation of the Liberator's stubborn refusal to exercise diplomatic tact with the sensitive Americans, and he resigned his office. Next, the younger and hotter bloods, high-spirited and anxious for action, broke off from the parent organization and established the Young Men's Repeal Society. The break came shortly after Thomas Mooney, just off the boat from the other side, stirred rapturous cheers with his florid oratory before the Repeal Society on July 20, 1841.

Mooney flitted in and out of the Catholic Irish communities in pre-Civil War America, more a character than a leader, a type familiar to the Irish, part promoter, part pitch-man, part showman, persuasive of tongue, quick of wit, fertile in ideas, gifted with the power of that flowing and exaggerated oratory peculiar to the race and before which it succumbed like the beloved in the arms of the lover. Mooney was restless and unstable, more charlatan than rogue, with unmitigated gall and full of brass.

Mooney became the central figure in the *cause célèbre* of the Repeal movement. Armed with the credentials of the Young Men's Repeal Association and forty dollars, he ventured into the West and the South to raise the prairie and bayou for the cause. His magniloquent reports of great achievements and of favor from great personages (Mooney dropped names luxuriantly) endeared the traveling delegate to his sponsors until a paragraph appeared in the May 21, 1842, issue of the *Catholic Telegraph,* official diocesan weekly of Cincinnati:

> How melancholy is the thought that so many should prove reckless of the high trust reposed in them, and instead of aiding to shield their helpless Ireland from the darts of her enemies, should add by their misconduct to her many afflictions.

The knowing read into this passage of clerical indirection the name of Mooney, and the New York society called upon him to answer two charges which had emerged: that he had attempted to seduce a married woman in Natchez and that he had accepted a suit of clothes from the Mobile Repealers, both derogatory of the society's good name.

After some time, Mooney responded, answering to the first charge:

> All I have to say is, that if asking a lady (whom I never saw before) for a glass of water and uttering a few commonplace observations in a space of time less than three minutes, can be tortured into such a crime, then my accusers have an advantage over me, which they are welcome to make the most of, if they think it is useful in the cause of Ireland.

As to the second charge, Mooney admitted he had accepted a suit of clothes from the "Reverend and Patriotic James McGarahan of Mobile, who, with other Good Friends, insisted on my accepting so substantial a token of their friendship." His Irish clothes looked seedy after twelve months of traveling "and if I did accept so good-natured a present, I hope, in the minds of good patriots I have not compromised either the Young Men, myself or the great cause of Repeal."

Mooney finally returned to New York and faced up to the society, but instead of refuting the charges he changed the subject and in a flaming speech recounted his services to Repeal. Rev. John Power was impressed into service as arbitrator of Mooney's conduct, but he returned an indefinite decision, on the basis of which the Mooney faction introduced a set of resolutions which completely absolved him, called his enemies treacherous liars and demanded the warmest thanks be endowed on Mooney. At a meeting packed with boys and non-members, the friends of Mooney howled down the opposition and adopted resolutions vindicating Mooney's character.

The officers of the society resigned. Factionalism appeared to have conquered over the cause of Irish freedom. But aroused and angry Irishmen frustrated the attempt of Mooney's party to reorganize the society. Healing forces, now quickened into action by the threat of debacle in the largest Irish community in the United States, appealed for peace and unity in the sacred name of Irish freedom. The old Irish patriot, Thomas O'Connor, was called into the breach, and out of the controversy arose a new and unified society. Mooney disappeared — temporarily.

4

During 1841, the Repeal movement speeded up as the Catholic Irish in every area of the country caught the enthusiasm and hopes first fired in Boston. In the cities Repeal societies held regular meetings and collected funds. In villages and rural areas, not sufficiently important to warrant the visit of a speaker or the formal organization of a society, the handful of Irishmen voluntarily met and forwarded the collection to the nearest large Repeal center. A letter received by the Boston *Pilot* from rural Oxford, Massachusetts, epitomized the character of these tiny gatherings:

> I enclose you the sum of eleven dollars, the subscriptions of a few Irishmen working in this village, and request you will have the kindness to hand it over to J. W. James, Esq., President of the Boston Repeal Association. If you will acknowledge the receipt of this, it will be a gratification to the subscribers:
> John Collins, co. Dublin, $1; Stephen Collins do 1; Mich'l Collins do 1; John Collins, Jr. do 1; Pat'k Jordan do 1; James Sheridan, city of Dublin 1; Wm Welsh co Meath 1; John Franey co Tipperary 1; John Delahanty do 1; Geoffrey Leahy co Waterford 1; John S. Carney, Queen's co 1.

It was the practice for subscriptions to be entered on the rolls of the society and published in the Catholic Irish press with the name of the donor, the county in Ireland of his origin, and the amount. O'Connell, fearing the English government would seize upon American aid as a pretext to suppress the Repeal movement, entered the American subscriptions in a separate account which he called the "Golden Book."

In communities which had a church, the local pastor invariably headed the subscription list with a donation of five or ten dollars. In the cities, Repeal wardens, assigned to the several wards, made the rounds monthly to collect the dues of members unable to attend the regular meetings.

Laborers on public works gave generously, like the workers pushing a railroad into western Massachusetts who met, under the chairmanship of the mission priest, Rev. John Brady, and contributed $145.70 through the treasurer, John Healy, a County Roscommon man, the section contractor. Irish soldiers and sailors in the armed forces held meetings in forts or on ships and sent their donations, usually with a rousing letter.

5

The wrath of the Repealers sprang at George P. Putnam of the book firm of Wiley & Putnam, in London buying, as an Irish-American weekly contemptuously put it, *"English* books." Mr. Putnam, in a letter to a London newspaper in the summer of 1841, suggested that the Repeal movement in the United States was confined exclusively to natives of Ireland, who, he added, were not worthy of being American citizens, "inasmuch as the recognized policy and practice of the American people, from Washington to the present time, has been opposed to all interference with the affairs of foreign states."

Repeal associations scurried through their rolls to refute the assertion of Mr. Putnam. While membership in the societies consisted almost exclusively of the Catholic Irish, Repeal brought forth active support or public approval from Americans with no Catholic Irish background. The instance of the faithful John W. James was an example. Governor William H. Seward spiritedly endorsed Repeal, and Andrew Jackson wished it success so long as it kept out of the internal affairs of other nations. Martin Van Buren wrote a letter in the double-talk for which he was famous. Senator James Buchanan of Pennsylvania, later to be President, told a St. Patrick's Day gathering in Pittsburgh that "with all my heart I wish the cause of Repeal success." Soul-searching John Quincy Adams sympathized with the Irish as against Great Britain but "upon the propriety or expediency of the specific measure of Repeal" he had formed no opinion. Senator Lewis Cass of Michigan, Democratic presidential candidate in 1848, who hated England, extended his blessing to the Irish. Gansevoort Melville, brother of Herman Melville, appeared frequently as a popular speaker on Repeal platforms. Horace Greeley was a firm friend of Repeal and Irish freedom, and upon his unexpected appearance at a Boston Repeal meeting with his whiskers, which the Irish called "Galway sluggers," the crowd gave an Irish welcome to the distinguished guest. George Bancroft, historian and Democratic politician, told the Irish they were right (and why) and urged them forward. Thurlow Weed, the mentor of Seward, wrote from Ireland: "An American who travels with unbandaged eyes through Ireland deserves no credit for being a Repealer."

But the fighting support that thrilled the Irish spirit came from Colonel Richard M. Johnson, a notorious frontier windbag, Vice-President under Van Buren and self-proclaimed hero of the Battle of the Thames in the War of 1812. Shattered as was his arm, he told a Repeal meeting in St. Louis, enfeebled as was his frame by age, fatigue, and exposure, worn by years of severe toil, he felt that he would rather "display his zeal in behalf of Ireland by charging upon her foes at the head of gallant columns than by pleading her cause in words." As he had fought for American honor, so he would fight for Irish independence. If the call came, Colonel Johnson would strap on his trusty gun and go forth to free Ireland. The Irish loved him and his frontier spread-eagle oratory, a kin of their own florid style. One of his speeches was printed on satin and distributed to the members of the Baltimore society.

The most impressive name, however, which took to the Repeal campaign was the President's son, Robert Tyler, poet, idealist, politician and earnest visionary, who enlisted in the cause in Washington and became its national leader. "All that I know is that I love Irishmen and hate tyranny in every form," he said in his first speech, and from across the water came the thanks of O'Connell.

6

The American Irish hoped that O'Connell would avoid the subject of slavery for the sake of their own position before American public opinion. How little these men really knew O'Connell!

Early in 1842 came the first of the series of O'Connell's outbursts. An "Address of the People of Ireland to their Countrymen and Countrywomen in America," signed by O'Connell, Father Mathew and sixty thousand other Irishmen, inspired by the Irish Quaker James Haughton and a few Abolitionist friends, called on the American Irish to go the whole distance with the American Abolitionists:

> Join with the Abolitionists everywhere! They are the only consistent advocates of liberty. Tell every man that you don't understand liberty for the white man and slavery for the black man; that you are for liberty for all, of every color, creed and country . . .

Bishop Hughes denounced the document as a forgery but added that should it prove to be authentic, then it became the duty of every naturalized Irishman to repudiate and denounce it with indignation not because of its doctrines "but because of their having emanated from a foreign source, and of their tendency to operate on questions of domestic and national policy. I am no friend to slavery, but I am still less friendly to any attempt of *foreign origin* to abolish it."

The Boston Abolitionists received the O'Connell address as manna from Heaven. "Come out! Come out! Join the Abolitionists!" they shouted to the Boston *Pilot*. They called a meeting and mingled praise to glory for its sentiments with sorrow for the wrongs of Ireland, in a spirited bid for local Irish favor. Very few Irish attended the meeting, whereupon the Abolitionists, with their finest battery of powerful speakers, including Edmund Quincy, Wendell Phillips, and Rev. George Bradburn, known friends of the Boston Irish, invaded a Repeal meeting. They were listened to with respect so long as they confined their speeches to the wrongs of Ireland but a dozen of more impulsive Irishmen challenged them from the floor when they slid from Ireland's woes into the evils of slavery.

7

In the midst of turmoil spread by O'Connell's apple of discord, the National Repeal Convention met in Philadelphia on Washington's Birthday, 1842, for a two-day session.

The Philadelphia convention was the first national gathering of Irishmen in behalf of the cause in Ireland and as such holds historic importance in the long campaign to exercise from the United States the weight-of-power influence against England that in the past had been conducted from the Continent of Europe.

The large hall of the Philadelphia Museum witnessed a meeting unique in the Republic — an assembly of men of one blood from the several sections of the country, with their friends, dedicated to changing the political relationships of a foreign country not as underground conspirators but in the open light of day, invoking the principles of the American Union as their precept and example and the principles of American freedom as their right to gather.

The opening roll call showed twenty-seven delegations from twenty-six cities or towns: New York (the original society and the Young Men's), Boston, Philadelphia, Baltimore, Washington, Worcester, Augusta (Maine), Albany, Sag Harbor, Rockaway, Jamaica, Brooklyn, Syracuse, Rochester, Newark, Trenton, Bordentown (New Jersey), Pottsville, Morristown, Conewago, Harrisburg, Lancaster (Pennsylvania), Frederick (Maryland), Lexington, Louisville, and Cincinnati. This was no convention of laborers and canal diggers. The delegations represented a cross-section of the substantial Catholic Irish population of the United States, many of the second and a few of the third generation, merchants, traders, shopkeepers, doctors, lawyers, journalists, and public works contractors.

Let it be perpetuated in the annals that the president of the first National Convention of Irishmen in the United States for the freedom of Ireland was a Boston Yankee, John W. James, unanimously named.

In the floundering preliminaries, it was apparent that no program had been arranged in advance: the inexperienced delegates came as testimony to a unified effort to back the Repeal agitation in Ireland and form a community of hearts. A committee on resolutions, chosen after much wrangling and conscious of the O'Connell manifesto, excluded other subjects from the convention by confining the resolutions to sympathy for Ireland, support of Repeal, praise of the American

Union as the exemplary model and advocacy of the ending of sectarian differences in Ireland.

But after the resolutions had been read, Isaac H. Wright, a furious
Democratic politician of Boston who had attached himself to the Repeal Society, launched into a bitter tirade against the Abolitionists —
and the balloon went up and, with it, the convention.

A passionate debate on Abolitionism, to which confusion was added
by the Irish love of parliamentary hair-splitting, so involved that the
convention became lost in discussion of whether or not "the previous
question" had precedence, consumed the first day until the purposeful
voice of J. T. Doyle, a lawyer in the New York delegation, cut
through the hurly-burly: "We have not come here to discuss slavery or
Abolition," and moved adjournment.

The next morning, the convention adopted a resolution fashioned
in nightly conferences which declared the original intention of the
meeting: to help Ireland regain its legislative independence and avoid
American controversial issues.

But a brooding row broke open when Mr. Doyle, who comprehended the possibilities of an appeal to the English people then
seething with domestic discontent, moved that an address to the people
of England be prepared, in addition to commissioned addresses to the
people of the United States and of Ireland. Off went the roof! An address to England! "We might as well," exclaimed Mr. Killion of
Philadelphia, "address the savages of Van Diemen's Land, or the man
in the moon." Petition England! "Never!" shouted Mr. Doherty, also
of Philadelphia. "When we petition the People of England, let us petition as we did before, in the thunders of our cannon, and in the
clashing of our bayonets!"

A resolution was adopted encouraging the use of Irish and American manufactures in preference to English, but a proposal to select a
committee of five to devise the best means of carrying the boycott into
operation was frustrated on the argument of Mr. Stokes of Philadelphia that it interfered with the tariff policy of the United States and
therefore stood in violation of the Constitution.

The convention's proceedings concluded with vigorous anti-English
attacks by a group of powerful speakers, and with three cheers for Ireland, O'Connell, Repeal, Philadelphia, and the ladies, respectively, the
convention adjourned, with much applause and waving of handkerchiefs.

The Boston *Pilot* immediately praised the convention as "worthy of the cause" and an inspiration to Ireland, but a year later, on sober second thought, labeled the Philadelphia meeting a "miserable abortion." Its vague purpose looked to a show of national solidarity behind Repeal through resolutions and speeches. In character with the Irish nature, the delegates suffered the word to stand for the deed. They neglected to consider the one tangible act which would have justified the convention — the organization of a national body.

8

The convention was ripped apart by the issue that the delegates, as advocates of Repeal, would have avoided but, as Americans, had had forced on them — the issue of Abolition. The American Irish correctly stated their confused situation to O'Connell: he could take a bold stand on Abolition in a land free of the peculiar institution of slavery, but a set of circumstances had put them in opposition to Abolitionism in a country where slavery was protected by the Constitution. The climate of America was affecting their Irish blood. They were thus torn between their love of Ireland and an eagerness to forward its freedom and their position as Americans in opposition to the strong stand of Ireland's leader on an American issue.

But O'Connell's anger had been mounting at the perseverance of the American Irish in what he called sin. Communications challenged his anti-slavery stand and informed him that if he lived in the United States his attitude would be different toward Abolitionists.

On May 10, 1843, he gathered a special meeting of the National Repeal Association for the sole purpose of receiving an address from the American Anti-Slavery Society and, to make his intent clear, barred all Repeal business from the proceedings. After the address had been read to frequent outbursts of approval and formally incorporated in the minutes of the Dublin society, O'Connell arose and let the American Irish have it — with the heavy thump of a hard Irish fist.

O'Connell vigorously answered the American arguments, warned the United States it was heading for civil war, and appealed directly to his fellow countrymen:

> Over the broad Atlantic I pour forth my voice, saying, "Come out of such a land, you Irishmen; or, if you remain, and dare counte-

nance the system of slavery that is supported there, we will recognize you as Irishmen no longer."

He then deliberately went up to the breaking point with the American Repealers:

> We may not get money from America after this declaration; but even if we should not, we do not want blood-stained money. If they make it a condition of their sympathy, or if there be implied any submission to the doctrine of slavery on our part in receiving remittances, let them cease sending it at once.

The Catholic Irish press refused to reprint the O'Connell speech, making it, said the New York *American*, which was both anti-slavery and anti-Repeal, "the more incumbent on American papers to publish it." The Boston *Atlas* challenged the Boston *Pilot* to print the address and received the reply: "We never publish such speeches from any source, as we are not specially engaged in the anti-slavery cause."

O'Connell had put the American Repealers in an embarrassing position. The Baltimore Repeal Society damned him effusively but resolved to continue to work for Ireland. The Charleston and Natchez Repeal associations dissolved, the latter characterizing O'Connell as a "base and hypocritical demagogue." William A. Stokes, whose wife owned slaves, resigned as president of the Philadelphia society, already riven by faction. An Abolitionist agent presented himself at a meeting of the New London society and tried to introduce a resolution praising O'Connell for his anti-slavery stand. He was asked to sit down.

Repeal societies all over the country twisted and squirmed upon the horns of the dilemma O'Connell had presented and, while dismayed and angered by O'Connell's blunt speech, nevertheless managed to hold the lines intact. The Boston *Pilot* set the popular tone by asking what Repeal had to do with Abolitionism: "Has this great question been commenced and carried out for Daniel O'Connell or for the Irish people?" The Abolitionists were blamed for the whole business.

9

In the United States, the first bright promises of Repeal had dimmed during 1842 into apathy and indifference. O'Connell's duties in the House of Commons and his election in 1841 as Lord Mayor of Dublin engaged much of the attention of a man now pushing toward seventy. Lack of constant action in Ireland thinned Repeal meetings, and remittances to Dublin dwindled to a trickle: even faithful Boston collected only $31.50 at the December, 1842, meeting. Unless the spirit of 1841 should be revived, the Boston *Pilot* felt "we have awakened hopes in the hearts of the patriots of Ireland which our present support and aid will not justify."

Then O'Connell proclaimed 1843 as "Repeal Year," predicting that before its end an independent Irish Parliament would sit in College Green in Dublin, the site of the old parliament. In February, 1843, he dramatically revivified the Repeal agitation by a speech of four hours in the Dublin Corporation (city government) in support of his own resolution affirming the right of Ireland to self-government.

He carried the agitation directly to the country, following his promise to appear in each county of Ireland. With his shrewd knowledge of the Irish love of the past, he tied in the Repeal agitation with revered memories by selecting sites enshrined in Irish history for the mammoth meetings. His appearance at Kells, once a famous monastic center, drew audiences that extended as far as the eye could see. At Tara, the capital of pagan Ireland, on August 15, a million people, according to contemporary estimates, turned out.

Sir Robert Peel, now prime minister, replying to a question of his plans to restrain the growing excitement in Ireland, said: "This bond of our national strength and safety I have already declared my fixed and unalterable resolution, under the blessing of Divine Providence, to maintain inviolate by all the means in my power." A coercion bill against Ireland was introduced in the House of Commons and troops started to move into Ireland. The excited Boston *Pilot* proclaimed that the crisis had arrived. "The noble, the magnanimous, the fearless strength of the people of Ireland for ten years is about to triumph or perish."

The Peel statement set the American agitation to blazing: the complacent assurance of British coercive power got under Irish skins. The New York society held five meetings in quick succession which amounted to public demonstrations, one in City Hall Park on June 14 drawing a crowd of twenty thousand and another raising a sum of a thousand dollars. Similarly, Philadelphia held three meetings, spaced a few days apart. Providence forgot its long-standing faction fight to unite. Lowell revived its disbanded organization. Colonel Richard M. Johnson renewed his offer to fight for Ireland. A music-loving

Irishman wrote a popular Repeal march. Poets took to their pens. Sailors on the U.S.S. *Ohio* wished Ireland success "and would *under orders* go to any length to elevate her to the rights and principles of a free people." Money started once more to flow to Dublin: $2500 from New York, $2100 from Philadelphia, $500 from Boston, $300 from Baltimore, $100 from Fall River. New societies appeared in towns which previously had neglected Repeal.

10

In the midst of great excitement and of blooming expectations for Ireland, the second national convention of the Repealers assembled on September 20, 1843, for a three-day session in New York. First plans had contemplated Boston as the meeting place, in honor of American Repeal's birth there, but the Boston members bowed to the superiority of New York — its leaders, wealth, and large Irish population. Henceforth New York would be the headquarters of the Irish patriotic movement in the United States.

At the calling of the roll in the large Broadway Tabernacle, 405 delegates from thirteen states responded, and Robert Tyler of the Philadelphia society was chosen to preside over the sessions. The last of the Old Guard of the United Irishmen 1798 exiles, Thomas O'Connor, John Caldwell, and General James Joseph McDonnell, were received with becoming awe. Congressman John McKeon opened the convention as temporary chairman, and Charles O'Conor and James T. Brady, already eminent at the American bar, worked as stabilizers to keep the impetuous Irish from the anarchy of Philadelphia.

The mistakes and omissions of the Philadelphia convention had been observed. Abolitionism would not disrupt the New York meeting if the directors could prevent it, and they had carried their wariness on the slavery issue to the extent of omitting O'Connell's name from the formal resolutions, a deliberate oversight, if not a calculated slight, corrected by the efforts of an angry delegate from Boston. The major failure of Philadelphia was overcome in New York by the establishment of a national executive committee of five, primarily to supervise national action quickly in the event the heightening crisis in Ireland broke overnight. It was Charles O'Conor who first compared this executive committee to the Directory of the Wolfe Tone revolutionary organization in 1798. When O'Conor first used the word, it dismayed the staunch advocates of O'Connell's moral force agitation and bloodless revolution.

The use of the words "physical force" in a resolution aroused Dr. Edmund O'Callaghan of the Albany delegation, the distinguished Irish-born scholar of the Dutch origins of New York and state historian, himself a refugee for his part in the 1837-1838 rebellion in Canada, to protest that such words opposed O'Connell's "moral force" principle and violated the laws of the United States.

But the show of Peel's threat of force against Ireland had stirred belligerency in the American Irish. A clamor developed to seize Canada if Ireland answered Peel with rebellion. The amateur strategists openly made plans for the quick invasion of Canada, with the help, they said, of rebellious French Canadians and Irish soldiers in the British army in the North American provinces. One wealthy Irishman offered to contribute a thousand dollars toward sending twenty thousand Irishmen to wrest Canada from John Bull. Lord John Russell in the House of Commons took note of the plans of the American Repealers "to disquiet the frontiers of Canada" in order to weaken British strength in Ireland. The convention contemplated a petition to the federal government for the intervention of American armed forces on the side of Ireland in case of war, on the same ground Britain justified her interference between Turkey and Greece — that the dictates of humanity required it.

At the convention even the gentle John W. James caught the excitement of the spirit to assist Ireland from America with arms. If action started in Ireland he favored the running of ten thousand stands of arms into the river Shannon to "the hands of the 'finest peasantry' in the world" — a declaration which set off the wildest tumult of applause and cheering during the three days. But the directors of the convention held it to the resolution which defined "physical force" as monetary contributions: the convention did not probe as to what use the money might be turned to.

The voice of the "physical force" men, the true disciples of Wolfe Tone as against O'Connell's moral agitation, started to grow louder among the rank and file of the American Irish. One spoke a rising thought by declaring that the British were not alarmed by the American Irish. "They think," he said, "there may be some money collected and a great deal of oratory wasted by the Irish party in this country and that it will end there." If civil war came in Ireland, he continued, America can give but one answer — "Arms!"

Even as he was speaking, the debacle had taken place in Ireland, of which the United States did not hear until days later because the speed of news was confined to the speed of ships carrying Irish and English papers. Another chapter of Irish frustrations had been written.

II

Sir Robert Peel had watched his ancient adversary, O'Connell, with the sharp eye of a hawk, waiting for the right moment to pounce and crush the agitation seething to the breaking point. O'Connell was striking at the foundations of the British Empire, as Tory sentiment furiously asserted. Peel would make no concession whatever upon the indissoluble union of Ireland and Britain.

O'Connell now prepared his most formidable test to determine if Peel would climb down before a demonstration of Irish unity and strength as he had in 1829. He announced a "monster meeting" to be held outside Dublin on Sunday, October 8, at Clontarf, where Brian Boru had almost a thousand years before broken the back of the Danish invaders and reasserted Irish rule.

At the very height of O'Connell's magnificent agitation, Peel struck. At three o'clock Saturday afternoon, just a few hours before the Sunday meeting, Peel's Lord Lieutenant in Dublin "proclaimed" the monster gathering, that is, forbade it under the Irish coercion statutes. Soldiers marched from the barracks to take their stations along the roads to Clontarf. Artillery guns were aimed point-blank at the approaches. An enlarged British fleet waited in Dublin Bay.

Peel had called O'Connell. It was the Liberator's move now and he responded consistently with his pacific agitation. He ordered the meeting canceled; riders were sent in all directions from Dublin to tell the people already on the tramp to Clontarf to go home. O'Connell issued a warning that not a shot must be fired, that the people must not rise and that whoever violated his orders for peace gave strength to the enemy. Ireland sullenly obeyed. A few days later O'Connell was arrested. Whether or not he was conscious of the fact, he had come to the end of the road with the collapse of Repeal at Clontarf, and though he later returned to the battle his sun had set.

Bishop Higgins of Ardagh, the patriotic prelate, at once wrote the epitaph of Repeal and the eternal defiance by the Irish of English rule:

> If the repeal meetings are put down, we will retire to our chapels, we will suspend all other instructions, in order to devote our time to teach the people to be repealers. If they beset our temples, we will prepare our people for the circumstances; if they bring us from that to the scaffold, in dying for the cause of our country, we will bequeath our wrongs to our successors.

12

The news of Clontarf was received with excitement — and confusion — by the Catholic Irish communities in the United States. First, O'Connell's dismissal of the meeting was hailed as a triumph of moral force over the brutal English with their superior power. Then it was declared that "O'Connell will strike when he is ready and not on invitation of the Tory government of England." Next, the O'Connell faithful, in hastily called meetings through the country, pledged their faith in the Liberator and renewed efforts for Repeal or whatever political campaign his wily mind proclaimed.

But the voice suppressed by the O'Connell peaceful revolution, the echo of Wolfe Tone, now took up the cry in full force:

> We may as well call a meeting of old women to menace the British Government with their indignation, depend upon it, it will be just as effective as our sympathy. . . . The Irish people expect something more from the people of America than second-hand editions of resolutions passed and fitted for the atmosphere of the Corn Exchange, Dublin [the Dublin Repeal headquarters]. . . . Is there any man now to be found blind enough to believe that the people of Ireland can acquire their liberty by means of peaceable agitation?

The writer quoted the words of Franklin, "The path to liberty is bloody," and warned that Ireland would not be freed by cabbage stalks as weapons or the sympathy of the American Irish. The turn of the "physical force" men was now coming.

A few days before the news of Clontarf reached the United States a correspondent from New York reported that even if the Irish there marked time on Repeal, they were not without local excitement. "One of the most important features in the present [election] campaign," he wrote, "is the establishment of another party — the Native American."

Blood on the Moon

UPON HIS RETURN, July 18, 1840, from a trip of nine months to Europe, Coadjutor Bishop John Hughes of New York found a matter awaiting his leadership that established him as the most influential Roman Catholic prelate for the next quarter of a century and the best-known man of his race in the United States. The matter was the bid of the Catholic population of New York City for a share of the public (or as it was called then "common") school fund for support of parochial schools.

2

The career of John Hughes cannot be isolated from the story of the Catholic Irish in the United States and confined to the history of the Roman Catholic Church, as would be possible with some other Irish-born prelates of the period. If a contemporary were asked to name the most important Catholic ecclesiastic, the answer would be, John Hughes. If he were asked to name the leading Catholic Irishman, the answer would be the same, John Hughes. As he was regarded by the country as the spokesman of the Church, so his Catholic Irish brethren looked to him as their chieftain.

The career of the Archbishop of New York stood for the most impressive success story among the multitudinous Catholic Irish emigrants.

John Hughes was born the son of a poor tenant farmer in a County Tyrone townland in 1797. As Catholics living in an Ulster Protestant neighborhood soaked with the Orange spirit, the Hughes family knew economic and social inferiority on the score of their religion still under the shadow of penal laws. John had wanted to be a priest from his earliest remembrance, but the father could afford him only a rudimentary education. "Many a time," he told a friend later, "have I thrown down my rake in the meadow, and kneeling behind a hay-rick, begged of God and the Blessed Virgin to let me become a priest."

Patrick Hughes emigrated to America in 1816 with his second son and settled in Chambersburg, Pennsylvania. The next year John, then twenty, was sent for and later the other members of the family. John worked as a laborer, a quarry hand, a road mender, a digger in gardens, any manual job he could find, to do his share in keeping a poor Irish emigrant family together.

Just over the border in Maryland was Mount St. Mary's Catholic college and seminary in Emmittsburg and there, again and again, young Hughes, still determined to be a priest, applied as a poor student, each time to be rejected because no vacancy existed. He moved to Emmittsburg to be near the college and toiled as a laborer on a mill-race and with a pickaxe and as a mason's helper on the construction of a bridge. In November, 1819, Father Dubois, the president, engaged him to be superintendent of the college garden in return for board and instruction. Thus was John Hughes, the laborer and gardener, set on the road to be the Archbishop of New York.

Unlike the generality of Irish-born members of the American hierarchy, Hughes had come out of the class of small Irish farmers and peasants who made up the large proportion of Catholic Irish emigrants. The hand that held the crozier had saved the hay in an Ulster meadow and swung a pick in America, to which he had come on an emigrant ship. His origins were quite different from the third-generation American John Carroll, cousin of the Signer, and from John England, son of a schoolmaster.

Whether education in the gracious atmosphere of Paris and Rome, like that of other members of the hierarchy, would have softened the hard Ulster angularity of John Hughes is like the familiar hypothesis of what would have happened to Abraham Lincoln had he gone to Harvard. He trampled on the prudence enjoined by John Carroll and rejected the diplomatic suavity practiced by John England, once saying that he did not hold with the "generally good, cautious souls, who believe in stealing through the world more submissively than suits a freeman." With the ascendancy of John Hughes rose the Church Militant.

His apprenticeship as a priest in Philadelphis sharpened the sword of the compulsive controversialist in Hughes. The absolutist in his nature which had battered down the obstacles in the way of his single-minded vow to be a priest turned into the steely inflexibility of the autocrat with the placing of the miter on his head.

To his admirers, Hughes was the strong prelate who led his people out of Egypt, the first to take an aggressive stand for their rights. To others who had less reason to reverence him, including his own clergy, his rule "has been the ambition and the politics of an alderman, and not the statesmanship of a prelate of the Church" and his administration spotted by "maladministration, nepotism, indolence, arrogance, a meddling and petty spirit." An Englishwoman, an Anglican, observed in an article eulogistic of Bishop Hughes in 1847 that "none ever regarded him with indifference; by some he is hated; by some feared, and by many loved; but his name is never pronounced unattended by some striking and expressive epithet."

He ruled his diocese with an unpitying discipline. "I will suffer no man in my diocese that I cannot control," he told Orestes Brownson, the famous Yankee convert. "I will either put him down, or he shall put me down." He was insensitive to the feelings of any who drew his wrath. "His rebukes were terrible," wrote his biographer. "He had the power of expressing scorn to a greater degree than any man I ever saw." Though he imposed discipline on others, he possessed no check-reins on his own impetuosity and could not restrain his pen from flying into the invectives of personalities under anger. An old hand at controversy, he expected his opponents to give as well as take. John Mitchel, the Irish patriot, who bitterly attacked Hughes, said "he deserved hard usage and could stand it and repay it."

Hughes was the most Irish of his contemporaries in the hierarchy, that is, he resembled the group of assertive and combative prelates in Ireland who came forward to rebuild the Church after Catholic Emancipation, with strong feelings on the rights of Catholics and on Irish nationality.

Archbishop Kenrick of Baltimore kept aloof from Irish issues and looked with less than ardor on O'Connell's Repeal campaign. Bishop Purcell of Cincinnati, an Irishman in a strong German diocese, won the affection of the Germans by de-emphasizing race. Bishop O'Connor was surrounded by a hostile nativist and Scotch-Irish climate in Pittsburgh. The American-born John Fitzpatrick in Boston maintained a strong policy of silence on Irish affairs.

Bishop Hughes, head of the most populous Irish diocese in the United States, became involved in the Irish national issue both by the tug of his nature and by circumstances he felt he had to face up to in all conscience.

But he fought the disposition of the Catholic Irish to retain native habits on this side of the water and struggled to translate them into Americans as speedily as possible. He was an apostle of Catholic exclusiveness but not of Irish clannishness. He scourged with anger the "red-hot Irishism" of politicians and editors. He disliked the Democratic monopolizing of the Irish vote and despised the professional Irish politicians. He voted for the presidency only once in his life — for Henry Clay in 1832 — and then, he later admitted, because the bulk of his Philadelphia congregation supported Andrew Jackson. He was conservative, even reactionary, in political views, and his sympathies aligned him with Whig and Republican principles, undoubtedly influenced in great measure by his admiration for Governor Seward and Thurlow Weed. It was ironic, because of his one unhappy venture into practical politics, that popular belief held him to be the Machiavelli who swung the Irish vote in New York as he pleased, whereas the Irish, bishop or no bishop, voted regularly, persistently (and, according to their detractors, with illegally repetitive enthusiasm) for the Democratic ticket.

In character with his countrymen, he was a confirmed newspaper reader. His interest in public affairs never ended. He probably addressed more letters to the public press than any Roman Catholic prelate before or since. Had he not been a priest, he would have made a spirited crusading editor: he was highly opinionated and commanded a forceful, driving and effective style. He rarely read a book.

His devotion to America was deep. "My feelings, my thoughts," he said, "have been so much identified with all that is American, that I have almost forgotten I am a foreigner." He sometimes misjudged American opinion, which led to serious mistakes, but he comprehended the character of Americans in relation to constitutional principles:

> Although you may quiz them on many peculiarities, they are too strict in their logic to admit a principle, and then cut off the consequences. They are not a people to tell you, "Here we have opened a fountain," and then say, "But the water must not flow." Therefore, admitting the universal right of man in this country to serve and worship God according to the dictates of his conscience, they are too logical and too just to quarrel with the consequences, however much some of them may, in their own way, deplore them, as evidence of the progress of that awful thing to so many — the spread of popery.

The Catholic Irish went through many tribulations because of racial and religious prejudices, but in their moments of despair after some

DANIEL O'CONNELL

ROBERT EMMET

THOMAS ADDIS EMMET

MICHAEL DOHENY

Dr. William J. MacNeven

Archbishop John Hughes

Father Theobald Mathew

Thomas Fitzpatrick

outrage, invariably their press, clergy, and leaders struck the same note as Hughes: the principle of religious liberty will see us through.

3

The principle of religious liberty was too deeply embedded in the foundations of the Republic ever to contemplate the proscription of a creed or sect by law. The spirit of proscription, however, worked in a variety of ways to impose discriminations upon the Catholics. Bishop England told the story of the rulers of Pennsylvania in colonial days who wrote to the Privy Council in London asking for directions when the Catholics wanted to raise a church as was their right under the liberal provisions of the charter. No legal power existed to prevent the Catholics from doing as they desired, the reply admitted, "but it is the wish of the council that as many difficulties as possible shall be raised." The Constitution protected the free right of worship by the Catholics, but there were "difficulties."

Town officers constantly refused their request for the use of the town hall or local schoolhouse in which to hold services, and owners would not rent public halls for Mass. Some societies rejected invitations to march in public parades with Irish and Catholic societies; and the Irish and Catholics frequently wound up in the least desirable places in processions. Five Boston military companies, as we have seen, marched off the Common on the appearance of the Irish Montgomery Guards.

Bishops and pastors often had to purchase land for church purposes through a friendly Protestant dummy because an owner preferred it idle to falling in papist hands. Catholic priests ran against obstacles placed in the way of religious observances, or even their presence, in public institutions — almshouses, infirmaries, prisons and houses of correction, orphan asylums, reform schools, and similar agencies of the state. Two influential Catholic Irishmen prevailed upon the commissioners to permit Mass every Sunday in the New York City almshouse late in 1839, but it was not until 1851 that authorities allowed a Catholic priest, for the first time, to visit a dying man in the Boston House of Correction.

The plight of the Roman Catholics presented itself dramatically in 1839. At the end of June in that year, Rev. Michael Gilbride of Carthage, Roman Catholic pastor of a mission in Jefferson County in upstate New York, appealed in desperation to Governor Seward.

Father Gilbride was denied hearing the confession of a Catholic Irishman sentenced to death for murder in the strict secrecy the Church requires because the law prohibited the doomed man from holding a conversation with another except in the presence of a prison officer. The priest asked Governor Seward to postpone the execution until the next legislature had been petitioned for the law's amendment. Instead, Governor Seward interpreted the law as not contemplating the exigency of a Roman Catholic confession and in effect ordered the sheriff to permit the priest access alone to the prisoner for confession.

4

The same generous-spirited Seward, friend of the emigrant Irish and of the minority Roman Catholics, in his annual message to the state legislature in 1840 raised the issue of public support for Roman Catholic schools and, though moved by the best of intentions, helped set in train the Native American movement of the 1840s.

Of all the "difficulties" under which the Catholic Irish labored, the one which touched the Church on its sensitive nerve was education. The Church held to the principle that inculcation of its religious doctrines was the foundation of education for Catholic youth.

The Catholic Irish, both clergy and people, had experienced organized Protestant proselytizing in Ireland and were suspicious in the United States. A prominent Catholic Irish orator in New York, Dr. Gaffney, compared in 1830 the proselytizing in Ireland with the exertions of ministers and "tract-hawkers" in New York to bring "poor Roman Catholics to their schools, that they may have a chance of stealing from them the faith of their fathers, and substituting that which they themselves profess." The Irish called this "kidnapping."

The supplanting of Protestant church schools by tax-supported public schools brought forward an issue of a different character from the uncomplex proselytizing forays. Public education avowed a secular and nondenominational character, but the long heritage of ministerial trusteeship of education and a powerful public opinion in support of homage to religion in the schools invested the classroom with practices acceptable to the Protestant sects. These included readings from the King James version of the Bible without notes or comments, the Protestant form of the Lord's Prayer, and sometimes the singing of Protestant hymns. Catholic ecclesiastics and opinion distrusted secular education, but secular education flavored with Protestant principles doubly offended their religious susceptibilities. Teachers were charged with openly sneering at or holding up to contempt the Catholic religion, turning children to deprecating and feeling ashamed of their faith. Textbooks carried hostile references to the Catholic Church on controversial subjects like the Reformation. School libraries had on their shelves, it was stated, attacks on Popery. A quick cause of anger to poor Catholic Irish parents was the mocking of their children as "Paddies," marked as a separate caste by their shabby clothes and frequently set upon by their school fellows.

Irish schoolmasters, like Bartholomew McGowan, A.M., or Bernard McAvoy, started schools, and genteel spinsters, like the Misses O'Keefe or the Misses FitzGerald, conducted select academies for young ladies, but the tuition ranged beyond the means of poor Catholic Irish parents. Individual Catholic churches tried to maintain free parochial schools, usually located in the basement of the church, with rude and makeshift accommodations, taught by the priest or by ill-paid and ill-prepared laymen. But the task was difficult, when the first call on the small revenues met the debt on the church itself and provided for its upkeep. The parish schools in New York City in 1840, according to Bishop Hughes, were crowded, even beyond their limits, by some four or five thousand pupils out of a Catholic child population estimated at between nine and twelve thousand.

Senator Gulian C. Verplanck, a solid man of Dutch ancestry and good friend of the Catholic Irish, told the New York upper house that Irish parents, though anxious for the education of their children, "yet they steadfastly — obstinately if you choose to call it — refuse to admit their children to attend the excellent schools gratuitously opened to them" when they feared the loss of their religion. They preferred, he said, taking such instruction as might be obtained in dark, crowded, and uncomfortable rooms from teachers paid from private bounty and their own scanty means. One Catholic Irishman said that he would rather that "his children should run in the streets without education than that they should go to these [public] schools where their regard for their own religion would be weakened."

5

Approximately one half the Catholic children in New York City ran in the streets when Governor Seward found children of foreigners deprived of education "in consequences of prejudices arising from differences of language or religion," and recommended in his 1840 message to the New York legislature "the establishment of schools, in which they may be instructed by teachers speaking the same language with them and professing the same faith." Seward declared: "I desire to see the children of Catholics educated as well as those of Protestants; not because I want them Catholics, but because I want them to become good citizens." The well-intentioned recommendation of Seward released deep passions and rancor in a bitter and prolonged fight.

A private, self-perpetuating organization, the Public School Society, established in 1805, administered the public schools in New York City with funds from both public and private sources.

Accepting Seward's message as an invitation, the trustees of seven parochial schools petitioned the Common Council for a share of the school fund in their support, and Vicar-General Power, in the absence of Bishop Hughes, organized the Catholic Association to forward the issue. But a committee of the Common Council rejected the bid on the ground that appropriations for schools "in which the religious tenets of any sect are taught to any extent" would be "a legal establishment of one denomination of religion over another" and violative of the Constitution.

The rabidly partisan Democratic *Truth Teller,* long the self-proclaimed defender of the Catholic religion and the Irish race, brought itself under ecclesiastical displeasure by precipitate condemnation of the Seward recommendation as a shrewd move to capture for the Whigs the New York Catholic Irish vote and attacked it as a political measure. On July 4, 1840, the New York *Freeman's Journal,* named after a famous Dublin paper and, as its prospectus declared, dedicated principally to secure "Catholic children a participation in the Public School Fund," appeared as a counter by the respectable Catholic Irish element, with the support of the clergy, to the battle-scarred Tammany sheet, the organ of the "Paddy" masses. It was initiated and edited by James W. White, a lawyer and member of a prominent Catholic Irish family, who later sat as a judge on New York's Superior Court.

The start of the *Freeman's Journal* in a way marked a new day for the Catholic Irish in the United States. The old leadership was dead or dying. Emmet and Sampson had gone; Dr. MacNeven died in 1841; and Thomas O'Connor remained as the venerable figure of the old guard Irish exiles. Mathew Carey had departed, full of years and honors, in 1839, the same year which had seen the passing of Luke Tiernan in Baltimore. Bishop England laid down the burden in 1842 and with him went the liberal statesmanship of what might be called gradualism in the Church's relationship to the still new Republic.

When Bishop Hughes arrived from Europe on July 19, 1840, he found awaiting him the issue of public support of Catholic education raised by Governor Seward, a Catholic Irish newspaper orthodox in character managed by a man he trusted, and an organization of Catholic men ready to follow his leadership. Two days later he presided over a meeting in the schoolhouse of St. Patrick's, and none doubted his sole command from now on, the director of strategy and tactics.

The emergence of Bishop Hughes and the *Freeman's Journal* in the New York school fight signalized a new and pronounced Catholic self-consciousness, assertive of the Church's rights and combative in direct assault to attain them. The vigorous activity of Bishop Hughes in the highly controversial area of public support of parochial schools aroused a formidable opposition and a passionate hostility in public opinion that betokened an awakening nativist spirit.

6

Late in October, 1840, Bishop Hughes himself argued the Catholic case before the Common Council against the phalanx of Protestant ministers and lawyers representing the Public School Society in a debate which mixed constitutional principles with "No Popery" speeches. Bishop Hughes stated the willingness of the Catholics to place parochial schools under the supervision of the Public School Society if permitted to share in the school fund but rejected the overtures of the society to remedy in the public schools the grievances of which the Catholics complained. On January 15, 1841, the Board of Aldermen, by a vote of 15 to 1, turned down the plea of Bishop Hughes.

Rising public excitement attended the controversy. Press and pulpit resounded with attacks on papal effrontery and what they called Hughes's avarice for public money to support Popery, while Catholics broke up two meetings called to support the Public School Society.

In his 1841 message, Seward repeated his recommendation, and Hughes took a new tack by turning to the state legislature with a petition to abolish the Public School Society and in its place create a system of state-controlled education. He disliked secular education but preferred state administration to the monopoly of the society which he believed responsible for sectarianism in the schools. John C. Spencer, Secretary of State and by virtue of his office superintendent of schools in the state, assigned by the legislature to make an inquiry, recommended the abolition of the Public School Society and the substitution of education commissioners in each ward, with local option as to religious instruction in the schools. But the state Senate postponed acting upon the Spencer report until the 1842 session. This threw the school problem, which became a Catholic-Protestant issue, squarely into the 1841 November election of state officers, with the whole matter seeming to hinge on the two senators and thirteen assemblymen to be chosen from New York City.

The Whig organization in New York City, saturated with nativism at odds with Seward's broad principles, endorsed a ticket thoroughly committed to the Protestant, or school society, cause, and the Democrats, with their ear to the ground, followed suit, with a few exceptions.

Bishop Hughes saw that the Catholic cause was headed for catastrophic defeat and that the almost solid backing by the two parties left no alternative for Catholics, if they voted at all, "but to vote for the Society and against themselves." He made a bold — and fateful — move to salvage what he could.

He called a meeting for October 30, four days before the election, at Carroll Hall, a Catholic assembly place, and placed before it an independent ticket of fifteen candidates drawn from both parties, which included the few regular candidates who had indicated they favored the Catholic measure.

If the bishop intended to use the Carroll Hall ticket to force the Democratic organization, which contained the bulk of the Catholic Irish vote, to change its stand or create a situation susceptible to trading, the reply came speedily. On the next day the Democratic candidates rejected Catholic support and Tammany organized a meeting of naturalized Catholic citizens "to rebuke, censure and denounce the conduct" of the bishop. James T. Brady presided and made the principal speech and on the platform sat such Tammany faithfuls as Hugh Mc-

Ginnis, James B. Nicholson, Thomas S. Brady, Patrick McCafferty, Patrick H. O'Neil, Charles P. Daly, John Ahern, John McGrath, and other Irish and a few German Catholic political figures, serving public notice that, despite the bishop, they stayed with the party. Incensed Catholic Irishmen passed strong resolutions stigmatizing "those unworthy individuals who have so far degraded themselves as Irishmen, disgraced themselves as Catholics, and dishonored themselves as Freemen" as to sanction the anti-bishop Tammany meeting, and the Boston *Pilot* printed the names of the officers within black borders, as dead to the faith and the race.

The Carroll Hall ticket polled 2200 votes in the election won by the Whigs with a thin margin of 290 votes. The number of Catholic voters at the time was estimated at between seven and ten thousand, which meant that the ticket put forward by Bishop Hughes received between one third and one fourth of the Catholic vote while the others maintained their party regularity. The Carroll Hall ticket vote was sufficient to defeat one Democratic candidate for the Senate and three candidates for the Assembly. It made the difference between a Whig and a Democratic victory.

The Carroll Hall ticket had demonstrated, at least to the practical minds of the hard-boiled Democratic Party in New York City, that the Catholic vote could be the balance of power in local politics.

But the price paid for the intervention by Bishop Hughes into the area of politics, heretofore rigidly proscribed by the hierarchy, came high. The bishop himself was characterized as a "political juggler" and a "political hack." He gave his bitter enemy, James Gordon Bennett of the New York *Herald,* himself reared in the Catholic faith, the opening to charge Bishop Hughes with attempting "to organize the Irish Catholics as a distinct party that could be given to the Whigs or Locofocos [Democrats] at the wave of his crosier," a phrase which resounded throughout the country. He furnished what anti-Catholic nativist sentiment considered clinching proof of the priest in politics and confirmed the fears of those who believed in Samuel Morse's *Foreign Conspiracy* that a Catholic party, aimed at subverting the liberties and free institutions of the United States for the eventual conquest of papal power, had at last come out into the open.

The 1841 elections had returned the Whig Seward to the governorship and a Democratic-controlled House and Senate. After frequent conferences by Governor Seward with Bishop Hughes, Horace Greeley, and Thurlow Weed, a bill incorporating the Spencer provisions was drawn up and introduced into the 1842 Assembly by William B. Maclay, a Democrat from New York City and son of a popular Baptist clergyman. Despite howlings from the city, the Maclay bill passed the Assembly by the sweeping vote of 64 to 16.

But the Senate balked. A city election was coming up in New York and to put pressure on the Democratic Party, a group of Catholic Irish delegates nominated a ticket of independent Democrats to fight on the school issue and oppose the regular organization. Candidate for mayor was the respected and venerable Thomas O'Connor. This ticket was immediately withdrawn, however, its purpose effected, when the New York Senate, by one vote, passed the Maclay bill.

Bishop Hughes had gained the day but he lost the war. The bill introduced public control of education into New York City by elected ward committeemen but a revision in the Senate provided that no school "in which any religious sectarian doctrine or tenet shall be taught, inculcated or practiced" could receive school funds. Bishop Hughes did not hide his disappointment and, realizing that the strength of opposition promised only further defeat, he turned to building a Catholic parochial school system, saying in 1850: "The time had almost come when we shall have to build the schoolhouse first and the church afterward."

7

On the day Governor Seward signed the bill, the New York City Whigs officially declared their opposition to it, and by this step the local Whig organization "became representative of nativism." A few days later, during the April city election, words passed at a Sixth Ward polling place and, according to the *Truth Teller,* "violence was offered to some peaceable Irishmen and promptly resisted." That night a gang of nativists stoned the windows and doors of the residence of Bishop Hughes, who was absent, and the mayor of New York stationed militia around Catholic churches as protection.

The year 1843 marked a definite turning point in the political fortunes of the Catholic Irish in New York City and, in the retrospect of their long association with its politics, must be ringed as an important date. That was the year they went on the city's payroll.

Up to 1842, the Catholic Irish vote had been so dependably Democratic that it was taken for granted by the Tammany chieftains and only a few graced the payroll.

The surprising vote rolled up by the Carroll Hall ticket had impressed upon the knowing political sense of the Catholic Irish that, as a balance of power, they had Tammany over a barrel and they concluded the time had come to invite themselves to the banquet table. The sachems also could add two and two and make it come out four. They were realistically appreciative of the faithful Catholic Democrats who had not left the Hall at the shepherd's call of their bishop and were ready to talk business when the prodigals returned in the city election of April, 1843, to roll up a sweeping Democratic victory.

The Democratic administration broke the monopoly of Americans on the butcher markets by granting licenses to Catholic Irishmen as competitors — a rich boon to the heretofore prohibited foreigners. The Democratic administration put Catholic Irishmen into a host of petty jobs, which it was their small ambition to hold: marshals, street inspectors, health wardens, lamplighters, firewardens, dock masters, weighers, clerks, inspectors of pawnbrokers, junk shops and meat markets, each vested with that official authority, no matter how small, which the Irish loved and by virtue of which they were raised to the white-collar class. The Democratic administration put the Irish on the police force, such as it was at the date, a night watch.

The 1843 parceling out of jobs settled the Irish unquestionably in the political life of New York City which in the years to come, by increased numbers through Irish fertility and massive emigration, they were to dominate, or, in the words of a disgruntled and bitter anti-Irish annalist, "the native and intelligent citizenship from that time onward being gradually more and more superseded by the foreign and the unintelligent in the control of offices." That literate snob, social careerist, and hard-shelled nativist, Philip Hone, wrote in his diary under date of June 8, 1843, that Bishop Hughes deserved "a cardinal's hat at least for what he has done in placing Irish Catholics upon the necks of native New Yorkers."

8

The sentiments written by Hone in the privacy of his library reflected the sense of grievance given voice to by a group of men who casually sat chatting in a New York City blacksmith's shop, and out of the meeting developed a political society in the Eleventh Ward, organized June 13, 1843, that spread rapidly to become the American Republican Party. The nativism which had flickered briefly in the middle 1830s and then died down now burst into a bright flame in New York City.

The lascivious anti-Catholic literature of the *Maria Monk* stamp, which marked the outcropping of nativism in the middle 1830s, had appealed to low elements but had disgusted the middle classes and passed into disfavor. The issue of public schools, however, symbolized by the reading of the Bible in the classroom, from which the nativist propaganda asserted the Catholics were trying to drive it, furnished a strong appeal to the respectable Protestant religious elements; and there existed an apprehension, with men of no sectarian connection as well as with religious people, that somehow all this stir menaced the principle of separation of Church and State.

The American Republican Party announced itself as the sentinel of free institutions against the papal power so recently exercised in the city, said its program, by the bartering of the public school system for the votes controlled by Bishop Hughes and against the same "dangerous influence" which had put "the large majority of the offices in this city" in the hands of the foreign-born. Once more the hard core of all nativist movements became its objective — modification of the naturalization law to require a residence of twenty-one years of future naturalized citizens. From its slight start, the American Republican movement so organized the opinion stirred up by the school fight that it put a full ticket of nativist candidates for state offices in the 1843 fall election, headed by the aspirant for state Senator with the fascinating name of Mangle M. Quackenboss. Though the party failed to elect any candidates, it impressed the professional politicians by attracting the surprisingly large vote of 8600 against 14,410 for the Democrats and 14,000 for the Whigs.

The American Republican Party was now really in business. Against the opposition of Governor Seward and the state Whig organization, the New York City Whigs struck an under-the-table alliance with the nativists. The American Republicans nominated a slate of candidates in the spring city elections of 1844. For mayor, it nominated James Harper, of the publishing house bearing his name (which a decade earlier had set up a dummy company to publish *Maria Monk*), Ameri-

can-born, of Scotch-Irish descent, a reformer by temperament.* Harper
was elected, with American Republican majorities in both branches of
the city government — a sweeping nativist victory. The jubilant American Republicans speedily fired the Catholic Irish officeholders.

But the feeling of triumph in New York City and the bright hopes
of a national future for the nativist party soon dissolved in the blackened ruins of Catholic churches burned in Philadelphia by mob violence turned upon the Catholic Irish and their houses of worship.

9

Philadelphia had a long Irish tradition, Protestant and Catholic, and
the mounting nineteenth-century emigration had added to the numbers
of both, primarily from the north of Ireland, by which fact the ancient
Orange-Catholic antagonism manifested itself more pronouncedly in
Philadelphia than in any other American community. Growing Catho-
lic Irish strength had submerged the once native dislike of Protestant
Irish into a common front against the Catholic Irish, and the alien-born
Protestant Irish were as nativist in feeling as the old Americans.
Aligned with this American-Orange combination were elements of the
German Calvinists.

At the head of this strange melange to save America for the Americans was a weird and fantastic creature named Lewis C. Levin, born
in the South Carolina Jewish community, an apostate from his people, a
former schoolteacher and peripatetic lawyer in the South, who had
settled in Philadelphia in 1838 and edited a nativist newspaper to forward his driving political ambition. He was a powerful orator, with a
singular mellifluousness which forced even the hostile to listen. Enemies asserted that Levin, a reformed drunkard, rose to emotional heights
under the influence of the opium he had substituted for whiskey.
Father Kerlin, writing of the church-burning riots, said that to this
wayward and wandering Jew "more than to any other man can be
ascribed the fomenting of the anti-religious spirit for his political purposes." He died hopelessly insane, and his wife and daughter both
joined the Roman Catholic Church.

---

* Bishop Hughes believed the municipal reform program, rather than nativist
prejudices, had caused the switch in votes to Harper and did not consider the
mayor a Native American, holding him in friendly regard.

10

Activities by the Catholic Irish had stirred a rumbling resentment that needed only the incitement of politicians to organize against them an already hostile public opinion.

Alderman Hugh Clark, boss of Kensington township north of Philadelphia proper, had taught the Democrats the political expediency of recognizing the Catholic Irish vote. Clark, born in Dublin, had settled in Philadelphia around 1820 and, as a driver of a Conestoga wagon between Philadelphia and Lancaster, had picked up a fluent command of German. This knowledge, together with shrewd political brains, had commended his usefulness to Democratic Governor Wolf, who named him alderman of the suburban Kensington district of Philadelphia in 1833, where he controlled the Catholic Irish vote.

Clark, a dour and brusque Irishman, nominated for office in 1839 on the Democratic ticket, had been defeated by nativist Democrats, who "spotted," or scratched, his name. Clark restrained his anger but three years later, with the circumstances favorable, he gave the word, a thousand Catholic Irish voters bolted the party and swung the election to the Whigs. Like the Carroll Hall ticket, Clark proved the Catholic Irish held the balance of power in the city and county of Philadelphia, but his coup also raised the wind of the nativists.

Without the assertiveness of Bishop Hughes and with no intent to force a controversy, the quiet Bishop Francis P. Kenrick had courteously asked the Controllers of the Public Schools in Philadelphia in 1842 to enforce the disregarded prohibition enacted in 1834 against the "introduction of any religious or sectarian forms as a part of the discipline of the Schools." He asked that the Catholic version of the Bible be used for Catholic children, as was the practice in the Baltimore schools, and that they be excused from participating in Protestant prayers and exercises. The Controllers honored Bishop Kenrick's request. Nativist sentiment and the newly formed Protestant Association, however, charged the Catholics with plotting to drive the Bible out of the schools. Hugh Clark, a commissioner of the Kensington school district, contributed to the furor, unwittingly, according to his story. Visiting a girls' grammar school, he noticed the departure of some pupils from the assembly hall at the reading of the Bible in the King James version and observed to the principal that if such confusion resulted from the reading of separate Bibles, it might be better if

Bible reading were eliminated altogether. The story spread abroad that he had arbitrarily commanded the teacher to stop reading the Bible, and she replied that she would give up her position first. A public meeting called in protest against this "Popish influence" resolved that the Reformation would not be undone in Philadelphia.

The heated Irish oratory of the Philadelphia Repeal meetings and the movement itself were condemned as the illegal use of American soil for a foreign cause. Levin insisted that Daniel O'Connell conspired behind the mask of Repeal to fix absolutism upon the United States and that the Liberator's interference in the American slavery issue was responsible for the birth of the American party in Philadelphia. (Levin was an ardent supporter of the South's "peculiar institution.")

II

The event which welded anti-Catholic Irish elements into the organization of a Philadelphia Native American party was the large vote of the New York American Republican Party in the November, 1843, election. The first Philadelphia meeting in December inspired branch associations in practically every ward.

From the outset, the Philadelphia organization concentrated its attacks upon the "Irish papists" and particularly upon the township of Kensington, the bailiwick of Hugh Clark and, through the girls' grammer school episode, a symbolic point in defense of the Bible in public schools.

Kensington was almost entirely inhabited by North-of-Ireland Protestants and Catholics, both native and foreign-born. There the Orange and Green frictions of the old country were continued; there the anniversary of the Battle of the Boyne was observed; there was heard "Boyne Water," whistled or played upon fife and flute, to the grim faces of the Catholic Irish. Scuffles were frequent.

The Catholic Irish from the Ulster counties had no illusions concerning the meeting of aggressive Native American partisans advertised for the afternoon of Friday, May 3, 1844, in the open lot next to the symbolic public school, at Second and Master Streets, in Kensington. This invasion was the familiar "Orange walk" of the old country and an invitation to trouble.

The outraged Gaels raided this first meeting, tore down the flimsy platform and dispersed the nativists. At the second meeting called for

ANTI-CATHOLIC (ANTI-IRISH) RIOTS IN PHILADELPHIA IN 1844

the following Monday, May 6, they changed their tactics: Irish carters drove their wagons in timed succession and dumped dirt in the midst of the crowd, without, however, breaking up the gathering. But while Lewis Levin was speaking, a sudden squall of gusts and rain drove the nativists to the shelter of the Kensington Market House, called the Nanny Goat Market, nearby on Washington Street, above Master, where the meeting resumed. Here the Philadelphia tragedy started to unfold its violent story.

The Market House stood in the midst of the Catholic Irish section of Kensington. Viewing the market on the west side stood the house of the Hibernia Hose, a volunteer fire company manned by Catholic Irish. Frame houses, occupied by Catholic Irish laborers and their families, ranged in rows west and east of the market and on adjoining streets.

Conflicting versions have left in doubt who fired the first shot, whether from the Hibernia Hose or after a scuffle in the market. The nativists swarmed from the market to attack the Hibernia Hose and the frame dwellings of the Irish, but the defenders fired from windows and alleyways and then rushed into the streets throwing rocks and brickbats supplied from the aprons of their women. In the general melee, George Shiffler, an eighteen-year-old nativist, described as an idler and roustabout, was mortally wounded when he stooped to pick up the flagstaff knocked from his hand.

That night a volley from the darkness frustrated a nativist attack upon a convent, and the belated arrival of the sheriff's force drove off bands that had started the sacking of Irish houses. Irish families fled the neighborhood and took refuge in a wood or started off with their small possessions to the safety of friends at a distance.

Early the next morning, Tuesday, May 7, Bishop Kenrick distributed placards regretting the outbreak and urging his people to avoid all public places. The nativists ripped these down. A procession displayed the flag carried by Shiffler, now a nativist hero-martyr, with a large sign, "THIS IS THE FLAG WHICH WAS TRAMPLED UPON BY THE IRISH PAPISTS."

The city seethed with excitement. That afternoon the Native Americans held a public meeting in the State House yard which attracted thousands by the incendiary notice in a nativist paper:

> Another St. Bartholomew's day is begun in the streets of Philadelphia. The bloody hand of the Pope has stretched itself forth to our destruction. We now call on our fellow-citizens, who regard free institutions, whether they be native or adopted, to arm. Our liberties are now to be fought for; — let us not be slack in our preparations.

After speeches and resolutions, a motion of adjournment to a later day was howled down in favor of an immediate adjournment to Second and Master Streets where the trouble had originated.

A procession of between two and three thousand men and boys invaded Kensington, tore the Hibernia Hose house to pieces, and set afire the dwellings from which they were unable to dislodge the armed Irishmen. The sparks from the twenty or thirty blazing houses set the Market House roaring into flames, which lighted up the battlefield of Kensington. Non-Catholics saved their property by hanging out an American flag or placards with the words "No Popery Here" or displaying a nativist newspaper. John Taggart, a Catholic Irishman, seized on the charge of fatally shooting a nativist, was knocked down by the maddened rioters and his face stomped out of recognition into a bloody mass; a rope was thrown around his neck and he was being dragged to a lamppost for hanging when the humane intervened. The rioting for that night ended with the arrival of the militia, who had been delayed by a debate among civic authorities over the legal power to resist a mob by arms and the reluctance of the militiamen to turn out unless assured of being paid.

By eight o'clock on Wednesday morning, May 8, feverish and agitated crowds assembled in Kensington and, despite the presence of militia, continued the organized burning of homes in search of armed Irishmen. At noon they gathered in front of St. Michael's Church on Second Street on the rumor it was filled with arms. The priest, who earlier had turned over the church to the protection of the military, fled, his life in danger. Inexperienced militia, drawn away by an excitement at a distance, left the church unguarded and at 2:30 in the afternoon it was fired, to the shouts of "To hell with the Pope and O'Connell" and the playing of "Boyne Water" by an improvised fife and drum corps. The house of the priest next suffered the torch, and the mob burned a convent on Second Street. The homes, side by side, of Hugh Clark and his brother Patrick were gutted, an Irish grocery store left in ruins, and homes in the neighborhood destroyed.

That night, despite the presence of Mayor Scott, who assured the mob the church was unarmed, a lad was sneaked through the cordon of police and military into St. Augustine's Church, on Fourth Street below Vine, and at ten minutes before ten o'clock flames leaped out of the windows. At ten o'clock, the church's bell, which had once rung out the good news of the Declaration of Independence, sounded the hour for the last time. At 10:20, the cross came hurtling to the ground with the collapse of the steeple, to the loud cheers of the mob. St. Augustine's Church, with its school, the Augustinian monastery and a library, with its rare collection of literature on the Fathers, was totally destroyed.

Philadelphia looked upon the desolated ruins of two Catholic churches, two Catholic rectories, two Catholic convents, and a Catholic library, property valued at $150,000. Philadelphia totaled the bill of disaster: forty lives sacrificed and more than sixty seriously wounded; eighty-one dwelling houses with their contents looted or destroyed, and two hundred families without homes; public property, to the amount of $150,000, wrecked.*

Devout Catholics saw as a judgment the uneffaced and clearly discernible line on the blackened wall high above where the ruined altar had stood: "The Lord Seeth."

It was noticeable that at no time during the rioting was a threat raised against, or an attack made upon, a German Catholic church: the mob's fury centered on the Catholic Irish, who chose to resist the

---

* Philadelphia, unlike Boston, later made restitution for the damage to Catholic property.

nativists. A city investigating committee placed the blame upon the Irish; and the grand jury, returning indictments, charged that the Native Americans, in the exercise of free speech, were "rudely disturbed and fired upon by a band of lawless, irresponsible men, some of whom had resided in our country only for a short period."

12

Nativist passions had not been spent by the riots and church burnings. Instead, they were vigorously capitalized, and the funeral of Shiffler, his coffin covered with the now famous Kensington flag, turned into a political demonstration. The Independence Day parade saw thousands of Native Americans marching and floats expressing Native American sentiments, including one with a serpent marked "Rome" hissing at the American flag. A tremendous picnic in a public park, addressed by nativist speakers, attested to a Philadelphia unafraid of the Pope and his Irish liegemen.

Then Philadelphia erupted once more, two months after the terrible May days, on the rumor that men had been seen carrying arms into the Church of St. Philip de Neri, the first Catholic free church (that is, without pew rents) in the country, in the district of Southwark, south of Philadelphia proper, near the waterfront.

The rumor was true. William H. Dunn, brother of the pastor of St. Philip's and a leading Repealer, had formed a volunteer company of Irishmen to protect the church after the May rioting, and Governor David Porter had allotted them a small amount of discarded arms. As a precaution against incitement which might arise from the elaborate nativist celebration of Independence Day, the company stood guard in the church. The guns carried into St. Philip's on Friday afternoon, July 5, had been of the disused lot returned from a repair shop. The gathered mob forced the sheriff and then an impromptu committee to search the church. The discovery of a small arsenal confirmed the popular belief that Roman Catholic churches were fortresses and, more than any other single event, gave long life to the legend that became part of American folklore of hidden guns and artillery in the basement of Catholic churches.

On Saturday, Sunday, and Monday, a Philadelphia mob went on the loose once more, intent on destroying St. Philip's. Paradoxically, the nativist leaders, who had felt the backlash of public opinion after the

May riots, joined with the police and military to quiet the mob. Lewis Levin himself dickered for the safe exit from the church of the Montgomery Hibernia Company, a Catholic Irish company assigned inside St. Philip's with two other military outfits for its protection. The mob fell upon the Irish company, which as it broke and fled let loose a volley of fire in self-defense. Several of the Irish militiamen were overtaken and badly beaten, and one youngster, Robert Gallagher, who ran into a house for safety, was smashed into a bloody mass and might have been killed had not a rescue party saved him.

Then the true face of a mob — any mob — presented itself. The situation changed. What had started out as an anti-Catholic Irish mob to wreck a church changed into a mob engaged in civil war with public authority. In anger against the military companies dispatched to break it up, the mob forgot its original purpose, skirmished in the streets with soldiers and fired cannons, taken from the wharves, upon the militia.

Governor Porter appeared in Philadelphia with a plea for peace, and military companies poured in from the several parts of Pennsylvania, finally restoring order.

The military and civilian casualties of the Southwark riot totaled fourteen killed and some fifty wounded.

The Kensington and Southwark riots revealed the breakdown in government and authority and, in consequence, Philadelphia adopted a modern form of government and adequate policing.

13

Bishop Kenrick had faced up to the burning of Catholic churches with the same dignified poise as Bishop Fenwick of Boston under the similar circumstance of the burning of the Charlestown convent, calling for no resistance from his people, urging them to bear their frightful burden of outrage with the spirit of Christian martyrs, depending upon respectable opinion and the public authority of the community to meet the issue of riotous lawlessness. When asked to give permission to Catholics to guard their own churches, he replied: "Never my people; I have placed my churches under the care of the Municipal authorities; it is their duty to protect them. Rather let every church burn than shed one drop of blood or imperil one precious soul."

The aggressive Bishop Hughes in New York was sorely out of patience with such submissiveness. In an article in the *Freeman's Journal*, undoubtedly written by himself, commenting on the Philadelphia riots, was the flat statement: "what we CANNOT understand is why the Catholics *did not* defend their Church." What "are rights good for, if men are not willing to FIGHT for them"? The burning of the Charlestown convent was recalled:

> When a band of ruffians destroyed the peaceful dwelling of unprotected families and children, in the neighbourhood of Boston, they trusted to the laws of their country whilst their own right arms might have exacted an instantaneous and bloody retribution. They did well; but the laws of their country have never vindicated them; and the black ruins of the Charlestown Convent are an abiding monument that the Commonwealth of Massachusetts have sanctioned the violation.

With a resolution that he maintained throughout the crisis which had communicated itself from Philadelphia to New York City, Bishop Hughes declared "there is one thing which should be understood all 'round, — that there must be no more sacking and BURNING OF CATHOLIC CHURCHES OR CONVENTS." Lest there be any mistaking of his firm purpose to defend the Catholic houses of worship, he made the public statement that "if a single Catholic Church were burned in New York, the city would become a second Moscow." This kind of talk, whether politic or not, the outraged Catholic Irish liked, and it increased the stature of Hughes.

Bishop Hughes followed what he called the "twofold front" that had worked successfully in the excitement attending upon the April, 1844, New York City election — of "calming excitement" by forbearance and of "quelling riot" by determination. He had cautioned the Catholic Irish before the election not to allow themselves to be provoked into retaliation by the taunts of the American Republicans and rowdy allies. For months before the election the Irish had been called "Greeks," "Irish rabble," "vagabond Paddies," and similar epithets. Yet the election passed off quietly, to the surprise of the press. At the closing of the polls on election day, an army of some twelve hundred victorious nativists, armed with canes, bludgeons, and other hurtful weapons, paraded through the Sixth Ward, shouting defiance, hurling insults, groaning and hooting at the grim-faced Irishmen who lined the streets, with the obvious intent of provoking a riot, in the same manner the Philadelphia nativists had invaded Kensington. The procession next walked through the Fourteenth Ward, only a little less strong in its Irish population than the Sixth, but here again the Irish restrained themselves. The marchers turned into the Bowery and swung up to Spring Street, within a stone's throw of the Catholic Cathedral, "but there halted," said Bishop Hughes, " 'for a reason they had.' " The "reason" was the sight of several thousand silent and sturdy Irishmen, well armed, gathered to protect the cathedral by Bishop Hughes.

The New York nativists, excited by the news from Philadelphia, organized a meeting on the night of May 7, shouted in approval of the anti-Catholic and anti-Irish orators, and offered rewards for the capture of the Irish rioters in Kensington. The meeting was adjourned to a public meeting to be held in City Hall Park two nights later, at which a delegation from Philadelphia promised to display the tattered Kensington flag.

Hughes knew that the meeting threatened rioting and possibly a repetition of church burning. He looked up the law and found no provisions for the compensation of property destroyed by mobs. He determined that only a tough line could save the city from the disaster that impended.

He issued an extra of the *Freeman's Journal* urging the Catholics to remain as peaceable as they could but to be prepared to act in their own defense. "We knew," he later explained, "the nature of a mob, especially a mob of church-burners, convent-sackers, and grave-robbers, that with it a firm front is the best peacemaker." He organized forces of one to two thousand men to protect each Catholic church in the city, "cool, collected, armed to the teeth, and with a firm determination, after taking as many lives as they could in defense of their property, to give up, if necessary, their own lives for the same cause."

The bishop called upon Mayor Robert H. Morris and advised him to prevent the nativist demonstration. In reply to the mayor's question as to what Bishop Hughes would have him do, he said:

> I did not come to tell you what to do. I am a churchman, not the mayor of New York; but if I were the mayor, I would examine the laws of the State, and see if there were not attached to the police force a battery of artillery, and a company or so of artillery, and a squadron of horse; and I think I should find that there were; and if so, I should call them out. Moreover, I should send to Mr. Harper, the mayor-elect, who has been chosen by this party. I should remind him that these men are his supporters; I should warn him that if they carry out their design, there will be a riot; and I should

urge him to use his influence in preventing this public reception of the delegates.

The mayor was apparently impressed, and a conclave of city officials agreed upon the wisdom of canceling the public meeting to preserve peace and order, a decision in which the leaders of the American Republican Party concurred.

Bishop Hughes was undoubtedly correct in his statement that had the meeting been held "the carnage that would have ensued is now utterly beyond calculation" and that the city had been spared "from the bloody scenes which have just been unfortunately enacted in Philadelphia." The tough-willed, Ulster-born Irishman had resolved a blood-on-the-moon emergency by forceful initiative and intervention, for which he was abused by his enemies, but the bishop felt justified in taking credit for saving New York City from a "fearful crisis."

14

The Native American movement was irreparably damaged by the Philadelphia riots and the name of "church burners" it henceforth carried. In April, even before the outbreak in the City of Brotherly Love and the crisis in New York, the Whig members of the New York state legislature had divorced themselves from the American Republican Party, repudiating the local Whig alliance. The Democratic members of the Legislature, on the same day, hailed the twenty thousand Democrats in New York City who had resisted the party of proscription. The Clay clubs in Syracuse complimented the five thousand Whigs for their fortitude in standing by the party against the lure of the nativists.

The word "Clay" was governing in this series of resolution. A presidential election loomed in November and Henry Clay was the central figure, his brilliance burnishing the burden of that unshakable ambition for the White House. In the 1844 election, the foreign vote pressed itself upon the nation's attention more noticeably than ever before in the Republic's history, unfavorably.

37
Intermezzo, 1840s

THE CATHOLIC IRISH in the 1844 presidential election staged a unique campaign — they turned out to defeat a candidate for Vice-President.

They fancied the blarneying Henry Clay personally, but his partner on the Whig ticket, former Senator Theodore Freylinghuysen of New Jersey, traveled in suspicious company. With a penchant for evangelism, he held high office in Bible, tract, Sunday School, foreign mission, and temperance societies that were associated with No-Popery agitation, and he presided over meetings at which No-Popery reverends attacked the Catholic Church as the dragon and beast of the sixteenth chapter of Apocalypse and the Pope as "the scaly tail of the rhinoceros." The tight-lipped Boston *Pilot* told its readers: "A Bigot shall never sit upon the chair of Washington."

The Boston weekly denounced Freylinghuysen in unmeasured language, and on the Sunday before election the Whigs posted placards around the city with excerpts from a *Pilot* editorial of the previous June 22, belaboring the Philadelphia church-burners, sneering at native courage and advising "those cowards and sons of cowards" to boast moderately. The Boston *Atlas,* leading Whig paper, stirred the apprehensions of the Catholic Irish community with an inflammatory article on election morning:

> They [Americans] will not tamely sit still and see their government controlled, and their country ruled by a band of paid, pensioned, ignorant and deluded foreigners, led on, in solid column, under the influence and the insignia of a foreign religious faith. . . . A countless host of ignorant, beggarly ragamuffins, who have no sympathy for our laws, or our institutions, are trampling our RIGHTS in the dust. ROME AND IRELAND ARE RULING AMERICA.

The familiar jargon of the anti-Catholic and anti-Irish vocabulary concerned the Irish less than the sinister recommendation of the *Atlas:*

> LET EVERY TRUE AMERICAN EMPLOYER AT ONCE REFUSE TO EMPLOY THE MISCREANTS, ON ANY TERMS, AND WE SHALL SOON

SEND THEM HOWLING BACK TO THEIR OWN BENIGHTED AND MISER-
ABLE COUNTRY.

After the election, in which the Whigs thumpingly carried Massachusetts, the Catholics of Boston in a public meeting disavowed the
Pilot as speaking for either the clergy or the people and recorded their
respect for the native-born Americans, who accepted the demonstration
as amends. The news that Bishop Fitzpatrick had canceled his subscription to the *Pilot* put the imprimatur of the Church on the Irish
will to appease.

2

The turbulent spirit behind this Irish brouhaha was the fledgling
junior editor of the *Pilot,* Thomas D'Arcy McGee, then just out of his
teens, embarked on his strange, brilliant, and erratic career that ended
a quarter of a century later with his body sprawled on a Montreal street
mowed down by the pistol of an Irish revolutionary assassin.

McGee had arrived in America at the age of seventeen. While looking for work in Boston, he listened to the patriotic observance of the
Fourth of July in front of Faneuil Hall, and in a burst of inspired
enthusiasm he stood on the tail of a cart and poured forth the meaning
to himself of America and liberty. An impressed crowd listened to the
native eloquence of the shabbily dressed boy, his homely dark Irish
face aglow. Within the week Patrick Donahoe, proprietor of the
Pilot, hired him.

McGee's mother had taught him love of the old Irish songs and
legends. With irregular and small formal education, he had shown
signs of prodigy by his absorption of extensive reading and facility
of literary expression. He carried with him on the emigrant ship a
batch of youthful poems.

Donahoe engaged McGee as a traveling agent to solicit *Pilot* subscriptions and, at the same time, to address and organize Repeal meetings throughout New England. McGee's speeches returned favorable
comment for his fresh talent: the "young genius," admirers called him.
The appreciative Donahoe moved him into the role of junior editor,
and he lifted the provincial *Pilot* to a national reputation among the
Catholic Irish.

With more fervor than discretion, he maligned Yankee pieties,
sneered at the revered Pilgrims and Puritans, and mocked the "gro-

tesque theology" of the Calvinist founding fathers. "Dear, delightful, bigotted New England . . . thou land of notions, and nice young parsons, thou oddity of the earth, thou eccentric museum of ill-assorted ideas." Boston seethed at the effrontery of this intruding "Paddy," but he forced Boston to pay him heed.

3

As if McGee were not enough in the land of Emerson, Thoreau, Hawthorne, Longfellow, Holmes, Whittier, and Bancroft, another Irish "genius" turned up in Boston — the talkative Mooney, who lay under the shadow of attempted seduction when he merely asked the woman for a glass of water. In Boston Mooney launched his history of Ireland, from fifteen centuries before Christ to 1845,* in a hired hall in the presence of the bishop, the clergy, and a crowded assembly with a program of Irish song and music. It was agreed that the Americans needed the correct story of Ireland to disabuse them of error. The Friends of Truthful Irish History was formed in Boston to promote the sale of Mooney's opus, not to protest against it.

Mooney's *History* was monumental only in size, 1651 pages weighing five pounds and selling for $3.50: it required a physically strong people like the Irish just to hold it. As history it was trash, a wholesale and uncritical pilfering from the pseudo-history which long beguiled the race, but it holds value as a social document for the glorified misinformation fed the Catholic Irish by the slick mercenary hack, Mooney. It told how the Irish race derived from the Egyptians and Phoenicians; how the Irish made war chariots for the Gauls to use against Caesar's legions; how the Irish came to the aid of the Carthaginians against Rome; how Latin was a product of the Irish language; how the Irish invented the violin; how Napoleon's grandfather was Gaul Burke, an Irishman; and so on. As the book had a wide sale, it helps explain the strange fantasies the Irish emigrants passed on to their children as the true story of Ireland.

* A History of Ireland, from Its First Settlement to the Present Time; Including a Particular Account of Its Literature, Music, Architecture, and Natural Resources; with upwards of Two Hundred Biographical Sketches of Its Most Eminent Men; Interspersed with a Great Number of Irish Melodies, Original and Selected; Arranged for Musical Instruments; and Illustrated by Many Portraits of Celebrated Irishmen; and a Series of Architectural Views. By Thomas Mooney, late of the City of Dublin, Boston: 1845.

After the enthusiastic introduction of his book in Boston, Mooney headed a traveling show, with himself as pitchman, to peddle it. "Was ever heard of a practice so monstrous as the organization of an agitation for the sale of a book?" asked the *Freeman's Journal,* which had given it a scathing review.

4

In contrast to the flashy showmanship of Mooney, with his unashamed flattery of the Irish, McGee straightforwardly analyzed the faults of the Irish emigrants as a prong to their self-improvement. McGee looked upon the state of the Catholic Irish emigrants in the United States and found it "heart-sickening." What he observed during two years in New England (he resigned from the *Pilot* in 1845 to join a Dublin paper) distressed his pride as an Irishman — and he blamed his own people.

If the Irish remembered the old maxim, "respect yourself and others will respect you," they might rise to a happier life and a higher station in society. The Irish had been flung among people *"seemingly"* very superior, he explained, and they therefore assumed the air and action of inferiors. Nothing was more foolish, more ungenerous to themselves, more cruel to their offspring and more dangerous to the existence of real democracy "than this wanton and willing prostitution."

The first duty of the Catholic Irish emigrant in America was to possess his self-respect, as a means of raising the regard of others for his Church, Ireland, and himself. McGee published with approbation an extract from a private letter:

> We Irish have a great penchant for the persons and views of strangers. Our long subjection induces us to think every one not of us, our superior; and to attach some ridiculous notion of respectability to the patronage of the Gentiles. This is low and mischievous. Half our force is lost by a want of concentration, and we accustom persons to think themselves masters, who would otherwise feel proud to be allies.

Catholic Irishmen frequently prefaced an undertaking with the query, "What will the Protestants think?"

McGee held the Catholic Irish press accountable in great part for the lack of progress in the emigrant masses:

Editors . . . have flattered them out of the knowledge of their
own failings; have persuaded them that they are the noblest yet
the most unfortunate of men, and by preaching up this species of
fatalism have benumbed the improving faculties of their own supporters.

A great fault with the Catholic Irish emigrants, McGee said, was
that they are "too *independent* with each other, and not sufficiently
so with other classes." This "false independence" led to quarrels
and controversies in their own ranks, and the "false submissiveness"
earned "general contempt out of them."

"That we have not yet fully realized our just expectations," wrote
McGee, "is our own fault." The Irish must cease acting "as if conscious of having intruded themselves upon America," a sensibility he
characterized as "the nursling of ignorance and the fruit of self-
abasement."

This was strong medicine. If you got what you deserved, the press,
leaders, and orators told the Catholic Irish, your merits would be
blazoned across the skies. You did get what you deserved, McGee
told them, and it was your own fault.

5

McGee's unflattering analysis of the state of the Catholic Irishman
prepared the way for the remedy he agitated on every possible occasion: Educate! Educate! Educate! "They [the Catholic Irish] must
. . . either be driven out by persecution," he declared, "or they must
gather sufficient knowledge here . . . to place them upon a nearer
social intercourse with the native." The lack of education, McGee
continued, was "the grievance which makes a white slave class amongst
us, and, consequently, creates an aristocracy in their employers."

McGee, taking the cue from the Young Ireland cultural movement
that paralleled Repeal, first advocated for emigrant education the
formation of mutual instruction clubs of six, twelve, twenty or any
convenient number of persons, each to subscribe twenty-five cents a
week to purchase books, magazines, and newspapers. He suggested
that prejudice against Catholicism and the Irish character had been
"the effect of the absence of mental culture in the Irish Catholic
population" and that removing the cause would in great part remove
the effect.

McGee's idea of mutual instruction clubs, however, did not reach to the roots of Irish deficiency in education, which was that great numbers could neither read nor write. A railroad contractor told Horace Mann, secretary of the Massachusetts Board of Education, that within a period of ten years he had employed about three thousand foreigners, mostly Irish, of whom only one out of eight could read intelligibly. It was estimated in 1845 that probably twenty thousand emigrants lived in Boston and vicinity, of whom eight thousand were reckoned as permanent residents. About four thousand were above the age of eighteen, of whom, perhaps, seven eighths lacked the lowest degree of a common school education. "The present generation of Irish emigrants still feel the effect of these [penal] laws," an Irishman told the Massachusetts Board of Education.

McGee's campaign for mutual instruction ran parallel with the Repeal agitation. John W. James, president of the Boston Repeal Association, was also a member of the State Board of Education, and the conjunction of his two offices inspired a deeper idea than McGee's. Why not strike first at the root cause of the Irishman's deficiency — illiteracy? Upon his initiative, two meetings of public-spirited Bostonians, including representatives of the Irish and German communities, launched the Boston Institution for the Education of Adults.

Its first object was to teach reading, writing, and arithmetic in evening schools, three nights a week from October to April, to females from sixteen on and to males from the age of eighteen, "at the least possible expense of time and money to the learner," ten cents a week for each pupil. Boston placed at the disposal of the society two schoolhouses, one for males and the other for females. Early in 1845, this experiment in adult education started. The Irish, hesitant at first, feared they would make laughable blunders and entertained the notion that if their children were educated in America, they had less reason for education themselves. But the willing and the bold took the plunge, and hefty Irishmen of mature years squeezed into the seats of children to learn the three R's. The report at the end of the first year showed such progress that at the beginning of the second year the City of Boston opened six schoolhouses for the increased number of applicants.

The idea of night schools for adults caught on in other communities, with adult classes in Troy, New Haven, Philadelphia, and in towns surrounding Boston. Classes were begun by Catholic pastors in church basements or parochial schools. For some reason not clear, the experiment expired after three years, but James S. Loring, writing in 1852 of the thousands benefiting from the night schools opened in New York and Philadelphia, moralized that "they and their posterity will have occasion to bless the generous Bostonians who originated . . . this new lever of moral power." The propaganda and search by McGee for a method of educating Catholic Irish emigrants, and the presidency of the Repeal Association by James, contributed to the origin of night schools.

6

When the Whigs shook off the stupor of shock and disappointment at Clay's defeat (it was as unexpected as Dewey's defeat by Truman in 1948) and examined the election returns, a howl went around the country. The burden of the complaint was that ignorant foreigners (that is, the Catholic Irish and the Germans), manipulated by professional Democratic politicians, had stolen the election by gross electoral frauds.

The grave Daniel Webster led off in a Boston address with the charge that illegal naturalization and fraudulent voting in the pivotal states of New York and Pennsylvania accounted for Polk's victory and convinced him of "an imperative necessity for reforming the naturalization laws of the United States." The ultra-nativist New York *American* asserted, *"the President of the United States has been chosen by foreigners, naturalized for the occasion . . . [who] thus have determined the policy of the country for years — it may be for all time."* Evidence substantiated the conclusion of McMaster, the American historian, "that at none of the fourteen presidential elections which up to that time had been held in our country was fraud so openly, so recklessly practiced as in 1844."

Illegal naturalization had developed noticeably in New York City with the careful spadework of his Democratic managers to elect Martin Van Buren president in 1836. A ship loaded with Irish emigrants consigned to Democratic Cornelius Lawrence, a prosperous shipping merchant, had landed in New York shortly after Mr. Lawrence had been chosen mayor in the spring election of 1834. "His Honor is early in the field," said a Whig paper. The New York *Evening Star,* taking note in June, 1836, of a thousand recently arrived

Irish emigrants, had no doubt that one half of the males over twenty-
one "will vote at our next fall elections," charging the fraud to Van
Buren and his spoilsmen. During the presidential campaign of 1836,
his enemies spread the story that Van Buren had opened electoral
offices in Dublin, Limerick and Cork to enroll Irish votes for the
Democrats. By 1844, Tammany had perfected a procedure for nat-
uralizing foreigners with the cooperation of amenable courts which
turned out certified citizens in mass production for the fees.

The Catholic Irishman had little in his Irish political experience
to label quick and illegal naturalization as wrong and much to recognize
it as familiar. Had not the great names in the Ascendancy paid for
the registration of their tenants as forty-shilling freeholders in order
to vote them when everybody knew that most of them had not a ten-
shilling interest, let alone forty shillings, in their holdings?

Naturalization abuses obtained because of lax enforcement of the
law and general popular indifference. Congress had failed, or refused, to establish uniform procedures or to standardize certificates.
The machinery of naturalization resided principally in local courts of
record. City machines avoided the strict federal courts. The federal
District Court in Philadelphia approved eighty-two naturalizations
in seven years while in the same period the court of general sessions
naturalized 4811.

In addition to illegal naturalization, a systematized calendar of
fraudulent voting procedures had been established in New York in both
parties by 1844.

7

Representative Clingman, a South Carolina Whig, arose in the
House to list the Democratic crimes in the 1844 election, dwelling
with mounting invective on the sins of the Empire Club of New
York City, organized in July of that year of "gamblers, pickpockets,
droppers, burners, thimble-riggers and the like" by Captain Isaiah
Rynders, who had come by his title on Mississippi River steamboats,
himself a thief and proprietor of a sporting saloon, who received
Tammany protection for his mob in return for thuggery at the polls.

Captain Rynders had copied his Empire Club from the Spartan
Band, organized in 1840 of Tammany malcontents by Mike Walsh,
who thus first introduced the organized gang into American politics, as

a challenge to Tammany Hall and not as an instrument of systematized corruption like the Empire Club. Mike Walsh was the most colorful political character of his day, the nation's leading demagogue, and his own worst enemy. The lively career of Walsh properly belongs in the history of workingmen's parties and American leftist movements, but as a Catholic Irishman born in Youghal, County Cork, and carried to the United States as a child by his emigrant father, he must be considered as a product of the race. Walsh showed only intermittent interest in Irish patriotic causes or in the matters which engaged the attention of his fellow countrymen. Though baptized a Catholic and educated for a brief time in St. Peter's parochial school in New York, he had early cut adrift from the Catholic Church and in his speeches often linked priestcraft with monopoly as oppressors of the poor. He entered so vigorously into the mainstream of American life that he lost contact with the life of the emigrant Irish, but no amount of saturation could wipe out his Irish nature.

Walsh was one of the early American anti-capitalist agitators: "The great and fruitful source of crime and misery on earth," he said, "is the inequality of society, the abject dependence of honest, willing industry upon idle and dishonest capitalists." He belonged to the rare breed which now and then deviates from the customary conservatism of the Catholic Irish — an economic and political radical. Because a Mike Walsh commanded a political gang, the assumption followed that his Spartan heelers were also Irishmen, when, on the contrary, the native-born for the most part made up his loyal legion.

As a coarse and eloquent rabble-rouser he was without superior. His preference was for that personal scurrility which made Irish journalism and politics terrible and fearful. Mike ran the *Subterranean,* a paper addressed to the working or subterranean classes, in partnership with George Wilkes, the well-known blackmailer, fellow traveler in radical causes, fancy man of the lady who ran a high-class brothel for the sporting gentry, and founder of the *Police Gazette.* An attack upon editors of the public press typified Mike's free-swinging style and content:

> And who are the spirits who preside over it and attempt to give a tone to public opinion? The mere supernumeraries of literature! A set of counterfeit blackguards, who can write about temperance with a gallon of punch in their bellies, upon honor with their backs

still smarting from the effects of a cow-skinning, and about honesty with a bribe jingling in their pockets!

"I will yet ride over all this rotten opposition," he shouted to an audience, "like a balloon over a dunghill." He had an imaginative feel for originating colorful slang phrases, including one which has persisted: "Everything is lovely — and the goose hangs high."

People whose testimony can be trusted never doubted the sincerity of Mike's feeling for the poor and downtrodden but they had no faith in his stability. His true character of the Irish playboy could not be suppressed, but he was no professional "stage Irishman." His strength as a humorist came from the genuine wellsprings of the Irish comic sense — the dead-pan treatment. To expose the pork and waste of public money in a rivers and harbors bill, he solemnly discussed an appropriation he introduced in Congress to build a lighthouse on the Erie Canal.

Had Mike been able to resist the impulse to clown and check the gregarious attraction of convivial companionship, he might have used his undoubted gifts for substantial and even enduring achievements. But his excessive and ill-balanced Irish nature betrayed him and sacrificed his talents in wasteful momentary satisfactions. Friends noticed the fits of melancholy which seized him and the sad face after bursts of rough humor, as though the truth of his own failure pressed upon him. He burned himself out in inconsequential living, the good fellow bolstered by the admiration of inferiors, aided and abetted by the bottle, frustrated, like so many other Irishmen of the same bright and unstable type, by forces within himself he lacked the character to control. His body was found early one morning after a night of carousing in the areaway of a shop, down which he had fallen, his head bloody and his watch missing. At first it was thought he had been murdered but further investigation concluded his death was the result of an apoplectic stroke. The writer of the Mike Walsh obituary summed him up: "Nobody exactly understood him; he did not understand himself. Spite of his undeniable ability, nobody highly respected him; and, spite of his many errors, everybody liked him."

8

The impression became widespread that Catholic Irish emigrants were met on landing piers by political runners and immediately rushed off to be naturalized as Democratic voters. Daniel Webster said that "masters of vessels having brought over emigrants from Europe, have within thirty days of their landing, seen those very persons carried up to the polls and give their votes for the highest offices in the national and state governments." But illegal naturalization was confined generally to the large cities, to New York in particular, and there the number fraudulently granted citizenship made a small total in proportion to the thousands of Catholic Irish pouring in from emigrant ships. It required constant effort to persuade the Catholic Irish to go through the regular process of naturalization.

We have seen how one priest advised young Irish girls not to marry their suitors unless they took out naturalization papers. Through councils and pastoral letters, church authorities hammered at the obligation of emigrants to become adopted citizens of the new country. Irish mutual benefit and other societies incorporated naturalization as a major purpose of their existence. The Hibernian Provident Society of New York in 1839 accepted as members only the naturalized or those who had taken out first papers, a quite common practice in Irish societies.

Irish groups organized themselves into naturalization societies. The Boston Naturalization Society was organized in 1839 after a spirited letter from an Irishman had appeared in the Boston *Pilot*:

> If Irishmen would become respected in Massachusetts, they must become a formidable political body; they must have a hand in making the laws by which they are to be governed, in a hundred fold a greater measure than they now enjoy.

Such a note became constant — and effective — in stirring the Irish to naturalization: for your own defense, protection, and interest, get naturalized and obtain the franchise.

The nativist agitations and discrimination against the religion or race of the Irish served the purpose just contrary to what the nativists contemplated — they drove the Catholic Irishmen into citizenship and the ballot.

The appeal to the national Irish cause provided ammunition to stir up the lagging Irish into citizenship. "In the event of a war with England," it was argued, "it will be a glorious privilege to work, fight and triumph for our native land, as well as for our adopted country."

Around 1840 there appeared the professional naturalization agent, with an office in a large center like Boston, who toured in towns and villages when the court was in session, filling out the first papers and attending the applicant in the final step of naturalization. Their first-hand information, together with the instructions of the Church and the Catholic press, dispelled the misapprehensions which held back the frugal and cautious among the unlettered Irish, the most prevalent being that the unnaturalized did not have to pay taxes.

So important did the leaders of the Catholic Irish hold naturalization of the race in the United States that the Boston *Pilot*, for instance, opposed a law in the Massachusetts legislature permitting foreigners to hold land, on the premise that it would discourage citizenship.

9

Rhode Island had so rigged electoral qualifications as not to be troubled by the intruding "foreigners," that is, the Catholic Irish. It simply disfranchised them by a property qualification in the Land-holders' Constitution drawn in 1842. The Landholders' Constitution supplanted the King Charles Charter of 1663 under which the state operated until 1841 when Thomas Wilson Dorr, an idealistic young Providence lawyer, led a popular uprising — the Dorr War — against oligarchic control, formed a rump government after a popularly elected convention had written a democratic constitution, and was forced to flee the state upon the suppression by the Charter government of the rebellion. Dorr returned to Rhode Island in October, 1843, and was committed to jail to stand trial for high treason. The Supreme Court calendar listed the trial of Dorr after the trial of John and William Gordon for murder.

The Gordons were charged with the murder of Amasa Sprague, who, with his brother, United States Senator William Sprague, had been a leader of the Law and Order party to down Dorr. But more than this, Sprague had been a magnate, one of the wealthiest men in the state, in the inner circle of the ruling powers of Rhode Island, and the accused were despised Catholic Irish emigrants.

Sprague's Village in the town of Cranston immediately south of Providence was a representative New England textile feudal barony with which Catholic Irish emigrants became well acquainted, dominated by the great and prosperous print works of the A. and W. Sprague Company. The operating overlord was Amasa Sprague, then forty-five years of age, a strong-willed Yankee, overbearing, dictatorial, plain-spoken, intolerant of opposition and, like his breed in the tough New England textile industry, a driving master but withal, his friends said, kindly.

The Sprague company owned the plant. It owned the company houses occupied by the "hands," as the Yankee and Irish employees were called. It owned the company store, where the hands found it advisable to trade. It owned the farms which supplied the company store. It even owned the church where the Protestant hands worshiped.

Sprague had disdain for the Irish but not to the extent of penalizing his own interests by drawing a racial barrier against the willing and hard-working Irish at low wages in his print works. An Irishman initiated a "greenhorn" into the ways of Amasa: "But see here, Mike, if ye don't obey his orders he will be after ye sure, wid those big boots of his, and woe be to the other side of ye if he overtakes ye. Remember that now." One Irishman he particularly hated — Nicholas Gordon. Nicholas reciprocated the hatred.

Sometime in the middle 1830s, Nicholas Gordon had emigrated from Ireland and settled in Cranston as the owner of a small store, with house attached, which sold groceries, notions, and candy for the children. The Cranston Town Council granted Nicholas a liquor license and his business flourished.

Nicholas Gordon, described as "a man of much talk, a sportive, swearing little Irishman, beneath the size of an ordinary man," and as "more genteel than the run of factory workers," was equally a fervent Catholic, worshiping in the Providence congregation, and an ardent Repealer. He had saved enough money to bring out from Ireland in July, 1843, the other members of his family — his aged mother Ellen, his sister Margaret, his three brothers, William, John and Robert, and the seven-year-old daughter of the widower William. The joy of embracing his family had been marred for Nicholas by an encounter with the power of Squire Amasa Sprague. The liquor counter of Nicholas's store began to interfere with the productivity of the print works, and Amasa blocked renewal of the license in June, 1843.

On the last day of December, 1843, a Sunday, Sprague left his manor shortly after three in the afternoon and started to walk to a large farm he owned in the next town of Johnston, about a mile and a half from Sprague's Village. He followed the short cut used by the

mill help across meadow, hollow, and thicket. Between dusk and darkness, Michael Costello, a handy man in the Sprague household, took
the same path and in the most secluded spot saw a body on its
hands and knees, face downward, in the blooded snow. The dead man
was Sprague. Reconstruction of the crime showed that he had been
shot in the right forearm, apparently from ambush, and then brutally
bludgeoned to death when he resisted his assailant or assailants. The
sixty dollars found in Sprague's pocket eliminated robbery as a motive.

Suspicion immediately centered on the Gordons. On circumstantial
evidence, John and William Gordon were indicted for murder, and
Nicholas, who had been indisputably placed in Providence at the
time of the crime, was indicted as an accessory before the fact, on
testimony that he had threatened to have revenge upon Amasa Sprague
and settle scores before the year was out. The design of the indictments set forth that Nicholas instigated the two brothers to commit
the murder in revenge.

The image developed in the popular mind of an Irish Whiteboy
agrarian outrage committed in the settled land of Roger Williams. The
"landlord," that is, Amasa Sprague of the Yankee gentry, had punished
"tenants" in his village, the Gordons, by imposing his political power
to harm the source of earnings of the head of the family, Nicholas,
and they had taken the law in their own hands, as in the Irish countryside, waylaid the offending master and murdered him.

Wagging tongues, incited both by the prevailing anti-Catholic Irish
prejudice and the lurid, biased newspaper reports, convicted the Gordons even before they stood trial. A fellow countryman was excused
from jury service when he admitted he believed in the guilt of the
Gordons from reading the newspaper accounts. A red-stained shirt
found in the Gordon house reeked with the gore of the innocent (and
wealthy) Amasa Sprague in newspaper stories; the blood later turned
out to be madder dye from a factory in which John had worked.

The Catholic Irish community in neighboring Providence immediately rallied to the support of the indicted Gordons and, poor as they
were, raised a defense fund for able counsel. The chief defense counsel was General Thomas F. Carpenter, who refused a fee, a leader of
the Rhode Island bar, but lost to the esteem of the respectable because
of his Dorrite sympathies and, more provocatively, of his recent conversion to Roman Catholicism, then a startling event. Others among
the defense counsel were also Dorrites.

Chief Justice Durfee of the Supreme Court, with three associates, sat on the case, and the transcript indicates that he, a strong partisan, looked with slight favor upon the accused and their counsel. He refused separate trials for each of the indicted Gordons but granted General Carpenter's motion that Nicholas be tried apart from John and William. The trial of the Gordons began on April 8, 1844.

The case against William Gordon collapsed with the dramatic reappearance of a Yankee who had left Rhode Island thinking William had been freed and for whom the Irish community had been frantically searching. He validated the testimony of Irish witnesses from Providence who had refuted the story of two reputable villagers placing William near the scene of the crime on that Sunday afternoon. The state concentrated its case on John Gordon.

John was a taciturn and rather sullen young man of twenty-one, who lived with Nicholas and worked as a laborer or in neighboring factories, since the doors of the Sprague company were closed to him. The case against him was entirely circumstantial, confused and conflicting, with testimony bearing on vital points from the village half-wit and a feather-brained prostitute. Nobody placed John, or even tried to place him, at or near the murder scene on that Sunday.

In his argument to the jury, after six days of testimony, Attorney General Blake laid the motive of the crime to Nicholas Gordon and presented a common conception of the Irish character then obtaining among Americans:

> He had two brothers who had come over from Ireland last summer, at his invitation and expense. They probably came with the idea which is common to many of their countrymen, that the laws here, in this free country, are less severe, and may be more easily evaded, than the laws of their own country. . . . Nicholas was the head of the family — he had prospered in the world; and there is a kind of pride which the members of a family feel for one of them who is more talented and successful than the rest — a pleasure in fulfilling his wishes and advancing his plans. . . . The Irish have strong propensities; strong attachments and resentments; qualities which, under a favorable development, tend to ennoble, but under an unfavorable one, to debase the mind. One of the strongest and most marked features of the Irish character, and to their honor be it said, is the strength of their national and fraternal feeling. The tie of kindred is to an Irishman almost an indissoluble bond.

This presentation to the jury by the Attorney General of a purported conspiracy in the Gordon family, still remaining to be proved in the trial of Nicholas Gordon, furnished the basis of a petition for a new trial by the defense, which the Court denied.

Chief Justice Durfee, in his charge to the jury, drew a distinction, which later students thought injudicious by its mere mention, between the testimony of native-born witnesses and "of the countrymen of William Gordon."

The jury left the box at 6:30 on the night of April 17 and returned one hour and fifteen minutes later with a verdict of guilty against John Gordon and freedom for William Gordon.

Then came an unusual development. William presented to the authorities the gun and pistol of Nicholas Gordon, which he said in an affidavit he had secreted in the garret of the Gordon home on the news of Sprague's murder. In Ireland, he explained, possession of firearms was a penal offense, and being new to the United States he feared that such a law was in effect here; therefore he hid them from the police, as people did in his native land. This new evidence challenged the validity of a basic point in the state's circumstantial case — the ownership by Nicholas of the broken murder gun found near the scene as testified to by key witnesses. But nothing came of it. The assistance of the Governor was sought, but, lacking the pardon power, he was prohibited from interference.

As the processes of the law had been exhausted, friends of John Gordon turned to the General Assembly with a petition for reprieve. The House debated the petition on January 14, 1845, with Wilkins Updike, a hardened nativist, taking a strong position in opposition, and by a vote of 36 to 27 the petition was rejected, a tight vote that suggested second thoughts and rising doubts to trouble the Rhode Island conscience in the trial of John Gordon.

John Gordon was hanged in the yard of the State Prison, on February 14, 1845, at eleven o'clock. He maintained his innocence to the end and showed no break in the steady and calm control of his emotions, which had distinguished his conduct from the moment of the arrest.

The funeral was held on Sunday afternoon, February 16. The procession of sorrowful and set-faced Irishmen took thirty minutes to pass a given point, six men abreast, from one to two thousand marchers, gathered from Rhode Island and from neighboring Massachusetts and Connecticut as a demonstration of faith in Gordon's innocence and massed protest against what they believed injustice. It would have been an even larger funeral procession had not some employers ordered their employees not to take part in it.

The belief to which the marching Irishman testified on that February Sunday in time became public opinion in Rhode Island. The trial had left many questions unanswered. But the compelling theme, which even those who thought John the murderer came to believe, was that, on a cold and impartial study of the trial, the young Irish lad had been convicted on insufficient and unsatisfactory evidence, a conclusion with which modern study concurs. John was sacrificed to a hostile climate in which he stood guilty from the moment the law took him into custody.

The hanging of John Gordon disturbed the conscience of Rhode Island and it became the cause which finally brought about the abolition of capital punishment in that state in 1852. With the case of John Gordon in mind, juries refused to return a single death penalty in murder trials from his execution to the abolition of capital punishment. An obscure and poor Irish emigrant, in the country less than a year when arrested for murder, served a humane end by his death. The Gordon case remains as an important argument in the continuing movement to abolish the capital penalty.

Nicholas Gordon, who was twice tried before juries which disagreed (in the second trial it was difficult to empanel a jury, so averse had public opinion grown to capital punishment), never recovered from the personal calamity of John's death, and taking to heavy drinking steadily declined until the mercy of death spared him further horror.

10

The first national organization of nativism gathered in convention on July 4, 1845, in Philadelphia, with 141 representatives from fourteen states — the high-water mark of the Native American movement in the middle 1840s. The American people saw this convention through the smoke of burning churches. Native Americanism prospered as a political force only locally and in areas of large emigrant populations as a resistance agency. It failed to take on nationally. A test in the House of Representatives demonstrated this.

Memorial after memorial from local bodies reached Congress petitioning for changes in the naturalization laws to restrict the vote of the foreign-born. As in the anti-foreign agitation of the 1830s, the Massachusetts General Court again took the legislative leadership to press action upon Congress. On December 17, 1845, Representative Robert C. Winthrop introduced the resolutions of the Massachusetts legislature seeking changes in the naturalization laws and measures to protect the purity of the ballot box.

Lewis C. Levin, elected to Congress from Philadelphia as a Native American in 1844, moved in an outburst of oratory that the resolutions be referred to a select committee rather than to the judiciary committee to which they would normally be assigned and there quietly buried. This touched off an unexpected debate on American nativism which surprisingly lasted until December 30 and grew hotter with each day's bout. Levin led the offensive and drew from both Whigs and Democrats a spirited arraignment of nativist purposes and a defense of the naturalized citizen and the foreigner.

On the vote, the voice of Native Americanism was proved stronger than its numbers and, after a weak showing in the count, the Levin motion was overruled and the Massachusetts resolutions referred to the judiciary committee and there the matter rested.

II

This congressional byplay on nativism came at a time when the United States concentrated its attention upon two heated issues — the dispute with Great Britain over the Oregon boundary and the annexation of Texas. On both these matters the Catholic Irish held strong opinions. The possibility of war with England over Oregon excited their imaginations to hope that out of the conflict would come Irish freedom, and their representative spokesmen placed the services of the Catholic Irish emigrants at the call of the American government. But once again Daniel O'Connell put them in an embarrassing position before American public opinion and once again the Catholic Irish in the United States angrily repudiated his leadership on an American issue.

In an address to the Repeal Association in Dublin early in 1845, O'Connell noted that England had shown no signs of conciliating Ireland until the war threat over Oregon arose. Would Ireland fight on the side of England against the United States? "Let them but conciliate us and do us justice," declared O'Connell, "and they will have us enlisted under the banner of Victoria. Let them but give us the parliament in College Green, and Oregon shall be theirs and Texas shall be harmless." In other words, if England granted Repeal, the Irish would fight the United States. Upon receipt of O'Connell's speech, the Baltimore Repeal Society dissolved itself in protest and Repeal associations throughout the country made it clear that O'Connell spoke not for them and doubted if on the matter of supporting England he spoke for Ireland.

The Catholic Irish favored the annexation of Texas not only because it was Democratic policy and opposed by the Abolitionists and because they suspected English intriguing in the area, but also because their strong Irish nationalistic instincts made them extreme American nationalists. They were 200 per cent Americans in shouting for American expansionism and the "manifest destiny" of the American nation. If disregard of other peoples whose rights would be trampled upon by American annexation of territory was inconsistent with the position of Ireland in forced association with England, then the Catholic Irish displayed a human failing and justified themselves on the ground that England wanted the territory the expansionists eyed. In the United States, they regarded chauvinism as true American patriotism.

12

It was in this national mood of expanding the territorial boundaries that Representative Felix Grundy McConnell of Alabama, himself an expansionist, offered his resolution for the annexation of Ireland to the United States.

Felix McConnell enjoys a footnote in American history as the author of the first homestead act — to give 160 acres of government land to any white man who would work them for five years. He was a popular member of Congress, of robust good humor, who could switch to slashing invective and raise the cry of "blackguardism" for his assaults. He was more often half swizzled than sober, a natural storyteller and colorful figure. His grandfather had been an eighteenth-century Catholic Irish emigrant who, without the ministration of the Church, had drifted away from the ancestral faith.

On January 6, 1846, in the opening days of the 29th Congress, McConnell offered his resolution on Ireland:

Resolved, That we hail the elevated feeling which now universally prevails in our glorious confederacy to strengthen and consolidate the principles of republican freedom, and extend the blessings of our free institutions in every practicable quarter of the
universe, in the spirit of Christian love and peaceful brotherhood.

Resolved, That while we hail the admission of Texas (which
fought its way to independence) as a sister State into our Union
and view with unaffected pride and satisfaction the patriotic resolution of the Executive Government and Congress to uphold our
title to Oregon, and also observe the growing desire to incorporate
Mexico, Yucatan, California, &c., in the confederacy, that *Ireland
is fully entitled to share the blessings of our free institutions.*

Resolved, That the Irish people, as a nation, have long been
ground down by the tyranny of British *misrule and misgovernment;*
and while her people for centuries have groaned under a foreign
monarchical yoke, they have always cherished the *democratic* principle of republican government, the only civilized institution that has
ever insured freedom to man.

Resolved, That this House receive with due attention and consideration any communication from that high-minded and liberty-
loving people, with a view to effect such an object.

Representative McConnell presumed that there would be no objection. But there were objections.

13

Representative McConnell undoubtedly had a mischievous look in
his eye while reading the resolution on annexing Ireland. But the tragedy had begun in Ireland which, before its exhaustion, caused more
than a million of Ireland's population to be annexed to the United
States in the space of seven years in one of the great mass migra-
tions of history.

The Famine was a watershed in Ireland's history and in the story of
the Catholic Irish in the United States. But it did not date the beginnings of the Catholic Irish settlements in the New World, as many
mistakenly conceive. By 1845, the Catholic Irish had become a familiar
and recognizable element in the population and were scattered from
Maine to Texas. They had become an important and valuable work
group. They had set a strong foundation to the Roman Catholic
Church in the face of opposition and given it an Irish character.
They had associated themselves as an increasingly strong component of
the Democratic Party. They enjoyed their own press. They had or-

ganized two campaigns to assist Irish freedom from the staging area of the New World. In marked ways, though still clannish in their huddles, they were being assimilated into American life more rapidly than thought by Americans, who failed to recognize the changes because their eyes had become fixed upon the exclusivist dwelling together of the Irish.

The incoming hordes of pauperized Famine emigrants acted as an economic setback to the Catholic Irish in the United States and posed a problem difficult to surround. But the Irish did not think of the Famine refugees in economic terms: they were their own flesh and blood, human beings reduced to starvation by the collapse of the upside-down social system of Ireland.

38
"The Hunger Is Upon Us"

YOUNG THOMAS MCMULLEN of Bailleborough, County Cavan, had gone to a lake in the mountains to collect a gallon of mud for a neighbor with a sore foot — "there was a cure in it," the people said. On the upward journey he had passed fields heavy with the life-sustaining potatoes of the poor, but coming back early in the morning "he felt a peculiar smell," as the Irish idiom put it. "It was the smell of the blight on the potatoes."

That was the way the potato disease, which had first appeared in America in 1844, struck: a rich promise of food on the land one day, the stalks healthy and natural, and on the morrow "they were as black as your shoe and burned to the clay," said the old people who remembered the blight or "the failure," as they called it, and the putrefactive odor of the corrupted plants.

The Boston *Pilot* of October 11, 1845, reprinted the poetical language of the literary *Nation* of Dublin, dated September 20: "The autumn is waning sunnily and cheerfully for the country. It is a busy and hopeful time. The husbandman is merry at his toil, because it has rich promise; and the beautiful Giver of all good has, by a guarantee of abundance in the bad food of the poor, given assurance against famine." At the end of November, the Boston weekly reprinted from an English paper the terrifying sentences: "Famine — gaunt, horrible, destroying famine — seems impending . . . In Ireland, matters look appalling."

The great Famine had started in Ireland, one of the terrible events of the nineteenth century. The misshapen social and economic system forced upon the native Irish in consequence of the great confiscations of the seventeenth century collapsed in the successive ruins of diseased potato beds. Ireland would not be the same after this soul-searing experience, and the scar remains to this day. Henceforth, a new dateline was established in the Irish mind: before the Famine and after the Famine.

The course of the Irish Famine ran five years. The disease first spotted the potato plants in the autumn of 1845 and ruined approximately one third of the crop. The cumulative effect deepened the disaster of 1846 when the blight destroyed the total crop everywhere in Ireland. In 1847, the damage added further ruin but the failure was not so comprehensive as in the previous year. The failure of 1848 was as absolute as in 1846. Some relief came in 1849, though the loss was great, and by 1850 the rot had spent itself.

In an exact and true sense, the Famine was not a famine. The only failure was the potato crop, the food of the poor. While the Irish died of starvation and of the parasitical diseases of malnutrition, the land produced sufficient food to sustain the population. But the carts rolled eastward toward the seaports with foodstuffs for England through villages reeking with death. Thousands of barrels of wheat, oats, barley, flour, oatmeal, and bread were exported from Ireland during the Famine years; tierces of beef, pork, and bacon and hundredweights of butter and lard filled the holds of outgoing ships.

"They call it God's famine!" exclaimed the distraught Bishop Hughes. "No! — No! God's famine is known by the general scarcity of food which is its consequence. There is no general scarcity . . . But political economy, finding Ireland too poor to buy the produce of its own labor, exported that harvest to a better market, and left the people to die of famine, or to live by alms." The Irish peasants put the anomaly of hunger in the midst of plenty in the pithy maxim that Almighty God sent the potato blight but the English created a famine.

The Irish knew from the past that pestilence followed the failure of the potato, and by December 13, 1845, the *Pilot* printed reports from Irish papers of the spread of fever, endemic in Ireland and virulent with the debility from lack of nourishment. Typhus and relapsing

FAMINE SCENE IN A HARD-HIT IRISH VILLAGE

fever became of epidemic proportions; dysentery resulted from scavenged food or from the change in diet to Indian meal, improperly cooked or often eaten raw by the starving; scurvy appeared with the loss of water-soluble vitamin C in the potato diet.

The Famine in Ireland wrote a chapter in human misery "to harrow up your hearts," as Captain Robert F. Forbes of Boston said after a short stay in Cork, where he excused himself from further sights following a brief walk with Father Mathew: "I saw enough in five minutes to horrify me — hovels crowded with the sick and dying, without floors, without furniture, and with patches of dirty straw covered with still dirtier shreds and patches of humanity; some called for water to Father Mathew, and others for a dying blessing."

Over Ireland there hung, as the people said, "the smell of the grave." In Boston, the Irish-born Rev. Henry Giles, a Protestant minister beloved by the Catholic Irish, spoke in Tremont Temple and moved the usually reticent Yankee audience with his invocation of the words of the prophet: "Oh that my head were waters, and mine eyes a fountain of tears, that I might weep day and night for the slain of the daughter of my people."

James H. Tuke, a Quaker relief officer, reflected on the state of a parish on the northwest coast of Ireland:

> Ten thousand people within forty-eight hours' journey of the metropolis of the world, living or rather starving upon turnip-tops, sand-eels, and sea-weed, a diet which no one in England would consider fit for the meanest animal which he keeps.

The contrast of the opulence of London with the "livid and death-set features" of the hungry in Ireland made more repugnant the English ruling system — "opposed to common humanity, common justice and common sense," Tuke called it.

Between 1846 and 1851, the records showed 21,770 people died of starvation. The Quaker Forsters heard in West-of-Ireland villages the same terrible words: "The hunger is upon us," and relief visitors to the Arranmore cabin of Widow Cooney, who had buried her husband and a child the day before, starved to death, saw on the five remaining children "a gaunt, unmeaning, vacant stare . . . their lips having become blanched and shrivelled from prolonged destitution."

Hundreds of thousands died of Famine diseases. If the driver of a cart felt a bump at night, he knew he had ridden over a dead body stricken on the highway.

Under normal expectancy, the population of Ireland in 1851 should have totaled over nine million. The Census of 1851 returned a figure of six and a half million — two million less than the estimated population of 1845. Ireland lost one quarter of her population during the Famine years, of whom over a million emigrated.

The cold figures of Irish Famine casualties spoke of the failure of the British government to come to grips with a major crisis that was its responsibility to meet. The blame lay principally with Lord John Russell, head of the Whig ministry which entered office in June, 1846, upon the defeat of Sir Robert Peel, a man of extraordinary common sense, who had responded realistically to the first appearance of the potato failure in the autumn of 1845.

Lord John Russell was the wrong man for a job which called for imaginative thinking, unorthodox procedures, decisive, ground-breaking action, and an unafraid bid to England's humanity. He was an imperturbable doctrinaire — a "political economist," in the contemporary term — who preached "business as usual" and non-interference by the state with the law of supply and demand while human beings perished. Had he humanity, or even common sense, he would have called Parlia-

A FUNERAL AT SKIBBEREEN IN THE FAMINE YEARS

ment into special session, placed the burden of quick relief on the imperial treasury and used English strength for Irish distress. Instead, he fumbled, dawdled and mismanaged. And Irish coroner juries sitting on bodies dead from starvation or disease returned the verdict: "Willful murder against John Russell, commonly called Lord John Russell."

The clearance system came into full force during the Famine. With tenants impoverished, eviction notices swamped Ireland. A clause in the outdoor relief measure finally sanctioned by the Russell ministry shut out from its benefits tenants who held more than a quarter acre of land, which amounted to duress upon the hungry to clear out of their small farms.

The emigrants who came to America burned with hatred from three major grievances against English policy during the Famine. The sight was in their eyes of carts hauling off food for England while the Irish people died. The idea was fixed that England had callously failed the relief responsibility. The recollection was bitter of forced clearance and eviction. They believed John Mitchel, the rebel and transported exile, when he told them that this was the design of calculated policy aimed to exterminate the Irish race and plant ruined Ireland with the English to work it as a garden plot for expanding English industrialism.

2

Relief for Ireland was the first great nationwide free-will extension of American generosity and benevolence to other people bowed down under a natural catastrophe. The quick, almost spontaneous, response of philanthropy when the terrible fact became known of the total loss of the Irish potato crop of 1846 and the dispatch and efficiency with which the bounty of the United States was organized to relieve suffering across the sea made a sight, as one comment said, "which men and angels may rejoice in." American relief for Ireland heralded the entrance of a great humane force into the affairs of the world.

The first relief movement started, as had so many other Irish causes, in Boston among the Irish when the *Britannia* from Liverpool arrived on November 20, 1845, with news of impending famine and a letter in the New York *Tribune* described the bleak prospects. Father Thomas J. O'Flaherty, once editor of the Boston *Jesuit,* first Catholic temperance crusader in New England and a central figure in the St. Mary's Church riot, organized the Irish Charitable Relief Fund at a meeting of December 2, which was followed by a great public meeting on December 8, the first public assembly in the United States for Irish assistance. The congregation of a laboring men's church in East Boston emptied its pockets on the first appeal, and "King" Daniel Crowley, the contractor, collected $1100 in nine days in Boston and East Boston.

But a letter from Thomas D'Arcy McGee, now active politically in Dublin, threw cold water on Boston relief as premature. He suggested that support of O'Connell's Repeal campaign provided the best means of aiding Ireland and thrust home a point bound to strike Irish sensibilities: do not force a feeling of pauperism on Ireland, he urged. An open communication in the *Pilot,* from a priest who signed himself "Clericus Hibernicus," advised Father O'Flaherty to abandon the whole business, return the money to the contributors and tell them "the Irish people will not accept the *beggars'* charity, and that you now glory in the national pride that dictated the *refusal.*"

Father O'Flaherty rejected the suggestion of McGee and the advice of the priest, but suddenly the controversy and the organization ended. Father O'Flaherty unexpectedly died. A year later, Rev. James O'Reilly, who had been active in the relief society, sighed: "Oh! what a glorious fund would have since been raised, did they but then hear us and cooperate with us!"

3

During the spring, summer, and autumn of 1846, no sense of urgency pressed for American relief. The Irish themselves held hopes of a good 1846 potato crop to reprieve the damage of 1845. Enthusiastic Repealers followed the McGee line that the surest guarantee against famine was an independent Irish parliament and expected the distress would bring England to terms.

By the middle of November, however, disturbing reports of another failure spread, and the *National Intelligencer* in Washington quoted from a Pittsburgh paper a call to Irishmen:

> How can we sit down at our tables ladened with the bounties of Providence and not reflect that hundreds of thousands of Irishmen are pining in hunger, and dying, yes, absolutely *dying of starvation!* We appeal to you. Will you do nothing for your suffering countrymen? Thousands of dollars were raised a few years ago for Repeal. Can nothing be raised for bread?

The first public meeting gathered on American initiative under the charge of Americans for Irish relief was held in Washington on November 24, 1846, with the venerable editor of the *National Intelligencer*, Colonel William W. Seaton, mayor of Washington, as presiding officer. This meeting started similar assemblies in Brooklyn, Jersey City, Philadelphia, Baltimore, Pittsburgh, St. Louis, Dubuque, and a large gathering in New York on the day after Christmas.

But it was the Quakers who impressed upon the United States the extent of the misery and needs of the Irish now faced with the total loss of the 1846 potato crop; and, of even more momentous service, they provided the machinery of administering relief as the connecting link with the increasing number of American local relief organizations. Americans had the will to share their bounty with Ireland, but they lacked the experience and the knowledge of the techniques to forward food, clothing, and money. The reputable Quakers willingly showed the way and filled the want. When American assistance responded generously, the Quakers in Ireland had organization perfected to receive and distribute it.

The Quakers of Dublin on November 13, 1846, organized the Central Relief Committee and issued an address of the Society of Friends in Ireland explaining its purpose. Copies were sent to Friends in America and with customary diligence and efficiency they set about soliciting funds from their own members. The *Freeman's Journal*, praising the work of the Quakers in Ireland, England, and the United States, wrote: "It is impossible to look on efforts of benevolence so modestly, and withal, so efficiently prosecuted, without experiencing emotions of pleasure." The untiring efforts of the Quaker body as a whole placed people of Catholic Irish blood in eternal debt to the Society of Friends.

The American relief campaign started rolling with will and vigor during February, 1847. The first ships to reach the United States in January, 1847, after a month's lack of news from abroad, brought confirmation beyond dispute of the total loss throughout Ireland of the potato crop and the gaunt distress in the land.

In Boston, Bishop Fitzpatrick mounted the pulpit of the Cathedral on Sunday, February 7, and read his sad and moving pastoral. At St. Mary's Church, the aged pastor, Rev. Patrick Flood, poured forth his love for his native land and as he told of her afflictions the congregation, all with personal ties in that darkened land, broke into tears and the pastor bowed his head under the emotional strain, his cheeks wet with uncontrollable sorrow and his voice stilled. That night a relief committee was organized at the Cathedral and on March 1 Bishop Fitzpatrick forwarded $20,000 to Archbishop Crolly of Armagh, the primate of Ireland, to be followed with $4000 two months later. Its historian estimated that the Boston diocese, in one form or other, sent $150,000 for Irish relief.

On the next day, an address from Boston on Irish relief, with an imposing list of sponsors from its business, social, and political leadership, was broadcast on the new electric telegraph and made a strong impression on the country. Two weeks later, urged forward by the Quaker poet, John Greenleaf Whittier, and the black news from Ireland, the civic and political leaders of Boston called a great public meeting addressed by President Everett of Harvard and Dr. Samuel G. Howe, the veteran of the Greek War of Independence. The business skill for which Boston was noted organized what was perhaps the most efficient body in America in the management of Irish relief. This work of mercy was carried on at a time when anti-Irish nativist spirit ran high and mobs invaded the Boston Irish quarters spoiling for a fight.

4

The most romantic episode of American relief developed from the Boston meeting. Captain Robert B. Forbes, who had skippered a ship in the China trade as a lad and was now a merchant prince of Boston, conceived the idea of using a sloop of war to carry a relief cargo to Ireland — "a vessel of wrath" converted into "a vessel of mercy fitted for glory."

Though engaged in the Mexican War, Congress put the man-of-war *Jamestown,* then in the Charlestown Navy Yard, at the disposal of the Boston relief committee and Captain Forbes came out of retirement to command its voyage to Ireland, "on her errand of mercy." Former captains of Forbes ships in the China trade came forward to act as mates, and he had no trouble in recruiting a voluntary crew. As befitted the trip, loading commenced on St. Patrick's Day by the freely given brawn of the Boston Laborers' Aid Society, all Irishmen, while Captain Forbes prayed that "all the good saints may bless the enterprise." The Irish came down to the wharf with sacks of wheat and flour and bags of potatoes, asking that he put it aboard, and many asked to be shipped as hands before the mast.

With the ship trimmed of her war fittings and the hold filled with eight hundred tons of foodstuffs, the *Jamestown* left the Charlestown Navy Yard on March 28, 1847, to the cheers of men and the waving of handkerchiefs by women who gathered along the banks to bid her a safe journey to the land of famine. Captain Forbes "cast anchor in Cork, outer harbor, *on the 12th April,*" as he underlined the date in his report, "exactly 15 days and 3 hours from the Navy Yard, Charlestown, without having lost a rope yarn," an unusually fast voyage.

British naval officers at Cork had had orders to give Captain Forbes every assistance; William Rathbone, the Liverpool Quaker, took over responsibility at Cork for the foodstuffs and arrangements for its distribution through the Roman Catholic clergy of County Cork; Father Mathew was on hand to greet Captain Forbes and express the gratitude of the Irish people. To them he represented the spirit of the great Republic in contrast with the niggling course of English rule. Children born in the Cork area at the time of the stay of the *Jamestown* were named "Forbes," "Boston," or "James."

The voyage of the *Jamestown* and the unassuming presence of Captain Forbes symbolized to the Irish people the American generosity which expected no reward and the spirit of magnanimity without ulterior motive. No compliment was too high, said the Cork *Advertiser*, "not for the *gift*: that is good, and for it we are thankful; but for the *feeling*, the *kindliness* in which it orginated."

5

On the day following the Boston address, a national call proceeded from Washington signed by Vice-President George Dallas and fifty members of Congress urging assistance to Ireland and appointing collectors of ports as agents of the executive committee to accept gifts. A tremendous crowd attended the public meeting at the Broadway Tabernacle on the night of February 17, and the substantial business community of New York put its influence behind relief. Subscriptions amounting to nearly $22,000 were entered that night. Relief headquarters was established in Wall Street where a committee sat daily to receive contributions, and a barge was fitted up in Lent's Basin for gifts of grain, provisions, and clothes.

Bishop Hughes ordered collections for Irish relief to be taken up in all churches of the diocese and transmitted the funds raised in Catholic churches to the Irish Quakers. He suspended subscriptions for the new seminary upon which he had set his heart. He announced that he would serve as a transmitting agent for all individual remittances for relatives and friends to Ireland above one pound sterling for those not handy to established agencies.

Late in February, Senator Crittenden of Kentucky and Representative Washington Hunt of New York introduced bills appropriating $500,-000 for the purchase of provisions to be tendered to Great Britain and transported on public ships of the United States for the relief of suffering in Ireland and in Scotland. In the midst of enthusiastic speeches in its support, Senator Niles introduced a word of caution. He feared that, without a parallel case in the legislative past, the Congress was setting a precedent. But what disturbed him mostly was that the United States government would, by the gift, take on an obligation that belonged to the British government. Were we to assume, he asked, that the richest nation in the world was not able to provide for its own subjects? Were we not sticking our noses in an affair that rightly did not concern us? Despite this warning, the Crittenden bill went sailing through the Senate by a thumping majority. The House, however, killed the appropriation by bottling it up in committee. Some powerful pressure had been exercised; it may have been by President Polk himself, who had a costly war on his hands.

By the end of February, the relief movement for Ireland engaged the whole United States, as William Lloyd Garrison wrote to his Quaker Abolitionist friend, Edward Allen, in Dublin:

> The number of public meetings that have been held on this subject is too great to be chronicled in this letter. Cities, towns, villages — whether near or remote — have been deeply stirred and are coming to the rescue in the spirit of universal brotherhood.

Protestant churches from one end of the country to the other held special collections for distress in Ireland. An appeal from the ladies of Dunmanaway, County Cork, to the ladies of America, was promptly answered: the first relief ship to sail for Ireland carried a cargo of foodstuffs purchased from funds raised by the women of New York. The golden voice of Henry Clay sounded around the United States pleading for generosity out of the national bounty.

A ball for Irish relief at Baltimore netted $2000. The cadets of West Point contributed $300. Irish laborers on the railroads gave one day's work, and contractors matched the sums. The Jewish synagogue in New York took up a large collection. The New York State legislators raised $1000 among themselves. Slaves on Southern plantations forwarded their mite through the owners or their slave churches. Soldiers on the Mexican war front passed the hat and were joined by the Mexican civilian populations in occupied towns. The Choctaw Indians met on their reservation and voted a gift to Irish relief. The officers and crew of the U.S.S. *United States* entered a subscription of $663. A little band of Boston Abolitionists collected $1000. Winchester, Virginia, announced a collection of three hundred barrels of corn and thirty barrels of flour. The members of the national House and Senate chipped in $1300, and the reporters in Congress raised $100 in a few minutes. The Boston *Pilot* exclaimed, "Well done, Porkopolis!" at the news Cincinnati had furnished five thousand barrels of provisions. The railroads carried all parcels and commodities marked for Irish relief free and the canals admitted cargoes of foodstuffs destined for Ireland without tolls.

6

As American relief for Ireland was organized by localities, without a national headquarters or central directing body, it is difficult to arrive at an accurate total of the cash collected or the value of the donations in kind. Incomplete returns published in the *American Almanac* toward the end of November gave a total of $651,712 contributed in cash and kind from sixteen cities and towns, with New York City the leader in donations but closely followed by Boston. These returns did not include cities like Newark, which fitted out its own ship, or St. Louis, Montgomery, Chicago or Hartford, which raised good sums, or the countless smaller communities. Indeed, in the spring, the Central Committee of Dublin had acknowledged the receipt of over $500,000 in money and food from the United States. The returns did not include the separate collection taken up by the Quakers or the collections in Catholic churches forwarded to the Irish hierarchy. An informed guess would put the total raised in the United States at over one million dollars. To a generation accustomed to think in astronomical terms of billions, this amount may seem trifling, but in the United States of 1847 it added up to a lot of money.

The Catholic Irish contributed to the general campaign in money or, as laborers and workers, by the cash equivalent of a day's work, and they put their bit into the collections on the Sundays set aside in Roman Catholic churches. But to them Irish relief did not represent, as to most Americans, personally disinterested aid to a faceless mass. Irish hunger, disease, and distress were stamped with clearly recognizable features of their own families and friends.

They responded to the Irish Famine in the ancient and traditional way of the race — they looked after their own. Putting money in a general pot for a general purpose of aiding the Irish was commendable in Americans, but the Catholic Irish tagged their assistance with a specific name in the form of a specific remittance to Ireland. The Catholic Irish laborer or female domestic made sure that his or her benevolence reached to the cabin he or she had in mind when Irish relief was talked. Benevolence was intimate and personal to him or her.

In 1846, before the general campaign started in the United States, the Irish in America had remitted $1,200,000 to relatives and friends in Ireland and each year until the crisis had been passed and until they had started relatives and friends for America, the amounts climbed

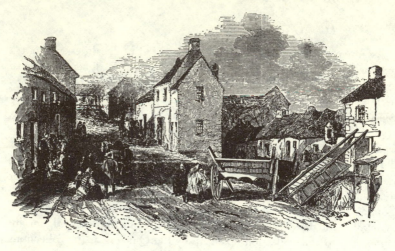

A FAMINE VILLAGE

higher and higher.* Servant girls mortgaged the future months to employers for an advance in wages to be sped off to Ireland and walked miles to a remittance agency so that more could be sent to a mother or brother by the savings in carfare. Laborers underwent sacrifices the more painful because of the small margin on which they existed.

They wanted to get their own out of Ireland to America. The most enduring effect of the Famine's cruel purge was the migration of Ireland's sons and daughters propelled in flight to other lands, principally America, which made the small and isolated Atlantic island one of the great motherlands of the Western World. Out of Ireland's pain and suffering was delivered a new estate removed from her hereditary acres.

3 9

"And Still They Come"

"In god's name, give us this generation out of the mouth of the Irish grave, to feed them, that they may live and not die!"

This was the anguished cry of the Boston *Pilot* in the middle of the

Famine emigration. Irish newspapers reported with growing apprehension the steady procession of people along the roads to the seaport towns, the crowded quays, the emigrant ships filled as soon as they had dropped anchor, the packed steamers for Liverpool. The tide of emigration was destined, they said, "to bear away on its bosom all that constitutes the bone and sinew of the country," leaving only "those whom destitution roots to the soil" to be a burden to the public. They counseled the people to stay. "For what?" asked the *Pilot*, "to show how desperately faithful, how bloodily beautiful a thing love of one's native soil is? 'Tis a cruel and false sentiment."

2

The New World had never seen the like before of the mass movement of emigrants from Europe to the United States in the decade and a half prior to the Civil War. They poured, or were dumped, into ports from Boston to New Orleans, but the concentration of the emigrant armadas on New York made that center of American shipping and commerce the great funnel from the Atlantic Ocean to the broad continent.

From May, 1847, when the New York Commissioners of Emigration first met and started to keep accurate records, to the end of 1860, Europeans to the number of 2,671,891 entered the United States by the port of New York. Of this total, 1,107,034, or nearly 45 per cent were natives of Ireland — the largest single nationality group. Of the Irish who arrived in New York during that period, 715,291, or nearly three fourths of their numbers, were bunched in the years 1848-1853, inclusive. The year 1851 was the peak, when the Irish quota amounted to 163,256, exceeding by 36,911 the whole number from other countries. Ireland, it was said, was "absolutely flinging herself on America." "And still they come," said the Americans.

3

The United States escaped the disaster of the 1847 Irish emigration to British North America that caught Quebec and Montreal unprepared. The American emigrant health record favorably contrasted with the black concentration of deaths at sea in English or Irish ships and in Quebec and Montreal in 1847.

Congressional legislation early in 1847 struck at the great evil of passenger transportation, overcrowding, but by raising the price of passage to the United States it forced Irish emigrants to take the cheaper route to British North America and contributed to the 1847 mass infected invasion of Canada and New Brunswick. Further legislation in 1848 required better ventilation on emigrant ships and adequate sea stores, water and cooking fuel against a distressed or prolonged journey.

The exposure of private emigrant poorhouses impressed New York with the need of a comprehensive public program to care for the thousands of newcomers. New York City required bonds of each emigrant passenger, which could be commuted by the payment of one dollar. Shipowners, not wanting to involve themselves with emigrants once landed from their ships, collected a dollar from each alien passenger and struck a bargain with professional bondsmen, usually passenger agents, who assumed responsibility for any who might be a public charge. This system developed into a larcenous racket. Rather than pay three dollars a week for the support of necessitous emigrants at the city almshouse, the rapacious bondsmen established their own poorhouses. An affidavit of the terrible conditions in one of these pens of squalor given by a group of Irishmen started an investigation which led to the state's responsibility for the emigrant. Through the hard work and political skill of Irish-born Andrew Carrigan, a produce merchant and treasurer of the Roman Catholic Orphan Asylum, and Thurlow Weed of the Albany *Journal,* the state legislature was persuaded to create in May, 1847, the New York Commissioners of Emigration.

Starting from scratch and learning from the lessons of experience, the Commissioners built up a complex of emigrant services and care that proved a valuable utility for directing the tide of emigration into the mainstream of America.

The state of New York hospitalized the emigrants ill with contagious diseases and erected a barrier at Quarantine against their spread. It furnished a haven for the ill and the exhausted until they had recovered. It offered a refuge for destitute aged, feeble and incapacitated. It took care of the young, the orphans and waifs. It provided an employment service for those looking for work and gave temporary help to the immediately distressed. It paid for the care of the mentally ill at the New York asylum.

This complex of care and services was maintained out of funds collected from the emigrants themselves and supervised by men, including the presidents of the German and Irish emigrant societies, who served without pay as a public-spirited duty.

The Commissioners of Emigration warred against the harpies and vultures who preyed on the emigrants along the New York waterfront, as in Liverpool. Only by isolating the emigrant from the fleecers could he be protected, and this was finally achieved in 1855, when the Commissioners leased Castle Garden, an old fort and public hall, and there established an all-inclusive emigrant depot under one roof. This predecessor to Ellis Island concluded the era of wide-open emigrant frauds. Men like Andrew Carrigan and Gregory Dillon, the dedicated president of the Irish Emigrant Society, had served the Irish emigrant well.

4

The first intimation in Boston of the character of the Famine emigration came with the arrival early in April, 1847, of the reeking *Thomas W. Sears* from Liverpool, loaded with iron, steel, hardware products and Irish emigrants "so weak and emaciated," wrote the Boston *Journal,* "that many of them could with difficulty crawl on shore," their condition "worse than that of any vessel which ever entered this port."

An Irish girl died on the way to the almshouse, and her father in the ensuing coroner's inquiry told of the death of his wife and four other children on the voyage from ship fever. A Liverpool passenger broker had cheated on fuel and provisions and because of secondhand casks he had furnished, a thousand gallons of water seeped out before discovery of the loss. Shortened food and water rations reduced the passengers to a suffering mass: of the 141 embarked, twenty-four died at sea and the poorhouse received sixteen ill with ship fever.

A week later Owen Drury, a newly landed emigrant from County Sligo, dropped dead in Hanover Street from the effects of fever, and the clothes of his two companions were so saturated with the stench of the steerage that the police at the station to which they were removed became sick. The Young Catholic's Friend Society took up a collection to bury an Irish emigrant who had died in the street, apparently from starvation. The increase of the poorhouse population to 480 included 181 cases of ship fever and a total sick list close to 350.

On May 17, the British brig *Mary* from Cork arrived in Boston with forty-six steerage passengers. As in New York, the state of Massachusetts levied on the emigrant passengers arriving by sea a two-dollar head tax or a bond of one thousand dollars against being chargeable. The officials, taking a look at the passengers, ordered the captain to post bonds. This he would not, or could not, do, and he directed the pilot to turn the ship around to sail for the British provinces, whereupon the passengers mutinied and a crew from a revenue cutter boarded the *Mary* to quell the Irish frustrated from landing.

About the time Captain Forbes returned with the *Jamestown* from its errand of mercy, the Boston Common Council, taking example from New York, built an improvised hospital and poorhouse for emigrants on Deer Island in Boston Harbor, which the Irish christened "Lord Nomanby's Palace," after a landlord who cleared his estate by shipping off tenants.

The pouring in of Irish emigrants by way of the New Brunswick-Eastport route and by sea direct from British and Irish ports — upwards of a thousand landed in Boston on one day, April 10, 1847 — provoked rising nativist hostility to demonstrations, adopting the Orange procedure. In the middle of June, the nativists, with flag, drum and fife, paraded through the streets of the crowded Fort Hill Irish section, organized a meeting in its heart, read resolutions and delivered harangues against the Irish, Catholics and emigrant paupers, then marched off again. Demonstrations continued during the summer and fall of 1847.

The climax of the 1847 anti-emigrant agitation came with a meeting at Faneuil Hall on November 14 over which the mayor presided. This meeting, not exclusively nativist in character, reflected the concern of sober Boston opinion over the destitution of the Famine emigrants which was piling up a social problem for Boston and a burden of relief costs. The emigrants who came in by sea paid a two-dollar head tax for the support of services, but hundreds entered the state by land without paying any tax and their support, if destitute, rested on the treasury of the commonwealth.

A resolution adopted at the Faneuil Hall meeting petitioned the Massachusetts legislature for a law making railroads, steamboats, and stages which transported foreigners into Massachusetts liable for bonds against their becoming public charges; that is, applying to overland emigrants the same requirement of bonding as those who entered by sea.

By the act of May 24, 1851, the General Court of Massachusetts did just that: it created a frontier guard against emigrants by land who might become public charges. Agents met trains of the several railroads converging on Boston and the New York line steamers at the Fall River terminal, lined up emigrants and recorded identifying data. If emigrants appeared likely candidates for public support, they were denied admission into Massachusetts and handed over to the railroads or steamship company, which returned them at their own expense to points of origin. Massachusetts presented bills to the companies for support of emigrants who had entered by their lines and later became public charges. But the 1851 provision had been written with the character of the unfortunate 1847 emigration in mind, since which the condition of Irish emigration had steadily improved in health and appearance. By 1854, the state concluded that the expense of the frontier guard cost more than the benefits and, besides, the objections of the carriers held merit.

The 1851 legislation, fashioned like the New York law to administer the emergency of extraordinary emigrant numbers, established Commissioners of Alien Passengers and Foreign Paupers, with oversight of newly created state almshouses and directions to weed out those able to support themselves, the supposition being, in line with nativist thinking, that the Irish preferred a poorhouse existence to work. Yet the reports showed two major classes of pauper Irish: orphans, and victims of that decimating scourge of the Irish, consumption, whom Dr. Charles A. Ruggles of the Bridgewater almshouse had heard say that "they come here to die; having expended their all in pursuit of health, now bereft of money and friends, they come here to be made as comfortable as the nature of the disease will admit."

Massachusetts hostility to the Famine emigration showed itself in the public pressure in 1849 to separate the Irish mental cases from the native-born in an institution solely for the Irish, which a Joint Committee of the legislature on the subject of insanity in 1849 honorably resisted as "an invidious distinction . . . not reconcilable with the humane and tolerant spirit of our age, and not in accordance with that lofty design of our institutions to make all who occupy American soil, American citizens."

5

The deep-grained nativist prejudice against the Irish emigrant in Massachusetts expressed itself ignobly in the deportation not out of the state but back overseas to their native land of Irish paupers and mentally ill that shocked the nation with its revelation in 1851. The practice was not new. Calvin Bailey, the Superintendent of Alien Passengers, appointed under the alien passenger act of 1837, had quietly used the emigrant head tax fund to deport destitute aliens instead of relieving them, as the act stipulated. British Consul Grattan in Boston reported to his government in 1843 that Bailey "never *relieves* the foreigners with money, but sends as many as he possibly can back to England and Ireland; and these are always persons entirely destitute."

Gregory Dillon of the Irish Emigrant Society in the spring of 1841 came upon the deportation of Eliza Sullivan, a native of Ireland, who had lived in the United States for eighteen years and the Massachusetts town of Southbridge for seven. She had applied twice for relief, and the selectmen got rid of her. Since the *Daniel Webster* from Boston to Liverpool had a full complement, an officer accompanied her and her child, an American citizen by birth, to New York and put them on the *Shannon* for Liverpool. Upon finding the pair, Dillon invoked a New York statute fixing a maximum penalty of ten years for anybody who seized a person against his will and shipped him out of the state, upon hearing which the Boston officer disappeared.

The anti-Abolitionists capitalized the Eliza Sullivan incident to belabor the Abolitionist "Christians," who had vowed to disobey the Fugitive Slave Act of 1850. These Massachusetts men, said one newspaper, "would dissolve the Union . . . sooner than give back a black bondsman to slavery" but "would give up to slavery, starvation and death the poor white bondswoman who had the' misfortune to be placed within their power, to sojourn amongst them, and mistake them for christians." The *Pilot,* in an extremely violent statement, regretted that Mrs. Sullivan was "not a black woman" but "only an Irishwoman" for whom the "fanatics . . . haven't a wink of sympathy."

Massachusetts, nevertheless, continued to deport Irish paupers, in one instance a batch of between twenty and thirty in one week from the Boston Police Court. The sickening story came back of six Irish women deported from the insane asylum in Worcester, five of whom were found wandering helplessly around a Dublin quay, not knowing where they were.

In 1855, a court order shipped Mary Williams and her infant child Bridget to Ireland. The Boston *Daily Advertiser,* in an article headed "An Infamous Case of Extradition," cried down shame on the people who in the previous year had staged a near-rebellion in an attempt to rescue Anthony Burns, a fugitive slave, from officers of the law in Boston and had decked the city in mourning when the frightened runaway was marched to a ship surrounded by companies of militia, while church bells tolled, but had neither pity nor help for an Irish pauper woman and her child, who were also being returned by the law.

But a voice with a Boston accent spoke up and said the banishment of Irish paupers and lunatics by the Commonwealth of Massachusetts was wrong. Peleg W. Chandler, descendant of an old New England family, a distinguished lawyer and scholarly law reporter, editor and author, was in 1854 a member of the Executive Council of Massachusetts and *ex officio* a member of the Commissioners of Alien Passengers and Foreign Paupers. He added a note to that body's report for 1854 which, exposing the dangerously arbitrary character of the law and its procedures and defending the cause of the depressed Irish, was a classic of the liberal Yankee's sense of justice and fair play.

"The undersigned," he wrote, "has no idea of keeping silence on this subject because the popular feeling is now swinging heavily against these unfortunate people, nor of yielding to prejudice what the law does not sanction."

After explaining that the law was so framed as to deny Irish paupers the due process of justice, he asked what offense they had committed to render them liable to transportation on the word solely of a justice of the peace. He wrote:

> Some of them have been laborious men, honest, useful citizens, and have in their small way contributed to the wealth of the State. Some of them have paid "head money" when they came here; and for some bonds have been given for their support in case they became paupers. If the Commonwealth desires to adopt the policy of preventing foreign immigration entirely, if she chooses to hold her sister States or foreign countries responsible for sending paupers here, let her do so in a suitable manner, with all proper firmness, *let her select antagonists about her own size,* and not wreak vengeance on poor wretches whose only fault is poverty and whose only heritage is misery.

He showed that every Abolitionist objection to the Fugitive Slave Act — that it was "unjust in principle, unnecessarily harsh in its detail, and cruel in its application" — applied with equal force to the deportation law.

While Massachusetts continued such a law, he said, its citizens could not very well declaim against the Fugitive Slave Act. "A black man," he concluded, "is no better, and is entitled to no more security as to his personal rights . . . than a white man, although the former may be a fugitive slave, and the latter a pauper and an Irishman."

It took courage to say this in the midst of heated Abolitionist emotionalism and anti-Irish prejudice.

6

The state of the emigrants arriving in 1847 stirred the formation of Irish emigrant societies on the model of the New York society. British Consul Grattan had organized an emigrant society in Boston in 1843, but the distrustful Irish refused their cooperation, suspecting it to be an agency to lure laborers to the plantations of Jamaica when in reality (and this the Irish did not know) Grattan hoped to drain off the surplus Irish in Boston to New Brunswick. As in New York, the Boston Irish, with the exception of the faithful reliables and the clergy, withheld support. They believed the head tax collected from arriving emigrants put the responsibility for their care on the state, and some took the individualistic attitude that as they had had to make their own way, let others who came after do the same. Not until 1850 were the means found to organize a Boston society, which survived until 1857, providing useful auxiliary service to the official commissioner of alien passengers.

A Jesuit, Rev. E. J. Barbelin, formed the St. Joseph's Society in Philadelphia to protect emigrants. After the arrival in April, 1847, of the ship *Hampden* with destitute Irish passengers, the well-established Hibernian Relief Society set up emergency aid in Baltimore and Rev. James Dolan raised subscriptions to start the Manual Labor School for the cure of orphans. The sight of Irish passengers on the *Stephen Baldwin,* "mere living skeletons," hastened the substantial Catholic Irish of New Orleans to organize a society, establish two depots for the distressed, and provide means for emigrants to proceed up the Mississippi to friends. Groups of Irishmen organized relief societies in St. Louis, Chicago, and Detroit.

7

Of all the frauds and swindles to victimize untutored Irish emigrants, none was more vile than the systematized robbery in remittances to Ireland and the sale of worthless passenger certificates by crooked or fly-by-night passenger agents. The tragedy was double-barreled: it robbed the emigrant in America of hard-earned money and cast down into despair and deeper destitution those who had looked forward to a remittance or certificate to escape from the famine-stricken land. They placed their money in the hands of a passenger agent "and lo! 'tis swindled," wrote Father O'Reilly of Woonsocket, whose whole Irish congregation had been fleeced by a dishonest agent.

A daughter had paid for the passage of the Connelly family from Ireland. They had sold out their possessions and waited for the certificates but, said Father O'Reilly, they had been for months "roaming houseless and penniless in a land of famine," now being "as a wieff on the world's wide common." Poor Irish laborers had worked for six months on the roads in Indiana, walked a hundred miles to Cincinnati to add the savings to the remittances, and the passenger agency had made off with the funds. The crash of supposedly reputable houses, which had overextended themselves in currency speculations, left a trail of misery.

The New York Irish Emigrant Society manfully fought frauds and exposed swindling agencies. The use by Bishop Hughes of the society's office to transmit individual remittances taught the Irish its good reputation. But as abuses continued with the Famine emigration, the society established its own fund in a bank in Ireland. Out of this experiment and with the advice of Bishop Hughes, the principal officers of the society established in 1850 a banking business, primarily for Irish savings, which today still flourishes as one of the best known American financial institutions, the Emigrant Industrial Savings Bank.

8

In 1855, when the migration had spent itself, the *Pilot* drew a broad conclusion of the character of the Famine emigration: "It is not so good

A CONTEMPORARY DRAWING OF FAMINE VICTIMS

an emigration as it was previous to the famine." Ten years before, prior to the beginning of the Famine, Thomas D'Arcy McGee had described the "previous to the famine" emigration as not so good as the Irish settlers of the Emmet-MacNeven-Sampson period. But the Irish settled in the United States before 1845 universally agreed that the Famine emigration was "not so good."

To the Americans who had looked upon the emigrants as they landed or saw them in city streets, the Famine emigration looked like a plague let loose in a fair land — bundles of disease, destitution, squalor, and hopelessness.

The Famine emigration represented a cross-section of depressed Irish life. If it included laborers, cottiers, and small tenant farmers, who had lacked the means, incentive and will to migrate in pre-Famine days, it also included strong and comfortable farmers, reduced by the exactions of the Famine, along with the sons and daughters of farmers, the class from which previous emigration had been considerably drawn. It included clerks, shopkeepers, mechanics, and teachers. It was primarily a rural emigration. It was poor, in an economic meaning, because the Irish countryside was poor, made even poorer by the Famine. Family groups migrated, aged parents as well as children.

The pre-Famine Catholic Irish communities and the Catholic Irish press entertained no illusions about this emigration, but they asked the humanity of America to give it asylum. They admitted the social problem of the emigration and its costs in relief, but they argued that what the distressed took from the wealth of the country for their care would be absorbed many times over in the wealth the strength of the emigrants would add in building America through labor. If the Irishmen did "the meanest portion," they said, " 'tis the most essential portion."

The parents and the elderly of the emigration were, as a general rule, a lost generation. In balancing the account of the emigration, wrote the *Pilot* in 1855, no political economist "can fail to observe the enormous entry which the children and grand-children of Catholic immigrants leave on the right side of the account."

The tremendous Famine emigration, crowded into a relatively brief number of years, contributed to the outbreak of the Know-Nothing agitation in the 1850s, but when the nativists demonstrated against them in 1847, the Irish tauntingly asked if they spoiled to fight, why didn't they go to Mexico, like the Irish.

4 0

They Fight Catholic Mexico

As THE MEXICAN WAR tested the young officers who would command large armies in the mighty civil strife less than a decade and a half away, so the battlefields of the Rio Grande and the Valley of Mexico proved the merits and loyalty of the Catholic Irish as fighting men in American service, in the numbers they furnished both to the regular army and in the volunteer companies, and in the casualty lists.

On January 1, 1846, with a new president of Mexico on the way to power sworn to redeem the national honor by driving the Americans out of Texas while President Polk in Washington awaited developments, the standing army of the United States numbered 7194 men in its rank and file. During the year 1845, the Register of Enlistments recorded 2135 natives of Ireland recruited or re-enlisted. With this number added to the Irishmen already in service, the Washington correspondent of *Freeman's Journal* hardly exaggerated when he wrote soon after the opening of the Mexican War: "It must be a source of pride to the Irish Catholic citizens to know that Gen. Taylor's army consists of more than one half of their countrymen."

From July, 1846, to May, 1848, that is, during the course of the Mexican War, the Irish-born who enlisted in the regular army numbered 2664 and, in addition, 1012 Irish-born enlisted for the duration of the conflict — a total of 3676. In the Register of Enlistments from July, 1846, to May, 1848, the enlistment of "Mc's" alone took a good eleven pages — three hundred names.

Starting in the 1820s, with the first wave of emigration, the Catholic Irish enlisted in American military establishments, following an ancient practice of serving under a foreign flag as an escape from the sodden countryside life of Ireland and in accordance with a nature that relished the occupation of soldiering. The casualty list of the long and botched war to put down brave Osceola and the Seminole Indians in the 1830s and early 1840s carried the names of the Dugans, O'Rileys, Bogans, O'Danaghs, and Egans massacred with Colonel Dade, killed at Lake Okeechobee or near Fort Micanopy, or dead in the fever hospitals of Tampa.

Americans held the rank and file of the army in open contempt and a military career as "the least honored." "Strangers to the soil, emigrants without home or hearth," wrote the editor of *Niles' Weekly* in 1846, "constitute the greater portion of the enlisted men." Irish and German emigrants constituted this "greater portion."

Want of employment was the main reason for emigrant enlistments. Adjutant General R. Jones in 1848, reporting for the year 1847, wrote that "in the States where the greatest number of men have been recruited, are situated our large commercial cities, where vast numbers of that class of men who enter the ranks of the army resort for employment, and where, also, vast numbers of emigrants are constantly arriving."

The Registers of the U. S. Army showed that enlistments of the Irish-born stepped up during the cold season, when work for the day laborer was scarce. The number of recruits signed up in Eastport and Houlton, Maine, in Oswego, in Sackett's Harbor and such points of emigrant entry from Canada and New Brunswick meant that the new soldiers were not far distant in space and time from an emigrant ship.

These Irishmen belonged to the regular army, but as soon as the call went out Catholic Irishmen volunteered from civilian life for the war. Adjutant General Jones reported that in many of the volunteer regiments enrolled during the Mexican War "not only natives of Europe singly entered . . . in numbers, but that entire companies of Germans and Irishmen were mustered into the service."

The Irish militia companies included the famous Jasper Greens of Savannah, under the command of Captain McMahon, proprietor of the City Hotel, which engaged in a memorable brawl on the Rio Grande, provoked by another Georgia company that taunted them as "Irish sons of bitches"; the Mobile Volunteers, headed by Captain Dasha; three full companies from New Orleans, described as strapping Irish lads, who departed after a rousing speech by Father Mullen, later a vigorous partisan of the Confederate cause; the Emmet Guards of Albany, the first company in New York enrolled under the orders of the Governor; four companies in Philadelphia, including one recruited from the Repeal Association; the Montgomery Guards of Cincinnati; the Montgomery Guards of Detroit; the Pittsburgh Hibernia Greens; an Illinois company under Captain Patrick Lawler; a St. Louis company outfitted by subscriptions raised by Bryan Mullanphy, son of old John and himself an officer in the war; the New York Volunteers, who, fighting under the command of General Shields, distinguished themselves at the Battle of Churubusco and the storming of Chapultepec. A Massachusetts regiment was formed, commanded by Caleb Cushing, with B Company made up of Boston Irish under Captain John Barry.

2

The army of Zachary Taylor, "Old Rough and Ready," a frontier veteran competent to fight Indians, marched from Corpus Christi on the Nueces River, which then marked the temporary boundary between Texas and Mexico, and arrived at the Rio Grande opposite the Mexican town of Matamoros on March 28, 1846. Washington described the move as precautionary against the Mexican threat of war. Detractors of President Polk regarded it as a design to provoke war and achieve his expansionist ambition to seize California as the nation's western boundary.

Mexican cavalry crossed the Rio Grande on April 24, 1846, and on the next day cut down the reconnoitering force of seventy-five sent out by General Taylor. "Hostilities may now be considered as commenced," Taylor reported on April 26, and on May 13 Polk signed the war bill.

In the first encounter, American casualties numbered sixty-three, including William Ryan, who formerly kept a tavern on Water Street in Philadelphia, killed; Private Patrick McLaughlin, wounded; and William McGinn, Patrick Linn, Dennis O'Neil, Barker O'Ryan, Peter O'Rafferty, James Gibbons, William Cunningham, Charles Burke, and Patrick Ward, captured.

The battles of Palo Alto and Resaca de la Palma early in May drove the Mexicans back across the Rio Grande. Officers in their reports mentioned, that is, commended, Sergeant McMaley, who was wounded, and Corporal McCauley for their part in the gallant charge of Captain May's dragoons; the "distinguished behavior" of Sergeant Major Maloney and Corporals Farrel and McFarlen, who, with six privates, captured a gun defended by a hundred and fifty Mexicans; the "conduct" of Corporal O'Sullivan, who seized a Mexican lieutenant as prisoner and later captured an enemy gun. The Irish had started well for American arms.

Sergeant Major Maurice Maloney, brevetted second lieutenant and later commissioned by the President, represented a familiar type of Catholic Irishman who loved soldiering. An emigrant from a County Limerick farm, he had enlisted at twenty-four and was serving his third hitch, a veteran of ten years, at the outbreak of the war. For "gallant and meritorious conduct" in the Mexico City fighting, he received promotion to first lieutenant and at the Civil War held rank as a lieutenant colonel in the regular army, an exceptional career for an enlisted man at that time.

An Irishman, who could not resist the temptation to crow, wrote to the Philadelphia *Spirit of the Times*:

> In the official dispatches from "Old Rough and Ready," giving the particulars of our recent brilliant success of the Rio Grande, I find that the name of every non-commissioned officer sounds awfully

Irish, if not *Catholic.* What can it mean? Surely men with such names cannot have acted so bravely!

The citizens of New Orleans raised a general subscription and had gold medals struck for the Irish noncoms cited in the opening battles of the war.

William F. Robinson, a Protestant Irish-born graduate of Yale and Washington correspondent of the *Buffalo Express,* hammered at the insubstantiality of nativist distrust of the loyalty of foreigners by publishing the casualty lists of the two battles of Palo Alto and Resaca de la Palma: of the total number of 152 noncommissioned officers and men killed or wounded, forty-three were Irishmen, seventeen Germans, seven English and five Scottish and, with individuals from other countries, added up to seventy-two foreign-born, or nearly one half of the casualties.

The Albany *Evening Journal* struck the same note in reply to the nativist assertion that Catholic soldiers would not fight against Catholic Mexico: "If any thing was needed to wipe out this vile calumny, we have it in the long and fatal list of 'Killed and Wounded.' It is only necessary to read the names to see that two-thirds if not three-fourths of all who shed their blood in that gallant action were Irishmen."

The Catholic Irish press, while regretting the human losses of war, universally upheld the American cause, "so long," said the *Freeman's Journal,* "as our country is dwelling, under tents, on the field of battle." It took a jab at the Abolitionists and Protestant clergy who opposed the war as a conspiracy of the slave power by declaring that a citizen had a right to express opinions on the war but not to throw obstacles in the way of its successful prosecution. The *Pilot,* with no direct religious ties, used the war performance of the Catholic Irish to lambaste the nativists, openly spoiling to fight the Irish in Boston. "In times of peace we Irish are not fit to enjoy 'life, liberty, and the pursuit of happiness,'" it mocked, "but when the country needs our aid, we are capital, glorious fellows." "Where is the valiant General Dearborn?" it asked concerning a prominent nativist, who used to say "We will do our own voting and our own *fighting!*" Each week it reprinted from the *National Police Gazette* the official list of deserters furnished by the Adjutant General's office, which invariably showed that American-born deserters outnumbered the total of foreign-born deserters.

The contribution of the Catholic Irish to the United States in the

Mexican War lay primarily in the fighting men of the rank and file and the sturdy backbone of every army — the noncommissioned officers. One cannot examine the Mexican War casualty lists without being struck by the prominence of Gaelic names among the killed and wounded, until at the Battle of Mexico, which exacted the severest toll of the war, the Donahues, Sullivans, Sheehans, Murphys, McMahons, and McGuires appear in profusion beside the familiar American names. They were buried in unhereditary graves beneath a warm sun far from the rain and mist of Cork, Kilkenny, and Donegal.

3

Of the many Catholic Irish officers who served in the Mexican War, three stood out for gallant and distinguished conduct.* They were Lieutenant John Paul Jones O'Brien, Colonel Bennet Riley, and Brigadier General James Shields.

Lieutenant O'Brien, born in Philadelphia in 1817 of Catholic Irish parentage and a graduate of West Point in 1836, had stirred the dovecotes of the army at Newport News in 1843 by refusing to march soldiers to a Sunday service conducted by a Protestant chaplain, because he believed they had the right not to enter if they pleased.

At the Battle of Buena Vista in northern Mexico, some 4700 American troops, mostly volunteers, under General Taylor faced an army of some 15,000 Mexicans commanded by the fantastic General Santa Anna, the "Napoleon of the West" and dictator of Mexico, on February 23, 1847. In the first major attack by the Mexicans, O'Brien's guns on the left of the American line had blazed away against the enemy in deadly fashion, but left alone when the infantry retreated upon order of their commander, O'Brien saved his guns by hauling them away with ropes. Later in the day, circumstances placed him in a somewhat similar position. With only a section of guns under his charge, supported by one gun in the rear by Lieutenant Thomas, of later Chickamauga fame, he found himself between a major offensive by the Mexicans and a vacuum behind yet to be filled by reinforcements. He had the choice: stand and fight and delay the Mexican advance until rein-

---

* *The Journal of the American Irish Historical Society,* XXVI, 257-259, contains a list of Irish officers, but they appear to have been chosen by name and are not differentiated by place of birth or by religion.

forcements came up and risk the loss of his guns, or save his guns and risk a swarming in by the Mexicans that might have turned the battle in their favor. O'Brien chose to stand and, though eventually he lost the guns, his decision delayed the enemy until Bragg and Sherman came up with batteries to drive the Mexicans back in disorder and, as General Taylor said, "saved the day." The guns, later recaptured, stand at West Point: "O'Brien's bull dogs," they are called. General Taylor mentioned Lieutenant O'Brien for coolness and courage under fire.

With the victory at Buena Vista, fighting ended in the north of Mexico and a new front was opened in the south, the first objective the port of Vera Cruz and then a march up the Cortez road to the capital city of Mexico, with General Winfield Scott, commander-in-chief of the American military forces, in personal charge. In the siege of Vera Cruz, General James Shields and Colonel Bennet Riley were prominent and from now on would be active figures in the succession of American victories.

Riley, born of Catholic Irish parents in St. Mary's County, Maryland, in 1787, had enlisted in the War of 1812 as an ensign of riflemen and remained in the army as a career. He was assigned to a regiment on the Mississippi frontier and spent the next quarter of a century fighting Indians, in the Dakota Territory, along the historic caravan route of the traders from St. Louis to Santa Fe, in the Black Hawk War and in the swamps of Florida against the Seminoles. At the opening of the Mexican War he had risen to the rank of colonel in command of the 2nd Infantry, but, as a soldier of experience and ability, he was speedily placed as head of a brigade in General Twiggs's division. In the same division was Brigadier General James Shields, who had arrived in Mexico in December, 1846.

General Shields, who became a national figure of heroic size by his personal bravery in battle, was the most distinguished Catholic Irishman to emerge from the Mexican War. His whole career furnished an interesting story, not least of which were the unique distinction of election as United States Senator by three different states and a certain immortality from his unfought duel with Abraham Lincoln.

James Shields, born in County Tyrone on May 12, 1806, came from a Catholic Irish family which had fought on the losing side of James II at the Boyne and lost its property. An uncle returned from America, a veteran of the Revolution and the War of 1812, gave him a taste for military life; a veteran of the Napoleonic wars taught him the use of the sword; another uncle, a priest, led him into the classics; and another old soldier grounded him in French.

In America, he worked for a while as a purser on a merchantman but gave up the sea to enlist in the Florida war. Shields settled in the then frontier town of Kaskaskia, the territorial capital of Illinois, to study law and supported himself by teaching French. Admitted to the bar in 1832, he was in 1835 elected to the legislature as a Democrat from the overwhelmingly Whig county of Randolph and took his seat in 1836 along with Lincoln and Stephen Douglas. After four years in the legislature, he was elected auditor of Illinois, whose capital had been removed to Springfield, and in this office challenged Lincoln to a duel.

In trying to straighten out the state's tangled finances from the panic of 1837 and overextension in canal building, Shields ordered that only silver and gold money be accepted in payment of taxes, which aroused a vigorous Whig attack upon the young Irishman. There appeared in the *Sangamo Journal* a coarse and vituperative article on Shields, deriding his manners and appearance as an Irishman. A second article similar in tone followed. They had been written by Julia Jayne and her friend, Mary Todd, to whom Lincoln was engaged, and when Shields asked the editor the name of the anonymous author he was told Lincoln took full responsibility. Shields immediately challenged Lincoln to a duel.

Lincoln's seconds named cavalry broadswords and the place a sand bar in the Mississippi River, on the Missouri side, to escape the Illinois law against dueling. While the seconds discussed procedure, the lanky Lincoln practiced swishes with the sword but that was the extent of the combat. Lincoln and Shields went into a conference and, instead of squaring off, emerged as good friends, which they remained. Lincoln later wrote what amounted to an apology in the *Sangamo Journal*.

While Shields sat as a justice of the Supreme Court of Illinois, President Polk called him to Washington to be Commissioner of the General Land Office in 1845. With the start of the Mexican War, Shields became restless and Polk appointed him a brigadier general of volunteers. Too many Whig generals hogged the spotlight, and Polk felt the country (and the party) needed the service of good solid Democrats to whip the Mexicans: Shields qualified by his earlier military experience but the general's commission wafted the Washington smell of Democratic politics. Shields, however, honored the appointment by gallant and brave conduct as a soldier.

When he took command of his companies, Shields was described as "a stout, soldier-like man with a heavy mustache, black hair and brilliant eyes." Reports uniformly referred to his urbanity of manner, pleasing speech, and native courtesy. He possessed a driving energy, and his courage at times bordered on the reckless.

At Cerro Gordo, both General Shields and Colonel Riley distinguished themselves in a surprise attack over difficult terrain on the flank of the Mexicans, and Shields went down with a bullet through his breast near his lung. Recovered, General Shields took part in the Contreras-Churubusco engagement on the outskirts of Mexico City where he and Colonel Riley were among the commanders who stormed the formidable convent-church of San Mateo, in the most stubborn fighting of the war. Inside San Mateo's walls and carrying the burden was the San Patricio Battalion, the so-called "Irish deserters," headed by Major John Riley, the most hated figure of the Mexican War, who was finally taken by another Catholic Irishman.

In his report on Churubusco, dated August 24, 1847, General Shields wrote: "In this last engagement, my command captured 380 prisoners, including 60 officers; of this number 42 had deserted from the American army during the war, and at their head was found the notorious O'Riley, who had fought against our troops at Monterey and elsewhere."

4

On that August day at Churubusco, seventy-two deserters in all, the remnants of the San Patricio Battalion, were captured; and their bizarre story, which has been told with more gilding than accuracy, holds particular pertinence here because at the time the American people believed the battalion to be composed solidly of Irishmen and because the legend persisted.

Outward evidence buttressed such a conclusion. The battalion's flag carried on one side a crude reproduction of St. Patrick, a shamrock, and a harp, and on the other side the arms of Mexico. Hence, Americans called it by the name of Ireland's patron saint, or the Irish Legion, though the Mexicans knew it by its rightful name, the Legion of Strangers or Foreign Legion, the title used during the court-martial

proceedings. The Irish character of the battalion was further emphasized by the man Americans connected with its leadership, Major John
Riley, an abjured figure, though he was not in fact its commander. Its
story properly begins with Riley, known variously as "Riely," "Reilly,"
"Ryley," "O'Riley," "O'Rielly," and "O'Reilly."

Charles M. O'Malley of Mackinac Island, Michigan, sat down on
February 5, 1848, and wrote to General Winfield Scott, enclosing "a
letter of the deserter John Riley," then an American prisoner in Mexico
City. "The said Riley," explained O'Malley, "worked in my employ off
and on for the space of two years, with whom I had more trouble than
all the other men who worked for me, and more particularly as a Justice of the Peace, for he was always in variance with every one he had
any thing to do with. Such was my opinion of him that I said when I
heared [sic] of desertions that Riley was one of the number."

O'Malley was hardly a man to condemn Riley's "variance" with
others. An irascible Irishman, born in County Mayo, he had studied for
the priesthood but settled in Mackinac in 1835 as a merchant and
entered politics. A leading Democratic member of the Michigan legislature, he was known as the "Irish dragon," a take-off on Lever's
Charles O'Malley, "the Irish Dragoon," after a quarrel with Henry R.
Schoolcraft, the explorer and Indian lore scholar, who constituted himself the guardian of Indian tradition in Michigan. To spite Schoolcraft,
the angry O'Malley put through the legislature a bill changing the
Indian names of five counties to Irish names after four counties in Ireland, Antrim, Clare, Roscommon, and Wexford, and after the Irish
national hero, Emmet, nearly breaking Schoolcraft's heart.

Riley, born in Ireland about 1817, appeared in Mackinac in 1843,
but mystery surrounds the intervening years, except that he had been a
soldier. At the height of Riley's notoriety during the Mexican War,
newspaper accounts placed him as a deserter from a British company in
Canada, but the British War Office admits of no such record. Rumor
described him also as an American recruiting sergeant in New York
City and a drillmaster of cadets at West Point, but court-martial proceedings made no mention of previous American army service and no
former comrades spoke up to recall him.

Riley's own testimony located him in the British army as probably a
noncommissioned officer. "I had never served as a private soldier in my
lifetime," he told the court-martial, "with the exception of 7 months
and 3 days I had served in the American army," that is, from his en-

listment until his desertion. He said he had lived in the United States two years before signing up at Fort Mackinac, which, from O'Malley's testimony that Riley had worked for him for two years, precluded American military service.

In the fact that Riley held higher rank in previous military service lay the answer to his desertion from General Taylor's army.

On September 4, 1845, Riley, who described himself as a "labourer," enlisted at Fort Mackinac and two days later left with the 5th Infantry as a private for Corpus Christi. He made the long march over the barren ground from Nueces, arrived on the Rio Grande on March 28, 1846, and went into camp with Taylor's army opposite Matamoros.

Riley was a striking figure, six feet one and three-quarters in height, with a soldierly bearing and the distinguishing features of the Gael — black hair, blue eyes, and a florid complexion. He held the reputation of a steady soldier. Riley was "a quiet and very good man," said Captain Chapman of the 5th Infantry, and Captain Merrill of his own company described his character as "very fair" and could not recall any occasion when Riley had had to be punished.

Riley was a mercenary, a true professional, not in the sense that he sold his services for money alone but in his prideful ambition for rank as an officer commanding men, regardless of the flag under which he fought. If you will recall, he wrote to O'Malley from Mexico City, "my last wourds [sic] with you and Thomas Chambers [a Mackinac friend] when last we parted which was if God spared me I would again attain my former rank or Die. . . ." Though a captive of the Americans and an execrated man in the United States, Riley had neither regret nor shame at his conduct. He had reached a rank in the Mexican army of major, higher than he had ever expected to hold and higher than any foreigner had ever attained in Mexico, he told O'Malley, and he wanted his friends in Mackinac to know that "the Mexicans has honoured me with a pair of epilitts" and he sorrowed "at not haveing them her [here] to share with me the honours the Mexicans has been kind enough to heap upon me." It never crossed his mind, obsessed with rank and honors, that his face, branded with a "D" on his cheek by a white-hot iron, would no longer be welcomed by old Mackinac companions. All that grieved him, he wrote to O'Malley, was "the death of fifty one of my best and bravest men who has been hung by the Americans for no other reason than fighting manfully against them." It was with a flourish, which no doubt he hoped would impress his friends, that he advised O'Malley to direct mail for Major John Riley "to his Excellency the president of the republic of Mexico."

For such a man as Riley, who felt himself born to leadership and honors, to remain a lowly private in the American ranks, with no prospects of promotion, was galling. From across the Rio Grande came the tempting seductions of the Mexican generals Arista, Ampudia, and Mejía promising favors to Americans who deserted. The suggestion that experienced soldiers might name their own terms if they took up Mexican arms hit his gnawing ambition at its most sensitive spot — "a pair of epilitts."

On the morning of Sunday, April 12, 1846, before war had started, Riley asked Captain Merrill to sign a pass that he might attend Catholic services, which he said a priest from Matamoros was holding in one of the buildings above the camps on the Texas side. Merrill signed, and Riley crossed over to the Mexicans. Desertions were so common at the time that General Taylor issued an order for sentinels to fire a warning shot at Americans seen crossing the Rio Grande to Matamoros and, if they did not immediately turn back, to shoot a second time to kill.

"I was never a deserter . . ." said Riley before the military court after Churubusco. "I went to hear services and was captured by the Mexicans, brought back as Prisoner to Matamoros, to the presence of General Ampudia." Riley then told a detailed story of the pressure the Mexican general put on him to extract information concerning Taylor's army, in the course of which Ampudia offered him a commission as a second lieutenant. Riley refused, saying he would not take up arms against "my Brothers and countrymen," whereupon Ampudia brought him out into the plaza of the city and said he was to be shot in twenty-five minutes. Just then, continued Riley, General Arista, Ampudia's superior, rode up and saved him, saying that such executions of American soldiers would not take place so long as he was in charge of the army.

Then Arista talked to Riley, trying to find out the constitution of Taylor's army, and "I made him an answer that I had not come there as an Informer." Arista told Riley that as a British subject and therefore alien to both the United States and Mexico he could be shot as a traitor to Mexico. Arista, said Riley, presented the choice: accept a commission as a second lieutenant or be shot and, as Riley rationalized before the board of officers, "if I was sentenced to death as a British subject that I would sooner serve as a commissioned officer and fight against my Brothers and countrymen [than] to receive death. No consul belonging to Great Britain being in that part of the Country at the time I thought fit to accept of the commission for fear of being immediately shot. I accepted of it."

His letter to O'Malley was pitched in a different tone. "I have had the honour," he wrote, "of fighting in all the battles that Mexico has had with the United States and by my good conduct and hard fighting I have attained the rank of major." He urged O'Malley not to be deceived by the prejudice against Mexico in the United States, "for a more hospitable or friendly people than the better or upper classes of Mexicans there exists not on the face of the earth that is to a foriner and espetically to an Irish man and a catholick."

A party of American deserters had been collected as soldiers for Mexico even before Matamoros had been evacuated; General Taylor reported that they had been behind guns which fired on his Fort Brown on the American side of the Rio Grande. They were among the troops at Saltillo and were prominent in the fighting at Monterrey, where they earned the reputation of being hardy and tough with their artillery batteries. At Buena Vista, they skillfully maneuvered a gun by hard exertion into a strategic point but were on the point of being overwhelmed by an American force when a short armistice was called, and they escaped, much to the anger of the Americans, who would have considered Monterrey a greater victory than it was had they bagged the deserters and their now known and familiar captain, Riley.

The Boston *Pilot* indignantly characterized as a nativist smear the stories the papers carried of the activities of Riley and his deserters. Far from being an Irishman, asserted the *Pilot,* Riley was not an Irishman at all but an Englishman named Ryder, and cited a New Orleans newspaper as authority. Instead of stirring anti-Irish and anti-Catholic rancor by dwelling upon this impostor, why, asked the *Pilot,* do not the nativist papers pay attention to another Riley, the brave and gallant colonel, who had distinguished himself so nobly at Vera Cruz?

In the meantime, Riley had gathered under him the core of a hard-fighting unit. He had found in another deserter, Patrick Dalton, born in Quebec, according to enlistment papers, but described by Riley as belonging "to Balina tiraly in the county of Mayo," another mercenary of his same breed, a professional, though just turned twenty-one, who had deserted on October 23, 1846, at Cormago, the Mexican town occupied by Taylor after he left Matamoros. He became Riley's closest friend and lieutenant and, like Riley, was a born fighting man, regardless of causes.

Early in the summer of 1847, the conception of a Legion of Strangers, a Mexican Foreign Legion, took shape, perhaps at the suggestion of Riley and Dalton. The American deserters grumbled at being mixed with Mexican troops and wanted their own unit. At that time, also, General Santa Anna had run into difficulties raising recruits among the disillusioned Mexicans. Scattered in Mexico City and throughout the country were strays from the American army, officially posted as deserters in time of war and sitting out the duration in enemy country, some of whom had found work, a German in teaching school, an Irishman in the mines, another Irishman as a guard.

Riley, Dalton, and a deserter named Batchelder talked the Mexican government into picking up these strays, depriving them of passports and the daily allowance granted by the government to sustain themselves, and putting them at the mercy of the Legion's recruitment. They were also given permission to round up alien civilians in Mexico City for possible enlistments. This was the genesis of the American-named San Patricio Battalion, two companies numbering some two hundred men, just a few months organized at the Battle of Churubusco. Colonel Francisco Moreno, a Mexican born in Florida, was assigned to be its commanding officer and Riley its major. Riley designed the banner, as he explained to O'Malley:

> in all my letter I forgot to tell you under what banner we fought so bravely it was that glorious emblem of native rights that banner which should have floated over our native soil many years ago it was St Patrick the harp of Erin the shamrock upon a green field.

The Legion of Strangers thus consisted of the deliberate deserters — for gain, better rank, resentment at or fear of punishment for breaches of military discipline — and the soldiers whom circumstances, rather than calculated decision, had made deserters: drunks, strays, isolated captives and AWOL's. After this flotsam and jetsam of the war had been collected in Mexico City, either Riley, with the soft approach, or Moreno, with the brutal fists, worked upon them to enlist in the Legion.

The defense of the deserters before the American military courts pleaded technical, not willful, desertion, and enlistment in the Legion of Strangers under duress, not voluntarily. They told the courts they got drunk or lost, or they picked up a woman and fell into the hands of the Mexicans. Some had fled the guardhouse or the harshness of an officer. The willful deserters merely pleaded guilty, accepting the inevitable.

The ragtag and bobtail of the Legion of Strangers, more dissolute, weak and ne'er-do-well than vicious, had been marched to their first battle of Churubusco with Mexican troops on either side (lest they bolt, some explained) and there, cornered in the Church of San Mateo, had given the now seasoned American army the most desperate fight of the war, conscious that no mercy awaited them if taken in combat.

When the battle was over, seventy-two deserters from the American army in the ranks of the Legion of Strangers had been captured. Of these, twenty-seven were natives of Ireland, fifteen of the United States, six of Germany, three of Scotland, two each of Quebec, England, and France, one who gave his birthplace as the Straits of Messina, and fourteen for whom no record of birth could be found. All were soldiers enlisted in the regular army.

Within less than a week after the Battle of Churubusco, two military courts were trying the prisoners. The scrupulously honest and fair General Scott assigned Colonel Bennet Riley, of Catholic Irish descent, to preside over one of the courts-martial at the little town of San Angel, the most important of which was that of the notorious Riley.

In the two sun-drenched, dusty Mexican villages, the course of strict military justice rolled on hour after hour to the inevitable verdict of "Guilty" of the charge of "desertion to the enemy" in case after case and the terrible sentence, "to be hanged by the neck until he is dead."

The supreme irony was that the man the army and the American public wanted above all the others to swing for his dishonor — John Riley — was spared the hangman's noose by the legal technicality of his having deserted before the war's declaration. Instead, the court ordered the strictest punishment that could be legally inflicted in peacetime — "fifty lashes with a raw hide whip, well laid on the bare back . . . with the addition that [he] be branded on a cheek with the letter 'D'; kept a close prisoner as long as this army remains in Mexico, and then drummed out of service." The newspapers howled at Riley's escape from the gallows. But General Scott said that he preferred to have his whole army "put to the sword" than violate the law to swing Riley.

Twenty citizens of different nations resident in Mexico City petitioned General Scott to pardon Riley, urging that "his misconduct might be pardoned by your Excellency in consideration of the protection he extended in this city to the persecuted and hounded American citizens whilst in concealment, by notifying an order he held to apprehend them and not acting on it," and adding their belief that Riley had "a generous heart admitting all his errors." The Mexican government intervened in an attempt to save the lives of Riley and the other deserters, unsuccessfully trying to make their pardon a condition of armistice terms.

To show its contempt of Riley, the army hired a Mexican muleteer to apply the lashes to his back and, according to the report, he failed to hold up stoically under the blows. Another current story related that the first branding of "D" on his cheek was botched and the iron had to be applied a second time.

And so the story of the Legion of Strangers, or the San Patricio Battalion, came to an end in the Valley of Mexico with forty-nine, of the original seventy-two captured, hanged in batches. Of those hanged, seventeen were natives of Ireland. But for years nativist and anti-Catholic Irish literature maintained the fiction of the solely Irish character of the battalion, one tale asserting it had consisted of Irishmen who deserted the American ranks in a body.

With the end of the war, Riley, drummed out of service, was appointed a colonel in the Mexican army. But he sided with the wrong crowd in a revolution and hurried out of Mexico. A report had it that Riley sued the United States government for the botched branding on his face but the Cincinnati federal court, where the trial reputedly took place, has no record of the case. Riley disappeared into the same mystery out of which he had come, certainly a fascinating, if discreditable, figure, a footloose Irishman who momentarily was cast in the villain's role of the United States at war.

5

The Mexican government had a fixation it could seduce the Catholic Irish away from the American ranks and directed appeals to them from the start. President Polk at the outbreak of war had named two Jesuits, one of whom was Father McElroy, remembered from the Baltimore & Washington Railroad riot, as chaplains, the first Catholic priests with the armed services, to minister to the Irish troops and to counter the Mexican propaganda. The Mexican government had used an Englishman named Sinnott in the north of Mexico to woo the Irish and an Irish priest in Mexico, Rev. Eugene McNamara, to try to buy Irishmen in Scott's army. But its strongest campaign followed the execution of the deserters. In an address from "Mexican to Catholic Irishmen," the government called to the Irish troops to listen to the accents of a Catholic people and remember the love the Spanish people had always borne for Irishmen. It dwelt upon the anti-Catholic outrages:

> Are Catholic Irishmen to be the destroyers of Catholic temples, the murderers of Catholic priests and the founders of heretical rites in this pious nation? . . . What? Can you fight by the sides of those who put fire to your temples in Boston and Philadelphia? . . . Irishmen! You were expected to be just, because you are the countrymen of that truly great and eloquent man, O'Connell, who has devoted his whole life to defend your rights, and finally, because you are said to be good and sincere Catholics. Why, then, do you rank among our wicked enemies?

General Taylor issued a general order on September 22, 1847, against the "false priests" serving the Mexican government, seeking "to entice our gallant Roman Catholic soldiers who have done so much honor to our colors, to desert, under a promise of lands in California." But the Irish troops were not tempted.

At the close of the Mexican War, the President of the United States conferred Certificates of Merit upon 238 privates for distinguished services in battle. Of these, at least eighty-six had distinctively Irish names.

6

Colonel Stephen Watts Kearny of the 1st Dragoons, commanding officer at Fort Leavenworth on the fringe of the Great Plains, knew what he had to do when the United States declared war on Mexico — march to Santa Fe and take over the province of New Mexico. Early in August, 1846, when Taylor's army on the Rio Grande prepared for the advance on Monterrey, the formidably titled Army of the West, which invoked a picture of corps with waving banners but which was in reality a hastily assembled body of some 1700 men, principally Missouri recruits, began the long trek over unfamiliar terrain.

The guide for the Army of the West through the difficult country was Thomas Fitzpatrick, who carried the nominal title of major and a solid reputation that made the exacting Colonel Kearny pleased and satisfied that the right man for the job rode by his side.

Here we pause to regard one of the greatest men in the story of the Catholic Irish race in the United States. It may be that his part in opening the vast imperial domain beyond the Missouri River to the Pacific will yet be accounted the greatest single contribution of a Catholic Irishman to the development of the United States. The deeper American historians probe into the Old West, the more impressive grows the stature of the men, like Tom Fitzpatrick, who pioneered the way to the wealth and with it the power that lay in the virginal lands beyond the bend of the Missouri.

Fitzpatrick, forty-seven years old when he rode out of Fort Leavenworth with the Army of the West, was already a legendary character along the frontier. Almost a quarter of a century before, he had left St. Louis with the second expedition organized by Lieutenant Governor William Henry Ashley of Missouri, the fur trader, to trap beaver in the Indian country around the Yellowstone in the Rockies. Fitzpatrick, then twenty-four, had come to the United States from his native County Cavan at seventeen and restlessly wandered to St. Louis, then the last town of civilization before the great unknown of the plains, mountains, and deserts, almost a million square miles yet to be tamed, part sweet land waiting for the first cut of the plow, part ferocious, full of natural menaces and the human savagery of Indians.

The life-story of this exceptional Irishman was, as his biographers wrote, "an epitome of the early history of the Far West." Knowing men would have spotted in his features the stamp of Ireland or, failing that, they would have recognized his origin in the Irish turn of speech. But race, creed or color had no reference to the character of a man among the collection of super-individualists who pressed across the uncharted line of civilization to the wild country. Alone, you worked your way out of bad spots by wits and spirit or you died. Together, you asked no questions of companions except that each do his share lest death touch them all by carelessness or imprudence. The frontier was intolerant of only the fool or the coward. This was no settled Boston.

In the quarter-century from his departure from St. Louis with the second Ashley party to the time he greeted Colonel Kearny at Fort Leavenworth, Tom Fitzpatrick had, in the Irish saying, won golden opinions as a pathbreaker to the empire of the West. That first journey into the wilderness by the young Irishman had ended in disaster when the expedition was raided and broken up by hostile Arikara Indians. But the conduct of Fitzpatrick had earned the approval of Ashley, who sent him out the next season with a trapping party on an expedition that made history.

Jedediah Smith, the upstate New Yorker, the "knight in buckskin," of the true breed of mountain men, as the trappers were called, headed the small party, with Fitzpatrick second in command. It included Jim Clyman from Virginia and William Sublette of Kentucky, both destined for high deeds, one as an explorer of the Great Salt Lake and the other as a great trapper and trader.

They trapped for beaver in the Upper Platte as they went ever westward with their pack animals in that season of 1823-1824, facing the incredible hardships that were routine in a mountain man's life — cold and snow, hunger, thirst, accidents — and the physical exactions of each day's tortured journey. Hafen and Ghent, the two dedicated students of the West and of Fitzpatrick, described the great moment of the discovery of the famous South Path in what is now southwestern Wyoming:

> They were approaching, almost imperceptibly, the Continental Divide. . . . For several days they moved westward, not knowing they had left the watershed of the Atlantic until they found streams flowing westward, when they realized they had traversed the long-sought South Pass. . . . The effective discovery of the pass dates from its crossing on a March day in 1824 by the party of Smith and Fitzpatrick. Little did these hardy pioneers dream that they were marking a trail destined to be, for nearly half a century, the most important route to the Pacific.

The little party entered California by the San Bernardino Valley. This was the vital life-saving and time-saving sector of the historic Oregon Trail.

For the next season, Fitzpatrick was in charge of a trapping colony on the present site of Ogden, and it was during this period that he had his first fight with Indians, a bad lot of Bannocks, horse-stealers and killers, whom he skillfully stampeded. But he had early learned the first maxim of the mountain men: never fight with Indians if you can make peace. Over the years he won so many friends with the various tribes and acted toward them in such good faith that his name became synonymous with trust and honesty to the Indians. They called him "Broken Hand" from the member crippled by a gun explosion.

They also called him "White Head" or "White Hair." Once he had been caught alone and pursued by a hostile tribe; he had been forced to abandon his horse and hide in a hole in the rocks for several days; he had escaped from the savages but faced further danger of death, first from wolves and then from hunger and thirst, as he plodded through forbidding territory looking for a refuge; he was finally picked up by friendly Indians, emaciated, gaunt, and barely alive. During these terrible days and nights, his once brownish black hair had turned snow-white.

He first met Kit Carson on an expedition to Santa Fe, during which his great friend, Jedediah Smith, out foraging with Fitzpatrick for water, disappeared over a hill and was never seen again: he had been taken unawares and killed by Comanches. Carson, who had just completed his first expedition with the Ewing Young party into California, was in Santa Fe looking for work, and Fitzpatrick signed him up. Carson, a born frontiersman, was still green, and his education developed under the tutelage of the man from County Cavan.

Fitzpatrick in 1830, with other leading trappers, bought out the old Ashley company, and he became head of the Rocky Mountain Fur Company, but the competition of stronger firms, like the Astor company, which was rapidly monopolizing the fur trade, proved too severe, and the beaver was being trapped to extinction. Fitzpatrick, like his friends Kit Carson and Jim Bridger — "the great triumvirate" of mountain men, De Voto called them — turned to other occupations, where their hardily acquired knowledge could be employed.

The day of the mountain men was drawing to an end. The first of the new type of pioneers, the settlers, families from the South and the East, began to move along the course of empire. But there were no canals and railroads; the journey to the land of promise had to be made by foot and wagon; and there was need of experienced guides to show the way, since lacking maps they would otherwise perish. Under these circumstances, Fitzpatrick entered upon the second stage of his remarkable career — as a guide to emigrant trains.

Fitzpatrick had guided some of the earlier missionaries to the Indian country. In 1840, he led the first expedition of Father Pierre DeSmet, the great Catholic missioner, from St. Louis to the land of the Blackfeet and formed a deep friendship with the humble explorer-priest. It was about this time that the traveler Dr. F. A. Wislizenus described the then forty-one-year-old Fitzpatrick: "I met the well-known Fitzpatrick, who has passed through many an adventure during his life in the mountains," he recorded. "He has a spare, bony figure, a face full of expression, and white hair; his whole demeanor reveals strong passions."

In 1841, John Bidwell, the schoolteacher of Weston, Missouri, captivated by the stories of California, organized the Western Emigration Society, which, after electing John Bartleson captain, prepared a wagon train for distant California. But none of the party knew the route. News arrived of the approach from St. Louis of a second DeSmet expedition, this time headed for the Flathead country in what are now Idaho and Montana, under the direction of the veteran Fitzpatrick, and the little Bidwell-Bartleson party decided to wait for it. About the middle of May, 1841, the joint Bidwell-Bartleson and DeSmet parties set out from Sapling Grove, near Independence, Missouri.

This was the first wagon train across the plains and mountains to California. Though the Bidwell-Bartleson wagon train was to bring fame to its organizer, John Bidwell, and encourage the westward flow by its example, the genius of its successful journey was the guide, Thomas Fitzpatrick, for without him, as Bidwell wrote, "probably not one of us would have reached California, because of our inexperience," and he continued:

> Afterwards when we came into contact with Indians, our people were so easily excited that if we had not with us an old mountaineer the result would certainly have been disastrous. The name of the guide was Captain Fitzpatrick; he had been at the head of trapping parties in the Rocky Mountains for many years.

Fitzpatrick quieted the fears of the distraught members at the first approach of Indians, saved the train from a buffalo stampede, safely ferried the train over swollen streams and sped them on safely to California.

Early in 1843, Lieutenant John C. Frémont, son-in-law of the leading expansionist Senator Benton and thirteen years later to be the first Republican candidate for President, was busy making preparations for his second expedition to the old trapper country, ostensibly to map the territory and pursue scientific studies but really, it was later charged, to spy out Oregon and California as desirable pieces of real estate for America's "manifest destiny." Since Kit Carson, the guide of the first Frémont expedition, from which he had received national fame in consequence of Frémont's writings, was not available, the pathfinder selected Thomas Fitzpatrick to be guide, adjutant, and quartermaster. On that historic party, which turned south from the Oregon Trail and entered California over the high Sierras in the blasts of winter, then returned by the southern route, Fitzpatrick was invaluable, as Frémont's praise for his skill, resourcefulness, and nobility testified.

But his ambition now centered in an appointment as an Indian agent, and it was while Fitzpatrick awaited the slow grinding of the federal machinery in Washington that Colonel Kearny asked him to be guide of the Army of the West to New Mexico. The army walked into Santa Fe, and Kearny, with Fitzpatrick still as guide, led a body of his troops for California upon reports of difficulties of the occupation forces. On the route, Kit Carson relieved Fitzpatrick, who had heard the news of his appointment as agent to the wild Indian tribes of the Great Plains in the Upper Platte and Arkansas area — the Cheyennes, Arapahos, divisions of the Oglala, Brule, Minneconjun and Sioux, and the violent Comanches, Kiowas and plains Apache. Fitzpatrick now entered upon the third and final phase of his full and adventurous life.

The record of Indian agents is not pleasant to pursue, but the nation would be free of its sense of guilt had the example of Fitzpatrick been followed. "In the dismal roll of America's corrupt and blundering Indian agents," wrote David Lavender in *Bent's Fort,* "his [Fitzpatrick's name] is one of the few that leaves no sour taste."

Fitzpatrick had no illusions or sentimentality about the Indians: he knew they were treacherous, ungrateful, and urged by savage violence; but he understood the obligation of the government to care for them. He steadily advocated a program of gradually training and settling them as agriculturalists and permitting the civilizing process to work by their contact with the marts of trade. He fought the beastly traffic in liquor by unscrupulous men with Indians.

But his greatest achievement was the treaty he drew with them, in the name of the United States, at the largest council of wild Indians heretofore gathered, near Fort Laramie in 1851. The Indians trusted "Broken Hand" and signed as a mark of confidence in his honor and integrity, but broken faith by both the United States and the Indians undid what he considered the crowning point of his career.

Early in January, 1854, Fitzpatrick arrived in Washington on official business and there had the pleasure of a reunion with his sister, a baby when he left County Cavan and now settled with her family in the United States. There he talked with Thomas D'Arcy McGee, now an editor of the *Celt* in Buffalo, who sat fascinated with his stories of the Indians. McGee also reported that Fitzpatrick was "half-way between 70 and 80" in age, which bespoke the ravages of the frontier on his face, since he was at the time only fifty-five years old. There he took cold and died on February 7 of pneumonia. The mountain man who had escaped death from cold, heat, exposure, wolves, and Indians died in bed at the splendid Brown's Hotel. He was buried in the Congressional Cemetery but for some unexplained reason his grave was not marked, "an unfitting end," remarked Lavender, "for one of the best men the mountains ever produced."

Tom Fitzpatrick's reputation had been won by hard achievement. "He was one of the greatest mountain men," wrote Bernard De Voto, "perhaps the greatest," a conclusion concurred in by other students. American history has suffered by his natural modesty, which forbade his writing of the years in the mountains and on the plains. He would have turned out a classic work, since he commanded powers of expression, observation, and analysis, as his reports as an Indian agent reveal. His taciturn personality did not lend itself to publicity or self-aggrandizement, and he was an unsmiling Gael of the breed of unbending prelates, top-flight politicians, and commanders of troops. People of his own blood today return a blank stare at the mention of his name while they recall some Irish windbag of the stump in the East of the same period. But the greatest tribute to Fitzpatrick is that students of the period, after long association with him, sound trumpets in his praise.

"It can hardly be doubted," wrote Hafen and Ghent, "that as the years pass he will more clearly emerge as a character of the first consequence on the frontier and in the wilderness — an epic figure, unique and incomparable."

7

Three weeks before Commodore John D. Sloat, on July 7, 1846, took the Mexican province of California in the name of the United States, Captain John C. Frémont initiated his own private conquest of that territory in the Bear Flag revolt that started a long controversy during which friends justified Frémont's unauthorized uprising as a foil to the activities of Rev. Eugene McNamara, described as "a native of Ireland, catholic priest, and apostolic missionary," a resident of Mexico

City and later employed by Santa Anna to try to seduce Catholic Irish troops to desert to Mexican arms.

The suspicious Polk feared that England would stake out a sphere of influence in California before the United States won it, and Senator John Dix of New York cited "the McNamara scheme" as part of the encroachment "deliberately entered upon and steadily pursued" by the British government to grab off territory surrounding the United States.

In the spring of 1845, Father McNamara petitioned the president of Mexico for a sizable grant of land in California for a Catholic Irish colony, with three objects in mind, he said: first, to advance the Catholic religion; second, "to contribute to the happiness of my countrymen"; and third, "to put an obstacle in the way of further usurpations on the part of an irreligious and anti-Catholic nation." He planned three separate Irish colonies, on San Francisco Bay, near Monterey and at Santa Barbara, which had they been granted would have made the prospective Irish colonists fabulously wealthy just by sitting on them and waiting for a rise in land prices. To Father McNamara's assertion that ten thousand Irishmen "will be sufficient to repel at the same time the secret intrigues and the open attacks of the American usurpers," some in Mexico skeptically suggested that in a showdown the Irish would more likely be found on the side of the Yankees repelling the Mexicans than the other way around.

The California legislature under Mexico authorized a grant to Father McNamara, but its location among Indian tribes made it of no value, and its uselessness was compounded by its legislative authorization on the same day Commodore Sloat raised the American flag over California. Little more proof of the perfidious English design behind "the McNamara scheme" was needed by Americans than the arrival of Father McNamara in California from Mexico on a British man-of-war and his departure by the same means, his mission a failure.

Bancroft, the historian of California, thought that McNamara was used as a Catholic priest in a Catholic country by a group of London speculators with the colonization scheme as a blind. Josiah Royce, the Harvard philosopher and historian of California, believed "the McNamara scheme" a sincere effort by the priest to aid Famine refugees and the British government aided him to that end. But Royce missed the point that a British government would never use Irish colonists for land it wanted for itself. Of that one can be sure.

8

The Frémont Bear Flag revolt began on the ranch of Martin Murphy the Younger near Sacramento. The Murphy clan, the first Catholic Irish party who entered California by the overland route, wafted history behind them in the first wagon train that completed the journey from Missouri to Captain Sutter's Fort by way of a path they blazed through the Sierra Nevada mountains that from then on became the well-trodden trail of wagons and eventually the route of the Union Pacific and Highway 40.

Martin Murphy the Elder, then past his sixty-first year, sold his farm in St. Joseph, organized supplies, gathered his clan together and early in 1844 set out for California to be shed of the damnable malarial climate of Missouri and to settle where he could attend Mass and have a priest instruct his children in the Catholic religion. The patriarch, who had come to Missouri from County Wexford after a spell of farming near Quebec, counted his sons and daughters and in-laws and grandchildren to the number of twenty and, with the Irish propensity for population, two more were born on the journey. Four other natives of Ireland started with the party: John, Michael, and Robert Sullivan and their sister Mary. Elisha Stevens, an old mountain man, guided the train.

The Murphys separated from the larger group headed for Oregon at Fort Hall, Idaho, and with some others struck out southwestward for California. After a winter's dangers, hardships, and near-disasters, which necessitated a separation of forces, the whole Murphy clan arrived without a loss in California then breaking into spring. The Murphys prospered, received homage as a pioneer family and the Stevens-Murphy train entered history.

In the winter of 1846, the now famous Donner party followed the same route and, entrapped at what is now Donner Lake, wrote one of the most grisly stories in our annals, too available elsewhere to be repeated here, except to mention Patrick Breen, his wife and their seven children and their bachelor friend, Patrick Dolan, emigrants from Ireland, who had sold their neighboring farms in Keokuk, Iowa, to join the ill-fated Donner party. Breen's diary, which he kept during the revolting weeks at Donner Lake, almost inhuman in its dispassionate objectivity, "one of the most soul-shocking documents in our literature," in the judgment of Bernard De Voto, was to another historian, Bancroft, "the most precious and fascinating record and relic of these events." Poor Patrick Dolan, merry and good-natured, with blue eyes and brown hair, started out with a group to seek help for the snowed-in Donner party. They were themselves caught in a blizzard. Dolan went insane, died, and was butchered for food for the remainder.

9

Late in September, 1848, the *Pilot* reported the inclusion of Irish soldiers among the many veterans of the Mexican War crowding into Washington for their reward of victory: 160 acres of wild Western land.

"Would there were many 'of the same sort' at home," sighed the disillusioned *Pilot*, "and Ballingarry would not have been the *first* and *last* battlefield in the revolution of 1848!"

While Catholic Irish troops fought on the winning side in America, England once more triumphed over the national cause in Ireland, and the fiasco that wound up in Mrs. McCormick's cabbage patch left the Irish in the United States disenchanted.

4 1

The Widow McCormick's Cabbage Patch

Sir robert peel's crushing of O'Connell at Clontarf in 1843 disillusioned the American Irish in the program of Repeal by moral power and strengthened the advocates of physical force. "I will . . . give 100 dollars to an association for the proviso of arms and the preservation of liberty," declared Rev. Terence Fitzsimmons, pastor in South Boston, after the bad news of Clontarf. "But I will not give *one cent* nor collect *one,* until I see an association formed for this purpose." In the summer of 1845, the Boston *Pilot* described the sorry state of the Repeal movement: "The hundreds and thousands who were wont tö congregate in our towns and large cities, have disappeared as if some strange and fatal magic had bid them from the cause."

The mounting tragedy of the Famine absorbed the interest of the Irish in America and diverted the funds of the mass of emigrants from Repeal to distressed relatives and friends in Ireland. But forces shaped up in Ireland during 1846 to change the character of the O'Connell

Repeal movement and give new direction and vitality to American aid for the Irish patriotic cause.

2

On a spring day in 1842, three young men sat in Dublin's Phoenix Park and agreed to start a weekly. They were Thomas Davis, a Protestant of the Established Church and descendant of Cromwellian settlers; Charles Gavan Duffy, an Ulster Catholic, son of a County Monaghan merchant; and John Blake Dillon of an old Catholic family in the west of Ireland. Out of that conference was born the Dublin *Nation*, which molded the ideas of Ireland with the same depth that the Federalist Papers had the United States.

Davis was the radiant figure of the *Nation*, a poet, a writer of incisive prose, a person of gentle and candid nature illumed by the spirit of Wolfe Tone, who conceived the idea of combining political agitation for freedom with "a Nationality of the spirit" through revival of Ireland's cultural heritage. The *Nation* appealed to the new generation of youth impatient with O'Connell's political clichés which after Clontarf sounded like hollow echoes. The cultural romanticism of the Dublin weekly, with its poems and ballads, raised a following called Young Ireland in differentiation from O'Connell's Old Ireland.

The *Nation* valiantly supported and informed O'Connell's Repeal agitation, which he resumed after the Clontarf setback, and the Liberator at first embraced the young men. But the aging warrior had changed after his defeat and a brief term in jail, showing obvious signs of the ailment that was to carry him to the grave. He failed, or refused, to understand, as the *Nation* said, that "a NEW MIND has grown up amongst us." Young Ireland deferred to O'Connell's leadership but refused to fall behind him as a subservient tail.

The whisperers with access to O'Connell's ear, notably his own son John, a small-minded and jealous counterfeit stamp of old Dan's greatness, buzzed their malice against the rising talent of Young Ireland, whom they feared as rivals. They incited O'Connell to a personal attack on Davis for Young Ireland's endorsement of Peel's measure to establish non-sectarian state-supported colleges bitterly opposed by the great majority of the Irish hierarchy, and they sought to taint Young Ireland with the label of "infidel" in an overwhelmingly Catholic country.

In the summer of 1846, John O'Connell introduced a series of resolutions that in a most craven manner pledged the Irish people never to resort to force under any circumstances and made acceptance of this extremist measure a test of Repeal membership.

The passionate eloquence of young Thomas F. Meagher, then in his twenty-fourth year, dramatically marked the break between Old and Young Ireland. In answer to the resolutions, he justified the use of force in the cause of freedom:

> Abhor the sword and stigmatise the sword? No, my lord, for at its blow a giant nation sprang from the waters of the Atlantic and by its redeeming magic the fettered colony became a daring, free republic. Abhor the sword and stigmatise the sword? No, my lord, for it scourged the Dutch marauders out of the fine old towns of Belgium, back into their own phlegmatic swamps, and knocked their flag, and laws, and sceptre, and bayonets into the sluggish waters of the Scheldt.

John O'Connell interrupted with the notice that, as Meagher's doctrines violated the peace principles of the Liberator, he would have to get out of the Repeal association or else it would disband. The Young Ireland leaders walked out.

The Meagher speech swept through Ireland and the Irish communities in America. Overnight the youthful orator became "Meagher of the Sword" and a hero.

As Meagher walked out of the hall, the cheers must have satisfied him that he had started a career — but hardly in the direction it took: penal exile, a leader of the Catholic Irish in the United States, a Union general in the Civil War, and death in the swirling waters of the Missouri River in the Territory of Montana, of which he was provisional governor.

The son of a wealthy merchant and mayor of the city of Waterford, educated in the Jesuit schools of Clongowes Wood in Ireland and Stonyhurst in England, where he excelled in literature and oratory, the apple-cheeked Meagher still looked like a schoolboy when he electrified an audience that had listened to the best talkers in Ireland.

The leadership of the Young Ireland party fell to William Smith O'Brien, the noblest figure of the Young Irelanders, a Protestant educated at Cambridge, a wealthy landlord, with a seat in Parliament, a member of the ennobled Inchquin family and a lineal descendant of Brian Boru. He possessed the Roman virtues — integrity, honor, fairness and justice — to such refined excess that he was in the end the victim of his own sterling character. He had come voluntarily into the Repeal movement from a sense of outrage at English unfairness and he led the seceders out of the hall outraged at John O'Connell's violation of the principle of free discussion.

Peacemakers of good will, concerned with Irish unity, failed to find a workable formula of reconciliation because John O'Connell preferred to be first man of the Repeal society in ruins than join with the gifted Young Irelanders who outshone him. The secession became permanent with the organization of the Irish Confederation early in January, 1847.

In February, O'Connell made his last appearance in the House of Commons, to the shock of the members, "a feeble old man muttering before a table," wrote Disraeli, his old Tory enemy, who remembered "the form of colossal energy, and the clear and thrilling tones that had once startled, disturbed, and controlled senates." In a voice scarcely audible, his final plea predicted that "one fourth of [Ireland's] population will perish unless you come to her relief." He then departed for the Continent and on May 15, in Genoa on his way to Rome, he died, his work for Ireland his monument.

The upswelling of national affection upon the death of O'Connell and the distrust of powerful bishops appeared to have isolated the Young Ireland Confederates as a faction of dissenters rather than the voice of a people. Dissent from the dissenters split their ranks with the resignation of John Mitchel from the staff of the *Nation* to start his own weekly, the *United Irishman,* on February 12, 1848.

Mitchel came the closest to Wolfe Tone in the fire that burned in his belly and his consuming hatred of England. The "Empire of Hell," he called "the greedy, carnivorous old monster," in whose final destruction he hoped to bear a hand, and his uncringing spirit served notice to the old enemy: "I expect no justice, no courtesy, no indulgence from you; and if you get me within your power, I entreat you to show me no mercy, as I, so help me God, would show none to you." England has been hated by some great and strong men in her long history but intertwined with that hatred usually went a respect for her power and talents, but Mitchel hated and had no respect; he made of this hatred a masterpiece of art, unrelenting up to his last breath.

Mitchel, the son of a Unitarian minister, was practicing law in the north of Ireland when Gavan Duffy brought him to the *Nation* to succeed Thomas Davis, who had died in 1845. Mitchel, a partisan of activism and violent in language, suffered under the constraint of Duffy's editorial direction and directed the new radical weekly to the maxim of Wolfe Tone: "If the men of property will not support us, they must fail: we can support ourselves by the aid of that numerous and respectable class of the community, the men of no property." Mitchel began to preach what he called Ireland's "glorious treason" and aimed not to repeal the Union but "to repeal the Conquest" through a republic won by force. With O'Connell dead less than a year, the revolutionary spirit of Tone returned to Ireland.

3

The Irish communities in the United States came alive, after months of apathy, at Meagher's speech and the quarrel in the ranks. This they could understand, as the *Pilot* lamented: "The facility with which a row can be created in an Irish crowd is proverbial; and the cordiality with which the people of that country will fight without knowing it is not more notorious than it is discreditable."

But conflicting loyalties left them bewildered and frustrated; they wanted to help Ireland, but how? A Boston Repeal meeting illustrated the American crosscurrents. A vehement speaker recalled the services of O'Connell, and he was vigorously cheered. The second speaker concluded with a passionate pledge to give his lifeblood for Ireland, and he was vigorously cheered. The third speaker upheld O'Connell's moral agitation but added that if the sword must be taken up then he would follow the sword, and he was vigorously cheered. This scene could very well be marked down as the disposition of an Irish audience to cheer emphatic assertions, no matter their nature, but now it marked authentic confusion as to which course to follow. Then things began to happen, and events made decisions for Irish Americans.

The bloodless downfall in 1848 of Louis Philippe and the establishment of the Lamartine republic in France set bonfires to blazing on the hills of Ireland. The *Nation* now struck out on the bold course of the *United Irishman* and seethed with "glorious treason," while the speakers of the Confederation began to stir a nation that, though weakened by the Famine, caught gleams of deliverance from the oppressors.

Sniffing the rising turbulence, the House of Commons passed a special law, the Treason-Felony Act, which reduced the capital crime of treason to a felony punishable by transportation to a penal colony, under which it convicted Mitchel with a packed jury and started him overseas as a felon and on his career as a patriot.

Events now moved even faster with the hopes aroused by the French example. The Confederates had been swept into a party of rebellion, while John O'Connell waked the coffin of the Repeal agitation. They started to enlist a national guard and all over the country political clubs that were really militia organizations drilled and prepared for the day the signal would be given. "When the harvest is over" — thus people spoke in the spring and early summer of 1848 in Ireland. Blacksmiths secretly made pikes; guns in hiding were polished. The poets and writers of romantic Young Ireland squared their shoulders for the colorful cloak of conspiratorial revolutionaries. The enthusiasm sped across the sea.

4

Events in Ireland regulated the temperature of the Irish in America. During 1847, bolters from Repeal societies followed the example of the Young Ireland Confederates and set up auxiliaries in several places, but confined their patriotic efforts for the most part to slandering the Repealers from whom they had parted.

Early in 1848, however, a new movement of far-reaching importance to the story of the Catholic Irish in America developed, though its significance was not fully grasped at the moment. A demonstration at the Shakespeare Hotel in New York on January 18, 1848, and the formation in February of the Emmet Club in Cincinnati, "a new association for old purposes," according to its initial statement, struck the roots of Irish revolutionary organization in the United States, the direct ancestor of Fenianism.

Late in March, the *Cambria* arrived in Boston from Liverpool with the news of the downfall of Louis Philippe. The American Irish interpreted the French constitutional revolution in terms of Irish aspirations and, like Young Ireland, found it good. Hereafter, proposed the *Pilot,* let no more money be sent to Ireland for Repeal but used in America to "equip volunteer militia, under the American Constitution, pledged to active service against Great Britain at any time the American Government may require." As no war with England darkened even the farthest horizon, the proposal boiled down to recruitment in the United States of Irish soldiers for eventualities on the other side. Mind you, said the *Pilot,* "we are recommending nothing but what is strictly constitutional, legal, and moral."

The Irish in New Orleans called upon their fellow countrymen, whether under the banner of O'Connell or the Confederation, to forget their differences, merge in unity through a proposed national convention in Albany, with its historic significance in the American Revolution, and raise a national fund.

Immediately after the news from France, the Irish Repeal Confederation held a mammoth meeting in Washington, presided over by an old friend of Irish freedom, George Washington Parke Custis. Among those seated on the platform, with other members of Congress, was a representative from Illinois, Abraham Lincoln, who had come to testify by his presence his support and sympathy for the cause of Irish liberation. Mr. Lincoln did not speak but he heard Senator Hannegan, the Protestant Irish firebrand from Indiana and the war hawk of the Oregon dispute, rise to the heights:

> I trust in God that before the sun shall again have reached this point in his yearly revolution, he will, as he brightens with his radiance the rich verdure of her soil, look down upon a still more glorious spectacle — her own Green flag floating free on every hill and rampart.

Mr. Lincoln undoubtedly joined in the "thundering applause" which followed Senator Hannegan's peroration.

There was no mistaking the intent of the American Irish now. With the pacific influence of O'Connell removed and the Confederates preparing for a rebellion, they talked openly of arms and fighting men for Ireland, not the money contributions of the earlier agitations.

The Shakespeare Hotel republicans proposed to ask France for permission to land arms from America there; they started to raise a regiment of a thousand men; they looked around for an armory to store weapons for the moment of crisis. The New Orleans Irish thought that the first use of funds should be the purchase of "the best war-steamers that can be obtained, armed and equipped in the most effectual manner, and sent forth in the service of the Irish Republic." Out of Louisville came the voice of the genius, Thomas Mooney, peddling his books from town to town: "I," he wrote, "am hastening along this busy valley

. . . with, as it were, a flaming torch in my hand to kindle up the beacon fires of liberty." He had already signed up "26 fine fellows" as recruits for the Irish Brigade and promised them fifty acres of the best land of Ireland when the victory had been won. Irishmen of Pennsylvania's coal-mining counties listened to an address: "Why Stand Ye Here Idle?" The *Pilot* advised the Irish how to fight a guerrilla war: "Irishmen can't be beaten," it wrote, "at the spade and pickaxe. The spade is not a bad weapon." Discussions praised the superiority of the Irish pike over the British rifle. The Rev. Mr. Purcell offered prayers for the delivery of Ireland from "the Empire of Hell." The Philadelphia society announced that soon a large fund would be placed to the credit of the "Provisional Government of Ireland," payable in merchandise — or metal.

The enthusiasm radiating from Irish hopes in the individual communities needed organization for effectiveness, and responsible Irishmen in New York came forward as leaders. At a public meeting on June 5, addressed by Horace Greeley, Dudley Field, the legal luminary, and a host of Democratic politicians, a resolution by Robert Emmet invited "a general system of communication, union and cooperation" among the Irish societies in the United States and Canada. A Directory of five men, modeled on the Directory of the United Irishmen in 1798, was empowered to raise funds and make decisions in secrecy during the emergency. The Directory carried on correspondence with one trusted member of each society in the country. The English government took note of the New York gathering, particularly of the inclusion of British North America in the American Irish plans, and reached a decision, so it was said, to act against the burgeoning rebellion in Ireland.

The Irish responded to the leadership of the New York Directory. After a love feast, the warring Irish societies in Boston forgot their differences and organized a Boston Directory to cover New England. A delegate from the Dublin Confederation, one Martin O'Flaherty, arrived in the United States — to coordinate efforts. General Shields pledged the consecration of his life to Irish liberty if the sword were unsheathed. The *Pilot* warned the politicians that Irishmen expected them "to press their sympathy, in the present Irish struggle, to the last bounds of the Constitution."

Early in August the news arrived that the British had started to move against the incipient rebellion. Police raided the offices of the Young Ireland publications and arrested the editors and writers. In his native

Waterford, Meagher was arrested and the excited populace raised a barricade to thwart the law, only to be told by the young orator to desist. The excited *Pilot* could hardly contain its riot of joy and hope: "The brain reels and reason whirls and passion bounds as we look upon, in imagination, THE FIRST IRISH BARRICADE." The following week came the news that the Lord Lieutenant had placed under martial law the city and county of Dublin and the surrounding countryside and several other danger spots.

On August 14 the New York Directory staged a monster meeting at Vauxhall Garden that reached the peak of Irish fervor in the United States for the cause of rebellion over the sea. The high point of the meeting was the appearance of Bishop Hughes, who after a long debate with himself had put aside his scruples as a prelate to testify publicly to his hopes for Ireland. He told the cheering audience he had come as a human being, who owed no allegiance to a government responsible for the death of a million Famine Irishmen. He predicted that in the battle the Irish would be brave and in the peace humane. The bishop contributed five hundred dollars, not as a sword, explained Charles O'Conor, but as a shield.

"As we write," pronounced the Boston *Pilot,* "polished pikes may glitter in the sun, and browned rifles be levelled with quick eye and steady hand by the Patriot Irish troops against the English foe. The wild hurrah of countless thousand . . . the eloquent and enthusiastic tribunes . . . may have buckled on the sword of vengeance . . . These things may be now! God grant it! God grant it!"

Even as the editor of the *Pilot* wrote his passionate lines that carried the hopes of every American Irishman, the Irish rebellion of 1848 lay in pitiful and pathetic ruins beside the little house of the Widow McCormick in the village of Ballingarry in County Tipperary.

5

Like Pitt and Castlereagh in the 1798 Rebellion and Peel at Clontarf, Lord John Russell struck with superb timing at the 1848 rebels, precipitating the uprising for which he was prepared and they were not. Before the Irish harvest got under way the British Parliament rushed through in less than three days a bill suspending the Habeas Corpus Act in Ireland, and on July 22 Lord John possessed the weapon he needed to break the back of Young Ireland. ("The maledictions of millions upon them!" cursed the *Pilot*. "They never made haste when any thing good was to be done for Ireland.")

Orders went out for the arrest of the Young Ireland leaders, who fled to the south to raise the countryside, led by Smith O'Brien. The Young Irelanders had neither plans nor preparations for the rebellion: they had concentrated their work in the cities and towns. The priests persuaded the half-starved peasantry in the countryside not to shed blood uselessly for a hopeless cause.

At Ballingarry, on July 29, Smith O'Brien stood at a crossroads watching the approach of the police. His "army," a few men armed with rusty old fowling pieces and mostly curious women and children, saw the police, not wanting to risk a pitched battle, take a cut-off and pile with great haste into the house of Widow McCormick. The "army" chased the police and surrounded the house, and the Widow Mc-Cormick, who had been in the village, rushed up and started shouting that her children were in the house. O'Brien, who was a brave man, walked up to the window to parley with the police for the release of the children, somebody in the "army" threw a brick through the window, the panicky police fired, two men were killed and several badly wounded. And that was the end of the '48 Rebellion, the one and only battle.

O'Brien and Meagher, with Terence McManus, a Liverpool merchant, and Patrick O'Donohoe, a Dublin solicitor's clerk, were convicted and sentenced to death by hanging, but special legislation commuted the punishment to penal transportation for life. By circuitous routes, the '48 leaders fled to American exile, accompanied by lesser figures, provincial journalists and captains of rebel militia companies, and they made a colony in New York.

After the glorious hopes built up, the debacle at Ballingarry shocked the Irish in the United States. Instead of an explosion of Irish valor, the rebellion was like the fall of a damp mop on the floor. Bishop Hughes was at first indignant "that the mountains of Irish patriotism had already labored, and the mouse of physical exertion had gone forth, to be the sport of Ireland's enemies." He wrote to Robert Emmet, head of the Directory, asking that his five-hundred-dollar contribution as a "shield" be turned over to the Sisters of Mercy. Irishmen felt sheepish at the knowing smiles of the Americans, and they sensed that after all the boasting of what Irish arms would do to the English, public opinion labeled them as gasconades.

The manly splendor of the rebels before their judges (Irishmen were at their noblest in the dock as prisoners) made the American Irish ashamed of their first quick disposition to blame and suggest cowardice on the part of Smith O'Brien and Meagher. The *Pilot* perhaps expressed the sober second thought in the United States on the rebellion early in December: "Now that the annoyance of disappointment is passing away, we are better pleased that the Irish Revolution did not come off. From the division of the Populace and the resources of the Government, the latter would have succeeded at a loss of an ocean of blood." The Irish priests had seen that.

The '48 Rebellion added fresh layers to the ancient deposit of hatred of English rule. Over a million anti-English propagandists left Ireland during the Famine years to take up a new life in America. Henry Grattan, the son of the Irish patriot, told of a conversation he had had with some Kildare men about to emigrate, and they said:

> We are going to another country to get that subsistence which we could not get in our own — our graves may be in a foreign land, but our children may yet return to Ireland; and when they do we hope it will be with rifles on their shoulders.

That bitterness ran through the Catholic Irish emigrants piling into the ships.

But the first thought of these men and women dwelt upon "that subsistence which we could not get in our own."

4 2

The Long and Dark Probation

THE IRISH WHO FLED the wretched cabins in Cork and Galway or the blackened potato gardens in Meath or the overpopulated estates in Mayo did not arrive at the journey's end of ancient hardships in the United States. They moved into a long probation of adversities, as raw labor for the most part, their status fixed in the lowest economic grade of free workers. Their weight dragged down the general economic level of the Catholic Irish in the United States.

In the great landing port of New York, they totaled 87 per cent of the foreign-born laborers in 1855; and more than one fifth of the gainfully employed Irish were laborers. A group of Boston Irish leaders in

THE LONG AND DARK PROBATION

1849 concluded that they dreaded not so much pauperism as the distress of the general laboring population in competition with the cheap labor of able-bodied newcomers. The percentage of Irish laborers to the total number of laborers in Baltimore had jumped from 11 per cent in 1842 to 25 per cent in 1858. In Washington, more than 23 per cent of the Catholic Irish families were listed as laborers in 1853 as against a percentage of between 6 and 7 up to that time, and "Foggy Bottom" became an Irish working-class section.

Once the Irish emigrant entered into the mass life of a city, unless he was a man of great ambition, unusual talents, or the beneficiary of fortunate circumstances, he became a captive of its poverty through his lack of education and skills. "The wonder is," wrote the *Irish American* of New York in 1849, "how thousands upon thousands weekly added by immigration to our teeming population, and that of all other sea-board cities, become swallowed up in the floating masses."

A popular Irish priest, Dr. Daniel W. Cahill, who visited the United States immediately prior to the Civil War, wrote in 1860: "A married man has a bad chance here; his first embarrassments with a wife and children are almost insurmountable."

The pitiful advertisements inserted in the Catholic Irish press by wives calling for husbands to return to deserted families meant that the pressures of adversity in the United States had broken even the strong bonds of Irish family life. Their ancient antagonists — poverty and its mean circumstances — followed the Catholic Irish from the dark heritage of their native land.

Modern students paint a fearful picture of Irish emigrant life in the slums of great cities and factory towns.* In the Five Points neighborhood of New York, the Irish emigrants occupied "the oldest, most ricketty, wooden buildings — open to the wind and the storm, and far less comfortable than the buildings used as barns or cattle stalls, by the great body of farmers throughout the country." Those unable to pay the rent of even these squalid tenements built squatter villages in the open country above 40th Street and in Brooklyn by the Navy Yard. The Irish Broad Street section of Boston was described as the most thickly populated place in the world, with the exception of an area in Liverpool. Lemuel Shattuck, the Census statistician, estimated

---

* See *Boston Immigrants 1790-1865* by Oscar Handlin, Cambridge: Harvard University Press, 1941; and *Immigrant Life in New York City 1825-1863* by Robert Ernst, New York: King's Crown Press, 1949.

the average of Irish life in Boston as not beyond fourteen years, but in the United States, as in Ireland, Irish fecundity conquered the grave. The ramshackle Irish "Acre" of Lowell would have seemed by 1850, according to a local historian, "like suburban luxury to an Irish immigrant." The Irish made up the populations of wretched Pennsylvania coal towns, swarmed in waterfront and industrial rookeries, lived near the railroad station on the wrong side of the tracks, and in the South undertook the heavy and dangerous work from which his master spared the slave.

Yet the visiting Father Cahill wrote back to the people of Ireland that "if you should come to this country, you will find it very difficult, under existing circumstances, ever to live again in Ireland."

The fact was that miserable life in the American city warrens impressed the Irish as better than the existence they had left. The Americans despised the Irish for accepting a standard of life so low as not fit for brute animals. They had no conception, or could have no authentic conception not having seen Ireland with their own eyes, of what the Catholic Irish had left behind them. By the American criterion, the Irish seemed beyond redemption in their poverty. The Irish, by the criterion of the heritage of their native land, thanked God for the new chance in the United States. "The freedom he [the Irishman] enjoys here," wrote Father Roddan of Boston, "contrasts so broadly with the slavery which chilled his blood at home, that if he do not cheerfully bear the burdens which the country lays upon his shoulders, he is no true man."

Comparatively few returned permanently to the land of their birth. Some, forseeing the end, went back, as they said, "to die" and to be buried in Irish soil. Those who returned for a visit were insufferably American in their boasting of the new land.

But the sights and sounds of Ireland never departed from the exiles. The land which had failed them became enveloped, through the enchantment of distance, with the mists of loveliness that softened the lines of grim reality, and a sentimental Ireland of green fields, silver lakes, pink dawns, and cloud-billowed skies — "first flower of the earth and first gem of the sea" — established itself in emigrant folklore. Homesickness for this vision must have been physical anguish when an Irishman read in the *Pilot:* "The cuckoo and corncrake are already heard in the fields near Limerick" or the "oak has burst into leaf before the ash this season."

Children born in America heard from their fathers (women were more realistic about such matters) tales of Ireland's beauty, her greatness, and wrongs of her soft earth:

> Oh! Erin dear, my fatherland.
> How dearly I still love thee.

Young John Turner, a budding boy orator, spoke on St. Patrick's Day in Worcester:

> Though I have never breathed the invigorating air of the land of happiness, or witnessed the recreation which so many experience in the land of virtue, yet, sir, from my infancy my father has instilled in my mind and impressed it so deep on my heart, that for his sake and in detestation of the wrongs inflicted by the hand of tyranny, it shall never be erased from my memory.

Though this sentiment of affection for his native land distinguished the Irishman in the United States, he did not go back: America was his home.

These Catholic Irish emigrants, as a class, worked hard and long hours for little, and the Americans used the expression in praise that "a good workman does as much work as an Irishman." Employers mercilessly exploited them, in the custom of the day.

The organization of a social conscience lay far in the future at the time of high Irish emigration: no settlement houses existed to direct them, no experienced social workers to help untangle their bewilderments, no trained advisers to guide their way into the new country. Only a few overburdened or intermittent emigration societies and head-tax-supported state commissions stood at the head of piers.

Emigrants in America depended upon their own system of social benevolence nurtured in Ireland — the poor helping the poor. They turned to their own mutual benefit societies, vastly expanded by the Famine numbers. In New York, Tammany Hall gave a helping hand. Or they fought their own fight, against horrible odds, as individuals and families, to keep above destitution. The experience through which the Irish emigrants passed made the entrance into the United States less onerous for the later flood of immigration.

The artistry of Eugene O'Neill has made the story of one family a representative picture of the hard course of the Irish emigrant without means in the new land. In *Long Day's Journey into Night*, Tyrone, the successful and prosperous actor, explained to his son the source of his compulsive penuriousness. For people of Catholic Irish descent dating from the pre-Civil War period, the passage strikes the deep wells of memory:

> My mother was left, a stranger in a strange land, with four small children, me and a sister a little older and two younger than me. My two older brothers had moved to other parts. They couldn't help. They were hard put to keep themselves alive. There was no damned romance in our poverty. Twice we were evicted from the miserable hovel we called home, with my mother's few sticks of furniture thrown out in the street, and my mother and sisters crying. I cried, too, though I tried hard not to, because I was the man of the family. At ten years old! There was no more school for me. I worked twelve hours a day in a machine shop, learning to make files. . . . And what do you think I got for it? Fifty cents a week! It's the truth! Fifty cents a week! And my poor mother washed and scrubbed for the Yanks by the day, and my older sister sewed, and my two younger stayed at home to keep the house. We never had clothes enough to wear, nor enough food to eat. Well I remember one Thanksgiving, or maybe it was Christmas, when some Yank in whose house mother had been scrubbing gave her a dollar extra for a present, and on the way home she spent it all on food. I can remember her hugging and kissing us and saying with tears of joy running down her tired face: "Glory be to God, for once in our lives we'll have enough for each of us!"

2

Americans believed that the Irish had only themselves to blame for poverty in the abundant American land. Were not the Irish improvident, wasteful in hospitality, lacking foresight and prudence? But the representative Irish emigrant was as close with a dollar as convention reputed the Scotsman to be; the transplanted peasant had not lost his hoarding instinct: if anything, the Irish handled money much too conservatively, preferring safety to risks for profits.

The millions remitted to Ireland by emigrants, their faithfulness in donations to the Church, the contributions to the Irish patriotic cause — these betokened both savings and self-sacrifice. A director of the New York Savings Bank, praising "a habit of economy" among the poor Irish, conjectured in 1838 that out of 23,000 persons holding about $3,000,000 in deposits, "more than one-half, and perhaps two-thirds are natives of Ireland, male and female." Lemuel Shattuck estimated that of the 19,007 open accounts, totaling $3,023,742 in de-

posits, in the Provident Institution for Savings in Boston in November, 1845, "more than one-half of the depositors . . . are Irish, or
persons immediately connected with our foreign population." Two
thirds of the depositors (1700 out of 2200) in the Emigrants Savings
Bank of New York in 1855 had enrolled themselves as natives of Ireland, and in 1859 Irish housekeepers, domestics, laborers, and clerks
owned a sizable portion of the total deposits of $1,669,322.

No statistics are available, but the assumption is valid from the reputation they bore in Ireland that Irish women encouraged the thrift
of the Catholic Irish, being great savers and managers of small
sums, and a strong husband-wife partnership accumulated funds.
Michael Crotty from County Clare, settled in Hornellsville, bequeathed
his considerable estate to his wife, also a native of Ireland, "remarking
that, as they had begun life together poor, and had toiled together
in early days to gain their possessions, everything should go to her at
his death." Those words encompassed the story of many Irish couples.
Mrs. Bradley of Manchester, New Hampshire, had three hundred
dollars in gold in the pocket of her voluminous skirts for the education of her son, Denis, who became a bishop.

3

An Irish woman remained a "girl" until she married; and the Irish
"girl" in the United States meant specifically to her own race, as she
came to mean to her American employer, a domestic servant or, as the
Irish described her "a living out girl," who might be almost any age.
Americans out of her earshot might call her "biddy," a contemptuous
diminutive of the name "Bridget" or, in the Irish affectionate use,
"Bridie."

But to the visiting Dr. Daniel W. Cahill they were the glory of
the Irish race. "Noble Irish girls! Children of God!" he wrote in 1859.
"The faithful children of their poor fathers and mothers!" The sons
might neglect to remit money; the girls never. Similarly, their generosity to the Church out of their small means never ceased and they gave,
not like some of the men, grumblingly, but with full and unquestioning devotion, as a duty they would not and could not shirk. Managers
of savings banks grew familiar with the faces of the Irish domestics,
who appeared regularly with their small deposits, frequently the total
wages for the week or the month. They were boarded and lodged

where they worked, and their clothes were hand-me-downs from their mistresses; hence, they put away their cash earnings.

Before the appearance of Irish girls in numbers, Americans with sufficient means complained of the difficulty of finding and keeping competent servants. Farmers hired girls from the neighborhood for household work, but being of the same stock and class as their employers they rated themselves as "help," not servants; they would have flown out of the door as fast as a chased cat if described or treated as servants: they had a home to return to if an employer slighted their independence.

The Irish girl was the answer to the prayer of the mistress. She had none of the inhibitions about entering domestic service which made an American girl toss her saucy head. In overpopulated and agricultural Ireland, employment as a servant maid was the only occupation open to her; and she thought herself fortunate to get work with a few pounds a year and food.

The Irish girls filled the vacuum in the United States of the want of domestic servants, and pleased they were to find work that paid them as much in a month as they received in a year in Ireland. Their lack of skills disqualified them from the picking and choosing of jobs; like the laborers, the need to find work at cash wages forced them into an occupation that had need of them. Dr. Cahill drew a picture of the girls fresh from Ireland in an economy entirely different from their own:

> These poor children, from their destitute condition, and from the nature of their social education and instruction, know, on their arrival here, scarcely anything about the work necessary in the houses of gentlemen or merchants, or any other class of wealthy persons. Being the daughters of laboring or needy tradesmen [artisans], or persecuted rack-rented cottiers, they are ignorant of the common duties of servants in respectable positions. They can neither wash nor iron clothes. They don't understand the cleaning of glass or silver plate. They cannot make fires expeditiously, or dust the carpets, or polish the furniture.

The result was that they had "to commence in the lowest places of house duties and work their way to the more elevated positions of knowledge, and trust, and wages." But it was "surprising," he added, how quickly they learned and "how soon they graduate and acquire this housecraft." The absence of the language barrier favored the Irish girls.

The character of Irish emigration also accounted for the strong trend of Irish girls to domestic service. Unlike the Germans, who moved to the new country in family groups, the Irish emigrated as individuals, and the single Irish girls regarded the protective and economic value of shelter and food in a private family as of great worth in comparison to the uncertainty of employment in other occupations and the drabness and loneliness of a shabby room. The story of the Irish girl who devoted her life to a family, becoming a part of it, not infrequently sacrificing marriage, was familiar. She transferred the closely knit loyalties of strong Irish family life to American households when treated with consideration and kindness.

The Irish girls obtained employment through an Intelligence Office, usually run as an auxiliary to another business, a Catholic bookstore, a fruit store, a passenger agency, a real estate business, or a loan office. Patrick Mooney in Boston advertised in 1829 that he had "Good Servants" at his Intelligence Office. He required that each application for a "situation," as domestic work was known among the Irish, exhibit "a Testimonial of moral conduct" from previous families or be recommended by a Roman Catholic clergyman for "honesty, sobriety, and the practical observances of the Duties which the Holy, Catholic Religion enjoins and enforces." The fact of the Irish girl's religion commended itself to Protestant employers, who, while they might entertain anti-Popery sentiments, nevertheless believed that the influence of the priests kept the girl obedient and, particularly, honest. Intelligence Offices in New York which supplied servants for the most substantial families preferred Catholic Irish girls; experience had proved their solid reputation for honesty. Hotels employed Catholic Irish help almost exclusively for that reason: sheets and pillow cases did not disappear when attended to by Irish girls, and lost articles in rooms invariably turned up in the manager's office. The strait-laced Irish domestics carried their own recommendation: mistresses disliked their disposition to be bold in answering back but, as one said, they were safer in the house where men were about.

The first public "No Irish Need Apply" proscription appeared in advertisements in New York for domestic servants and later appeared elsewhere. Generally, this form of advertised discrimination was confined to domestic service. This early prejudice against the Catholic Irish girl, while never entirely dispelled, gradually withered under the force of two circumstances: a spreading prosperity increased the number of families able to employ domestic help, and Irish emigrant girls were the major available source; next, the Irish girl filled the specifications, outlined by one mistress, for "faithfulness, obedience, honesty and capability, and a general regard for my interests."

By 1860, estimates placed the number of Irish girls employed as domestic servants at seventy thousand in New York and Brooklyn, and fifteen thousand in Philadelphia; they enjoyed practically a monopoly in Yankee households in Boston and New England; and in smaller cities and towns in the North they presided over kitchen and chamber. In the South, they worked in hotels, since slave help predominated in private homes.

A word must be said about Irish cooks, the sovereign of the kitchen. No more radical transplanting took place among the Irish emigrants than the stationing of an Irish country girl, who knew how to boil potatoes and fry a bit of bacon, in command of an American cook-stove. "Many of them never in all their lives," wrote Dr. Cahill, "saw a leg of mutton boiled or roasted. Several of them cannot even prepare for their own dinner a pound of bacon, or pork, or cabbage from the miserable lot and the inextricable poverty in which these creatures of persecution and sectarian scorn have been steeped." The English historian A. L. Rowse observed that "cooking is not a strong point with any of the Celts."

But the Irish came among a people that had not yet been educated to the niceties of fine cooking. When they arrived, the United States was still essentially agricultural and even the cities set the table by rural standards: quantities of simple and heavy food. The Appletons and Lawrences, who ruled Boston business and society, had been born on farms. The rising middle class of wealth and influence had not shaken off their rural antecedents. On farms, the owner and the hired hands ate at the same table of the same food. Their sons in the cities had still the countryman's taste in food. The wealthy William Sprague, owner of a great industry, died when a bone from spareribs for breakfast became lodged in his throat. The Irish cook catered to a simple American table, and she learned enough to satisfy the hearty appetites of the magnates.

American households needed cooks, chambermaids, nurses for children, upstairs help, and general girls of all work to meet a rising standard of living. The untutored and single Irish girls needed jobs as speedily as they landed. The bargain struck was mutually beneficial, and both parties moved to a higher level.

4

A drunk staggered along the street. "Oh, he's an Irishman, nothing better can be expected of him."

The sight and the comment reflected a side of Irish life that established an unfavorable reputation for the race in the new land. Americans marked down drunkenness as natural to the Irish as their brogue and held them in disdain for their open lack of self-control. It was not that the Americans themselves were not a hard-drinking people: the temperance movement, incorporated in Boston in the middle 1820s, was directed against the excesses of the native-born, who loved the gurgle of the jug. But the campaign against the Demon, carried on by the churches and the moral reformers, had so propagandized powerful middle-class opinion as to make open drinking scandalous and drunkenness a barrier to respectable society. In addition, drinking reduced economic usefulness and harmed profitable productiveness. Known intemperance violated middle-class mores. The lower classes continued their traditional indulgence, but the drinking members of the higher classes bowed to the social dictates and confined tippling to the home or club.

"When an American gets drunk," it was said, "he commonly hides himself and he keeps still, at any rate. The Irishman, in similar circumstances, rushes out into the street, and under the very nose of the police."

His intemperance added a fourth dimension to the original disqualifications of being Catholic, Irish and a foreigner. Apologists traced Irish intemperance to poverty, but, as suggested earlier, deeper compulsions toward the dreams in the bottle lay buried in the Irish nature. As a matter of fact, the poverty of the Irish emigrant in the United States was, relative to Irish poverty, an improvement. A laborer in Ireland received from 8 to 16 cents a day, in the United States from 75 cents to $1.25 a day. While rent and food were higher in the United States, the price of whiskey was lower, selling at 28 cents a gallon. So, sardonic as it seems, the "prosperity" of the Irish emigrant laborer contributed to his drinking. A man explained:

Six shillings and eight pence sterling used to be the price of a gallon of whiskey at the distillery at Clonmel, in the County of Tipperary, while a shilling a day was better wages than many could obtain, scarcely enough, at that rate, to enable a poor fellow to be drunk for a single day with the wages of six. Here, with the means of getting drunk, at 28¢ per gallon, and wages at a dollar per day, with the wages of a single day a man may be drunk, for a month.

Too often, tragically for the family, a man's wages disappeared in a grog shop.

Fellow countrymen ran the grog shops in Irish areas. The 1839 satire upon Irish officeholders described the Irish Sixth Ward in New York:

> So fam'd for dens for selling brandy,
> In every second house, so handy.

"Look at South Cove; look at Ann street; good God! look at Hamilton street," exclaimed a Boston Irish temperance advocate. "At every place where the Irish were located, were not bar-shops to be found?" For the one Yankee who kept a shop on Tremont Road in Roxbury, there were no less than twenty-eight run by Irishmen, he added. In 1852, Marshal Tukey of the Boston police reported that nearly two thirds of the grog shops were owned by the Irish. The New York *Tribune* in 1854 estimated that one fourth of the population was Catholic and that from one half to three fourths of the groceries were kept by Catholics. "Catholics," it said, "sell much more than their proportion of the liquor drank in this country."

No social stigma attached to the selling of liquor in Ireland, legally or otherwise. An Irishman considered himself favored by fortune if he set up a grog shop in the United States; it was one way of improving his economic status and with many, because of American proscription against the Irish, the only way. It was a business congenial to the social gregariousness of the Irish nature.

But the tavern keeper enjoyed no social immunity in the United States. Extremist Catholic Irish temperance men (and they were as fanatical as the American reformers) granted no tolerance to the sellers of liquor. Dennis O'Brien, a leader of total abstinence in Boston, proclaimed that a rum dealer was worse than a murderer or the keeper of a brothel (a horrible accusation among the Irish) and urged the Irish to get out of the business. The effect of the agitation began to appear. In 1855 an Irishman, requesting a license of the excise board, was questioned as to his moral fitness and replied: "Ah, sure, it is not much character a man needs to sell rum."

During the 1830s, the interdependence of the Irish liquor seller and Tammany Hall, which secured him a license, related the Irish and liquor to politics. The charge of the relationship arose in a different way in New England. The Catholic opposition to sumptuary legislation — a restrictive law in Massachusetts and the Maine prohibition on the manufacture and sale of liquor — identified the Irish, in the eyes of the reform elements, with the liquor interests.*

The realistic and shrewdly observant Matthew P. Breen, in his sourcebook of practical politics, *Thirty Years of New York Politics,* concisely explained the relationship and attitude of the Irish liquor dealer to politics:

> As a rule the liquor dealer in politics makes headway by no false pretenses. He is no better or no worse than he appears. He is free from hypocrisy and cant. He is in politics as a matter of business, and he makes no disguise of it. He laughs to scorn those who sanctimoniously publish to the world that they accept political station for the benefit of the people, and that the sole object of their existence on earth is to see that the taxpayer is protected and the citizen upheld in all his inalienable rights. Such declarations he regards (and justly in most cases) as the merest sham. He is open, frank, free of expression, generous and hospitable. He never dreams that his methods of conducting local politics are otherwise than in harmony with the highest principles of political science, adhered to because of precedent, and justifiable because of example.

The interrelationship of politics and liquor was not a cultivated thing with the Catholic Irish in the United States; it came out of their Irish background and was natural in the order of things, a part of the pattern they understood. Generally speaking, it struck them as strange that Americans made a moral issue of it.

The sad side of Irish intemperance rested in the fine and decent men it entrapped, for the racial curse refused to confine itself to a careful selection of damaged souls. The obituary praise of a glassworker accidentally killed while drunk wrote the epitaph of many a good man: the compassionate Irish had a saying that drink was a good man's weakness. *"If we except one thing,"* the obituary said, "he was a valuable

---

* Respectable Catholic opinion advocated strong licensing laws and their vigorous enforcement rather than prohibition legislation.

man, ingenious, industrious, and always ready and willing to do his part in any difficult work." That "one thing" added a further burden to poverty-bowed backs. It helped increase the Irish population of poorhouses with distressed families. That "one thing," if pursued, brought an Irish emigrant to his grave in seven years, the statisticians said.

5

The most relentless foe of that "one thing" among the Irish was the Roman Catholic clergy. They succeeded, wrote the historian of the New York diocese, "not only in diminishing its ravages, but in affixing to the saloon business a stigma which remains to this day."

Rev. John Shanahan, who had been a mission priest during the building of the Erie Canal, organized the first Irish temperance society at Troy in the late 1820s, and similar societies followed in Utica (1830), Albany (1831), and Rochester. The initiative for a temperance movement of wider dimensions than a local society came from the Boston Irish, who at a public meeting on April 7, 1836, laid plans for the Irish Temperance Society of Boston and issued an address to their countrymen in the United States.

Temperance reform was the one subject upon which Catholics and Protestants found common ground of accord in those days. Catholic priests mounted Protestant pulpits to preach on temperance, and Protestant reformers gave encouragement to Catholic efforts. But fundamental differences on the theology of temperance and deep-seated distrust intervened against joint cooperation and set up separate movements. The Church looked sourly then on the fanaticism of Protestant reformers, who preached that even the moderate use of alcohol was sinful, and made total abstinence an article of religion. The very name of "temperance," said the *Jesuit,* is a "bull," for to the sectarians it signified "total abstinence." The Catholic Irish, too, recognized among the temperance reformers many of the men who engaged actively in anti-Popery campaigns, distributed anti-Catholic tracts and zealously proselytized among poor Catholics.

When the zeal of the Protestant reformers called in the police power of the state with prohibition legislation in 1839 in Massachusetts, the Catholic Irish bristled with hostility, and the *Pilot,* reflecting Catholic teachings as well as sentiment, said:

We cannot but regard any *law* on the subject as an impudent interference with the habits of individuals, and a desperate attempt to carry points by main force, which can never be carried out in that manner. Laws were designed to guard the persons and property of the community against direct attacks; and not to root out vice from the hearts of men and women. The grace of God alone can destroy our vile propensities; and hence the law is unreasonable, and calculated to create confusion, without being of any advantage to the public.

It characterized the reformers behind the law as "busy bodies, who are fond of novelty . . . who care not so much to ascertain what is right, as to run on their own account, without pausing to inquire — whether they are sent or not."

This first open break set off the Catholic Irish in the minds of the Boston moral improvers as a force in the community hostile to progress and reform and prepared the stage for vigorous clashes later and the alienation of the two cultures.

6

The Catholic Irish temperance movement, faltering and feeble, burst out into a flaming crusade in the United States with the sudden emergence of Father Theobald Mathew in Ireland as the inspiration of one of the most remarkable movements of the nineteenth century — the temperance evangelizing of a man who had none of the characteristics of the evangelizer, a humble, diffident, self-effacing, and unworldly Capuchin friar.

Interestingly, Father Mathew's extraordinary mission was an indirect outgrowth of the American temperance movement. He was a priest in the city of Cork, a devoted worker among the poor, founder of an industrial school for boys and another for girls, and a member of the Board of Guardians of the Cork Workhouse. The Quakers, taking example from the American movement, had founded the Cork Total Abstinence Society and under the persuasions of William Martin, a fellow member of the workhouse board, Father Mathew signed his name on April 10, 1838, with the remark, "Here goes, in the name of God." Clerical eyebrows were raised at the news of a Capuchin friar associating himself with a Quaker society.

The Boston *Pilot* of November 2, 1839, carried the brief news item: "The success of a Catholic clergyman, the Rev. T. Mathew, who has become an apostle of Temperance in the South [of Ireland], appears to have been extraordinary and unparalleled. The people flock to him in great multitudes, and the number of those whom he has induced to abandon the horrible vice of drunkenness is beyond calculation."

Father Mathew started giving the pledge of total abstinence to the poor in Cork, but soon groups walked in from the adjacent country-side to receive it and cities at a distance invited him to visit them. What the impressed observers called a "moral revolution" swept all Ireland. The simple appeal of the radiant character of a priest captured the attachments of an emotional people.

His miracle in evangelizing Ireland to temperance without hysteria originated in a native innocence and saintly self-abnegation that made Father Mathew the best-known Irishman in the world, next to O'Connell. He gave the pledge personally to more than half the population of Ireland in massive open-air meetings and extended his work to England and Scotland. Millions wore Father Mathew Temperance medals or joined Father Mathew Temperance societies; every Irish town had its Father Mathew band and marching banners.

The fame of Father Mathew reached across the Atlantic in reports of the Catholic Irish press and the stories of the emigrants, many of whom had taken the pledge from him. The year 1840 marked the start of the real temperance movement among the Catholic Irish in the United States under the inspiration of Father Mathew, now called the Apostle of Temperance. The economic stake of insurance kept an Irishman's interest in temperance from flagging; the local organizations encouraged a fuller social life to take the place of the grog shops through picnics and entertainments; the Father Mathew literary institutes developed cultural improvement as a corollary of the pledge against intoxicating drink.

Catholics and Protestants pressed invitations upon Father Mathew to visit the United States. When he finally arrived at Staten Island on July 29, 1849, his visit turned into a national reception by all creeds and classes. New York staged a welcome to the Irish Capuchin un-equaled since the testimony of American affection for Lafayette a quarter of a century before. The priest who symbolized the great virtue of temperance was borne down by the excesses of American hospitality. Levees, dinners, and receptions followed one another, and the temperance New York *Tribune* finally suggested an expedition to rescue Father Mathew from "the windy compliments of winebibing dignitaries" and permit him "to do the good work for which he has come among us." When he shook himself free of the ceremonies, Father Mathew began giving the pledge, from eight o'clock in the morning until nine o'clock at night: more than twenty thousand took the total abstinence pledge from him during his stay in New York.

Boston, the birthplace of American temperance, took Father Mathew into its Puritan arms. Hon. Josiah Quincy, Jr., in the chair at a Faneuil Hall meeting, wondered what the Puritan Fathers would say at the sight of their offspring zealously welcoming a Roman Catholic priest — and an Irishman to boot. Bishop Fitzpatrick set down his thought of the Puritan-Irish consorting in the description of a public meeting addressed by Father Mathew: "The platform was . . . covered by sectarian fanaticks, Calvinistic preachers and deacons and other such who also made their speeches. The appearance of fellowship between a Catholic priest and such men can hardly be without evil results." An unhappy and embarrassing scene, the most disagreeable episode of Father Mathew's visit to America, occurred in Boston, fulfilling Bishop Fitzpatrick's "evil results" and the apprehensions of Bishop Hughes over the innocent Mathew in enemy country.

Father Mathew had signed, with Daniel O'Connell, the famous address to the Irish in America to come out from under the slaveholders and join the Abolitionists. William Lloyd Garrison, a master of propaganda, well remembered the famous signature on the adddress and calculated to turn Father Mathew's presence in Boston to the advantage of the anti-slavery cause.

Three days after Father Mathew's arrival, Garrison visited him and, recalling the earlier address, invited the Irish priest to attend a meeting in Worcester on August 3 of the Massachusetts Anti-Slavery Society to celebrate the anniversary of West Indian emancipation. Father Mathew replied:

> I have as much as I can do to save men from the slavery of intemperance, without attempting the overthrow of any other kind of slavery! Besides, it would not be proper for me to commit myself on a question like this, under present circumstances. I am a Catholic priest; but, being here to promote the cause of temperance, I should not be justified in turning aside from my mission for the purpose of subserving the cause of Catholicism.

Garrison thought this "essential jesuitry" and suspected that Bishop Hughes, "that slavite," had warned Father Mathew against the Abolitionists. Father Mathew told Garrison that he was no friend of slavery but feared the ruin of his temperance mission were he dragged into the partisan fury of a domestic issue.

In a series of articles in the *Liberator*, Garrison belabored Father Mathew for betraying the Abolitionist cause and refusing to admonish his countrymen to be true to liberty by unlocking the slave's dungeon to which he asserted they held the key by their balance of political power. The *Pilot* called Garrison "a fierce-hearted son of an Inquisitor" and asked, "In the name of common sense, why should Garrison force himself or his views upon the Irish missionary?" Father Mathew, it said, did not come to America "to be hawked about" by Garrison. Even strong Abolitionists, like George Bradburn, denounced Garrison and justified the refusal of the old Irish priest to be made an anti-slavery partisan. Garrison exploited the Father Mathew incident for weeks and further convinced the Catholic Irish that Abolitionism stood for fanaticism and anti-Catholicism.

Then Southern anti-Abolitionist fanaticism had a whirl at the kindly priest who had come to preach temperance. After an extended tour through the Catholic Irish communities of New England, Father Mathew visited Philadelphia and Baltimore and arrived in Washington on December 18.

Governor Lumpkin of Georgia, president of the Georgia State Temperance Society, had second thoughts upon the cordial invitation issued to Father Mathew to visit Georgia and in the light of the Garrison incident demanded to know if the priest stood against slavery. Father Mathew told him, as he had told Garrison, that in the United States he stood neutral, whereupon the governor withdrew the invitation.

In Washington, the House unanimously voted Father Mathew the honor of a seat on the floor, but in the Senate members from slaveholding states resisted a resolution affording Father Mathew the same courtesy as the House. Jefferson Davis led a slashing attack on Father Mathew as an enemy of slavery and others followed in the same vein. But Henry Clay, William H. Seward, and General Cass rose in spirited behalf of Father Mathew, and the invitation won by a good margin. Up to that time, General Lafayette had been the only foreigner so honored by Congress, and the distinction spoke public opinion's approval of Father Mathew's temperance work.

In all, Father Mathew spent two years and four months in the United

States, visited most of the states east of the Mississippi and gave the
pledge to an estimated five to six hundred thousand people in an extraordinary crusade, marred only by his unwilling involvement in the
passionate issue of the day.

Had the Father Mathew pledge wrought a change in the habits of
the Catholic Irish? John F. Maguire, the Irish journalist, who visited
the United States after the Civil War, wrote: "Were I asked to say
what I believed to be the most serious obstacle to the advancement of
the Irish in America, I would unhesitatingly answer — *Drink*." But
Father Stephen Byrne, who compiled a handbook and guide to newcomers, *Irish Emigration to the United States*, wrote in 1873 of
Father Mathew's work: "Millions now living, if not in opulence, at
least in independent circumstances and enjoying the comfort of
peaceful homes, are indebted to him for all they possess."

By the time of the Civil War, the Father Mathew movement appeared dead, hastened to its grave by the hard times of 1856-1858,
which increased intemperance. The temperance societies founded under the spell of his name withered away. But a new generation of
bishops and clergymen revived the temperance cause after the Civil
War on the principles and in the name of Father Mathew, with a
particular appeal to the young. Throughout the nineteenth century and
even up to World War I, the impression of Father Mathew remained
with the Catholic Irish in the United States and his labors bore rich
fruits.

7

The effect of liquor on the nervous system of the Catholic Irish, together with their disposition to hit first and repent later, piled up
impressive statistics of court cases and jail commitments that suggested
a lawlessness more arithmetical than vicious.

Statistical reports, wrote the *Freeman's Journal* in 1845, indicated
the natives of Ireland "as having furnished the largest number of
criminals — indeed more than all of the other countries put together."
Police returns for six months of 1845 showed 1492 arrests in one section, of whom 844 were Irish, 454 Americans and 26 English — a pre-
possessing record at first glance, but the *Freeman's Journal* took a
second look:

> Whereas on reference to the criminal docket, it will be seen that more than two-thirds of the Irish persons who are arrested are charged with assaults and other minor offences, so that but comparatively few of them are left to commit the other higher offences, such as forgery, &c. It is seldom we hear of an Irishman being arrested for forgery, burglary, packing pistols, &c. Their acts being confined to mere breaches of the peace, assaults, &c. of the most trifling nature.

The New York *Journal of Commerce* reporter of Police and Sessions' courts observed: "You will scarcely ever find an Irishman dabbling in counterfeit money, or breaking into houses, or swindling; but if there is any fighting to be done, he is very apt to have a hand in it." Even though Pat might " 'meet with a friend and for love knock him down,' " noted a Montreal paper, the fighting usually resulted from a sudden excitement, allowing there was "but little 'malice prepense' in his whole composition." The *Catholic Telegraph* of Cincinnati in 1853, saying that the "name of 'Irish' has become identified in the minds of many, with almost every species of outlawry," distinguished the Irish vices as "not of a deep malignant nature," arising rather from the "transient burst of undisciplined passion," like "drunk, disorderly, fighting, etc., not like robbery, cheating, swindling, counterfeiting, slandering, calumniating, blasphemy, using obscene language, &c."

Why, exclaimed the Boston *Pilot* in 1852, the sum of $205,718 embezzled from the Suffolk Bank by Brewer and Rand, two native-born citizens, was more money "than has been stolen in goods and money by the Irish population since the settlement of Boston!"

The eagerness of the police, usually nativists, to run in the Irish foreigners for drunkenness, fighting, and resisting their authority added to the statistics of Irish lawlessness. The *Pilot* acknowledged with shame the truth of the record cited by a nativist paper that seven eighths of the arrests for drunkenness were foreigners, that is, Irish, but asserted that "if the native constables and watchmen of this city looked as sharp after natives as they do foreigners," the story would be different. Constables shushed native boisterousness; they arrested the boisterous Irish. They helped home a native drunk; the Irish drunk landed behind the bars.

Non-Irish newspapers testified to the police discrimination against the Irish. A Boston judge sentenced four Irishmen to a year's imprisonment and upward, leaving their families subject to the almshouse, for tangling with the police: his honor felt the "necessity of example."

A month and a half later two young Boston bloods, sons of rich men, involved in precisely the same situation, were freed without examination. "If the offender had been a poor Irishman," moralized the *Daily Bee,* "he would as surely have been imprisoned for months."

Violations of liquor or licensing laws enjoyed the support and even the connivance of public opinion in Ireland and hence a steady procession of Irish offenders in American courts, especially for illegal selling on Sunday. The Irish thought it an outrage on common sense and Christian charity for the police to arrest a poor woman who tried to make both ends meet by keeping an illicit bottle for the use, at a price, of friends and friends' friends; besides, it was a service they appreciated. Early prohibition laws, like the Maine law, stimulated the Irish to bootlegging. Father O'Donnell of Portland said that probably not more than eight among the Irish population had obeyed the Maine law by giving up the liquor business; instead liquor selling and shops had increased twofold, and tenements and houses were being turned into "striped pigs," the contemporary name for speakeasies. A race of people familiar with the tricks of illegal poteen distillers to frustrate revenue agents in Ireland had ways of making evidence disappear in the prohibition state of Maine. The city marshal of Portland inspected the premises of a liquor seller named Noonan. He discovered a lead pipe under a stairway leading to a cask of cherry brandy cached in the structure of the house but by the time he set the hands of the law upon it, Noonan's friends outside had pumped out the brandy through another pipe.

8

Settled American communities expected the worst of the Irish and resolved no doubts in their favor. "Indeed, the most simple crime, if well seasoned with Irish blood," wrote the *Pilot* in 1839, "swells into an offence of immense magnitude. Thus, the plundering of a hen-roost, when accomplished by an Irishman, assumes the gigantic front of a plot against the government, and an attempt to bring over the Pope." A good deal of this sentiment traced to the suspicions of respectable Americans that all foreigners were criminals or, at any rate, they were different from the law-abiding citizenry and therefore up to no good. The Court House in the solid Yankee town of Concord blazed with an incendiary fire on June 9, 1849, and the blame fell upon Irishmen until a native confessed and implicated another native. One Pullen was murdered in Providence in 1852, and the police arrested "almost every Irishman in the city, who was in the habit of being out after dark." During the Know-Nothing agitation in 1855, when true Americans were determined to put and keep down the Catholic Irish, the Providence *Journal* wrote satirically of a small Yankee Rhode Island town that had grown excited over a murder:

> The good people of Glocester arrested their Irishman last week on suspicion of being concerned in the late murder, but finding no evidence against him, discharged him. They have only one, we believe, in that town, but they make the most of him, and have valiantly determined that he shall not *rise*. With these views, some of them go constantly armed, and have even carried their anti-popery so far as to astonish by their presence a Protestant church.

Hosea Gardner, postmaster of Hingham, Massachusetts, was poisoned by his wife, who fancied another man, and it was revealed that she had instructed the boy, who had been sent on the errand to buy the arsenic, to return to the apothecary shop and say that "it was a paddy woman who had sent for it."

Newspapers, without intending to do so, put the general character of Irish offenses against the law in the proper perspective as minor, trivial, and not essentially serious. Reporters early seized upon the colorful, talkative, and individualistic Irish characters enmeshed in the law to write lively stories that, though they burlesqued them as "stage Irish" and exaggerated the details, at least removed the Irish from the sordid run-of-the-mill cases of the courts. Their interest and attention perked up when an Irishman or woman appeared before a judge. Invariably the Irish, in themselves or by the twist of the offense or by their excuses, gave color to the drab court proceedings.

Daniel Shanahan was called to account for his assault on an officer. It seemed that Shanahan and some fellow Irishman watching a dog fight fell to swinging on one another when differences of opinion arose. But they forgot their own quarreling to turn together upon a policeman who tried to interfere.

An example gives an idea of how Irish "crime" was handled by newspapers in an earlier day:

> Police Court — *Yesterday* — Justice Rogers. — The court, during the morning, had several spicy cases before it. . . .
> *Wm. Murphy* — a poor, God-forsaken looking man — was

charged with stealing a butcher's knife from the cart of Joshua
Law. William was seen to take the knife, put it under his coat
and start off; but he was followed, and "the knife was covered up
under his coat" — so the witness said.

"Wasn't it under the left wing o' me coat?" asked William.

"Yes," replied the witness.

"An' so it *was;* I know bether 'an take the whole o' me coat to
hide a small knife like o' that. But I didn't stale it; I only *took* it
an' was on me way home wid it to cut a pace o' rope, an' thin it was
meself that was to bring it back in the marnin'."

"Three dollars and costs," said his honor.

"*What,* sir! — *Thraa dollars* an' divil a cent have I to pay it wid."

Pat Rooney, c.d., 2 m. H.C. [common drunk, two months in the
House of Correction] "Gard bliss me! From the likes o' this defind
me hereafter!," and away he went.

The Catholic Irish press and respectable Irishmen protested against
the newspaper practice of turning the Irishman on the stand into a
comic stage character and by the Civil War, with the exception of
some incorrigible sheets, like Bennett's New York *Herald,* had reduced its use. They also raised their voices against the custom of national description in newspaper accounts, like "John O'Brien, Irishman" or "James Murphy, foreigner." That, too, disappeared.

9

But the most interesting and significant relationship of the Catholic
Irish to the law was in its enforcement — as policemen. In 1848 the
Pilot said, in regretting the appearance of "the well-known Celtic
names" in police cases (*"not deep-dyed* crime," it explained, requiring
"method and deliberation"): "Could they but get rid of those crimes
and vices which naturally beset an excitable temperament, victim to
too many social temptations, and too many social wrongs, the Irish
would present a fair moral face to the world." Within not too many
years, that face was surmounted by a policeman's helmet.

The Irish satisfied the requirements of police duty: they were
physically strong and physically courageous; at any time it is dangerous
procedure to challenge the physical courage of an Irishman. They had
carried from Ireland, as O'Connell had told an English parliamentary
commission, a deep respect for the station of policeman: it marked a
substantial advance in status; it gave the man who wore the uniform

a position in the government and vested him with a sense of authority, which the Irish nature cherished. In America, the lot of policeman elevated a man from the ranks of the hand workers and provided him that warm glow of self-importance and dignity that a hod carrier, for example, would not possess. A policeman had caste.

The logic of appointing the Irish to the police force was as clear as that of Drummond in Ireland when he threw open the constabulary to Catholic Irish merit: an Irishman was the best choice for patrolling and supervising his fellow countrymen. As Irish populations increased in the cities, the wisdom of Drummond's judgment commended itself to municipal authority. An even more compelling fact joined this ordinary common sense: Irish politicians grew in influence with the expanding Irish vote, and they saw to it that they had a share in the distribution of jobs, including the police.

The Irish Democrats in New York were awarded jobs as watchmen for their loyalty in the 1844 municipal elections, though there had been Irish constables long before that date. By 1855, of the 1149 policemen in New York's uniformed force, 718 were natives of America, 305 natives of Ireland, and 51 natives of Germany. The creation of a unified police force in Philadelphia opened the door for more numerous Irish officers. By 1850, in the growing city of Chicago, six of the nine men on the police force were Irish and by 1860, 49 of the 107 on the police force carried Irish names. Chief O'Leary headed the police force in New Orleans and Malachi Fallon (or O'Fallon), former New York saloonkeeper, was chief of police of San Francisco.

Even Boston appointed an Irishman to the police force, one Barney McGinniskin, named by Mayor Bigelow in the fall of 1851 after a petition by prominent citizens urged the wisdom of putting the stick in the hand of a son of Erin. A nativist storm broke over Barney's head. Newspapers complained of an Irishman on the force; an alderman attempted to force a reconsideration of the appointment; and the nativists held a demonstration of protest in Faneuil Hall. Barney, who had been the driver of a hack stationed in the Irish Ann Street section, was recalled as having paid a ten-dollar fine for his part in the St. Mary's Church riot; and the nativists said he was a no-good drunken Irishman. Marshal Tukey, who investigated Barney for the mayor, cleared him as a "temperate and quiet man." Two months later Tukey described him as "a noisy, quarrelsome, meddlesome Ann Street cabman," and wanted him discharged. Tukey said he regularly reported himself for duty as "Barney McGinniskin, from the bogs of Ireland," which the marshal thought was designed to provoke trouble. It was only his Irish good nature, retorted Barney. The marshal wrote a letter to the papers on Barney's disqualifications, and Barney sued him for libel. The marshal fired Barney when Mayor Bigelow went out, but the new mayor restored him. The marshal refused to recognize Barney as a member of the force, and Barney refused to recognize the marshal. This standoff was finally broken when the Know Nothings forced out Boston's first Irish policeman.

The "crime wave" which trembling Americans anticipated from the floodtide of Catholic Irish foreigners ended up with the Catholic Irish entrenched as the guardians of the law.

10

The light at the end of the dark tunnel of Catholic Irish emigrant poverty beckoned as the typically American vision of middle-class respectability, if not for the emigrants themselves, at least for their children. Where he wished to see the Irish people, wrote John Ryan, the woolen manufacturer in 1855, "is in the great, numerous, industrious, intelligent, and independent class of people in the United States, who live in comfort and independence, by their labor, sobriety, industry, and frugality." The Church, too, encouraged this ideal of success. A Church poor in means equated success in terms of wealth, like the emigrants themselves.

The first generation of emigrants, however, were unprepared for the commercial life which brought rewards in the bustling United States, and they had inhibitions from Ireland which needed to be overcome before ambition entered into play. The Catholic Irish press chided the newcomers for their lack of economic and social progress in comparison to the steady improvement of other emigrant peoples, the Germans notably. "Laborers remain laborers," said one critic, "and hod-carriers continue hod-carriers, and tradesmen [artisans] do not become 'bosses' as adopted citizens from other nations or native citizens do." Americans noted the stagnation of the Irish in their poverty and ascribed it to the characteristic backwardness of the race.

But Orestes Brownson, the Yankee convert, comprehended the difference America would make to the children of the emigrants bowed down in the captivity of poverty. "Out from these narrow lanes, blind courts, dirty streets, damp cellars, and suffocating garrets," he wrote, "will come forth some of the noblest sons of our country, whom she will delight to own and to honor."

The *Pilot,* which had invoked the Deity for the refuge in America of the Famine thousands, again called upon the name of God, this time to get the Irish emigrants out of the cities, "from the over-crowded and tax-oppressed seaboards." Go to the West, it advised, "and lay the foundations of future comfort and prosperity. . . . Even as *paupers,* the new comers would have a far better chance in the cities and settlements of the interior."

43

On the Course of Empire

THE CATHOLIC IRISH EMIGRANT was no Daniel Boone: neither his nature nor his circumstances equipped him for the pioneering life of the frontier.

Yet he managed to get around the Western country in considerable numbers. "The West is full of colonies of Dutchmen, Norwegians, Portuguese and Hollanders," wrote an Irishman from Michigan in 1859, "while the Irish, though they are *everywhere* in units, are nowhere together." Their impact or presence was hardly so noticeable as in the East, but their numbers and characteristics built an Irish tradition in Michigan, Wisconsin, Illinois, Indiana, Minnesota, Iowa, and particularly in California, dating from pre-Civil War days.

The Catholic Irish movement westward generally followed the unorganized pattern of the emigration from Ireland to the United States. At no time before the Civil War was there a continuing design, carefully planned and adequately financed, such as obtained with the Germans, to move the Irish from the overcrowded Eastern cities to the West. When the Irish went West, they followed their noses, as they had in crossing the Atlantic.

Father Roddan in 1855 described the nature of Irish migration as having been "for some years small in details, but steady, and, in the course of a few years, it amounts to a body very respectable in weight and numbers. And the persons who go are precisely the persons whom we can ill afford to spare." These were the Irish who made a conscious decision to move from the settled communities of the East with the hope of improving their lot.

The body of urban floating labor, the hod carriers, the draymen, the diggers of foundations and the like, whom the clergy, press, and emigrant societies exhorted to get out of the cities, remained unbudged. This population, the *Pilot* said, "cannot, taking one man with another, raise money enough to pay their fare to Canada or to the West." Insolvency explained in part the apathetic response of the emigrants to the bombardment of the Go-West campaign, but other considerations also weighed against the trek.

Lack of means as a reason failed to impress Mooney, the traveling bookseller: "Let the Irish in New York and Boston who cannot find work in those cities strike out on foot for the Great West — yes, on foot." With regular work, he explained, the Irish emigrant can "save the price of an acre and a half of the finest land in the world every week!" and in less than a year he would have sufficient funds to start to the West and take up an eighty-acre farm, "which will be your own for ever." A letter in the *Western Pioneer* of Michigan in 1849 by Edward Gillon, the traveling agent of the *Pilot,* put the case for Irish migration succinctly and sensibly:

> Any man who intends to make this country his home, and who must earn his bread by the sweat of his brow, the West is the ground for him, and the sooner he goes the better. There is no danger of starving in the West, and any man who has his health can do well, if not it is his own fault.

2

Thoughtful men in retrospect have regretted the poverty and other retarding circumstances which fixed the Catholic Irish along the Atlantic Coast. But examination of the forces which kept the bulk roosting in the East inevitably comes to the comprehensive cause which illumines the other reasons: the emigrants lacked a decisive will to move to the new country of the West.

They were sick and tired and thought themselves well shed of the farm and the countryside. They had had their fill of miserable rural life in Ireland and they turned full circle to another kind of life in the United States. The Irish propagandists for the blessings of the West urged the emigrants not to dally a day in the cities. They knew, consciously or unconsciously, that once the contagion of the city took hold of the emigrant from rural Ireland the attractiveness of a homestead in the West dimmed. "The settler will recollect," wrote an Irishman extolling the advantages of Wisconsin, "that on the moment he makes his purchase *he is the undisturbed lord of the soil*, henceforth, and for ever, that he need not fear rent, rate, or taxes, bailiffs, drivers, or rectors, agents, bribe men, or canters." An Irishman in Ireland would describe such a state of affairs as paradise. But his orientation shifted in the United States and what seemed paradisiacal in Ireland had not the same appeal in a new land where a man could earn a living without digging the soil.

3

The Catholic clergymen in the East agreed, almost to a man, upon the wisdom of moving the emigrants out of the cities, but they sharply divided as to where they should locate. One school, of which Father Roddan, editor of the Boston *Pilot,* could be considered a representative spokesman, encouraged migration to the West. Bishop Timon of Buffalo represented the school of more prudent Irish migration, that is, to settled farm communities in the East and Middle States. Bishop Timon, the son of Irish emigrants, had come to Buffalo out of the West and his recommendation carried authority. Numerous Catholic Irish farm settlements dotted his diocese in western New York. In urging these upon Irish city-dwellers, Bishop Timon said:

> In years past, ministerial duties forced me to travel widely over the West and South of our country. From facts there noted, I feel convinced that the Irish Catholic emigrant of sober, industrious habits and but moderate means, can find no *safer,* perhaps no *better,* location than in some of the districts I have mentioned. There indeed, life will be less of a lottery; few great prizes can be drawn, but then *also there need be no blanks.*

The timid school of Eastern clerics feared the loss of faith by the Catholic Irish in the West. Father E. Dillon of the Buffalo diocese emphasized "the consolation of their holy religion" to the Irish who settled in western New York and warned: "In the Western States there are many places in which the emigrant must of necessity settle down, destitute of churches and pastors. In such places he will fall into the disuse of his religion, and from disuse into indifferentism, till he finally makes a complete wreck of his faith." This school thought the Catholic Irishman would fare better on a farm that had been cleared and worked, with a house and outbuildings already raised, than in virgin territory starting from scratch.

4

The Boston *Pilot* was the most influential medium in the East for the promotion of Catholic Irish Western emigration. Its traveling agent, Edward Gillon, an interesting figure, who left Hartford to journey with his horse ("Old Boney") and buggy through the Western country signing up subscribers and who ended his days in the religious community of the College of Notre Dame, forwarded intelligent information for the prospective Irish emigrant to the West.

The letters to newspapers in the East from the traveling historian peddling his own wares, Thomas Mooney, carried vivid pictures of the fatness of the land, the wealth that awaited the industrious and diligent Irishman and the glory which would redound to Ireland by the prosperity of her sons, whose success in the West was in itself an incitement to migrate. Despite his charlatanism, Mooney conferred a real benefit upon his countrymen by his unceasing and vigorous propagandizing of the West.

Responsible and conscientious Irishmen in the West, who felt the obligation to inform emigrants in the East of the West's splendid opportunities, used the columns of the Catholic Irish press for their communications. In these letters was found the quick adaptability of the Irishman to his surroundings: they boasted of the little cities and settlements they had adopted as home, and one even admitted that Wisconsin made better butter than Ireland.

5

The most indefatigable drum-beaters in the West for Irish emigrant recruits were Bishop Mathias Loras and Judge Charles Corkery of Dubuque, who between them spread the name of Iowa throughout the East. Bishop Loras, a native of France and first bishop of Dubuque in 1837, contemplated the West as a home of rising Catholicity, and he hoped to people it with Irish emigrants, then the largest source of supply.

He induced a group of Irish Sisters of Charity to leave Philadelphia and open an academy in Dubuque in 1844. He struck it off splendidly with Brother Ambrose, who sought a location in America for an overflow of monks, in consequence of which new Melleray Abbey established itself in Vernon Township, twelve miles from Dubuque, in 1849 as a branch of the famous Mount Melleray Abbey of Irish Cistercian Trappists in County Waterford. Within two years, the abbey had become the center of a flourishing congregation. As the knowing Bishop Loras had foreseen, the Irish monks attracted Irish settlers, and in 1860 a correspondent wrote that Catholic Irish farmers filled the surrounding countryside. He constantly circularized Irish emigrants through the Catholic and Irish press of the East; he kept in touch with transportation companies; and he carried on correspondence with Irish emigrant societies.

Charles Corkery, a pioneer settler of Dubuque, a Democratic officeholder and a leading man of the Irish group active in early Iowa affairs, deserves credit as father of publicity for Irish emigration to the West. Two letters addressed from Dubuque, in 1838 and 1841, in the *Catholic Herald* of Philadelphia, systematically specified land and job opportunities in the Iowa country for the Irish. Corkery's reply to the questionnaire sent out by the newly formed Irish Emigrant Society, widely publicized in the Eastern Catholic Irish newspapers, was loaded with exactly the precise information wanted in the East by Irishmen considering emigration.

The Census of 1850 listed 4885 Irish-born in Iowa; by 1860, the number had jumped to 28,072.

In 1851, four new counties in Iowa carried the names of Irish heroes — Emmet, O'Brien, and Mitchel, after the patriots, and Mathew, after the Apostle of Temperance. Irish place names reflected the Irish influence in pre-Civil War Iowa: Derrinane (the ancestral home of O'Connell), Tara, Garryowen, Melleray, Glasnevin (the Dublin cemetery), all in Dubuque County; Erin, Wexford, Burke, Belfast, the Reilly Settlement, Waterford Township, the Irish Settlement near Des Moines, Emmetsburg and Brophy's Creek elsewhere.

While Irish artisans and laborers settled in the larger towns, Iowa also had a respectable Irish farming population. Dennis Mahoney, the newspaper editor and politician, renamed the 1838 Irish settlement at Makokiti after the Garryowen section of his native city of Limerick. Father Hore's unhappy colonization project of Famine emigrants from County Wexford finally lighted on the prairie in Allamakee County, a few miles distant from Prairie du Chien, eighteen families out of the several hundred people who started. Out from Fort Dodge were two Catholic Irish settlements established in the middle 1850s, one on Lizard Creek and a second at Emmetsburg, on the wild frontier.

The background of the Lizard Creek settlement group can be taken as representative of Catholic Irish migration to the West. Unlike German, Scandinavian, and Hollander emigrants, who moved directly from transatlantic ships to farms, the Catholic Irish made an initial stay in the East. The Lizard Creek Irish, mostly young men with families or young unmarried men, had come to Iowa from Maine, New York, the Pennsylvania coal mines, Ohio, and St. Louis. The magnet which attracted them was free government land. Apparently they had started West as single families with no fixed destination in mind and had merged as a group along the line of journey. Once settled, they had been joined by other Irish families.

Sister M. Justille McDonald, in her exemplary study of the Irish in Wisconsin,* examined the backgrounds of 150 Irish-born farmers, businessmen, and professional men from about twenty-five Wisconsin counties and found that they averaged seven years in other states before they moved to new homes, that Massachusetts and New York led as previous residence and that a rather large number had come through Canada.

A common design appeared in the emigration westward of Irish engaged in the same occupation, even in the same factory. The Pennsylvania coal mines furnished quotas of Irish settlers. The panic of 1837 speeded unemployed textile workers from Fall River to be the pioneer Irish settlers of Milwaukee. The decision of a popular foreman encouraged some twenty Irish families to leave the powder mills near Wilmington and follow him to Wisconsin's Portage County. The township of Conception, Missouri, was settled by fifty-eight Irish people from the vicinity of Reading, Pennsylvania, who had been thrown out of work on the railroads and railroad shops by the 1857 depression.

6

Minnesota Territory early attracted Catholic Irish settlers. When St. Paul in 1851 had a population of less than two thousand, the mission-

---

* *History of the Irish in Wisconsin in the Nineteenth Century,* Washington: The Catholic University of America Press, 1954.

ary priest, Rev. James Moran, urged his countrymen to come to this land, better than which, he said, he had never seen. Richard Fewer of St. Anthony's Falls (now Minneapolis), a persistent booster of the Territory, wrote in 1854 that many respectable Catholic Irish from Fall River had made new homes there and more were expected to follow. The St. Paul *Pioneer* sought to win the Irish as settlers by describing the prolific crop of potatoes the soil yielded. Before 1855, the Catholic congregation of St. Paul numbered between 370 and 380 members in the new church. In 1856, the Benevolent Sons of Erin was organized and on March 17 paraded through the streets, with two bands, two green banners and an American flag, to the residence of the territorial governor, Willis Gorman.

Richard Ireland, a carpenter, and his family settled in Vermont for over two years after landing from Ireland and in 1851 made the break for Chicago. By chance, Ireland met an old friend, John O'Gorman, on a Chicago street and they concluded that Minnesota Territory offered better prospects. The two families moved by hired prairie schooners to Galena, Illinois, and there embarked on a steamboat for St. Paul, then not far removed from a frontier log-cabin village. Ireland built a rough shack for the two families and started a campaign through letters to the *Pilot* to get the Irish out of the cities to St. Paul, "where under the care and guidance of our holy Bishop they could enjoy the happiness of good moral and religious education for their children, and peace and plenty for themselves." The Irish carpenter's contribution to St. Paul was his son John, one of the great figures of the Roman Catholic Church in the United States, who, as Archbishop Ireland, worked with another settler, James J. Hill, to harness their great energies to build Minnesota and left their stamp on the state. Thomas O'Gorman, the son of Ireland's companion, also entered the priesthood, taught at Catholic University, wrote a history of the Catholic Church in America, accompanied the Taft mission to Rome for the settlement of the Friars' claims in the Philippines and was first bishop of Sioux Falls, South Dakota.

General James Shields was rewarded by a grateful government for his services in the Mexican War with large grants of land in Rice and Lesueur Counties, which he organized into the townships of Shieldsville, Erin, Kilkenny, and Montgomery, and with Alexander Fairbault founded the town of Fairbault. He traveled in the East advocating in the Irish communities emigration to his holdings.

7

Wisconsin had a particular appeal for the Catholic Irish. Indeed, they said it looked like Ireland, with its soft, green fields, many lakes and rolling landscape. It was a rich dairy country, not too far west, and access to it presented no difficult journeying. Wisconsin systematically encouraged Irish emigration: an agent of the Wisconsin State Emigrant Agency, John A. Byrne, met Irish newcomers in New York and urged upon them the advantages of the state, until the department was discontinued in 1855.

By 1860, approximately 12,900 natives of Ireland were engaged in agriculture in Wisconsin, 10,500 as owners or proprietors of farms and 2400 as farm laborers. In contrast to the proportions elsewhere, more Irishmen were farmers in Wisconsin than laborers: there were 6200 Irish laborers in 1860. Milwaukee was the great port of entry into Wisconsin, and there many Irish remained, concentrated in the Third Ward and active in city and state politics. The Irish community of Milwaukee, however, suffered a tragedy from which it never recovered. The Union Guards, an Irish military company, sponsored an excursion to Chicago on September 7, 1860, to attend a rally at which Stephen Douglas, the idol of the Catholic Irish, spoke. On the return trip, the chartered steamer, *Lady Elgin,* plowing through the fog and rain was slashed into by a lumber freighter, the *Augusta,* and of the some four hundred passengers, all but ninety-five were lost, mostly healthy young Irish men and women. "This September 8," wrote Sister M. Justille McDonald, "marked the beginning of a decline in the Irish population of Milwaukee."

8

Irish emigration to Illinois deviated from the pattern, in that the emigrants moved from the ships directly, first, to labor on the Illinois & Michigan Canal and in the 1850s on the great Illinois Central Railroad construction job and the other lines radiating out of Chicago.

Chicago called to their gregarious nature. By the canal developed the Bridgeport Irish district, noisy, crowded, belligerent, unhealthy, corresponding in character to the Sixth Ward of New York and Fort Hill in Boston. Aldermen Hogan, Ward, Murphy, Carney, Carroll, Brady, Morrissey, McDonough, and Kehoe, who introduced the brogue into municipal affairs from 1837 to 1846, testified to the Irish interest in politics and the beginning of the long Irish familiarity with the City Hall. Leading Irishmen started the Hibernian Bank in 1853; James W. Sheahan edited the Douglas Democratic Chicago *Times* and John Ryan edited the weekly Chicago *Tribune*. The Irish community had its military companies — the Robert Emmet Guards and the Shields Guards — and the typical Irish benevolent societies.

By 1860, natives of Ireland numbered 19,889 or 18.2 per cent of Chicago's total population of 109,260 and totaled 87,573, or 5.12 per cent of the population of Illinois.

In 1855, at the peak of Know-Nothing nativism in the East, a correspondent, apparently a priest, wrote from Chicago on the live-and-let-live spirit of the West:

> Indeed, there appears to be a happy blending of kindly influences, and a disposition in all to submerge minor differences of country and race, and to become in manners, as well as in fact, Americans and men of the West. And this has a happy effect in promoting charity and the absence of those senseless outcries against foreigners which have become the disgrace of other cities. This change of feeling is refreshing to one who has lived for years in the East, and had to feel the cutting lash of persecution, and the sting of anti-Catholic prejudice.

It could be set down almost as an axiom that the ratio of religious and racial prejudice diminished in proportion to the distance from the older and settled communities of the East, so that on the West Coast it hardly existed. This is not to say that in the new states in the pre-Civil War period intolerance lacked vitality: anti-Popery had its apostles in the Mississippi Valley. But it lacked the virulence of the settled East.

9

In the Dubuque diocese a young Irish-born, American-educated priest, Father Jeremiah T. Treacy, matched the zeal of Bishop Loras to colonize the West with Irish. In the spring of 1855, Father Treacy led eight faithful followers out of Garryowen, where he was priest, over the length of Iowa to Sioux City, thence across the Missouri River and along the west bank until they arrived at the entrance of the great Elk Valley. Here they staked out ground, named it St. John's as a future Irish colony and began work on a church in the first parish in Nebraska.

As he pitched in with the others to break the silence of this lonely land, Father Treacy had no thought of the shadow of powerful Archbishop Hughes in populous New York across his colony, but events piled up in the East that were to invite the wrath of that willful prelate on the unwitting head of the obscure pioneering priest.

The anathematizing under dramatic circumstances by Archbishop Hughes of Irish Western colonization must be related to the context of a lengthy prelude. What seemed to later detractors to have been an arbitrary and unhappy act, hurtful to the Irish, had its grounding in a series of errors and bad judgments on the part of Catholic Irish colonizers, notably Thomas D'Arcy McGee.

Archbishop Hughes neither liked nor trusted McGee. He believed the worst of him with almost peasant suspicion. He remembered McGee's incendiary language in 1844. He spotted him among the defectors from O'Connell in the Young Ireland movement. He had driven him out of New York when McGee, after the 1848 debacle, set up a weekly paper and put the blame for the uprising's failure upon the priests. McGee had wound up with another Catholic Irish weekly, the *American Celt*, in Buffalo, and he started a love affair with Canada just across the border.

The Know-Nothing movement, then climbing to the height of its power, made McGee seethe. He compared the lot of the bulk of Catholic Irish emigrants crowded in Eastern cities and laboring as hod carriers and draymen with the situation of Irish emigrants in Canada located on farms. Resentment against the movement governed his thinking on Irish colonization and led him into two initial errors of judgment which he never completely retrieved. He urged that a hundred thousand Catholic Irish leave the cities of the United States and take up residence on the land in Canada. He related this movement, which the *Pilot* called a "stampede," to Know-Nothingism on two points. He argued that the Catholic Irish as workers and consumers were more valuable to the Yankees than the Yankees were to the Catholic Irish. The one way to hurt them, in return for the hurt they were inflicting upon the Catholic Irish, McGee argued, was to hit them in their most precious possession — their pocketbooks — by showing them "that a part of us *can* do without their insolent patronage, and *can* retreat beyond their savage hatred." If the Irish moved from New England and took their savings with them, he said, they could collapse the economy of that area. Next, the excitable and highly imaginative McGee urged the flight as a measure of self-protection, predicting that Know-Nothingism would end up either with a "massacre" of the Catholics or penal laws against them.

The Catholic Irish responded unfavorably to McGee's idea of an exodus to Canada. It seemed like a cowardly running away from the Know Nothings instead of standing up and fighting out the issue. Father Roddan, who favored the removal of the Catholic Irish from the cities for different reasons from McGee's, summed up succinctly the fundamental opposition to the exodus. It was unpatriotic: native son or adopted citizen, he said, we Irish have sworn an oath of allegiance to the Constitution and, speaking for himself, "we would rather have our head cut off than do or say anything to injure America. So say all real Catholics. . . ." It was un-Catholic "because the men most likely to go are the men whom the Church, here, may in a certain sense be said to stand in need" of, to fulfill her high mission.

Thus, right at the start, McGee's expansive colonization scheme carried the stigma of an unpatriotic and un-Catholic flight to a British possession. But McGee's plan offended in still another way. McGee was an apostle of what Archbishop Hughes called "red-hot Irishism." McGee had steadily grown disillusioned with the United States: he never, for example, took out naturalization papers. He wanted to keep the Irish in America Irish, believed in exclusiveness and feared the Irish would lose their nature in American surroundings.

McGee carried his "red-hot Irishism" into his colonization principles of establishing separate Irish settlements, which the *Freeman's Journal* opposed as undesirable, saying that "the attempt at any exclusive settlements, any social segregation of Catholics in tracts of country by themselves, will prove a ruinous failure" and put the Catholics in the same category as the Mormons, as "socially inimical."

10

Resistance to McGee's principles of organized and separate colonization of the Catholic Irish in the West and to him personally as an unstable and divisive factionalist had developed in influential Catholic opinion even before the Buffalo Convention gathered. There was also, generally, a wide indifference or lack of interest.

The Buffalo Convention was the outcome of the discussion in the Catholic and Irish press during 1855 started by McGee's original article. Rev. Dean Kirwin of London, Canada West, early in 1856 proposed a meeting to organize systematic Irish colonization, raise means to carry out the project, and select favorable sites "on the Continent." On February 12, the Irish Catholic Convention for the Promotion of Agricultural Settlements in America gathered at Dudley Hall in Buffalo with seventy-two delegates, thirty-two of whom were clergymen, from the United States and Canada. They represented parishes, societies, Catholic Irish communities, and some came on their own as individuals out of interest in the project. The roll call showed delegates from New York, Illinois, Massachusetts, Michigan, Iowa (including Father Treacy of St. John's settlement and Charles Corkery of Dubuque), Ohio, Missouri, Connecticut, New Jersey, Pennsylvania, and fourteen communities in Canada.

The sanguine Irish nature, when seized by grandiose projects on paper, floated like a cloud at the convention in high expectations of mighty achievements. Talk filled the air of an Irish state in the West. McGee, for the committee on finance, reported that in the savings banks of the ten oldest states the Catholic Irish possessed forty-eight million dollars, a fantastic sum which the wishful thinking of the arithmetic of McGee, who never gave his own cause the worst of it, had added up and which would have been challenged had the delegates been more practical than visionary. Other delegates gave rosy descriptions of possible colonization sites in the United States and Canada. The convention set up a joint stock company to purchase land to be sold to active settlers at a price just enough above cost to pay the expenses of the organization. The stock company was to be financed by the sale of shares at fifty dollars each, and when five hundred shares had been taken up, the $25,000 was to be invested in land. Agencies were to be opened in New York, Boston, Pittsburgh, Buffalo, Chicago, and St. Louis. A board of five directors, including Patrick Donohoe of the *Pilot*, was named.

The *Freeman's Journal*, in a violent editorial, characterized the Buffalo gathering as "another empty, noisy Irish convention" and the clerical and lay delegates as "the fungi of the Catholic body" and "the barnacles that grow to the ship of the Church." It flatly asserted that the convention's purpose was "to encourage Irish citizens to leave the United States for Canada" and charged that American citizens in attendance had compromised their citizenship to become "political catspaws to British subjects." It rang the charges on McGee's Irish separatism as Know-Nothingism, "which calls itself Irish and assumes to be Catholic," and denied that the Irish in America were "a pusillanimous race," to take to their heels away from the cities in fear of the nativists.

Bishop Michael O'Connor of Pittsburgh, an intelligent and clear-headed man, singularly free of the Irish disposition for personalities, tried to free the directed colonization idea, which he favored, from the controversial excrescences that had grown up on it. To the sensitive point, that Catholics in the West might lose their faith, he applied his massive common sense: "The success of your society," he said, "will have the effect of enabling the emigrant to take the Church, as it were, with him into the wilderness; to obtain his lands at first cost, and yet secure to himself the opportunity of practising his religious duties." As a testament of his convictions on directed colonization, he paid the first installment on $500 worth of shares. Bishops Loras, Cretin of St. Paul, and Whelan of Wheeling, West Virginia, also came forward with their approval.

The Buffalo Convention had created the St. Patrick's Agricultural Association to select the land in the West and plot out the township. The township for the first settlement was officially named St. Patrick's and on the map of the hypothetical colony the streets carried good Irish names, like Dublin and Kilkenny: this was to be Ireland in the United States. Unfortunately, two obstructions stood in the way of carrying out the plan: the association had no land and it had no money.

The United States government in 1856 had shut down its land offices in the West, for two reasons: to give the railroads the opportunity to select the territory through which to lay the tracks and the adjoining sections which Congress had voted to the roads as a form of subsidy; and to shut down the frantic speculation in government lands by profit-mad interests.

But even more frustrating than the government's moratorium was the refusal of the Irish to invest their savings in the Buffalo Convention project.

On August 20, 1856, a report was made by the directors on the progress of the movement from the Buffalo Convention to the present date. While 347 shares of capital stock, worth $17,350, had been subscribed to, the report stated, only $1950 had been paid in, and of this $562 had been consumed in expenses. In short, the association had $1388 to realize the colonization dream of Buffalo, and the movement was obviously a failure, collapsed primarily by the lack of interest by the Irish. St. Patrick's Township, with its Kilkenny and Dublin Streets, never came into existence.

Father Treacy returned to Garryowen after the Buffalo Convention and in the spring of 1856 started out with twenty-five families which had engaged themselves to move to the town of St. John's he had staked out the year before. Father Treacy did not spend the terrible winter of 1856-1857 with the Nebraska Irish colony. Late in March, 1857, he was in New York on a propaganda trip for Irish Western colonization. There he publicly felt the lashing tongue of Archbishop Hughes.

II

Hughes favored the movement of Irish emigrants out of cities, but he preferred that they proceed by easy stages, learning as they went, rather than go westward in one bound and not even know how to handle an axe. He opposed directed colonization in consequence of a disillusioning experience in 1843 with the Catholic Emigrant Society of Ireland which had proposed a grandiose scheme that came to nothing as men of practical experience had warned Hughes it would, saying it was "all nonsense."

The record of directed Irish colonization was hardly inspiring. The O'Connor-Kernan settlement early in the century in Steuben County, New York, had fallen apart; the united effort of New York, Philadelphia, and Baltimore Irishmen, concerted by Emmet, MacNeven, Sampson, and O'Connor, to secure land in Illinois from Congress had been voted down; Bishop Fenwick's colony in Benedicta, Maine, had petered out. In Ireland, the same story repeated itself: the grandiose Godley scheme to settle Irish emigrants, with their priests, in Canada had been ripped apart by the Catholic hierarchy; the Father Hore Wexford colonization party to the United States had dissipated itself on the docks of Liverpool, in Arkansas, in St. Louis, and only a handful of the original members settled in Iowa; Father Maher's Leinster Emigration Society proved barren as did the Catholic Emigrant Society of Ireland.

Archbishop Hughes liked nothing about the Buffalo Convention movement, its impractical men, its Irish exclusivist principle, its possible involvement of the Church in failure. He suspected that the

hands which moved it belonged to shifty and calculating land speculators.

Father Treacy in New York called upon Archbishop Hughes and
discussed Western colonization, in which the prelate seemed interested, but the priest failed to inform Hughes of the public meeting to
promote Western colonization he was to address. When the archbishop
heard of it and the report he favored Western colonization, he put on
his hat and muffler and walked to the Broadway Tabernacle. On that
night of March 26, 1857, Hughes sat in the gallery and as he looked
on the platform he saw there, among the clerical and lay figures,
Thomas D'Arcy McGee, come to lend his support.

When Father Treacy finished his talk, the muffled figure in the gallery arose and exclaimed: "Wait a moment; I have a word to say."

"Come on the stand, then," rasped a voice from the audience.

"No, I shall not," came back the answer. "I would rather be by myself." The archbishop, not lacking a sense of drama, removed his
muffler and surprise rippled through the audience.

The wisdom of Archbishop Hughes's public declaration against
directed colonization that night has since been a subject of controversy
among Catholics, but debaters have passed over his harsh chastisement
of Father Treacy in public. Father Treacy may have been at fault for
failing to tell Hughes of the meeting, but Hughes lacked charity in
the imposition publicly of his powerful ecclesiastical authority on a
poor and dedicated mission priest from the Nebraska shanties. Father
Treacy sought to defend himself, only to feel the even harsher ex-
coriation of Hughes. It was a heavyhanded and unedifying exercise
of episcopal power.

Archbishop Hughes, in his impromptu talk, charged that the Buffalo
Convention was a land-selling scheme. He asserted that men ought to
make their own decisions about going West and not be advised by
others. He denied that priests opposed Western migration for fear of
losing their congregations, saying that he could fill ten more churches
if he had them in New York. Then addressing himself directly to Father Treacy he came to what he called "the touching point of the question." He wished for himself and the priests of the diocese, he said,
"that religion might not be debated by being brought into questions of
this kind."

Later advocates of directed colonization, like Archbishop Ireland and
Bishop Spalding of Peoria, have sighed over what they called the

shortsightedness of Hughes, but the indictment was unjust in the light of contemporary realities. The Buffalo Convention was dead when he condemned it, killed by the indifference of the Irish themselves. Hughes cannot be blamed for the unwillingness of the Irish to go West. The obvious impracticality of the Buffalo Convention men justified Hughes in opposing them. It was not Hughes but McGee who tainted directed colonization with his initial blunders.

Father Treacy returned to Nebraska and he probably told his experience to the Creighton brothers, Edward and John, Ohio-born sons of poor Catholic Irish emigrants of Omaha. Edward was superintendent for the Western Union in pushing the magnetic telegraph westward from Omaha. John was one of the founders of the great beef-packing industry in South Omaha. Together they amassed varied interests and were pioneer builders of Nebraska. Devout Roman Catholics, they were generous benefactors of the Church and left a family monument in Creighton University. But they were of true pioneer stock, and the same could not be said of the mass of Catholic Irish.

12

John F. Maguire, the Irish journalist who visited the United States at the close of the Civil War, wrote in 1867:

> There is not a State in the Union in which the Irish have taken deeper and stronger root, or thriven more successfully, than California, in whose amazing progress — material, social, and intellectual — they have had a conspicuous share.

If the Catholic Irish arrived late in the older states, they arrived early in California and grew up with the country. In the gold rush, as Maguire observed, "every social distinction was trampled under foot . . . the hodman and the doctor, the labourer and the lawyer, standing upon exactly the same level. . . . In such a competition there was a glorious chance for the humblest or most recently-arrived of the Irish newcomers." In California no such social or economic inhibitions as stood in his way in the older settled communities of the East bothered the Irishman. On the West Coast he entertained a different state of mind, or psychology, from his fellows in the stratified East, and felt at home in the tradition he had helped to build and not like an unwanted stranger. The California Irishman was different from the Boston Irishman.

Catholic California under the Mexicans welcomed the Irish, like Jasper O'Farrell, who laid out the first survey of San Francisco, and Timothy Murphy, called Don Timoteo, a Wexford man up from Peru as an agent for beef and hides, who became mayor of San Rafael, an administrator of mission lands, and as a prosperous rancher enjoyed a fabulous reputation for his hospitality.

The Irish banking crowd in San Francisco grew into national names. Eugene Kelly and Joseph A. Donohoe, Irish-born, switched from dry goods into the banking house of Donohoe, Ralston & Company, and Kelly acted as Eastern agent in the New York house of Eugene Kelly & Company. John Sullivan, the emigrant who came overland with the Murphy party, succeeded in merchandising, teaming, and real estate and, joining with other Irishmen of means, established in 1859 the Hibernia Savings and Loan Society. James D. Phelan, born in Ireland, was a merchant in New York, with branches in Philadelphia and the South, before he came to San Francisco in 1849 with a cargo of goods and then established the wholesale liquor house of J. and M. Phelan. His career as a banker and that of his son as U. S. Senator belong to a later period. William Shoney O'Brien and James C. Flood ran a famous bar and free lunch on Washington Street in San Francisco and one day their association with John W. Mackey, the grubstake miner who became for a time the wealthiest man in the United States, turned them into bankers and millionaires, but that remarkable story developed after the Civil War.

Peter Donahue, machinist and millwright, set up an improvised blacksmith and boiler-making shop in a tent with his two brothers, veterans of the Mexican War, and out of this adventure in primitive industrialism built the Union Iron Works, the first heavy industry in California. He organized the San Francisco gas company in 1852 and the first omnibus street railway company and extended his interests to include steamboating, railroads, and shipbuilding. California had that kind of opportunity for the son of Irish parents, born in Glasgow and hard at work in a Glasgow factory at the age of nine.

These men of affairs tended to the Irish formalism of middle-class respectability, while San Francisco relished colorful characters like Tom Maguire, the theater man, who had started as a hack driver in New York and then progressed to the status of a bartender in a saloon palace connected with a theater and never got the stage out of his blood. He came in the rush and opened a saloon and gambling joint, but his real passion was in the Jenny Lind Theatre he started on the second floor. Though Tom died broke, Maguire's Opera House wrote a fascinating chapter in the story of the American stage.

13

A Catholic Irishman, James P. Casey, was the immediate cause of the organization in 1856 of the Vigilantes in San Francisco.

A lot of men who arrived in San Francisco left their home community for that community's good, of whom Ned McGowan, a glib operator, served as a pertinent example. Ned, a police captain in Philadelphia, was indicted for robbing a bank while on his lawful duties and following an inconclusive trial headed for California in 1849. His admirers denied any relationship, except coincidental, between San Francisco's perpetual crime wave and Ned's position as assistant justice of the court of sessions.

Ned organized a smooth-functioning political machine with a caravan of "shoulder pushers" and ballot-box stuffers who had learned their trade as Tammany hangers-on in New York. His righthand man was "Yankee" Sullivan, born Francis Murray in Ireland and shipped from London by the police as a common thief to the convict camp at Sydney, from which he escaped to reach America by way of the Hawaiian Islands. Sullivan manufactured a ballot box with a false bottom and a false side into which ballots were stuffed before the polls opened and which by deft shuffling superseded the honest votes of the citizens.

Allied with Sullivan in San Francisco's replica of Tammany were such gamy characters as "Billy" Mulligan, a stray from New York, a fighting bantam of a man, adept in shouldering undesirable elements from the polls and, in reward for services, keeper of the city jail; Mike Brannigan, who drove a hack; Tom Cunningham, the coroner, who was not above putting a stone in a coffin and charging the county for a legitimate funeral and who had a reputation as a counterfeiter; Martin Gallagher, night watchman at the Custom House and pollster bully; Billy Carr, "king of the wharf-rats" and handy fistman at primaries and elections; Woolly Kearny, a common thief, whom "Billy" Mulligan thought too low for his company; James Maloney, the black-sheep son of decent Irish people; Jim Burke, always called "Activity" Burke; and James Cusick, an inveterate disturber of the peace.

Prominent in politics was James P. Casey of the Sixth Ward, which held the balance of power in city and county elections. Casey had been released from Sing Sing in September, 1851, after a term of two years at hard labor for grand larceny. He started for California to begin life over again. Though with scant education, the lean, delicately featured and sandy-haired Casey had an active native intelligence, and he never shirked brazen enterprise. He found his milieu in the Mc-Gowan-"Yankee" Sullivan crowd of political adventurers and, as a member of a fire company, proved a bonny fighter against rival companies. He made the most of his office of inspector of elections in the Sixth Ward. In the autumn election of 1855, the results from the Presidio district, where "Yankee" Sullivan managed the ballot box, were delayed for five days and then the announcement came that James P. Casey had been chosen by the people to the Board of Supervisors, which governed the county. Naturally surprise was expressed, since Casey had not been a candidate for the office and did not even live in the district! Strange things happened when Sullivan's electoral genius paired up with Casey's boldness. Casey, on the way to political power, founded a small weekly, the *Sunday Times,* for his ends.

That same autumn, Charles Cora, an Italian professional gambler, stabbed to death U. S. Marshal William H. Richardson, a hard-drinking man, who went looking for trouble on the fancied slight of his wife by Cora's light-of-love, the leading lady of a brothel. A jury disagreed in the trial of Cora for murder, and he was waiting in jail for a second trial when James Casey shot to death James King of William, editor and owner of the San Francisco *Bulletin,* on Wednesday, May 14, 1856. As officers placed Casey in the next cell, Cora told him fatalistically: "You have put the noose around the neck of both of us."

In the course of a bitter exchange between Casey's *Sunday Times* and the *Bulletin,* King, in an editorial which stated that Casey deserved to have "his neck stretched" for ballot-box stuffing, touched upon the latter's most sensitive point — his Sing Sing record. Casey, then twenty-nine, stalked into King's office to demand he stop raking up the past, only to be shown the door. Casey brooded in a black, bitter mood and, as he said later, "Whenever I was injured I have resented it. It has been part of my education, during an existence of twenty-nine years." Casey took the law in his own hands by shooting King, and then walked to the police station to give himself up.

On the day after the shooting of King by Casey, the Vigilance

Committee was organized and, with thousands as members, took over physical control of the city, hiring a large hall as headquarters. John Nugent, the courageous editor of the San Francisco *Herald,* who had had as his partner William Walker, the filibusterer, protested against the usurpation of legal authority by a kangaroo committee but for his pains suffered loss of advertising and circulation and eventually had to suspend.

In succession, the Vigilance Committee marched its armed men to the jail, seized Casey and Cora, tried them before the executive committee, and on an improvised platform erected from the second floor of the headquarters, publicly hanged them. The Irish community gave Casey a tremendous funeral and friends erected an elaborate monument in the graveyard of the Mission Dolores church, with the inscription that he had been murdered by the Vigilance Committee and may God forgive his persecutors.

The Vigilance Committee set about methodically to drive the Casey and McGowan hangers-on from San Francisco as "disturbers of the peace of our city, destroyers of the purity of our elections, active members and leaders of the organized gang who have invaded the sanctity of our ballot boxes, and perfect pests to society."

"Yankee" Sullivan was laid by the heels and thrown into the committee's jail. The hard-drinking Sullivan (it was reported he took at least eighty shots a day) was shut off from his supply and, in his trembling, nervous state, bordering on hallucinations, became possessed of the fear that a mob was set on hanging him. Guards found him one morning sprawled in his own blood, a suicide.

One by one the spotted political mercenaries of the McGowan-Casey-Sullivan outfit were seized by the Vigilance Committee, given a drumhead trial and escorted to the ships that carried them away from San Francisco. Civil authorities dared not challenge the self-appointed guardians of order. The committee failed to nab Ned McGowan, the man it wanted the most, who was passed along to safety and protected by Irish friends. The committee even started proceedings against the powerful Dave Broderick, boss of the Democratic Party in California, but he was different company from the small-bore ward heelers the committee arbitrarily hustled out of the city.

14

David C. Broderick was a man of great personal power and will, a political organizer of drive and skill. Nobody ever regarded him in terms of the stereotyped Irishman. A dark brooding mood troubled his thoughts; a smile rarely crossed his swarthy bearded face; his chilling blue eyes declared a hard purposiveness. He acted like a man who had to prove something to himself, and that showed itself in his sole ambition — the eminence of a seat in the United States Senate.

His father, a Kilkenny man, had been hired from Ireland for skilled stonework in the interior of the Capitol then building in Washington, where David was born in 1820. He learned the craft of stonework in New York, but politics had the first call on his interest. He attracted a following by his prowess as a volunteer fireman, opened a political saloon and by the time he reached his majority ran the Ninth Ward. Defeated for Congress, he declined renomination two years later, closed his saloon, dumped the liquor in the street and vowed never to drink, smoke or gamble again. He set out for California to make a political career for himself, first securing his financial independence as a partner in an assaying and coining firm in San Francisco.

Broderick sat as a member of the first state Senate and took over control of the Democratic Party at the time of its organization in 1851. He worked steadily toward his objective and in 1857 the California legislature elected Broderick to the United States Senate. "The purity of his life," wrote James Ford Rhodes, the American historian, "and his scrupulous honesty, associated with pride, energy, and ambition, commanded respect from men of both sections and of all parties."

Just when Broderick concluded that slavery was a wrong cannot be traced, but opposition to the extension of the peculiar institution became an obsession with him. He stood with Stephen Douglas for the free-state constitution of Kansas and against the Buchanan administration on the slavery issue. President Buchanan removed California patronage from Broderick and favored his pro-slavery fellow, Senator William H. Gwin, who accepted it despite an agreement that Broderick should dispense it.

The pro-slavery Democrats in California, mostly men from the South, held Broderick in contempt for his humble origins and set out to destroy him for his anti-slavery principles. He represented to this "chivalry" the mean rank of men who had labored with their hands, "the very mudsills of Society," as Senator James H. Hammond of South Carolina called the wage earners of the North.

In the 1859 gubernatorial election, the bitterness of the two Democratic factions came to a boiling point. Judge David S. Terry of the California Supreme Court, a fire-eater of extremist pro-slavery views, calculatingly insulted Broderick in a public speech and Broderick responded in kind. It was apparent that the Southerners designed to bait Broderick to the field of honor.

On the day after the election, which the pro-slavery faction won, Judge Terry resigned from the bench and challenged Broderick to answer for his remark. A meeting was arranged on September 12, 1859, in San Mateo County, outside San Francisco, but Chief Martin Burke and his police interfered and broke up the party. The next day they met again. Broderick appeared uneasy and nervous, as though the whole business was distasteful to him. Broderick and Terry faced each other and raised their guns, but Broderick's gun had a sensitive trigger and fired before he had taken true aim, the bullet plowing into the ground some distance from his antagonist. Terry took sure aim, fired, and Broderick slumped to the ground. Three days later he died, saying to friends who came to comfort him: "They killed me because I was opposed to the extension of slavery, and a corrupt administration."

The whole country was shocked. With the slavery issue on the point of explosion, Broderick was lamented as a martyr of his pro-Union and anti-slavery convictions. San Francisco turned out in its greatest funeral procession to the leader who had come a long, long way from the brawling streets of New York. But the Church, of which he had not been a faithful member in his life, denied him, by its strict laws against dueling, burial in consecrated ground, though a priest accompanied the remains as far as the gates of the Lone Mountain Cemetery. Over his grave the people of California erected a stately monument. When the forces inside the so-called "black Irishman" are comprehended, then the strange Broderick will be understood.

Governor Latham succeeded Broderick in the Senate, and Lieutenant Governor John G. Downey of Los Angeles, a devout Catholic Irishman from County Roscommon, a wholesale druggist who prospered in real estate, ranching, and banking, was elevated to the chief magistracy. Downey's great act was his veto of a measure that would have constituted one of the greatest steals in our political history, nothing less than the San Francisco waterfront by a parcel of freebooters. "Governor John G. Downey," wrote one historian, "was not considered a man of great talent, intellect, or ability — but he was honest, a rarity in politics in California in those days."

15

It was almost axiomatic that the farther away from Ireland a native son dwelt, the more vehement were his anti-English sentiments and the more vigorous his shouts for the cold steel as the radical solution of the Irish problem. The San Francisco Irish stored great faith in revolution, and they went wild with joy when, one by one, the Irish patriots of 1848, escaped from their penal confinement in the Australian colonies, entered the United States by the West Coast on their way to New York, the headquarters of the Ballingarry exiles.

44
The Birth of Fenianism

THE 1848 REVOLUTIONARY UPHEAVALS in Europe started the Catholic clergy and press in the United States off on a Red hunt that ran contrary to the almost universal American hope for the triumph of the Kossuths, Mazzinis, and Garibaldis. "Your European democracy," wrote the Boston *Pilot*, "is a cut-throat affair, it is bloodthirsty, it is Red, it is socialist, it only *aims* to destroy, never to build up, it is atheistical, it is devilish, it *is* criminal *per se*." The *Freeman's Journal* described Louis Kossuth, president of the short-lived Hungarian Republic, and his Red allies in Germany, Italy, and France as the enemies of God, man, laws, order, property, the family, and society.

The interesting fact in this violent American Catholic reaction to 1848 European liberalism, or Red Republicanism as the Catholics called it, was that converts to Catholicism, ex-Protestant intellectuals, directed it, who in their zeal became more Catholic than the Catholics and more papal than the Pope.

Orestes A. Brownson, the biggest fish that Peter's net had caught in American infidel waters, had made the circle from a Congregationalist household in Vermont through the Presbyterian Church, the Universalist ministry, a spell of freethinking and Unitarian pastorates to a settlement in the arms of the Catholic Church in 1844, where he remained faithfully, if not always easily, until his death. His writings expounded "stern, austere, uncompromising Catholic orthodoxy" and as the champion of the authority of the Church, which alone, he said, gave sanction to law, he saw in the consequences of Protestantism "the extremest forms of Radicalism, Revolution and Red Republicanism."

Brownson's most ardent disciple was the young American-born priest of Irish ancestry, Rev. John T. Roddan, who, educated in Rome, became editor of the *Pilot* and popularized Brownson's logic in strong anti-Red Republican articles. Father Roddan made the *Pilot* the leading Catholic scourge of Red Republicanism, and he was at his best, if unfairest, in making the Irish Reds, or "Pinks," as McGee called them, the butt of his joshing and priestly censure.

Quite different from Brownson and Roddan was the eccentric James Alphonsus McMaster, editor of the *Freeman's Journal*, which he purchased from Bishop Hughes in 1848. McMaster's father, a Presbyterian minister of the orthodox Westminster dispensation, had reared James with the expectation he would enter the kirk. Instead, converted to Catholicism, he enrolled in the Redemptorist Order in Belgium as a postulant and novice. There the fathers persuaded him that his vocation did not lie in the priesthood but in journalism as a defender of the faith. As an editor, he fancied himself the last word in theological purity, and the zeal of the Middle Ages still lived so long as McMaster breathed.

McMaster and Brownson had something very much in common — they believed in the supremacy of the Pope and were, in the words of Maurice Francis Egan, "ultramontane of the ultramontanes." They set the intellectual tone of the ultra-Catholic party. They had something else very much in common — they never understood the Catholic Irish.

2

The Catholic Irish clergy and press gave sound whacks to the freethinking Germans, the Italian secret societies, and the French republicans but they saved their hardest blows for the '48 Irish exiles who had turned professional revolutionaries, saying that as practicing Catholics the exiles should know better than to align themselves with Red Republicanism.

The exiles had no sooner landed than bitter feuding broke out among themselves. They pushed aside the pre-Famine leadership in the United States and took upon themselves the initiative of directing American Irish opinion. They struck a harsher note of implacable hatred of England than had previously been heard on this side of the Atlantic. They made the Irish cause an issue in American politics with a new assertiveness and called upon the Famine emigration numbers to back them up. Their violence of conduct, factionalism, and language troubled the settled American Irish. They plotted to revolutionize Ireland from the staging ground of the United States. With them a new element entered into the story of the Catholic Irish in the United States.

"Previously to the arrival of the first 'refugee' in Philadelphia, in the autumn of 1848," wrote the *Irish American* in 1850, "there had been a remarkable unanimity among the sons of Erin on these shores; but ever since that ill-fated moment it has been, with the Irish in America, a regular succession of gales of anger, bitterness, passion and dissension."

Thomas D'Arcy McGee, the "first 'refugee'" referred to, had with the aid of a bishop been secreted out of Ireland disguised as a priest and had not taken part in the uprising, an omission which laid him open to accusations by fellow Irishmen reflecting on his honor and courage. In New York he started a weekly, the *Nation*, blamed the clergy for the collapse of the rebellion and brought on his head the wrath of Bishop Hughes, who accused McGee and Young Ireland of botching up a noble conception in the execution of the uprising, while McGee called the bishop a power-drunk prelate.

McGee also conducted warfare on a second front, with the bellicose republicans of the military companies. McGee's weekly supported the movement organized in Ireland by Gavan Duffy for Irish land reform through parliamentary action. To the uncompromising revolutionaries this meant only one thing — McGee had sold out his country's cause. Any Irishman who treated with England on a lesser basis than the "cold steel" of a bayonet marked himself as a traitor in the opinion of these passionate men.

Michael Doheny headed the anti-McGee faction in the New York military companies. Doheny, a Tipperary plowboy, had by hard work and self-sacrifice become a lawyer and then turned to radical journalism in the cause of Young Ireland. He took part in the uprising, and he told how he eluded his British pursuers in a minor classic of revolutionary literature, *The Felon's Track*. When Doheny landed in New York from France, the military companies welcomed him with open arms as a patriotic hero.

3

The Irish revolutionary movement in the United States centered in the New York military companies. Their organization began in the radical Irish Republican Union of the Shakespeare Hotel that wanted to assist Ireland in 1848 with more than talk and money. Michael Phelan, the Willie Hoppe of his day, the billiard champion of the United States, and an unreconstructed Gael, proposed the formation of a regiment, if not a brigade, "for the purpose of going to Ireland to aid in the good cause."

The first company, mustered from among the Irish dealers in Washington Market, called itself the Mitchel Guard in honor of the republican revolutionary. The Ballingarry fiasco failed to discourage revolutionary enthusiasm: another day would come and the Irish in America would be prepared. Company after company appeared in green uniforms and distinctively Irish names: the Wolfe Tone Guards, the Napper Tandy Light Artillery, the Emerald Rangers, the Irish Patriot Fusileers. These numerous New York companies had nothing in common with the social and political military companies of an earlier day. Veterans of the United States Army drilled them; Oliver Byrne of the Shields Guard of Philadelphia, a '48 exile, wrote several textbooks designed to put them into efficient military posture, suggesting that targets for rifle practice be set up in the form of British kings, queens, and nobles to perfect Irish aim.

In April, 1850, the Irish Volunteer Regiment was mustered into the New York State Militia as the 9th Regiment, the first Irish regiment in the United States, composed of Irishmen or the sons of Irishmen. On November 14, 1851, after the formation of further Irish companies and their consolidation on November 1, General Ewan of the State Militia delivered commissions to the second regiment of Irish volunteers, officially designated the 69th Regiment, which became historic. By 1853, of the six thousand uniformed militiamen in New York, four thousand were of foreign birth, the Irish numbering twenty-six hundred. They dominated in the 75th Regiment and were

JACKSON,
MONTGOMERY,
SULLIVAN, BARRY,
FITZGERALD.

69

GENTLE WHEN STROKED   FIERCE WHEN PROVOKED

FLAG OF THE 69TH IRISH REGIMENT, NEW YORK STATE MILITIA

prominent in the 10th, 11th, 14th, and 70th Regiments. Formed as an expeditionary force for eventual use to free Ireland, they never attained their original purpose but they died on American battlefields.

4

One Irish company rejected McGee's application for membership; another company, on the other hand, elected Doheny as its commander. Doheny called McGee treacherous, and McGee described Doheny as a drunk. One day the two met on the street, Doheny punched McGee and paid a ten-dollar fine in court. McGee twice organized public meetings in support of Gavan Duffy's Irish Alliance and twice the followers of Doheny invaded and broke them up. The older Irish had had their factional quarrels but nothing to compare with the rasping recriminations of the exiles.

An ancient who said he had worked in America for Ireland from the first meeting in 1828 for the relief of Harry Mills, the patriotic forty-shilling freeholder, to the great Vauxhall meeting of 1848, compared in 1850 the creditable conduct of the earlier Irish with the "BRAGGARTS AND BRAWLERS!" of the exiles, and he disavowed them: "the real Irish inhabitants of New York know them not, and trust them not." The *Freeman's Journal* frostily dissociated the "respectable" Irish from the new men.

A stronger spirit of assertiveness among the Irish expressed itself in a touchiness always vigilant for slights, real or fancied, on the race, and in the watch they set upon the encroachments of English perfidy. Officers of the military companies provoked a scene at the annual St. Patrick's Day dinner of the Friendly Sons of St. Patrick, the elite society in New York of mixed Catholic and Protestant Irish, when the health of Queen Victoria was drunk. The editor of the New York *Day Book,* described as "a very mean paper," compared the Irish unfavorably with the Negroes, and Captain O'Callaghan of a military company waited upon the editor for satisfaction on the field of honor or an apology. Sir Henry Bulwer, British minister to the United States, spoke in uncomplimentary terms of the Irish as "savages," and at a public meeting of indignation in New York Doheny called upon the President of the United States to throw the minister out of the country, while Sir Henry explained he had meant the semi-barbarous Celts of ancient times, not the modern Irish; indeed, his own daughter had married an Irishman.

The Irish revolutionaries in New York joined with Italian, French, and German republicans in supporting Louis Kossuth and the Hungarian revolution against Austria. Irish military companies participated in demonstrations for Hungary, and Doheny addressed meetings in its behalf. The secular *Irish American,* which appealed particularly to the Famine emigration Irish, upheld the liberal cause everywhere in Europe.

The Catholic press, however, as one voice denounced Kossuth as a Red Republican and enemy of the Church. He represented a Protestant cause, wrote the *Pilot,* which noted the zeal of the Protestant clergy in acclaiming Kossuth on his arrival in the United States in the middle of December, 1851. Bishop Hughes described him as a "humbug." It did not go unobserved that only the Catholic press spoke in the language of European reaction and made a solid front in opposition to the man whom the country believed inspired by American principles. But the people turned their back on Kossuth after the first fer-

vent greetings when he interpreted popular cheers as a mandate to
seek the physical intervention of the United States on the side of Hungary against Austria and Russia. Liberty-loving America hailed the romantic apostle of freedom, but isolationist America speedily disposed
of him upon his prompting of an entangling alliance.

5

In the meantime, the Irish undertook an interventionist movement
of their own, for the use of the good offices of the United States to
intercede with the British government for the release of the Irish political prisoners of '48 in the penal colony of Van Diemen's Land —
now Tasmania.

This movement reached its peak in 1852 as one of a series of
significant events which marked that year as a watershed in the story
of the Catholic Irish in America for its seminal firsts.

In April, 1851, the *Pilot* suggested that with a presidential election
scheduled for 1852, the pressure of the Irish vote might be used in behalf of the seven prisoners. The escape of McManus, the patriot who
had given up a prosperous Liverpool business to join the rebels, and
the universal Irish joy on his arrival in San Francisco on June 5, 1851,
gave the matter great impetus. On the night of September 10, a public
meeting of between five and six thousand in Baltimore's Monument
Square, presided over by the mayor, memorialized President Fillmore
for assistance.

The "Baltimore movement," as it was called, spread from city to
city, and petitions and memorials piled up. Early in January, 1852,
delegates from the several cities met in Baltimore and arranged to send
a deputation to petition the President personally. Accordingly, on January 22, 1852, a delegation of two hundred and fifty Irishmen marched
to the White House and in the East Room met President Millard Fillmore. This deputation, said the *Pilot*, was "the first that has ever appeared in Washington from Irish Americandom."

Fillmore gave the self-conscious and solemn-faced Irishmen a glib
line of double-talk that, after the spell of the White House had worn
off, turned out to be upon analysis a brushoff. But T. D. McGee
summed up the sentiments of the deputation and of American Irish
opinion generally: if we got nothing out of the President, he said in
effect, at least we got into the White House, and that was a triumph,

amounting to official recognition of the Irish. The deputation fared much better when, after leaving the White House, they called upon Secretary of State Daniel Webster, who acted more friendly than had Fillmore. The upshot of the meeting was that Webster wrote a private letter to London, setting forth the Irish case but without an official commitment. The Irish had little faith in the Whigs, anyway, though their loyal friend, Senator Seward, delivered the best speech of the debate when Congress took up the petition of Michigan politicians for the cause.

The Irish Left Wing (Red Republicans, Radicals, or Revolutionaries) boycotted the Baltimore movement. To petition the Queen for mercy on men who had intended no good for her rule in Ireland struck them as cowardice. The military companies would have broken up any meeting called in New York to petition Congress for the prisoners. But the military companies in the year 1852 established an Irish first that survives today in all its glory — the St. Patrick's Day procession in New York.

6

Observance of St. Patrick's Day had been honored by the Protestant Irish in the American colonies as far back as 1737, when the first Irish society, the Charitable Irish Society of Boston, was formed. With the increase of the Catholic Irish and the multiplication of their societies, the day began to enter the American calendar as an Irish holiday. Canal and railroad contractors resigned themselves to accepting the day as workless for Irish laborers, and understanding employers granted the day off for the Irish in shops and factories. At first each Catholic Irish society held its own dinner. In New York, each formed its own little parade, careful to avoid crossing one another's path lest mutual taunts start a brawl. Gradually, the Irish communities evolved a pattern of observance: societies met in their halls, paraded to the church for Mass and a St. Patrick's Day oration, then marched through the principal streets of the town to a dinner in their own rooms or the local hotel.

The numerous military companies in New York laid plans for a mighty display on St. Patrick's Day in 1851, but the weather turned up so miserable, with driving rain and sleet, that only the most hardy appeared. The year 1852, however, was different, even if the weather

was not ideal. New York stood in openeyed wonder at the first
massed St. Patrick's Day procession. One bystander exclaimed "testily,"
according to the report: "Why, sure these can't be all Irish; there are
not so many in this city, at least."

Green filled the eye everywhere, girls in green dresses and bonnets,
men with broad green scarves, the military companies in green uniforms, and banners, flags, and emblems waving in the wind.

First came the horse commands, the Irish light artillery and companies of dragoons. The volunteer military companies, headed by the
Emmet Guard under Lieutenant John Kelly, later the boss of Tammany Hall, made up the second section, bearing such names as the
Irish Rifles, the Smith O'Brien Guard, and the Montgomery Rifles. A
lively band played "Garryowen" and with professional precision paraded
the companies of reputation, the joy of the New York Irish, the seven
companies of the 9th Regiment under Major Shea. Next followed the
69th Regiment, the first public appearance in their new uniforms. Mana-
han's Band headed the third of the Irish regiments, the 75th.

St. Patrick's Day Parade forming in New York in 1858

After the military display, hundreds of the Irish societies kept coming on, the burial, benevolent, temperance, and workingmen's societies, each with its distinctive banner declaring an Irish sentiment or its purpose. Bringing up the long parade were the carriages with the ladies.

The parade proceeded up Broadway to 23rd Street, down 23rd to Eighth Avenue, then to Hudson and West Broadway, up Chambers to Broadway and around to City Hall Park where the mayor and the city council reviewed it. It took nearly one hour and a half to pass the stand. The marching Irish on that 1852 St. Patrick's Day had started something the end of which is not in sight. The New York Irish agreed with Father O'Reilly that "the Irish had this day established a character for themselves."

7

The third significant event in 1852 was that for the first time on a national scale, not alone in New York and Pennsylvania, the two major parties, Democratic and Whig, made a particular drive for Catholic Irish votes in the presidential election. "For the first time in America," wrote the *Pilot* of the contest between Democratic Franklin Pierce and Whig General Winfield Scott, "Catholics have been recognized as a Power in the State." There was also a diligent concentration upon the German vote, and 1852 marked the entrance of racial blocs as an element of power in national politics.

The Whigs sought to discredit General Pierce with the Catholic Irish by tying him in with the constitutional disqualification of Catholics to hold office in New Hampshire, his native state, but convincing evidence showed the sincere effort of Pierce for the provision's repeal. The Democrats resurrected a sympathetic letter by General Scott to an 1841 convention of the Native American Party, but he repudiated this earlier errancy with a ringing declaration that the bravery and patriotism of Irish and German soldiers on the bloody battlefields of Mexico had cleansed him of prejudice. He remarked in an eloquent letter that "perhaps no man — certainly no American — owes so much to the valor and blood of Irishmen as myself. Many of them marched and fought *under my command* in the war of 1812-1815, and many more — thousands — *in the recent war with Mexico*, not one of whom was ever known to turn his back upon the enemy or a friend."

During a campaign speech in Cleveland, a son of Erin asked General Scott why he had changed his mind on nativism, whereupon Scott replied with warmth: "I hear that rich brogue — I love to hear it; it makes me remember noble deeds of Irishmen, many of whom I have led to battle and victory." At Madison, Indiana, he repeated the sentiment. The sight of "Old Fuss and Feathers" blarneying the Irish struck the country as amusing and his reference to the "rich brogue" of the Irish made it laugh.

Father Roddan of the *Pilot* expressed his disgust at the crude and blatant appeals for the Catholic Irish vote:

> Politicians would talk sensibly before an American audience, but when they came to speak before Irishmen, they lost their wits in supposing that we had lost ours. We heard of nothing but Catholic Emancipation [that is, the New Hampshire issue], rich Irish brogue — bigoted Protestants, — and so on to the end of a sickening chapter. . . . They did not know that their Irish hearers understood them and despised them.

Proud and sensitive Irishmen resented the particularized appeal to their Catholicity as an insult. McGee's Buffalo *Celt* blasted the practice:

> Such a man "is a friend of your folks"; such another "sent his daughter to a Convent"; a third contributed to a Catholic charity; a fourth had "a grandmother who was a Catholic." What a contemptible estimate of our intelligence they must have who address us with such *arguments* and give us such *reasons!*

"Are we unworthy of being reasoned with?" the *Celt* asked at another time. "Are we dogs only to be coaxed and driven?" "Beware of the windbags!" warned Father Roddan.

The Church, as in the days of Bishop England, frowned on the "bribery of the affections" of the Catholic Irish by calculating voteseekers. It resisted the campaign of the two parties to appeal to the Catholic Irish as a body isolated from the American mainstream. "The *Catholic* vote is first sought out," wrote the *Pilot,* "and it is attempted, for the first time in America, to make it a *partizan* vote." Observing the Whig attacks on Franklin Pierce for the failure of the religious test to be expunged in New Hampshire, the *Pilot* forcefully exclaimed:

> No use, gentlemen, no use. The Catholic voters will go to the polls, not as Catholics, but as American citizens. . . . The question is: — does the candidate uphold American principles?

The stress by the politicians was on the appeal to nationalities principally, to "the Irish vote" and "the German vote," not to religion. As "Catholic" and "Irish" were at that time synonymous, the "Catholic vote" meant "the Irish vote" and has remained so in the American political vocabulary. There were thousands of German Catholics but political attention was directed to them not as Catholics but as Germans. "Irish" and "Catholic," however, were interchangeable.

8

The temperamental defects of Michael Doheny — an unrestrained impetuosity, an instinctive affinity for faction and an undisciplined disposition to turn differences into personalities — unfitted him for American leadership. The hero the Irish had awaited walked into the office on William Street in New York of the law firm of Dillon & O'Gorman, both '48 exiles, on the morning of May 27, 1852. Thomas Francis Meagher, "Meagher of the Sword," had escaped from the British penal colony in Australia and now presented himself to his countrymen in the United States hungry for a luminous figure.

Meagher was in his thirtieth year when he arrived in New York, a handsome man, of straight, soldierly bearing, below six feet in height, with the contrasting raven black hair and pale blue eyes so distinctive of a Gaelic type and the high cheekbones that accentuated an unmistakably Irish face. Irish Americandom received Meagher with the warmth and affection it had always in reserve for a man who had suffered under the British government in the national cause, compounded in his case by a romantic escape from British captivity.

But Meagher's refusal to conform to the ultra-Catholic political creed by his praise of Kossuth and his preference for mixed rather than Catholic audiences at his public lectures set the Catholic press off against him, the Irish revolutionaries and the 1848 exiles. Its burden was that the radicals should cease trying to free Ireland by force and settle down to be pacific Catholics. During the embroilment, the authentic voice of the historic Gael spoke up saying he was not interested in Red Republicanism or Kossuth or recrimination over 1848; he was interested in the freedom of Ireland and wanted to know when something was going to be done on that score. Were Irishmen ready to go to Ireland to fight? "I will go," he said simply.

Next appeared another Irish hero and patriot in America — John Mitchel, the Ulster rebel, the revolutionary journalist, the first of the Irish Confederates to be arrested, convicted by a packed jury of sedition and transported overseas, first to the hulks in Bermuda and then to Van Diemen's Land.

American funds provided the means for Mitchel's escape from the English penal colony. The New York Directory, finding it impracticable to return the contributions collected for the '48 Rebellion, used the money to aid the political prisoners to their freedom. Patrick J. Smyth, a '48 exile who had edited a newspaper in Pittsburgh and later wrote for the New York *Sun,* had been dispatched to Australia by the Directory and with ample sums at his disposal arranged for Mitchel's escape.

Mitchel arrived in New York on the ship *Prometheus* from Nicaragua on November 19, 1853, and once more, as on the landing of Meagher a year and a half previously, the Irish community went wild. Throughout the country, the Irish forgot their factional and political differences in the formation of committees to invite Mitchel to visit them, and New York City gave him a public reception.

With the Crimean War between England and Russia inevitable, Mitchel hastened to organize a weekly newspaper to direct the Irish in America how to make England's difficulty Ireland's opportunity. On January 7, 1854, appeared the first issue of the *Citizen,* with Mitchel as editor assisted by Meagher, John McClenahan, former editor of the Limerick *Reporter,* and John Savage, a rebel journalist and poet, all exiles.

Mitchel made the *Citizen,* in the one year he conducted it, a lively, forceful, and controversial weekly, "without the least regard to the wrath it might provoke in the subscribers it might lose," as he said. He built the *Citizen* into a circulation of fifty thousand and then watched it dwindle under the violence of his opinions.

Though only in the country a few weeks he read a savage lecture to Secretary of State Marcy and disturbed the Democratic politicians by advising his countrymen not to allow themselves to be manipulated as the "Irish vote." "I have no other claim on you," he told the New York public dinner, "than simply as an advocate of liberty." No Irishman ever described the clanking of chains upon what he called "Irish serfs and slaves" by the tyranny of England in more vivid language than Mitchel. Yet he was a fanatical apologist of Negro slavery and, in what was called a "very frank declaration of his admiration for slavery," Mitchel wrote in the *Citizen:*

> We are not abolitionists — no more abolitionists than Moses or Socrates or Jesus Christ. We deny that it is a crime, or even a peccadillo, to hold slaves, to buy slaves, to keep slaves to their work by flogging or other needful coercion. "By your silence," says Mr. Haughton, "you will become a participator in their wrongs." * But we will not be silent when occasion calls for a speech; and as for being a participator in the wrongs, we, for our part, wish we had a plantation well stocked with healthy Negroes in Alabama.

The brutality of the candor, "not very creditable to the head or heart of the author," said the *Pilot,* shocked even the conservative sentiment in the North sympathetic to the slaveholding interest. The Catholic Irish held no such positive views on the virtue of slavery as Mitchel entertained, and they too recoiled in shock. Doheny published a letter repudiating Mitchel, writing "I detest and abhor the slavery of an African Negro, a Hill coolie or any other coolie, precisely as I detest and abhor the slavery of a white Irishman. The pretences called arguments that are based on the inferiority of race and the distinctions of color, I utterly repudiate and stigmatize as fraudulent, barbaric, brutal and contemptible." A correspondent who signed himself "Young Irelander" wrote to the New York *Tribune* that Mitchel did not speak for Young Ireland. One paper observed that if Mr. Mitchel could not get the Alabama plantation well stocked with Negroes, he would take one in Ireland well stocked with Irishmen. Mitchel's extremism harmed the Irish in the United States by adding to the existing prejudice against them a feeling that a representative spokesman had placed them with the inhumane.

In a series of public letters in the *Citizen,* Mitchel savagely attacked Archbishop Hughes, in an attempt to prove, he said, "that while the Irish Catholic laity in America are capable of being good Republicans, and want to have nothing to do with persecution, the Irish Catholic clergy in America (including Your Grace) are not to be trusted." Mitchel's ill-tempered accusations, including one that Archbishop Hughes would burn heretics in City Hall Park if he had the power, offended the Catholic Irish, and the circulation of the *Citizen* dropped. Catholic Irishmen, with the deepest respect for Mitchel's sacrifices

---

* Haughton was the Irish Quaker Abolitionist, the great friend of Daniel O'Connell and the author of the famous petition urging the Catholic Irish in America to come out from under slavery and join the Abolitionists.

in the cause of Irish freedom, regretted that he attacked Hughes at the time the Church was under the heavy fire of the Know Nothings — though Mitchel gave the Know Nothings the rough side of his fist.

Years later Mitchel wrote of the unnecessary and unhappy episode that "I would if I could erase from the page and all men's memory, about three-fourths of what I then wrote and published to the address of Archbishop Hughes. This I say not by way of atonement to his memory — for he deserved harsh usage and could stand it and repay it — but by way of justice to myself alone."

9

Mitchel lost hope of turning the Crimean War to Ireland's advantage after a call upon the Russian minister to the United States, Baron Stockl, in Washington. Mitchel explained that the Irish in Ireland and in America wanted to "make a diversion for Russia — and for themselves — if some material aid could be only furnished them to make a beginning." The minister listened attentively to Mitchel's persuasive argument but, pointing to a map, showed that the combined fleets of Britain and France had blocked up the Baltic and Black Seas. Russia cannot even get out of her inland seas, he stressed. Money to purchase arms for Ireland would therefore be of no value because they could not be run in without a covering fleet. And Russia, said the Baron with a shrug of finality, had not a covering fleet. The only effect of this Washington talk was that it gave the British government a bad case of the jitters.

A few weeks before the outbreak of the Crimean War in March, 1854, Lord Palmerston, the English Foreign Secretary, announced that since Smith O'Brien had faithfully abided by his parole, and thus acted the role of honorable gentleman, the government would permit him to apply for a pardon. It was neither magnanimity nor regard for his personal honor that prompted the British to move to release Smith O'Brien. The British recruiting sergeants in Ireland reported the rejection of the Saxon shilling, and a gesture to the Irish in the release of a national hero was demanded to stimulate interest in the British army.

The Irish in the United States, by resolutions, public statements, letters, and other means of communication, vigorously urged the Irish in Ireland not to enlist in the British army for war in the Crimea. The

New Ireland in America, strengthened by the Famine numbers, now
began the campaign that was to continue for years of blocking, embarrassing, and hurting, if possible, the British government upon every
occasion it could make its influence felt.

The Galway *Packet* explained the lack of British recruiting success
by pointing out that the class of people who formerly enlisted in the
British army no longer lived in Ireland. "If the British Government require Irish recruits," it wrote, "they must try New York or Boston."

That idea also occurred to the British government. The heavy casualties rocked England, but the Irish in America noted the heavy losses
among the Irish soldiers in the British reverses. Conflicting emotions
tore them: they found satisfaction in British defeats but sorrow in the
number of natives of Ireland killed or wounded. Weekly the *Pilot*
printed the location of the fighting regiments so that the Irish in
America could address their relatives and friends, and it took note of
the anomalous position:

> There is scarcely an Irish family that has not more or less rela-
> tions in the army, and however they may wish the fall of England,
> they cannot help but sympathise with their countrymen who are
> falling there to uphold a power that has been their relentless perse-
> cutor.

Under special legislation creating a foreign legion, the British started
recruiting in the United States in violation of the 1818 neutrality act.
The *Pilot* exposed the recruiting activities of Hon. Joseph Howe,
member of the Nova Scotia provincial parliament and chairman of the
Nova Scotia Railroad, who hired Irish laborers in Boston for construction work on the road and when they arrived in Halifax tried to enlist
them for military service. The British consul in New York issued a
handbill announcing a British recruiting station in Pearl Street, which
brought prompt action from United States District Attorney John
McKeon. The British established a recruiting system under the direction of the minister in Washington and consuls designed to avoid technical violation of the law. Expectations of ensnaring the Irish into
enlistment generally failed, though the Irish dug a pit for one British consul. Daniel Conahan, founder of the Emmet Society of Cincinnati, trapped Charles Rowcroft, the British consul there, into advancing money for the forwarding of fifty mythical Irish recruits to
Canada, and involved him with the law. President Pierce in the end
asked for the recall of the British minister and three consuls, includ-

ing the gentleman at Cincinnati, for their illegal recruiting activities.

When James Buchanan, American minister to Great Britain, protested against British recruiting in the United States, Lord Clarendon, the Foreign Secretary, remonstrated on Irish plots being hatched on American soil to invade Ireland. Secretary of State Marcy informed Clarendon that the United States Government had no knowledge of "any such Irish plots," recalling only a meeting of a few persons held at Boston to discuss the condition of their countrymen at home and offer suggestions touching "the ameliorations of the condition of the land of their birth." He could not help adding as a poke at Clarendon that the Boston meeting "will probably rejoice at having effected much more than they anticipated" by stirring the apprehensions of the British government.

10

The Boston meeting of which Secretary Marcy spoke assembled in answer to a demand among the Irish for some sort of action lest the opportunities of the Crimean War be lost. By the unwillingness of such leaders as Mitchel, Meagher, and McGee to initiate an organization, John McClenahan, who had taken over the *Citizen* from Mitchel, and Patrick Lynch of the *Irish American* started the Irish Emigrant Aid Society. The title of the society was adopted from the New England Emigrant Aid Company, which ostensibly helped settlers take up land in Kansas but had as a corollary purpose the colonization of Kansas with anti-slavery voters. So the Irish society looked not to aiding the emigrant in America but to sending him back to Ireland with a gun.

The first meeting was held on August 14, 1855, at Dooley's Merchants' Exchange Hotel in Boston, with delegates from fifty-five Massachusetts towns and twelve invited guests representing seven states. The ambiguous language of the platform, together with the addresses, failed to hide the fact that the Irish Emigrant Aid Society, an oath-bound secret society, looked to sending men to Ireland for revolutionary purposes. During the summer and fall of 1855, the Irish Emigrant Aid Society spread auxiliary associations through the United States. Its total numbers were small in comparison with the total Catholic Irish population, but historically the Irish revolutionary movements attracted only a minority of the people, either in Ireland or the United

States. That minority, however, constituted a hard core of bitter-end absolutists, uncompromising and with no concessions in their bones.

On December 4, 1855, some hundred delegates representing twenty-four states met in the Astor House in New York for the first national convention of the society, drew up a constitution and elected Robert Tyler, the old Repealer, president. Bitter personal differences marked the convention. Doheny, who declared he spoke for two thousand Irish revolutionaries in the military companies, contested the right of John McClenahan of the *Citizen* to speak for the Irish, charging that he was a British spy, and McClenahan in response called Doheny "a thug." In the showdown, Doheny and his faction were outvoted and left the meeting.

On January 7, 1856, eleven members of the Robert Emmet branch of the Irish Emigrant Aid Society in Cincinnati appeared in the United States District Court of the city to stand trial on an indictment charging violation of the neutrality law in setting on foot an expedition against a country with which the United States enjoyed peaceful relations. Two Orangemen, members of the American Protestant Association, an ally of the Know-Nothing organization, infiltrated the Robert Emmet branch for the purpose of exposing it, but the judge decided that talking about an invasion of Ireland was quite different from actually making plans to invade, and released the prisoners. That was the fault of the Irish Emigrant Aid Society — it constantly talked of what it was going to do to England without doing anything, and it collapsed of its own squabbles, the ending of the Crimean War and the disappearance of funds.

II

Another society now came to the front to pick up the remains of the Irish Emigrant Aid Society. The Emmet Monument Association was of a different character: through it originated the historic Irish revolutionary movement known as Fenianism.

At the end of 1853, John O'Mahony arrived in New York from Paris soon after John Mitchel. O'Mahony, a gentleman farmer and scholar of ancient Gaelic culture (in New York he translated Keating's *General History of Ireland*), had been a leader of a Tipperary rifle club in the 1848 uprising and after its collapse continued guerrilla warfare until forced to flee to France, where he lived in poverty.

O'Mahony, described by John O'Leary, the O'Leary of "Romantic Ireland" in Yeats's poem as "perhaps the manliest and handsomest man" he ever saw and "the soul of truth and honor," was an inflexible Irish revolutionary. He joined Mitchel, Doheny, and the leaders of the military companies in New York. Early in 1854 he organized the Emmet Monument Association, a secret society within the military companies, and himself became captain of the Edward Fitzgerald Guard of one hundred men. The significance of the association's name was not lost on the knowing. In his speech from the dock Robert Emmet commanded that no monument be raised to him until free Ireland had taken her place among the nations of the world. It appealed to single-minded, dedicated men. When the Emmet Monument Association was in existence, according to one local historian, there were more armed, disciplined, and determined Irishmen in New York pledged to Irish freedom than at any other time. The association of the military companies with secret societies angered the more vehement of the clergy. Father Kelly of Jersey City ordered out of the Church Captain Farrell of the Montgomery Guards.

Early in June, 1855, Joseph Denieffe, a member of the association, received news of his father's illness in Ireland and booked passage for return. Doheny commissioned him to make connections with revolutionary nationalists in Ireland, and when young Denieffe asked to whom he should report, Doheny replied: "We have no one there as yet. So we give you carte blanche to do what you can for the organization and yourself." Denieffe was both amazed and shocked, as he had been led to understand, with the other members of the association, that an invasion from the United States was scheduled for the following November.

This excellently characterized the unreality in which the Irish revolutionaries in the United States moved. With typical Irish disregard of hard facts, they took the dream for the deed. They thought so wishfully of freeing Ireland that the image of the event became alive. Though no liaison had been made with forces in Ireland and no preparations arranged for the invasion, Doheny, when asked by Denieffe what date to give for the descent, gravely informed him: "You may assure them the time will be in September. We have thirty thousand men ready now, and all we need is money, and arrangements are under way to provide it. We propose to issue bonds and some of the wealthiest men of our race are willing to take them."

"That was my commission," Denieffe wrote, "and I went with a cheerful heart, although I had no one in Ireland to report to. Oh, what a charming period is youth, when nothing seems impossible."

The Cloud Cuckoo Land of the United States was repeated in Ireland. When Denieffe met with the revolutionaries on the other side, they had not even heard of the society which had sent him as the advance agent of the invasion. Still, so infinite was the capacity of the Irish imagination for unreality that the Irish nationalists waited expectantly for the invasion to take place in September, and when it failed to materialize they still hoped on. They concluded that delay in raising money from bonds accounted for the postponement.

In the meantime, the end of the Crimean War had dissolved the Emmet Monument Association and the plan of invading Ireland from the United States. A committee of thirteen was created as a continuing body, empowered to revive the revolutionary society in the United States if the need developed.

Denieffe took a job in the north of Ireland. Two days before Christmas, 1857, he received word from James Stephens to come quickly to Dublin. Stephens, the railway engineer from Kilkenny who had been wounded in the '48 uprising, had become a professional revolutionary and, without formal organization, kept together a band of faithful Irishmen, who had only the eternal Irish hope and the unreconstructed Gaelic spirit to sustain them in the midst of an Ireland politically barren.

The excited Stephens had received a letter from Doheny. Was Ireland ready for revolutionary organization? asked Doheny. If so, would Stephens take the lead in recruiting members? And finally, how much money would be required for the work? Stephens replied that the country never offered better prospects for organization. If the American financiers would put up a hundred pounds for three months, he thought the revolutionary organization could be started. Not trusting the mails, regularly searched by British authorities, Stephens asked Denieffe to act as a courier with the letter to New York. Stephens lacked the money to pay young Denieffe's passage, but the American managed to rustle it up in Dublin.

In New York, Denieffe discovered that Doheny and associates had queried Stephens out of full and patriotic hearts but that they had neither money to finance revolutionary organization in Ireland nor prospects of raising any. The Irish in America had lost faith in movements to free Ireland and confidence in the trustworthiness of the leaders.

Denieffe, after waiting two months, took the four hundred dollars raised by the committee and returned to Ireland. He arrived in Dublin on St. Patrick's morning, 1858, and turned the money over to Stephens. That night the Irish Revolutionary Brotherhood, which henceforth would have to be reckoned with in Ireland, was born. Thomas Clarke Luby, a graduate of Trinity College and a Protestant Irishman like Stephens, drafted the oath of membership, which pledged allegiance to the Irish Republic, "now virtually established," and "implicit obedience in all things, not contrary to the laws of God, to the commands of my superior officers."

In the United States, John O'Mahony reached into his store of Irish knowledge and called the new revolutionary society the Fenians after the heroic band of warriors, *Fianna Eireann,* who followed the legendary Finn McCool. Thus out of Doheny's idea and American financing was developed the revolutionary brotherhood idea in the two countries that eventually accomplished the design initiated by Wolfe Tone and carried forward by the '48 rebels: an Irish republic established by rebellion.

45
"Life, Liberty, and the Pursuit of Irishmen"

JOHN MCKEON, the former Congressman, pressed two questions on prospective jurors. Are you prejudiced against foreigners? Do you belong to the Order of United Americans?

McKeon was counsel for eleven members of the Ancient Order of Hibernians standing trial in New York for rioting in the Ninth Ward on the Fourth of July, 1853.* The Hibernians, according to their own story, staged a parade to honor the birthday of American freedom but a rowdy nativist drove an omnibus through the line of march and when the Irish resisted, a nativist mob — the "spawn of Orangemen" — fell upon the procession.

* The Ancient Order of Hibernians, organized in 1836 by members of St. Patrick's Fraternal Society of New York, a burial society, as an American auxiliary of the Ribbon Society of Ireland, had become a benevolent, mutual-aid organization which steadily attracted membership in the 1850s.

McKeon's two questions had pertinence to the heightening sentiment under organization against the Catholic Church and the Irish
called Know-Nothingism. Like many others of the day, McKeon confused the Order of United Americans, a sizable nativist society, with the
Supreme Order of the Star Spangled Banner, a secret, oath-bound
society, dedicated to the political purpose of putting and keeping in
office native-born Protestants, of opposing the Catholic Church and
of frustrating the Irish. Its popular name came from the pledge of the
members to "know nothing" when queried concerning the society. It
accepted only native-born Protestants as members, and ties by blood or
marriage with a Roman Catholic acted as automatic disqualification
for membership. Its slogan was that "Americans must rule America."

Organized in 1849-1850 as one of a spate of nativist Societies then
mushrooming, the Know-Nothing or American Party, as it formally
called itself, was a political phenomenon of the 1850s. It had become a
national force by 1854. It seemed likely in 1855 to elect its candidate
for president in 1856. At the opening of 1857 it lay in ruins.

While this third and most vigorous nativist movement in pre-Civil
War days still had anti-Catholicism as its core, religious exclusivism
alone failed to account for the dazzling, if brief, success of the Know-
Nothing Party. Its secrecy and paraphernalia of mystification — hand
grips, passwords, oaths, recognition signals, notice of meetings by distribution on the streets of distinctively cut paper and such mumbo-
jumbo, similar to that of the Irish Ribbon Society — attracted members who otherwise would have had no interest in organized nativism;
this secrecy, said one observer, constituted "a charm, a vitality . . .
that draws men into it, without much reference to the whys and where-
fore of the case."

The main reason, however, for its unusual rise was the disintegration
of the two major parties and the temporary shelter the Know-Nothing
Party afforded until the political convulsions, like geological corrections
beneath the earth's surface, had come to rest in changed alignments in
accommodation to new circumstances. The historic Whig Party collapsed into a waiting grave after the disaster of General Scott's defeat
for the presidency in 1852. The Democratic Party split into Northern and Southern wings on the issue of slavery. In lieu of the discipline of two strong national parties, the Know Nothings, as a well-
knit minority, benefited from the dispersed strength of local frag-
mentations, splinter groups, and fusion coalitions. The controversial

Kansas-Nebraska Act of 1854 made slavery the all-absorbing political issue and the Republican Party inevitable. The Know-Nothing Party acted as a bridge between the decline of the Whig and the rise of the Republican Party for the confused, the frustrated and the perplexed. The professional politicians seized upon it because — like the later Anti-Saloon League — it could deliver votes and they needed a going organization to which to attach themselves.

2

The part of the Roman Catholic Church and of the Irish in contributing to the revival of the nativist spirit out of which Know-Nothingism developed lay in several directions.

The growth of the Roman Catholic Church pressed itself on the consciousness of the country. In 1800, one bishop ruled the Church in America, with perhaps not more than forty clergymen in the land. Thomas O'Connor, who lived until 1855, remembered the one Catholic church in New York City and the clergymen whose number could be counted on one hand. In 1850, there were six archbishops, twenty-six bishops, thirty-four dioceses, 1245 churches and 1303 priests. The period of the greatest emigration coincided with the awe-inspiring advance of the Church. In the decade 1840-1850, the number of priests and of churches had been more than doubled and the number of dioceses nearly doubled. The ratio of increase in that period was as great as during the previous forty years.

At mid-century the Church, in addition to numbers — or (as the nativists said) because of numbers — had taken on a combative and challenging assertiveness quite markedly in contrast to the soft-voiced approach of Bishop England. Archbishop Hughes set the tone for the new aggressiveness and Orestes Brownson gave it intellectual texture. Hughes later justified himself to a friend in Rome: "The gentle language of meekness and forbearance which, in ordinary circumstances, should flow from the lips and the pen of a Christian bishop," he wrote, "would have no effect upon the class of adversaries that I have had to deal with." He explained that he had had to stand up among his people as "their bishop and chief" and "to contend for their rights as a religious community." Because, he said, New York enjoyed "a certain kind of general predominancy in the minds of the Catholics," other places followed his lead. The Know Nothings of the day accepted

Hughes's estimate of his own Catholic leadership, but unfavorably. The bible of the Know Nothings, *Republican Landmarks,* by John P. Sanderson, said of him: "No man in the country has done more to cause excitement among the Americans, and unite them against all attempts at innovations upon their institutions by foreigners, than Archbishop Hughes."

The Catholic euphoria which set in at the middle of the century stemmed not so much from the arrogance of European Catholicism transported to the United States, as one historian has suggested,* as from the sanguine Irish temperament which now dominated the Church in the United States. As the clergy of Irish blood looked at the astounding resurrection of Catholicism in Ireland since Catholic Emancipation in 1829, observed the remarkable growth of the Church in the United States, and traced its spread throughout the British Empire thanks to the efforts of Irish priests, the ancient Irish sense of mission burst into full flame and Irish excess in zeal to convert America gave rise to hopes not warranted by the hard facts.

Nativists blamed Archbishop Hughes for originating what seemed a concerted movement by the hierarchy to demand a share of public funds for the support of parochial schools. Catholic apologists miscalculated the profound regard and pride of the United States in the public school. They sought to build up the argument for public support of parochial schools by knocking down public schools as atheistic, godless, and infidel — a maneuver that while rooted in Catholic conviction nevertheless tactlessly offended Protestant sentiment and aroused a resentful stubbornness.

Nativists interpreted the petition of Catholic bishops that Catholic children in public schools be excused from the reading of the King James version as a conspiracy to drive the Bible from the classroom. They responded with the slogan of spiritual freedom, a free Bible, and free schools. They echoed the sentiment of Hon. Joseph Choate: "Never shall the Bible be shut out of our schools. No! never! while there is enough of Plymouth Rock left to make a gunflint out of."

But the really powerful impetus to Know-Nothingism was the growing number of Catholic Irish, their belligerent assertiveness and, as a capstone, their intensive political activities, directed (according to nativist ideology) by a "Foreign Priesthood" for the service of the Roman Catholic Church.

---

* Professor Ray Billington in *The Protestant Crusade, 1800-1860,* pp. 289-292.

"And here we are in the middle of the Nineteenth Century," wrote the *Pilot* early in 1850, "as numerous a nation on this soil, as we were, on that of old Ireland, in the beginning of it!" As the total Catholic population of all nationalities in the United States was in the vicinity of two million, the *Pilot* editor indulged his sanguinary Irish nature in the claim. But Irish bustle made the numbers seem larger than they were.

The accusation that the Irish became voters illegally through fraudulent naturalization, degraded the purity of the ballot by electoral corruption and used physical violence at the polls in a frenzy of partisan zeal grew louder with the Whig defeats.

"All that is demanded of foreigners," wrote John P. Sanderson, the Know-Nothing propagandist, "is to lay aside their national peculiarities and prejudices, to deport themselves with becoming modesty and propriety, and, instead of at once mixing in political brawls, and attempting to regulate and control public affairs, mind their own private business."

Once upon a time, wrote the *Pilot* in the summer of 1850, we acted in the servile manner the nativists thought befitting for Catholics, adopting in the manner of Bishop England an apologetic tone — and we received only scorn for our pains. But now, continued the *Pilot*, the Catholic, thanks to the teachings of Brownson, bowed to no man and asked no favor of his Protestant neighbor. Its advice to the Catholic in America was plain: "Be a MAN, ask for no more than your rights, but demand them firmly and temperately."

3

The first rumblings of the third go, in three decades, of nativism against the Roman Catholic Church and the foreigner, came out of the stronghold of Protestant Irish rancor — Pittsburgh. A violent, profane, drunken, and rowdy street-corner anti-Popery preacher, one Joseph Barker, had been thrown into jail for offenses against peace and order and, emerging as a martyr, was elected mayor of the city. Soon after he took office in 1850, he ordered the arrest of Bishop O'Connor, a humble and retiring prelate, on the charge that a sewer connecting the Roman Catholic hospital with the main sewer constituted a nuisance. He fined the bishop twenty-five dollars and denied him an appeal to a higher court. Pittsburgh came to realize that anti-Popery and efficient management of the city's business had no relationship, and retired Barker after he served one term.

The next manifestation of rising anti-Catholic Irish feeling appeared with the revival of "Paddy making," the taunting effigies of St. Patrick's Day, in New Jersey, Massachusetts, Maine, and New York during 1852 and 1853.

The Hannah Corcoran affair in Charlestown early in March, 1853, revealed no change in the mentality that almost twenty years before had conspired to destroy the Ursuline convent. Her Protestant employer persuaded Hannah, a young girl fresh from Ireland, to join his sect in Charlestown. Her mother speedily removed the girl from this environment and, on the advice of a priest, dispatched her to Philadelphia. The rumor circulated that priests held Hannah imprisoned for her apostasy and that she might even have been killed. Handbills announced a public meeting on March 2 in the vicinity of the Catholic church in Charlestown, with the ultimatum: "SHE MUST BE FOUND." For almost a week, military companies and the police kept constantly on the alert to prevent a mob from burning the church. Even the reappearance of Hannah, unharmed and under the protection of her Protestant sponsors, failed to deter the mob from its incendiary design, but the obvious intention of the militia to shoot to kill in protection of the church finally quenched the upflaring of anti-Catholic hostility. The five days of tension in Charlestown demonstrated an explosive nativist temper ready for the fuse.

4

The arrival in New York on Sunday, March 6, 1853, of Father Alessandro Gavazzi on the steamer *Baltic* from England ushered in the period of anti-Catholic and anti-Irish violence that marked the rise of the Know-Nothing Party and its satellite nativist societies. A series of events that fell into an undesigned relationship set the bad feelings of nativism into excitable operation.

The pattern began with the assignment by Rome of Archbishop Gaetano Bedini, a pleasant, agreeable, and urbane Catholic diplomat, to visit the United States to settle a revival of trusteeism in the dispute between the Irish-descended Bishop John Timon and the German trustees of St. Louis' Church of Buffalo over title to the church property. Rome made a mistake in sending a papal nuncio into Know-

Nothing United States at this particular time and with Father Gavazzi on the demagogic loose against the Catholic Church.

Gavazzi was the advance guard and prototype of the nativist storm troopers who took to the streets in rioting and church burning to save the United States from the Pope of Rome. Gavazzi, an Italian Barnabite monk, was a fanatic. He had been active in the Italian liberation movement of 1848 and 1849 and blamed the Church for its failure. He left his priestly calling and vowed to annihilate the Church. The zeal for the patriotic cause he diverted into uncompromising hatred of the Church, and he found a sympathetic audience in England to which he had repaired. Reports of his success as an anti-Catholic rabble-rouser inspired the American and Foreign Christian Union, dedicated to opposing the errors of Rome and spreading truth among the Romanists, to invite him to the United States. Father Gavazzi assured Monsignor Bedini of the wrong kind of warm reception in the United States.

He stigmatized Bedini, who had been governor of Bologna by appointment of the Pope, as the executioner of Ugo Bassi, a priest with Garibaldi's forces, indeed that Bedini himself had tortured Bassi, and had sent other Italian republicans to their death.* He fixed upon Bedini the title of "the bloody butcher of Bologna." In consequence of Gavazzi's passion, crowds burned Bedini in effigy, threatened his life, and posted warnings against him as a monster as he journeyed through the United States. German '48 exiles, radical freethinkers bitterly hostile to the Catholic Church, staged the most riotous demonstration against Bedini in Cincinnati. Police broke up a procession of Free Germans on the way to burn Bedini's effigy and a number were injured in the ensuing street battle. Outraged nativist sentiment placed the responsibility for the interference of the police upon Catholic influence, and so angry and raw had sentiment grown against the papal nuncio that friends secreted him aboard the steamer taking him back to Europe to escape the angry mob awaiting his appearance on a New York dock.

It was paradoxical that an intense and dramatic foreigner, Gavazzi, with imperfect command of English, ushered the nation into a period of disturbance and rioting against the foreigner.

---

* Bedini had tried to save Bassi from the death decree of the Austrian military rulers of Bologna.

5

Gavazzi's success as a rabble-rouser encouraged a rash of street preachers, unlettered porters, carpenters and the like, who felt the evangelical call to war on Romanism. At first the contortions of these open-air Savonarolas evoked amusement and ribaldry but trouble hovered when they set up their pulpits in the vicinity of Catholic Irish neighborhoods. Bishops in pastorals, priests from the altar, and the Catholic press warned the people to avoid these meetings and above all not to be baited into physical reprisals. By and large, the Catholic Irish showed unusual restraint under extreme provocation.

The most notorious of these street gospelers was John S. Orr, who described himself as the "trumpeter of the approaching King" and "publisher in the open air of the tidings of the glorious Majesty of the approaching Kingdom and its King." People dubbed him the "Angel Gabriel" from the white gown in which he dressed himself and the horn he loudly blew to attract listeners. "Gabriel" linked Popery and slavery as "twin sisters" and cursed the Irish. American-born Negroes were treated like cattle and not allowed to vote, he preached, while thousands of white men who came from the Green Isle to plot against the United States were put into office. The Negro had a black skin outside, he shouted, but the Irishman was black inside.

"Gabriel's" sentiments and language found favor in New England to which he journeyed from the streets of New York in the spring of 1854. His crusade resolved itself into a contest by the police and militia to forestall the riots urged against the Catholic Irish by the agitated preaching of the crazed "Gabriel." He set a mob to attack a settlement of Irish workers in Chelsea and take down the cross on the Catholic church for burning. On the next Sunday, seven hundred and fifty troops stood guard in Boston as a precaution against his incendiarism. At Worcester the police clapped him in jail and when the mob demanded his release the mayor called out the local militia. At Lowell he organized a demonstration against a convent but a protective cordon of determined Irishmen warded off the attack. At Nashua, New Hampshire, "Gabriel" incited a mob to action against an Irish colony located on the Acre, but the police interfered. His greatest triumph in New England was in Bath, Maine, where after listening to his ravings of hatred, a mob battered down the door of the Catholic church and then burned it to the ground. In between his visits to New England,

"Gabriel" preached at Palmyra, New York, and an attempt was made to burn down the Catholic church. He met his Waterloo at Charlestown, where a magistrate placed him under bonds to keep the peace after his following had twice unsuccessfully tried to release him from jail. Thenceforth, authorities denied him a speaking permit and he faded out of the American scene.

Ellsworth, Maine, needed no "Angel Gabriel" to keep its wind up against the Catholic Church and the Irish so long as a newspaper editor named Chaney, the boss of the town and of an unlovely gang of nativist ruffians, operated. Bad feelings against the Irish spilled over in the ruling of the school committee that Catholic children must read the Protestant Bible, whereupon one Lawrence Donahoe removed his daughter from the public school and sent the bill for private instruction to the town, which boiled up anti-Catholic sentiment. Several physical attacks upon the church, together with open signs of ill will against Father John Bapst, S.J., the Ellsworth priest, caused diocesan authorities to remove him to Bangor, and the local nativists publicly issued the warning to Father Bapst not to return to the town. But he did, one Saturday night in October, 1854, to hear confession and say Mass. News of his appearance gathered a vicious mob who seized the priest, robbed him of his wallet and watch, stripped him of his clothing, smeared him with a coating of hot tar, applied a coating of feathers, rode him on a jiggling sharp-edged rail, and left him unconscious on a wharf. This mob manhandling of a defenseless priest was one of the most sickening anti-Catholic outbreaks of the Fierce Fifties.

Anti-Catholic street preachers in New York and Brooklyn turned each Lord's Day into a day of potential rioting and bloodshed by the violence of their attacks on Catholicism, the Pope, and the Irish. The prank of a boy tumbled Preacher West, by occupation a carpenter, from his rickety pulpit one Sunday in November, 1853, and the following Sunday a Know-Nothing guard appeared to protect him. Daniel "Sailor" Parsons, an evangelical porter, was arrested, by the influence (it was said) of prominent Catholics. A mob rushed to the house of the mayor demanding the "Sailor's" release, and a police justice discharged him because he had spoken on private property and not on a public highway. Irate Protestants called a public meeting late in December to protest against the arrest of Parsons as a violation of civil and religious liberty. The electric sense of riot filled the air. But the mayor issued a proclamation urging citizens to remain in their homes and Archbishop

Hughes, in a special appeal, asked Catholics to stay away from public meetings. Though twenty thousand turned out for the demonstration, no disturbance ensued. People blamed the Know Nothings for the trouble, saying they paid the preachers to attack the Catholics.

An auxiliary of the Know Nothings composed of young men, who came to be known as the "Wide-Awakes," from their rallying cry, sprang up to protect the street preachers. Their white hats with broad brims distinguished these lads of the Order of the American Star, and the Irishman responded to the hats with a clout at its wearer just as his fist instinctively doubled at the sight of the Orange war flag.

During the spring of 1854, Brooklyn enjoyed no repose on Sunday. The trouble arose when a crowd of New York Know Nothings crossed over by ferry to act as sentinels of a street preacher and invited the wrath of the Irish by parading through an Irish neighborhood on their way back. The battle was resumed on the following Sunday and this continued for several Sundays until the militia called out by the mayor finally quieted the heated antagonists.

The poisoned air of the United States in the years 1854 and 1855, the peak of the Know-Nothing disturbance, acted upon men's minds to unhinge civilized restraints and let loose destructive religious and racial passions.

Nativist conspirators destroyed a block of marble sent by the Pope for the Washington Monument, then under construction. Mobs swarmed through the Irish sections of Manchester, New Hampshire, and Lawrence, Massachusetts, and smashed windows in Catholic churches. They attacked Catholic churches in Clinton and Southbridge, Massachusetts, and burned one down in Raritan, New Jersey. A fight between an Irishman and a nativist at the polls in St. Louis on September 11, 1854, started a two-day riot that left damage to Irish homes and grocery stores to the amount of $50,000 in its wake.

The lodges of the American Protestant Association, a nativist society (if an Irish bull may be used) composed of foreigners, mostly Protestant Irish of the Orange disposition, gathered in Newark on September 5, and during the procession members fired shots at a German Catholic church, killing an Irishman, and then wrecked its interior, causing the New York *Tribune* to say that while the Newark was the fifth or sixth Catholic church devastated by mobs, "there is no instance on record where a Protestant house of worship has been ravaged by Catholics." Know Nothings from New York seized control of the

Williamsburg section of Brooklyn after an electoral fracas between Irishmen and nativists and would have burned down the Church of SS. Peter and Paul had not four Irishmen staved off their rushes until the arrival of the militia.

The most violent outbreak in 1855 occurred in Louisville where Know Nothings took control of the polls in an election, drove off the Irish and Germans, then stormed an Irish section, destroying twelve frame houses and leaving eleven Irish casualties. In Providence, nativists, stirred by rumors of a young girl held against her will in a convent, gathered menacingly in its vicinity, but well-armed Irishmen warned them off, and the influence of the mayor and the Providence *Journal* quieted misinformed opinion. New Orleans had its normal election riot and the Know Nothings strengthened their hold on Baltimore.

The low life in New York was divided into American "sons of bitches" and Irish "sons of bitches," as the respective factions called each other. John Morrissey, an Irish tough from Troy, a Tammany mercenary, heavyweight champion of the world and a prodigious drinker, who was later to be a member of Congress, a famous gambler and organizer of the Saratoga race track, led the Irish of the so-called sporting fraternity. William Poole, a butcher and saloonkeeper, a brutal street brawler, notorious as an eye gouger, was the hero of the Know Nothings. Late in February, 1855, Poole had beaten the drunken Morrissey in a saloon brawl and police had removed the Troy rowdy to his room where he passed out. Later the same night friends of Morrissey returned. A cocky, fighting little Irishman, Patrick "Paudeen" McLaughlin, baited Poole, started a free-for-all and when police broke up the affair, Poole lay badly wounded. Eleven days later he died, his last words being, so it was said, "I die an American." The Know Nothings gave him a tremendous funeral, and the nativists translated this gutter gladiator into a hero-martyr, whose memory drew American tears and anti-Irish curses.

In Portland, Maine, a priest declared that he dared not go out on the street after dark, fearing for his life. Wild rumors spread that Irish servant girls had been provided with poison by priests to do away with their Protestant masters and mistresses on a given day. A Know-Nothing school committee in Philadelphia discharged all Catholic teachers. A gang of nativists threw an inoffensive young Irishman into a pond at Newburyport because he was "a damned Paddy." Sisters of Charity were assaulted on the streets of Providence, and in Mobile they received orders to get out of the City Hospital. The clergy recommended that St. Patrick's Day celebrations be held indoors in 1854. They resurrected O'Connell's old political slogan to restrain the impetuous Irish under severe provocation: "He who commits a crime gives strength to the enemy." Daniel O'Rourke raised a toast at the March 17 observance of the Charitable Irish Society of Boston: "Bad luck to our foes. May the devil cut off their toes, that we may know them by their limping."

6

In November, 1854, the Know Nothings won their greatest triumph in, as might be expected, Massachusetts, electing Henry J. Gardner, a wholsesale dry goods merchant and former Whig, as governor, a full state ticket, every seat in the Senate, and 376 out of 379 seats in the House, casting 63 per cent of all the ballots.

Resentment against the Catholic Irish in Massachusetts intensified rather than lessened as the second half of the nineteenth century opened. A dismayed Yankee might well worry over the future when the figures showed that in Boston the native-born vote increased by only 14.72 per cent from 1850 to 1855 against an increase in the foreign-born of 194.64 per cent in the same period, while the ratio of births to the foreign-born was far in excess of births to the native-born.

The reformist elements in Massachusetts angrily blamed the Catholic Irish for turning back the clock. A coalition of progressives in a constitutional convention in 1851 had written amendments fashioned to break the hold of wealthy Whig conservatism on the state. But the Irish concluded that the reforms aimed to penalize them rather than the Whigs. One amendment would have denied the use of public funds for sectarian education, a gratuitous fling at the Irish since they had not raised the issue in Massachusetts. A second amendment to gerrymander Massachusetts would have given more power to the smaller towns, the centers of anti-Catholic Irish sentiment and the source of the defeat of the convent indemnification bills, at the expense of Boston, where Catholic Irish strength lay. A third amendment would have made the judiciary elective, and if Massachusetts raised the same type to the bench that it sent to the General Court, then the warning of Orestes Brownson made sense, that popularly chosen judges threatened their rights. The Catholic Irish aligned themselves with the Whigs in rejecting the amendments.

The Catholic Irish supported the controversial Kansas-Nebraska Act, which repealed the Missouri Compromise and established popular sovereignty as the principle to govern whether or not a new state should countenance slavery. It had been managed in Congress by their favorite Democrat, Senator Stephen A. Douglas of Illinois, whom New England burned in effigy. They believed that, in supporting Douglas's measure, they upheld the Constitution, as in their support of the 1850 Compromise, with its provision for the return of fugitive slaves. The *Pilot* spared no feelings in calling to account the three thousand New England ministers who had memorialized Congress against the Kansas-Nebraska Act. The abomination of Popery, unsmiling New Englanders believed, had struck hands with the abomination of the slave power.

In the spring of 1854, officers seized Anthony Burns in Boston as a runaway slave and despite the strong legal talent which came to his defense he was ordered returned to his master in Virginia. Plans of the anti-slavery rescue party to release Burns by force went awry and in the storming of the jail a deputy marshal was killed. Boston closed down its business, went into mourning black, pealed its church bells and stood in impotent rage as militia companies escorted the frightened Burns through the streets to a waiting man-of-war assigned to carry him back to Virginia. The bleak eyes of Boston looked with cold fury upon two of the militia companies called out to serve as escort — the Irish Columbian Artillery and the Sarsfield Guards. A handbill incited the populace against the Irish:

AMERICANS TO THE RESCUE!

AMERICANS! SONS OF THE REVOLUTION!

A Body of Seventy-five Irishmen

known as the

"Columbian Artillery"

have volunteered their services to shoot down the citizens

of Boston! and are now under arms to defend Virginia

in kidnapping a Citizen of Massachusetts!

Americans! These Irishmen have called us

"Cowards and Sons of Cowards"!

Shall we submit to have our citizens shot

down by a set of Vagabond Irishmen?

The Irish companies had not volunteered.

And so Governor Gardner, the Know Nothing, in his inaugural message to the 1855 General Court recommended the disbandment of foreign military companies, along with a general program of nativist legislation, including the prohibition of public funds for sectarian education, a constitutional amendment requiring twenty-one years' residence before naturalization, a literacy test for voters, on the policy that America should "nationalize before we naturalize."

But the moral and ultra-patriotic Know-Nothing regime had been in power only a few weeks when it was hit in the face by the Joseph Hiss case.

7

Late in March, 1855, two horse-drawn omnibuses stopped before a dwelling on the heavily traveled Dedham Turnpike in Roxbury and disgorged seventeen men. This was the Joint Special Committee on the Inspection of Nunneries and Convents authorized by the august General Court of the great Commonwealth of Massachusetts, come without advance notice to "visit and examine," as the law specified, a convent and school conducted by seven Belgian nuns of the Notre Dame order for twelve young lady pupils between the ages of ten and fifteen, all Americans by birth. Actually only five of the party were members of the committee; the others were friends curious about the inside of a convent or just along for the ride. Previously the committee had visited the Jesuit college of Holy Cross in Worcester and given it a clean bill.

Now the visitors proceeded to examine the convent-school from attic to cellar. Their entrance excited the children, who, being told the men were Know Nothings, feared the worst. The young girls were asked by these grown men if they entertained boys at the school. The nunnery committee and friends tramped through all the rooms, including one where a Cuban child lay sick, though they had been advised of her sickness. They closely inspected the chapel and probed the basement with lights.

Particularly active, if not in the inspection, at least in making his presence felt, was one Joseph Hiss, a Know-Nothing legislator and member of the "smelling committee," as the body came to be known. Hiss, born in Baltimore, was an insolvent tailor from a Massachusetts town and a former Grand Worshipful Instructor of the Know-Nothing or-

der in the state, who had ridden into legislative office on the Know-
Nothing sweep of 1854. Hiss insinuated himself into an unwanted
confidential chat with a nun. Giving his name as that of another legislator, he told her of his studies for the priesthood in Baltimore and of a
sister even now there in a convent. He patted the nun familiarly on the
back, examined the rosary beads hanging from her waist, asked if she
liked her "situation" and suggested a trip with him to Montreal —
conduct which one newspaper characterized as the "salacity and goat-
ish propensities" of Hiss.

After inspecting the convent-school, the committee and their friends
repaired to the Norfolk House, ate a turkey dinner, drank champagne
(then illegal in Massachusetts) and presented the bill — $72 — to the
state.

Nathan and Charles Hale, staunch Whigs and owners of the Boston
Advertiser, despised the Know Nothings and felt they were performing
a public duty in publishing a full account of the visit and editorializ-
ing on the shame these Know-Nothing snoops had brought to the
name of a supposedly enlightened commonwealth. Bishop Fitzpatrick
no sooner read the story than he was at his desk writing a letter of
protest. The Massachusetts General Court ordered a joint House-
Senate investigation.

In the meantime, the nunnery inspection committee had been off
on another junket, this time to a convent of the Notre Dame order in
Lowell. The members put up at the Washington House and included
in the party was a lady friend of Hiss, not his wife, a certain "Mrs.
Patterson," whose board and keep was charged to the state. According
to the chambermaid, the bed in Hiss's room appeared to her to have
been unoccupied while "Mrs. Patterson's" bed looked as though it had
been occupied during the night by more than one person. That same
night a member of the committee who had started on a jag in Lowell
continued it on his return to Boston and ended up in a crib where he
was robbed of his wallet. The newspapers took delight in refreshing
the public with the record of this erring Know Nothing as a strong
temperance advocate.

The joint investigating committee whitewashed the inspection of
the Roxbury convent and found insufficient evidence to convict in the
Lowell instance. But a special House committee looked into the conduct of Hiss, voted him unworthy of membership, ordered him expelled, and a sergeant-at-arms bodily tossed him out of the legislative

chamber upon his refusal to budge. A creditor clamped Hiss into jail for a ninety-dollar debt, and Hiss disavowed the Know-Nothing Party as having sold out to the Abolitionists and the Maine Law prohibition reformers. After a few lectures he disappeared from sight.

The Hiss case revealed the extent of hypocrisy in the Know-Nothing movement and its penetration by careerists and opportunists exploiting religious prejudice for self-serving ends. The Know-Nothing legislature, characterized by the *Pilot* as the "Praise-God Barebones" legislature, had hardly got off to an edifying start.

8

Now appeared what was perhaps the most fantastic paradox of the whole nativist movement of the 1850s — Catholic Know-Nothing-ism, undertaken by Orestes Brownson in cooperation with his admiring disciple, the Boston *Pilot*.

Brownson, being a native-born American of English antecedents, and a Roman Catholic by conversion, felt qualified to interpret the sentiments of honest American nationality (as distinguished from its extremist and prejudiced form of political nativism) to the Roman Catholic foreigners, that is, the Irish. Brownson never ceased avowing his affection for the Irish, but he would have loved them better were they less Irish, and he regretted, as a convert who hoped to spread the faith, that the American mind considered the Roman Catholic religion to be synonymous with Irish nationality: an American did not turn Roman Catholic; he turned Irish.

In an article, "Of Native Americanism," in the June, 1854, issue of *Brownson's Quarterly Review,* Brownson suggested that the Irish cease being Irish and conform as quickly as possible to the Anglo-American nationality of the United States. The English stock, he explained, comprised "the original germ of the great American people," and other peoples, so long as they remained distinct and separate, remained foreigners. "No nationality can stand for a moment before the Anglo-American." Let the Irish, he advised, give up their political activities, cease fighting their country's battles in the United States, desist from forming military companies, disavow journals and associations formed for foreign political purposes; let their journalists and politicians avoid engaging even in the struggle against anti-foreign and anti-Catholic nativism because their extremism in the attack made the lot of their countrymen the more difficult. In short, the policy for the emigrant to follow, said Brownson, was to be as quiet in conduct, demeanor, and language as well-behaved servants; the emigrant should in effect accept a second-class status until he was assimilated into the prevailing and dominant Anglo-American life.

In asking the Catholic Irish to put aside their deepest feelings and strip themselves of their Irish nature, Brownson showed a naïveté (as well as a miscomprehension of the race) that sharply contrasted with his shrewd analysis of the character of American nationality. But he entirely parted with reality by the course of action he pressed upon the Irish. Brownson, author of the American Catholic intellectual case against foreign radicalism, that is, Red Republicanism, now appealed to the Irish in the name of that case to succumb voluntarily to Know-Nothingism.

The Catholic Irish have been the principal targets of native Americanism, he wrote, "partly because the popular feeling of the country is anti-Catholic, partly because they have less than others in common with the American national character, and partly because they come into more immediate contact with our countrymen, and are represented by journals in the English language." But the Catholic Irish, he said, were not a threat to the United States. The most dangerous class consisted of non-Catholics from Continental states — Germans, Hungarians, and Italians, "imbued with the infidel and anarchical principles of the mad European revolutionists."

He then asked the Catholic Irish who had not as yet been naturalized to make the sacrifice of excluding themselves from citizenship so that through a revised naturalization law the Red Republican foreigners could be denied "a footing of equality with natural-born citizens" and thereby their menace would be ended. What the American Know Nothing wanted to do to the Catholic Irish he wanted the Catholic Irish to do to the Germans, Hungarians, and Italians.

The Boston *Pilot*, which took up the Brownson suggestion favorably, showed more practicality (or expediency) than the Yankee logician. It pointed out that the sacrifice on the part of the Catholic Irish would not be great: already Irish emigration had diminished to a trickle while the German was on the increase; the Germans would be hit by an amended naturalization law, not the Irish. But it also suggested that the amendment be withheld until all the Irish not yet naturalized had gone through the process and become citizens.

The Irish hit Brownson with everything they found at hand. The universal response was a shriek of outrage and indignation. Not one journal endorsed the idea. One Sweeney, a Boston publisher, collected the Catholic comments on Brownson's article, which made Brownson compare himself to O'Connell as "the best abused man in the country." He was chastised for giving aid to the Know Nothings and the Whigs, who made much of the article; he was called a Know Nothing. The Catholic Irish resented his criticism of their foibles and faults; they would take the same criticism from McGee, one man shrewdly said, but not from the Yankee Brownson. Brownson had been consistent with his own logic but had written himself right out of the affections of the Catholic Irish, who did not forgive him for his well-meant, if unreal, suggestion; and he wondered at times if the Catholic religion was broad enough to contain both himself and the Catholic Irish. Certainly Boston had not enough room for both, and Brownson moved to New York.

9

Soon after the opening of the 1855 session of the General Court, Governor Gardner ordered all Irish volunteer military companies disbanded: Columbian Artillery, Webster Artillery, Shields Artillery, and Sarsfield Guards of Boston, Jackson Musketeers of Lowell, Union Guards of Lawrence, and Jackson Guards of Worcester — seven companies in all. Governor Gardner, like Governor Everett with the Montgomery Guards of a decade and a half previously, had sacrificed the companies to anti-Irish opinion and appeased the Abolitionists for the part two Irish companies had played in upholding the federal law in the Anthony Burns case. Captain Cass of the Columbian Artillery, in anticipation, had called a meeting of the company several days previous to the governor's act and the members voted to surrender the charter voluntarily. A month later the company reorganized as the Columbian Literary Association, for the day when Know-Nothingism would have passed away. Benjamin F. Butler, the Lowell demagogue, colonel of the 5th Regiment of Light Infantry, refused to order the Irish company under his command disbanded, and Governor Gardner removed Ben, which made that weather-wise politician more popular than ever with the Catholic Irish. "The time will come," said the *Pilot*, "when Massachusetts will need their services," although the vehement Irish politician, John C. Tucker, predicted in the legislature that Irishmen could not be expected to risk their lives in defense of the proscription-ists. In Connecticut six Irish military companies were disbanded by the order of the governor, and in Cincinnati the arms of the Irish and German companies were seized.

IO

The Know-Nothing order reached its greatest power in 1855, widely extending its lodges and numbers. That year it carried every state in New England except Maine; it won in Maryland and Kentucky; it showed surprising strength in New York, Pennsylvania, California, and in the South.

But the Know-Nothing Party carried its own destruction within it-self. The artificiality of exclusivist nativism as a vital or enduring issue was proved when the issue of slavery, stirred by the Kansas-Nebraska controversy, absorbed and destroyed Know-Nothingism. The Know-Nothing national convention of 1855 could not avoid facing up to slavery, and it endorsed a pro-slavery resolution, whereupon the North-ern anti-slavery members, under Henry Wilson of Massachusetts, sepa-rated themselves from the organization. Henry Wise showed that the Know Nothings were vulnerable by running on an anti-Know-Nothing platform and winning the governorship of Virginia, while Andrew Johnson beat the order in Tennessee. The 1856 election killed off the "dark lantern" party. Instead of putting its candidate into the White House, as freely predicted a year before, the Know Nothings carried only the state of Maryland.

Know-Nothingism ingloriously petered out in its last stronghold, Baltimore, where gangs with such unlovely names as Plug-Uglies, Blood Tubs, Rip-Raps, Rough-Skin Blackguards, and Red Necks co-alesced to hold corrupt political power from 1854 to 1860, keep a Know-Nothing ruffian, Mayor Swann, in office, and cheer the gifted eloquence of Hon. Henry Winter Davis, who used Know-Nothingism to further his political ambitions. The symbol of Baltimore's Know-Nothing gangs was the awl, which members wore strapped to their knees and pressed against decent citizens who sought to exercise the franchise. The Blood Tubs got their name from the practice of squeez-ing a sponge filled with animal blood collected in tubs from butcher shops over the heads of Germans and Irishmen who ventured to the polls. Regularly in the Eighth Ward, the Irish Democrats resisted the violence of the Know Nothings, but it was not until the patience of the people had been exhausted at Know-Nothing excesses that a reform party won back control of the city and the nativism of the 1850s ended.

The Know Nothings sent sizable delegations to Congress, but attempts to alter the naturalization laws against the alien, extend the probation period and restrict the franchise failed as completely as had the earlier measures of the 1830s and 1840s. The national temper thus on three successive occasions rejected narrow nativism. The failure of Know-Nothingism meant the refusal of the United States to give continuing sanction to a set of prejudices.

II

The Catholic Irish took Know-Nothingism in their stride. Two previous experiences had ruggedly conditioned them to endure nativism in the 1850s, and they were stronger in numbers. Their clerical and lay leaders taught them not to condemn the United States and the American people for the narrowness of a minority faction. With the Know-Nothing spirit still active, Archbishop Hughes wrote that in the annals of Church history "there has never been a country which, in its civil and social relations, has exhibited so fair an opportunity for developing the practical harmonies of Catholic faith, and of Catholic charity, as the United States." Their leaders told them to hang on patiently and this nativist aberration would pass. The bishops urged the people, in the words of Archbishop Kenrick of Baltimore, to stay "far away from scenes of danger, from tumult and bloody strife." The Irish did not always exercise restraint, but against the record of damage by nativists to Catholic lives and property the conduct of the Irish was exemplary.

The Irish abided by the principle that the Know Nothings warred not upon the foreigners but upon the American people by their un-American creed and actions. This, they said, was not a problem for Catholics or Irish to settle; it was a problem for the American people to handle and solve. The clergy and the press warned the Irish not to let the Know Nothings maneuver them into taking a stand either as a Catholic party or an Irish party, thereby isolating themselves as a direct and specific target.

The contrast of the hysterical fears raised by the Know-Nothing agitators and literature with the cold facts relating to the Catholics and Irish helped to put Know-Nothingism out of business when the people regained common sense. Out of a population of thirty million in the United States, some one million were Irish; out of 38,000 churches, 1221 were Catholic; out of eighty-seven million dollars in church property, the Catholics owned nine million. There was not one Catholic governor in the thirty-three states; of the five thousand legislators in those thirty-three states, not fifty were of foreign birth. One foreign-born Irishman, Shields of Illinois, adorned the Senate, and during the height of the agitation, when Americans trembled over the menace of the Irish, only John Kelly, native-born of Irish emigrant parents, sat in the House.

The Catholic press described Know-Nothingism as "a sort of fever — a phase of madness which has seized the country." Of representative Catholic Irishmen, only McGee gave way to panic, with his plan to move the Irish to Canada and his fear that Know-Nothingism would end in penal laws or a massacre of Catholics.

Indeed, in the Catholic Irish literature of the times, good humor constantly erupted along with the sledge-hammer condemnation of Know-Nothingism. The *Pilot*, in the very citadel of Know-Nothingism, jibed, joshed, and ribbed its reliable old adversaries as they scrambled for place in the new opportunity; it poked fun at the synthetic mystification with which the "dark lantern" brigade surrounded itself.

The Irish engaged in levity at the expense of the nativists. An Irish boy, in one popular story, who was being whipped by his father for stealing money said he did not mind being whipped for that "but that it hurt his feelings, being a *native*, to be lathered over the head by an infernal foreigner." A Catholic religious paper reprinted a contemporary saw: " 'It always gives me great pleasure,' said an official ruffian to a poor boy who asked a coffin for the body of his father, 'to give a coffin to bury an Irishman.' " The Catholic Cincinnati *Telegraph* said that now that the Irish were excluded from office, "some of them will find time to make their Easter Communion."

The Irish enjoyed the widely circulated jest that the "Know-Nothings have altered a portion of the Declaration of Independence, making it read thus, 'Life, Liberty and the pursuit of Irishmen.' "

Like every persecuting movement founded on discrimination, Know-Nothingism strengthened the attachment of the Catholic Irish to the

Church, brought the wayward and the indifferent back into the fold, and increased the non-Catholic respect for the demeanor of the Church under heavy siege. At the same time it chastened the assertiveness of both churchmen and the Irish which had cropped out at the mid-turn of the century. And it confirmed the Catholic Irish in their loyalty to the Democratic Party.

The first political figure of national stature to condemn the Know-Nothing order was Democratic Stephen A. Douglas. While other politicians had wetted fingers in the wind to catch the flow of opinion, Douglas, straightforwardly and with great courage, spoke up at Philadelphia's Independence Hall on July 4, 1854: "To proscribe a man in this country on account of his birthplace or religious faith," he declared, "is subversive of all our ideas of civil and religious liberty. It is revolting to our sense of justice and right." The Catholic Irish had had warm affections for Douglas up to this time: after the Philadelphia speech, they followed him without question.

Such a statement as the following, issued when Know-Nothingism was riding high in strength and power, had much to do with the loyalty of the Catholic Irish to Tammany Hall despite its sins:

> Resolved, That it is the glory and pride of old Tammany Hall that she has never, at any period of her history, avowed aught but truly republican doctrines . . . proscribing no man for opinion sake, discriminating neither for nor against any on account of birth or religion, but opening the door wide to the oppressed of all climes, and to the downtrodden of all monarchies.

Undoubtedly this was smart and shrewd politics, but to the Catholic Irishman, under proscription by a powerful group, his Church reviled and his race held up to contempt, the resolution was the voice of friendship and good will when he needed solace; and be sure that he reminded his children of Tammany's fidelity in the dark and forbidding times.

The Democratic platform on which James Buchanan ran in 1856 was vigorous and forthright in opposition to Know-Nothingism. The abridgment of the naturalization privilege, it said, "ought to be resisted with the same spirit which swept the alien and sedition laws from our statute-books." In declaring opposition to all secret political societies, the platform declared that "a political crusade in the nineteenth century, and in the United States of America, against Catholic and foreign-born is neither justified by the past history or the future prospects of the country, nor in unison with the spirit of toleration and enlarged freedom which particularly distinguishes the American system of government." The Democratic Party had taken a further mortgage on the affections of the Catholic Irish, particularly since the Republican Party avoided the issue altogether, not wanting to alienate those who had deserted the sinking Know-Nothing craft for the new party.

Events now headed toward civil war, on the eve of which we might inquire into the state of the Irish countryman translated from his hereditary fields to the broad United States.

46
"Give Me Again My Harp of Yew . . ."

AN IRISH GIRL in Philadelphia wrote back to her parish in Ireland that "when I see the young Irish priest here in most of our churches, and listen to the flood of eloquence he pours forth with all his native feeling and enthusiasm, I oftentimes begin to think that I am still in the loved Ireland of Sorrow, the dear old land of my birth and St. Patrick." Rev. Dr. Cahill, coming from Ireland just before the Civil War, described the Church in America as "an Irish plantation" and its career in the new land "the second volume of modern Irish history."

The Roman Catholic Church, the predominating cultural influence in nineteenth-century Ireland, continued its cultural direction of the Irish in the United States. The Irish character of the Church lent a familiarity that made the new and different American environment less difficult for the Irishman to adjust to. But the Church could not preserve the traditional cultural pattern of the Irish countryside, and the Irishman accommodated himself to the new tempo and emphases of a bustling, progressive, and materialistic civilization.

2

The folk life of the Irish village belonged to a cycle of time that had passed from Western Europe even before English colonists sank roots in America. "We are a primitive people," wrote a literate Irishman in America, "wandering wildly in a strange land, the Nineteenth Century." The Irish in America, a literary '48 exile wrote to the Dublin *Nation,* "are, in fact, the very same people you see from your office window, with better food in their stomachs, some money in their pockets, the right to vote, to meet, and to bear arms." America supplied their material wants, even on a low level, to a degree they could never expect in their native land, but the Irish abandoned at the same time what the writer called "the nobler part."

The Irish, separated from their tradition-bound villages, suffered a loss in values that encompassed a grace more poetic than cash-and-carry in worth. They had an unsophisticated innocence that the worldly called ignorant credulity — vices common to an advanced civilization were not in their experience. They weighed life by religion in a sense of wonder and awe that the superior called unenlightened superstition. They had an uncomplex love of and feel for tradition which the go-ahead spirit derided as unprogressive and reactionary. The Irish had to encounter the increasing complexities of the nineteenth century and in the process they parted company with cultural integrity. Paddy Kit Molloy, honoring the ancient and unwritten Gaelic pieties in a Donegal or a Kerry village, had other and less vulgar venerations than Patrick Molloy, a coal miner in Pennsylvania or a railroad laborer in Illinois or a factory worker in Massachusetts. He had a distinctiveness of character in his native village that became fogged in America. One '48 exile sensed this change and regretted it: "Ireland is the country for the Irish," he wrote; "there God intended them to bide." But better a live Irishman in America than a starved Gael dutifully worshiping ancestral ways in his native land.

3

Americans generally accepted the conventional judgment that Irish wildness erupted from the abuse of American liberty and the laxity of American law enforcement in comparison to strict British policing in Ireland, as the Attorney General of Rhode Island explained to the jury in the Sprague murder case. But the Americans neglected the even more valid and compelling reason: the uprooting of the Irishman from his village released him from the discipline and restraints

upon his conduct of a public opinion he respected and from its punish-
ments by moral censure, amounting to moral coercion.

The freedom of the host culture, however, exaggerated and excited temperamental characteristics of the Irishman that seemed natural in the background of his own tradition: his urge to boast, for example, his excess of blarney or an unlettered assertiveness or his capacity for footless noise. It was paradoxical that the uninhibited animal
vitality of the Catholic Irish vexed a people themselves bouncy with
vitality. Apparently a distinction held between American and un-
American vitality.

The Catholic Irish clustered together in America too closely in
clannishness. They would have been far better off, and avoided considerable misunderstanding, had they mixed with others in a freer
manner. An Irishman made more rapid economic progress, learned
more quickly, and divested himself of unfortunate Irish practices, like
intemperance, more easily when he separated himself from the time-
consuming and unambitious gregariousness of the Gaels. The instinct
of the Americans to spread out the solid Catholic Irish mass was correct but not always for the right reasons — the urge to divorce them
from their religion, for example, only brought the Irish into stronger
cohesiveness. The more vigorous the pressure against Irish clannishness, the stronger Irish clannishness resisted it. It was true in this as in
other departments of life that, as was said: "The Catholics [that is, the
Irish] are a stiff-necked generation, obstinate as asses and dogged as
she asses — they neither will be driven or drawn against their will,
and the man who attempts both or either, will have his labor for his
reward." Yet the Irish refused to believe they were clannish; the Germans were clannish, they said.

4

Next to the Church as a cultural influence was the Catholic Irish
newspaper.

The newspaper stood to the Catholic Irishman as school and college
in one, his library, guide and companion. The impress of the Catholic
Irish weekly upon the emigrants cannot be overemphasized. The
United States introduced the newspaper to the Irishman as a habit,
and it had a tremendous effect on his growth and change. Critics have
dwelt upon the untoward influences of the Catholic Irish press: that it

kept alive Irish sentiments, that it agitated Irish passions, that it flattered the Irishman instead of telling him the truth, that its results were
divisive and exclusivist inside the American community. Let the truth
of these accusations be granted and yet the benefits of the Irish press in
pre-Civil War years outweighed its faults. It hammered into the Irishman's head the need and advisability of naturalization without delay.
It never ceased preaching to him that while he owed love to his native
land, his unshakable allegiance belonged to the country of his adoption. It dwelt, perhaps with Irish excess, upon American patriotism. It
fought valiantly the Irish weakness for drink. It crusaded to get the
Catholic Irish out of their city warrens into the country. It encouraged
self-improvement and acted as a lyceum to lecture the emigrants on
American middle-class standards, which it offered them for emulation.
The literature of the Catholic Irish emigrant was the newspaper.

5

Of the numerous Catholic Irish journals in the United States, many
of which had only a brief and fitful life, the best and most important
was the Boston *Pilot*.

The association of John Boyle O'Reilly with the *Pilot* in the later
nineteenth century has obscured the solid record of the paper for the
more than three decades before he assumed its editorial direction. The
first *Pilot*, which grew out of Bishop Fenwick's *Jesuit* and its successors and which was named after a famous Catholic newspaper in
Dublin, failed, but the undiscouraged Patrick Donahoe picked himself
up from the wreckage and on January 27, 1838, launched the reorganized *Pilot* which has continued to this day — at present the official
organ of the Archdiocese of Boston, one of the oldest papers in the
United States and among the few remaining that originated in the
immigrant press.

At the end of the first year, Donahoe announced that the *Pilot*
would have to suspend unless friends came to its aid. Loyal Irishmen
in New England held meetings, solicited subscriptions, and on July
20, 1839, the *Pilot* proclaimed it had weathered the storm. By the end
of 1842, the *Pilot* began to build a national circulation and in 1847
boasted it "circulates largely in every town in the United States,
Canada, British Provinces, Mexico, &c., where there is an Irishman."
It was available "at every Periodical Depot in the United States."

By the opening of the Civil War the *Pilot* was (and had been for years) the representative Catholic Irish weekly and the newspaper bible of the Gaels. Not even the *Freeman's Journal*, published in cosmopolitan New York, the center of Irish wealth, position, and numbers, could compete with the *Pilot*, published in provincial Boston, in the affection and loyalty of the Catholic Irish throughout the country.

The secret of the *Pilot's* success was the smart, vigorous, knowing and tightfisted emigrant from County Cavan, Patrick Donahoe, who landed as a lad in Boston in 1821, learned the trade of printer and branched out as owner and publisher of the *Pilot*.

Pat Donahoe was an unusual and useful man. Some day the descendants of the Irish in Boston will erect a monument to his memory befitting his labors for the race during a long life. Editors came and departed, but Donahoe kept the *Pilot* together, just as he had formed and molded its character. What distinguished him was that he knew what the Irish, emigrant and settled, wanted to read, and he furnished it.

"We wish it to be distinctly understood," said the *Pilot* in 1841, "that our paper is emphatically an *Irish* and *Catholic* journal." But it made it also distinctly understood that the *Pilot* was not a theological journal and denied it was the organ either of the bishop or the Pope. By virtue of its secular control, the *Pilot* could keep free of the involved theological discussions which clerical editors of the Catholic weeklies felt compelled to indulge in or relished as the lawyer a legal argument. They pleased fellow priests by their expositions, but theology ran the business office into the red. The Irish loved to read the human stories of priests who had been martyred by Cromwell or the heroism of bishops in the penal days, and they never tired of the old saints, but theological excursions left them cold. The *Freeman's Journal* was forbidding to many because its lay theologian McMaster spread his specialized erudition over its pages. The *Pilot* stuck to news, features, and sentimental entertainment pitched for the Irishman. If the *Freeman's Journal* reviewed a work by a French theologian at length, the *Pilot* added more news of County Roscommon.

Before the telegraph and cable, the *Pilot* depended for its foreign news on Irish and English papers transported on transatlantic vessels, and often during the winter months readers were without information from Ireland for as long as two months. Starting in 1840, the *Pilot* enjoyed an advantage over its competitors by the establishment of Boston as the terminal port of the fast Cunard steamers, which gave it priority in foreign journals.

Issues of the *Pilot* left the impression that the United States was a suburb of Ireland rather than a different country. Irish news included political events and speeches and a full coverage of elections; births, deaths, and marriages; the state of the crops, farm prices, and reports on the fairs; the goings and comings of the prelacy and clergy; accidents, fires, and murders; evictions and outrages — in short, the news the emigrant would be interested in were he in Ireland, including the wonders of the land such as an oldster of a hundred and seven years who still had all his teeth. American news of interest and concern to the Irish was also covered but not to the extent of the Irish news for the simple reason that the American press, upon which the Irish-American weeklies relied, generally gave sketchy coverage of Irish events. Paid and volunteer correspondents forwarded intelligence that was not always reliable. A great deal of attention was paid to editorial articles, generally forthright in character.

The *Pilot* was at times scurrilous, poetic, bigoted, generous, subtle, naïve, ham-fisted, eloquent, sentimental, radical and reactionary, Democratic in its leanings and, more often than not, interesting and lively. It could not escape Irish bulls: "We never publish anonymous communications without knowing the author"; or mixed figures: "this goose's egg, if it be hatched out, will throw a wet sack over the trade of Boston completely"; or Irish idiom: "It feels very like the smell of a rat." While often it gave way to Irish vehemence and violence in language and opinion, as often its good nature broke through. If the No-Popery people insisted on calling the Church nasty names, the *Pilot* saw to it that every Protestant reverend involved with a female choir singer or taken with a fair member of the congregation not his wife got full publicity in its columns. It carefully noted, as a judgment of Heaven, every Protestant meetinghouse burned or struck by lightning.

But, in character with Catholic Irish journalism of the day, the *Pilot* reserved its choice spleen for fellow Catholic or Irish papers. At no single moment up to the Civil War were all the Catholic Irish weeklies on speaking terms with one another at the same time. McMaster returned from the Baltimore Council of 1849 and informed his readers he had learned "a great deal of modesty, humility, and charity." "God knows," commented the *Pilot*, "it was much wanted."

It called the New York *Irish American,* the organ of the '48 exiles, the "Whiskey Advertiser," because it accepted advertisements of Noonan's mountain dew and Monongahela strong waters.

It picked up rare and juicy correspondents, including one C. Manus O'Keeffe, who wrote a letter from Dublin and nursed a round, full, implacable, and satisfying hatred of England. Has it occurred to you, he wrote, that the Irish have not had one saint since the coming of the English? Of course it was well known, he said, that the angels spoke Irish in Heaven. He devastated Ralph Waldo Emerson in an eloquent but incomprehensible article. He urged that the Irish fit out the wheels of their carts with scythes and sickles, like the ancient Scythians, and employ these "war machines" to mow down British infantry in war. The *Pilot* finally had to dispense with his services after his whistle got stuck on the one note of boycott in the United States of Belfast goods to punish the North.

An experienced newspaperman would have found the surest proof of the national character of the *Pilot* in the fascinating department called "Information Wanted," in which for a small fee the Irish all over the country and in Canada advertised for relatives or friends from whom they had become separated or with whom they wanted to communicate: parents looking for children, children seeking out parents, wives landing in America and searching for husbands who had come out before, brother trying to locate sister and sister hunting for brother, neighbors from the same townland wanting information of one another — a reflection of the confusion, mishaps and misadventures of a large emigration, of which the following was representative:

> *Philip McGovern,* Co. Cavan, left Dublin in Dec. 1848 in ship *Sarah,* landed in New Orleans in March, 1849. In June following he left New Orleans in steamboat *Belvidere* to go to his aunts, Mrs. Kernan and Mrs. Pim, near Zanesville, Ohio; since which time he has not been heard from by his wife, who is in New Orleans, and has written many letters without getting an answer. She heard from others that he lived in Ironton and wrote for her, but she never got the letters. Any one knowing him will confer a favor on his wife by letting him know this, or by writing to Mrs. Margaret McGovern, c/o Mr. O'Donnell, New Orleans, Louisiana.

Such standardized and routine search for information was now and then interrupted by the raising of a hue and cry for an Irish rogue:

Tom Daniel, Co. Tipperary, who came to this country about 15 years ago, — was last living in a little groggery in Jackson St., Brooklyn, and taking up with a woman, who passed as his wife. If the Catholic clergy, or laity, of Brooklyn, know of his whereabouts, they will confer a favor by writing to his wife, whom he forsook after having robbed her of all her property. Please address Mrs. Thomas Daniel, Boston, Ms.

The Irish continued in the advertisements the country custom of addressing a woman by her maiden name after she was married. A "Mrs. John Lally" remained known to her friends as "Mary Murphy."

Just as a sizable classified advertisement section in the modern newspaper speaks of a large circulation, so did the columns of "Information Wanted" vouch for the readership of the *Pilot* everywhere in the United States. No other Catholic Irish weekly carried such volume in this department as did the *Pilot*. The fact that some two thirds of the advertisements resulted in the reuniting of the separated testified to the vast channel of communication among the Irish afforded by the *Pilot*. The Irish in Iowa or Wisconsin or Pennsylvania awaited its word on candidates during an election campaign, and the politicians recognized its influence.

The *Pilot* tried to carry out its stated purpose: "the elevation of the Irish character in this country, the Independence of Ireland, and the overthrow of sectarian prejudice." The highest tribute to the value of the *Pilot* is to say that no history of the Catholic Irish in the United States can be written without it. Its pages were in the marrow of the Catholic Irish.

His enemies said that Pat Donahoe was illiterate, but he wrote in a vigorous and masculine prose full of common sense. His enemies said Pat Donahoe loved the dollar too much, but no lay member before the Civil War served the Boston Irish community so devotedly and faithfully. He joined actively in every movement and society to raise the station of the Catholic Irish. The Yankees may not have liked the Irish collectively; they not only liked but they also respected Donahoe; indeed, he was the link between the two communities. He had a Yankee drive in him: he branched out from the *Pilot* into a successful book publishing business and into a passenger and remittance agency. He was a charter member of the Young Catholic's Friend Society, organized in 1835, which added to its funds for charitable work by promoting a series of public lectures each season.

6

The early Catholic Irish societies, notably in New York, fell into three general categories: the mutual benefit society, with burial insurance, like the Hibernian Provident Society; the society which combined mutual benefit features with the simplest form of trades unionism, like the Mechanics Benefit or Cordwainers societies; and the socio-political club, like the Brian Boroihme (Boru) Association, promoted by ambitious politicians. These societies were practical in purpose, and they allowed for the social companionship the Catholic Irish nature required.

But with the rise of societies like the Young Catholic's Friend Society of Boston developed the movement for the mental and moral improvement of the Irish. The YCFS lecture series, modeled on the Yankee lyceum for popular culture, presented an imposing list of speakers, like Joseph Choate, Wendell Phillips, George Bancroft, and George Curtis on subjects that included the Constitution, law, medicine, travel, history, literature, natural history, and science; the series always included lectures on Ireland and the Catholic Church, and by the middle '40s the lecturers were all Catholics, principally priests, on Catholic subjects. In time the Catholic Irish built up a lecture circuit, extending from Boston to Cincinnati, Chicago, and St. Louis, with Orestes Brownson the most popular of the lecturers. Regional circuits, composed of smaller towns, rotated inside the national circuit with lesser-known speakers. But only a small minority attended the lectures, and the sponsoring societies usually ended up with deficits, according to T. L. Nichols, a professional lecturer and a convert to Catholicism.

In March, 1842, another form of cultural expression was organized, the Catholic Literary Society of New York, under the presidency of Rev. John McCloskey, later to be the first American cardinal. The purpose officially contemplated a systematic defense of Catholicity against its detractors. A library of carefully selected Catholic works for the instruction of members was purchased out of funds raised through initiation fees and dues. Beyond the stated defense of Catholicity was the goal of raising up a strong generation of Catholics in America, firmly indoctrinated in the tenets of the faith and protected by the selective reading from the free-and-easy religious and philosophical ideas of a latitudinarian land.

The Father Mathew temperance crusade established the Catholic literary institute in the United States as a cultural apparatus for Irish self-improvement. Father Mathew organized reading rooms throughout Ireland on the theory they were needed for the increased moral, spiritual, and intellectual activities of the Irish who had taken the pledge. The John England Institute of Baltimore, started early in 1845, set the example for others. As its base was a circulating library. It sponsored lectures. It staged debates among its members, encouraged the preparation of literary papers for reading at meetings, and set out its purpose, in the prospectus of the Fenwick Literary Institute of Boston, "to combine pleasure with improvement and to instruct while it gratifies."

These literary institutes were preparatory schools for fledgling politicians among the ambitious young Irishmen. There they trained in public speaking, sharpened their wits in debates, learned the principles of parliamentary procedure and improved their store of knowledge; in addition, the institute provided a ready-at-hand organization to support the prospective candidate for office. The saloon was generally accepted as the proving ground of Catholic Irish politicians, but perhaps as many, if not more, entered politics by the door of the literary institute; this held particularly true outside of New York. But a constant complaint was that the institutes, organized so vigorously in the fall and the winter, dissolved and broke up in the summer.

7

The Church exercised an alert vigilance over the reading matter of the Irish faithful, with the cooperation of the faithful themselves. St. Joseph's College in Buffalo allowed no books to circulate among the students "unless previously examined by the President." Richard C. Doran of Providence advertised that his bookstore was conducted on Catholic principles, "admitting no religious works not duly approved, nor works of any kind contrary to faith and morals." The New York Catholic Library Association submitted a list of its books to the bishop who might, in his own discretion, strike out those he considered objectionable. The clergy warned the people not to buy a book on religion from a peddler until assured it carried the bishop's approval. Circulating libraries confined their books to safe and standard Catholic literature. The non-Catholic friends of Orestes Brownson were startled at his disclosure that he submitted all his writings to Bishop Fitzpatrick, or his theologian, for approval. Catholics were cautioned against books recommended in secular journals. The press warned against "a bad book," containing heresy, ridiculing religion, censuring ceremonies and scoffing at priests, as it defined one.

The extent of the fear that the young might be affected by non-Catholic ideas was nervously noted by the *Pilot* in comment in 1858 on the Holy Cross Commencement orators, saying:

> It was quite apparent that the writers had, perhaps unconsciously, borrowed expressions from the current non-Catholic literature of the day. The occurrence of this defect indicates that the dangerous process of assimilation, which the real Know-Nothings have so much at heart, as essential to the perpetuity of American institutions, is really taking place, through lack of vigilance on the part of those who have by nature, or the civil law of the country, the direction of the rising generation of Catholics.

8

Orestes Brownson trembled not so much at the possible infection of the Catholic Irish by intellectual interests as their want of intellectual interests of any kind, though influential clergymen argued in justification of the lack of intellectual curiosity among the Irish. Brownson's magazine thought Catholic colleges a failure and raised the question of how many men of prominence and influence had been turned out by Catholic education. But the Catholic college of the date made no pretense to give what was called a "polite" education; it was more a commercial school than an institution for classical learning.

Realistic observers reasoned on the absurdity of attempting to educate unlettered Catholic Irish emigrants overnight or translate a race, still scarred by the penal laws, into lovers of the intellectual within a generation. The largest proportion of the emigrants, they stressed, were "honest, hard-working men, who must at first establish for themselves and children a *status*," before they could turn their minds to intellectual pursuits. "It will require the slow and progressive work of two or three generations," concluded the *Pilot* in 1860, "before the Catholic community will have attained a high state of consolidation." Then, and only then, it said, could it be appreciative of the intellectual. Very few Irish, wrote the practical John Ryan in 1855, "possess the means to

give their children what is termed 'a first-rate education.'" Hugh Cummisky, the successful first-generation Irish contractor, could send his
son to Holy Cross College, but the generality of the emigrants held
out no greater advance for their children than a primary education
and learning a trade or getting a foothold in a commercial house:
among the very poor every hand had to be turned to help the whole
family. Like the Irish in the old country, the emigrant placed great
value on the status earned with a priest or a lawyer in the family.

9

A reading of the *Pilot* in the pre-Civil War years underlines the
wide gulf between cultured Boston and the Irish community. The
Golden Age of New England letters coincided with the years of the
greatest Irish emigration. Nothing in the *Pilot* indicated that the great
literary figures of the time exercised the slightest influence on the
Boston Irish, worlds apart in education, cultivation, and literacy. The
most painful cut to the humble and uneducated Irish of the emigrant generation came from the towering figure of the literary Brahmins. The anti-Popery and the Know-Nothing attacks aroused the
Irishman's anger, but Ralph Waldo Emerson hit him where it hurt. In
his essay, *Fate,* Emerson wrote:

> The German and Irish millions, like the Negro, have a great
> deal of guano in their destiny. They are ferried over the Atlantic,
> and carted over America, to ditch and to drudge, to make corn
> cheap, and then to lie down prematurely to make a spot of green
> grass on the prairie.

"If Mr. Emerson's sentiments were those of the best portion of the
community (thank God they are not)," wrote the *Pilot,* "the only reply that we could wish to make to them, would be to obtain such a
decree (were it possible) that would sweep the whole Irish race away
from the land. In that case it would appear whether the Irish millions
have a great deal of guano in their destiny." There was missing in the
Pilot's response the Irishman's instinctive resort to scurrility, the hard
swing against an opponent from the floor, the nut-cracking sound of
the shillelah. Instead in it was a sense of sadness and pain at Emerson's
cruel and insensitive judgment of the Irish — his "heathenist, soulless,
immoral remarks."

10

The Irishman as a stage character was as old as the American drama, and the part of the Irish in the development of the American theater was historic. The most substantial contribution by the Irish to the cultural pattern of the United States in the pre-Civil War years was in the field of entertainment; they gave it an Irish flavor and an Irish tradition.

The affinity of the Catholic Irish for the stage was natural: their love of make-believe, their susceptibility to the power of the human voice, their imaginative capacity to identify themselves with the play and players, their disposition to entertain and be entertained, attracted them to the theater as participants and audience. It has been observed that the Irish would not make good Protestants because of the simplicity and austerity of the reformed services in contrast to the color and drama of Catholic liturgy.

The Irish play entered into the American repertory in the 1820s. The "stage Irishman" began to flourish in the 1830s. Plays of liberty-loving nationalism in Ireland took hold as a theme in the 1840s. The Irish emigrant and his relationships with the Yankees reflected in the 1850s the rise in Famine numbers and introduced the emigrant milieu that was to be so important a part of the theater as successive waves brought new European nationalities to the Republic.

A popular farce of the English theater, *The Irish Tutor*, first appeared in New York's Park Theatre in 1823. The Irish historical drama brought the Irish hero-king to the American stage in 1827 through *Brian Boroihme, or the Maid of Erin* by James Sheridan Knowles, the Irish playwright. In the following year the New York stage saw two more plays built around the Irish king, *Brian the Brave* and *Ireland Redeemed*. George Pepper, the Irish journalist, was the author of the latter, and he also wrote *Kathleen O'Neill, or A Picture of Feudal Times in Ireland* and *The Red Branch Knight, or Ireland Triumphant,* all praised for construction, characterization, and eloquence.

Master Joseph Burke made his American debut on November 22, 1830, and proceeded from New York on a triumphal tour of the United States. An Irish prodigy of about twelve, dubbed "the Irish Roscius," Master Burke amazed American audiences by his versatility. They delighted to watch him, with his pretty child's face, bright blue eyes and light hair, enact scenes from popular melodramas and Shakespeare; portray an old man, a young hero, an Italian music master, and a rollicking Irishman; lead the orchestra between the acts, play the violin and sing in a sweet voice. "His countrymen," wrote the *Truth Teller*, "may well be proud of this extraordinary child."

In the meantime, one Boyle introduced the Irish tenor voice to the Americans, and they took to themselves that ethereal, light-as-air pitch, as perfect an organ as was ever dreamed of for sentimentalism to wring the eyes and the heart. The American people, though gone as so many were in nativism, never could resist the sweet Irish voice, the tender Irish melodies and the rowdy Irish ballads. The pretty tunes of *Kate Kearney* set all New York to singing. A Know Nothing would knock an Irishman down and yet weep at "The Last Rose of Summer."

Tyrone Power made his first appearance in America on August 28, 1833, as Sir Patrick O'Plenipo in *The Irish Ambassador,* to be followed by *Teddy the Tiler,* a hardy perennial. Early in January, 1837, he played Phelim O'Flannigan in *O'Flannigan and the Fairies, or a Midsummer Night's Dream, Not Shakespeare's.* Here was the broad Irish farce in all its uproariousness. Here was the "stage Irishman" in perfect stereotype, dressed in frieze clothes, battered caubeen and heavy brogans, swinging his shillelah in a fight at the fair, smoking a foreshortened clay pipe, a heavy drinker, a jollier of the ladies, a believer in the little people, improvident, happy-go-lucky, a buffoon, lacking nothing but a pig tied to a string. A coarse play, *O'Flannigan and the Fairies* offended the sensitive and self-conscious Catholic Irish. A decade later, when James Hudson, an Irish actor, revived it in New York, a Mr. Molony and a Mr. Donnelly hissed him and were ejected from the theater, but Mr. Hudson apologized to the Irish citizens of New York. "These foolish and stupid representations of Irish character," said the *Pilot,* "deserve nothing but hisses." But Pat Donahoe was more puritan than any descendants of the original Puritans in Boston. He refused to review plays in his weekly and told the Irish they would be better off attending lectures than going to the theater.

Power toured the United States on his several visits with a repertory which included *The Irish Lion, Rory O'Moore, How to Pay the Rent,* and other Irish comedies, and he wrote an interesting account of his travels. He sailed from New York City in March, 1841, on the steamship *President* and went down with that vessel. "If Mr. Power has ever been equalled on our stage in the character of the Irish gentleman," wrote a commentator, "he unquestionably never had a rival or competitor in parts of lower grade."

In the 1840s, Irish plays and players so bedecked the American stage that in 1849 the *Irish American* reported "the largest number of Irish actors ever assembled, together, are at present amongst us." John Brougham, born in Ireland, both wrote and acted, specializing in burlesque — not of the Minsky school. He played *Hamlet* with a heavy brogue and he guyed the serious drama of the day. In *The Game of Love,* he satirized the social-climbing wife who had changed the family name from Murphy to De Merfie when her emigrant husband struck it rich — the ancestor of Mr. and Mrs. Jiggs. George Mossup, the Irish comedian, made his American debut as Mickey Free in *Charles O'Malley.* The career of Thomas Flynn, an excellent Irish comic actor and prominent theater manager, came to a premature end by the combined ravages of melancholia and dissipation. John Collins, compared to Tyrone Power, first appeared in 1848 in the Irish roles now become standardized, like Paudeen O'Rafferty in *Born to Good Luck,* Terence O'Grady in *The Irish Post,* Captain O'Rourke in *Soldier of Fortune, or The Irish Settler,* and McShane in *The Nervous Man.* John ("Rascal Jack") Dunn, born Donohue, earned a favorable reputation as a sound character actor. Mr. and Mrs. Thomas Barry built up a popular American following. The Irish complained that the admission fee to readings by Samuel Lover, the Irish writer, were so high as to bar them. Joseph Jefferson thought John Drew, father of the later matinee idol, the equal of Tyrone Power as an Irish comedian, but Barney Williams was the favorite.

Barney Williams, born Bernard Flaherty in Cork and brought early to New York City by his emigrant parents, held dominating place on the American stage as the portrayer of Irish comic roles from the middle 1840s till the 1870s. He graduated to the legitimate theater from Negro minstrels, the circus, and song-and-dance variety. He played the standard Irish parts and American playwrights wrote Irish plays for him, like *Brian O'Linn,* on the theme of which — a man playing dead to test his beloved — Synge many years later fashioned a drama, *In the Shadow of the Glen.*

Williams started in the plays of Irish nationalism — the honest Irish peasantry opposed to the black villainies of English landlordism, hackneyed in theme, stereotyped in character and stilted in language, but popular. In the 1850s, he turned to the character of the Irish emigrant in America and with his wife, who was American-born, exploited the Yankee-Irish theme. From all accounts Williams possessed the true Irish spirit of the comical: he could make an audience roar by his pantomimic excellence. William Carleton, the Irish novelist and sure student of Irish character, saw Williams in Dublin and thought his acting equal to Power's. Williams, he wrote, spoke the "true Irish brogue," not the coarse accent of the mere buffoon, and he created the illusion that he was not acting.

William Jermyn Florence, born Bernard Conlin in New York, was considered in his day one of the great actors on the American stage and certainly he was one of the most popular. He played both American roles and, with his wife, the sister of Mrs. Barney Williams, the role of the Irishman in the successful Irish-Yankee play, *The Irish Boy and the Yankee Girl*.

Dion Boucicault, born in Dublin and trained in the English theater, arrived in New York from London in 1853. He specialized in the Irish play, though he contributed to the growth of the American theater in a variety of useful ways. His tremendous dramatic success on the eve of the Civil War, *Colleen Bawn*, adapted from Gerald Griffin's novel *The Collegians*, introduced into Irish melodrama a side of Irish life hitherto neglected — the Catholic Irish gentry or middleman of wealth. The play, which was to enjoy a half century's popularity, was characterized as "gross trumpery" by the *Freeman's Journal*, which was also the judgment of time.

Barry Sullivan appeared in America in the late 1850s in Shakespearean roles in which, according to contemporary opinion, he fared none too well but shone in costume dramas, like *Richelieu*. He was the idol of the Irish emigrant masses and the hero of the Irish military companies.

It would be footless to list the numerous plays of Irish nature, long since forgotten, that made the New York stage of 1860 far more Irish than Dublin's stage, but a few will suggest the variety: *The Gentleman from Ireland*, by Fitz James O'Brien, the wit and bohemian; *The Irish American; The Irish Fortune Hunter; The Irish Stew; Paddy the Piper; The Irish Know-Nothing; Shandy Maguire; Andy Blake; Ireland and America; The Irish Emigrant; Irish Assurance; Phelim O'Donnell and the Leprechaun; How to Get Out of It, or The Irish Free Lover; The Irish Heiress; Ireland As It Is; The Irish Valet; The Irish Attorney*, and so on.

These plays drew as accurate a picture of Ireland and the Irish as that which was in the mind of the British official who, ordered to Dublin for the first time, requested his agent to hire a house in the city that was not thatched. These "miserable productions," wrote the *Freeman's Journal,* "are no more Irish in tone or sentiment than were their authors." The succession of Irish plays and characters of stock nature left an incorrect and unhappy impression of the Irishman in the American mind that hurt the race, more deeply than was comprehended at the time. Audiences accustomed to guffaw at the Irish on the stage could not be blamed for guffawing at them in real life.

Often the plays merely served as a framework for Irish singing and dancing — and Irish jigs, reels, and breakdowns entered into the variegated culture of America. In 1844, a New York entrepreneur conceived the idea of an entertainment of singing and dancing divorced from a play. Matt Brennan opened Novelty Hall, at Pearl and Centre Streets, described as "a humble place of amusement," for stage-struck Irish lads in what has been characterized as the first variety show in New York City. There Luke West, Matt Peel (Matt Flannery), one Slavin and George Reed danced and sang in individual acts, Dick Carroll gave an exhibition of high kicking and Joe Miles won neighborhood fame as a jig dancer. Within a few years some, like Luke West, Matt Peel, and Dick Carroll, graduated into the minstrel shows, then extremely popular; and Irish entertainers, like Richard Hooley, Joe Murphy, and T. Prendergast, put burnt cork on Celtic faces, sang of the old plantation home down South and danced the Negro walk-around — an interesting amalgamation of an emigrant people and the culture of the depressed blacks. Just before the Civil War, the Bryant Brothers' Minstrels was a leading Ethiopian show, the Bryant Brothers being Dan, Neil, and Jerry Bryant, born O'Brien. Irish lads in the Irish section of New York City began the long tradition of the Irish in the vaudeville theater.

II

Kitty Hayes from Limerick, billed variously as "the Irish Thrush" and "the Irish Swan," gave her first concert at Tripler Hall on September 23, 1851, and of course the Irish thought she sang much better than Jenny Lind. Her lovely Irish face more than compensated for lack of strength in her voice and when she gave forth with "The Emigrant's Lament," hearts melted. Like all wise performers, Kate went West to San Francisco and there, under Tom Maguire's patronage, amassed a sizable fortune.

12

Whether or not Father Mathew's crusade inspired it, like the temperance bands in Ireland, at least the pause of the Irish from drinking in America coincided with the rise of Irish bands — brass, cornet, reed, and bagpipe bands. Growing references in the *Pilot* spoke of the popularity of P. S. Gilmore and his band. Though not a Catholic himself, Patrick Gilmore, the first of the great bandmasters, lived close to the Boston and Salem Catholic Irish communities and enjoyed both their affection and patronage.

13

In another department of life, the Catholic Irish made a great name for themselves that, however, shamed the respectable. They dominated in the noble art of fisticuffs or prize fighting.* Every emigrant ship that sailed, they said in Ireland, carried a potential world champion in its hold.

Even O'Connell had to take second place before the Irish love of sports when a prize fight, in which Simon Byrne, "The Emerald Gem," participated, attracted a larger audience than turned out to hear the Liberator. This Byrne, the first of the Irish professional fighters, so damaged Sandy McKay, the champion of Scotland, in 1830, that McKay died from the punishment. No Marquess of Queensberry rules guided the conduct of a prize fight in those days. The boxers fought with bare fists and slugged it out until one man dropped. It was permissible to fall on an opponent when he was down, and gouging, kicking, and biting were fair play.

By the early 1840s, a crowd of pleasure lovers, fond of drinking, gambling, and sports, made New York a lively, colorful, and rascally city. They loved to watch and gamble on prize fighting and cock fight-

---

* In other forms of sporting contests, the Irish longshoremen of Boston engaged in boat races on the Charles with Harvard varsity crews and visiting boats from Nova Scotia, an Irishman, Michael Phelan, held the billiard championship, and Irish were noted walkers, like the Boston Buck.

ing, both illegal. Their habitat was a round of saloons, where fighters, managers, trainers, and hangers-on greeted friends. Fighters contested for a certain sum a side — $500 or $1000 or $2000 — according to their reputations. Even then prize fighting had been pretty well organized with seconds and trainers of fascinating names, like Dublin Tricks and Country McCloskey, with training camps before big fights and sites for the matches chosen at a distance from the arm of the law.

The brutality of these early prize fights was sickening. In 1842, one McCoy died in the ring at the hands of Chris Lilley after 121 rounds. A bruiser named Kelly killed a fighter named Cox in New Orleans. No scheduled number of rounds set the length of fights: John Monaghan and James Hart fought 44 rounds; Dan Callaghan fought a local boy in New Orleans for 116 rounds in three hours; Harry Lazarus won over Dennis Horrigan in 102 rounds, or three hours and two minutes; Dominick Bradley beat Samuel Rankin, both of Philadelphia, after 150 rounds; Dan Cunningham knocked out John Hooly near New Orleans in 143 rounds. The Bradley-Rankin fight attracted high attention because, with the Know-Nothing spirit then riding, it posed a Catholic Irishman against a native-born Protestant in which the superiority of their respective religions was tested by bare fists.

As apparent from the names, Irish prize fighters dominated in these primitive beginnings of the American ring. They came from a physically strong race; manual labor toughened their frames; and they had astounding courage. The Irish prize fighters naturally enjoyed large followings among their own people, accustomed to spectator sports in their native land; and the role of the Irish in building up professional sports and spectator attendance was pioneering. The long connection of the emigrant with professional sports began with the Catholic Irish. Until the swarming Irish emigration, native Americans paid scant attention to spectator sports, with the exception of horse racing.

After native-born Tom Hyer retired from the ring, the American heavyweight championship fell successively to three Irishmen in the bare-knuckles period. (Boxing records have no status until the championship of John L. Sullivan, long after the Civil War.) "Yankee" Sullivan, the Liverpool Irishman, convict and scum, held the title after Hyer, but John Morrissey won it from Sullivan in 1853 at Boston Four Corners, where New York, Connecticut, and Massachusetts meet, in the thirty-seventh round. Morrissey, born in Tipperary and reared in Troy, held the reputation of the Irish Strong Boy long before John L.

He was rough and tough, had served an apprenticeship along the New York waterfront and feared no man in a saloon brawl.

Brought up as a neighbor of Morrissey in Troy was John C. Heenan (the C standing for "Carmel") born of Irish emigrant parents. After a falling out of their parents, Morrissey heartily disliked the brawny Heenan and his fistic ambitions. Heenan had gone to California to try his luck and had picked up work swinging a 32-pound sledge hammer for the Pacific Mail Steamship Company in its shops at Benicia from which he got his fighting name of "the Benicia Boy." A trainer of fighters, Dick Cusick, saw the possibilities of Heenan and when the Vigilantes began to get rough Heenan moved eastward to New York and challenged Morrissey. In a brutal fight in Canada, Morrissey defeated Heenan in 1858 and then, like Hyer, retired from the ring, which passed the title to his defeated opponent.

Heenan was the first of the great popular heavyweight champions, from his amiable manner, pleasant address and native friendliness. The country seized upon him as a national idol after his fight in England in 1860 with the British champion, Tom Sayers, whose parents had come from Ireland. Even Queen Victoria, they said, was interested in the fight, though it was banned by the police. In what was perhaps the wildest and most ferocious battle in the history of boxing, Heenan and Sayers committed mayhem on each other until the thirty-seventh round when the attempted interference of the police brought the spectators into action against the law. The crowd held off the bobbies from breaking up the fight for five more rounds. Heenan had Sayers strangled against the ropes when somebody cut them, the mob came pouring into the ring and the fight was declared ended. The Americans felt that Heenan had been victimized by English bad sportsmanship, and they lavished their affection and purses on the Irish boy from Troy. He signed a contract and took to the stage and married the notorious Adah Isaacs Menken.

The *Pilot* turned a sour eye on the parade of low-life prize fighters among the Irish and if it had its way would have put them in jail. Though Catholic Irish in origin, they had long since forgotten how to bless themselves and certainly offered no edification to Catholic Irish youth. Yet an ambivalence prevailed among the respectable Catholic Irish: they disliked the linking of the name of the race with the bruisers, but they could not contain a certain pride in the knowledge that the Irish were the best prize fighters in the world.

T. D. McGee related the fighters to the San Francisco ballot-box stuffers and eschewed them both as "a horde of hardy, vulgar ruffians, unmatched in any former state of society." Then McGee made an interesting observation: "Most of these wretches are young men born here or in the English manufacturing towns of Irish parentage. Such was the notorious Sullivan, such was the Kelly* in this last tragedy. Surely, surely, some one has a terrible account to give of our neglected first and *lost second generation* in the English and American cities." This fitted the McGee theory that the Catholic Irish lost their spiritual nature by the blighting atmosphere of the United States and England.

Archbishop Hughes rapped McGee's remarks as "insolent and untrue" and added that he whined over "moral results which he himself had contributed in no small degree to bring about." The implacable Hughes had not yet forgiven McGee.

But another kind of fighting than Heenan's strong fists in the ring menaced the peace and order of the United States. No release from the deadlock over the issue of slavery now seemed likely except civil war.

47
"The Union – It Must Be Preserved"

THE BOLD SOARING IMAGINATION of Archbishop Hughes contemplated the vast design with that tenacity of purpose which had raised him from the hayfield of an Ulster farm to the eminence of the see of New York. His unblinking sense of realism informed him that not many years remained for him on this earth, and he wanted to round out his unusual career with grandeur. His mind pictured the culmination of his life's work that would be at once a testament to the permanency of the Roman Catholic religion in the United States, a hymn in stone glorifying his dearly beloved native land and, not unmindful of his own worth, a memorial to Archbishop John Hughes. He would build a Gothic cathedral in New York under the patronage of St. Patrick that would match the great cathedrals of Europe and stand unique in the United States.

* An Irish fighter who died from the beating visited on him in a prize fight.

On August 15, 1858, Archbishop Hughes laid the cornerstone of St. Patrick's Cathedral, in far uptown New York, anticipating that the city would grow to its walls and then flow around it, perhaps eventually setting this triumph of Catholicity at the center and heart of the great metropolis. Archbishop Hughes had no fear of the future.

Over a hundred thousand people gathered to watch the ceremonies on the Sunday of the Feast of the Assumption. Hughes had persuaded 103 wealthy men to pledge a thousand dollars each to start the cathedral, and he hoped to finish it in five years by an organized system of contributions. He did not live to see it completed.

Hughes left no doubt in the minds of his hearers that afternoon of the role of the Irish in spreading the Catholic faith. He traced their history from St. Patrick down through the penal laws, and he continued:

> Since then they have become the outcasts of their native land, and been scattered over the earth. You can trace their path of life through all the civilized countries of the world. You can trace them through England itself, through America, through India, through Australia, and though there may have been no mark to designate the graves in which they slumber, still, the churches which they have erected, either wholly or in part, all round the globe to the same faith by which St. Patrick emancipated them from heathenism; these churches, I say, are the most fitting headstones to commemorate the existence, and I had almost added, the honorable history of such a people.

Had they known the phrase at the time the Irish would have said that this was their finest hour thus far in the United States. Old men at the exercises remembered the Church when it was practically a hidden sect, with its small numbers meeting in a hole-in-the-corner house of worship. Association with this enterprise compensated for the slanders and disdains of the Know Nothings; and an Irishman, so the people thought, would have been a poor thing not to make sacrifices for the erection of the cathedral. The Irish were not the kind of people who worried over the debt Hughes incurred to build a cathedral; they said among themselves what a great man Archbishop Hughes was to go ahead with St. Patrick's.

It was a remarkable fact that the Church, associated with the poor and the emigrant masses, planned a cathedral that would put into the shadow the churches of the wealthy Protestant sects. It was not without psychological meaning that the driving force to build a towering edifice in New York was the Catholic Irish race, who only a generation before had not a cathedral that it could be proud of in its native land. The growth and expansion of the Church paralleled the career of Archbishop Hughes and the generation of Irish to which he belonged was now dying out.

2

"The early pioneers," sighed the *Pilot*, "are fast disappearing from the midst of our Irish population." Thomas O'Connor, the oldest Irish settler in New York City, had died in 1855 and two years later Dr. Hugh Sweeney, who tended the Irish and fought their battles, passed on. Michael Quarter died in Utica at the age of ninety-two: three of his sons had entered the priesthood, one to become bishop of Chicago. When Edward Quigley, who died in Lowell at the age of eighty-four, had arrived in Boston fifty years before, the only Catholic church in New England, the Cathedral of the Holy Cross in Boston, had just been completed. Terence McHugh, the coal and wood merchant in Boston, who had been a member of the first society to agitate for Catholic Emancipation and active in all Irish and Catholic causes, departed.

In true accord with the tradition in Ireland that went back beyond memory, the old men said that the people of the new generation were hardly to be compared with the breed now going to its reward. The Irish body of a quarter of a century ago, it was declared, "was more of a body then than now, more full of life, and energy, and action, more united, more closely bound together, had leading men who directed matters, while now, alas! though ten times as numerous, it is ten times as easy to wrong us." The generation against which the Irish complaint was made would, in its own time, say that the succeeding generation could not compare with the race of giants departing. Thus it had been with the Catholic Irish, and thus it would be. It seemed that the epitaph of an epoch was written not in the death of a Gael but of a Yankee, John W. James, in 1861, the true and faithful James.

Thomas Reed died at Manayunk, Pennsylvania, in February, 1859, and in this "very unassuming but true and faithful Catholic Irishman" we catch a glimpse of the life and character of the first generation of nineteenth-century Irish emigration. Thomas was a native of the city of Kilkenny and he emigrated in the spring of 1827, which made his stay in America just short of thirty-two years. In Boston "he was most kindly received, and kindly treated by the very worthy and respectable class of Irishmen, who then were foremost in extending friendship and good offices of every kind to the newly arrived Irish emigrant," first and foremost among those worthies being the tailor father of Bishop Fitzpatrick. Thomas left Boston and worked in Billerica Mills for Messrs. Faulkner. "These are sad and mournful things to reflect on and record," said his obituary, "as they tell us too forcibly that those very intelligent Irishmen, who 30 and 40 years ago might be found in the then few manufacturing villages of New England, are now fast passing from time to eternity."

Many of these men wandered into other parts to get away from the intolerance of the land of the Pilgrims. "We have known many of these in years now far gone by," wrote the commentator, "and have often talked over with them the insupportable sufferings of that class in those times." Thomas Reed often rejoiced at the rapid and wonderful progress of the Catholic faith "among the cold and formal people of New England." Though he laughed and joked about New England and her people, he by no means regarded them unfavorably. He admired their many fine traits of character: skill, industry, and perseverance under obstacles that to others would have appeared insurmountable.

Thomas had what his eulogist called "the most childish fondness for Ireland." "He loved warmly the dear and venerable old land. The old round tower of his native city, and the venerable and ivy clad Cathedral beside it, spoke a language more eloquent to his soul than the tongues of men. But there was that in Ireland more dear to him than even the round tower and abbey; namely, the skylark. The cuckoo, he often remarked, he liked to hear, in connection with the whistling of the Irish plowman; but even that did not so entrance him, as the lark of a fine May morning, when it arose from its nest on the sward, and never ceased its music until it disappeared in the distant cloud. This to Thomas Reed was the greatest of all charms of Old Ireland."

John Waters, of Haddington, who more than forty years before had taught catechism and prayers to a few poor Catholics at Ned Howard's woolen factory in the then town of Dudley, now Webster, though he was now advanced in years, traveled many miles on a severe winter's

WHAT BEFELL THEM IN AMERICA

day to attend Tom Reed's funeral. Mr. Scanlan, the bookseller in Fifth
Street, Philadelphia, who thirty years before had been an active Irishman in New England, also was present.

It was the largest funeral ever seen in Manayunk. Father Mulhol-
land gave the last rites and he got carried away with emotion over the
death of his dear friend: "Tom," he exclaimed from the altar, "you are
fast approaching your God, and you were a true and faithful Irishman." He spoke a good obituary, through Tom, of the first-generation
Irish who had borne the heat of the struggle and now left the work to
others. Many did not live out their days like Tom Reed but died on
Civil War fields.

3

The pastoral letter of the archbishop and bishops of the Province of
Baltimore issued after the ninth provincial council in 1858 proclaimed
a neutralist position on the slavery issue, stressed the absence of agitation among the Catholics on the subject and left the faithful to make
their own judgments. The year before, while the Northern anti-slavery
people grew grimmer around the mouth on hearing the news, Catholic
Irish opinion generally sided with the Supreme Court in the Dred Scott
decision — "that juridical masterpiece," the *Pilot* called it.

Abraham Lincoln wrote to a friend that the folly of the Massachusetts Republicans would lose the party the foreign vote in the
Northwest. They pushed a constitutional amendment in the General
Court prohibiting the naturalized citizen from voting for two years
after he received his final papers. Lincoln saw that the Massachusetts
former Know Nothings, though aiming the amendment at the Irish,
had angered the Germans, now good Republicans on the question of
slavery; and Carl Schurz had hastened to Massachusetts to reason with
the leaders. (Smith O'Brien, the '48 leader and exile, who made a triumphal tour among his countrymen in America in 1859, said no state
in the Union treated the Irish worse than did Massachusetts.)

Lincoln suspected that the footloose Irish he saw, or heard of, in
Illinois, ostensibly railroad workers, were really floaters imported to vote
for Senator Stephen A. Douglas; and his forthright law partner, Bill
Herndon, told Rev. Theodore Parker of Boston, no lover of the Gaels,
that if Lincoln lost to Douglas the blame would rest on the "thousands
of wild, roving, robbing, bloated, pock-marked Irish, who are thrown

in on us by the Douglas Democracy for the purpose of out-voting us."
But other forces than the Irish vote defeated Lincoln in that memorable
1858 Illinois senatorial battle.

No political figure since Andrew Jackson had so won the affection,
even the love, of the Catholic Irish as Stephen Douglas. He had proved
his friendship for the Catholic Irish emigrant time and again. His best
man when he married a second time, to a Catholic woman, was General Shields; and one of his closest advisers was Jim Sheahan, editor of
the Chicago *Times*. The Irish admired the fighting spirit in a man his
size, the "Little Giant." They believed he had found the formula to
save the Union in his principle of popular sovereignty, which, after all,
was what the Irish in Ireland asked of the English government — the
right to make their own domestic decisions.

The Catholic Irish neglected politics and slavery talks in the spring
and summer of 1859 to bathe in the reflected glory of General Mac-
Mahon, who, after defeating the Austrians at Magenta, was promoted
by Napoleon III to be a marshal of France. The Irish press took the occasion of his fame to recall the number of fighters and statesmen, descendants of Irish exiles, who had served other nations with distinction
— the barons, dukes, counts, and marshals; and the humble Irish
proudly rolled the courtly names on their tongues: they had always had
a weakness for noble titles. The military companies of New York began a fund to buy a blooded horse for the marshal, and they openly
hoped that Napoleon III would deliver Ireland from the English bondage.

4

John Brown's raid on Harpers Ferry shocked the Catholic Irish as it
did conservative opinion in the North. A missionary priest from All
Hallows College stationed in the town gave the last rites to a Catholic
shot by the raiders and to a Marine named Quinn fatally wounded in
trying to dislodge Brown and his men. The priest, Father M. A. Costello,
interviewed John Brown, and he wrote later:

> I visited "Old Brown" . . . some time previous to his execu-
> tion, and he informed me that he was a congregationalist. He said
> that he would not receive the services of any minister of religion,
> for he believed that they, as apologists of slavery, had violated the
> laws of nature and of God, and that they were as bad as murderers,

fornicators, adulterers, etc.; hence that they ought first to sanctify themselves by becoming abolitionists, and then they might be worthy to minister unto him. Let them follow St. Paul's advice, he said, and go and break the chains of the slave, and then they might preach to others. I told him that I was not aware of St. Paul's ever giving any such advice, but that I remembered an epistle of St. Paul to Philemon, where we are informed that he sent back the fugitive slave Onesimus from Rome to his master. I then asked him what he thought of that, and he said that he did not care what St. Paul did, but what he said, and not even what he said if it was in favour of slavery!

The Irish vigorously supported Stephen Douglas in the 1860 presidential election, and then wondered if President-elect Abraham Lincoln had the powers to pull together the rapidly disintegrating Union. The *Pilot* spoke for Catholic Irish opinion in the North with its proclamation: "The Union — It Must Be Preserved! The *Pilot* Knows No North, No South." As the lines tightened and the hour for men to declare themselves started to strike, the Catholic Irish position was sharply defined: "We Catholics have only one course to adopt, only one line to follow. Stand by the Union; fight for the Union; die by the Union." They made it clear that the Union, not slavery or the slave, was the issue they stood upon.

Archbishop Hughes explained the position of the Catholic in the United States as civil war drew near: "If, being on the south side of Mason and Dixon's Line, that he ought to fight there, let him fight; and if we, living here, think the other way, why we will fight too." But the Catholics on both sides of the Line, he felt sure, no matter how wide and deep the political chasm between the North and the South, "will, as far as religion is concerned, throw a bridge over that chasm."

5

In February, 1861, the *Pilot* thought Lincoln had failed to shape up adequately to the emergency and predicted an embarrassed government, unable to meet its debts, "unless the Chicago platform is at once abandoned by Lincoln's administration" and the fanatical Republicans discarded. But its hope in Lincoln rose by the candor of the inaugural address, though it said: "If we criticized him in a literary point of view, we should find him no brilliant model in composition."

Fort Sumter surrendered and on April 15, 1861, President Lincoln called for seventy-five thousand men. The 69th Regiment immediately offered its services, and the commanding general called off the court-martial of Colonel Corcoran, who resumed command of the regiment and in his first order declared his pride in rallying the men to support of the Constitution and the laws. Six thousand Irishmen sought to enlist in the 69th, but the governor's order confined the regiment to a complement of one thousand. On April 26, 1861, the 69th formed and marched through vast multitudes of excited Irishmen and handkerchief-waving Irishwomen on the way to the steamer that was to carry the regiment to the defense of Washington. A few days after arrival the members started the construction of Fort Corcoran.

What would the Catholic Irish do in Massachusetts where twice in the past their military companies had been humiliatingly suppressed? "Every member of those insulted companies that we have exchanged a word with on the subject of the disbandment of 1855," the editor of the *Pilot* reported, "has shown a disposition to throw the remembrances of the affront to the winds" and they were prepared to march "side by side with the native-born volunteers." "The flag of our Union is not to be abandoned," it continued, "because the Know-Nothings and republicans six years ago acted with stupid malignancy." The Boston Irish, under Captain Thomas Cass of the disbanded Columbian Artillery, began to recruit a regiment with the blessing of Governor Andrew.

All over the country Irish companies were mustered into service and Irish volunteers swarmed into recruiting offices. They proved that they had meant what they said all along, that they would fight to defend the Union. "This is their real country," a spokesman proclaimed, and in the Civil War the ordeal by blood sealed the Catholic Irish and the Republic indissolubly.

And mind you now, warned the *Pilot* in a final word as the troops began to march, we Catholic Irish did not intend to fight in support of the Republican Party, but we "will stand up for the Union, and surround it like a wall of fire, wherever the hostile hosts of rebellion make their appearance in battle array."

Index of Names

(In this index, the abbreviation "Fr." is used for Roman Catholic clergy, "Rev." for Protestant clergy.)